Garfield
FAT CAT 3-PACK
VOLUME 4

BY
JIM DAVIS

BALLANTINE BOOKS • NEW YORK

2009 Ballantine Books Trade Paperback Edition

Copyright © 2009 by PAWS, Inc. All Rights Reserved.
GARFIELD MAKES IT BIG copyright © 1985, 2005 by PAWS, Inc. All Rights Reserved.
   "GARFIELD" and the GARFIELD characters are registered and unregistered trademarks of PAWS, Inc.
GARFIELD ROLLS ON copyright © 1984, 1985, 2005 by PAWS, Inc. All Rights Reserved.
   "GARFIELD" and the GARFIELD characters are registered and unregistered trademarks of PAWS, Inc.
GARFIELD OUT TO LUNCH copyright © 1986, 2006 by PAWS, Inc. All Rights Reserved.
   "GARFIELD" and the GARFIELD characters are registered and unregistered trademarks of PAWS, Inc.
Based on the Garfield® characters created by Jim Davis

Published in the United States by Ballantine Books, an imprint of Random House, a division of
Penguin Random House LLC, New York.

BALLANTINE and the HOUSE colophon are registered trademarks of Penguin Random House LLC.

NICKELODEON is a Trademark of Viacom International, Inc.

Originally published as three separate titles: Garfield Makes It Big, Garfield Rolls On, and Garfield Out
to Lunch. This edition was subsequently published in slightly different form in 1995.

ISBN 978-0-345-49171-8

Printed in China

randomhousebooks.com

18

Garfield
makes it big

BY JIM DAVIS

Ballantine Books • New York

Garfield's Loves & Hates

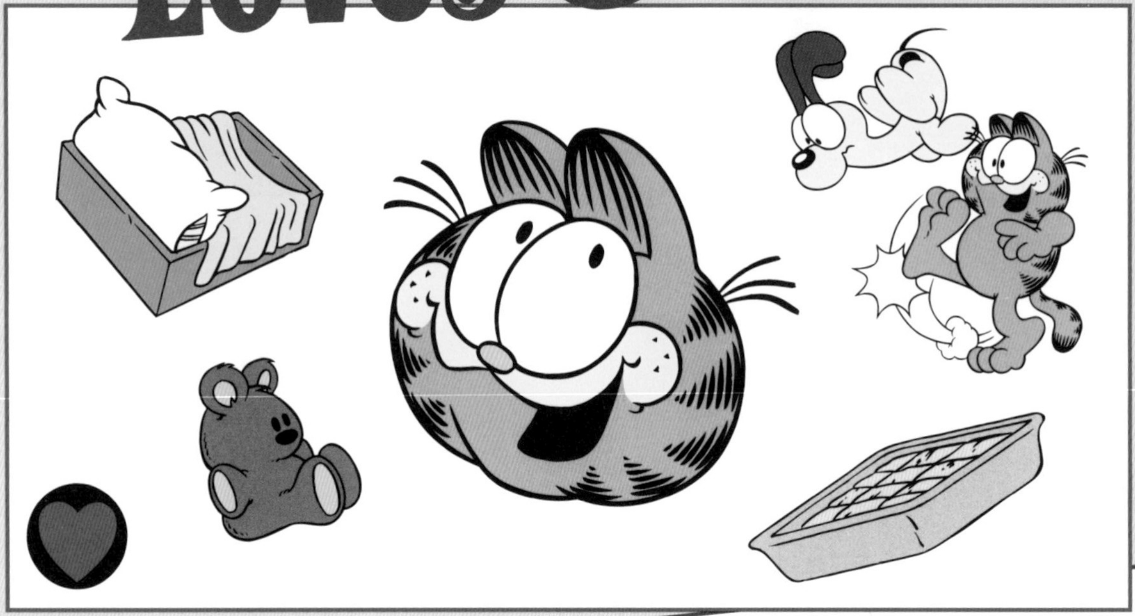

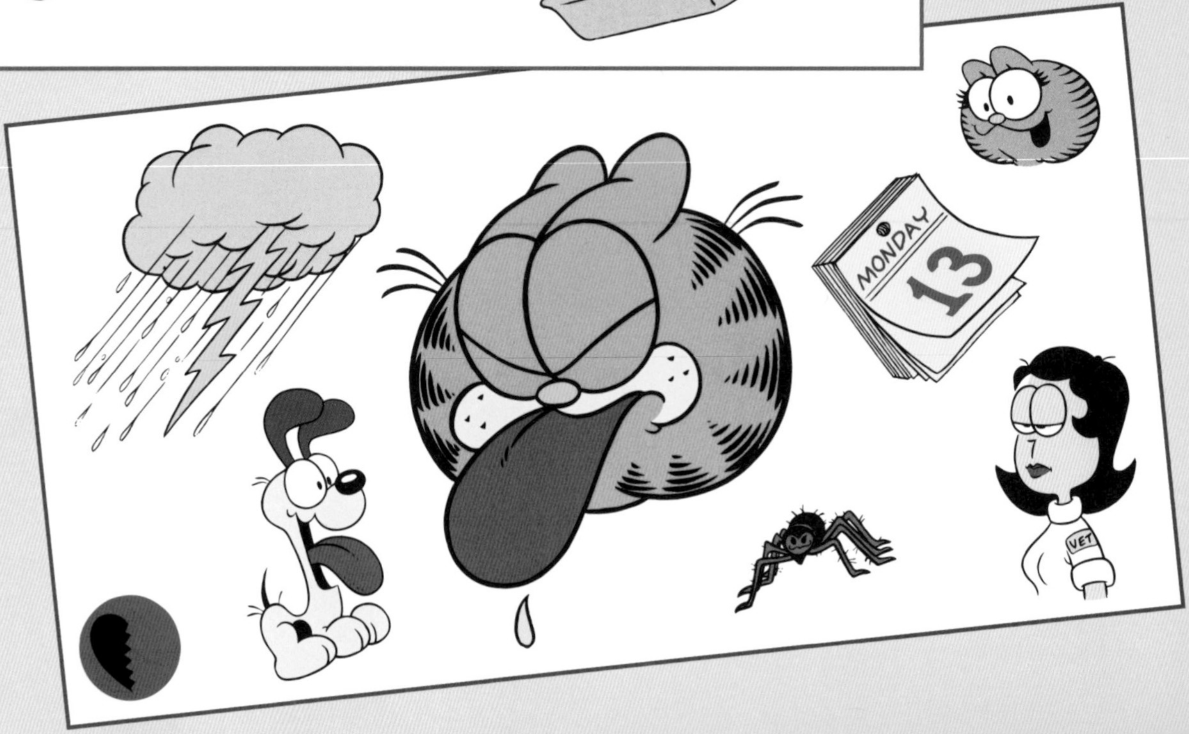
MONDAY
13
VET

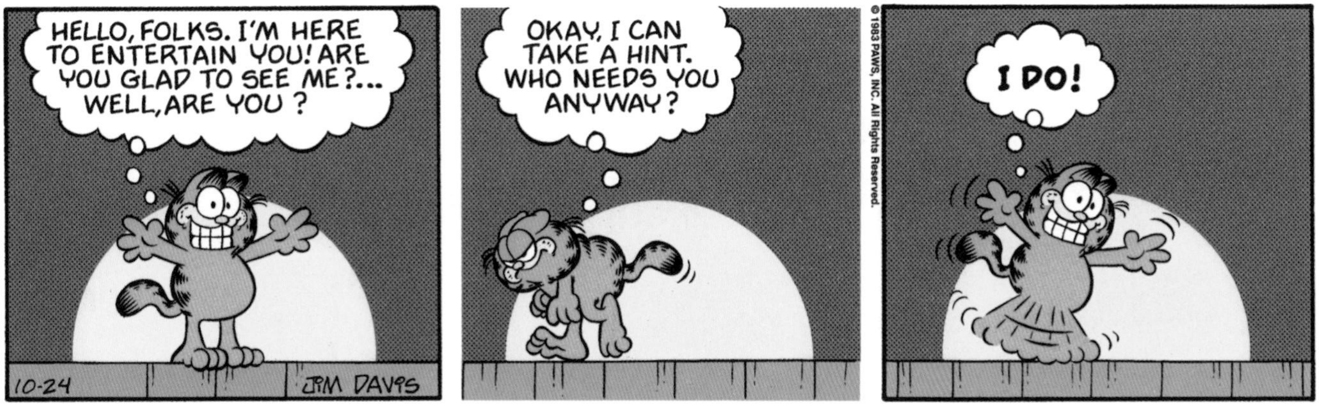
HELLO, FOLKS. I'M HERE TO ENTERTAIN YOU! ARE YOU GLAD TO SEE ME?... WELL, ARE YOU ?
10-24
JIM DAVIS
OKAY, I CAN TAKE A HINT. WHO NEEDS YOU ANYWAY?
© 1983 PAWS, INC. All Rights Reserved.
I DO!

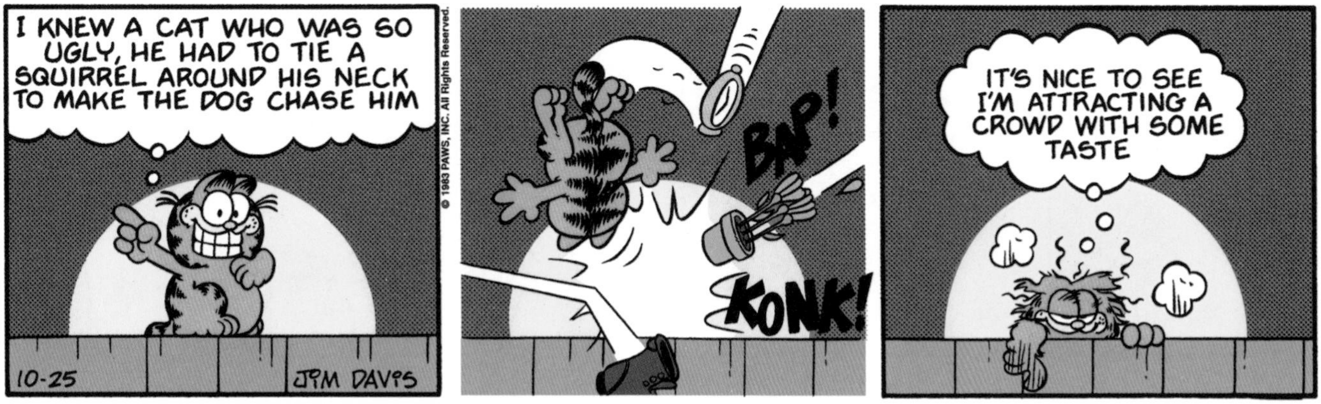
I KNEW A CAT WHO WAS SO UGLY, HE HAD TO TIE A SQUIRREL AROUND HIS NECK TO MAKE THE DOG CHASE HIM
10-25
JIM DAVIS
© 1983 PAWS, INC. All Rights Reserved.
BAP!
KONK!
IT'S NICE TO SEE I'M ATTRACTING A CROWD WITH SOME TASTE

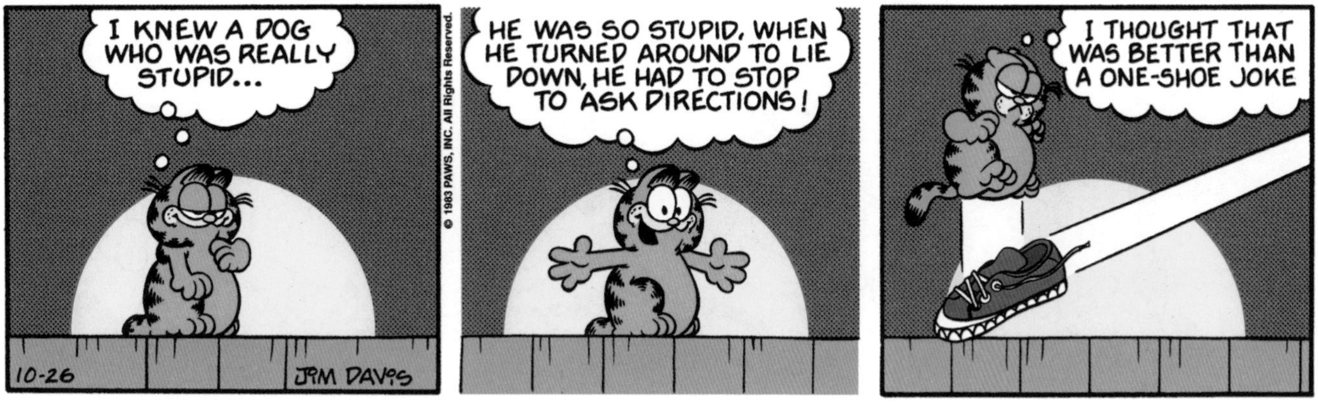
I KNEW A DOG WHO WAS REALLY STUPID...
10-26
JIM DAVIS
© 1983 PAWS, INC. All Rights Reserved.
HE WAS SO STUPID, WHEN HE TURNED AROUND TO LIE DOWN, HE HAD TO STOP TO ASK DIRECTIONS!
I THOUGHT THAT WAS BETTER THAN A ONE-SHOE JOKE

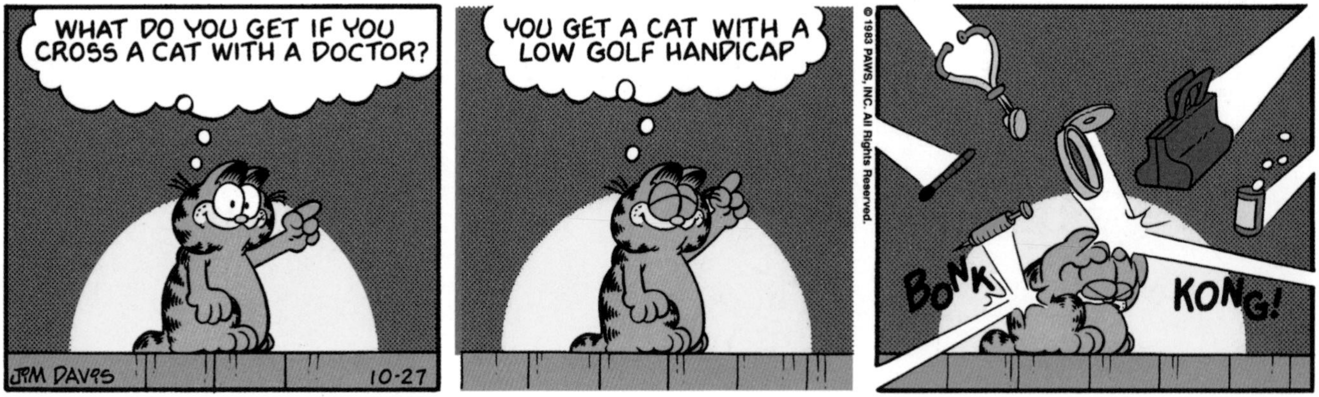
WHAT DO YOU GET IF YOU CROSS A CAT WITH A DOCTOR?
JIM DAVIS
10-27
YOU GET A CAT WITH A LOW GOLF HANDICAP
© 1983 PAWS, INC. All Rights Reserved.
BONK
KONG!

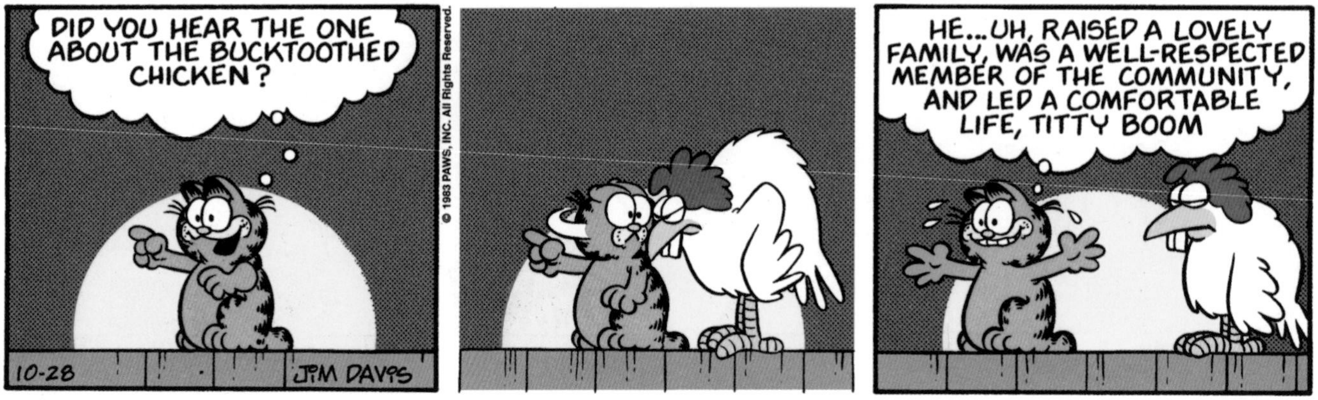
DID YOU HEAR THE ONE ABOUT THE BUCKTOOTHED CHICKEN?
10-28
JIM DAVIS
© 1983 PAWS, INC. All Rights Reserved.
HE...UH, RAISED A LOVELY FAMILY, WAS A WELL-RESPECTED MEMBER OF THE COMMUNITY, AND LED A COMFORTABLE LIFE, TITTY BOOM

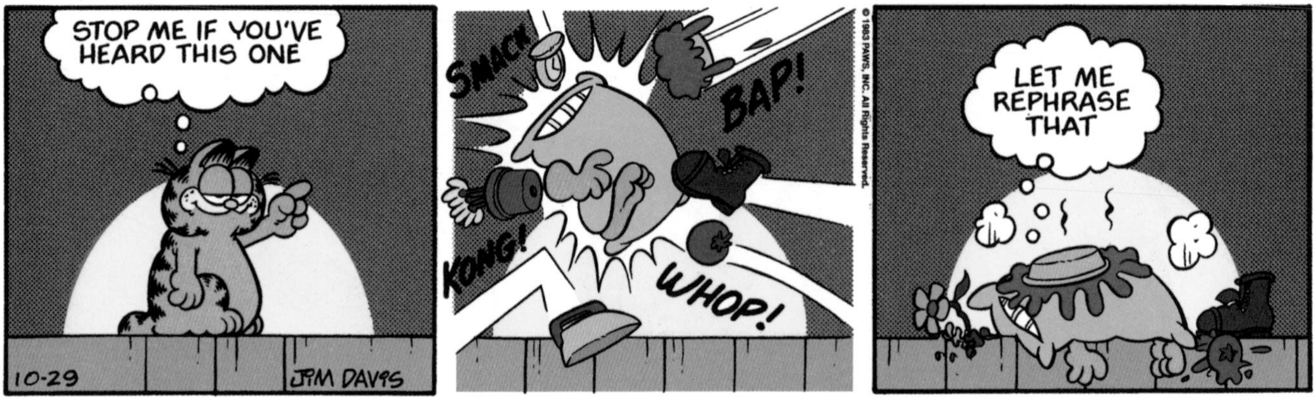
STOP ME IF YOU'VE HEARD THIS ONE
10-29
JIM DAVIS
SMACK
BAP!
KONG!
WHOP!
© 1983 PAWS, INC. All Rights Reserved.
LET ME REPHRASE THAT

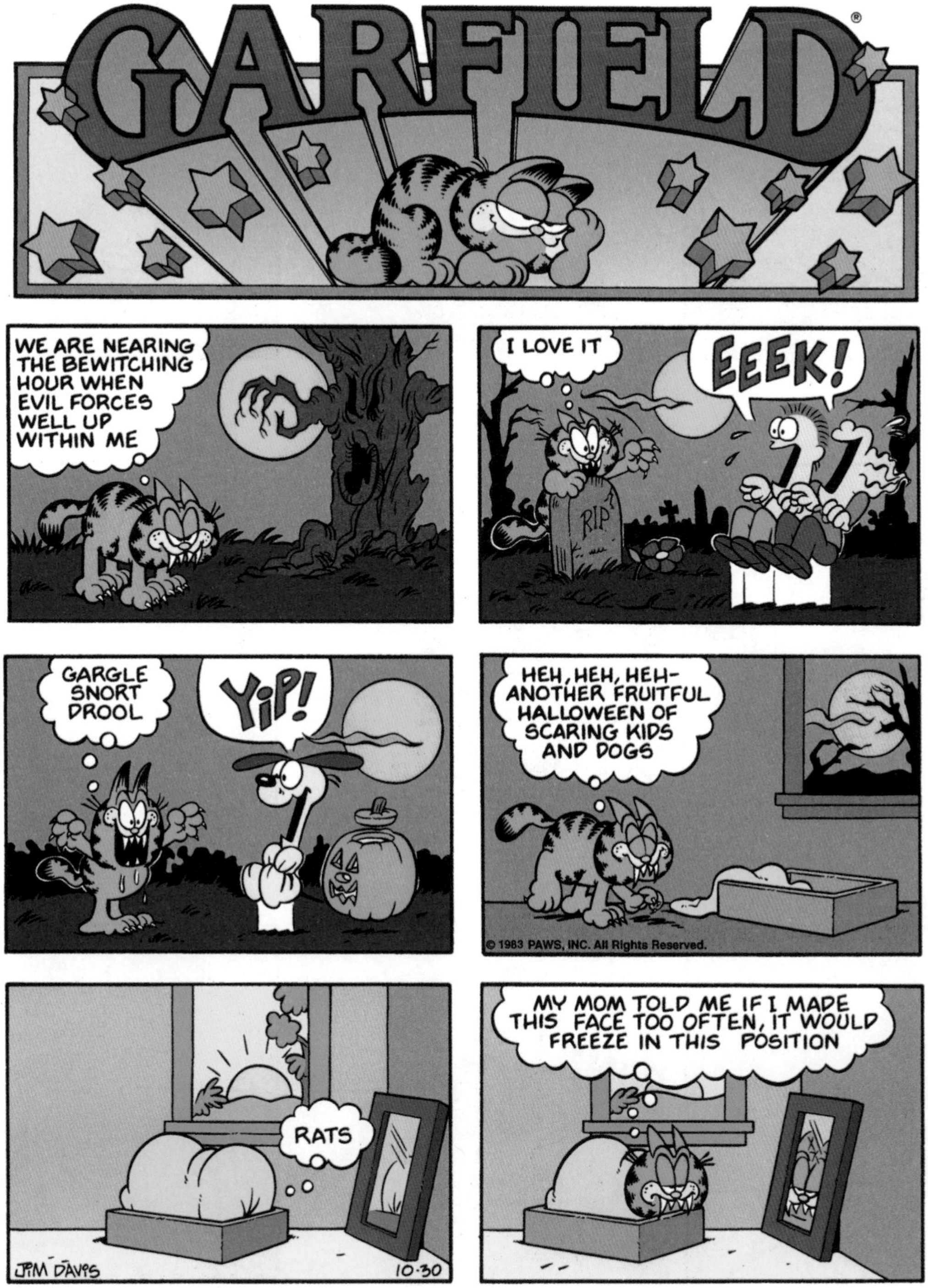
GARFIELD
WE ARE NEARING THE BEWITCHING HOUR WHEN EVIL FORCES WELL UP WITHIN ME
I LOVE IT
EEEK!
RIP
GARGLE SNORT DROOL
YIP!
HEH, HEH, HEH- ANOTHER FRUITFUL HALLOWEEN OF SCARING KIDS AND DOGS
RATS
MY MOM TOLD ME IF I MADE THIS FACE TOO OFTEN, IT WOULD FREEZE IN THIS POSITION
JIM DAVIS
10-30

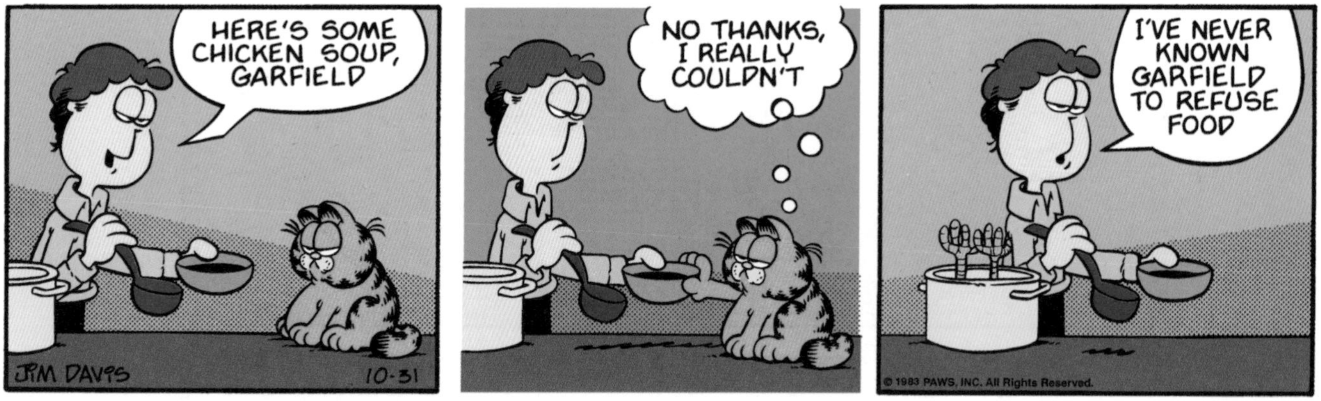
HERE'S SOME CHICKEN SOUP, GARFIELD
NO THANKS, I REALLY COULDN'T
I'VE NEVER KNOWN GARFIELD TO REFUSE FOOD
JIM DAVIS
10-31
© 1983 PAWS, INC. All Rights Reserved.

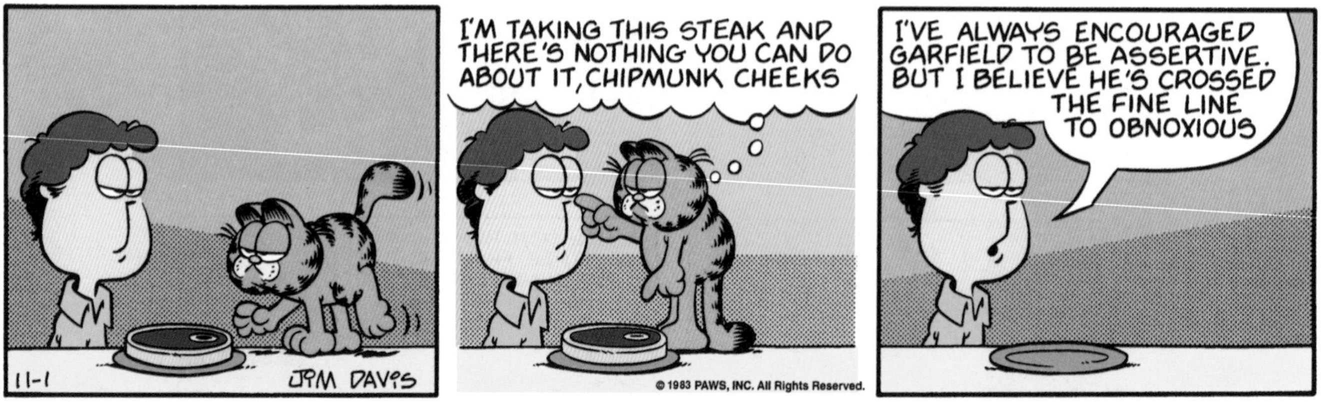
I'M TAKING THIS STEAK AND THERE'S NOTHING YOU CAN DO ABOUT IT, CHIPMUNK CHEEKS
I'VE ALWAYS ENCOURAGED GARFIELD TO BE ASSERTIVE. BUT I BELIEVE HE'S CROSSED THE FINE LINE TO OBNOXIOUS
11-1
JIM DAVIS
© 1983 PAWS, INC. All Rights Reserved.

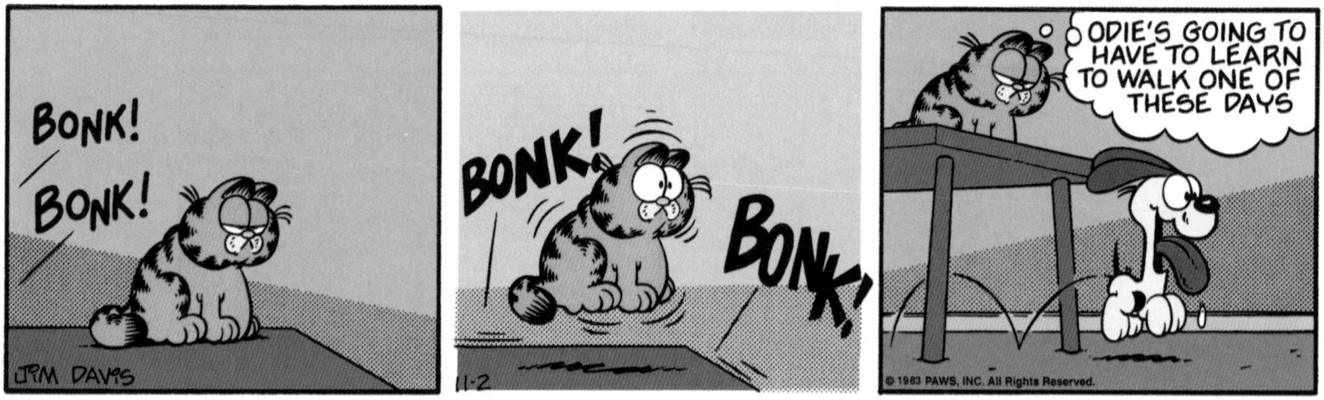
BONK!
BONK!
BONK!
BONK!
ODIE'S GOING TO HAVE TO LEARN TO WALK ONE OF THESE DAYS
JIM DAVIS
11-2
© 1983 PAWS, INC. All Rights Reserved.

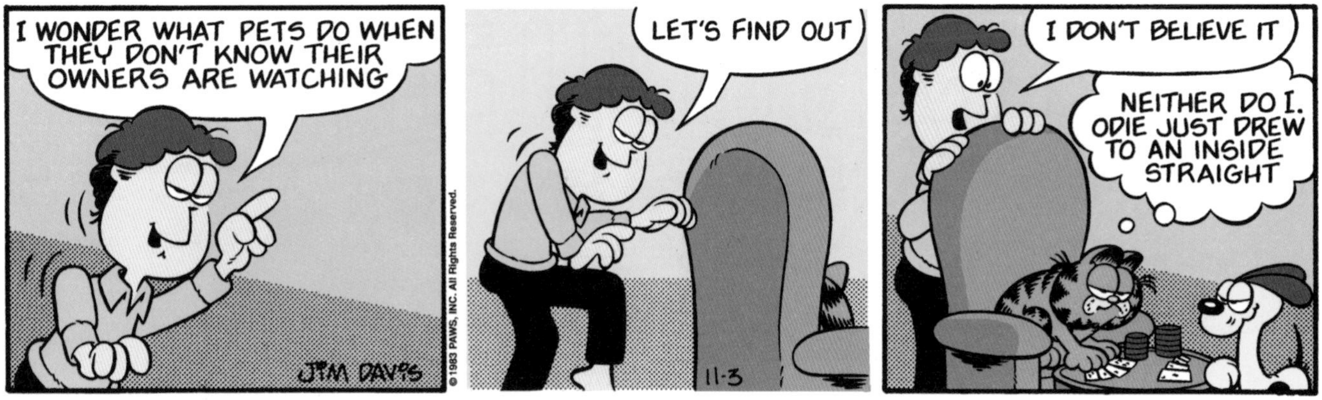
I WONDER WHAT PETS DO WHEN THEY DON'T KNOW THEIR OWNERS ARE WATCHING
JIM DAVIS
LET'S FIND OUT
11-3
I DON'T BELIEVE IT
NEITHER DO I. ODIE JUST DREW TO AN INSIDE STRAIGHT

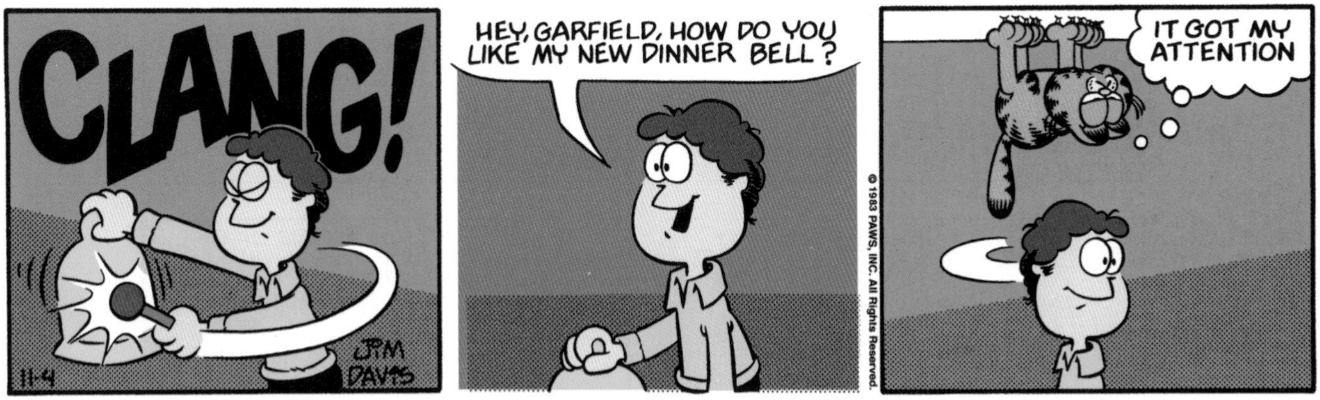
CLANG!
11-4
JIM DAVIS
HEY, GARFIELD, HOW DO YOU LIKE MY NEW DINNER BELL?
IT GOT MY ATTENTION

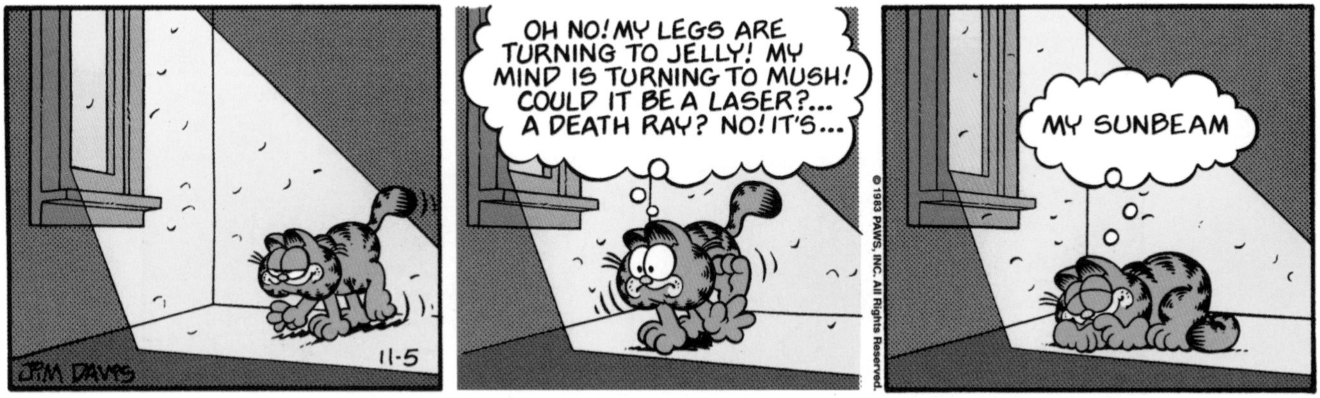
JIM DAVIS
11-5
OH NO! MY LEGS ARE TURNING TO JELLY! MY MIND IS TURNING TO MUSH! COULD IT BE A LASER?... A DEATH RAY? NO! IT'S...
MY SUNBEAM

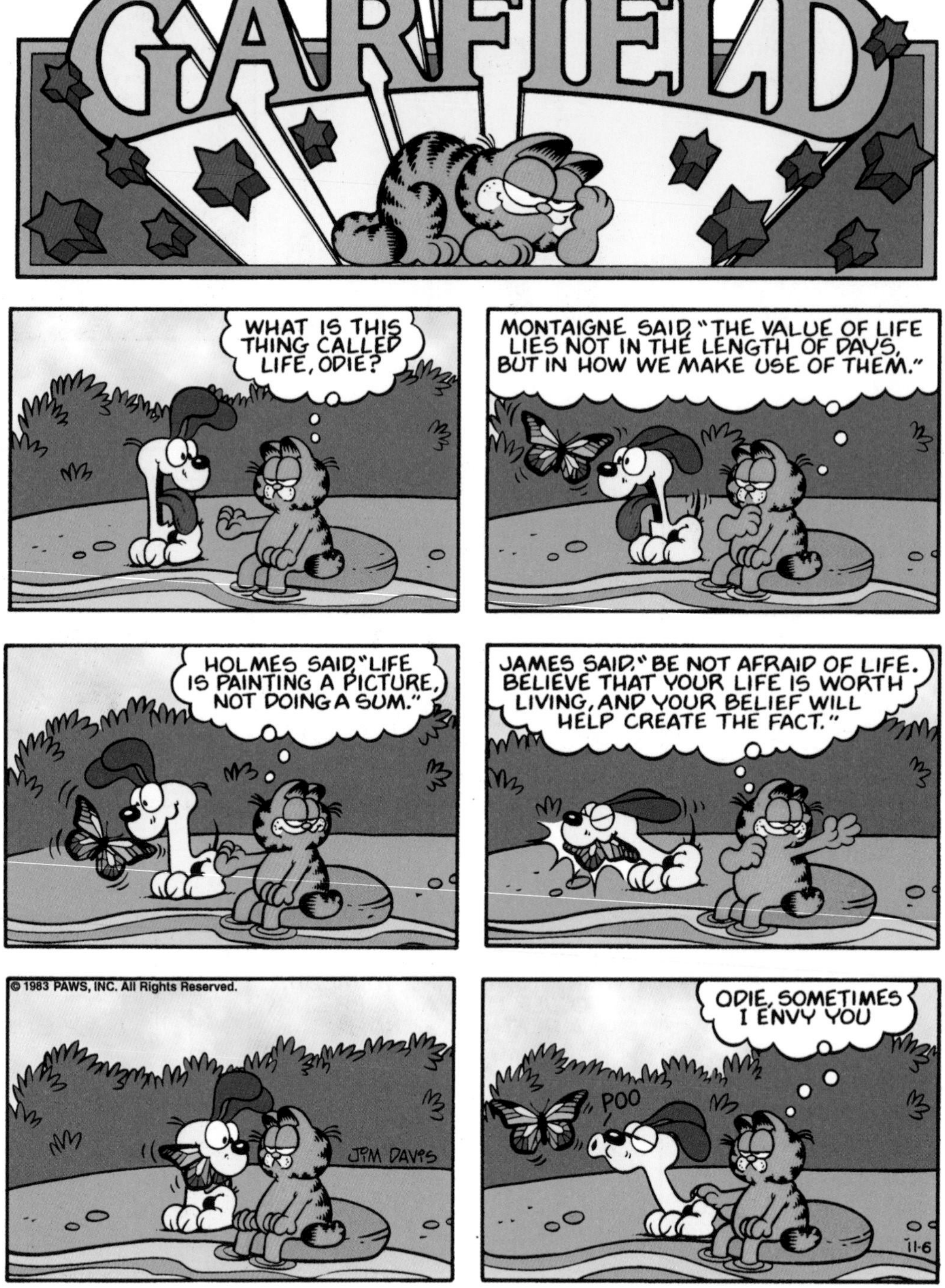
GARFIELD
WHAT IS THIS THING CALLED LIFE, ODIE?
MONTAIGNE SAID, "THE VALUE OF LIFE LIES NOT IN THE LENGTH OF DAYS, BUT IN HOW WE MAKE USE OF THEM."
HOLMES SAID, "LIFE IS PAINTING A PICTURE, NOT DOING A SUM."
JAMES SAID, "BE NOT AFRAID OF LIFE. BELIEVE THAT YOUR LIFE IS WORTH LIVING, AND YOUR BELIEF WILL HELP CREATE THE FACT."
© 1983 PAWS, INC. All Rights Reserved.
JIM DAVIS
ODIE, SOMETIMES I ENVY YOU
POO
11-6

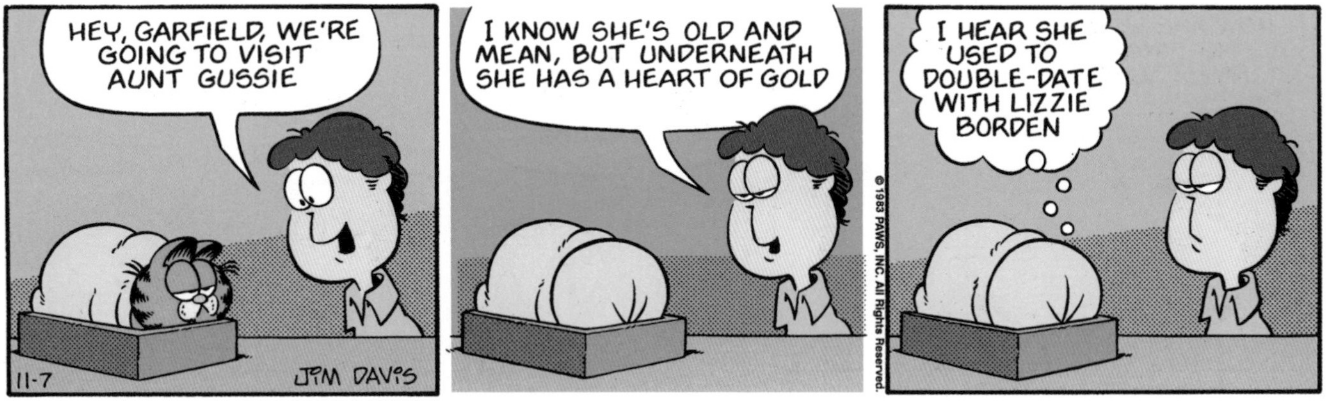
HEY, GARFIELD, WE'RE GOING TO VISIT AUNT GUSSIE
I KNOW SHE'S OLD AND MEAN, BUT UNDERNEATH SHE HAS A HEART OF GOLD
I HEAR SHE USED TO DOUBLE-DATE WITH LIZZIE BORDEN
11-7
JIM DAVIS
© 1983 PAWS, INC. All Rights Reserved.

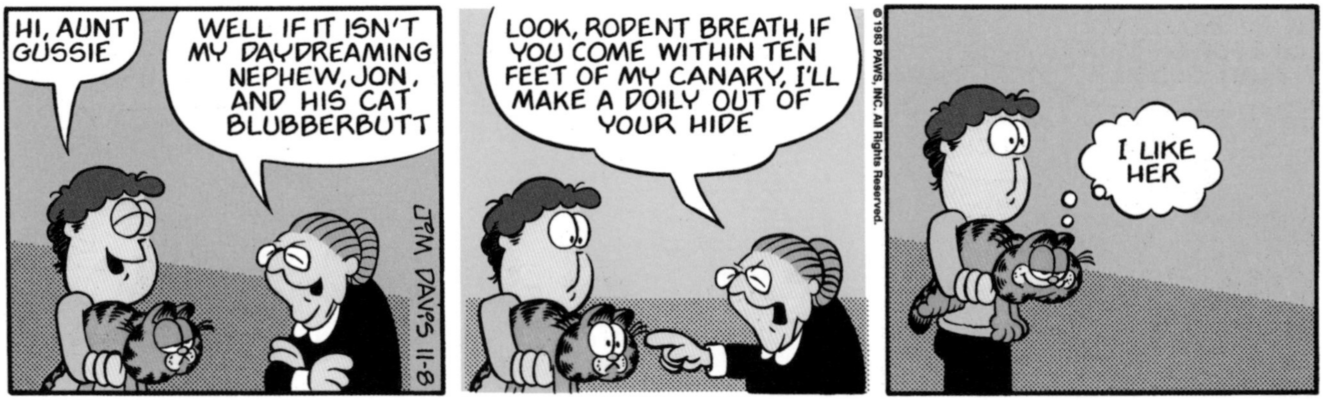
HI, AUNT GUSSIE
WELL IF IT ISN'T MY DAYDREAMING NEPHEW, JON, AND HIS CAT BLUBBERBUTT
LOOK, RODENT BREATH, IF YOU COME WITHIN TEN FEET OF MY CANARY, I'LL MAKE A DOILY OUT OF YOUR HIDE
I LIKE HER
JIM DAVIS 11-8
© 1983 PAWS, INC. All Rights Reserved.

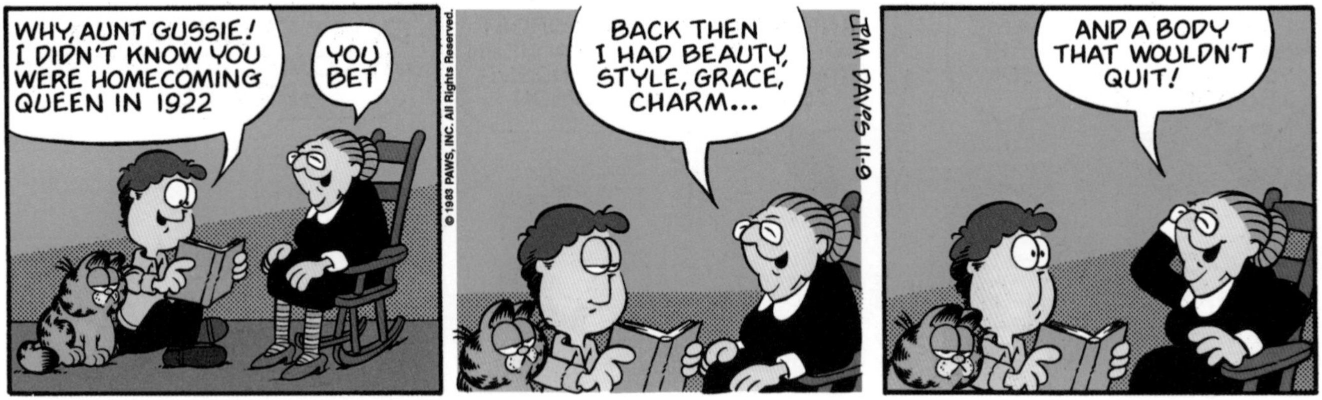
WHY, AUNT GUSSIE! I DIDN'T KNOW YOU WERE HOMECOMING QUEEN IN 1922
YOU BET
BACK THEN I HAD BEAUTY, STYLE, GRACE, CHARM...
AND A BODY THAT WOULDN'T QUIT!
JIM DAVIS 11-9
© 1983 PAWS, INC. All Rights Reserved.

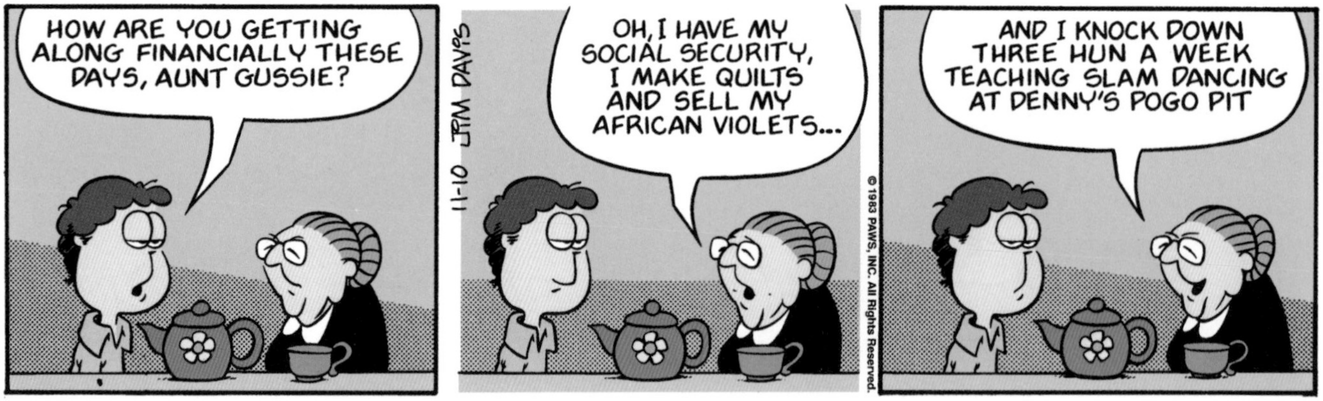
HOW ARE YOU GETTING ALONG FINANCIALLY THESE DAYS, AUNT GUSSIE?
JIM DAVIS 11-10
OH, I HAVE MY SOCIAL SECURITY, I MAKE QUILTS AND SELL MY AFRICAN VIOLETS...
© 1983 PAWS, INC. All Rights Reserved.
AND I KNOCK DOWN THREE HUN A WEEK TEACHING SLAM DANCING AT DENNY'S POGO PIT

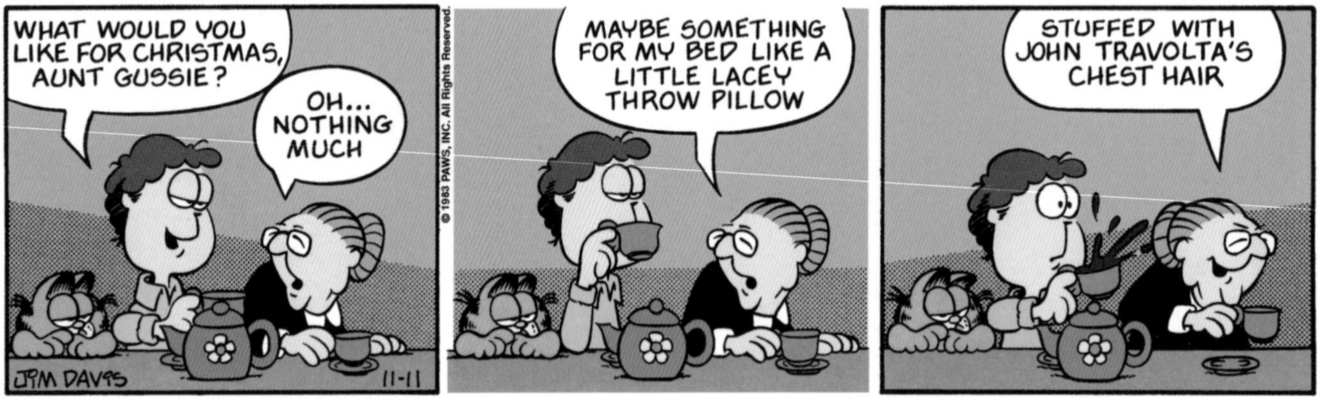
WHAT WOULD YOU LIKE FOR CHRISTMAS, AUNT GUSSIE?
OH... NOTHING MUCH
JIM DAVIS 11-11
© 1983 PAWS, INC. All Rights Reserved.
MAYBE SOMETHING FOR MY BED LIKE A LITTLE LACEY THROW PILLOW
STUFFED WITH JOHN TRAVOLTA'S CHEST HAIR

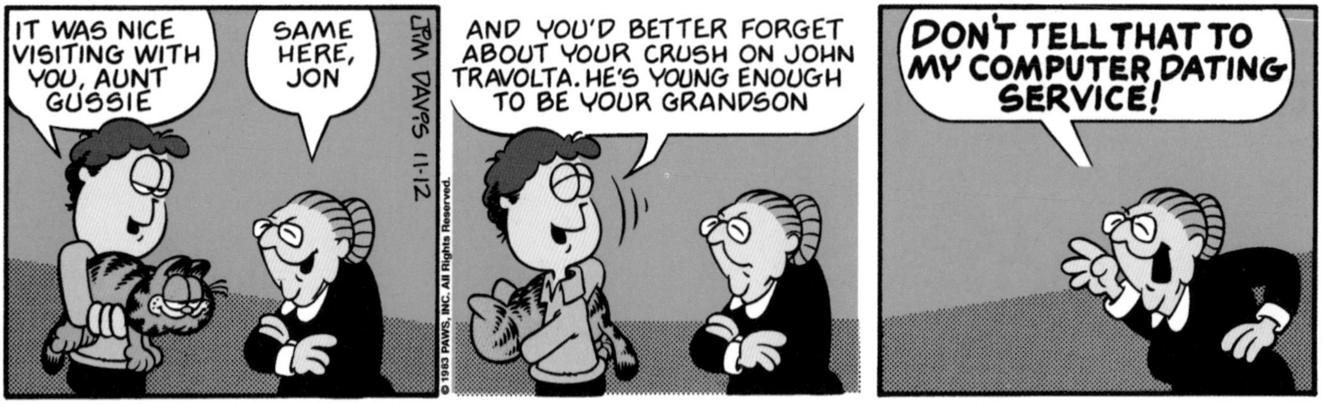
IT WAS NICE VISITING WITH YOU, AUNT GUSSIE
SAME HERE, JON
JIM DAVIS 11-12
© 1983 PAWS, INC. All Rights Reserved.
AND YOU'D BETTER FORGET ABOUT YOUR CRUSH ON JOHN TRAVOLTA. HE'S YOUNG ENOUGH TO BE YOUR GRANDSON
DON'T TELL THAT TO MY COMPUTER DATING SERVICE!

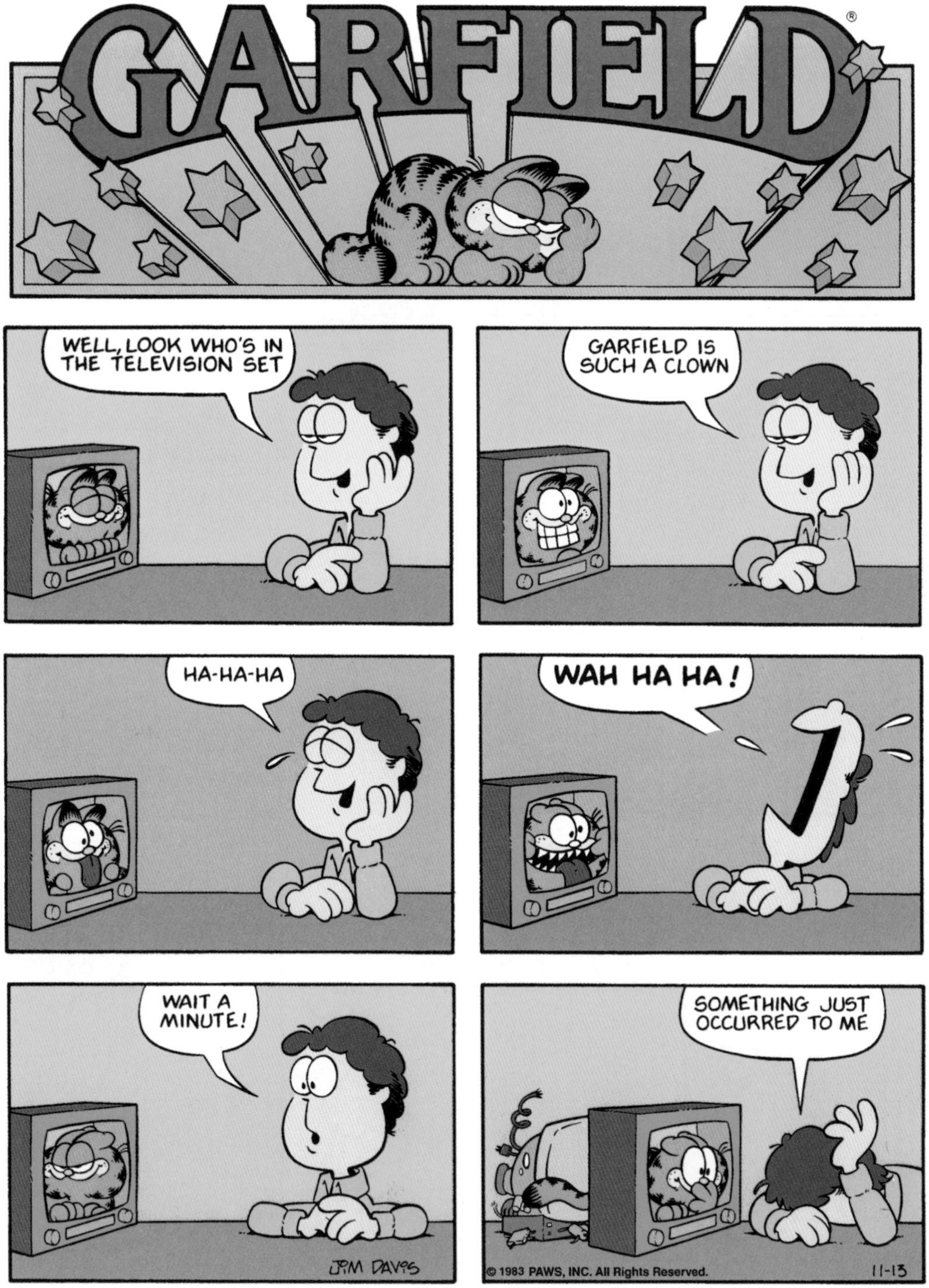
GARFIELD®
WELL, LOOK WHO'S IN THE TELEVISION SET
GARFIELD IS SUCH A CLOWN
HA-HA-HA
WAH HA HA!
WAIT A MINUTE!
SOMETHING JUST OCCURRED TO ME
JIM DAVIS
© 1983 PAWS, INC. All Rights Reserved.
11-13

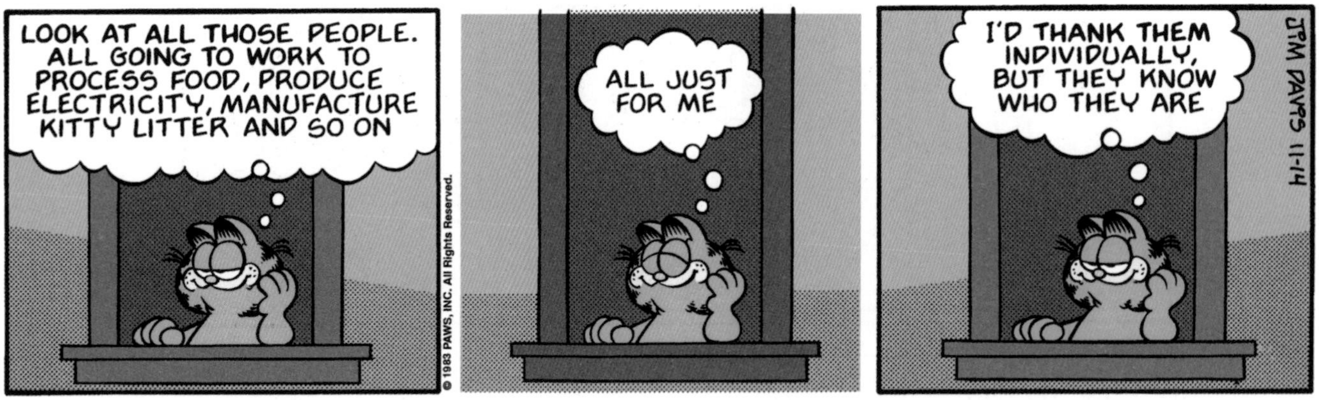
LOOK AT ALL THOSE PEOPLE. ALL GOING TO WORK TO PROCESS FOOD, PRODUCE ELECTRICITY, MANUFACTURE KITTY LITTER AND SO ON
© 1983 PAWS, INC. All Rights Reserved.
ALL JUST FOR ME
I'D THANK THEM INDIVIDUALLY, BUT THEY KNOW WHO THEY ARE
JIM DAVIS 11-14

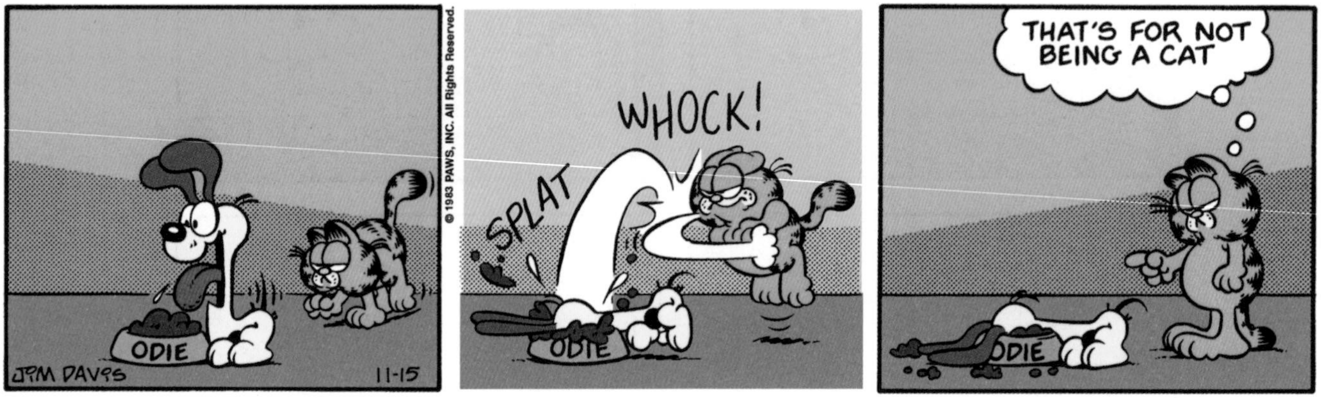
ODIE
JIM DAVIS
11-15
© 1983 PAWS, INC. All Rights Reserved.
WHOCK!
SPLAT
ODIE
THAT'S FOR NOT BEING A CAT
ODIE

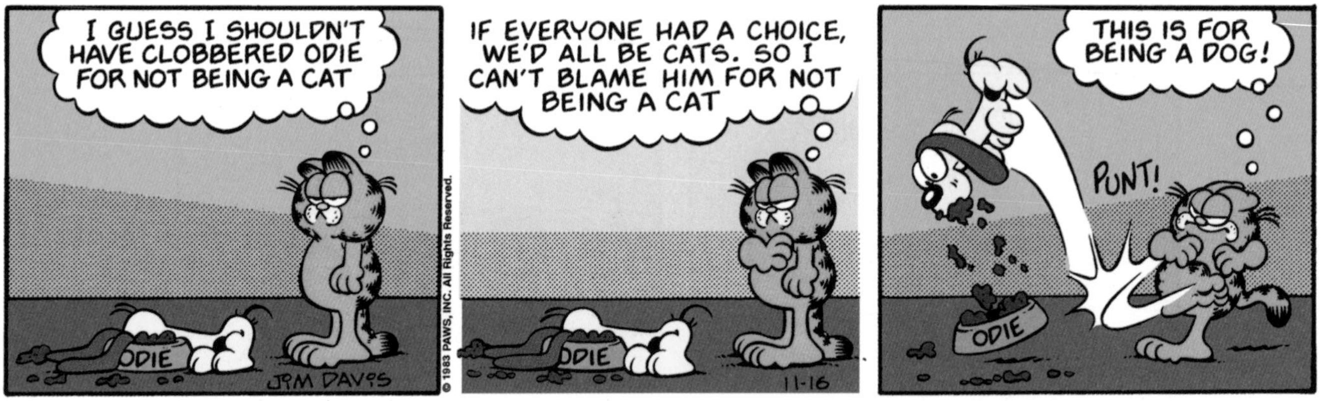
I GUESS I SHOULDN'T HAVE CLOBBERED ODIE FOR NOT BEING A CAT
ODIE
JIM DAVIS
© 1983 PAWS, INC. All Rights Reserved.
IF EVERYONE HAD A CHOICE, WE'D ALL BE CATS. SO I CAN'T BLAME HIM FOR NOT BEING A CAT
ODIE
11-16
THIS IS FOR BEING A DOG!
PUNT!
ODIE

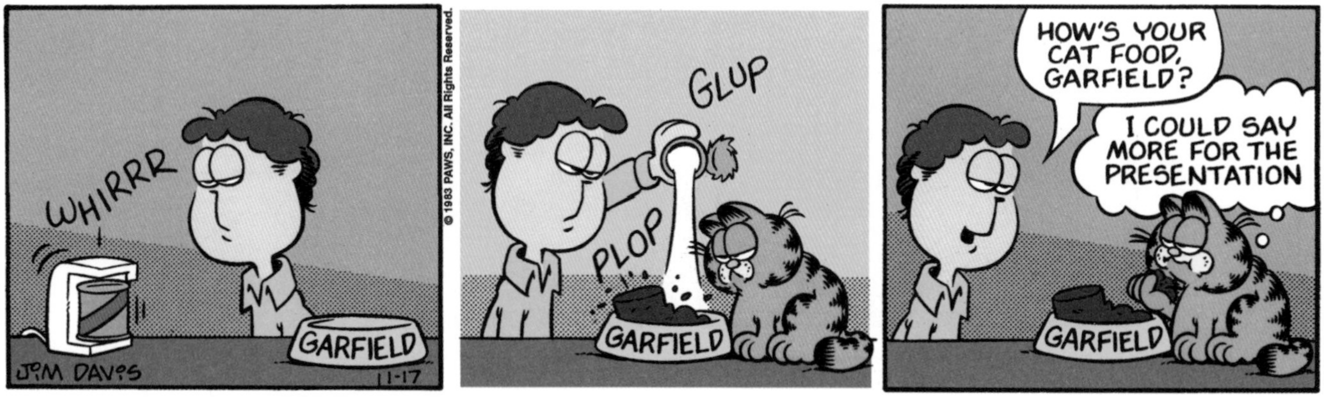
WHIRRR
JIM DAVIS
11-17
© 1983 PAWS, INC. All Rights Reserved.
GARFIELD
GLUP
PLOP
GARFIELD
HOW'S YOUR CAT FOOD, GARFIELD?
I COULD SAY MORE FOR THE PRESENTATION
GARFIELD

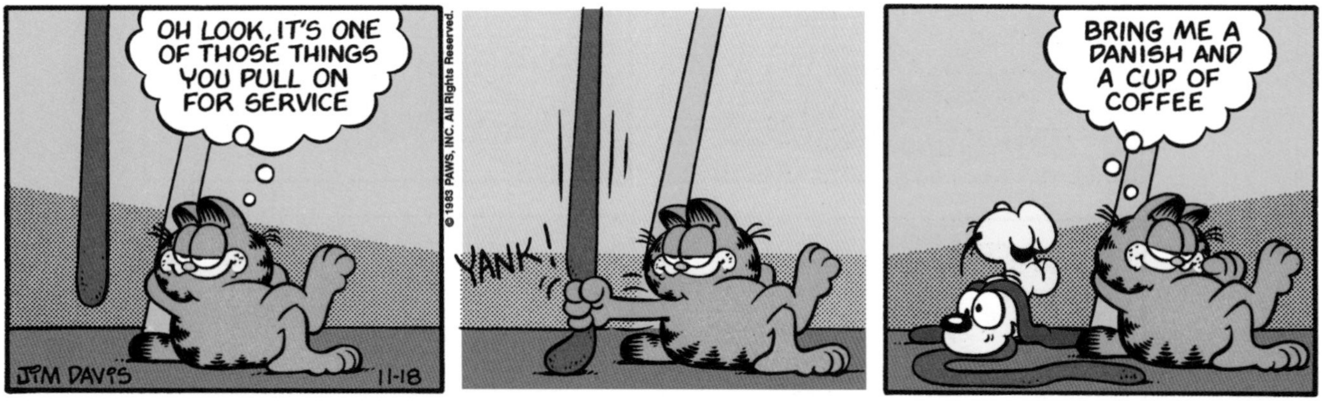
OH LOOK, IT'S ONE OF THOSE THINGS YOU PULL ON FOR SERVICE
JIM DAVIS
11-18
© 1983 PAWS, INC. All Rights Reserved.
YANK!
BRING ME A DANISH AND A CUP OF COFFEE

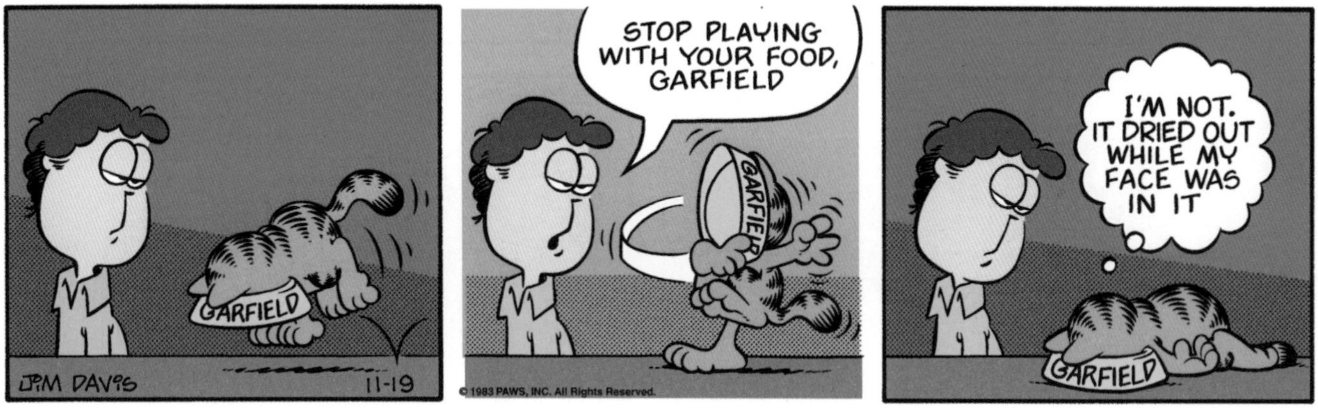
GARFIELD
JIM DAVIS
11-19
STOP PLAYING WITH YOUR FOOD, GARFIELD
GARFIELD
© 1983 PAWS, INC. All Rights Reserved.
I'M NOT. IT DRIED OUT WHILE MY FACE WAS IN IT
GARFIELD

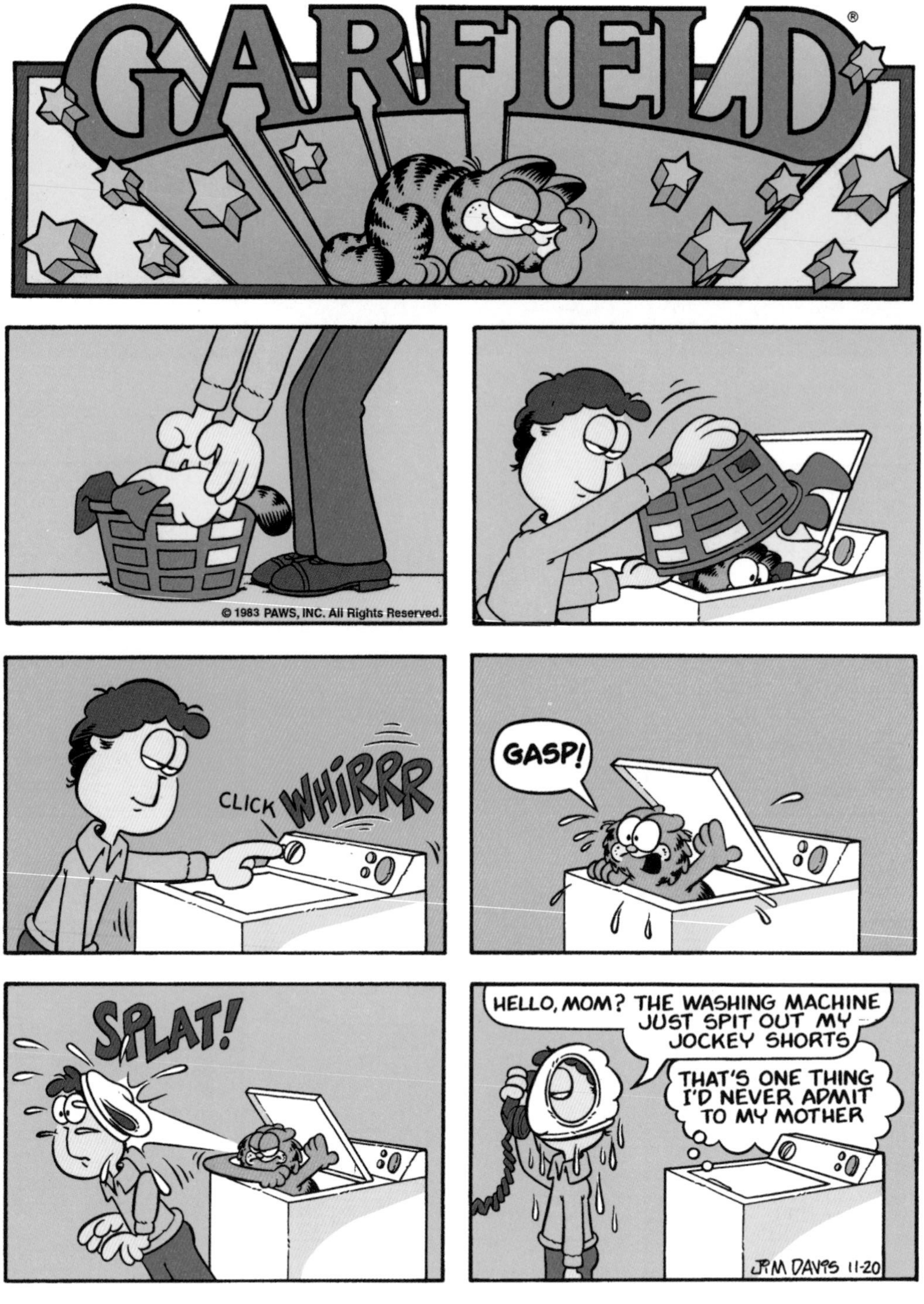
GARFIELD®
© 1983 PAWS, INC. All Rights Reserved.
CLICK
WHIRRR
GASP!
SPLAT!
HELLO, MOM? THE WASHING MACHINE JUST SPIT OUT MY JOCKEY SHORTS
THAT'S ONE THING I'D NEVER ADMIT TO MY MOTHER
JIM DAVIS 11-20

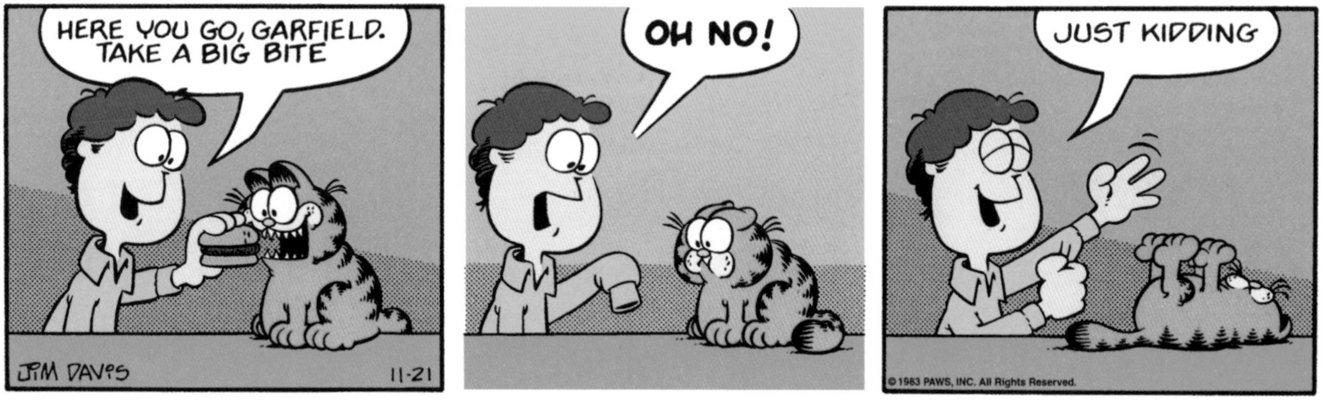
HERE YOU GO, GARFIELD. TAKE A BIG BITE
JIM DAVIS
11-21
OH NO!
JUST KIDDING
© 1983 PAWS, INC. All Rights Reserved.

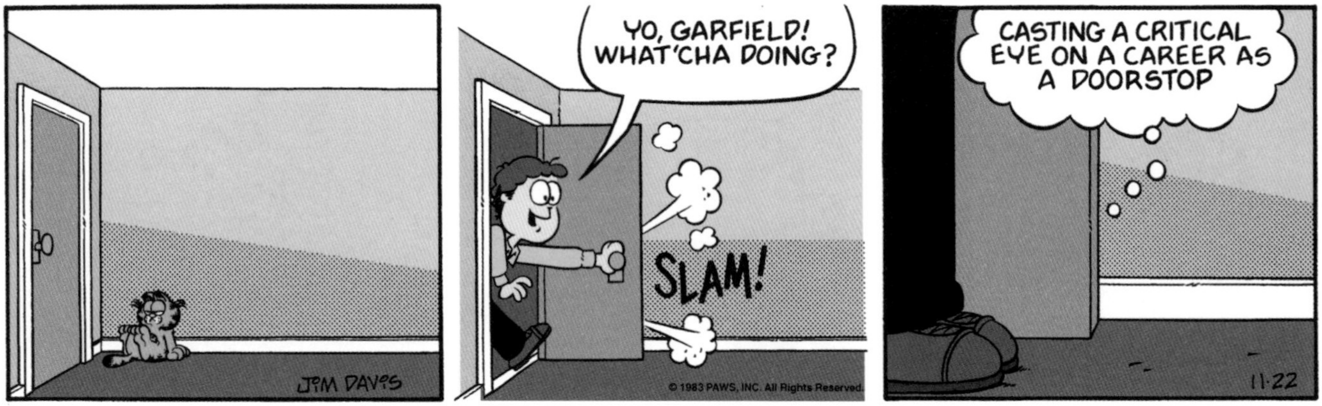
JIM DAVIS
YO, GARFIELD! WHAT'CHA DOING?
SLAM!
© 1983 PAWS, INC. All Rights Reserved.
CASTING A CRITICAL EYE ON A CAREER AS A DOORSTOP
11-22

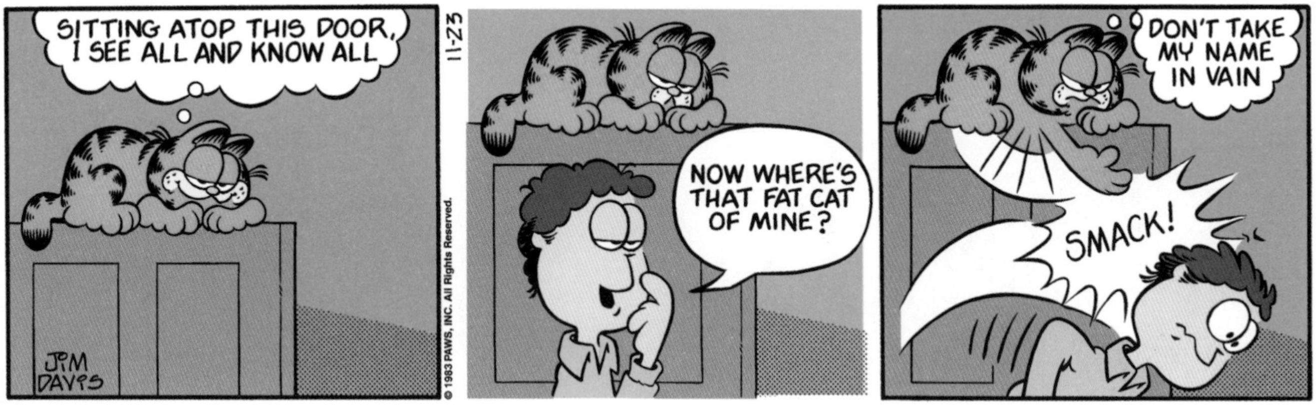
SITTING ATOP THIS DOOR, I SEE ALL AND KNOW ALL
JIM DAVIS
11-23
© 1983 PAWS, INC. All Rights Reserved.
NOW WHERE'S THAT FAT CAT OF MINE?
DON'T TAKE MY NAME IN VAIN
SMACK!

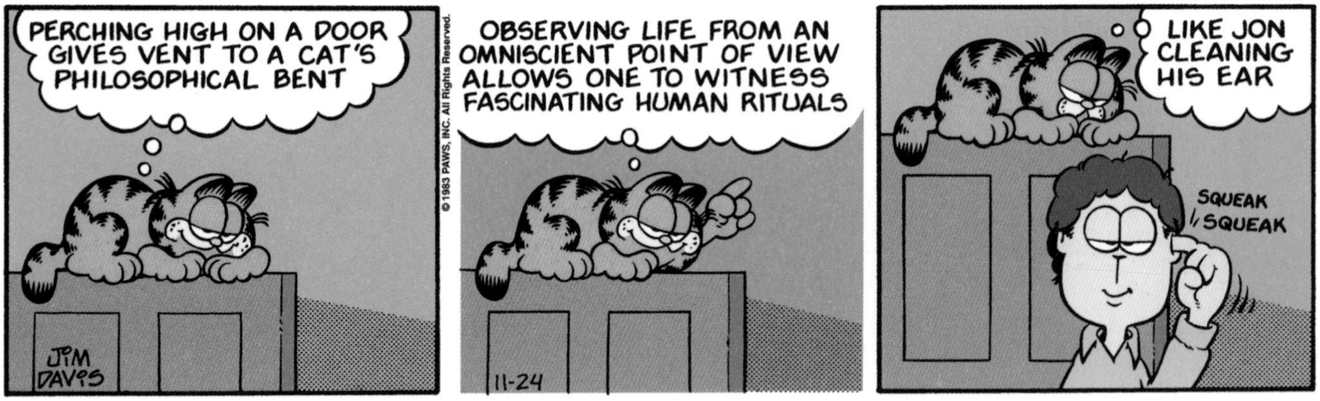
PERCHING HIGH ON A DOOR GIVES VENT TO A CAT'S PHILOSOPHICAL BENT
JIM DAVIS
© 1983 PAWS, INC. All Rights Reserved.
OBSERVING LIFE FROM AN OMNISCIENT POINT OF VIEW ALLOWS ONE TO WITNESS FASCINATING HUMAN RITUALS
11-24
LIKE JON CLEANING HIS EAR
SQUEAK SQUEAK

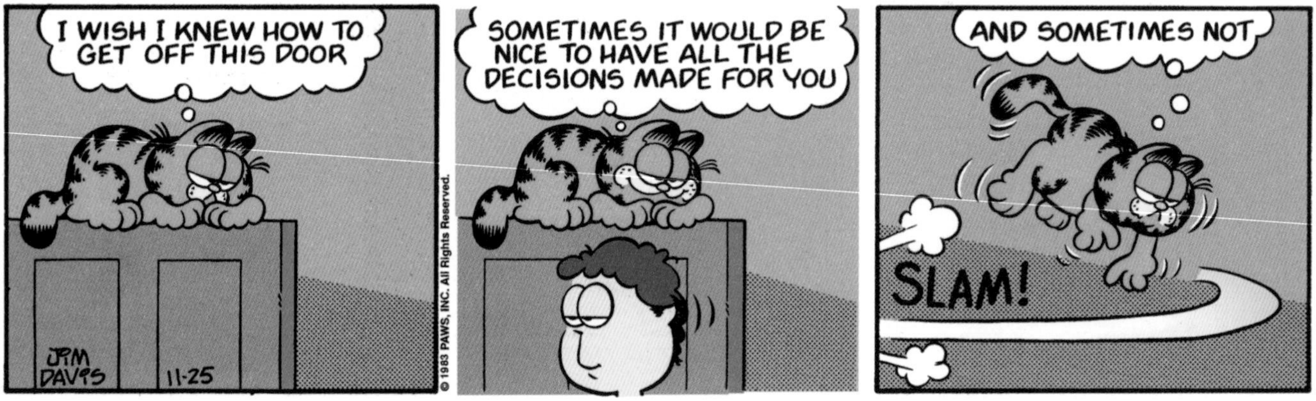
I WISH I KNEW HOW TO GET OFF THIS DOOR
JIM DAVIS
11-25
© 1983 PAWS, INC. All Rights Reserved.
SOMETIMES IT WOULD BE NICE TO HAVE ALL THE DECISIONS MADE FOR YOU
AND SOMETIMES NOT
SLAM!

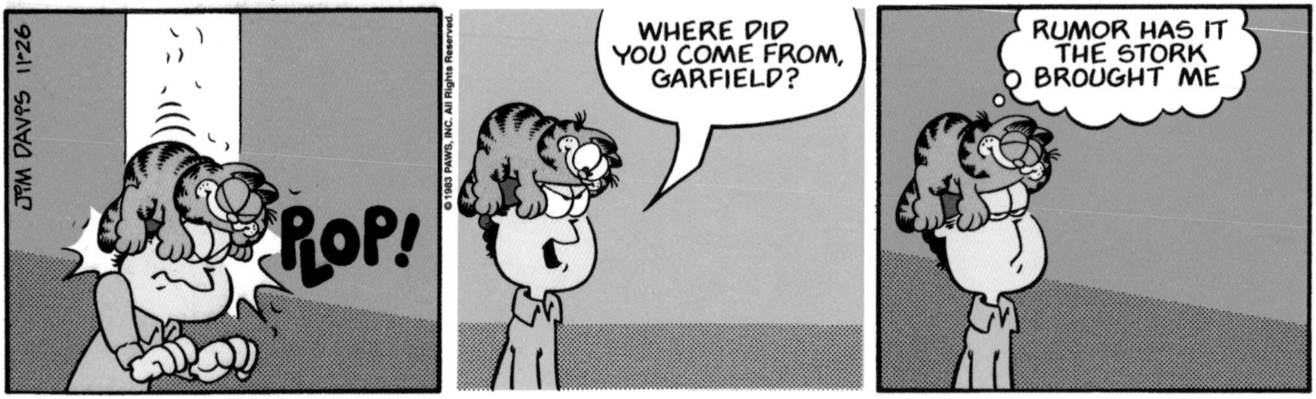
JIM DAVIS 11-26
PLOP!
© 1983 PAWS, INC. All Rights Reserved.
WHERE DID YOU COME FROM, GARFIELD?
RUMOR HAS IT THE STORK BROUGHT ME

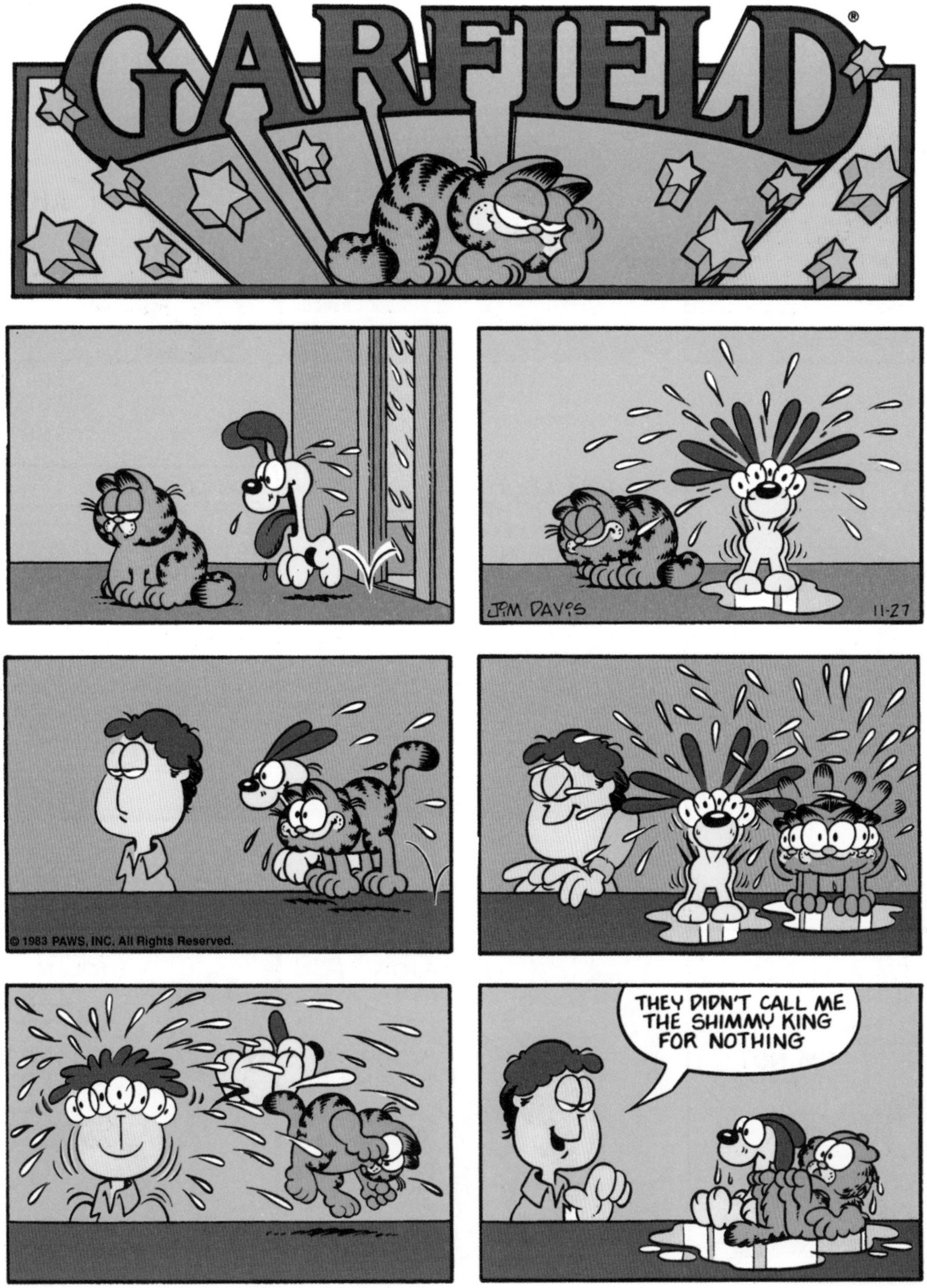
GARFIELD
JIM DAVIS
11-27
© 1983 PAWS, INC. All Rights Reserved.
THEY DIDN'T CALL ME THE SHIMMY KING FOR NOTHING

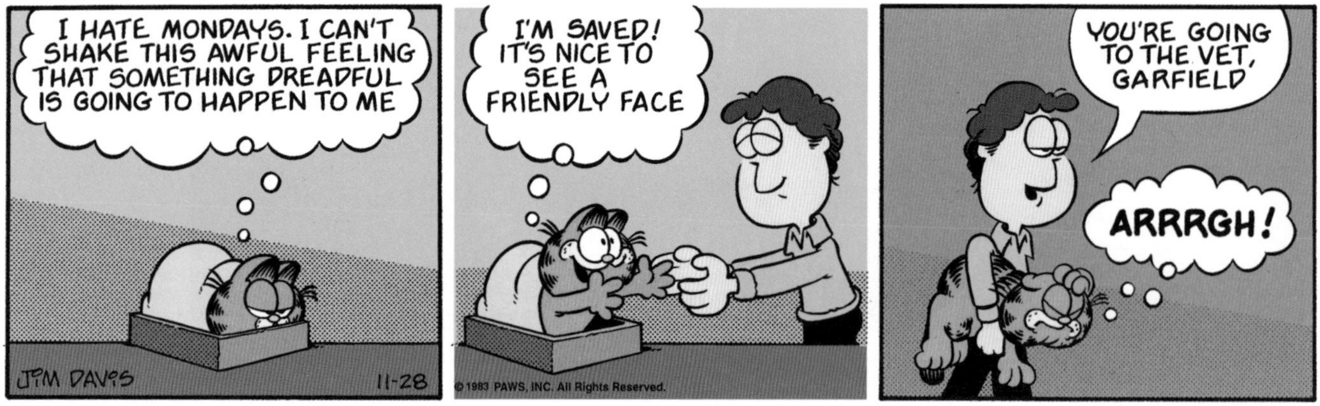
I HATE MONDAYS. I CAN'T SHAKE THIS AWFUL FEELING THAT SOMETHING DREADFUL IS GOING TO HAPPEN TO ME
JIM DAVIS
11-28
I'M SAVED! IT'S NICE TO SEE A FRIENDLY FACE
© 1983 PAWS, INC. All Rights Reserved.
YOU'RE GOING TO THE VET, GARFIELD
ARRRGH!

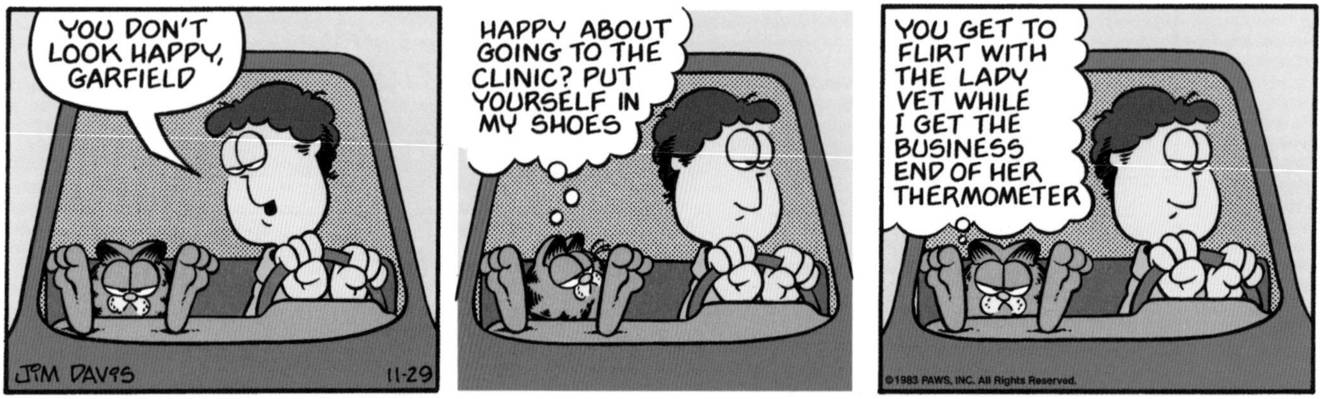
YOU DON'T LOOK HAPPY, GARFIELD
JIM DAVIS
11-29
HAPPY ABOUT GOING TO THE CLINIC? PUT YOURSELF IN MY SHOES
YOU GET TO FLIRT WITH THE LADY VET WHILE I GET THE BUSINESS END OF HER THERMOMETER
©1983 PAWS, INC. All Rights Reserved.

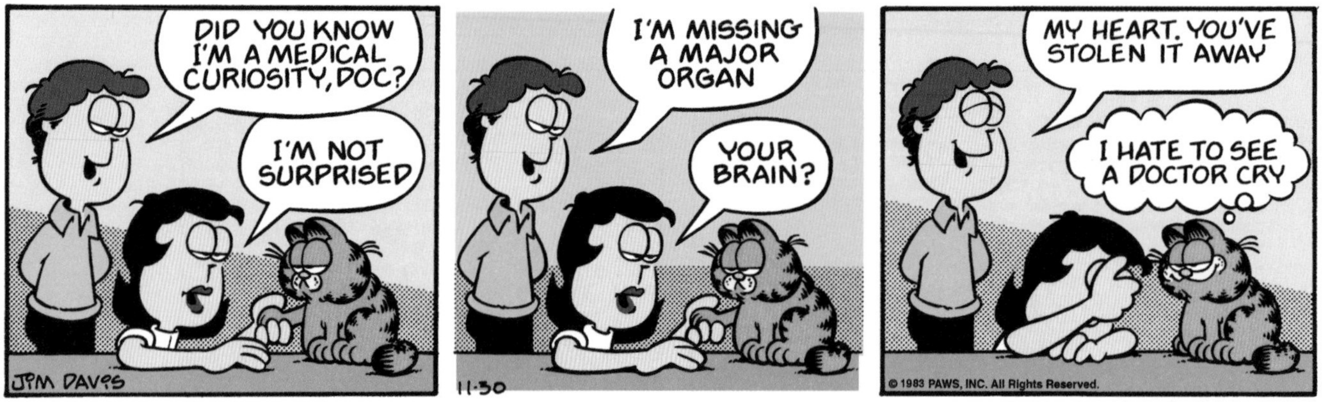
DID YOU KNOW I'M A MEDICAL CURIOSITY, DOC?
I'M NOT SURPRISED
JIM DAVIS
I'M MISSING A MAJOR ORGAN
YOUR BRAIN?
11-30
MY HEART. YOU'VE STOLEN IT AWAY
I HATE TO SEE A DOCTOR CRY
© 1983 PAWS, INC. All Rights Reserved.

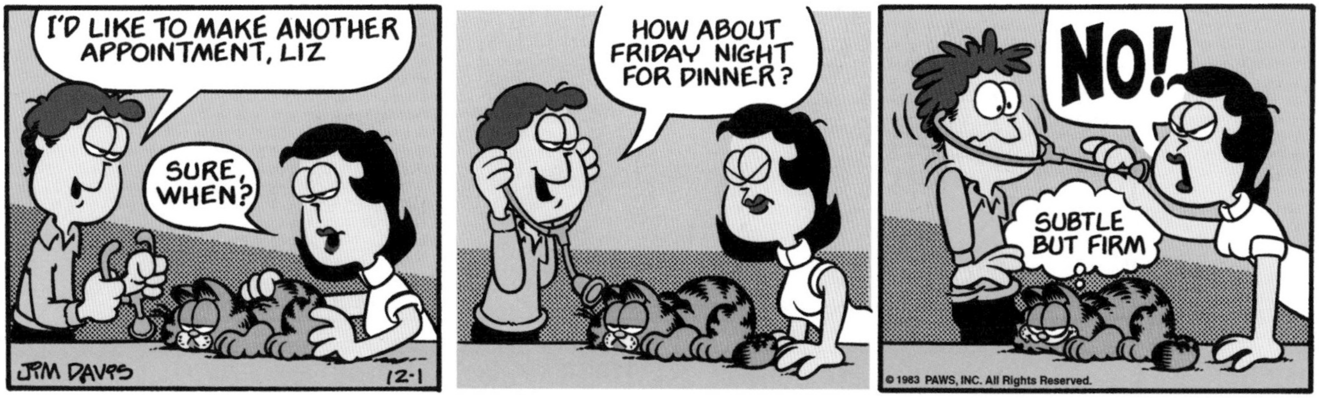
I'D LIKE TO MAKE ANOTHER APPOINTMENT, LIZ
SURE, WHEN?
JIM DAVIS 12-1
HOW ABOUT FRIDAY NIGHT FOR DINNER?
NO!
SUBTLE BUT FIRM
© 1983 PAWS, INC. All Rights Reserved.

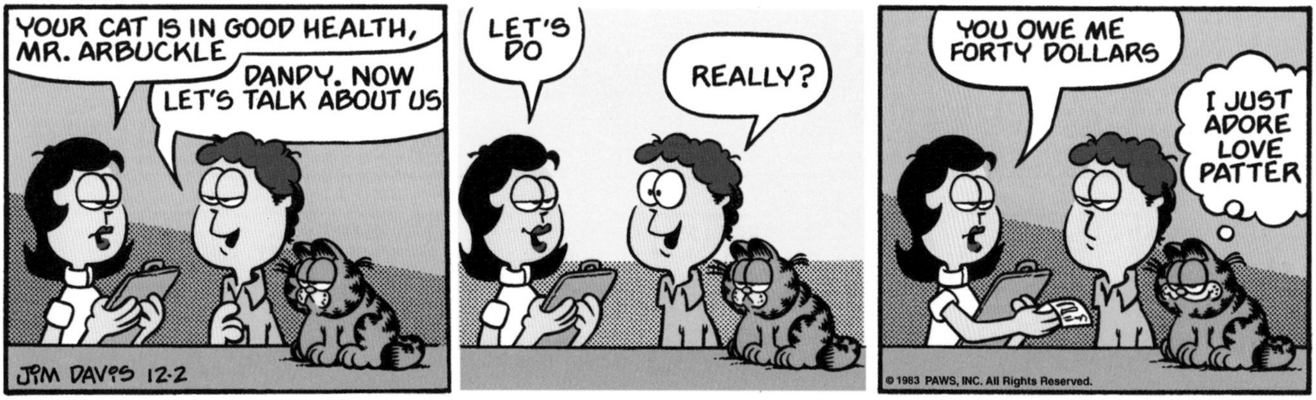
YOUR CAT IS IN GOOD HEALTH, MR. ARBUCKLE
DANDY. NOW LET'S TALK ABOUT US
JIM DAVIS 12-2
LET'S DO
REALLY?
YOU OWE ME FORTY DOLLARS
I JUST ADORE LOVE PATTER
© 1983 PAWS, INC. All Rights Reserved.

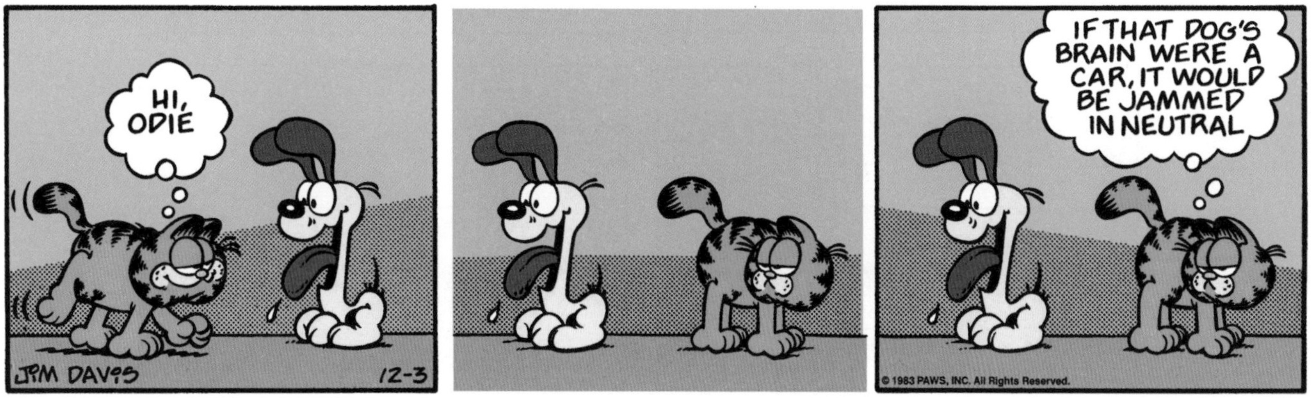
HI, ODIE
JIM DAVIS 12-3
IF THAT DOG'S BRAIN WERE A CAR, IT WOULD BE JAMMED IN NEUTRAL
© 1983 PAWS, INC. All Rights Reserved.

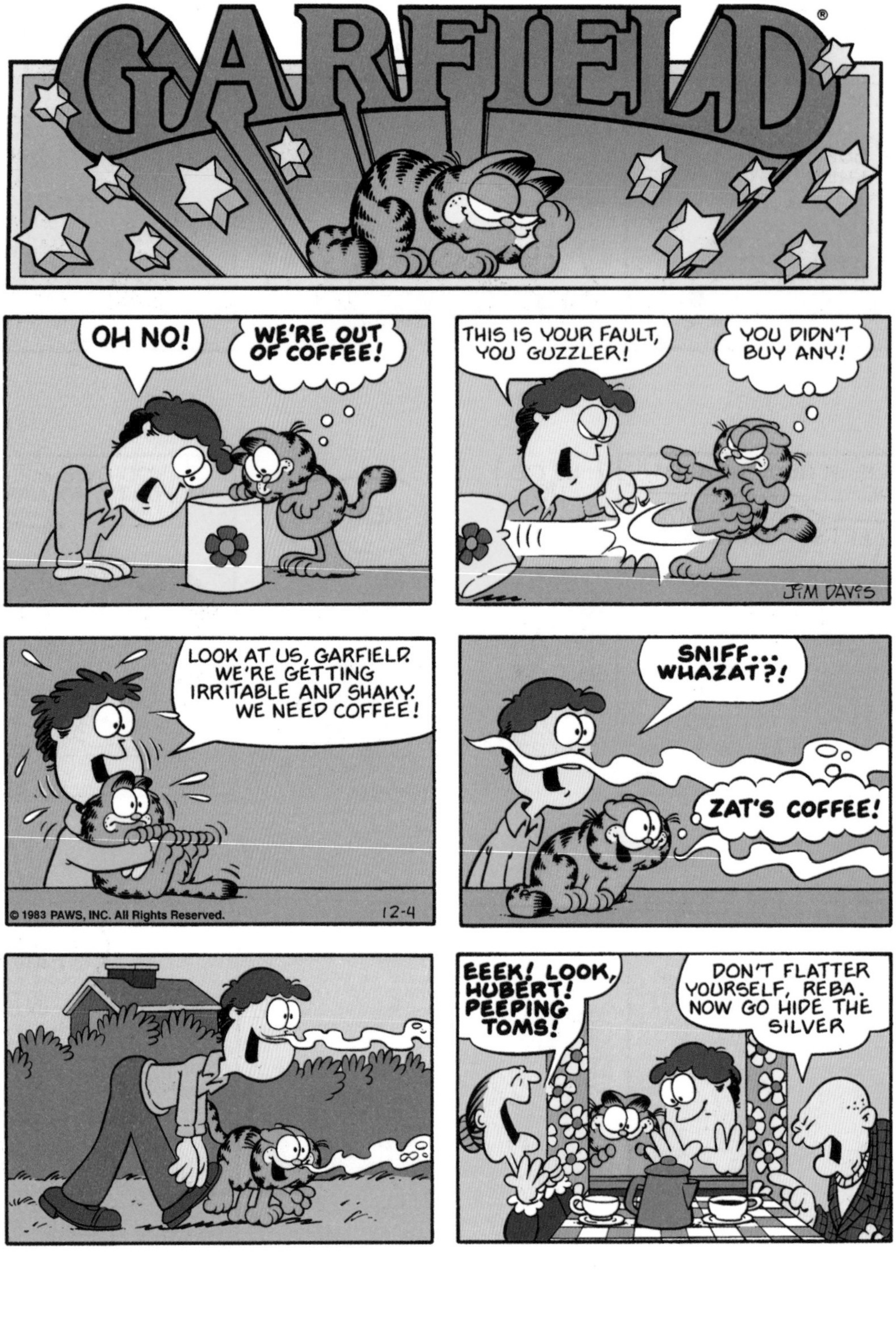
GARFIELD®
OH NO!
WE'RE OUT OF COFFEE!
THIS IS YOUR FAULT, YOU GUZZLER!
YOU DIDN'T BUY ANY!
JIM DAVIS
LOOK AT US, GARFIELD. WE'RE GETTING IRRITABLE AND SHAKY. WE NEED COFFEE!
© 1983 PAWS, INC. All Rights Reserved.
12-4
SNIFF... WHAZAT?!
ZAT'S COFFEE!
EEEK! LOOK, HUBERT! PEEPING TOMS!
DON'T FLATTER YOURSELF, REBA. NOW GO HIDE THE SILVER

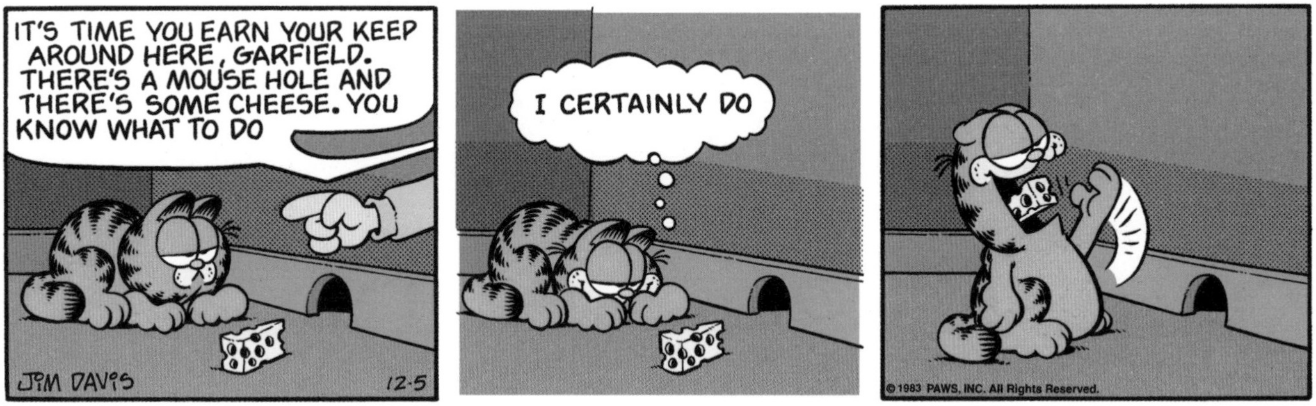
IT'S TIME YOU EARN YOUR KEEP AROUND HERE, GARFIELD. THERE'S A MOUSE HOLE AND THERE'S SOME CHEESE. YOU KNOW WHAT TO DO
JIM DAVIS
12-5
I CERTAINLY DO
© 1983 PAWS, INC. All Rights Reserved.

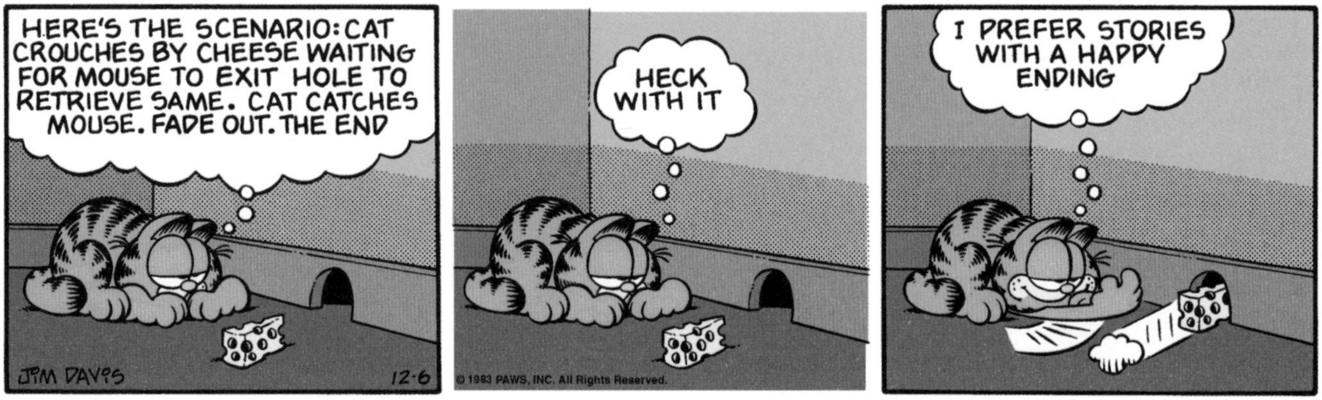
HERE'S THE SCENARIO: CAT CROUCHES BY CHEESE WAITING FOR MOUSE TO EXIT HOLE TO RETRIEVE SAME. CAT CATCHES MOUSE. FADE OUT. THE END
JIM DAVIS
12-6
HECK WITH IT
© 1983 PAWS, INC. All Rights Reserved.
I PREFER STORIES WITH A HAPPY ENDING

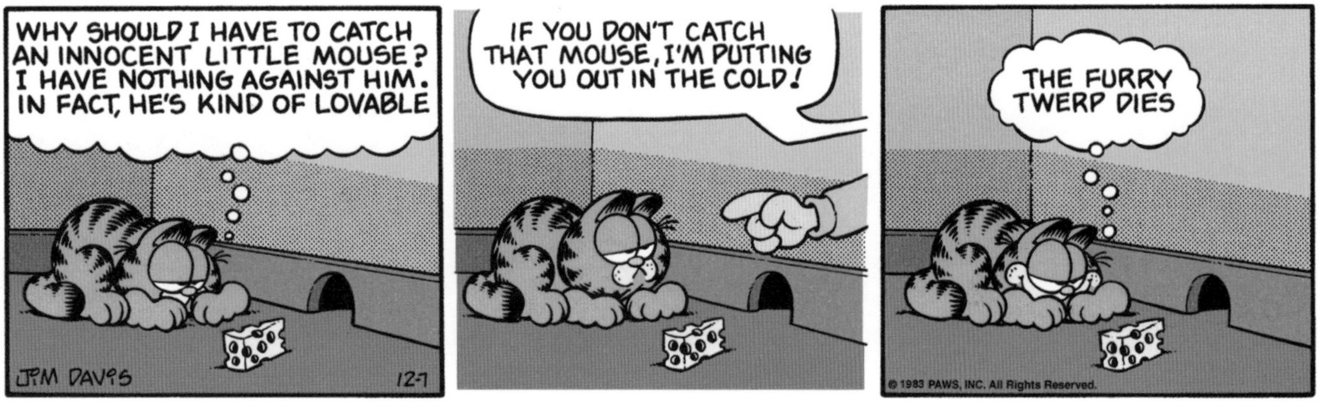
WHY SHOULD I HAVE TO CATCH AN INNOCENT LITTLE MOUSE? I HAVE NOTHING AGAINST HIM. IN FACT, HE'S KIND OF LOVABLE
JIM DAVIS
12-7
IF YOU DON'T CATCH THAT MOUSE, I'M PUTTING YOU OUT IN THE COLD!
THE FURRY TWERP DIES
© 1983 PAWS, INC. All Rights Reserved.

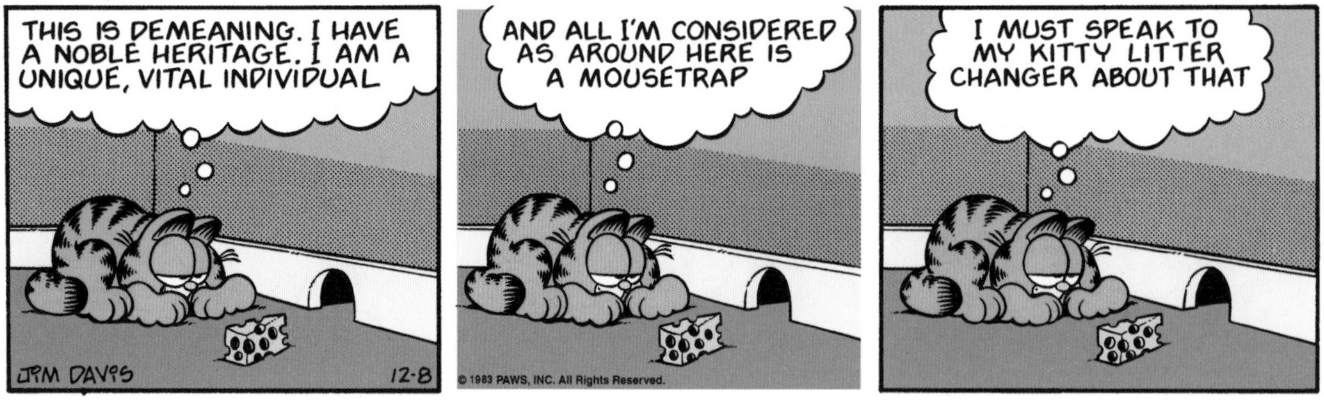
THIS IS DEMEANING. I HAVE A NOBLE HERITAGE. I AM A UNIQUE, VITAL INDIVIDUAL
JIM DAVIS
12-8
AND ALL I'M CONSIDERED AS AROUND HERE IS A MOUSETRAP
© 1983 PAWS, INC. All Rights Reserved.
I MUST SPEAK TO MY KITTY LITTER CHANGER ABOUT THAT

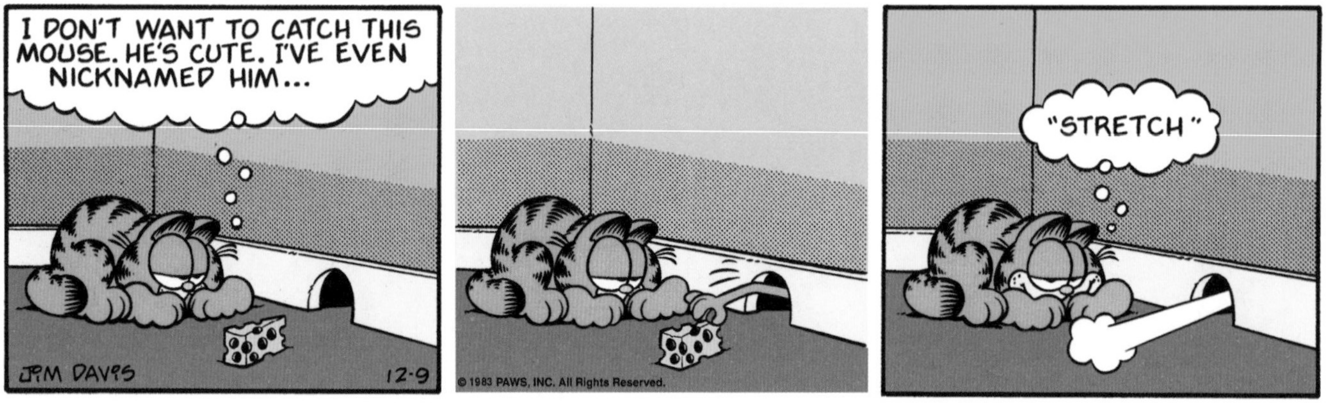
I DON'T WANT TO CATCH THIS MOUSE. HE'S CUTE. I'VE EVEN NICKNAMED HIM...
JIM DAVIS
12-9
© 1983 PAWS, INC. All Rights Reserved.
"STRETCH"

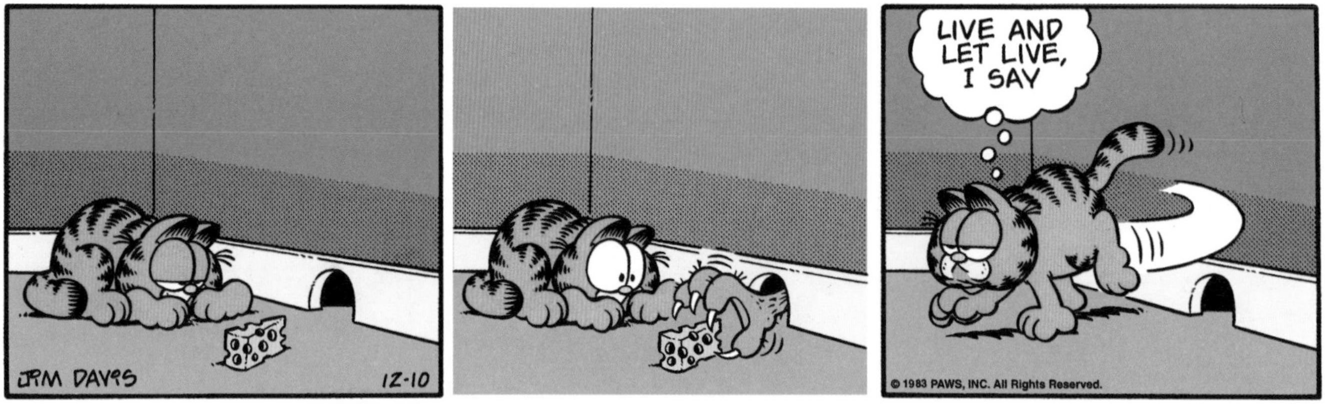
JIM DAVIS
12-10
LIVE AND LET LIVE, I SAY
© 1983 PAWS, INC. All Rights Reserved.

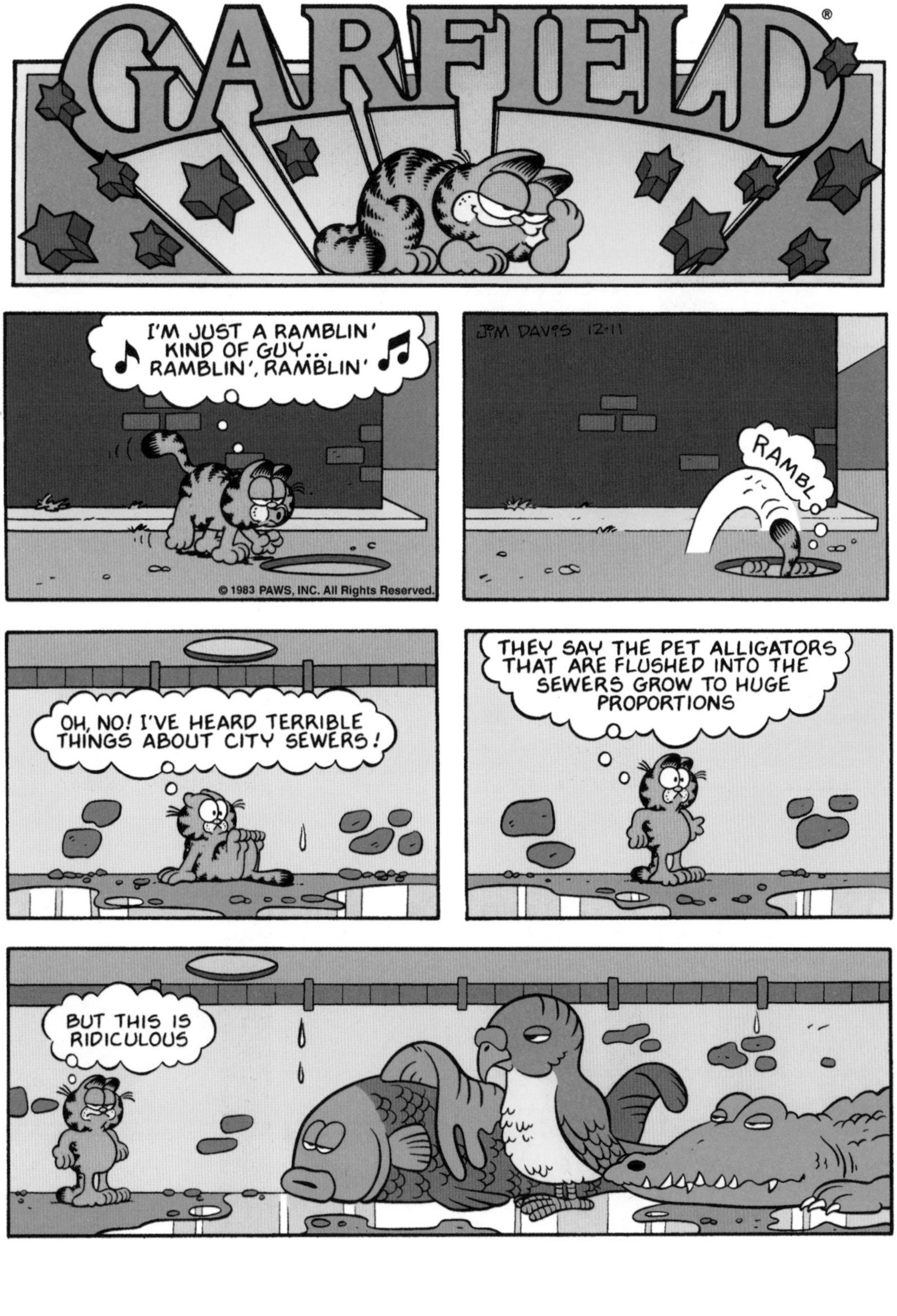
GARFIELD®
I'M JUST A RAMBLIN' KIND OF GUY... RAMBLIN', RAMBLIN'
© 1983 PAWS, INC. All Rights Reserved.
JIM DAVIS 12-11
RAMBL
OH, NO! I'VE HEARD TERRIBLE THINGS ABOUT CITY SEWERS!
THEY SAY THE PET ALLIGATORS THAT ARE FLUSHED INTO THE SEWERS GROW TO HUGE PROPORTIONS
BUT THIS IS RIDICULOUS

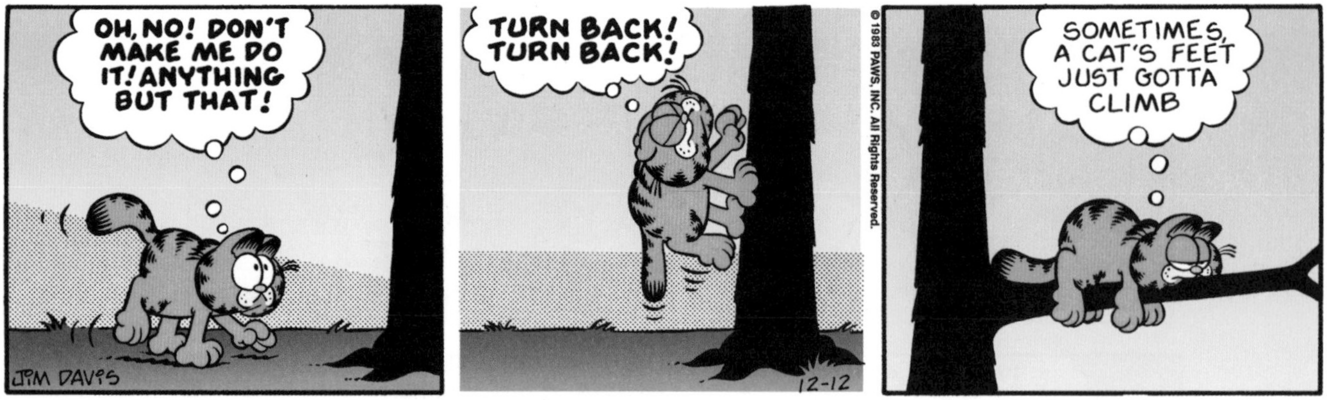
OH, NO! DON'T MAKE ME DO IT! ANYTHING BUT THAT!
JIM DAVIS
TURN BACK! TURN BACK!
12-12
© 1983 PAWS, INC. All Rights Reserved.
SOMETIMES, A CAT'S FEET JUST GOTTA CLIMB

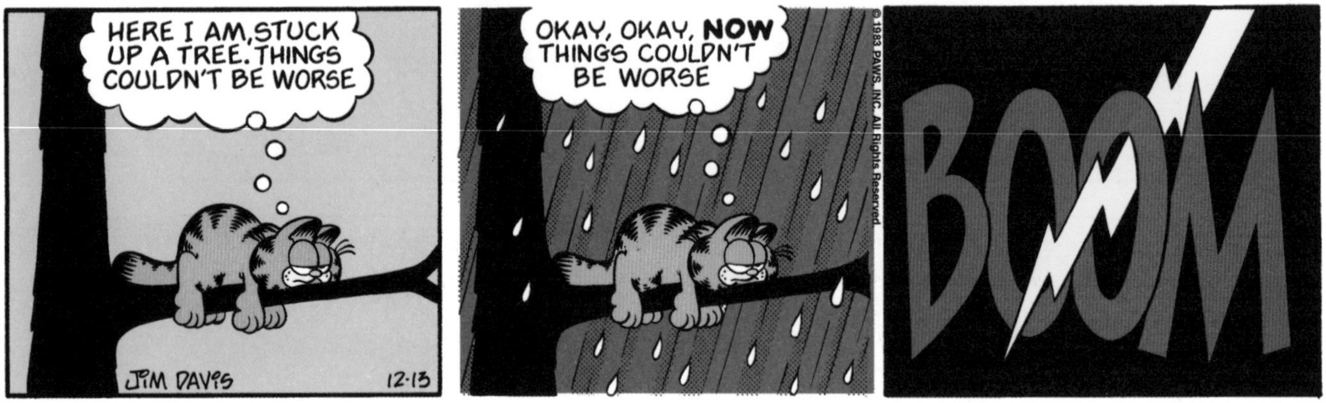
HERE I AM, STUCK UP A TREE. THINGS COULDN'T BE WORSE
JIM DAVIS
12-13
OKAY, OKAY, **NOW** THINGS COULDN'T BE WORSE
© 1983 PAWS, INC. All Rights Reserved.
BOOM

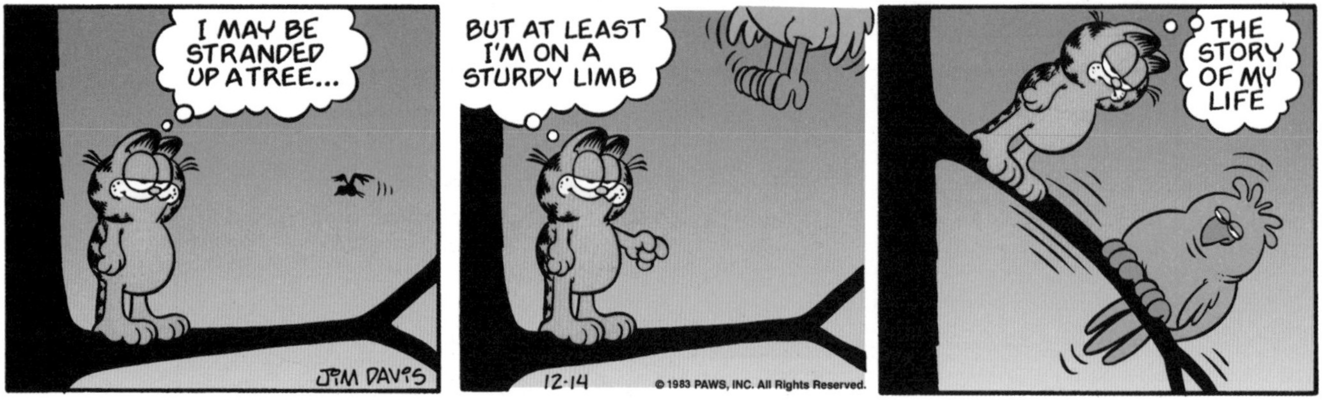
I MAY BE STRANDED UP A TREE...
JIM DAVIS
BUT AT LEAST I'M ON A STURDY LIMB
12-14
© 1983 PAWS, INC. All Rights Reserved.
THE STORY OF MY LIFE

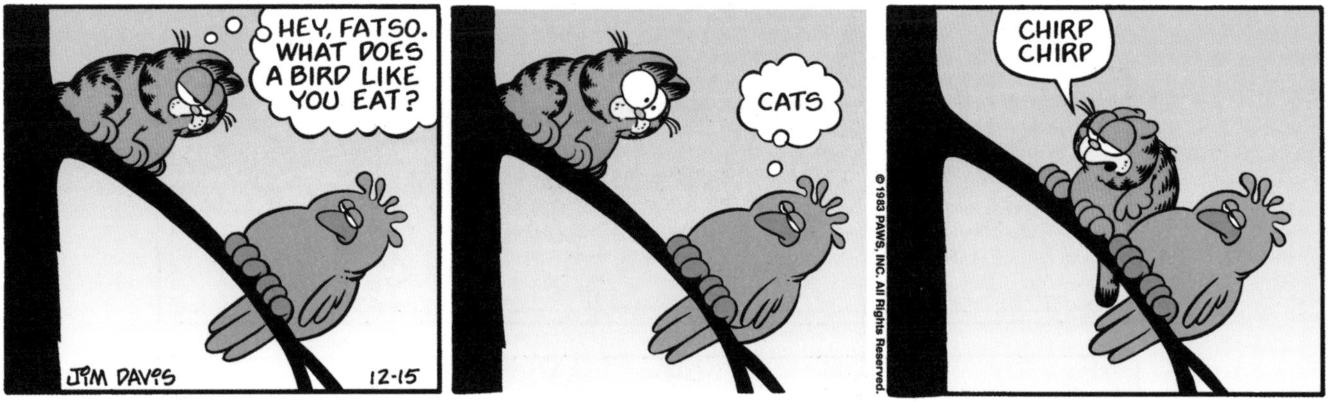
HEY, FATSO. WHAT DOES A BIRD LIKE YOU EAT?
JIM DAVIS
12-15
CATS
© 1983 PAWS, INC. All Rights Reserved.
CHIRP CHIRP

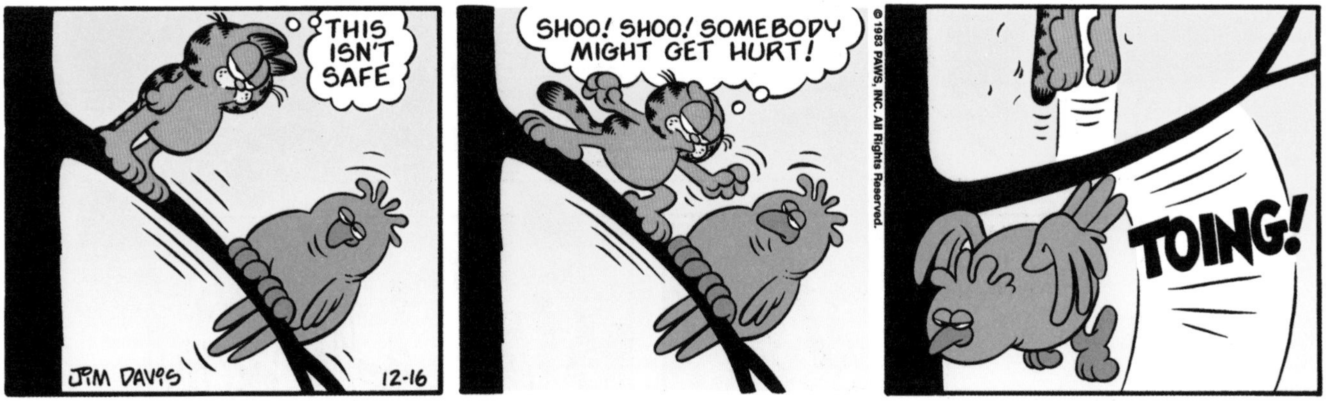
THIS ISN'T SAFE
JIM DAVIS
12-16
SHOO! SHOO! SOMEBODY MIGHT GET HURT!
© 1983 PAWS, INC. All Rights Reserved.
TOING!

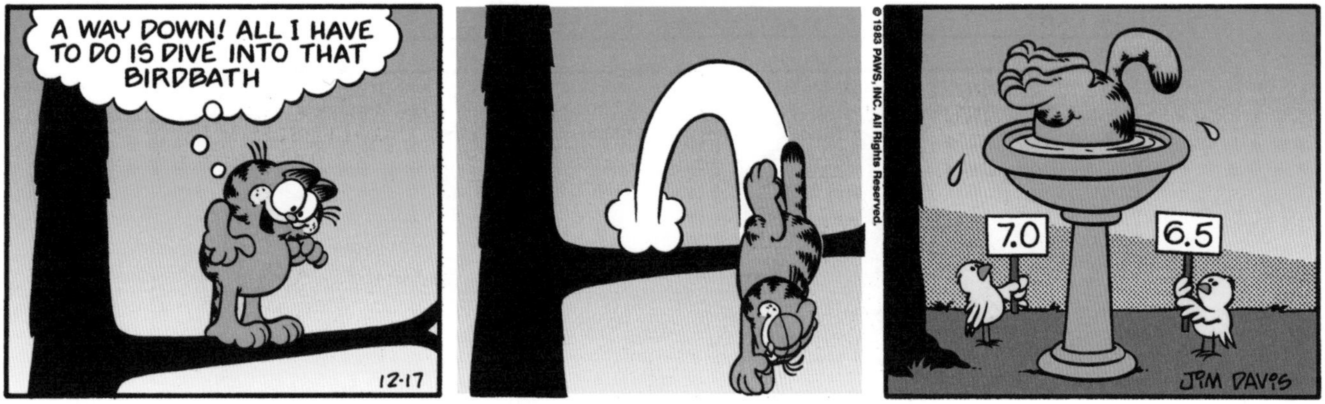
A WAY DOWN! ALL I HAVE TO DO IS DIVE INTO THAT BIRDBATH
12-17
© 1983 PAWS, INC. All Rights Reserved.
7.0
6.5
JIM DAVIS

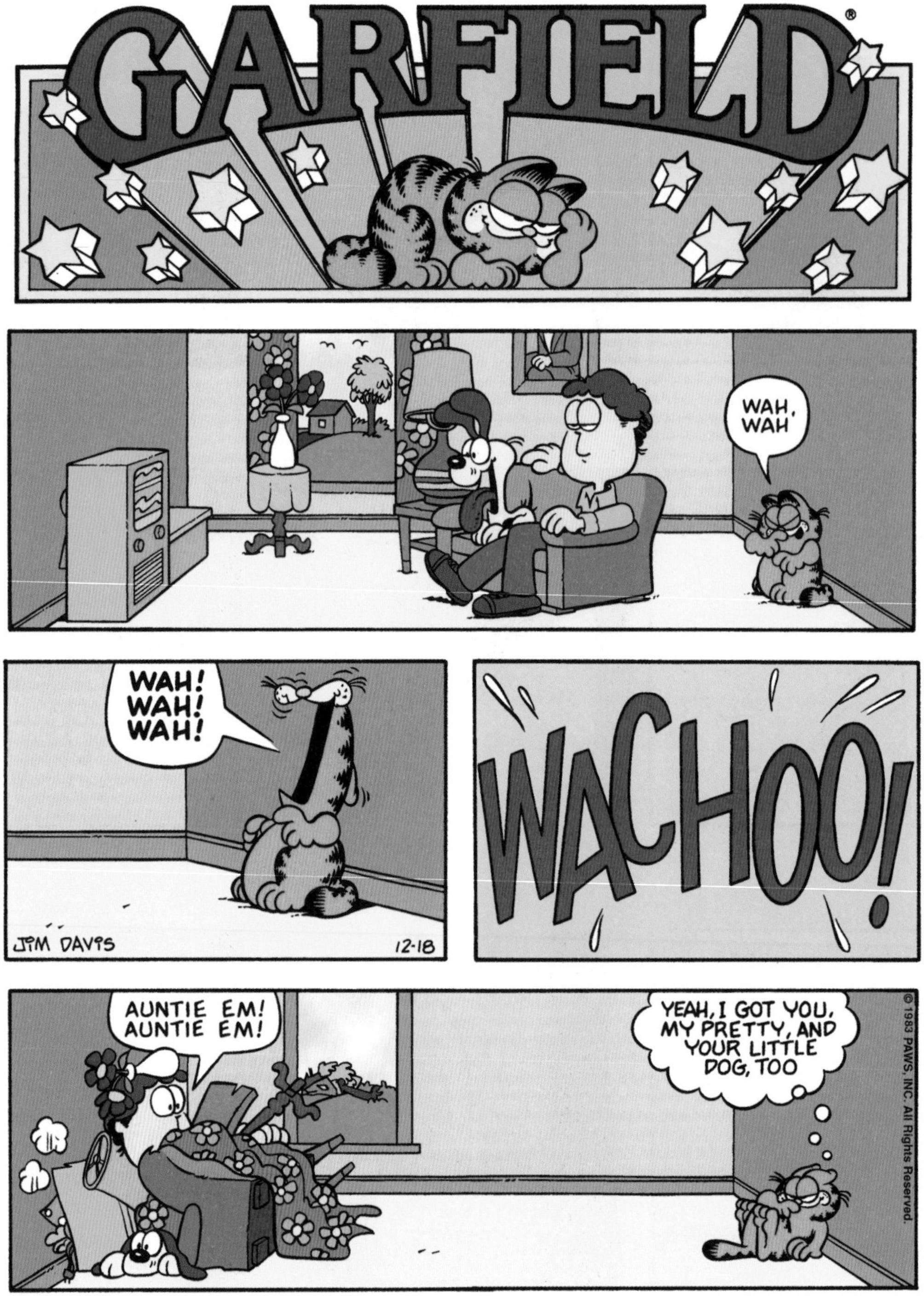
GARFIELD®
WAH, WAH
WAH! WAH! WAH!
JIM DAVIS
12-18
WACHOO!
AUNTIE EM! AUNTIE EM!
YEAH, I GOT YOU, MY PRETTY, AND YOUR LITTLE DOG, TOO
© 1983 PAWS, INC. All Rights Reserved.

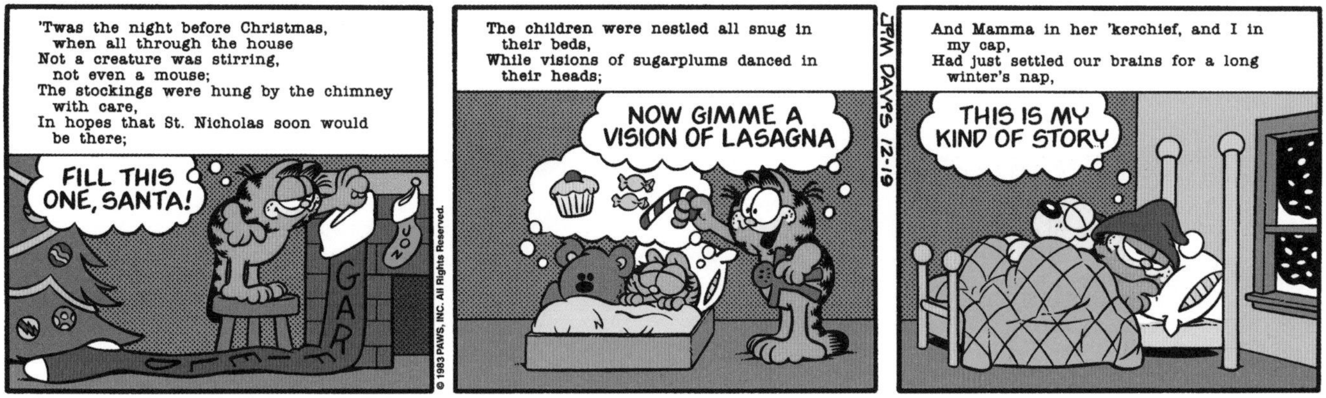
'Twas the night before Christmas, when all through the house
Not a creature was stirring, not even a mouse;
The stockings were hung by the chimney with care,
In hopes that St. Nicholas soon would be there;
FILL THIS ONE, SANTA!
© 1983 PAWS, INC. All Rights Reserved.
The children were nestled all snug in their beds,
While visions of sugarplums danced in their heads;
NOW GIMME A VISION OF LASAGNA
JPM DAVPS 12-19
And Mamma in her 'kerchief, and I in my cap,
Had just settled our brains for a long winter's nap,
THIS IS MY KIND OF STORY

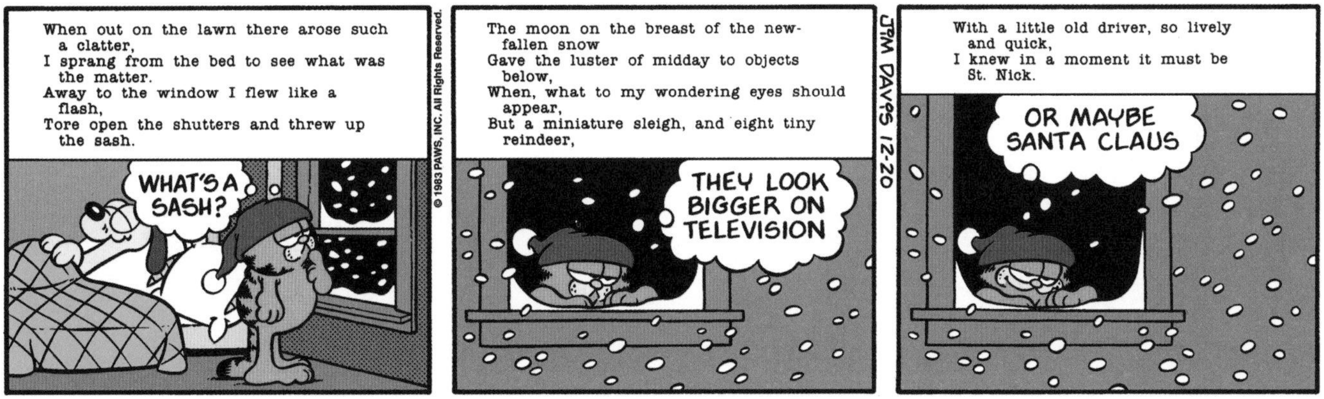
When out on the lawn there arose such a clatter,
I sprang from the bed to see what was the matter.
Away to the window I flew like a flash,
Tore open the shutters and threw up the sash.
WHAT'S A SASH?
© 1983 PAWS, INC. All Rights Reserved.
The moon on the breast of the new-fallen snow
Gave the luster of midday to objects below,
When, what to my wondering eyes should appear,
But a miniature sleigh, and eight tiny reindeer,
THEY LOOK BIGGER ON TELEVISION
JPM DAVPS 12-20
With a little old driver, so lively and quick,
I knew in a moment it must be St. Nick.
OR MAYBE SANTA CLAUS

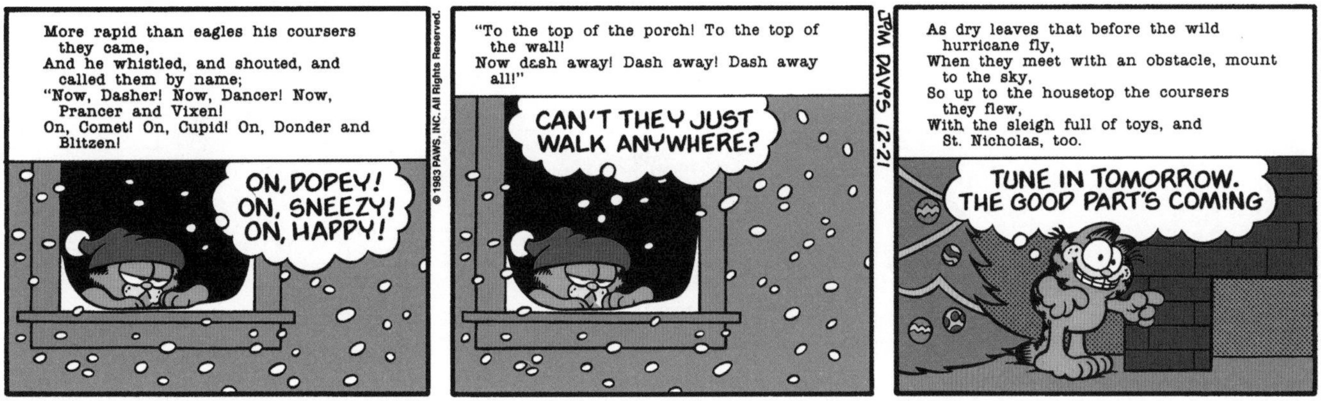
More rapid than eagles his coursers they came,
And he whistled, and shouted, and called them by name;
"Now, Dasher! Now, Dancer! Now, Prancer and Vixen!
On, Comet! On, Cupid! On, Donder and Blitzen!
ON, DOPEY! ON, SNEEZY! ON, HAPPY!
© 1983 PAWS, INC. All Rights Reserved.
"To the top of the porch! To the top of the wall!
Now dash away! Dash away! Dash away all!"
CAN'T THEY JUST WALK ANYWHERE?
JPM DAVPS 12-21
As dry leaves that before the wild hurricane fly,
When they meet with an obstacle, mount to the sky,
So up to the housetop the coursers they flew,
With the sleigh full of toys, and St. Nicholas, too.
TUNE IN TOMORROW. THE GOOD PART'S COMING

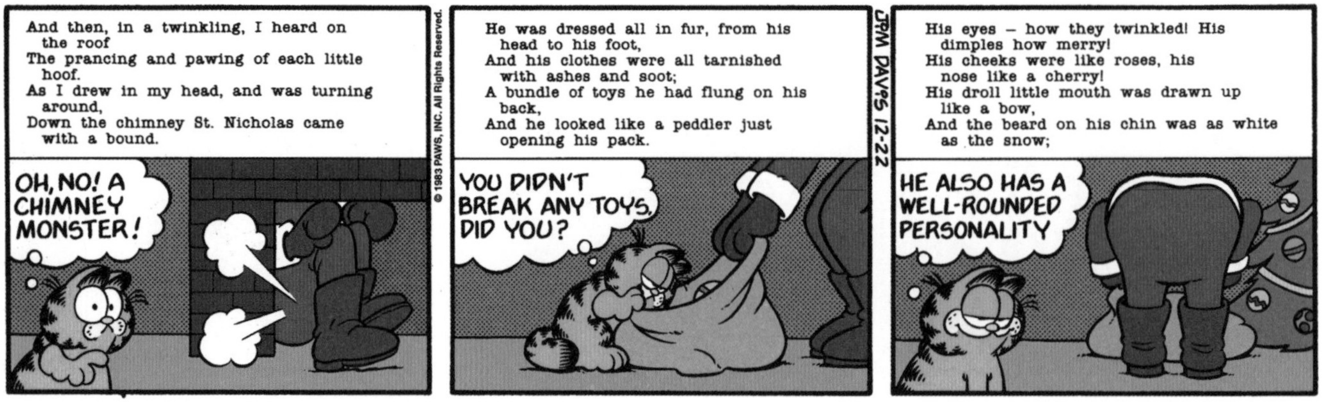
And then, in a twinkling, I heard on the roof
The prancing and pawing of each little hoof.
As I drew in my head, and was turning around,
Down the chimney St. Nicholas came with a bound.
OH, NO! A CHIMNEY MONSTER!
© 1983 PAWS, INC. All Rights Reserved.
He was dressed all in fur, from his head to his foot,
And his clothes were all tarnished with ashes and soot;
A bundle of toys he had flung on his back,
And he looked like a peddler just opening his pack.
YOU DIDN'T BREAK ANY TOYS, DID YOU?
JIM DAVIS 12-22
His eyes – how they twinkled! His dimples how merry!
His cheeks were like roses, his nose like a cherry!
His droll little mouth was drawn up like a bow,
And the beard on his chin was as white as the snow;
HE ALSO HAS A WELL-ROUNDED PERSONALITY

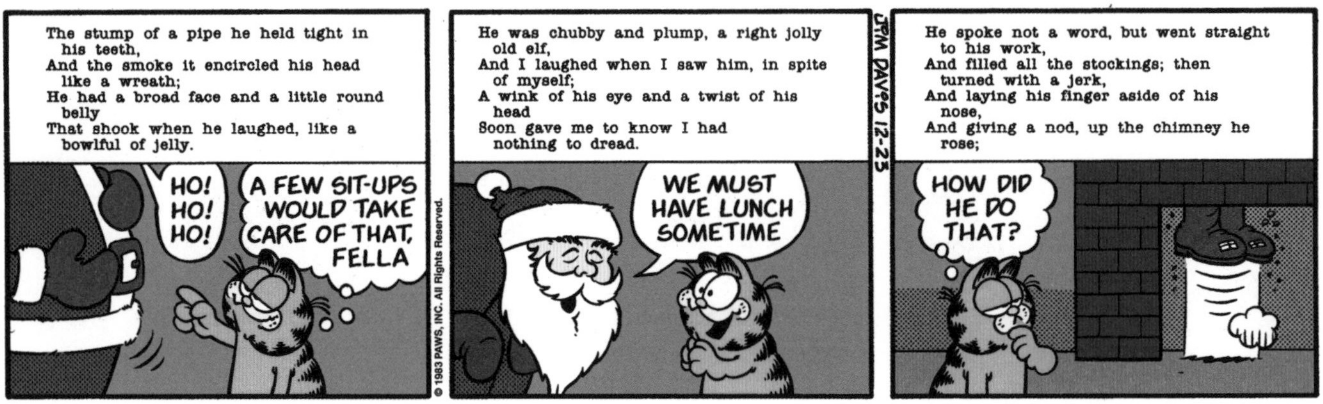
The stump of a pipe he held tight in his teeth,
And the smoke it encircled his head like a wreath;
He had a broad face and a little round belly
That shook when he laughed, like a bowlful of jelly.
HO! HO! HO!
A FEW SIT-UPS WOULD TAKE CARE OF THAT, FELLA
© 1983 PAWS, INC. All Rights Reserved.
He was chubby and plump, a right jolly old elf,
And I laughed when I saw him, in spite of myself;
A wink of his eye and a twist of his head
Soon gave me to know I had nothing to dread.
WE MUST HAVE LUNCH SOMETIME
JIM DAVIS 12-23
He spoke not a word, but went straight to his work,
And filled all the stockings; then turned with a jerk,
And laying his finger aside of his nose,
And giving a nod, up the chimney he rose;
HOW DID HE DO THAT?

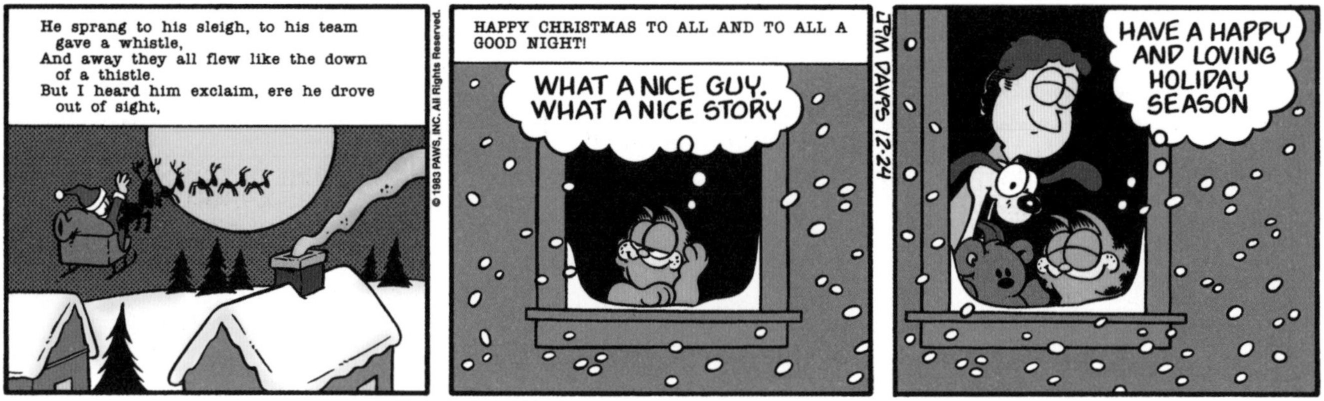
He sprang to his sleigh, to his team gave a whistle,
And away they all flew like the down of a thistle.
But I heard him exclaim, ere he drove out of sight,
© 1983 PAWS, INC. All Rights Reserved.
HAPPY CHRISTMAS TO ALL AND TO ALL A GOOD NIGHT!
WHAT A NICE GUY. WHAT A NICE STORY
JIM DAVIS 12-24
HAVE A HAPPY AND LOVING HOLIDAY SEASON

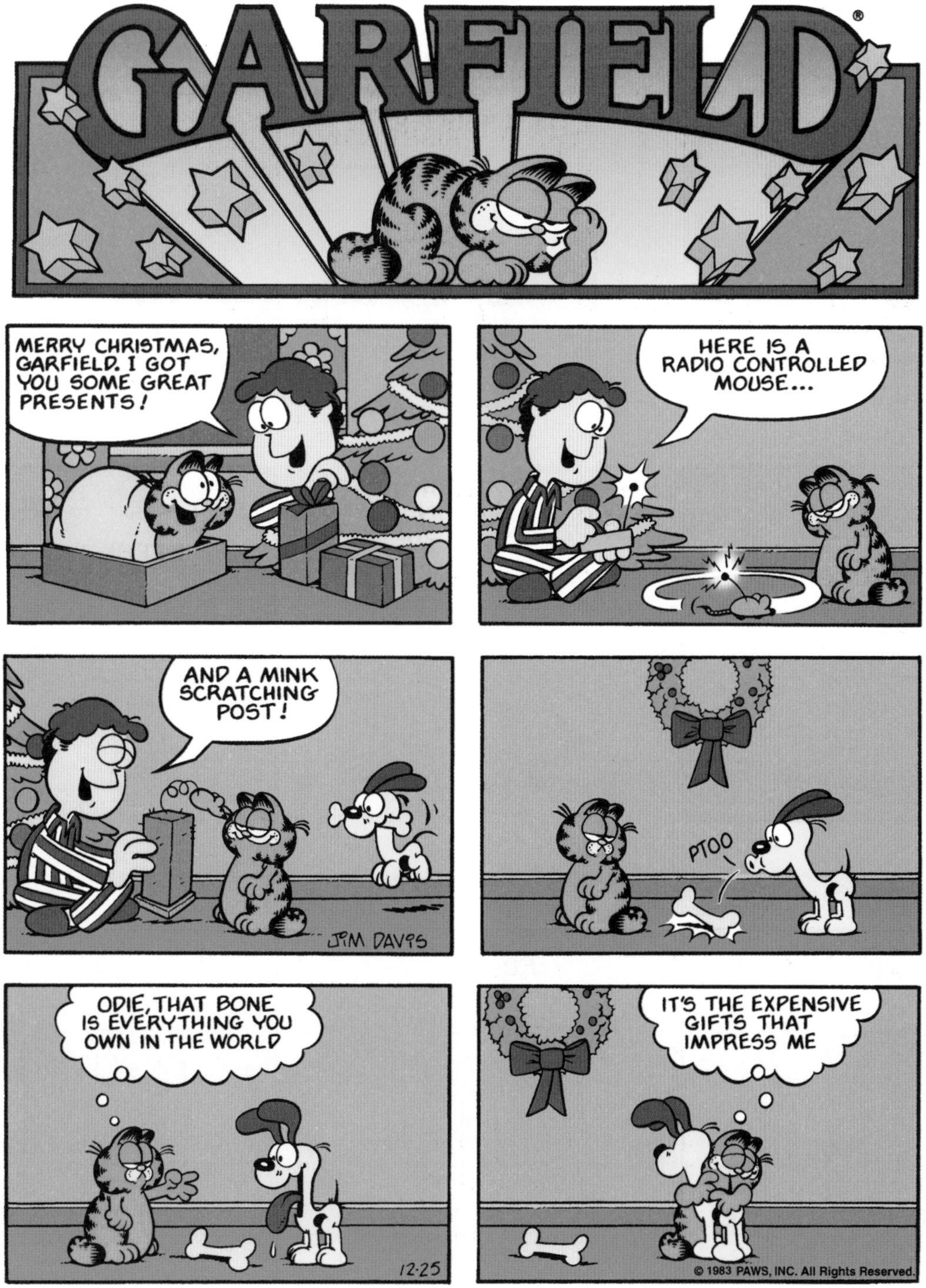
GARFIELD®
MERRY CHRISTMAS, GARFIELD. I GOT YOU SOME GREAT PRESENTS!
HERE IS A RADIO CONTROLLED MOUSE...
AND A MINK SCRATCHING POST!
JIM DAVIS
PTOO
ODIE, THAT BONE IS EVERYTHING YOU OWN IN THE WORLD
12-25
IT'S THE EXPENSIVE GIFTS THAT IMPRESS ME
© 1983 PAWS, INC. All Rights Reserved.

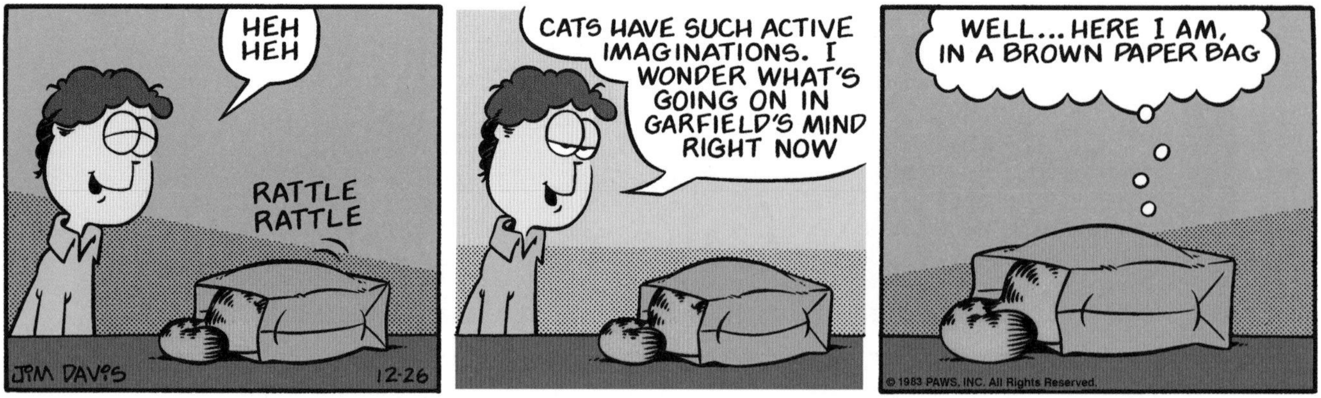
HEH HEH
RATTLE RATTLE
JIM DAVIS
12-26
CATS HAVE SUCH ACTIVE IMAGINATIONS. I WONDER WHAT'S GOING ON IN GARFIELD'S MIND RIGHT NOW
WELL... HERE I AM, IN A BROWN PAPER BAG
© 1983 PAWS, INC. All Rights Reserved.

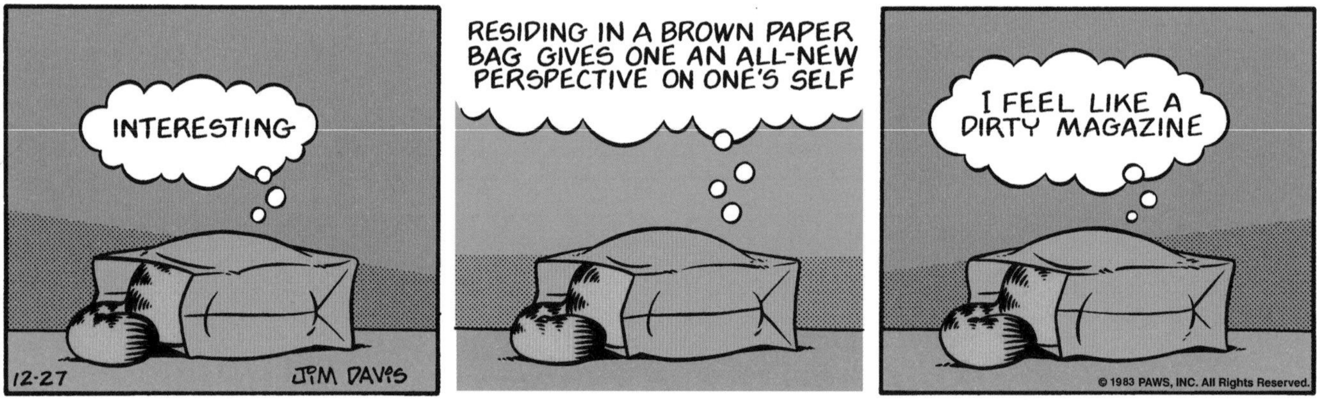
INTERESTING
12-27
JIM DAVIS
RESIDING IN A BROWN PAPER BAG GIVES ONE AN ALL-NEW PERSPECTIVE ON ONE'S SELF
I FEEL LIKE A DIRTY MAGAZINE
© 1983 PAWS, INC. All Rights Reserved.

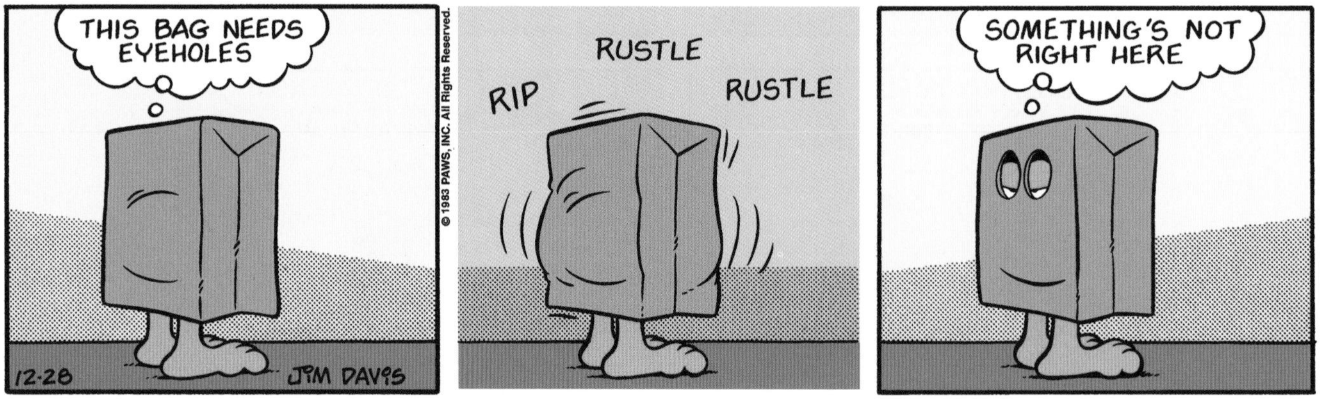
THIS BAG NEEDS EYEHOLES
12-28
JIM DAVIS
© 1983 PAWS, INC. All Rights Reserved.
RUSTLE
RIP
RUSTLE
SOMETHING'S NOT RIGHT HERE

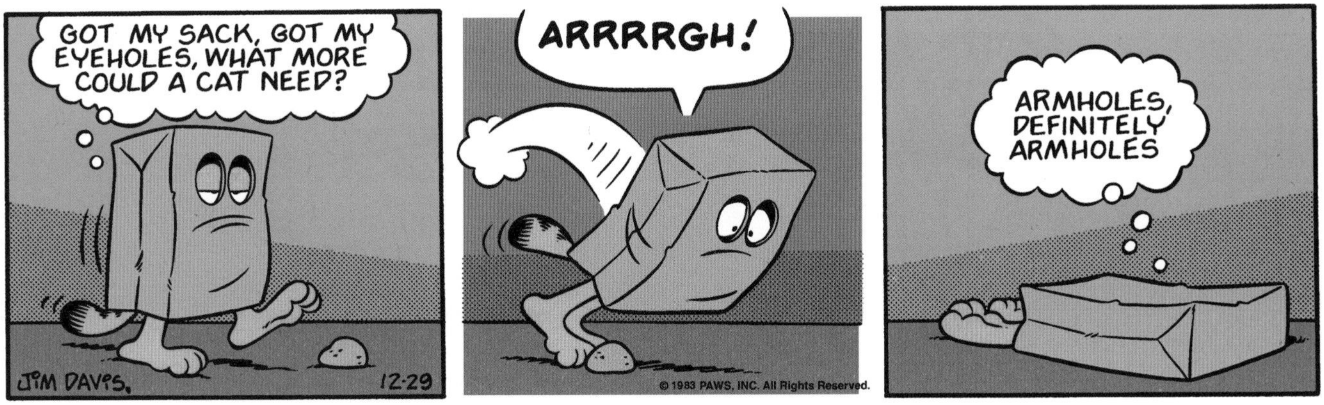
GOT MY SACK, GOT MY EYEHOLES, WHAT MORE COULD A CAT NEED?
JIM DAVIS
12-29
ARRRRGH!
© 1983 PAWS, INC. All Rights Reserved.
ARMHOLES, DEFINITELY ARMHOLES

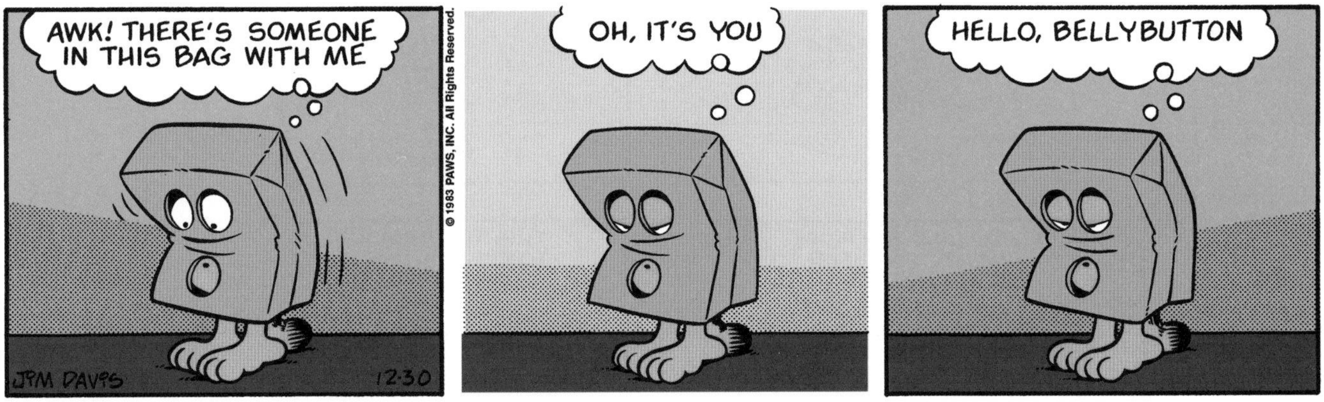
AWK! THERE'S SOMEONE IN THIS BAG WITH ME
JIM DAVIS
12-30
© 1983 PAWS, INC. All Rights Reserved.
OH, IT'S YOU
HELLO, BELLYBUTTON

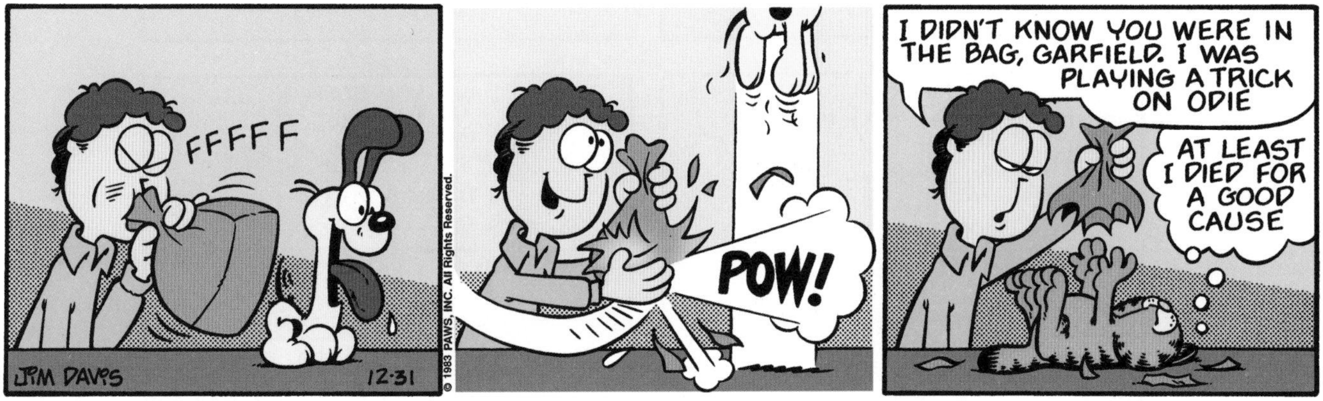
FFFFF
JIM DAVIS
12-31
© 1983 PAWS, INC. All Rights Reserved.
POW!
I DIDN'T KNOW YOU WERE IN THE BAG, GARFIELD. I WAS PLAYING A TRICK ON ODIE
AT LEAST I DIED FOR A GOOD CAUSE

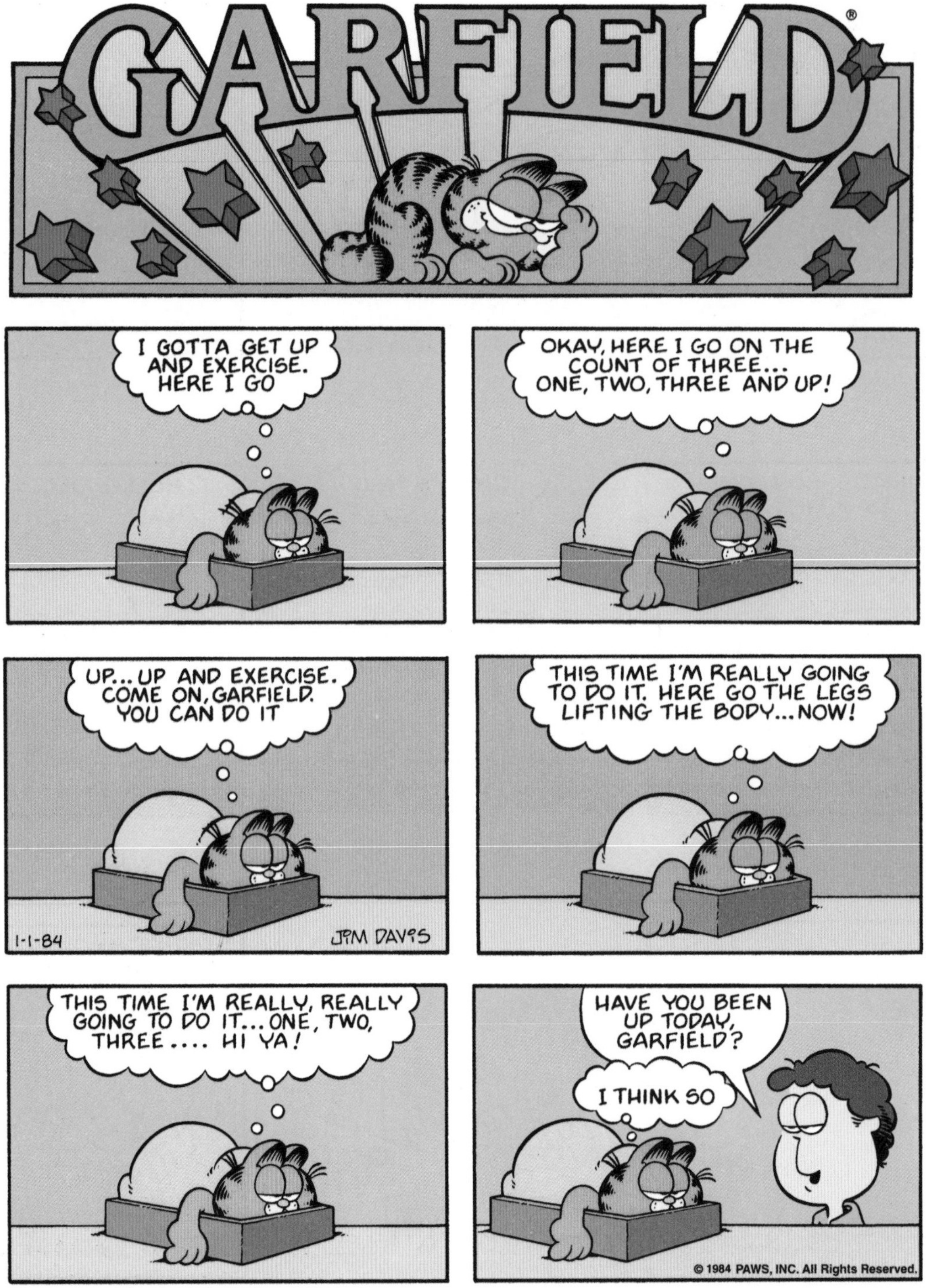
GARFIELD®
I GOTTA GET UP AND EXERCISE. HERE I GO
OKAY, HERE I GO ON THE COUNT OF THREE... ONE, TWO, THREE AND UP!
UP... UP AND EXERCISE. COME ON, GARFIELD. YOU CAN DO IT
1-1-84
JIM DAVIS
THIS TIME I'M REALLY GOING TO DO IT. HERE GO THE LEGS LIFTING THE BODY... NOW!
THIS TIME I'M REALLY, REALLY GOING TO DO IT... ONE, TWO, THREE.... HI YA!
HAVE YOU BEEN UP TODAY, GARFIELD?
I THINK SO
© 1984 PAWS, INC. All Rights Reserved.

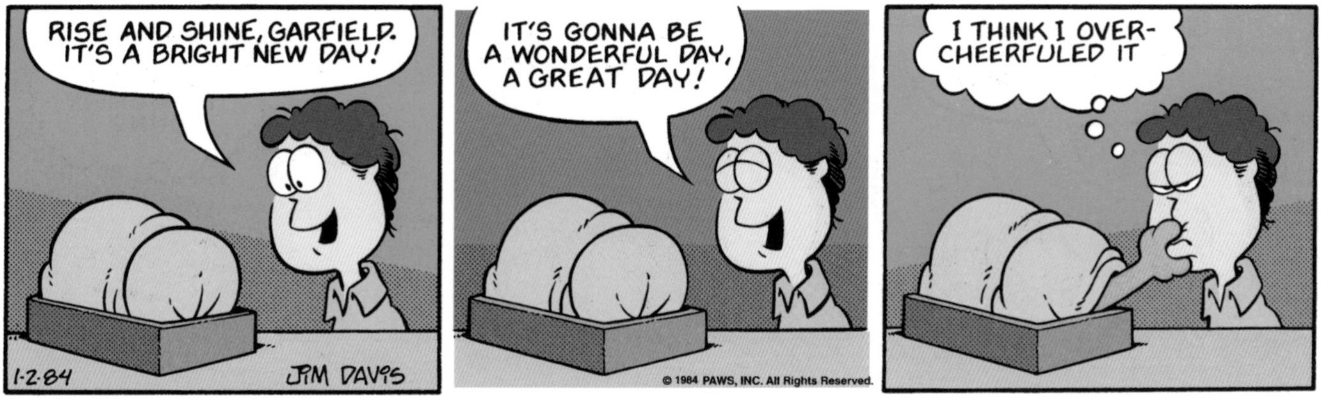
RISE AND SHINE, GARFIELD. IT'S A BRIGHT NEW DAY!
1-2-84
JIM DAVIS
IT'S GONNA BE A WONDERFUL DAY, A GREAT DAY!
© 1984 PAWS, INC. All Rights Reserved.
I THINK I OVER-CHEERFULED IT

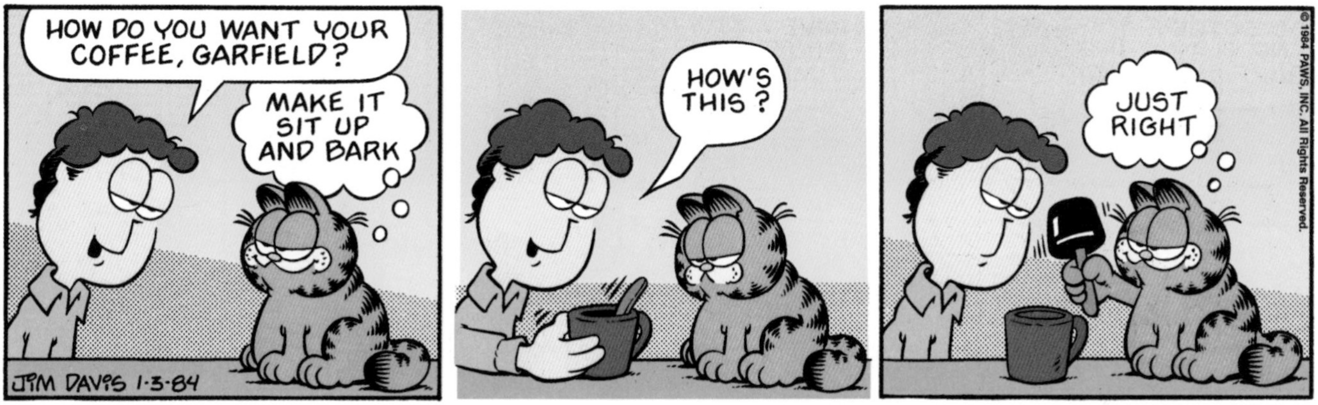
HOW DO YOU WANT YOUR COFFEE, GARFIELD?
MAKE IT SIT UP AND BARK
JIM DAVIS 1-3-84
HOW'S THIS?
JUST RIGHT
© 1984 PAWS, INC. All Rights Reserved.

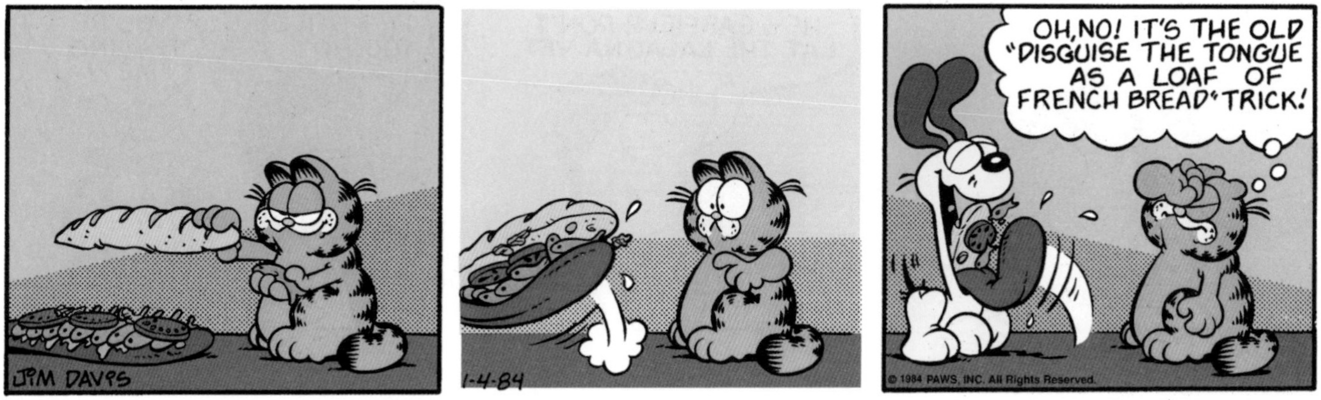
JIM DAVIS
1-4-84
OH, NO! IT'S THE OLD "DISGUISE THE TONGUE AS A LOAF OF FRENCH BREAD" TRICK!
© 1984 PAWS, INC. All Rights Reserved.

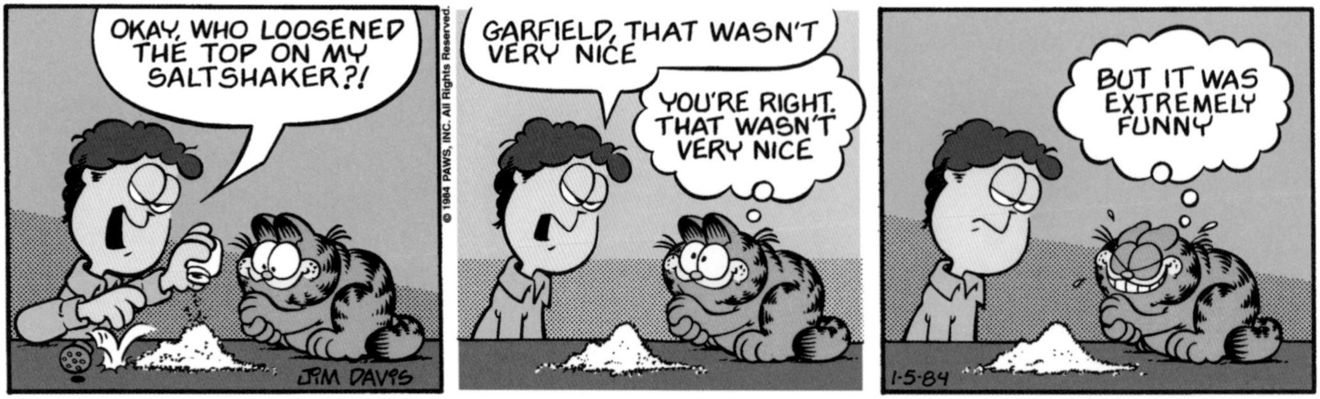
OKAY, WHO LOOSENED THE TOP ON MY SALTSHAKER?!
JIM DAVIS
© 1984 PAWS, INC. All Rights Reserved.
GARFIELD, THAT WASN'T VERY NICE
YOU'RE RIGHT. THAT WASN'T VERY NICE
BUT IT WAS EXTREMELY FUNNY
1-5-84

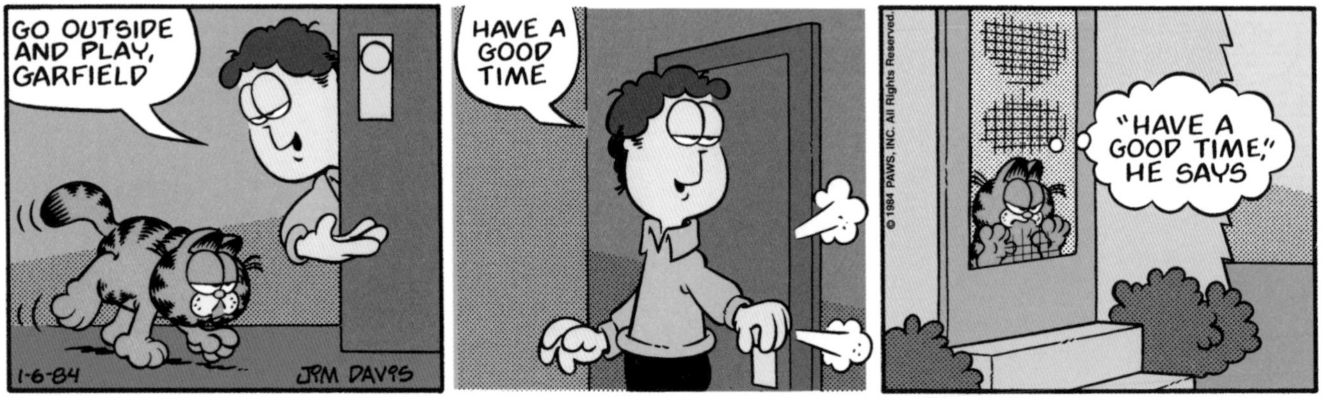
GO OUTSIDE AND PLAY, GARFIELD
1-6-84
JIM DAVIS
HAVE A GOOD TIME
© 1984 PAWS, INC. All Rights Reserved.
"HAVE A GOOD TIME," HE SAYS

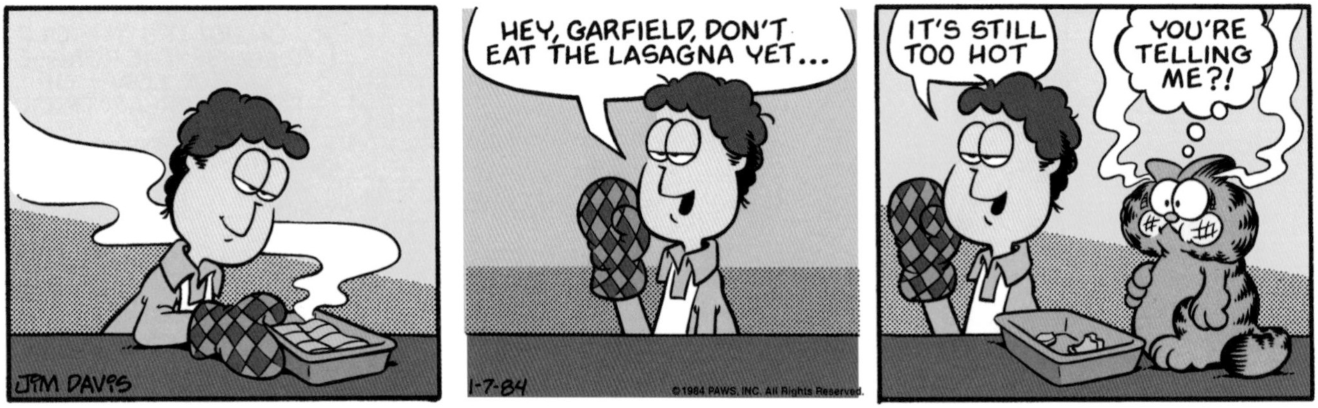
JIM DAVIS
HEY, GARFIELD, DON'T EAT THE LASAGNA YET...
1-7-84
©1984 PAWS, INC. All Rights Reserved.
IT'S STILL TOO HOT
YOU'RE TELLING ME?!

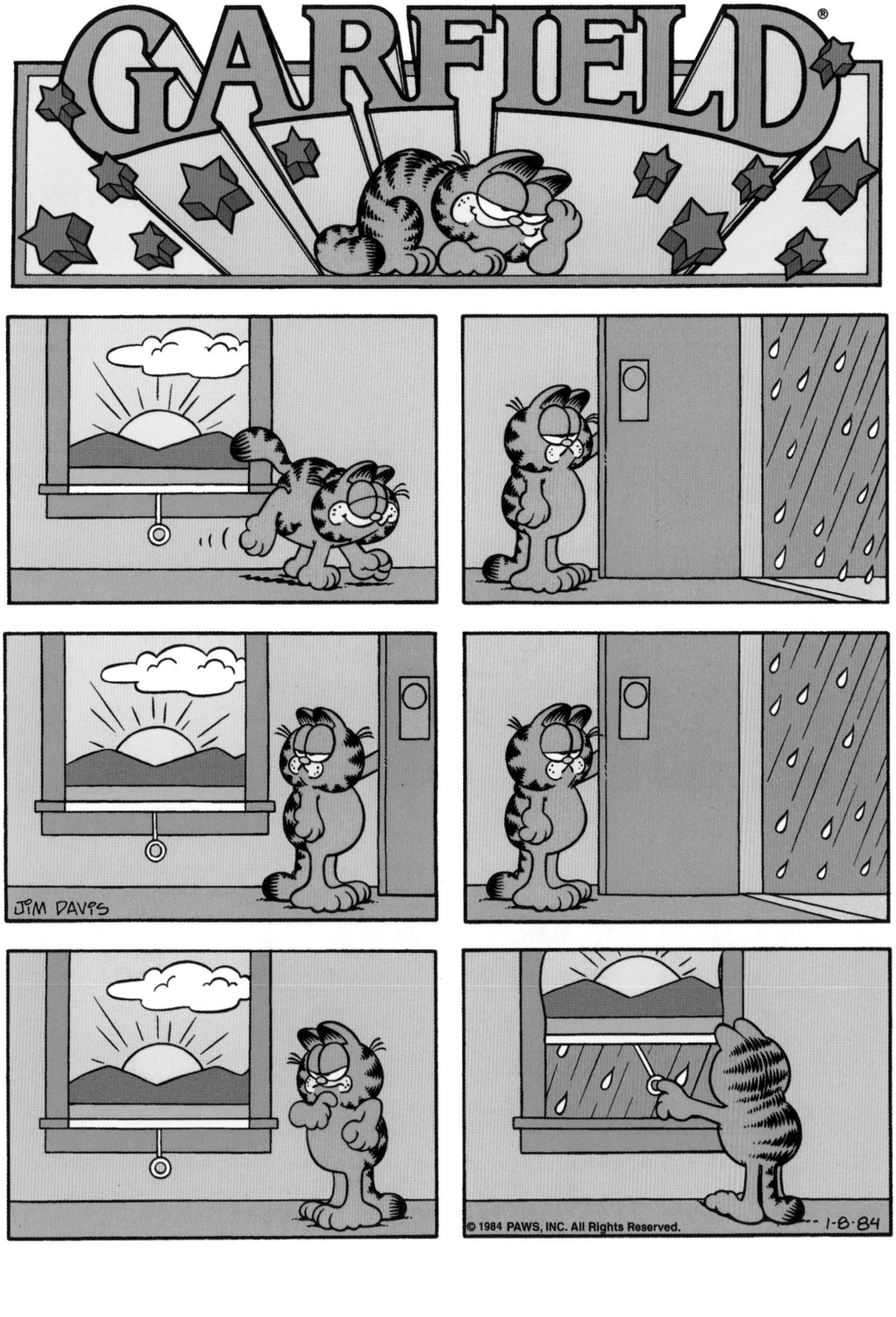
GARFIELD®
JIM DAVIS
© 1984 PAWS, INC. All Rights Reserved.
1-8-84

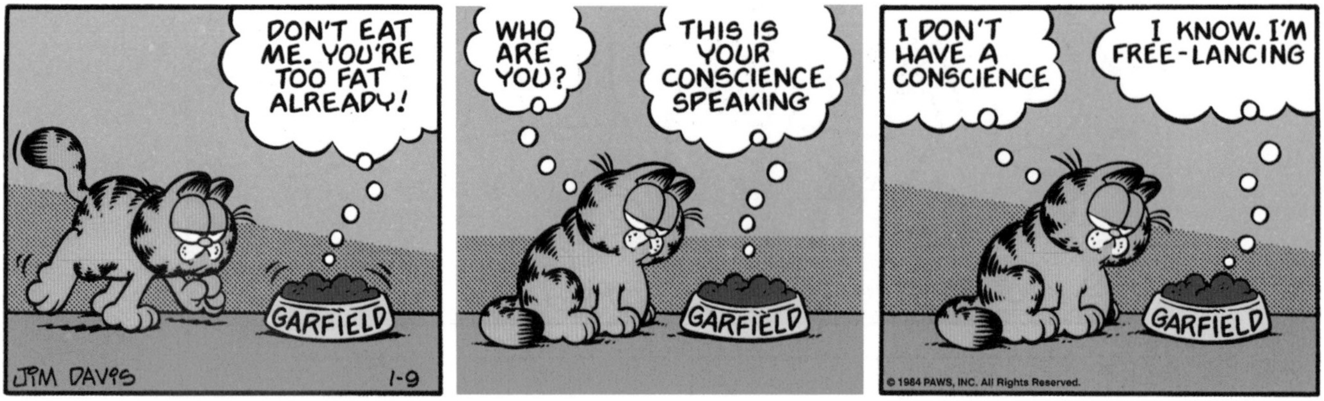
DON'T EAT ME. YOU'RE TOO FAT ALREADY!
JIM DAVIS
1-9
WHO ARE YOU?
THIS IS YOUR CONSCIENCE SPEAKING
I DON'T HAVE A CONSCIENCE
I KNOW. I'M FREE-LANCING
© 1984 PAWS, INC. All Rights Reserved.

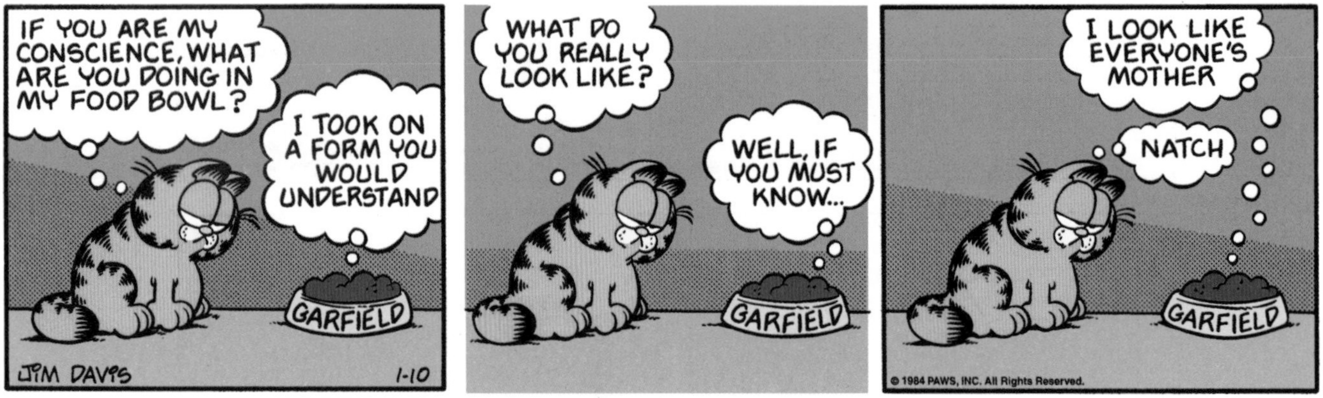
IF YOU ARE MY CONSCIENCE, WHAT ARE YOU DOING IN MY FOOD BOWL?
I TOOK ON A FORM YOU WOULD UNDERSTAND
JIM DAVIS
1-10
WHAT DO YOU REALLY LOOK LIKE?
WELL, IF YOU MUST KNOW...
I LOOK LIKE EVERYONE'S MOTHER
NATCH
© 1984 PAWS, INC. All Rights Reserved.

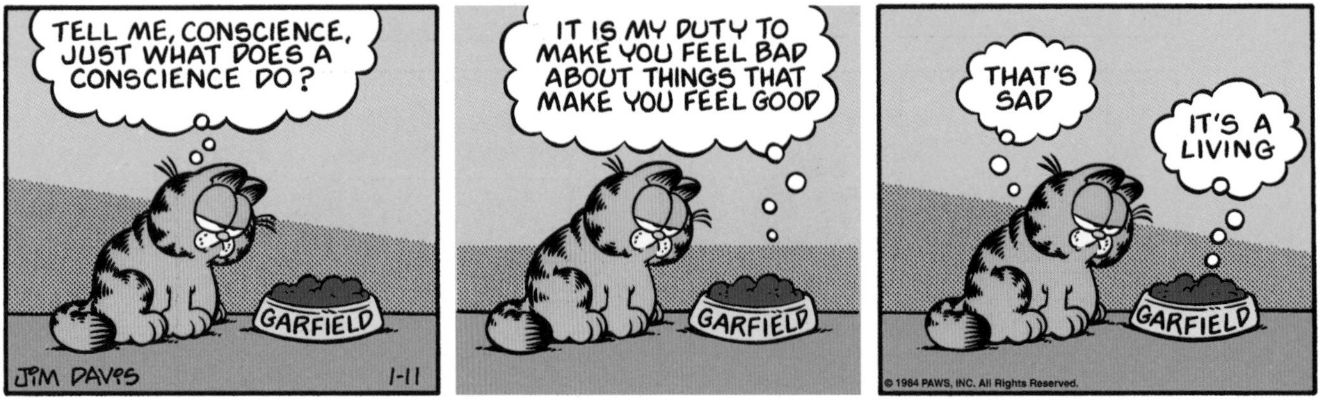
TELL ME, CONSCIENCE, JUST WHAT DOES A CONSCIENCE DO?
JIM DAVIS
1-11
IT IS MY DUTY TO MAKE YOU FEEL BAD ABOUT THINGS THAT MAKE YOU FEEL GOOD
THAT'S SAD
IT'S A LIVING
© 1984 PAWS, INC. All Rights Reserved.

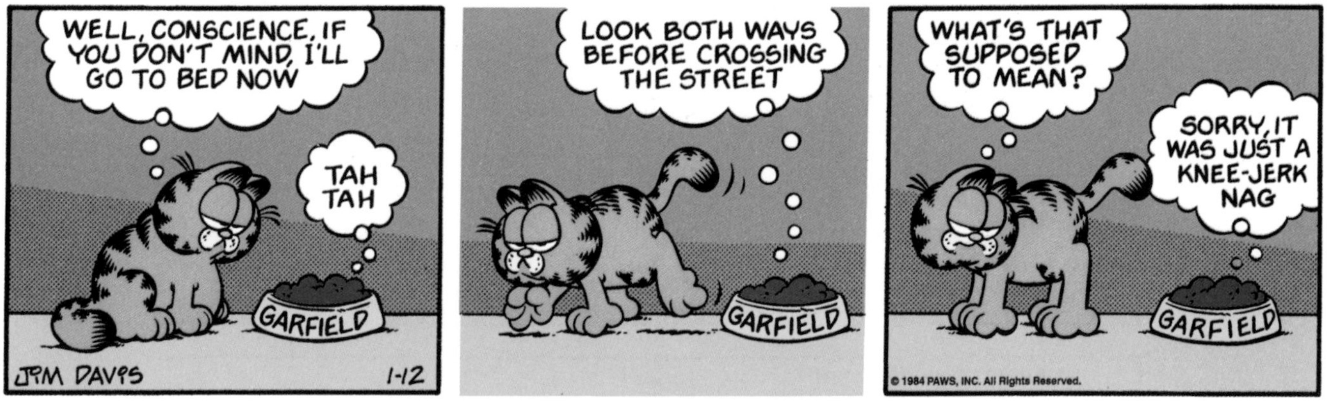
WELL, CONSCIENCE, IF YOU DON'T MIND, I'LL GO TO BED NOW
TAH TAH
GARFIELD
JIM DAVIS
1-12
LOOK BOTH WAYS BEFORE CROSSING THE STREET
GARFIELD
WHAT'S THAT SUPPOSED TO MEAN?
SORRY, IT WAS JUST A KNEE-JERK NAG
GARFIELD
© 1984 PAWS, INC. All Rights Reserved.

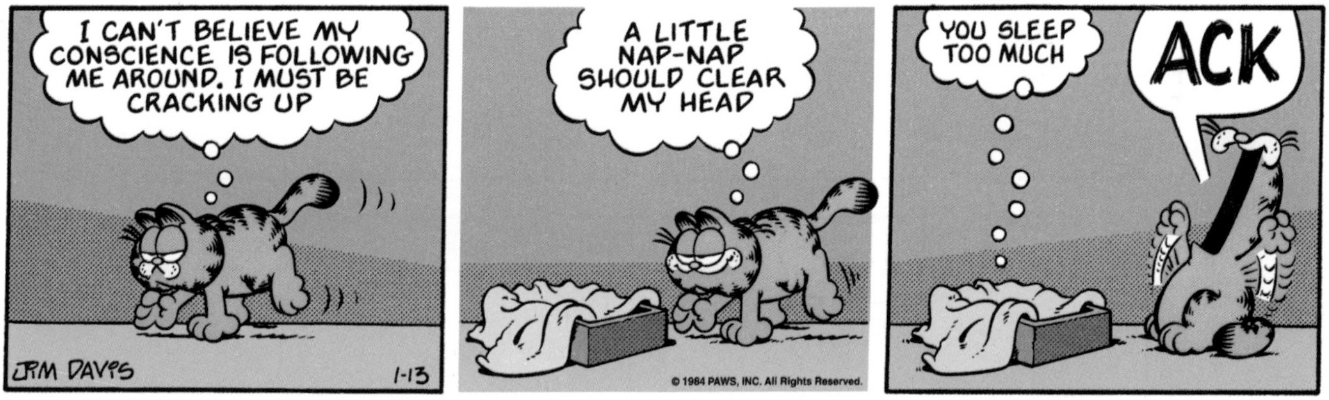
I CAN'T BELIEVE MY CONSCIENCE IS FOLLOWING ME AROUND. I MUST BE CRACKING UP
JIM DAVIS
1-13
A LITTLE NAP-NAP SHOULD CLEAR MY HEAD
© 1984 PAWS, INC. All Rights Reserved.
YOU SLEEP TOO MUCH
ACK

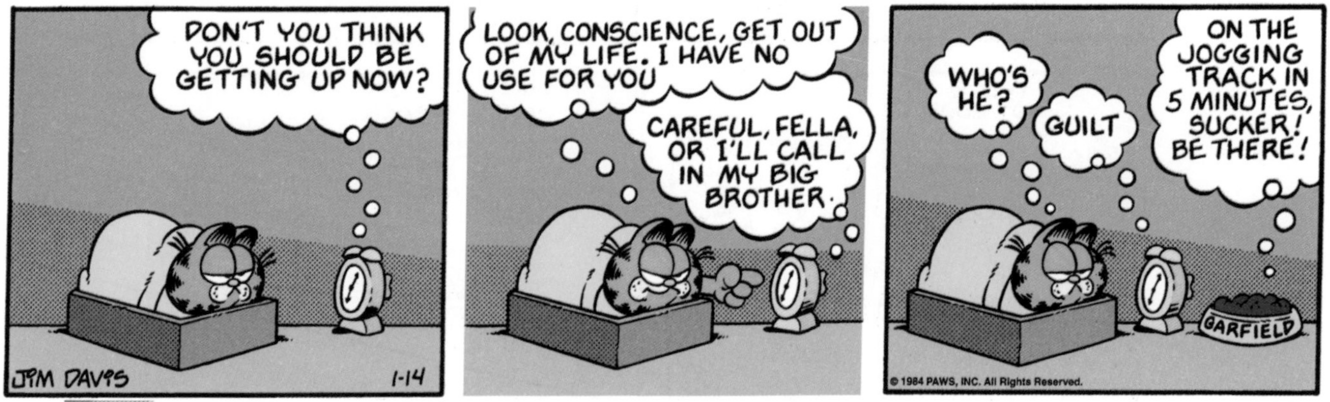
DON'T YOU THINK YOU SHOULD BE GETTING UP NOW?
JIM DAVIS
1-14
LOOK, CONSCIENCE, GET OUT OF MY LIFE. I HAVE NO USE FOR YOU
CAREFUL, FELLA, OR I'LL CALL IN MY BIG BROTHER.
WHO'S HE?
GUILT
ON THE JOGGING TRACK IN 5 MINUTES, SUCKER! BE THERE!
GARFIELD
© 1984 PAWS, INC. All Rights Reserved.

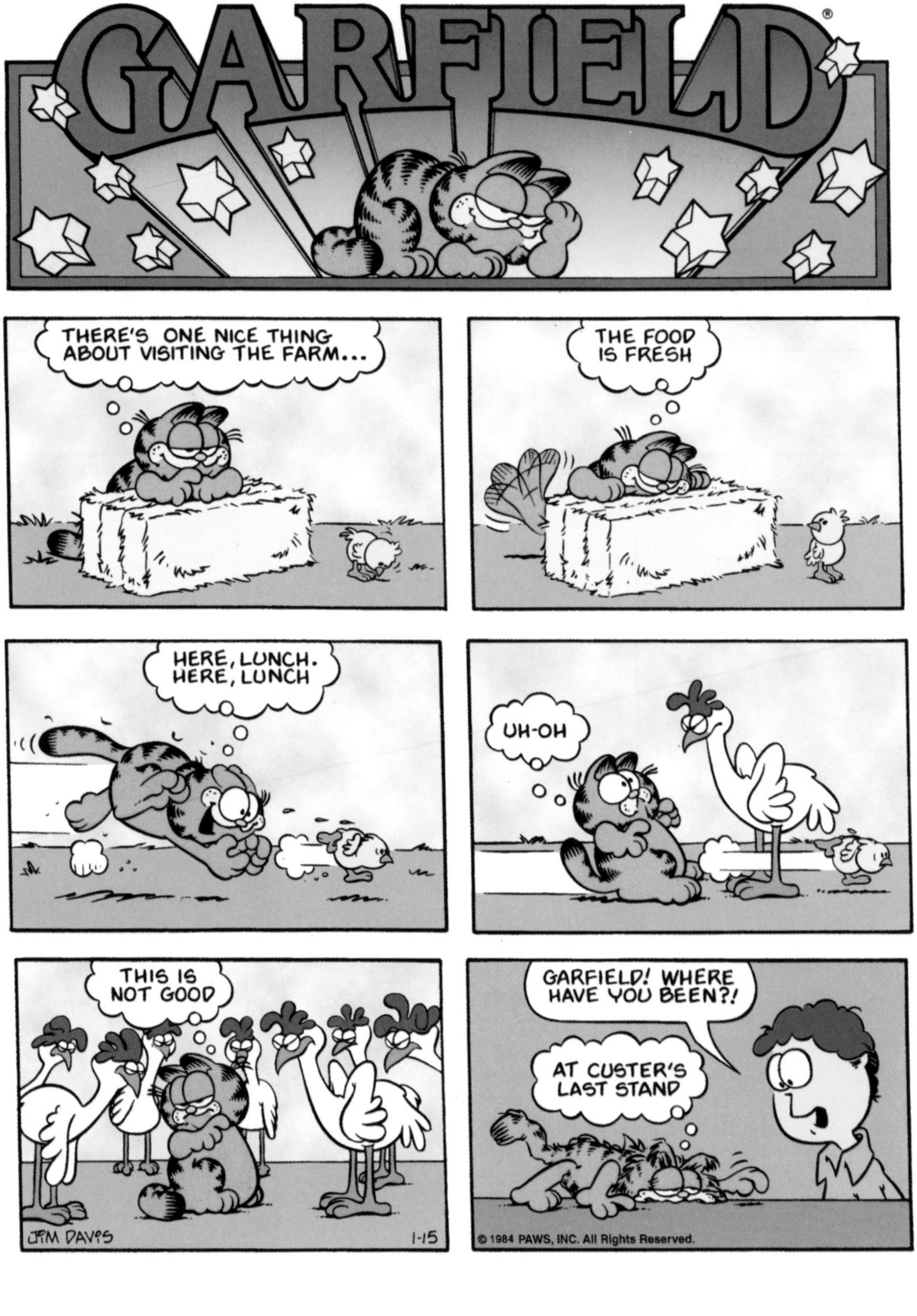
GARFIELD®
THERE'S ONE NICE THING ABOUT VISITING THE FARM...
THE FOOD IS FRESH
HERE, LUNCH. HERE, LUNCH
UH-OH
THIS IS NOT GOOD
GARFIELD! WHERE HAVE YOU BEEN?!
AT CUSTER'S LAST STAND
JIM DAVIS
1-15
© 1984 PAWS, INC. All Rights Reserved.

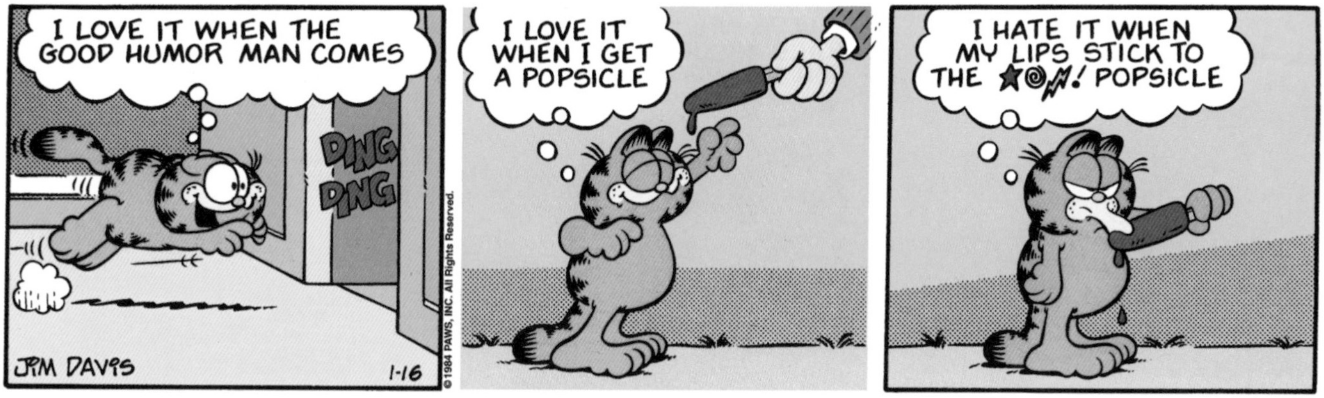
I LOVE IT WHEN THE GOOD HUMOR MAN COMES
DING DING
JIM DAVIS
1-16
©1984 PAWS, INC. All Rights Reserved.
I LOVE IT WHEN I GET A POPSICLE
I HATE IT WHEN MY LIPS STICK TO THE ★@#! POPSICLE

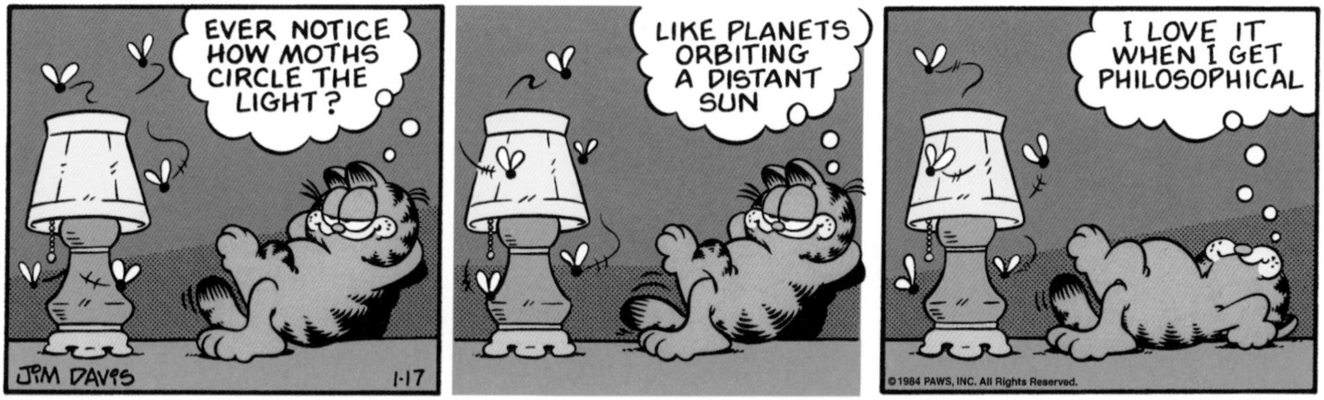
EVER NOTICE HOW MOTHS CIRCLE THE LIGHT?
JIM DAVIS
1-17
LIKE PLANETS ORBITING A DISTANT SUN
I LOVE IT WHEN I GET PHILOSOPHICAL
©1984 PAWS, INC. All Rights Reserved.

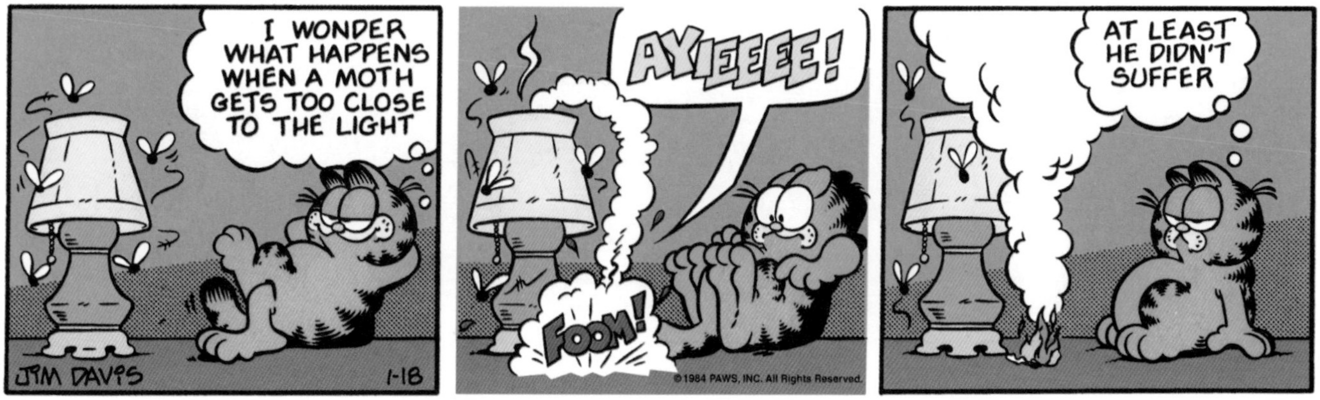
I WONDER WHAT HAPPENS WHEN A MOTH GETS TOO CLOSE TO THE LIGHT
JIM DAVIS
1-18
AYIEEEEE!
FOOM!
©1984 PAWS, INC. All Rights Reserved.
AT LEAST HE DIDN'T SUFFER

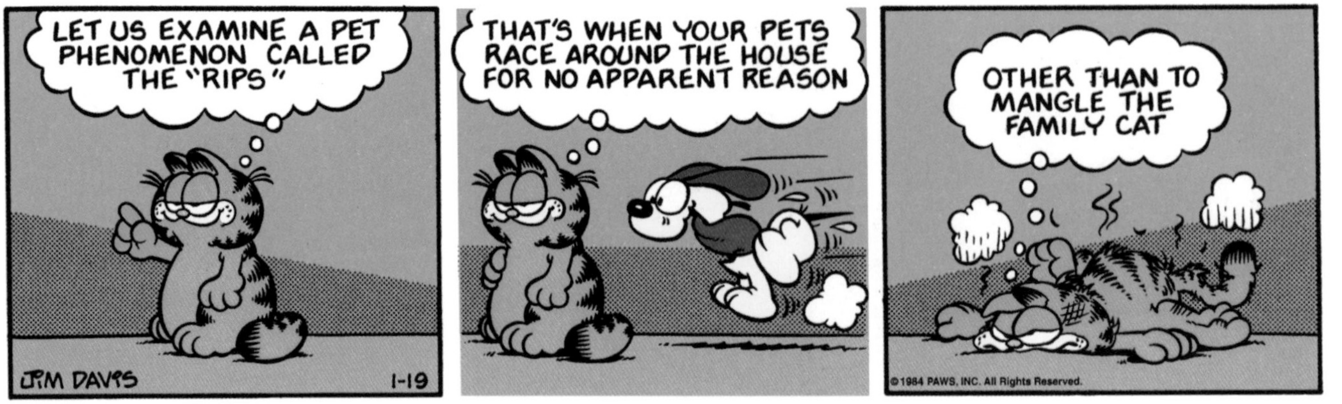
LET US EXAMINE A PET PHENOMENON CALLED THE "RIPS"
JIM DAVIS
1-19
THAT'S WHEN YOUR PETS RACE AROUND THE HOUSE FOR NO APPARENT REASON
OTHER THAN TO MANGLE THE FAMILY CAT
©1984 PAWS, INC. All Rights Reserved.

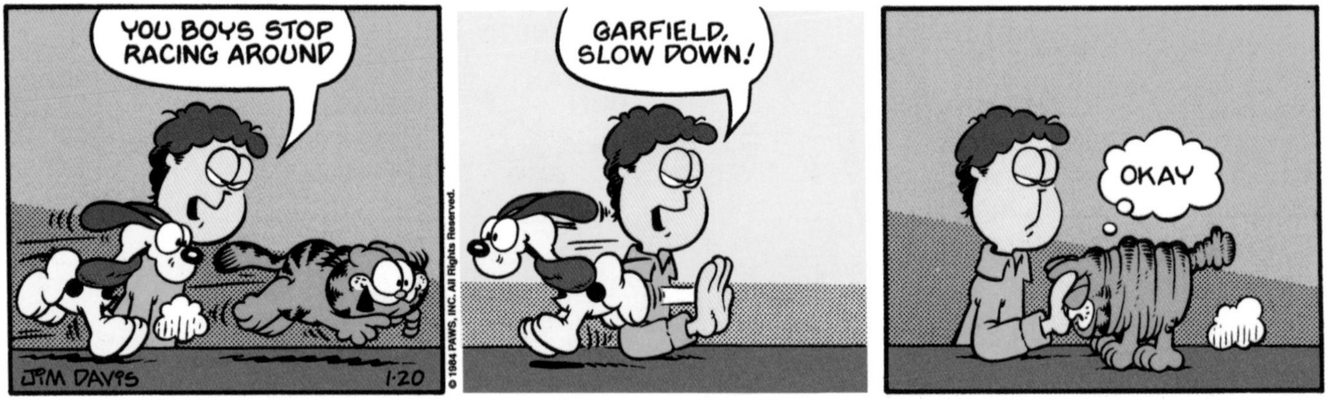
YOU BOYS STOP RACING AROUND
JIM DAVIS
1-20
© 1984 PAWS, INC. All Rights Reserved.
GARFIELD, SLOW DOWN!
OKAY

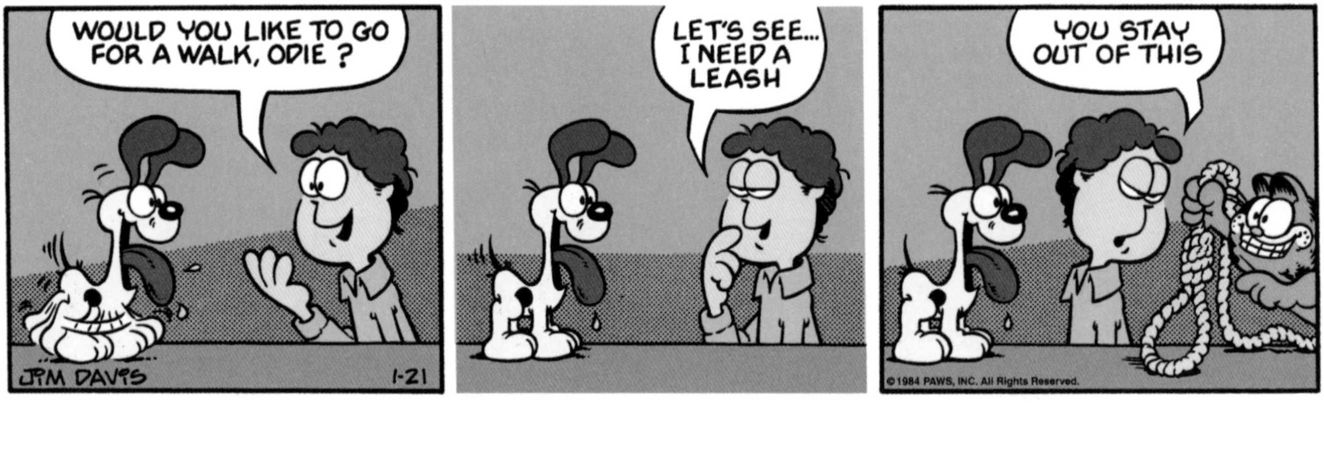
WOULD YOU LIKE TO GO FOR A WALK, ODIE ?
JIM DAVIS
1-21
LET'S SEE... I NEED A LEASH
YOU STAY OUT OF THIS
©1984 PAWS, INC. All Rights Reserved.

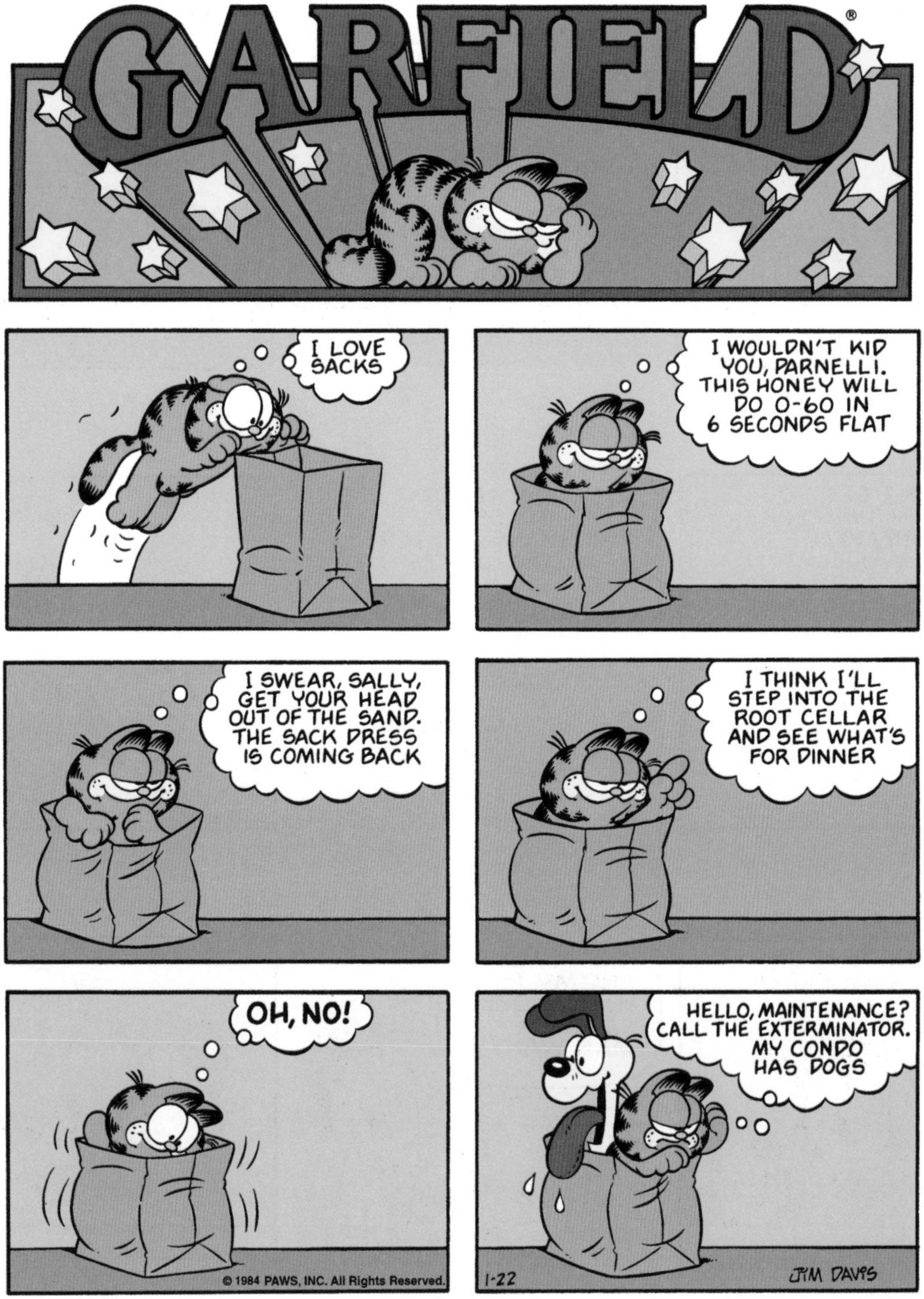
GARFIELD®
I LOVE SACKS
I WOULDN'T KID YOU, PARNELLI. THIS HONEY WILL DO 0-60 IN 6 SECONDS FLAT
I SWEAR, SALLY, GET YOUR HEAD OUT OF THE SAND. THE SACK DRESS IS COMING BACK
I THINK I'LL STEP INTO THE ROOT CELLAR AND SEE WHAT'S FOR DINNER
OH, NO!
HELLO, MAINTENANCE? CALL THE EXTERMINATOR. MY CONDO HAS DOGS
© 1984 PAWS, INC. All Rights Reserved.
1-22
JIM DAVIS

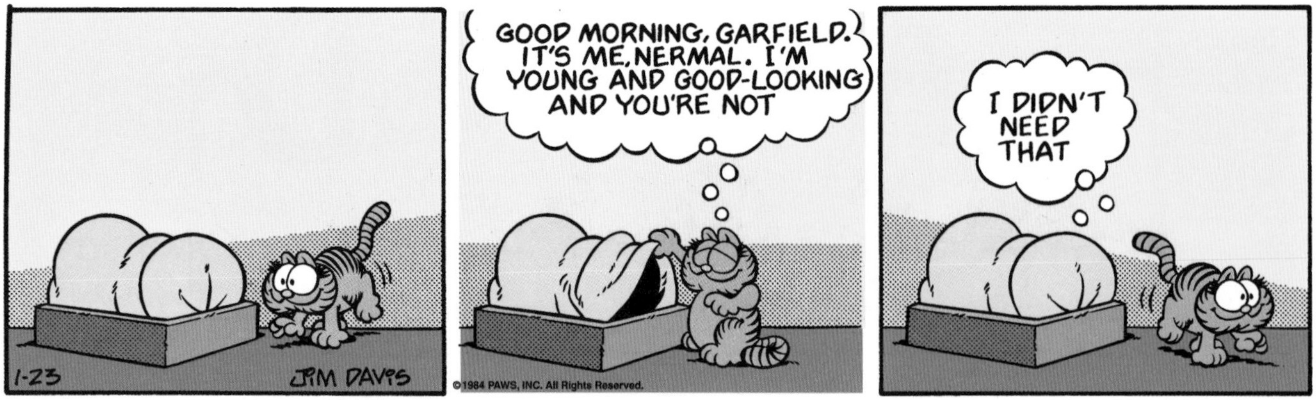
1-23
JIM DAVIS
GOOD MORNING, GARFIELD. IT'S ME, NERMAL. I'M YOUNG AND GOOD-LOOKING AND YOU'RE NOT
©1984 PAWS, INC. All Rights Reserved.
I DIDN'T NEED THAT

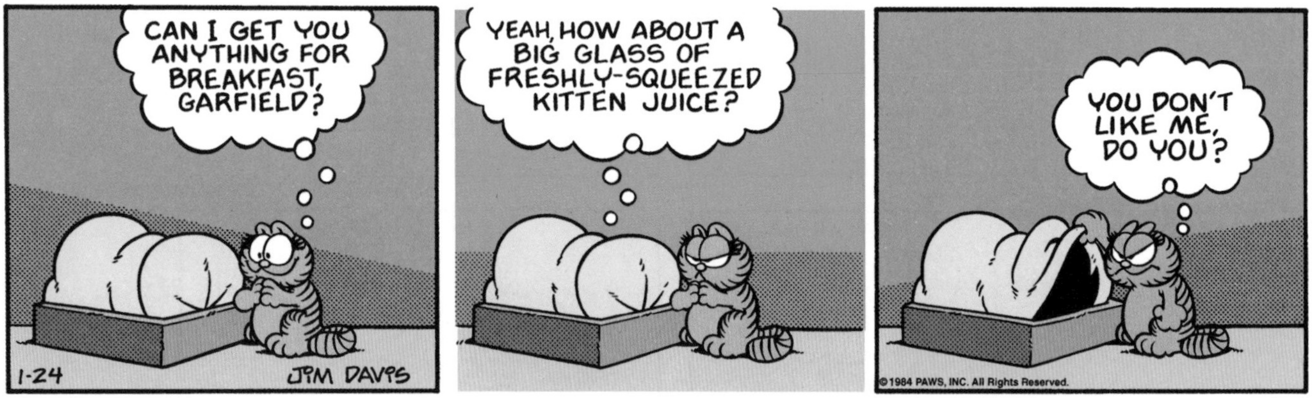
CAN I GET YOU ANYTHING FOR BREAKFAST, GARFIELD?
1-24
JIM DAVIS
YEAH, HOW ABOUT A BIG GLASS OF FRESHLY-SQUEEZED KITTEN JUICE?
YOU DON'T LIKE ME, DO YOU?
©1984 PAWS, INC. All Rights Reserved.

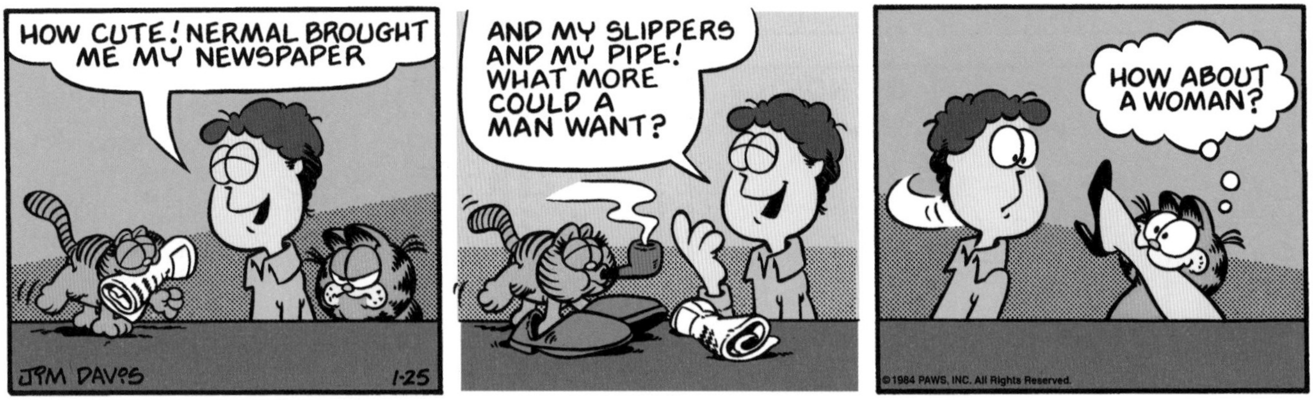
HOW CUTE! NERMAL BROUGHT ME MY NEWSPAPER
JIM DAVIS
1-25
AND MY SLIPPERS AND MY PIPE! WHAT MORE COULD A MAN WANT?
HOW ABOUT A WOMAN?
©1984 PAWS, INC. All Rights Reserved.

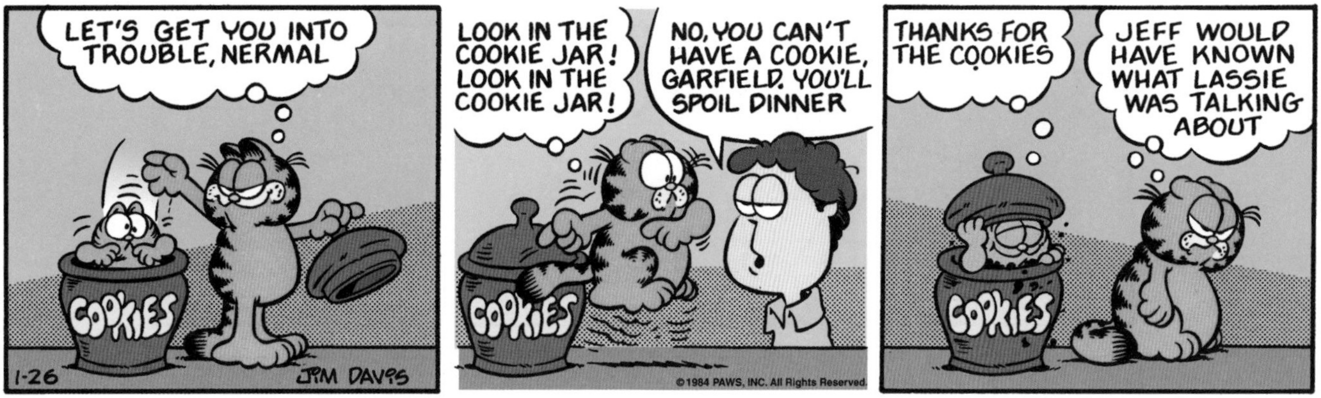
LET'S GET YOU INTO TROUBLE, NERMAL
1-26
JIM DAVIS
LOOK IN THE COOKIE JAR! LOOK IN THE COOKIE JAR!
NO, YOU CAN'T HAVE A COOKIE, GARFIELD. YOU'LL SPOIL DINNER
COOKIES
© 1984 PAWS, INC. All Rights Reserved.
THANKS FOR THE COOKIES
JEFF WOULD HAVE KNOWN WHAT LASSIE WAS TALKING ABOUT

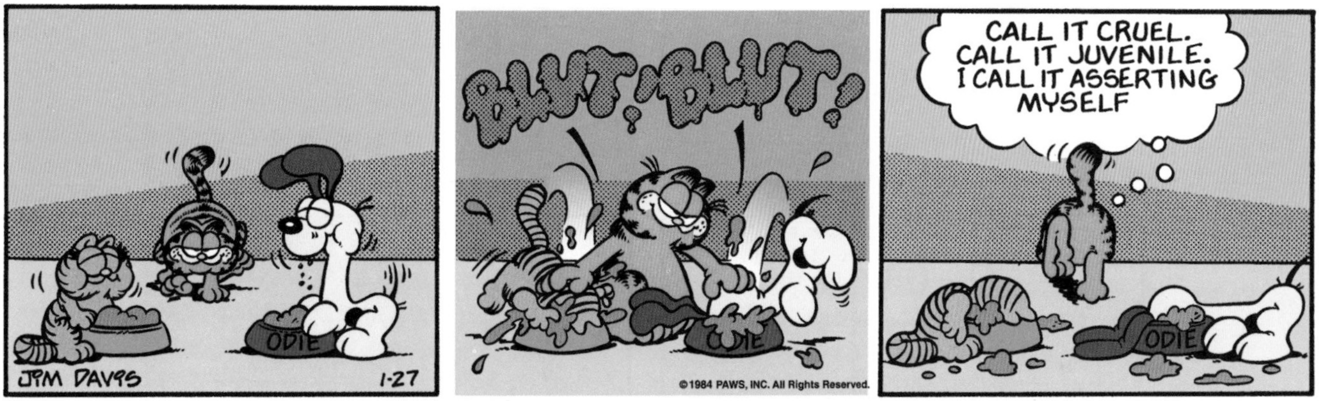
JIM DAVIS
1-27
ODIE
BLUT! BLUT!
© 1984 PAWS, INC. All Rights Reserved.
CALL IT CRUEL. CALL IT JUVENILE. I CALL IT ASSERTING MYSELF

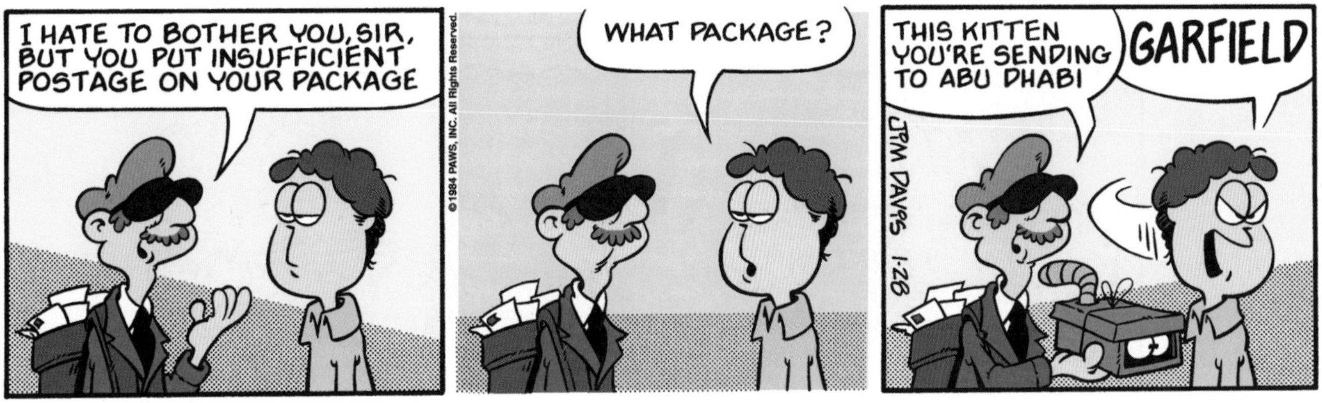
I HATE TO BOTHER YOU, SIR, BUT YOU PUT INSUFFICIENT POSTAGE ON YOUR PACKAGE
© 1984 PAWS, INC. All Rights Reserved.
WHAT PACKAGE?
THIS KITTEN YOU'RE SENDING TO ABU DHABI
GARFIELD
JIM DAVIS 1-28

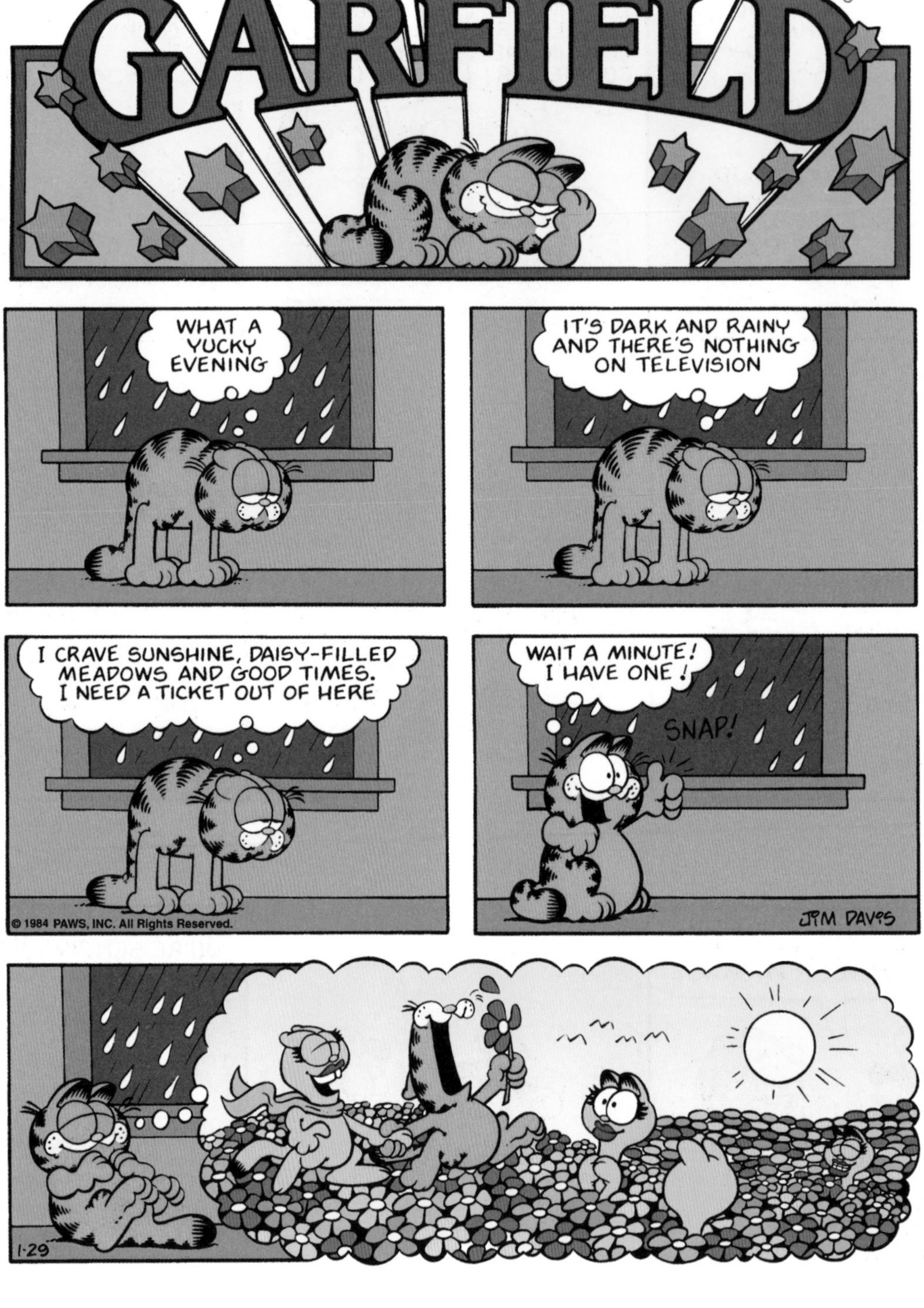
GARFIELD®
WHAT A YUCKY EVENING
IT'S DARK AND RAINY AND THERE'S NOTHING ON TELEVISION
I CRAVE SUNSHINE, DAISY-FILLED MEADOWS AND GOOD TIMES. I NEED A TICKET OUT OF HERE
WAIT A MINUTE! I HAVE ONE!
SNAP!
JIM DAVIS
1·29

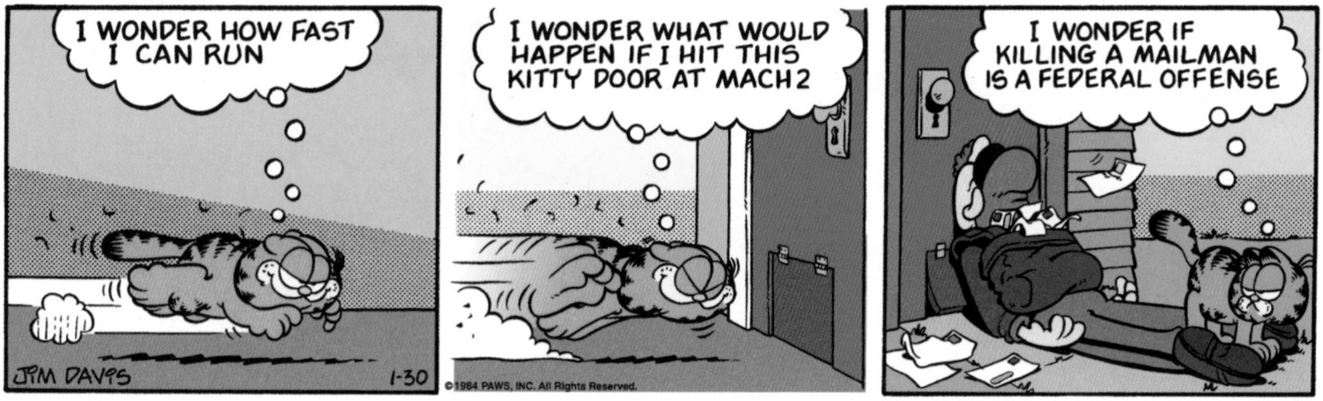
I WONDER HOW FAST I CAN RUN
JIM DAVIS
1-30
I WONDER WHAT WOULD HAPPEN IF I HIT THIS KITTY DOOR AT MACH 2
©1984 PAWS, INC. All Rights Reserved.
I WONDER IF KILLING A MAILMAN IS A FEDERAL OFFENSE

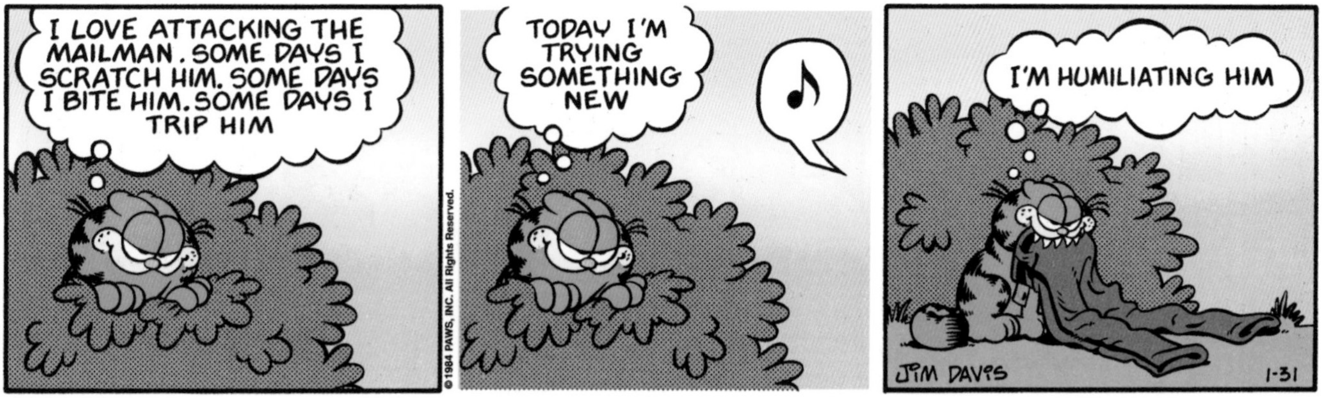
I LOVE ATTACKING THE MAILMAN. SOME DAYS I SCRATCH HIM. SOME DAYS I BITE HIM. SOME DAYS I TRIP HIM
©1984 PAWS, INC. All Rights Reserved.
TODAY I'M TRYING SOMETHING NEW
♪
I'M HUMILIATING HIM
JIM DAVIS
1-31

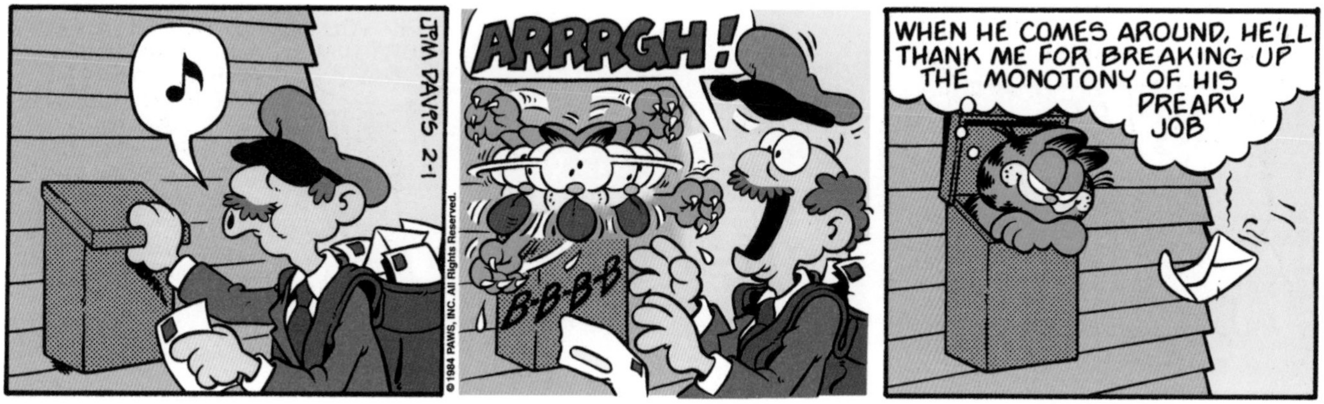
♪
JIM DAVIS 2-1
©1984 PAWS, INC. All Rights Reserved.
ARRRGH!
B-B-B-B
WHEN HE COMES AROUND, HE'LL THANK ME FOR BREAKING UP THE MONOTONY OF HIS DREARY JOB

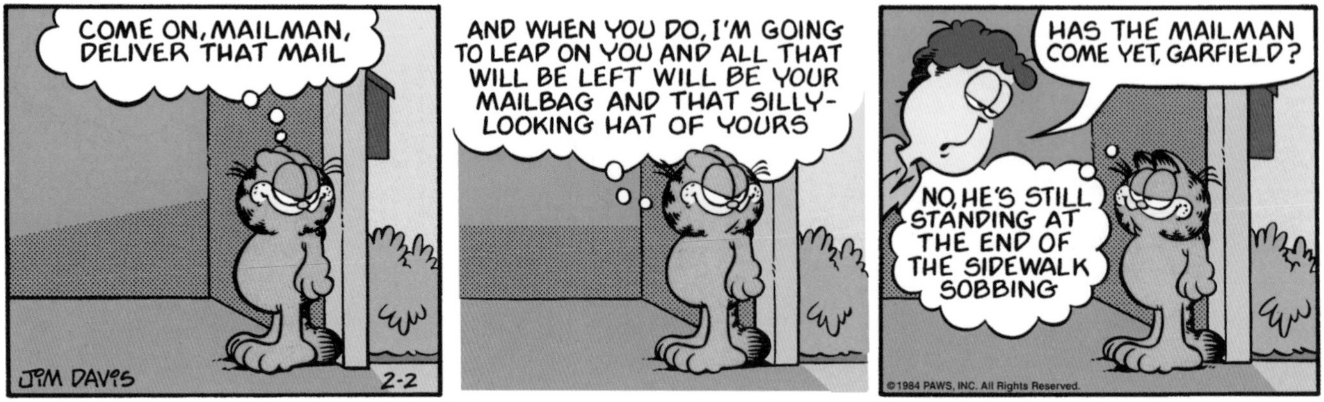
COME ON, MAILMAN, DELIVER THAT MAIL
JIM DAVIS
2-2
AND WHEN YOU DO, I'M GOING TO LEAP ON YOU AND ALL THAT WILL BE LEFT WILL BE YOUR MAILBAG AND THAT SILLY-LOOKING HAT OF YOURS
HAS THE MAILMAN COME YET, GARFIELD?
NO, HE'S STILL STANDING AT THE END OF THE SIDEWALK SOBBING
©1984 PAWS, INC. All Rights Reserved.

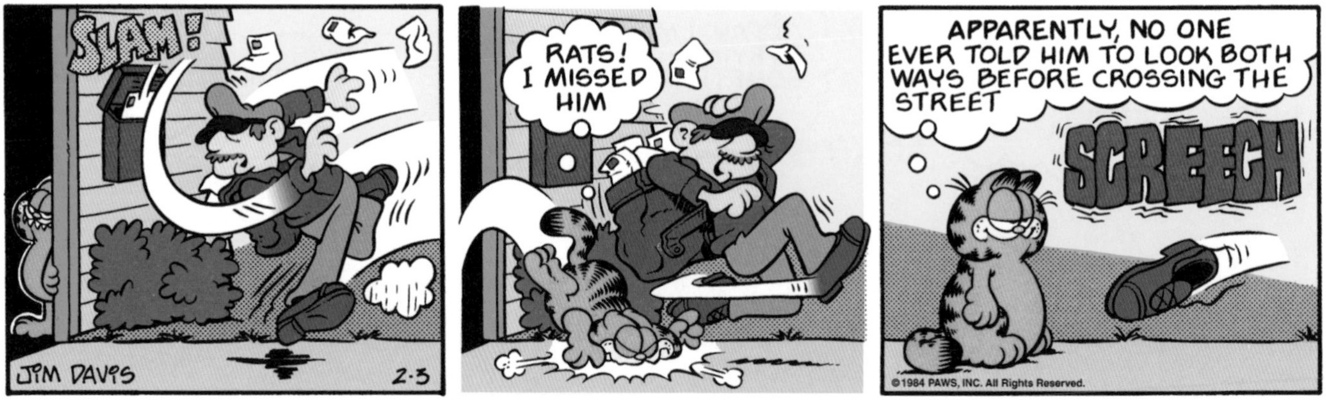
SLAM!
JIM DAVIS
2-3
RATS! I MISSED HIM
APPARENTLY, NO ONE EVER TOLD HIM TO LOOK BOTH WAYS BEFORE CROSSING THE STREET
SCREECH
©1984 PAWS, INC. All Rights Reserved.

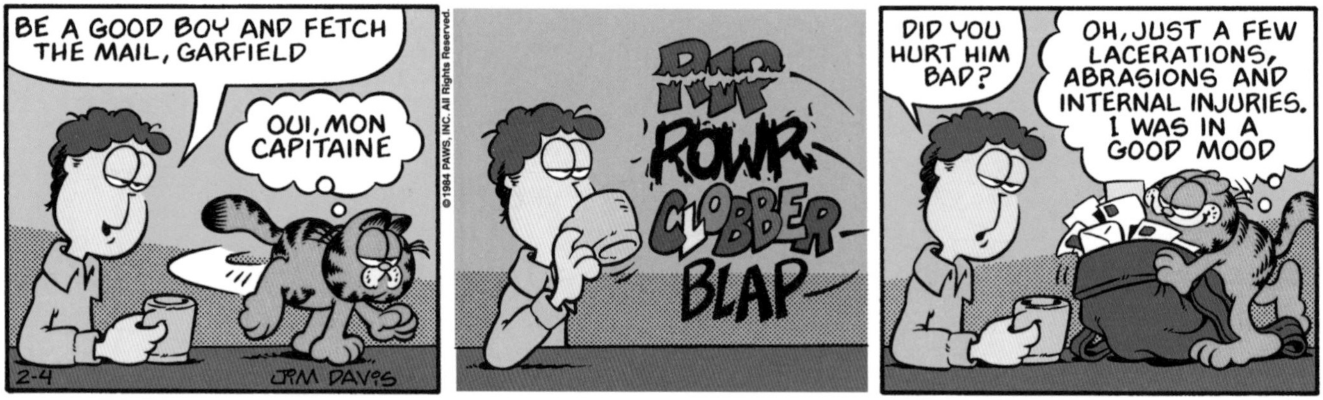
BE A GOOD BOY AND FETCH THE MAIL, GARFIELD
OUI, MON CAPITAINE
2-4
JIM DAVIS
©1984 PAWS, INC. All Rights Reserved.
ROWR
CLOBBER
BLAP
DID YOU HURT HIM BAD?
OH, JUST A FEW LACERATIONS, ABRASIONS AND INTERNAL INJURIES. I WAS IN A GOOD MOOD

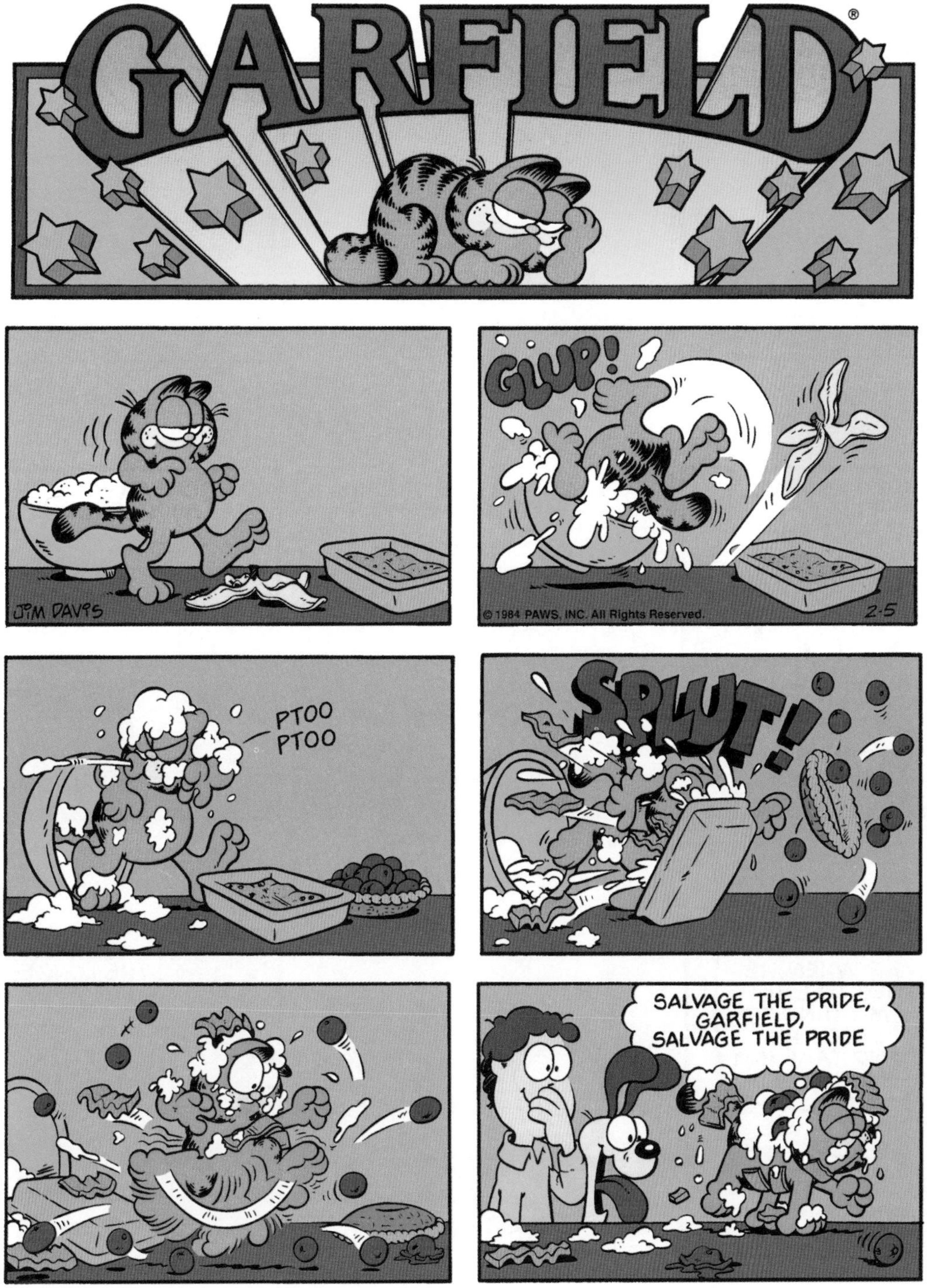
GARFIELD
JIM DAVIS
GLUP!
© 1984 PAWS, INC. All Rights Reserved.
2-5
PTOO PTOO
SPLUT!
SALVAGE THE PRIDE, GARFIELD, SALVAGE THE PRIDE

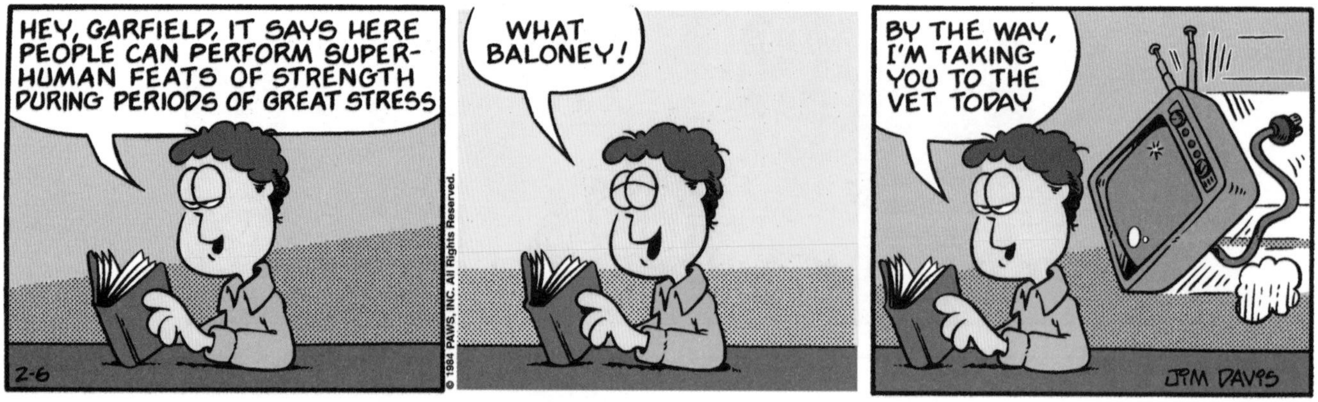
HEY, GARFIELD, IT SAYS HERE PEOPLE CAN PERFORM SUPER-HUMAN FEATS OF STRENGTH DURING PERIODS OF GREAT STRESS
2-6
© 1984 PAWS, INC. All Rights Reserved.
WHAT BALONEY!
BY THE WAY, I'M TAKING YOU TO THE VET TODAY
JIM DAVIS

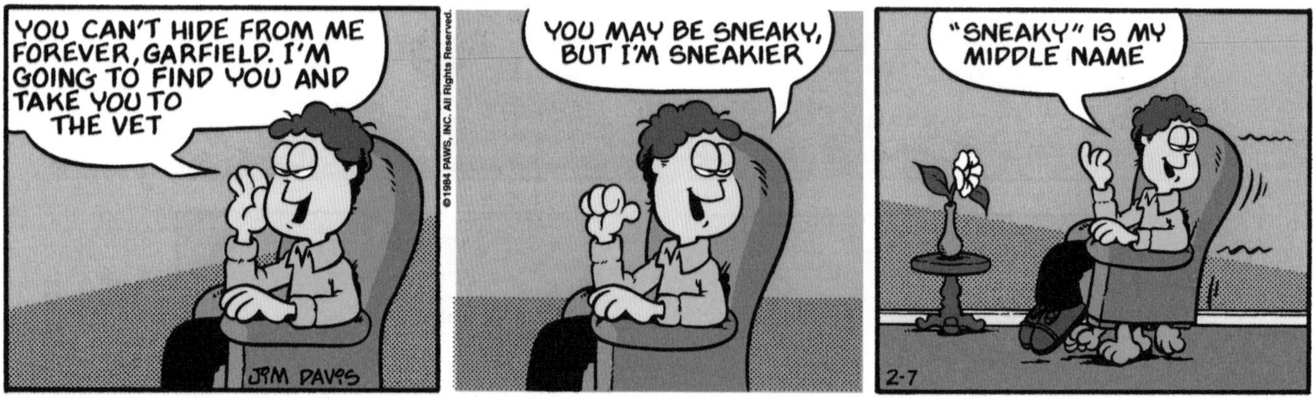
YOU CAN'T HIDE FROM ME FOREVER, GARFIELD. I'M GOING TO FIND YOU AND TAKE YOU TO THE VET
JIM DAVIS
© 1984 PAWS, INC. All Rights Reserved.
YOU MAY BE SNEAKY, BUT I'M SNEAKIER
"SNEAKY" IS MY MIDDLE NAME
2-7

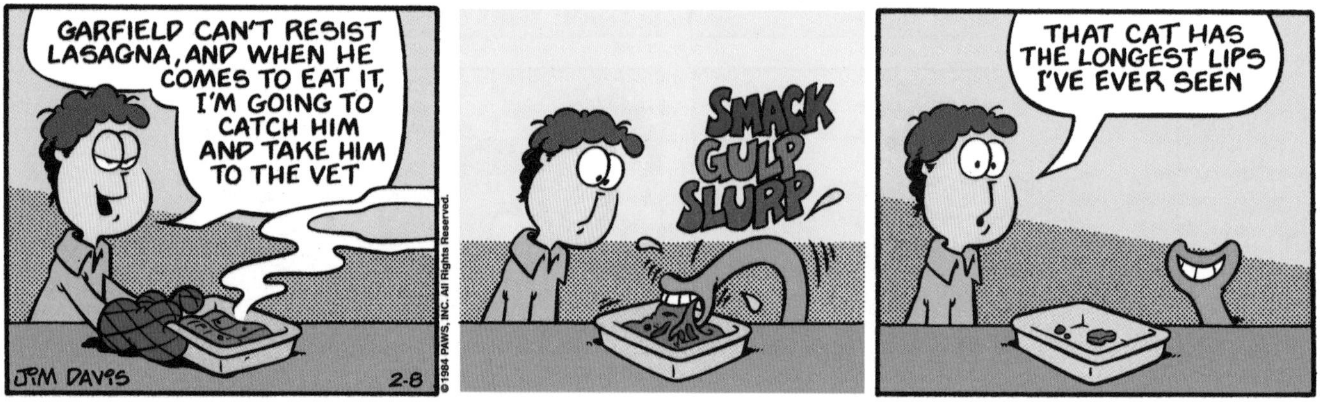
GARFIELD CAN'T RESIST LASAGNA, AND WHEN HE COMES TO EAT IT, I'M GOING TO CATCH HIM AND TAKE HIM TO THE VET
JIM DAVIS
2-8
© 1984 PAWS, INC. All Rights Reserved.
SMACK
GULP
SLURP
THAT CAT HAS THE LONGEST LIPS I'VE EVER SEEN

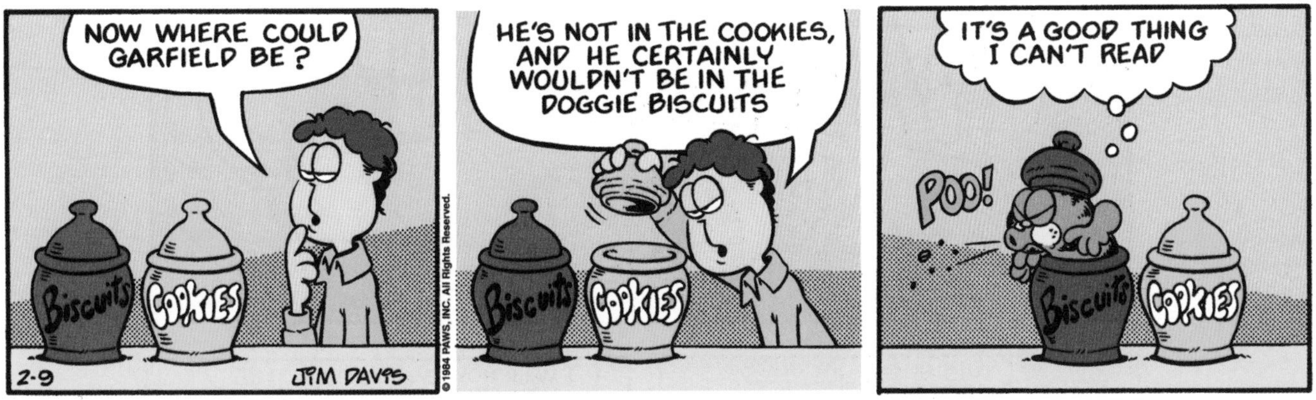
NOW WHERE COULD GARFIELD BE ?
2-9
JIM DAVIS
© 1984 PAWS, INC. All Rights Reserved.
HE'S NOT IN THE COOKIES, AND HE CERTAINLY WOULDN'T BE IN THE DOGGIE BISCUITS
BISCUITS
COOKIES
POO!
IT'S A GOOD THING I CAN'T READ

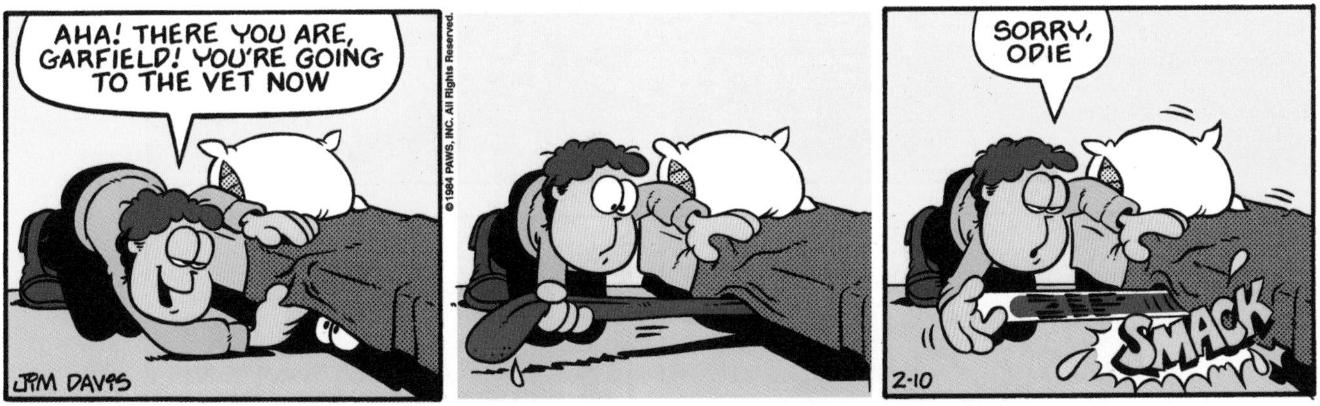
AHA! THERE YOU ARE, GARFIELD! YOU'RE GOING TO THE VET NOW
JIM DAVIS
© 1984 PAWS, INC. All Rights Reserved.
SORRY, ODIE
SMACK
2-10

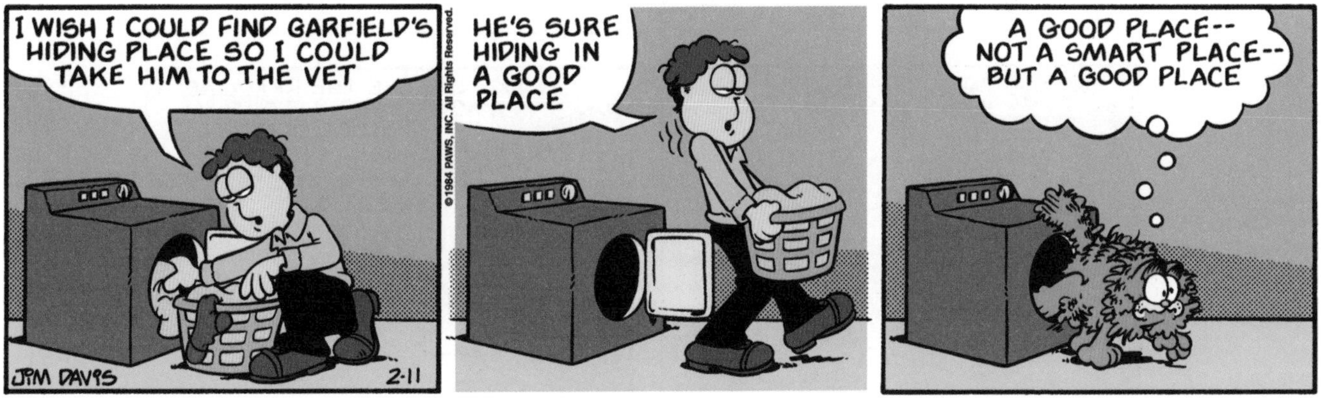
I WISH I COULD FIND GARFIELD'S HIDING PLACE SO I COULD TAKE HIM TO THE VET
JIM DAVIS
2-11
© 1984 PAWS, INC. All Rights Reserved.
HE'S SURE HIDING IN A GOOD PLACE
A GOOD PLACE-- NOT A SMART PLACE-- BUT A GOOD PLACE

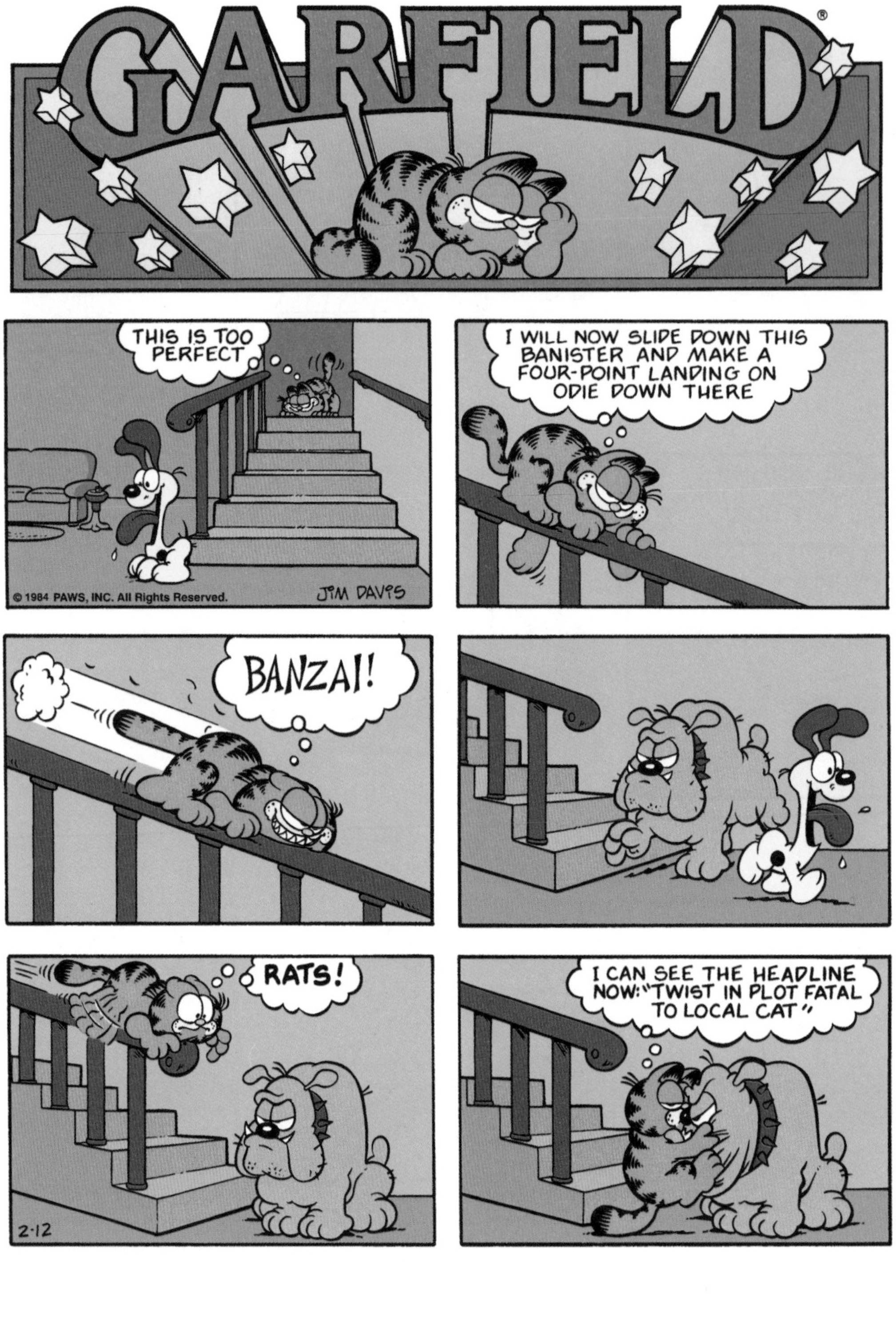
GARFIELD®
THIS IS TOO PERFECT
© 1984 PAWS, INC. All Rights Reserved.
JIM DAVIS
I WILL NOW SLIDE DOWN THIS BANISTER AND MAKE A FOUR-POINT LANDING ON ODIE DOWN THERE
BANZAI!
RATS!
2-12
I CAN SEE THE HEADLINE NOW: "TWIST IN PLOT FATAL TO LOCAL CAT"

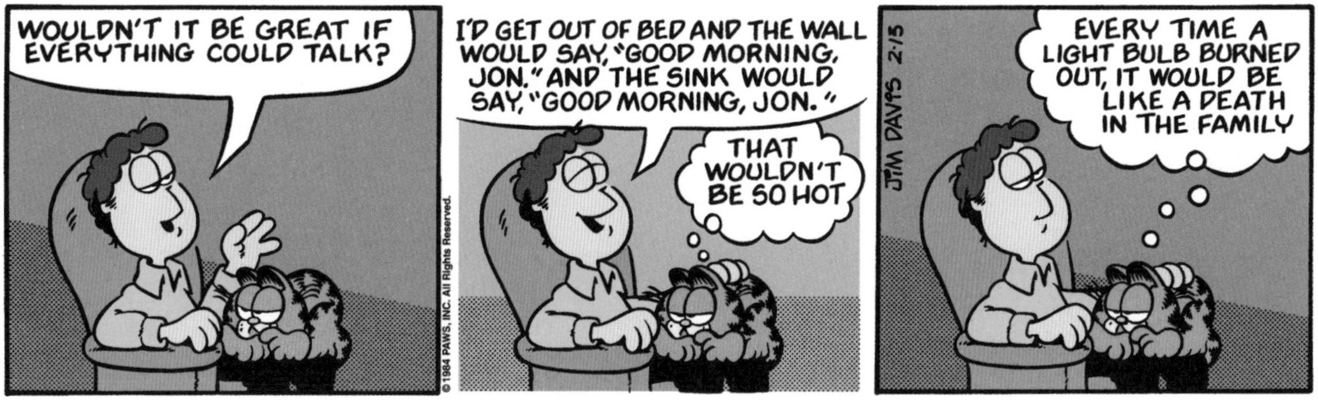
WOULDN'T IT BE GREAT IF EVERYTHING COULD TALK?
©1984 PAWS, INC. All Rights Reserved.
I'D GET OUT OF BED AND THE WALL WOULD SAY, "GOOD MORNING, JON." AND THE SINK WOULD SAY, "GOOD MORNING, JON."
THAT WOULDN'T BE SO HOT
JIM DAVIS 2-13
EVERY TIME A LIGHT BULB BURNED OUT, IT WOULD BE LIKE A DEATH IN THE FAMILY

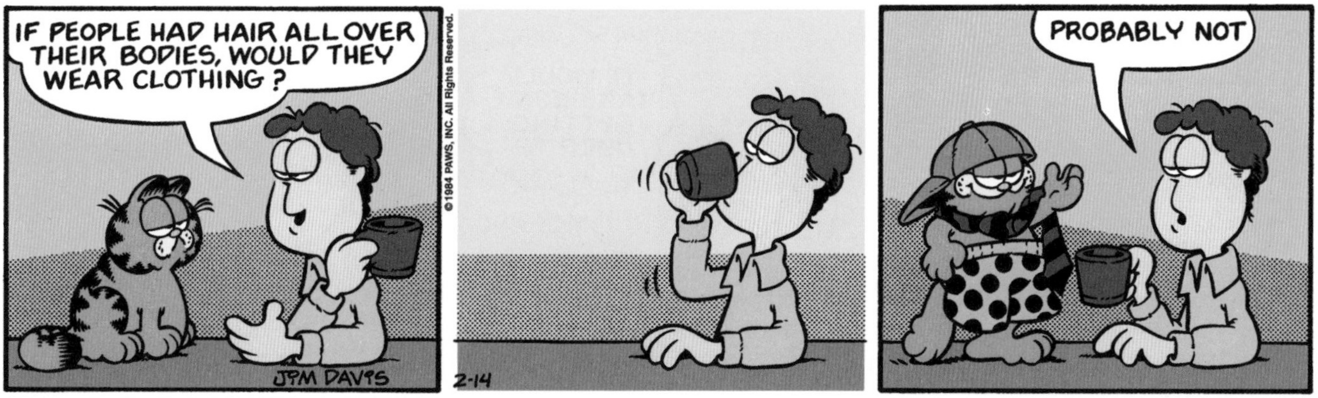
IF PEOPLE HAD HAIR ALL OVER THEIR BODIES, WOULD THEY WEAR CLOTHING?
JIM DAVIS
©1984 PAWS, INC. All Rights Reserved.
2-14
PROBABLY NOT

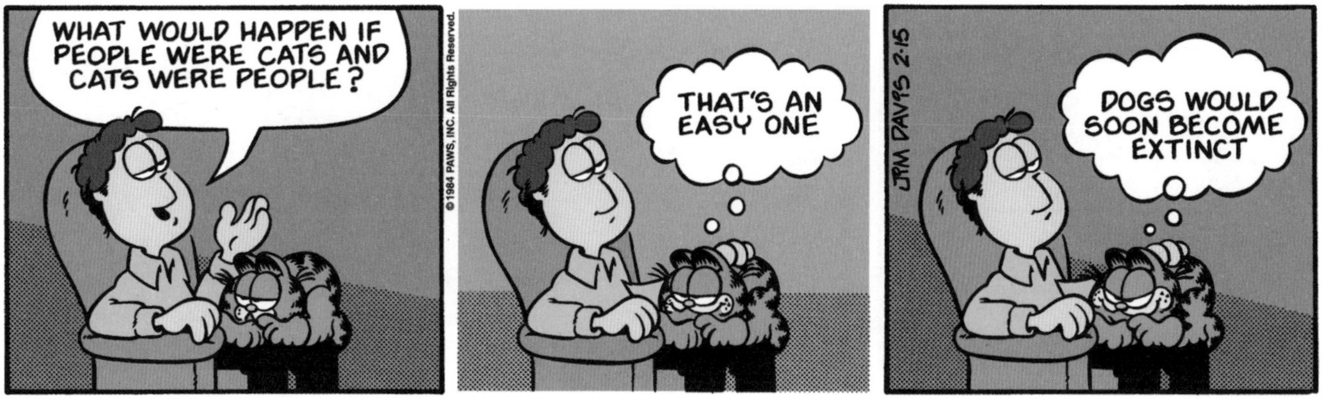
WHAT WOULD HAPPEN IF PEOPLE WERE CATS AND CATS WERE PEOPLE?
©1984 PAWS, INC. All Rights Reserved.
THAT'S AN EASY ONE
JIM DAVIS 2-15
DOGS WOULD SOON BECOME EXTINCT

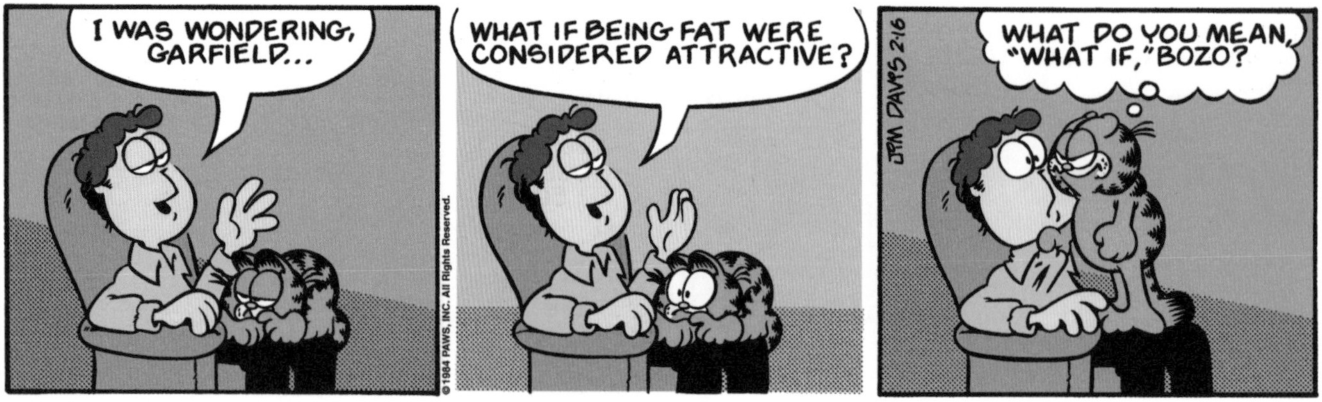
I WAS WONDERING, GARFIELD...
WHAT IF BEING FAT WERE CONSIDERED ATTRACTIVE?
©1984 PAWS, INC. All Rights Reserved.
JIM DAVIS 2·16
WHAT DO YOU MEAN, "WHAT IF," BOZO?

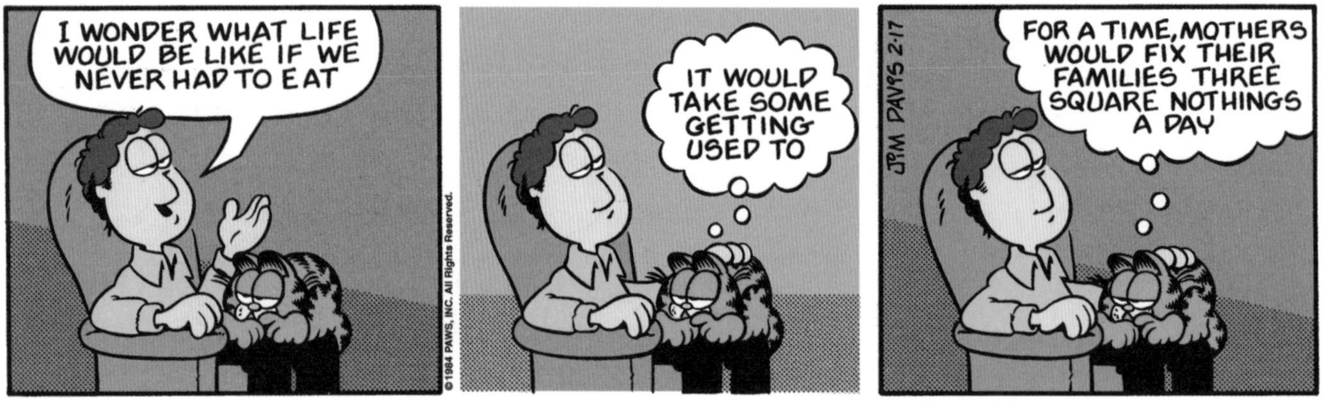
I WONDER WHAT LIFE WOULD BE LIKE IF WE NEVER HAD TO EAT
©1984 PAWS, INC. All Rights Reserved.
IT WOULD TAKE SOME GETTING USED TO
JIM DAVIS 2·17
FOR A TIME, MOTHERS WOULD FIX THEIR FAMILIES THREE SQUARE NOTHINGS A DAY

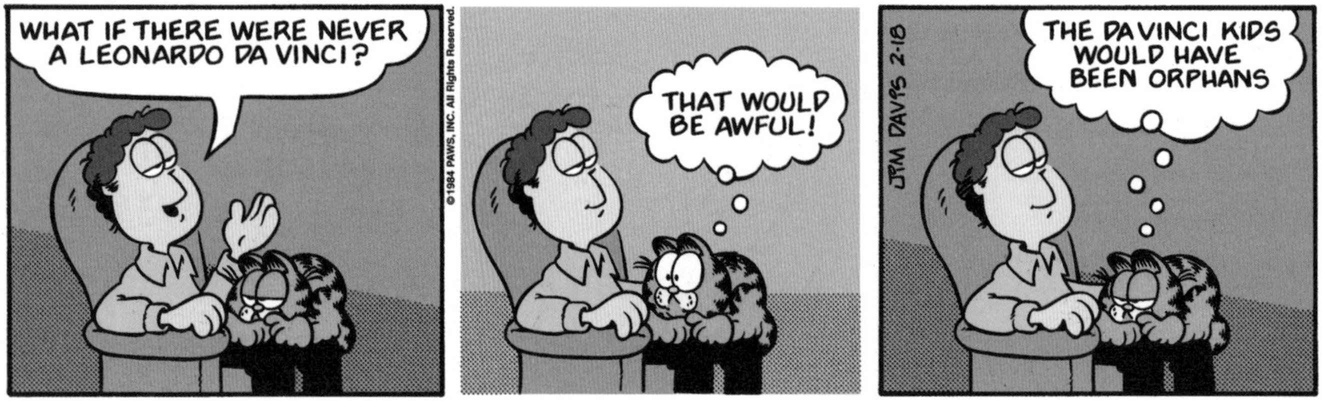
WHAT IF THERE WERE NEVER A LEONARDO DA VINCI?
©1984 PAWS, INC. All Rights Reserved.
THAT WOULD BE AWFUL!
JIM DAVIS 2·18
THE DA VINCI KIDS WOULD HAVE BEEN ORPHANS

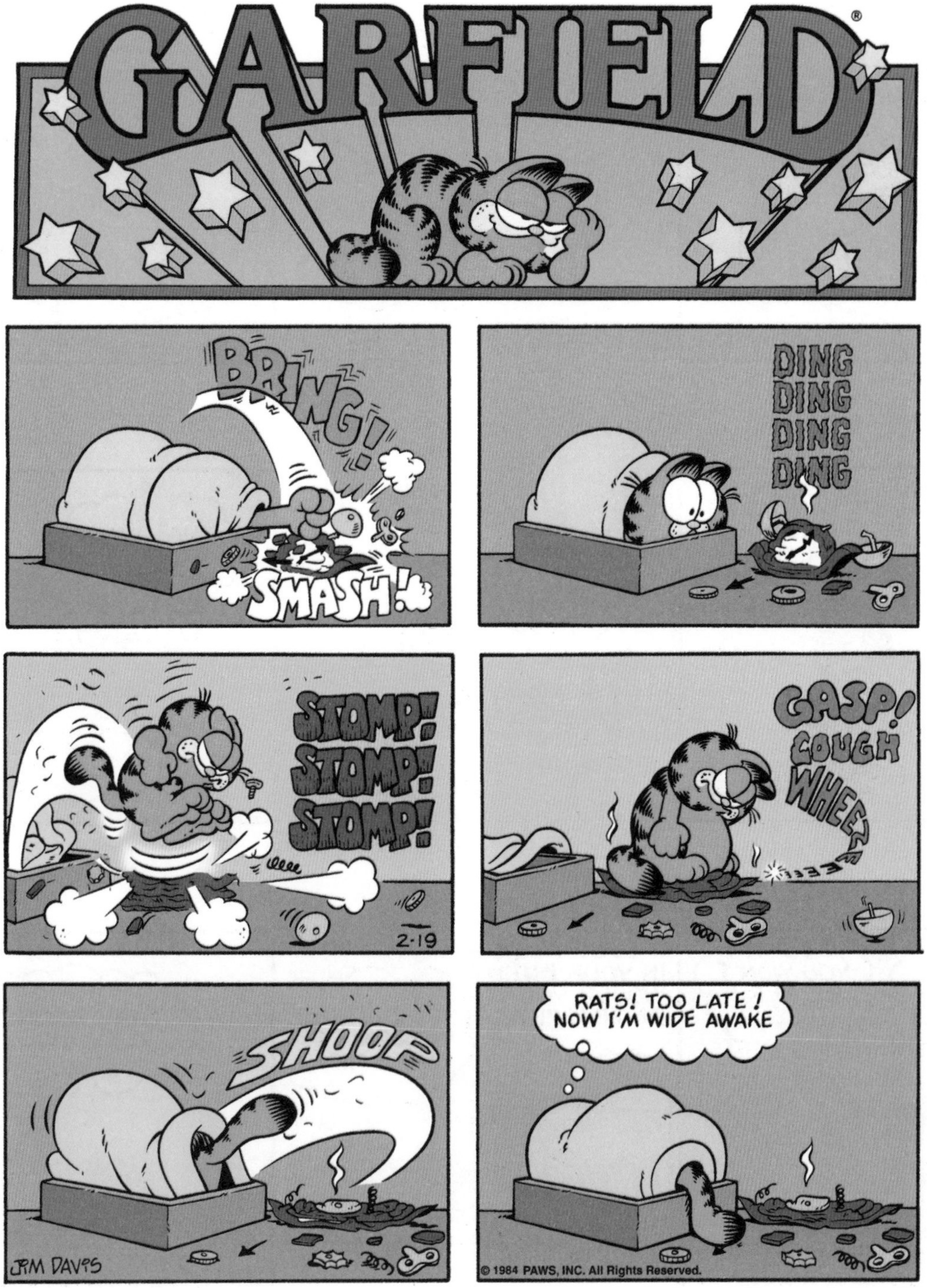
GARFIELD
BRING!
SMASH!
DING
DING
DING
DING
STOMP!
STOMP!
STOMP!
2-19
GASP!
COUGH
WHEEZE
SHOOP
RATS! TOO LATE! NOW I'M WIDE AWAKE
JIM DAVIS

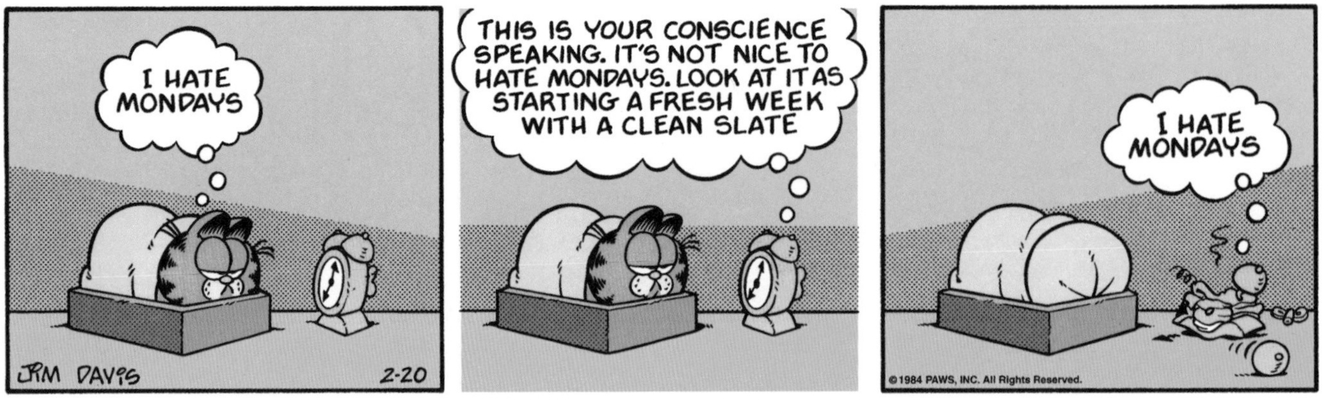
I HATE MONDAYS
JIM DAVIS 2-20
THIS IS YOUR CONSCIENCE SPEAKING. IT'S NOT NICE TO HATE MONDAYS. LOOK AT IT AS STARTING A FRESH WEEK WITH A CLEAN SLATE
I HATE MONDAYS
©1984 PAWS, INC. All Rights Reserved.

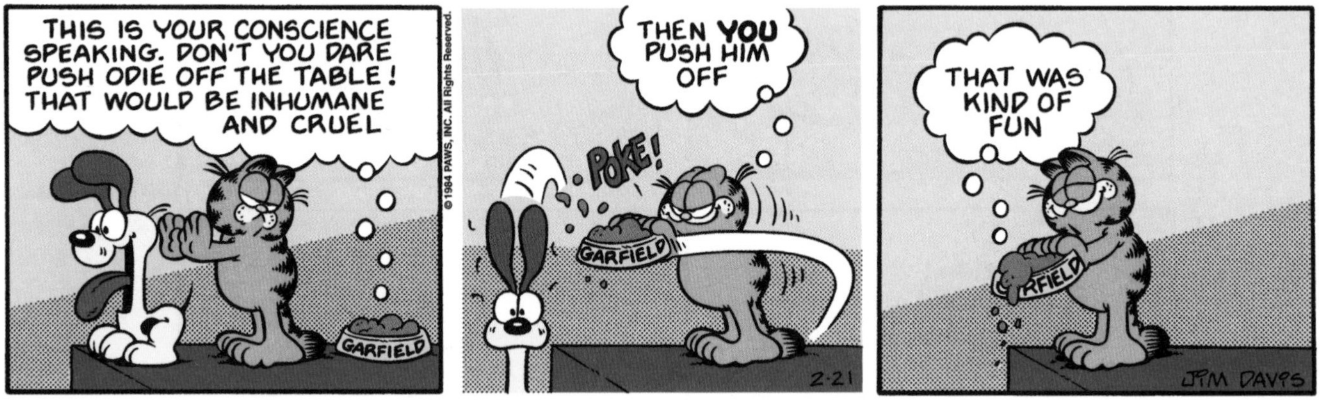
THIS IS YOUR CONSCIENCE SPEAKING. DON'T YOU DARE PUSH ODIE OFF THE TABLE! THAT WOULD BE INHUMANE AND CRUEL
GARFIELD
©1984 PAWS, INC. All Rights Reserved.
THEN **YOU** PUSH HIM OFF
POKE!
GARFIELD
2-21
THAT WAS KIND OF FUN
RFIELD
JIM DAVIS

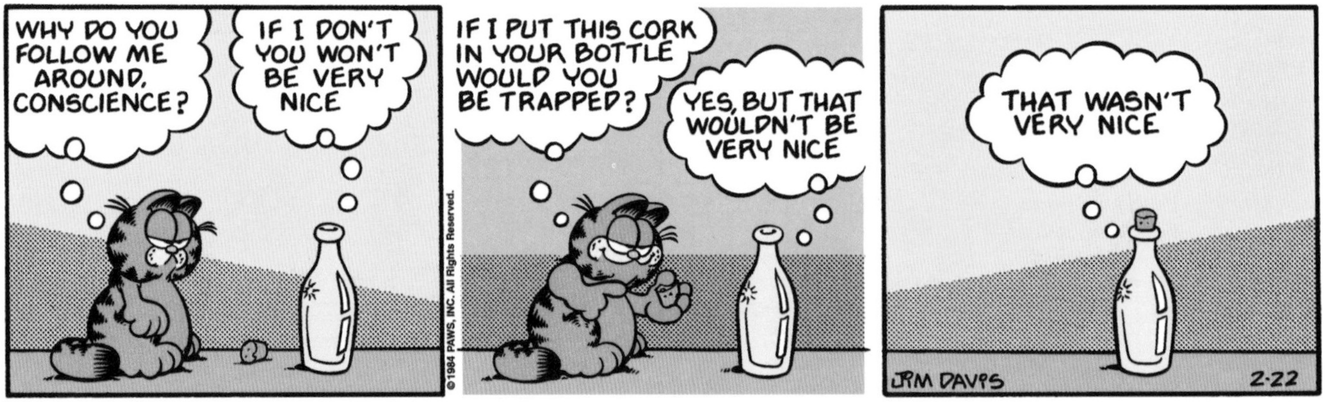
WHY DO YOU FOLLOW ME AROUND, CONSCIENCE?
IF I DON'T YOU WON'T BE VERY NICE
©1984 PAWS, INC. All Rights Reserved.
IF I PUT THIS CORK IN YOUR BOTTLE WOULD YOU BE TRAPPED?
YES, BUT THAT WOULDN'T BE VERY NICE
THAT WASN'T VERY NICE
JIM DAVIS 2-22

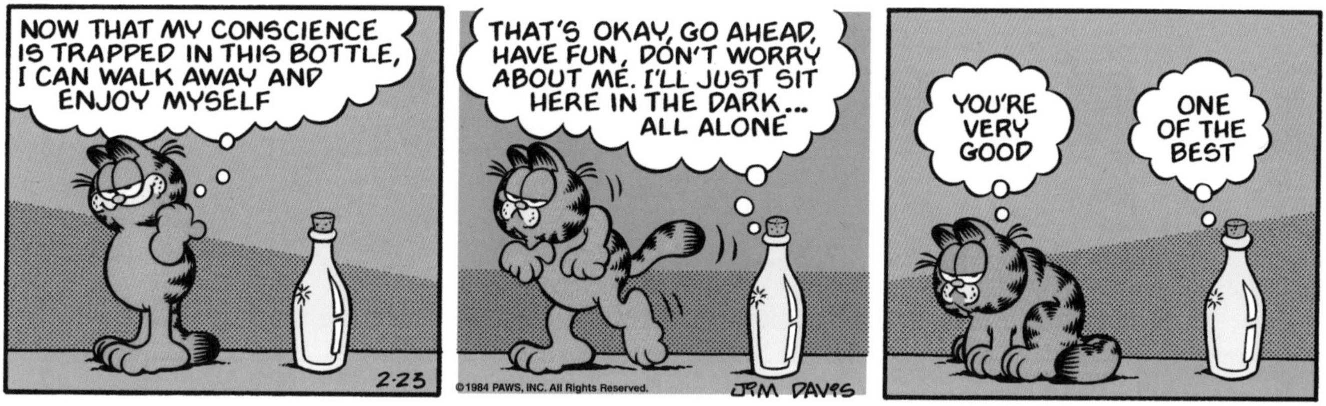
NOW THAT MY CONSCIENCE IS TRAPPED IN THIS BOTTLE, I CAN WALK AWAY AND ENJOY MYSELF
2-23
THAT'S OKAY, GO AHEAD, HAVE FUN, DON'T WORRY ABOUT ME. I'LL JUST SIT HERE IN THE DARK... ALL ALONE
©1984 PAWS, INC. All Rights Reserved.
JIM DAVIS
YOU'RE VERY GOOD
ONE OF THE BEST

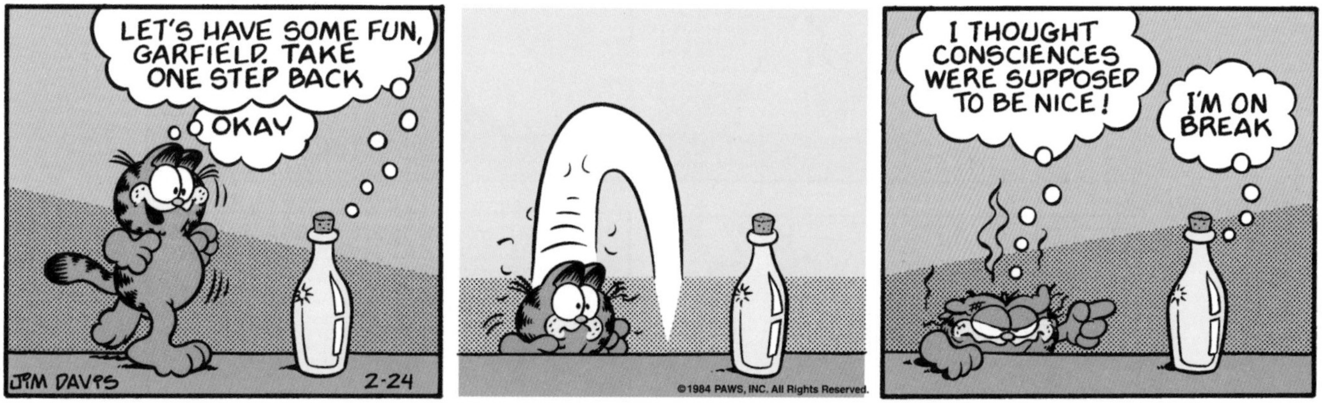
LET'S HAVE SOME FUN, GARFIELD. TAKE ONE STEP BACK
OKAY
JIM DAVIS
2-24
©1984 PAWS, INC. All Rights Reserved.
I THOUGHT CONSCIENCES WERE SUPPOSED TO BE NICE!
I'M ON BREAK

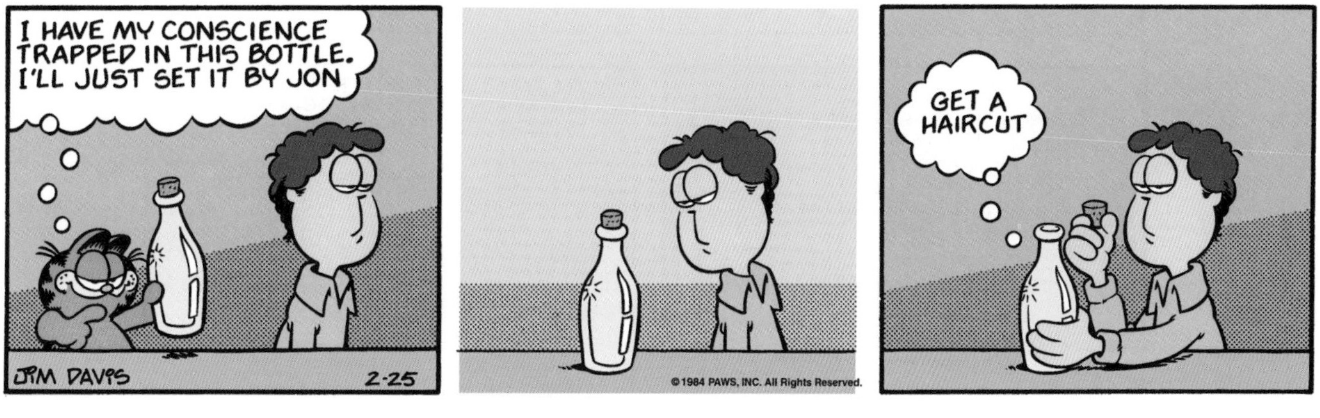
I HAVE MY CONSCIENCE TRAPPED IN THIS BOTTLE. I'LL JUST SET IT BY JON
JIM DAVIS
2-25
©1984 PAWS, INC. All Rights Reserved.
GET A HAIRCUT

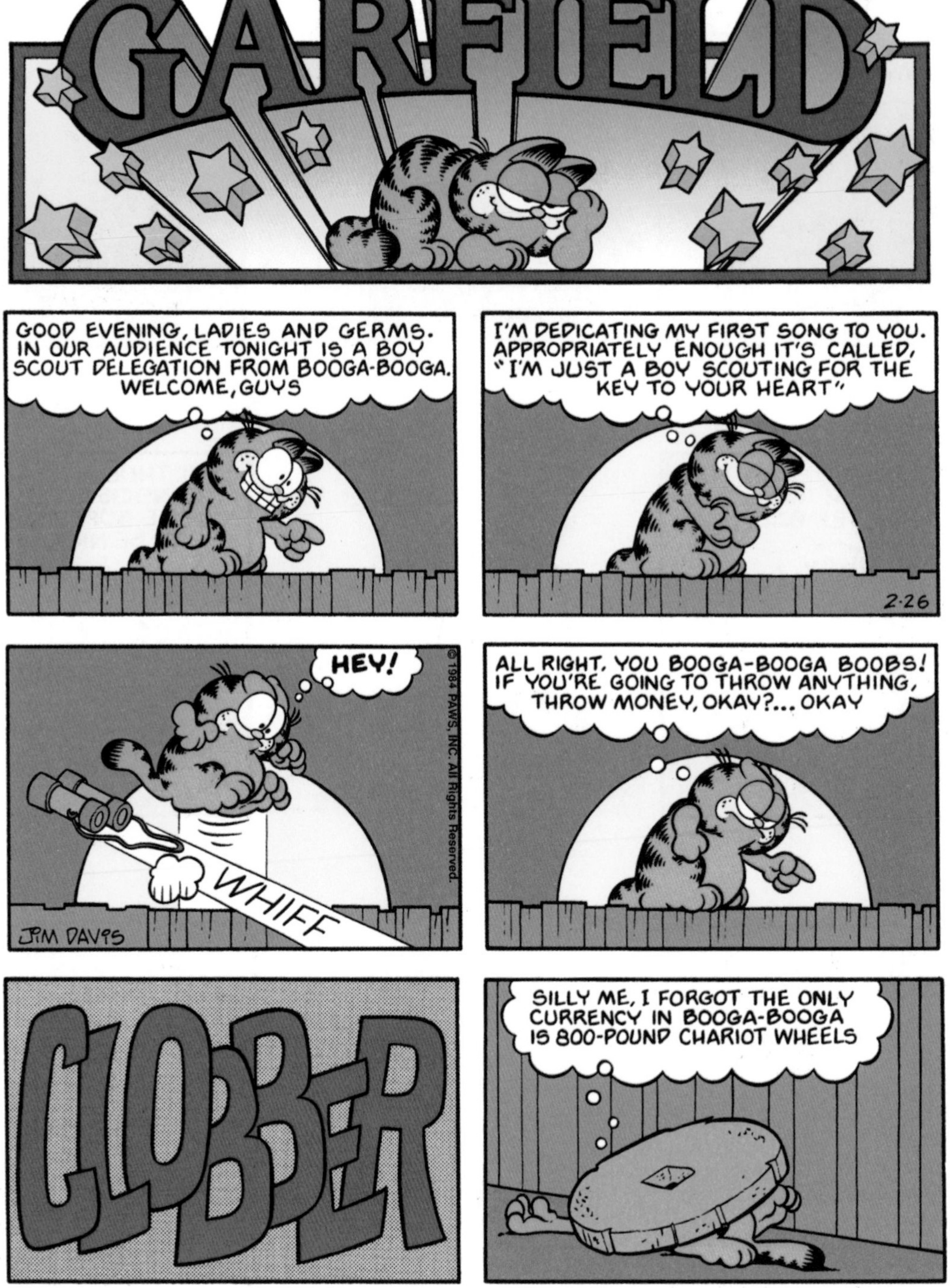
GARFIELD®
GOOD EVENING, LADIES AND GERMS. IN OUR AUDIENCE TONIGHT IS A BOY SCOUT DELEGATION FROM BOOGA-BOOGA. WELCOME, GUYS
I'M DEDICATING MY FIRST SONG TO YOU. APPROPRIATELY ENOUGH IT'S CALLED, "I'M JUST A BOY SCOUTING FOR THE KEY TO YOUR HEART"
2-26
HEY!
WHIFF
JIM DAVIS
© 1984 PAWS, INC. All Rights Reserved.
ALL RIGHT, YOU BOOGA-BOOGA BOOBS! IF YOU'RE GOING TO THROW ANYTHING, THROW MONEY, OKAY?... OKAY
CLOBBER
SILLY ME, I FORGOT THE ONLY CURRENCY IN BOOGA-BOOGA IS 800-POUND CHARIOT WHEELS

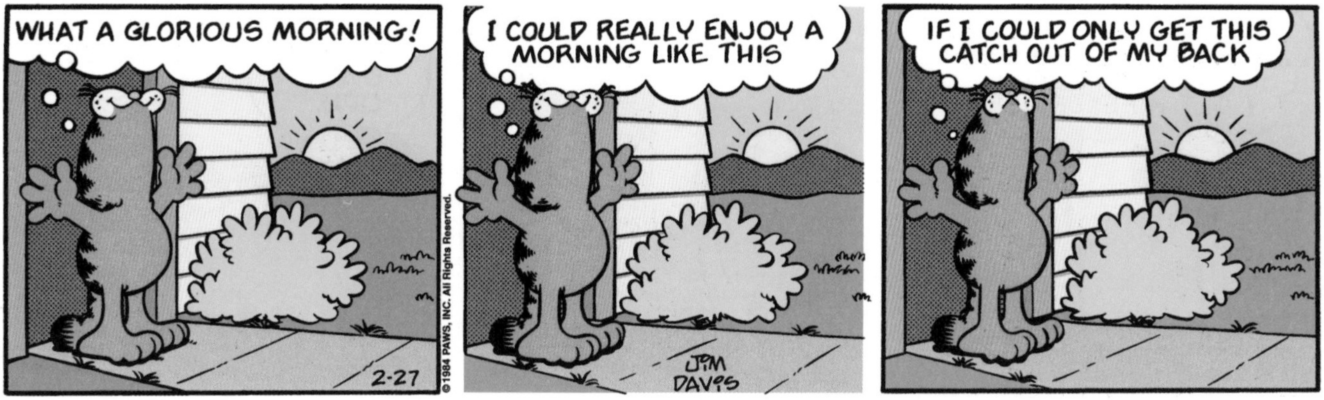
WHAT A GLORIOUS MORNING!
2-27
©1984 PAWS, INC. All Rights Reserved.
I COULD REALLY ENJOY A MORNING LIKE THIS
JIM DAVIS
IF I COULD ONLY GET THIS CATCH OUT OF MY BACK

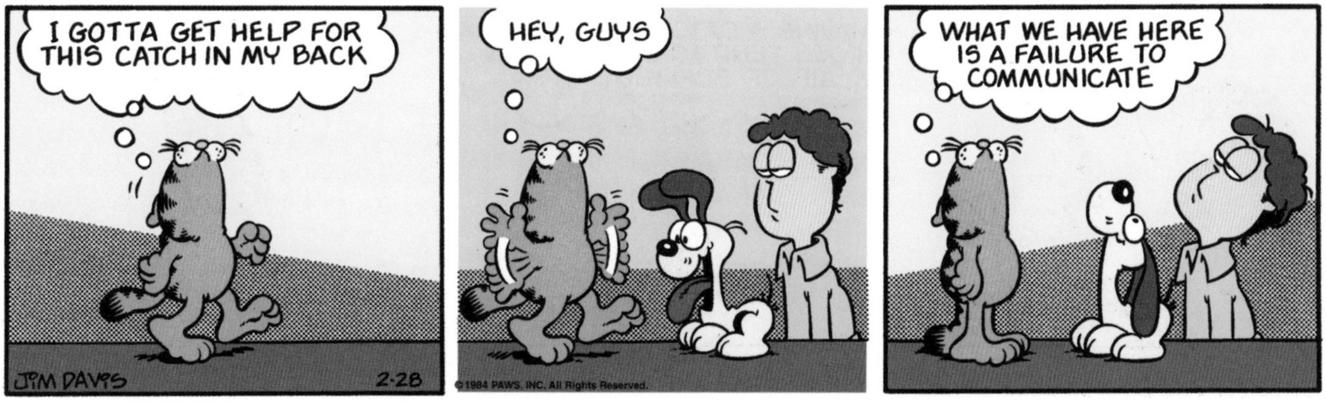
I GOTTA GET HELP FOR THIS CATCH IN MY BACK
JIM DAVIS
2-28
HEY, GUYS
©1984 PAWS, INC. All Rights Reserved.
WHAT WE HAVE HERE IS A FAILURE TO COMMUNICATE

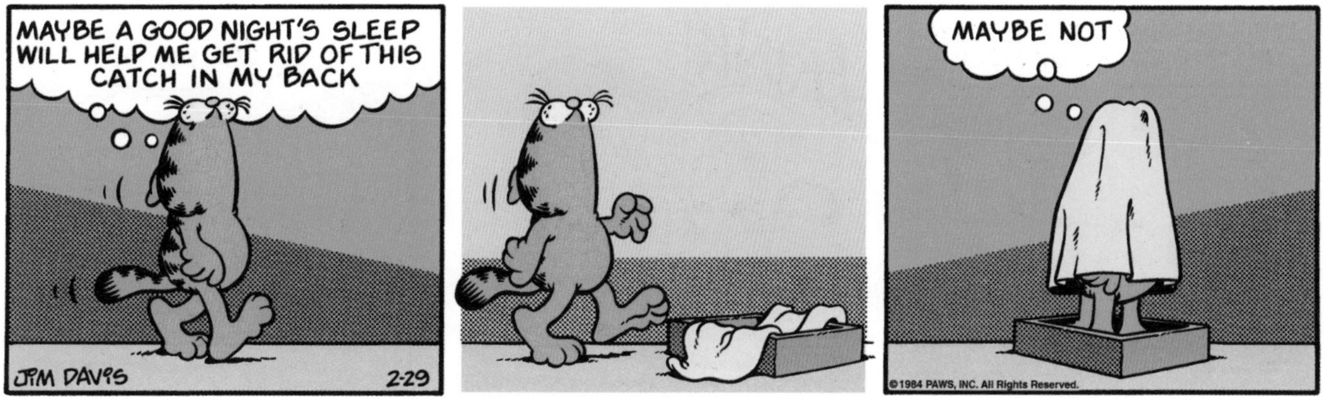
MAYBE A GOOD NIGHT'S SLEEP WILL HELP ME GET RID OF THIS CATCH IN MY BACK
JIM DAVIS
2-29
MAYBE NOT
©1984 PAWS, INC. All Rights Reserved.

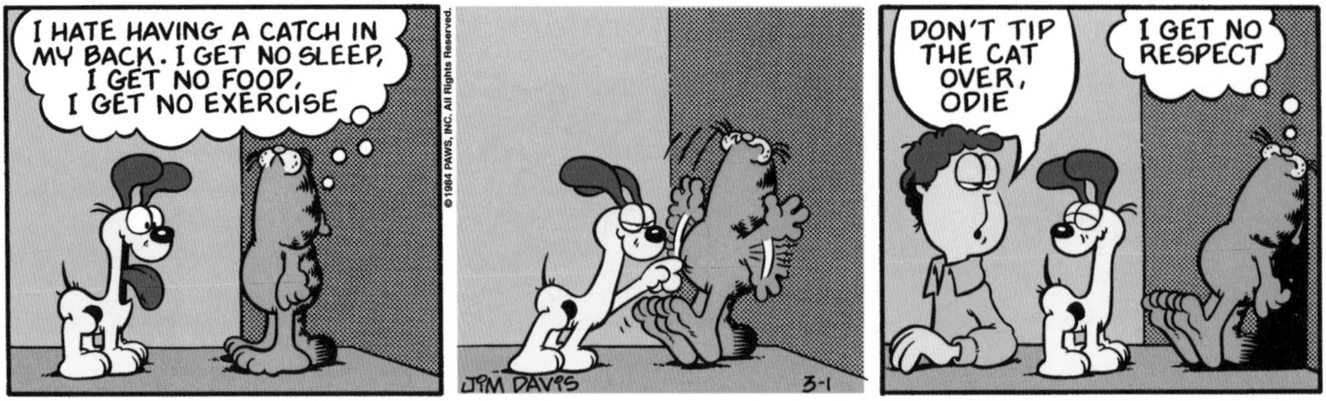
I HATE HAVING A CATCH IN MY BACK. I GET NO SLEEP, I GET NO FOOD, I GET NO EXERCISE
© 1984 PAWS, INC. All Rights Reserved.
JIM DAVIS
3-1
DON'T TIP THE CAT OVER, ODIE
I GET NO RESPECT

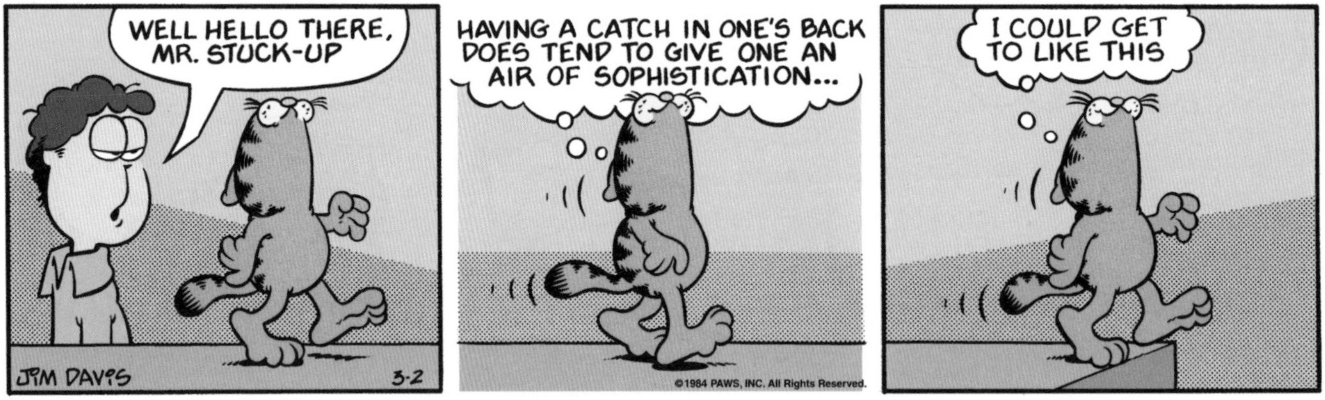
WELL HELLO THERE, MR. STUCK-UP
JIM DAVIS
3-2
HAVING A CATCH IN ONE'S BACK DOES TEND TO GIVE ONE AN AIR OF SOPHISTICATION...
© 1984 PAWS, INC. All Rights Reserved.
I COULD GET TO LIKE THIS

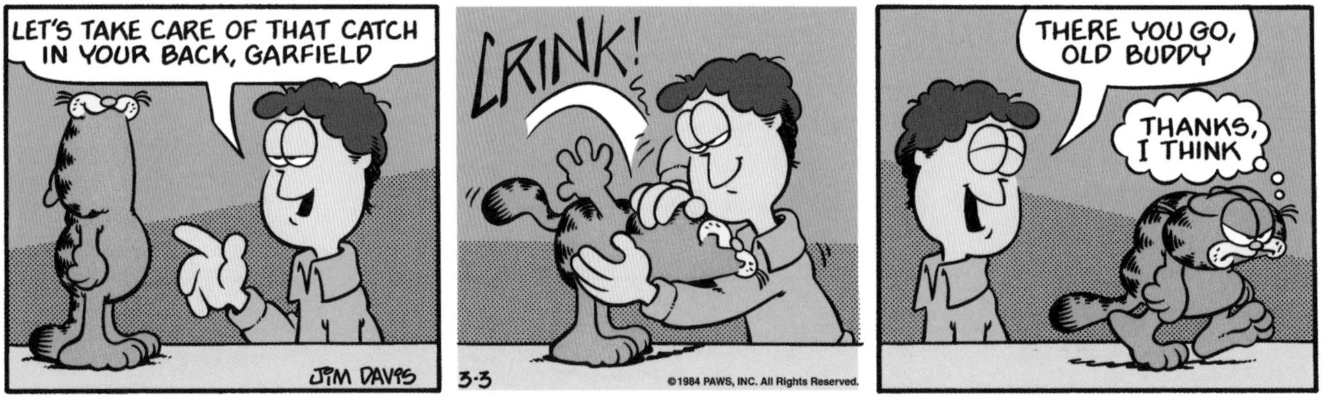
LET'S TAKE CARE OF THAT CATCH IN YOUR BACK, GARFIELD
JIM DAVIS
CRINK!
3-3
© 1984 PAWS, INC. All Rights Reserved.
THERE YOU GO, OLD BUDDY
THANKS, I THINK

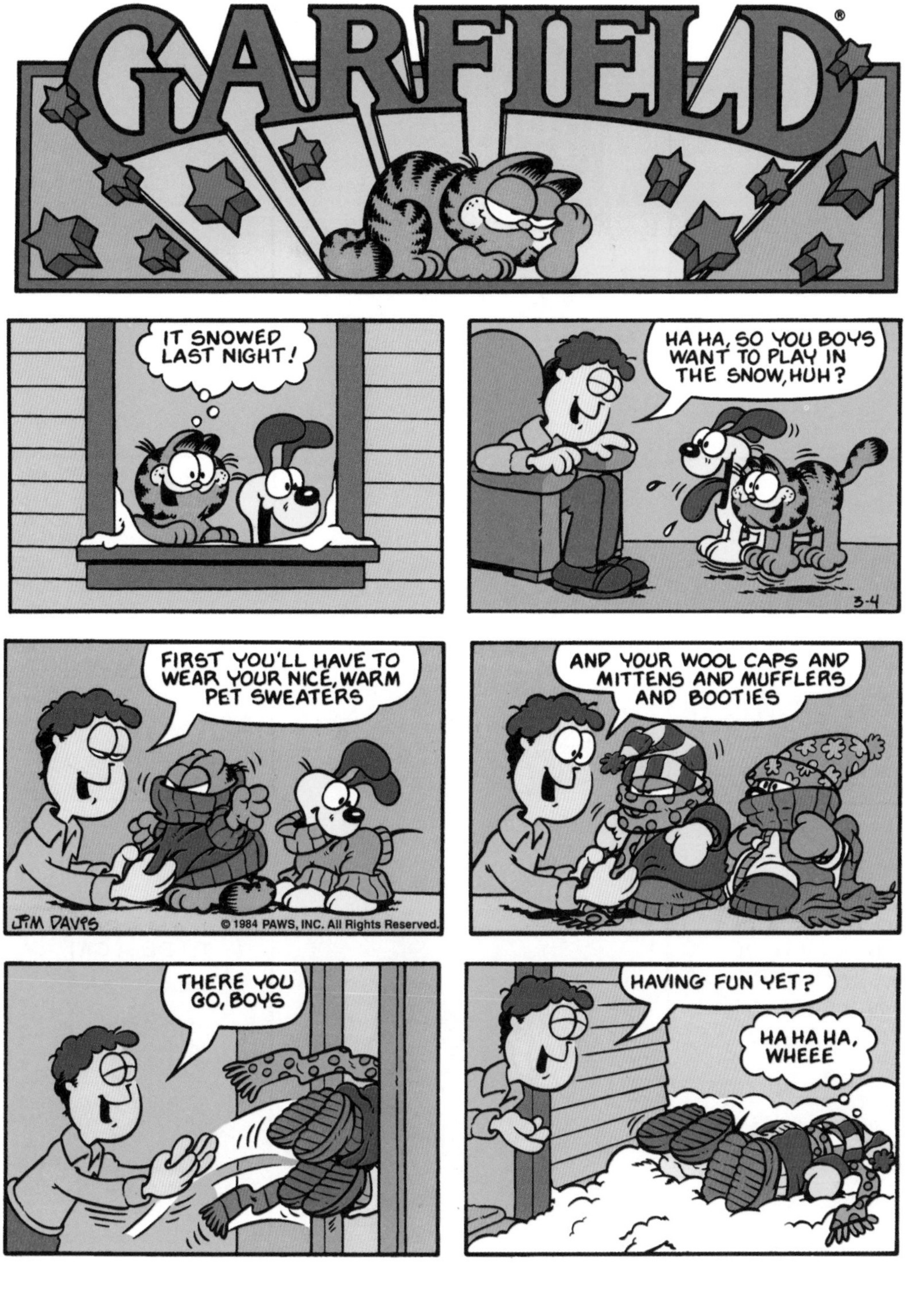
GARFIELD®
IT SNOWED LAST NIGHT!
HA HA, SO YOU BOYS WANT TO PLAY IN THE SNOW, HUH?
3-4
FIRST YOU'LL HAVE TO WEAR YOUR NICE, WARM PET SWEATERS
AND YOUR WOOL CAPS AND MITTENS AND MUFFLERS AND BOOTIES
JIM DAVIS
© 1984 PAWS, INC. All Rights Reserved.
THERE YOU GO, BOYS
HAVING FUN YET?
HA HA HA, WHEEE

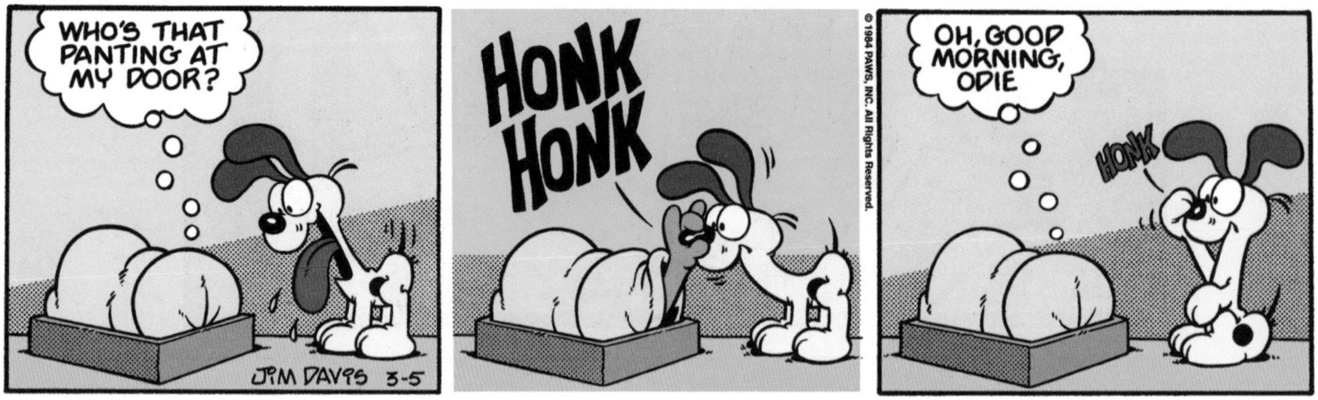
WHO'S THAT PANTING AT MY DOOR?
JIM DAVIS 3-5
HONK HONK
© 1984 PAWS, INC. All Rights Reserved.
OH, GOOD MORNING, ODIE
HONK

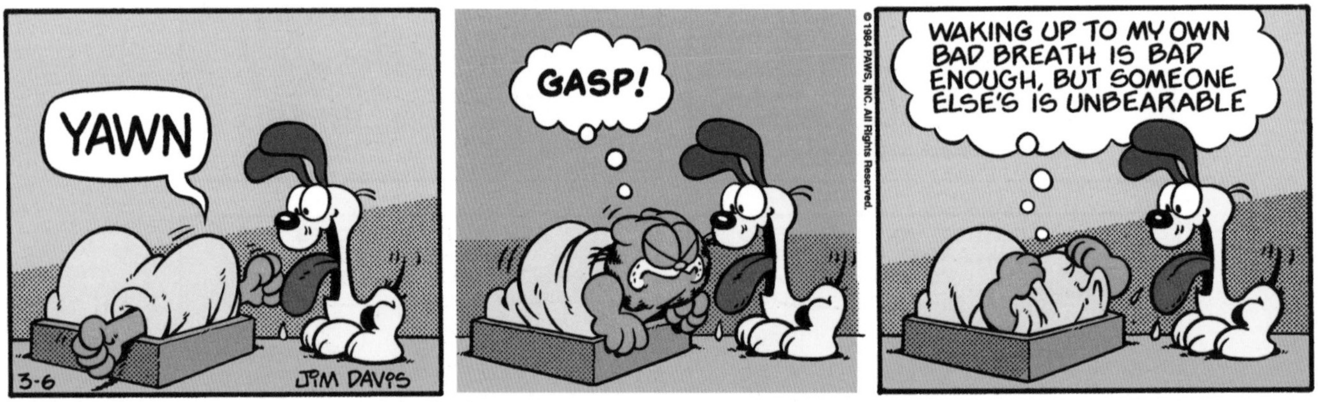
YAWN
3-6 JIM DAVIS
GASP!
© 1984 PAWS, INC. All Rights Reserved.
WAKING UP TO MY OWN BAD BREATH IS BAD ENOUGH, BUT SOMEONE ELSE'S IS UNBEARABLE

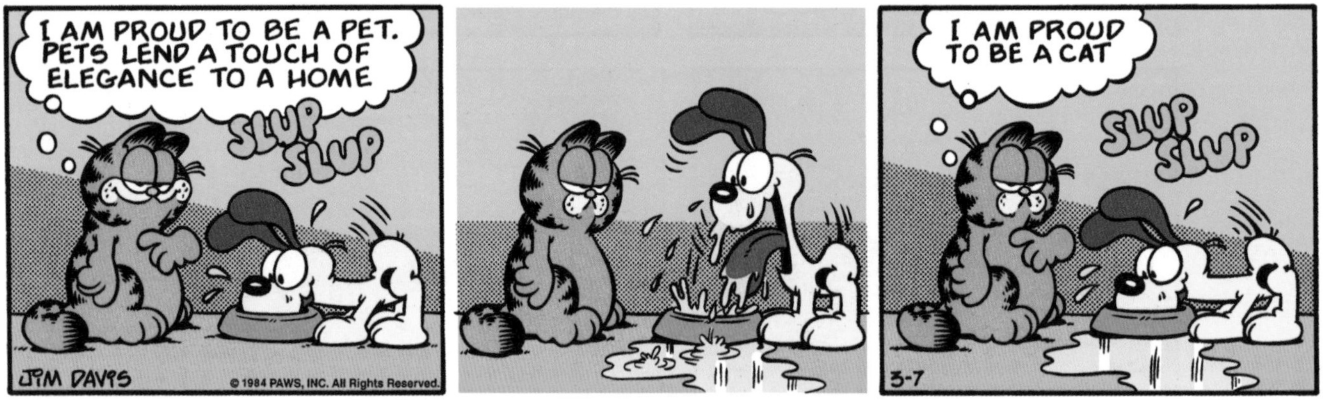
I AM PROUD TO BE A PET. PETS LEND A TOUCH OF ELEGANCE TO A HOME
SLUP SLUP
JIM DAVIS
© 1984 PAWS, INC. All Rights Reserved.
I AM PROUD TO BE A CAT
SLUP SLUP
3-7

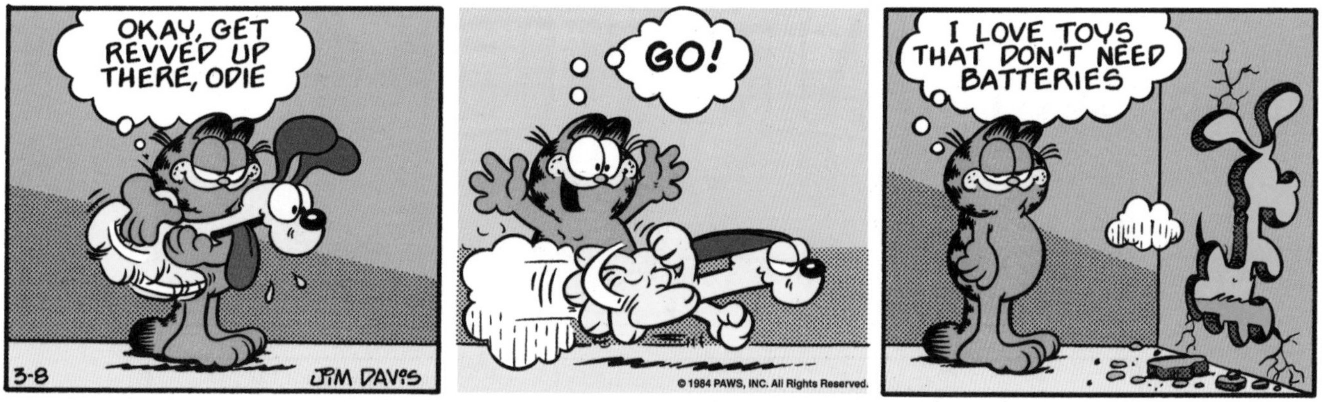
OKAY, GET REVVED UP THERE, ODIE
3-8
JIM DAVIS
GO!
© 1984 PAWS, INC. All Rights Reserved.
I LOVE TOYS THAT DON'T NEED BATTERIES

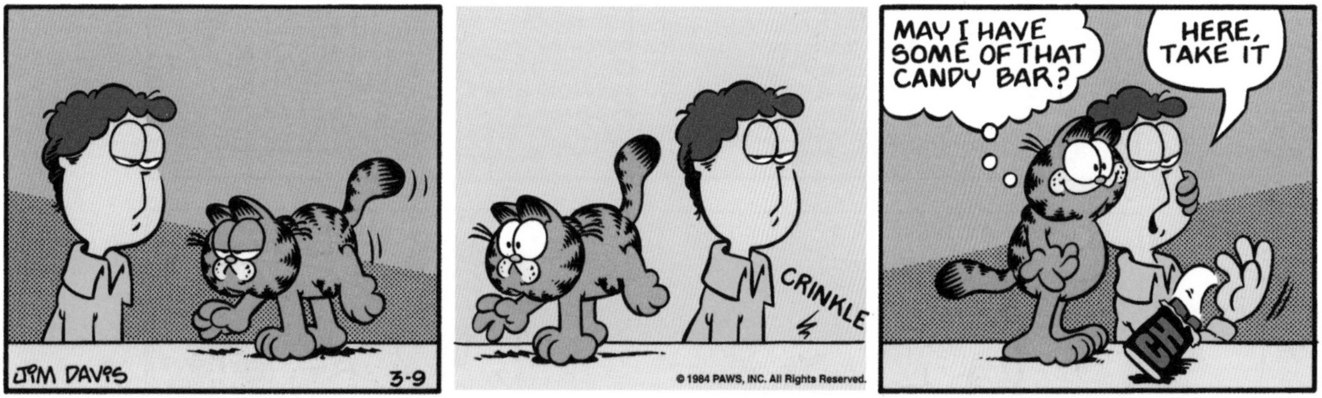
JIM DAVIS
3-9
CRINKLE
© 1984 PAWS, INC. All Rights Reserved.
MAY I HAVE SOME OF THAT CANDY BAR?
HERE, TAKE IT

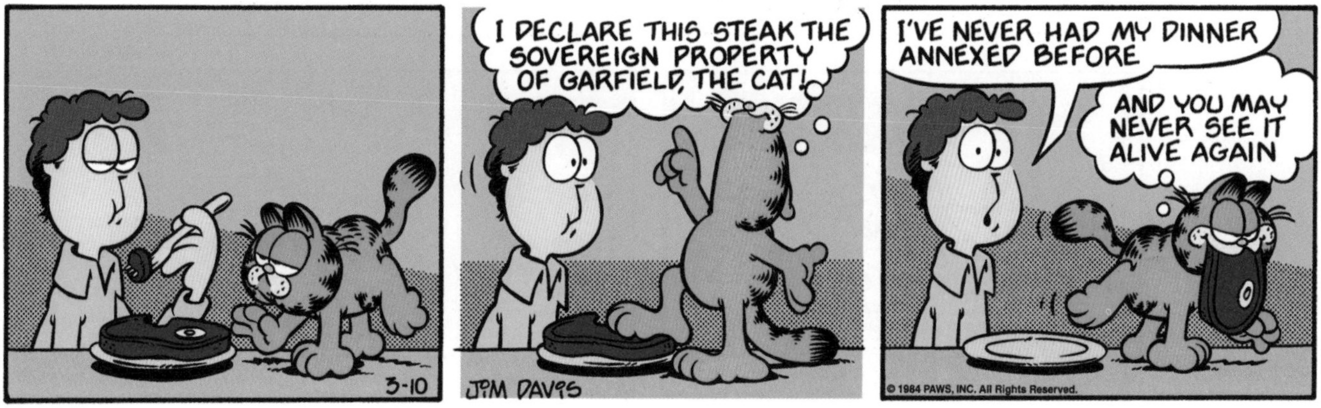
3-10
I DECLARE THIS STEAK THE SOVEREIGN PROPERTY OF GARFIELD, THE CAT!
JIM DAVIS
I'VE NEVER HAD MY DINNER ANNEXED BEFORE
AND YOU MAY NEVER SEE IT ALIVE AGAIN
© 1984 PAWS, INC. All Rights Reserved.

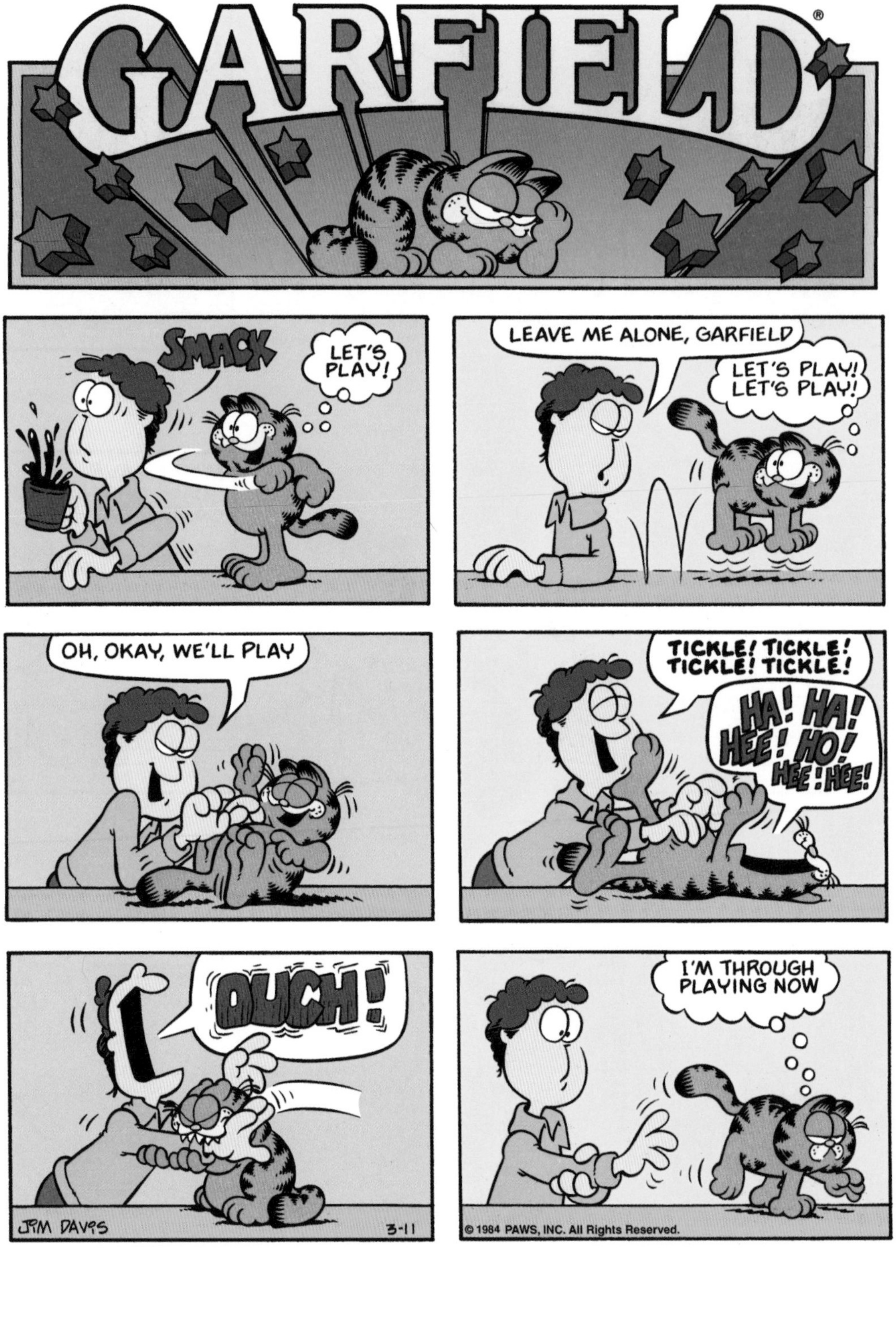
GARFIELD
SMACK
LET'S PLAY!
LEAVE ME ALONE, GARFIELD
LET'S PLAY! LET'S PLAY!
OH, OKAY, WE'LL PLAY
TICKLE! TICKLE! TICKLE! TICKLE!
HA! HA! HEE! HO! HEE! HEE!
OUCH!
I'M THROUGH PLAYING NOW
JIM DAVIS
3-11
© 1984 PAWS, INC. All Rights Reserved.

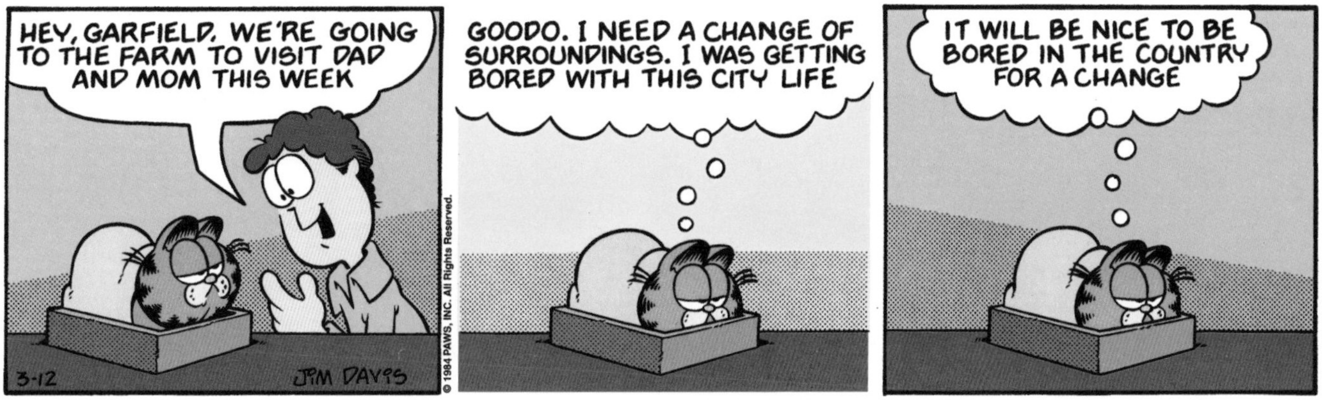
HEY, GARFIELD. WE'RE GOING TO THE FARM TO VISIT DAD AND MOM THIS WEEK
GOODO. I NEED A CHANGE OF SURROUNDINGS. I WAS GETTING BORED WITH THIS CITY LIFE
IT WILL BE NICE TO BE BORED IN THE COUNTRY FOR A CHANGE
3-12
JIM DAVIS
© 1984 PAWS, INC. All Rights Reserved.

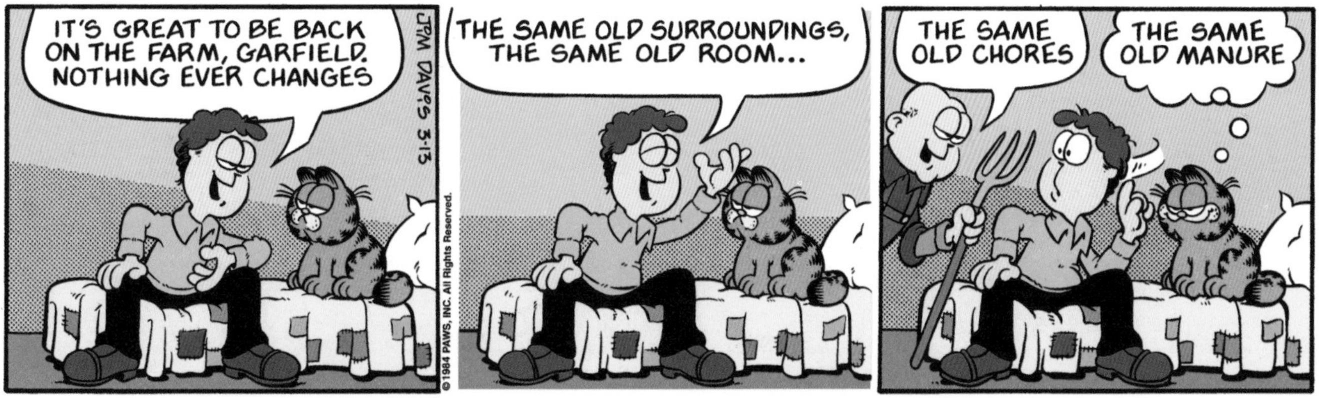
IT'S GREAT TO BE BACK ON THE FARM, GARFIELD. NOTHING EVER CHANGES
JIM DAVIS 3-13
© 1984 PAWS, INC. All Rights Reserved.
THE SAME OLD SURROUNDINGS, THE SAME OLD ROOM...
THE SAME OLD CHORES
THE SAME OLD MANURE

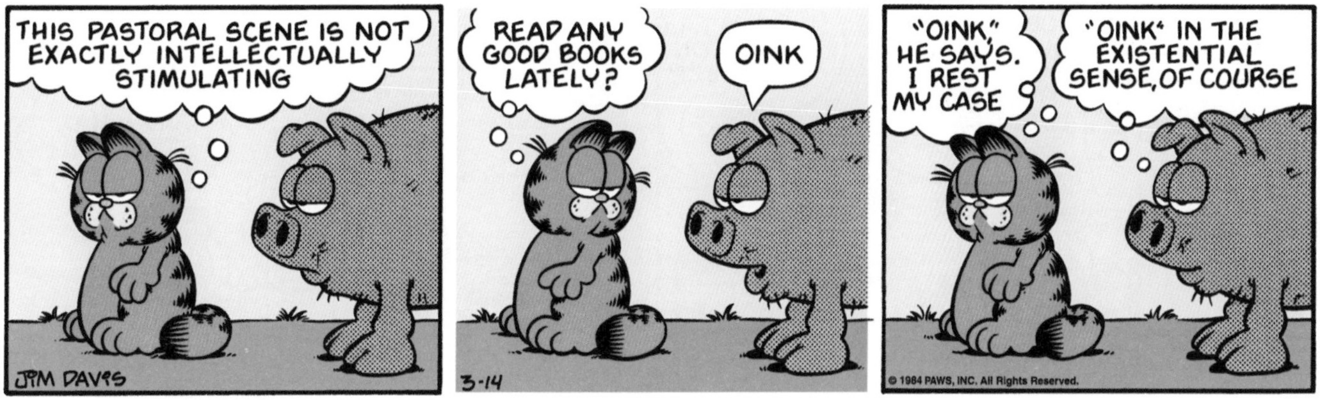
THIS PASTORAL SCENE IS NOT EXACTLY INTELLECTUALLY STIMULATING
JIM DAVIS
READ ANY GOOD BOOKS LATELY?
OINK
3-14
"OINK," HE SAYS. I REST MY CASE
"OINK" IN THE EXISTENTIAL SENSE, OF COURSE
© 1984 PAWS, INC. All Rights Reserved.

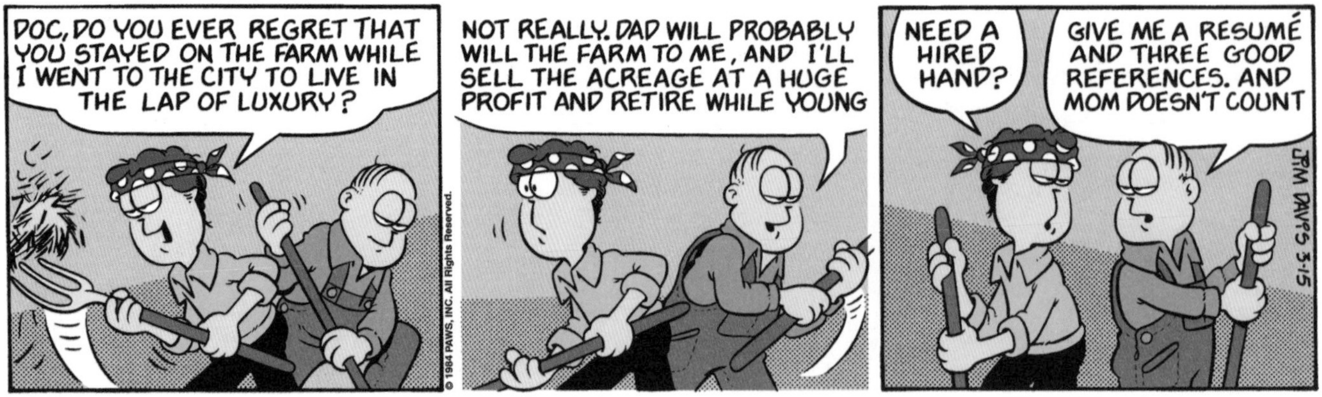
DOC, DO YOU EVER REGRET THAT YOU STAYED ON THE FARM WHILE I WENT TO THE CITY TO LIVE IN THE LAP OF LUXURY?
© 1984 PAWS, INC. All Rights Reserved.
NOT REALLY. DAD WILL PROBABLY WILL THE FARM TO ME, AND I'LL SELL THE ACREAGE AT A HUGE PROFIT AND RETIRE WHILE YOUNG
NEED A HIRED HAND?
GIVE ME A RESUMÉ AND THREE GOOD REFERENCES. AND MOM DOESN'T COUNT
JIM DAVIS 3-15

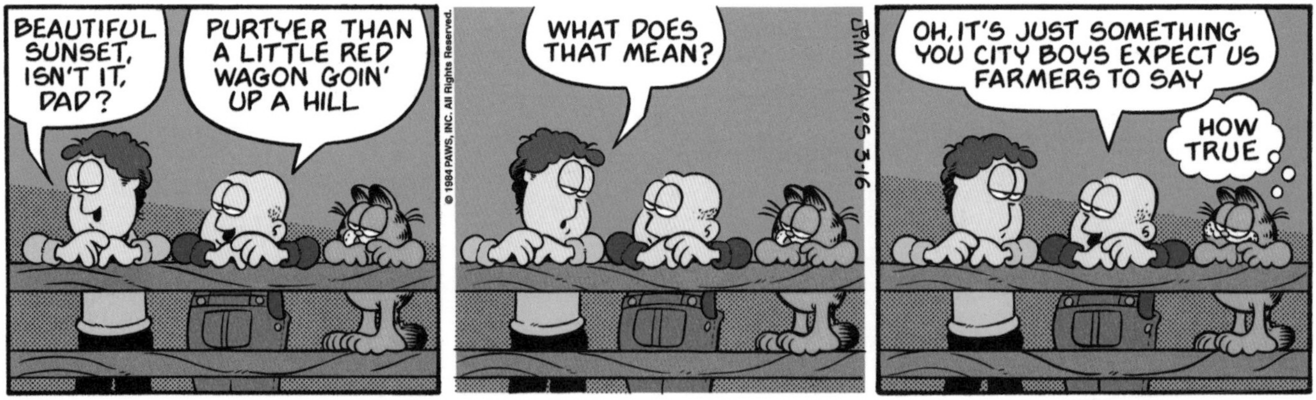
BEAUTIFUL SUNSET, ISN'T IT, DAD?
PURTYER THAN A LITTLE RED WAGON GOIN' UP A HILL
© 1984 PAWS, INC. All Rights Reserved.
WHAT DOES THAT MEAN?
JIM DAVIS 3-16
OH, IT'S JUST SOMETHING YOU CITY BOYS EXPECT US FARMERS TO SAY
HOW TRUE

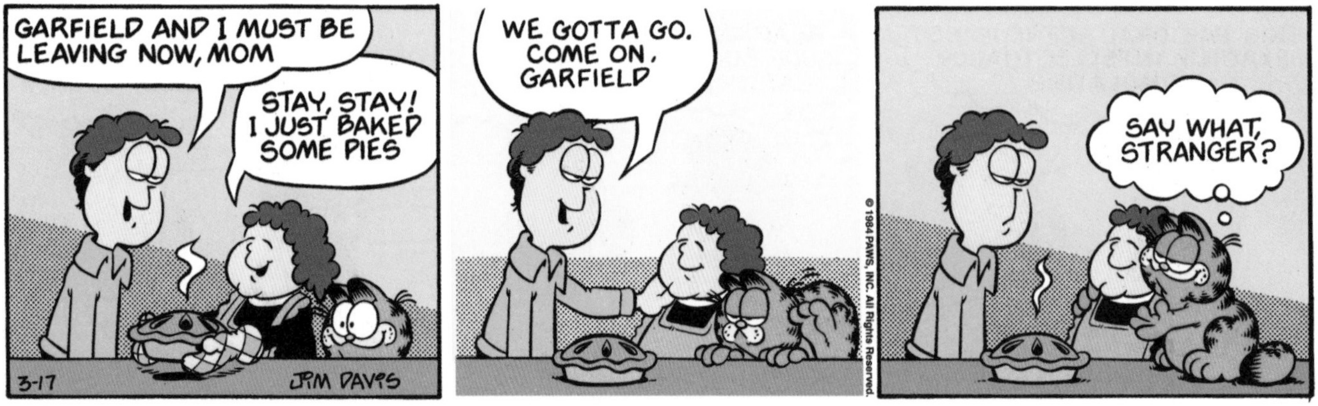
GARFIELD AND I MUST BE LEAVING NOW, MOM
STAY, STAY! I JUST BAKED SOME PIES
3-17
JIM DAVIS
WE GOTTA GO. COME ON, GARFIELD
© 1984 PAWS, INC. All Rights Reserved.
SAY WHAT, STRANGER?

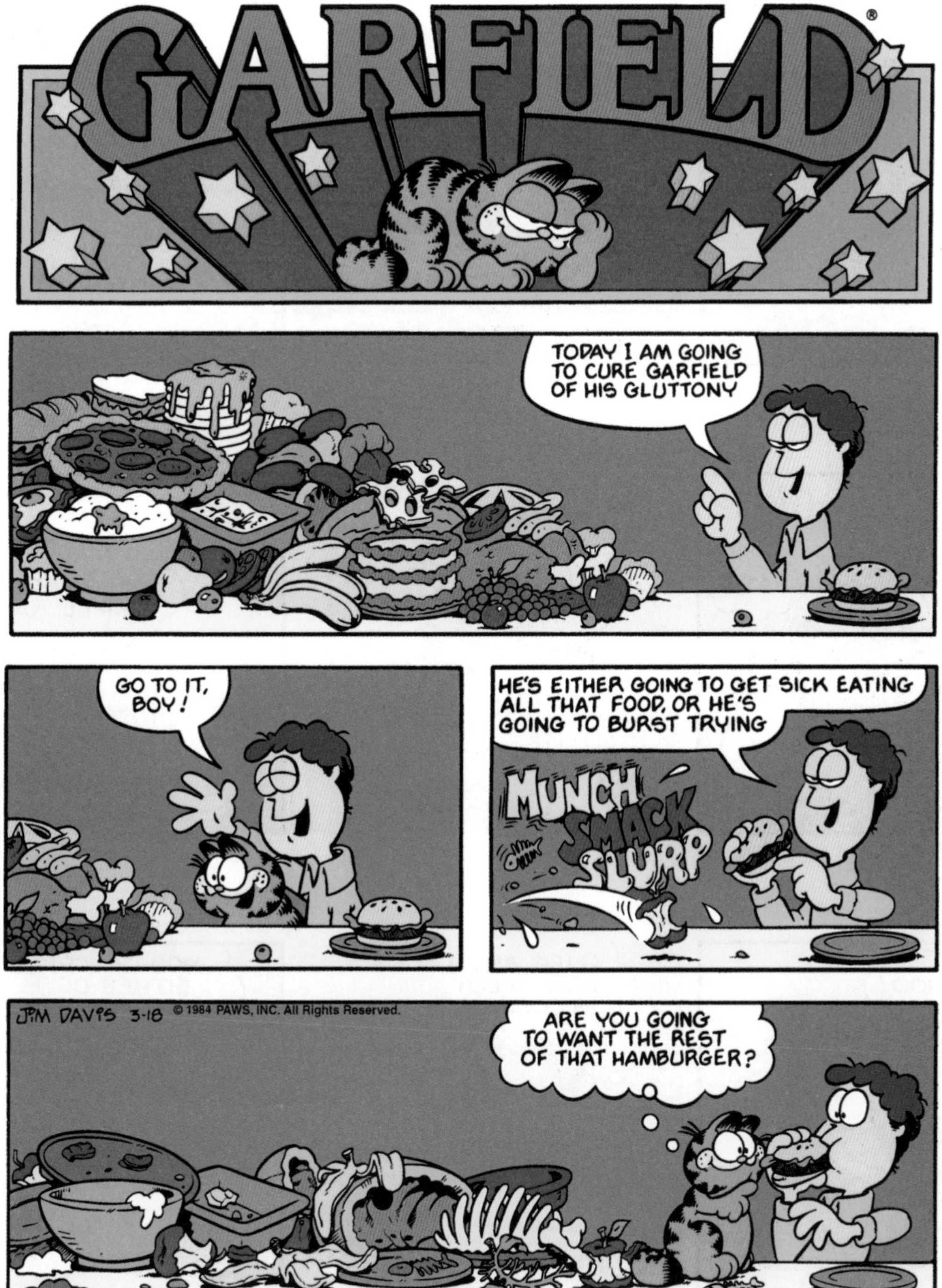
GARFIELD®
TODAY I AM GOING TO CURE GARFIELD OF HIS GLUTTONY
GO TO IT, BOY!
HE'S EITHER GOING TO GET SICK EATING ALL THAT FOOD, OR HE'S GOING TO BURST TRYING
MUNCH
SMACK
SLURP
JIM DAVIS 3-18
© 1984 PAWS, INC. All Rights Reserved.
ARE YOU GOING TO WANT THE REST OF THAT HAMBURGER?

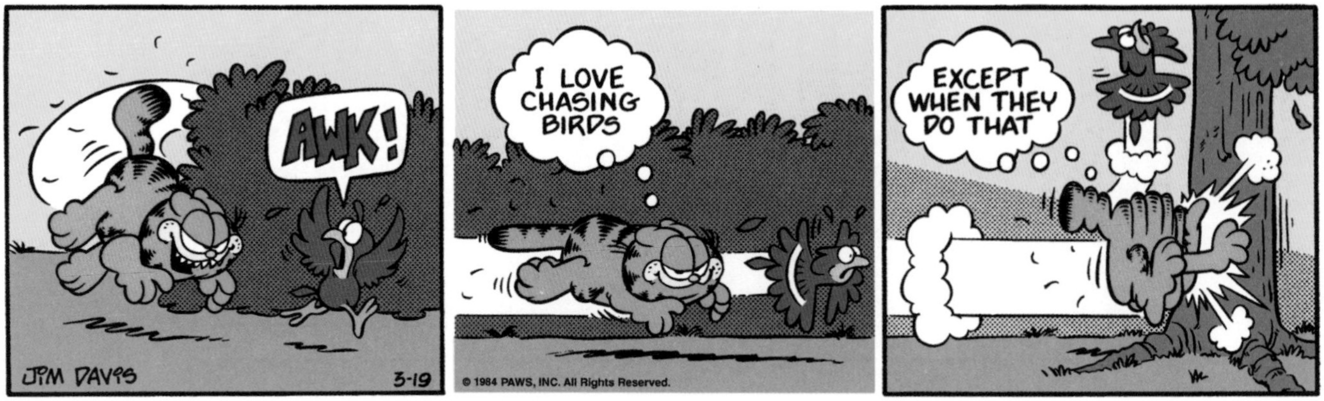
AWK!
JIM DAVIS
3-19
I LOVE CHASING BIRDS
© 1984 PAWS, INC. All Rights Reserved.
EXCEPT WHEN THEY DO THAT

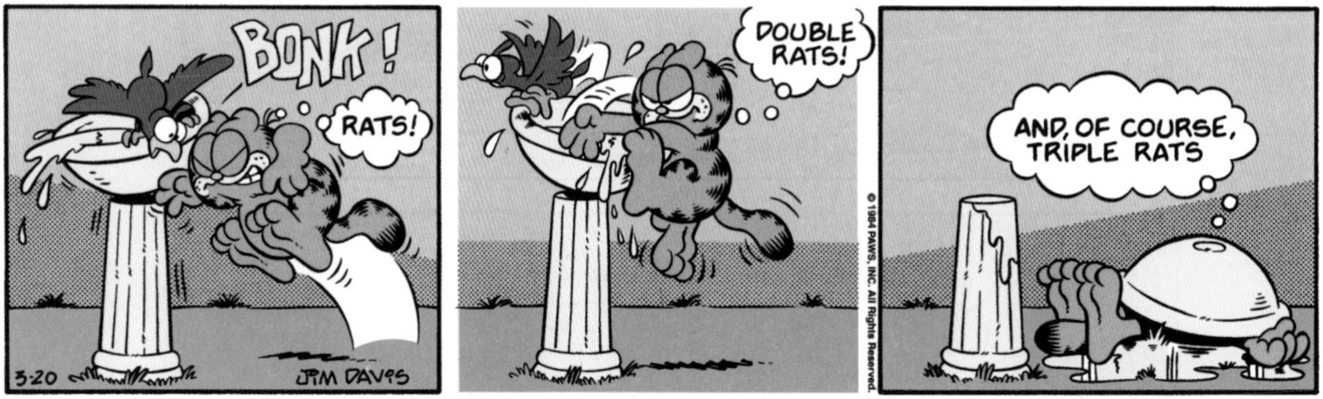
BONK!
RATS!
3-20
JIM DAVIS
DOUBLE RATS!
© 1984 PAWS, INC. All Rights Reserved.
AND, OF COURSE, TRIPLE RATS

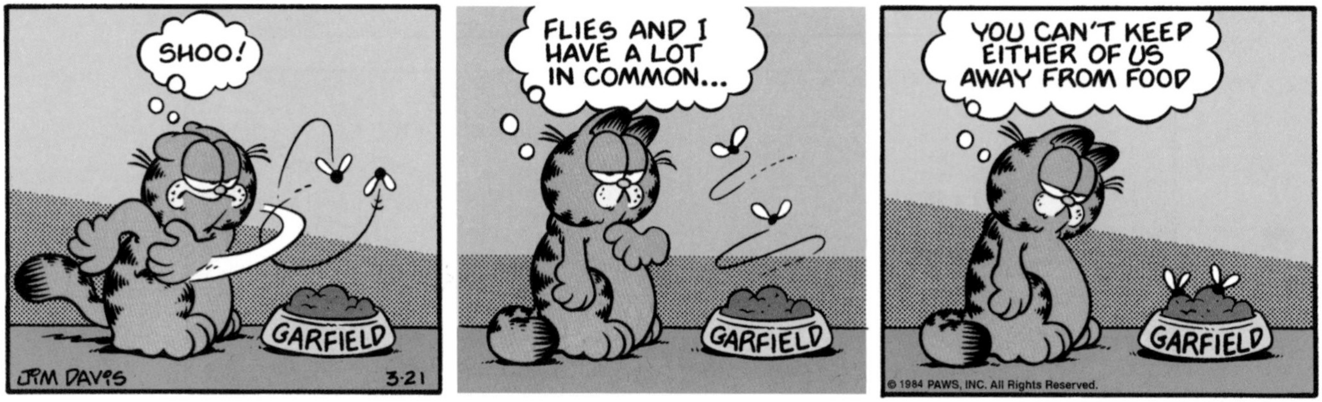
SHOO!
GARFIELD
JIM DAVIS
3-21
FLIES AND I HAVE A LOT IN COMMON...
GARFIELD
YOU CAN'T KEEP EITHER OF US AWAY FROM FOOD
GARFIELD
© 1984 PAWS, INC. All Rights Reserved.

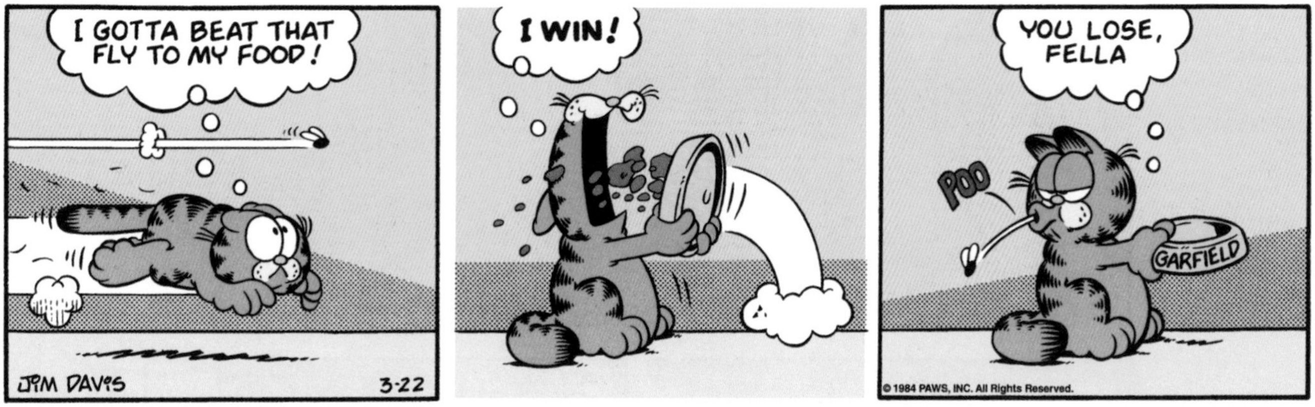
I GOTTA BEAT THAT FLY TO MY FOOD!
JIM DAVIS
3-22
I WIN!
YOU LOSE, FELLA
POO
GARFIELD
© 1984 PAWS, INC. All Rights Reserved.

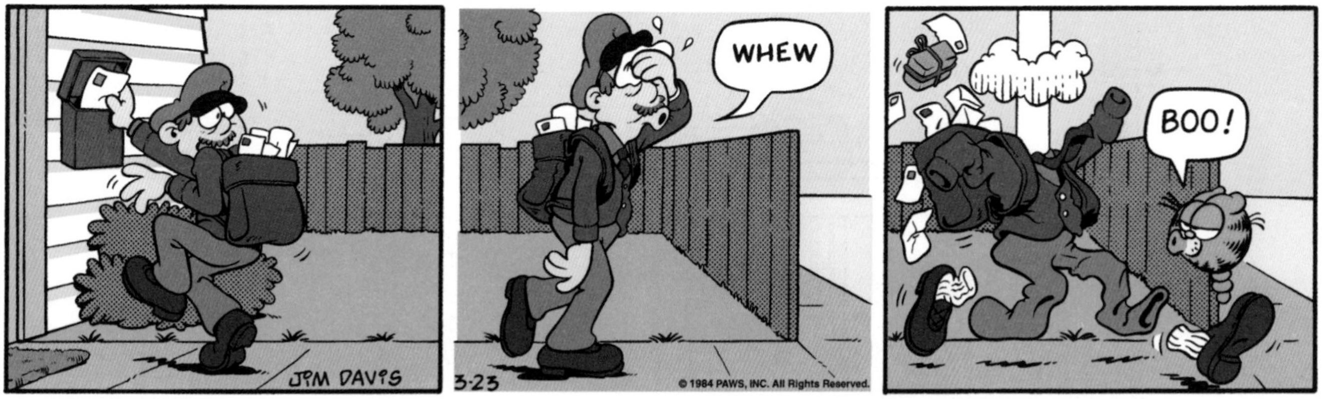
JIM DAVIS
WHEW
3-23
© 1984 PAWS, INC. All Rights Reserved.
BOO!

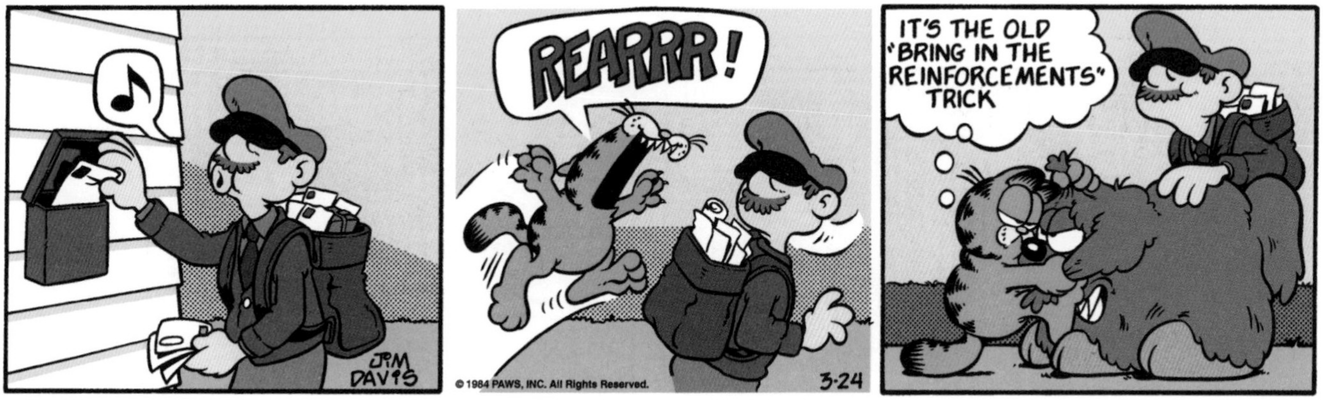
♪
JIM DAVIS
REARRR!
© 1984 PAWS, INC. All Rights Reserved.
3-24
IT'S THE OLD "BRING IN THE REINFORCEMENTS" TRICK

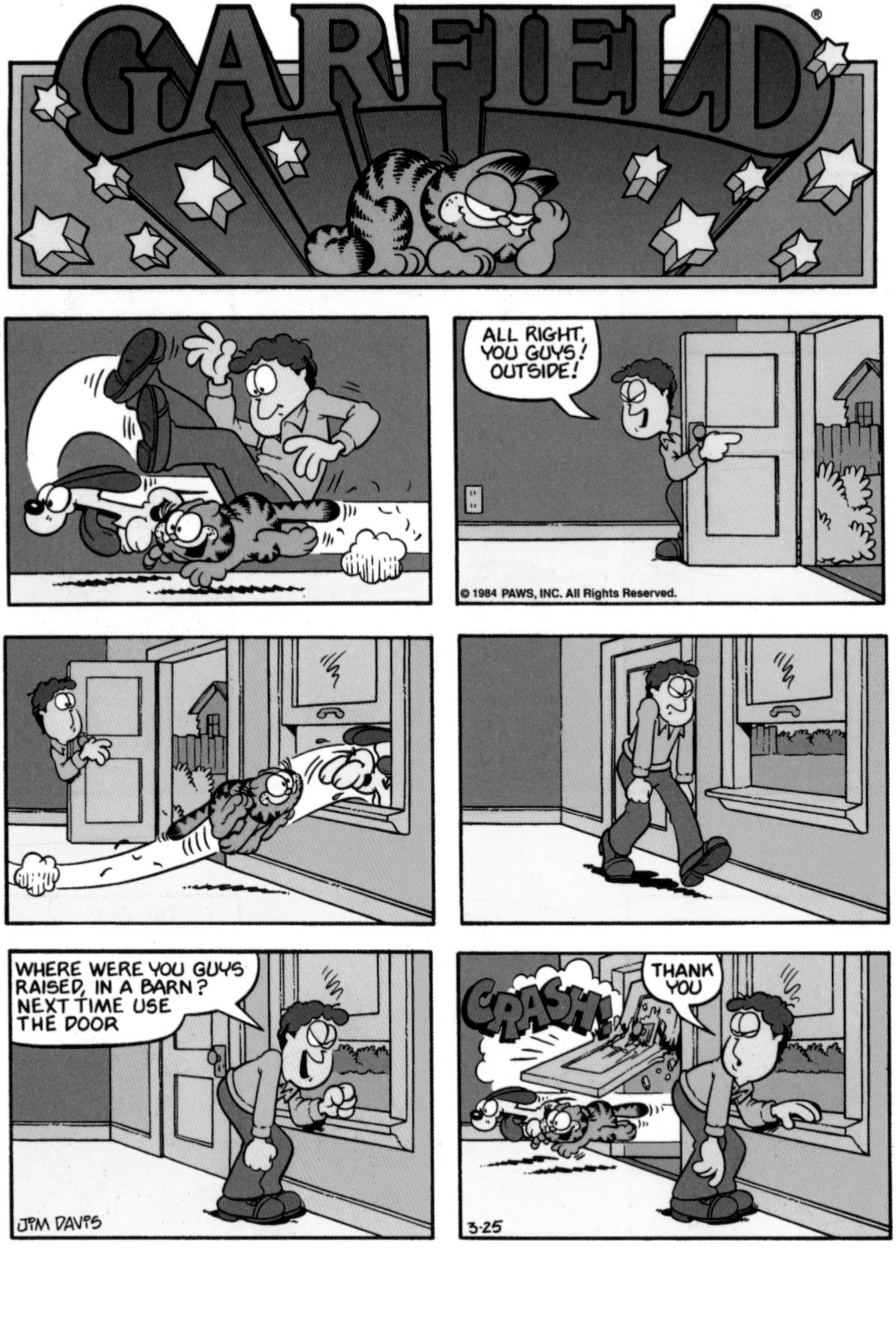
GARFIELD®
ALL RIGHT, YOU GUYS! OUTSIDE!
© 1984 PAWS, INC. All Rights Reserved.
WHERE WERE YOU GUYS RAISED, IN A BARN? NEXT TIME USE THE DOOR
JIM DAVIS
CRASH!
THANK YOU
3-25

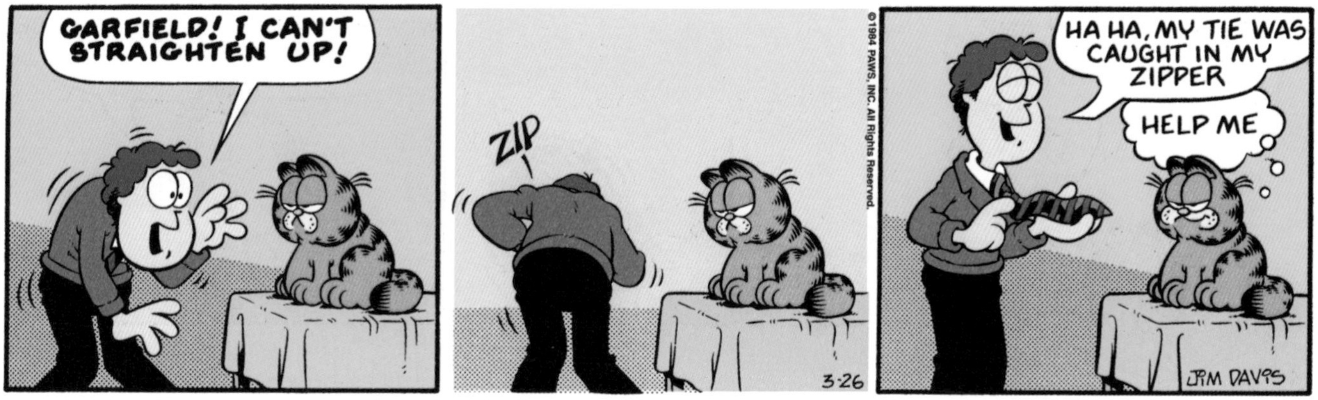
GARFIELD! I CAN'T STRAIGHTEN UP!
ZIP
©1984 PAWS, INC. All Rights Reserved.
3-26
HA HA, MY TIE WAS CAUGHT IN MY ZIPPER
HELP ME
JIM DAVIS

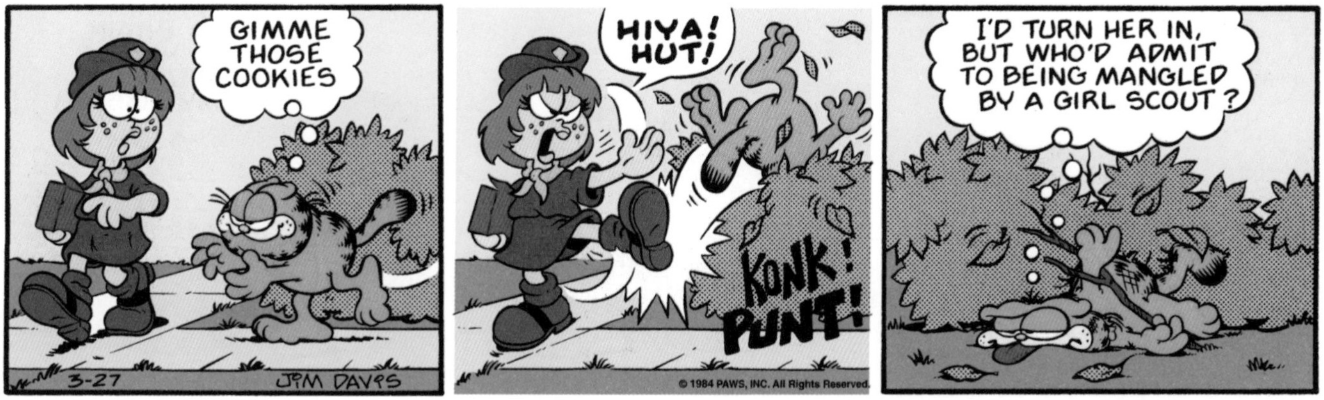
GIMME THOSE COOKIES
3-27
JIM DAVIS
HIYA! HUT!
KONK!
PUNT!
© 1984 PAWS, INC. All Rights Reserved.
I'D TURN HER IN, BUT WHO'D ADMIT TO BEING MANGLED BY A GIRL SCOUT?

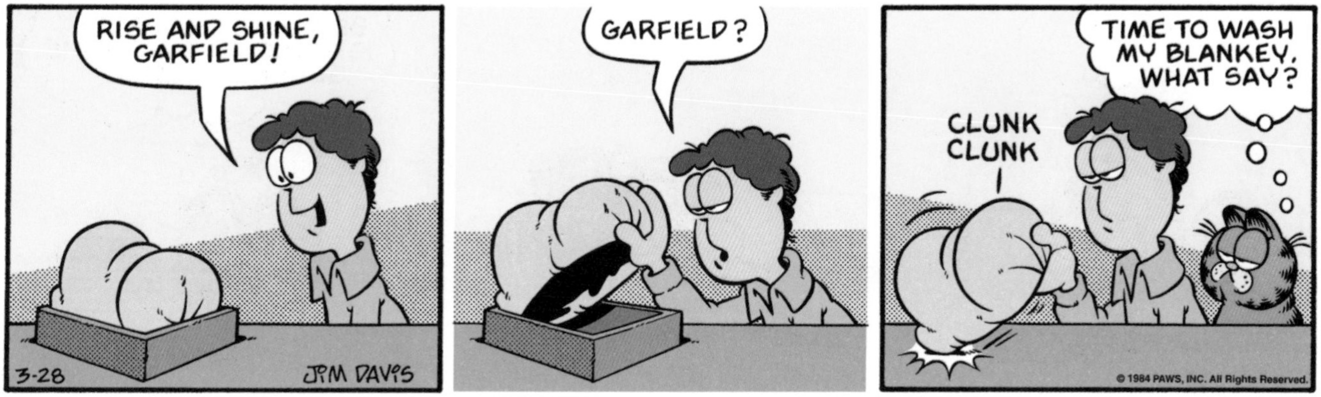
RISE AND SHINE, GARFIELD!
3-28
JIM DAVIS
GARFIELD?
CLUNK CLUNK
TIME TO WASH MY BLANKEY, WHAT SAY?
© 1984 PAWS, INC. All Rights Reserved.

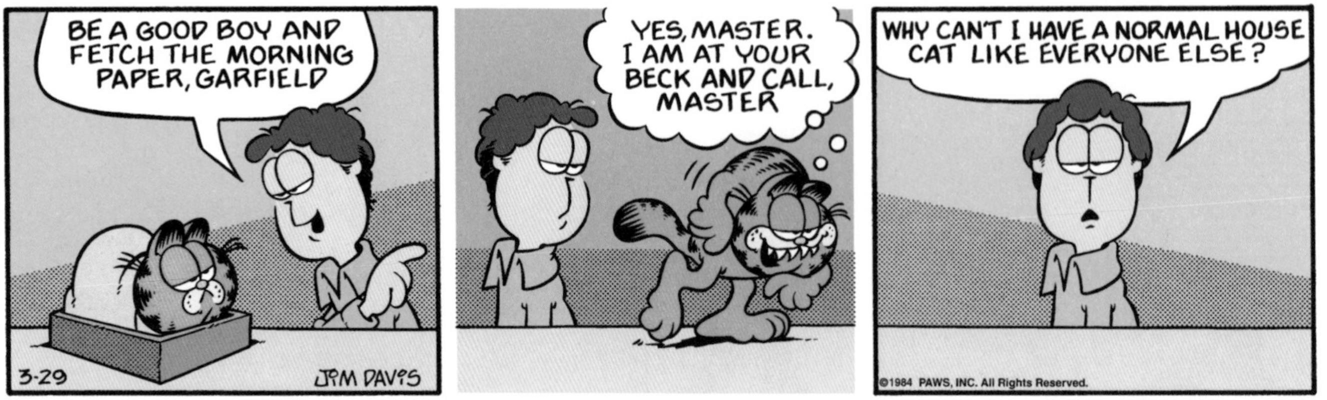
BE A GOOD BOY AND FETCH THE MORNING PAPER, GARFIELD
3-29
JIM DAVIS
YES, MASTER. I AM AT YOUR BECK AND CALL, MASTER
WHY CAN'T I HAVE A NORMAL HOUSE CAT LIKE EVERYONE ELSE?
©1984 PAWS, INC. All Rights Reserved.

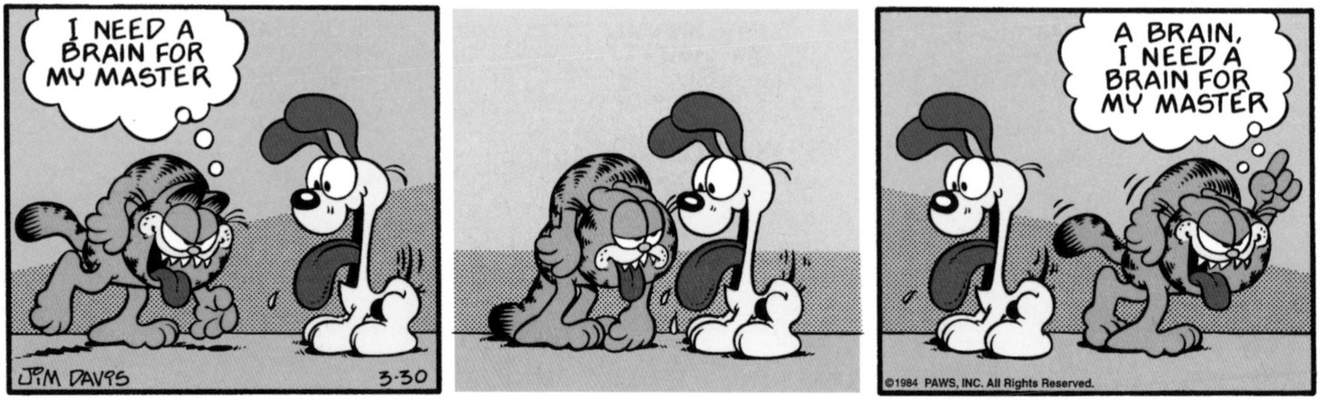
I NEED A BRAIN FOR MY MASTER
JIM DAVIS
3-30
A BRAIN, I NEED A BRAIN FOR MY MASTER
©1984 PAWS, INC. All Rights Reserved.

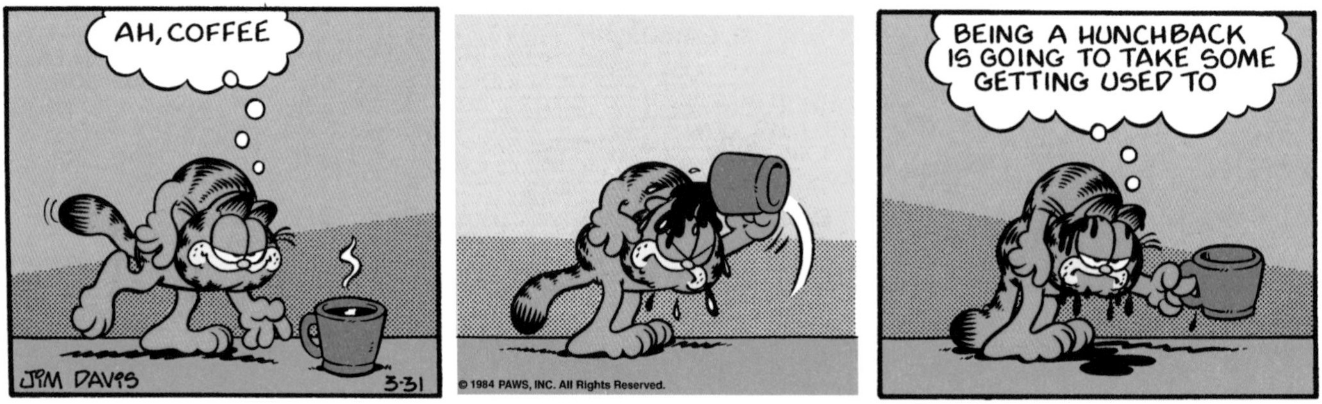
AH, COFFEE
JIM DAVIS
3-31
© 1984 PAWS, INC. All Rights Reserved.
BEING A HUNCHBACK IS GOING TO TAKE SOME GETTING USED TO

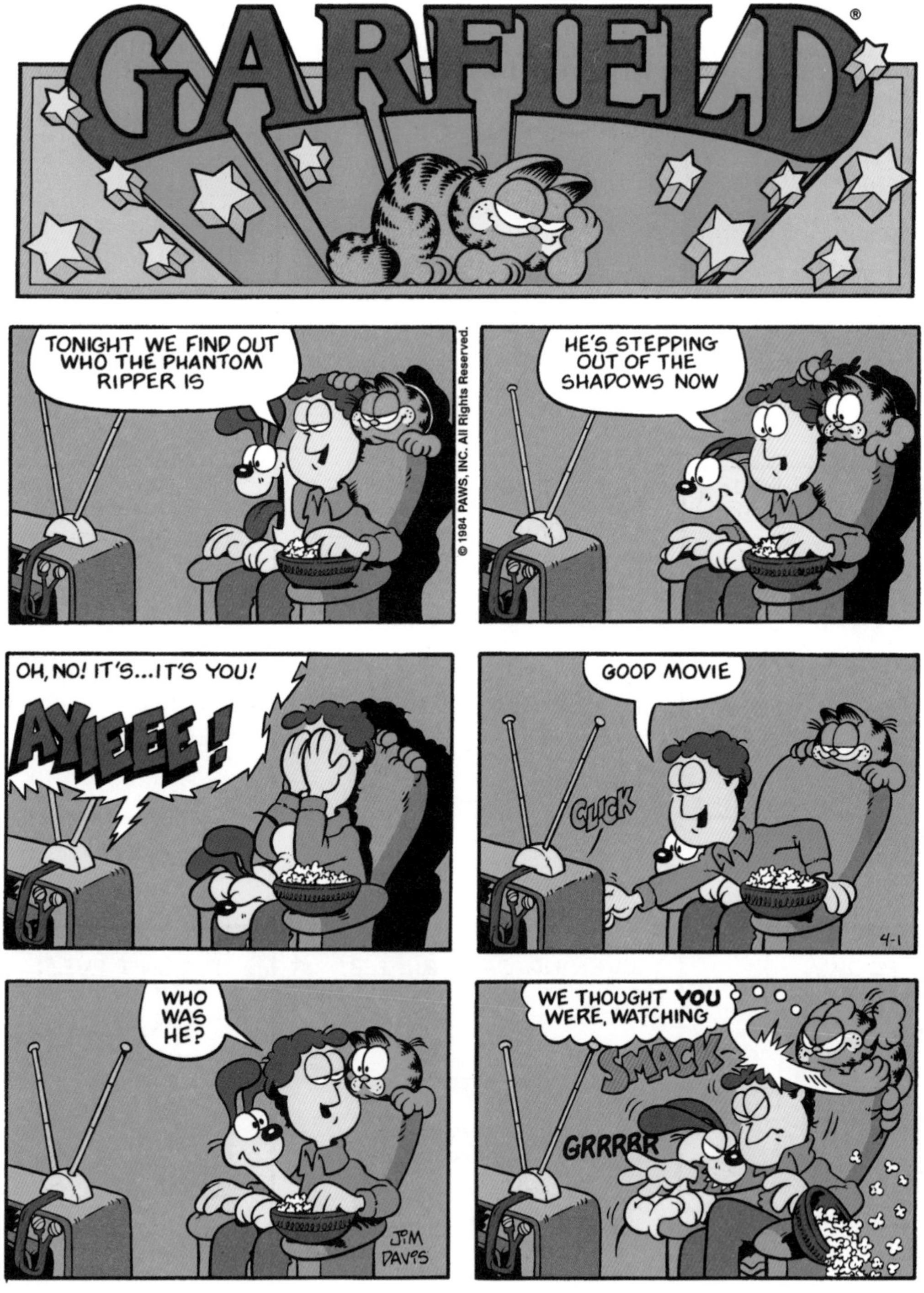
GARFIELD®
TONIGHT WE FIND OUT WHO THE PHANTOM RIPPER IS
© 1984 PAWS, INC. All Rights Reserved.
HE'S STEPPING OUT OF THE SHADOWS NOW
OH, NO! IT'S...IT'S YOU!
AYIEEE!
GOOD MOVIE
CLICK
4-1
WHO WAS HE?
JIM DAVIS
WE THOUGHT YOU WERE, WATCHING
SMACK
GRRRBR

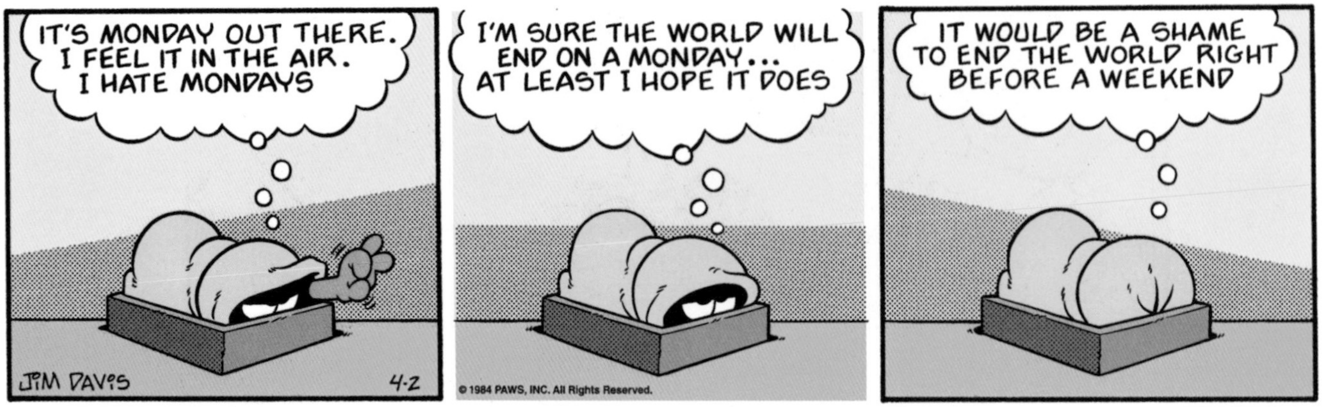
IT'S MONDAY OUT THERE. I FEEL IT IN THE AIR. I HATE MONDAYS
JIM DAVIS
4-2
I'M SURE THE WORLD WILL END ON A MONDAY... AT LEAST I HOPE IT DOES
© 1984 PAWS, INC. All Rights Reserved.
IT WOULD BE A SHAME TO END THE WORLD RIGHT BEFORE A WEEKEND

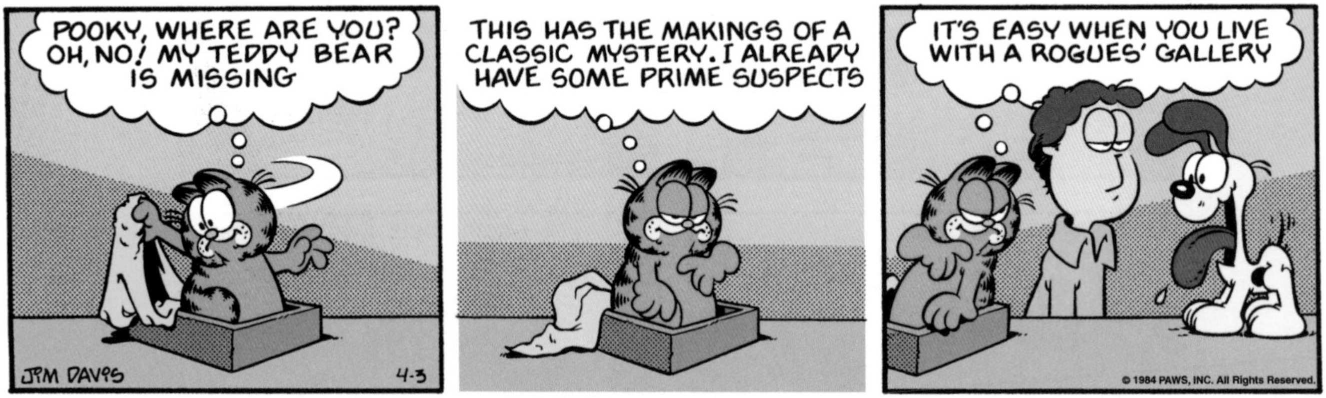
POOKY, WHERE ARE YOU? OH, NO! MY TEDDY BEAR IS MISSING
JIM DAVIS
4-3
THIS HAS THE MAKINGS OF A CLASSIC MYSTERY. I ALREADY HAVE SOME PRIME SUSPECTS
IT'S EASY WHEN YOU LIVE WITH A ROGUES' GALLERY
© 1984 PAWS, INC. All Rights Reserved.

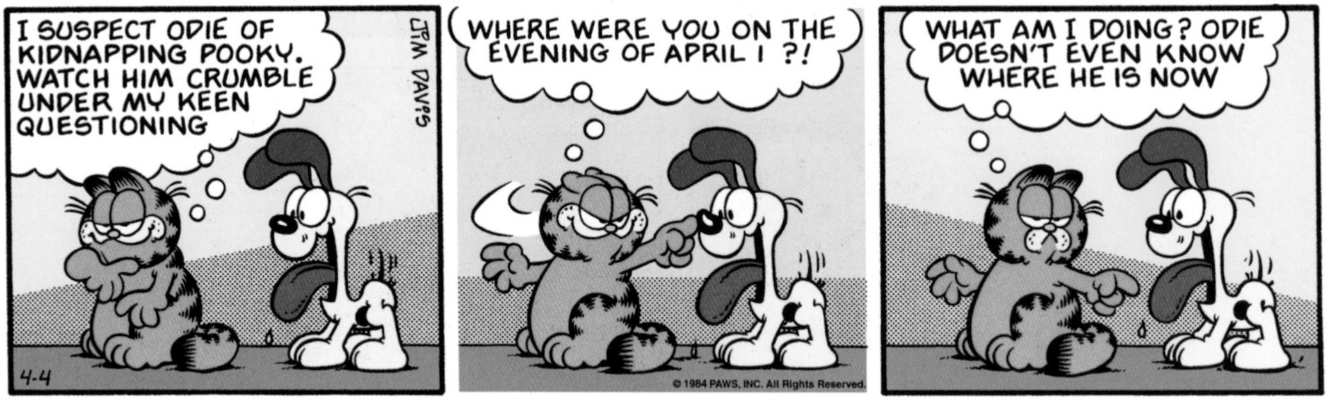
I SUSPECT ODIE OF KIDNAPPING POOKY. WATCH HIM CRUMBLE UNDER MY KEEN QUESTIONING
JIM DAVIS
4-4
WHERE WERE YOU ON THE EVENING OF APRIL 1 ?!
© 1984 PAWS, INC. All Rights Reserved.
WHAT AM I DOING? ODIE DOESN'T EVEN KNOW WHERE HE IS NOW

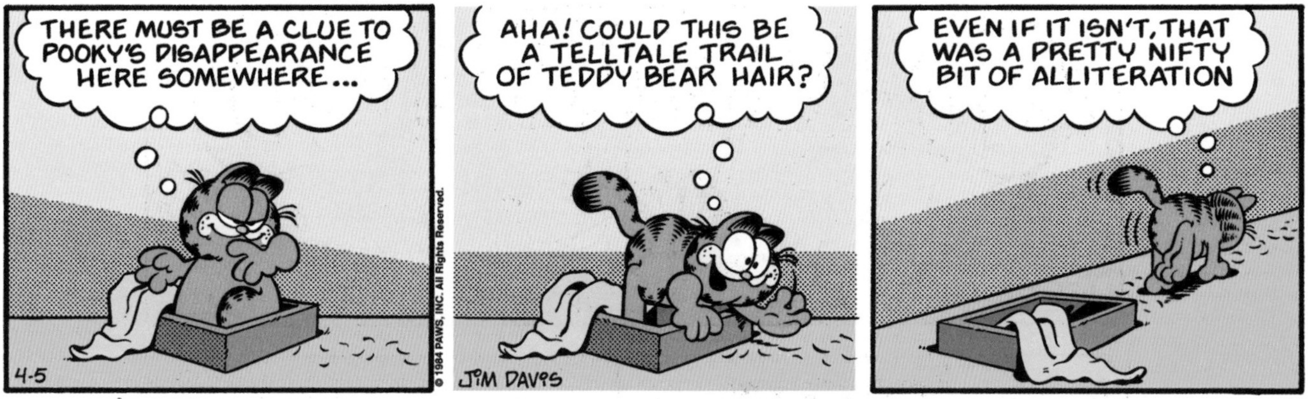
THERE MUST BE A CLUE TO POOKY'S DISAPPEARANCE HERE SOMEWHERE...
4-5
AHA! COULD THIS BE A TELLTALE TRAIL OF TEDDY BEAR HAIR?
© 1984 PAWS, INC. All Rights Reserved.
JIM DAVIS
EVEN IF IT ISN'T, THAT WAS A PRETTY NIFTY BIT OF ALLITERATION

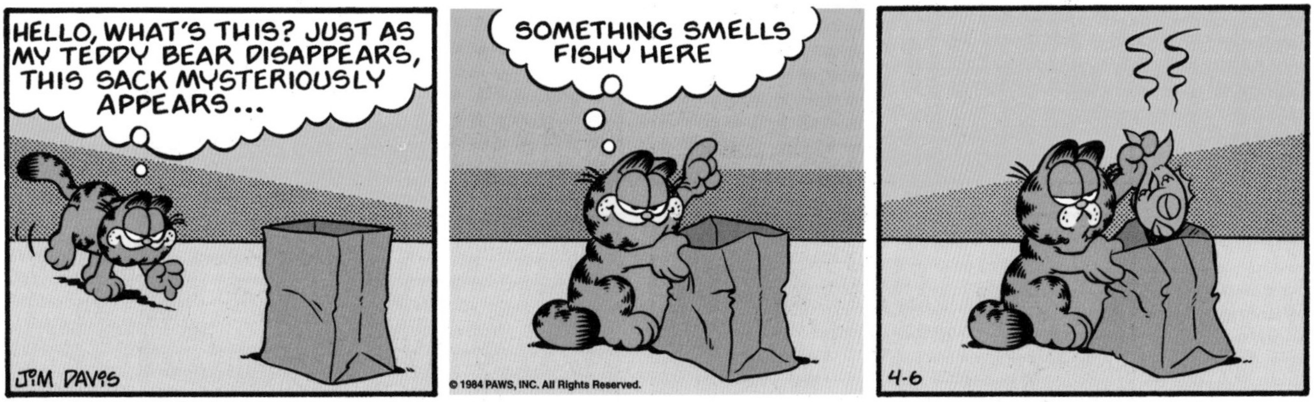
HELLO, WHAT'S THIS? JUST AS MY TEDDY BEAR DISAPPEARS, THIS SACK MYSTERIOUSLY APPEARS...
JIM DAVIS
SOMETHING SMELLS FISHY HERE
© 1984 PAWS, INC. All Rights Reserved.
4-6

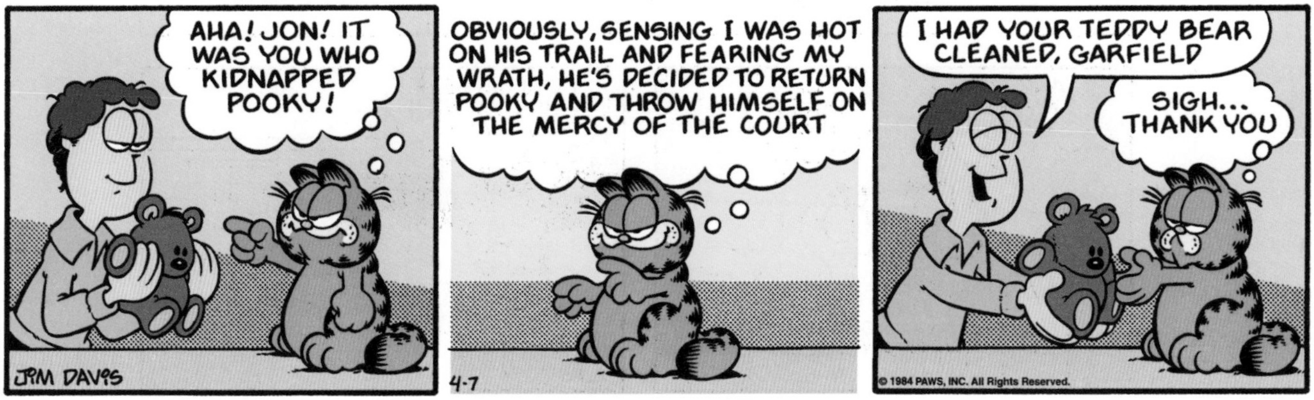
AHA! JON! IT WAS YOU WHO KIDNAPPED POOKY!
JIM DAVIS
OBVIOUSLY, SENSING I WAS HOT ON HIS TRAIL AND FEARING MY WRATH, HE'S DECIDED TO RETURN POOKY AND THROW HIMSELF ON THE MERCY OF THE COURT
4-7
I HAD YOUR TEDDY BEAR CLEANED, GARFIELD
SIGH... THANK YOU
© 1984 PAWS, INC. All Rights Reserved.

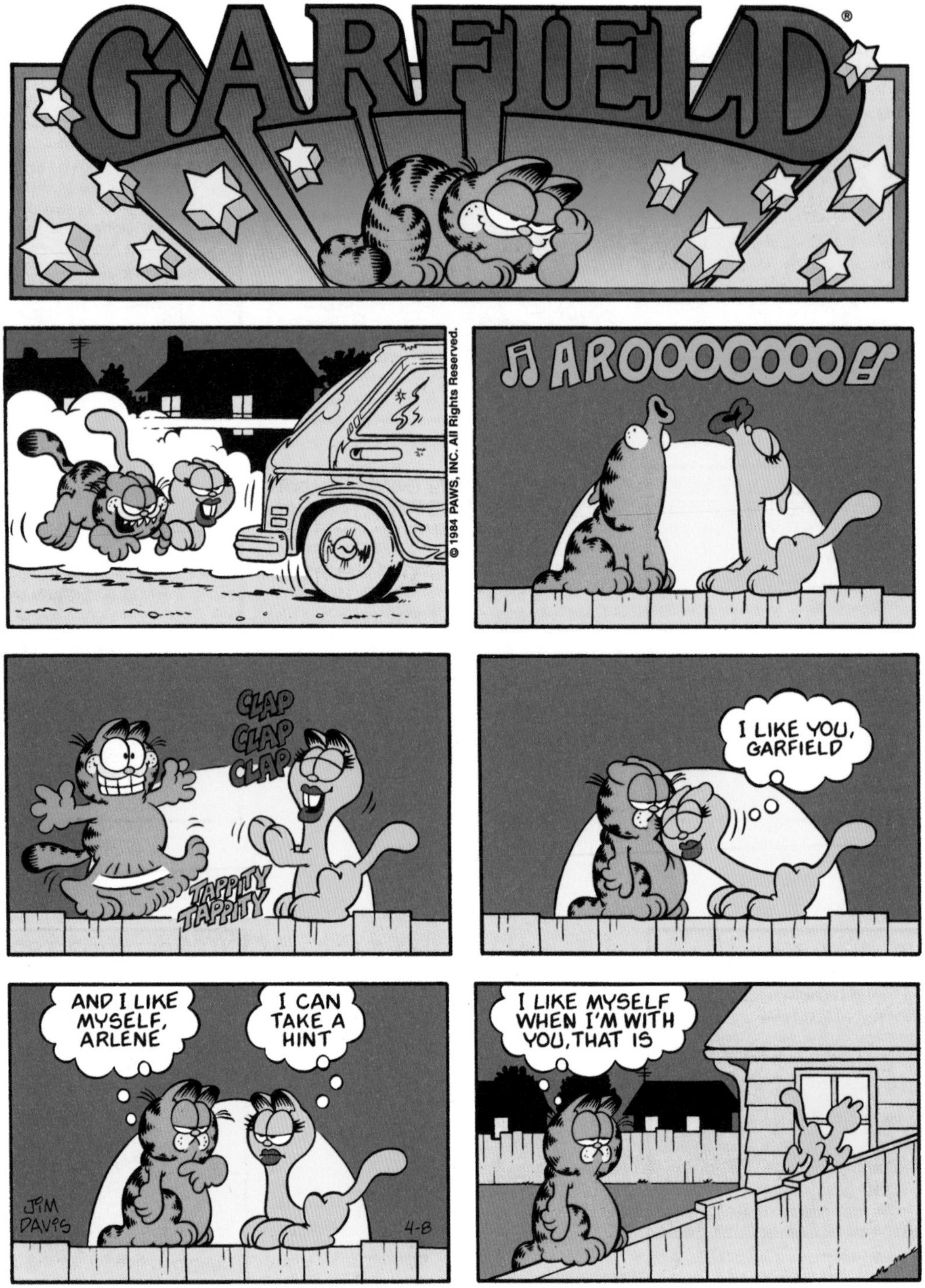
GARFIELD®
© 1984 PAWS, INC. All Rights Reserved.
AROOOOOOOO
CLAP
CLAP
CLAP
TAPPITY
TAPPITY
I LIKE YOU, GARFIELD
AND I LIKE MYSELF, ARLENE
I CAN TAKE A HINT
JIM DAVIS
4-8
I LIKE MYSELF WHEN I'M WITH YOU, THAT IS

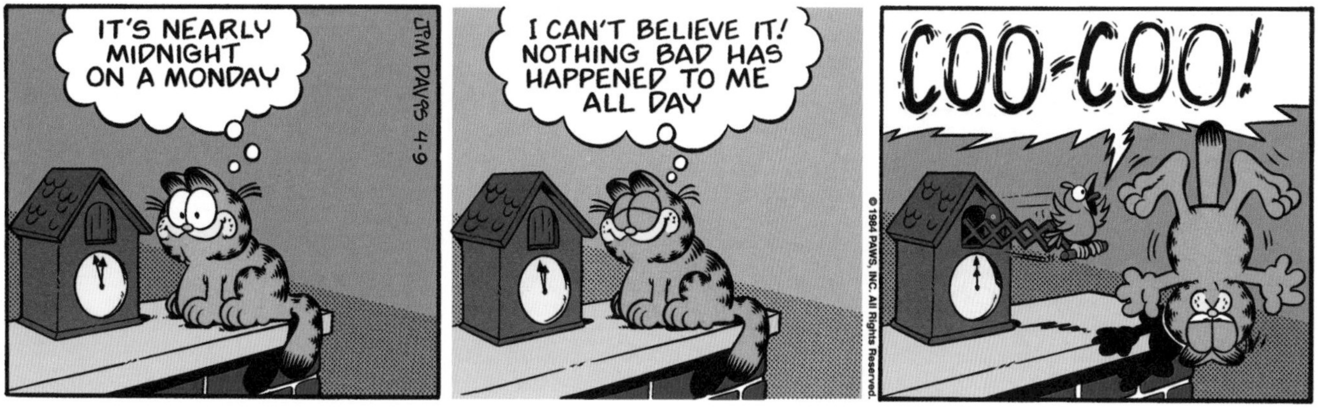
IT'S NEARLY MIDNIGHT ON A MONDAY
JIM DAVIS 4-9
I CAN'T BELIEVE IT! NOTHING BAD HAS HAPPENED TO ME ALL DAY
© 1984 PAWS, INC. All Rights Reserved.
COO-COO!

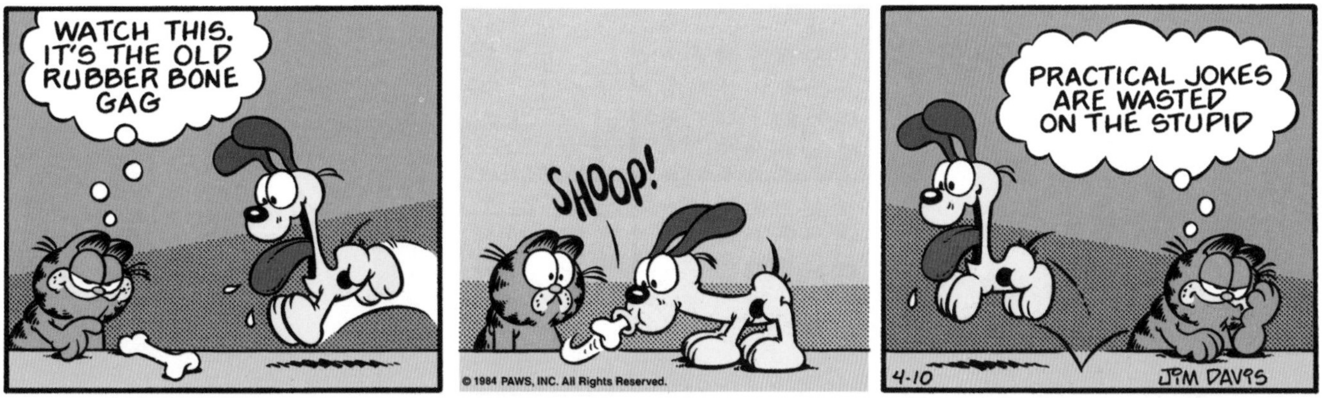
WATCH THIS. IT'S THE OLD RUBBER BONE GAG
SHOOP!
© 1984 PAWS, INC. All Rights Reserved.
PRACTICAL JOKES ARE WASTED ON THE STUPID
4-10
JIM DAVIS

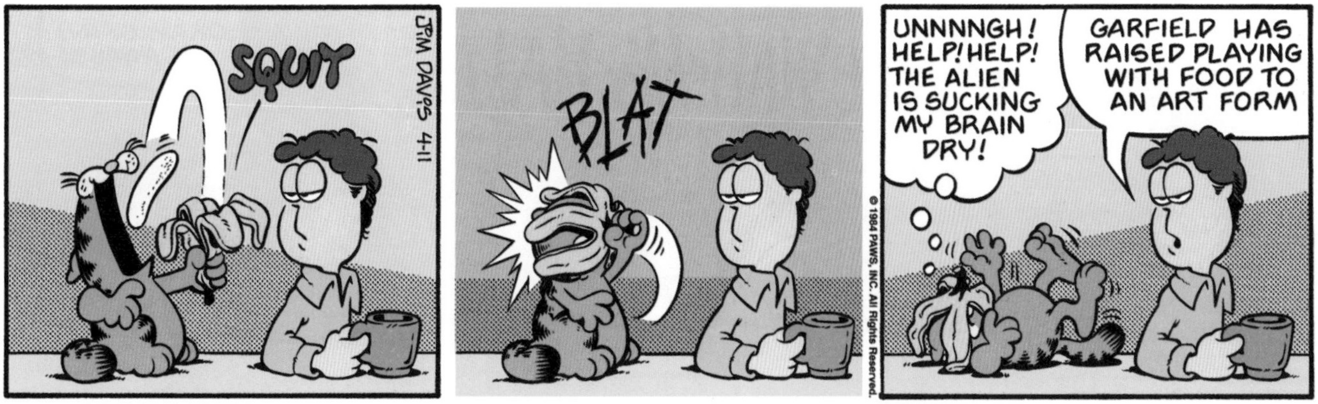
SQUIT
JIM DAVIS 4-11
BLAT
© 1984 PAWS, INC. All Rights Reserved.
UNNNNGH! HELP! HELP! THE ALIEN IS SUCKING MY BRAIN DRY!
GARFIELD HAS RAISED PLAYING WITH FOOD TO AN ART FORM

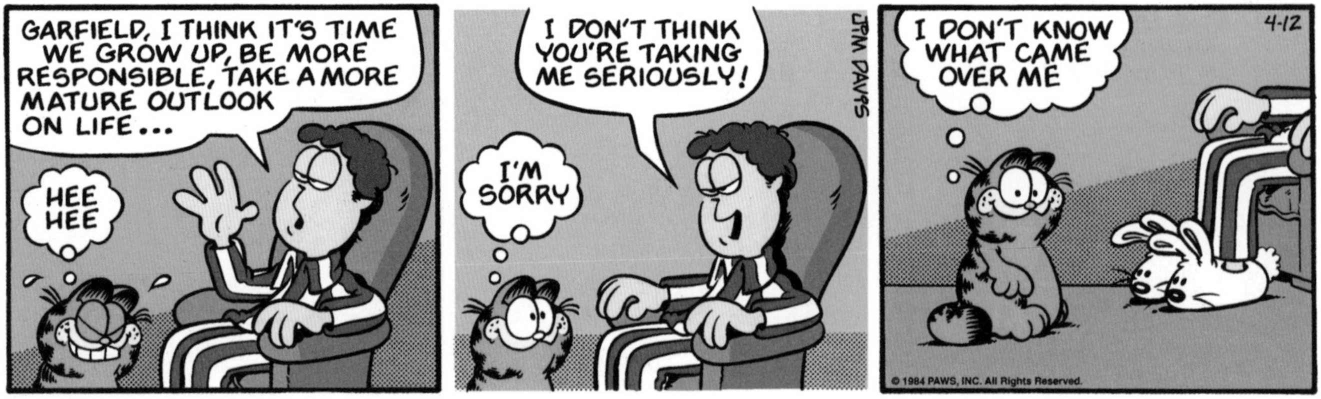
GARFIELD, I THINK IT'S TIME WE GROW UP, BE MORE RESPONSIBLE, TAKE A MORE MATURE OUTLOOK ON LIFE...
HEE HEE
I DON'T THINK YOU'RE TAKING ME SERIOUSLY!
I'M SORRY
JIM DAVIS
4-12
I DON'T KNOW WHAT CAME OVER ME
© 1984 PAWS, INC. All Rights Reserved.

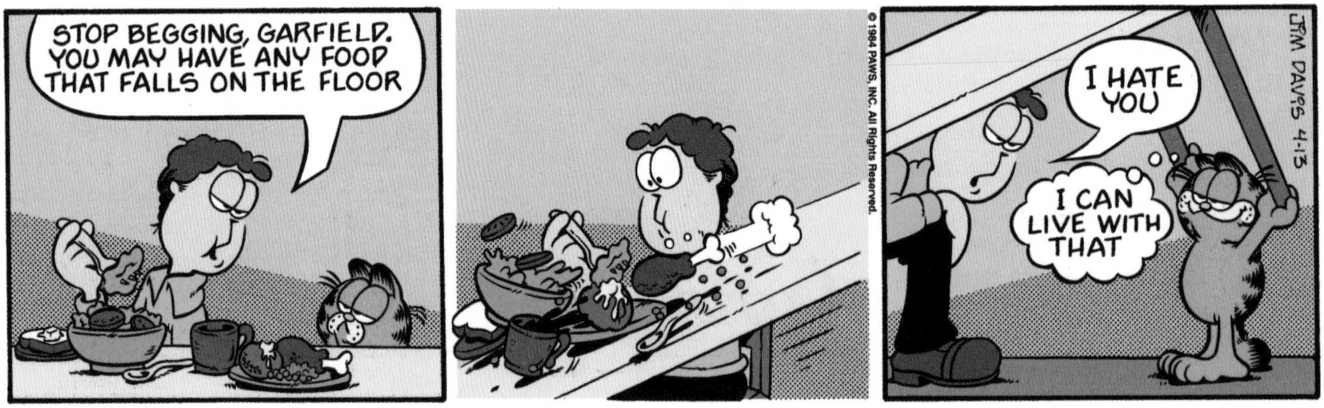
STOP BEGGING, GARFIELD. YOU MAY HAVE ANY FOOD THAT FALLS ON THE FLOOR
© 1984 PAWS, INC. All Rights Reserved.
JIM DAVIS 4-13
I HATE YOU
I CAN LIVE WITH THAT

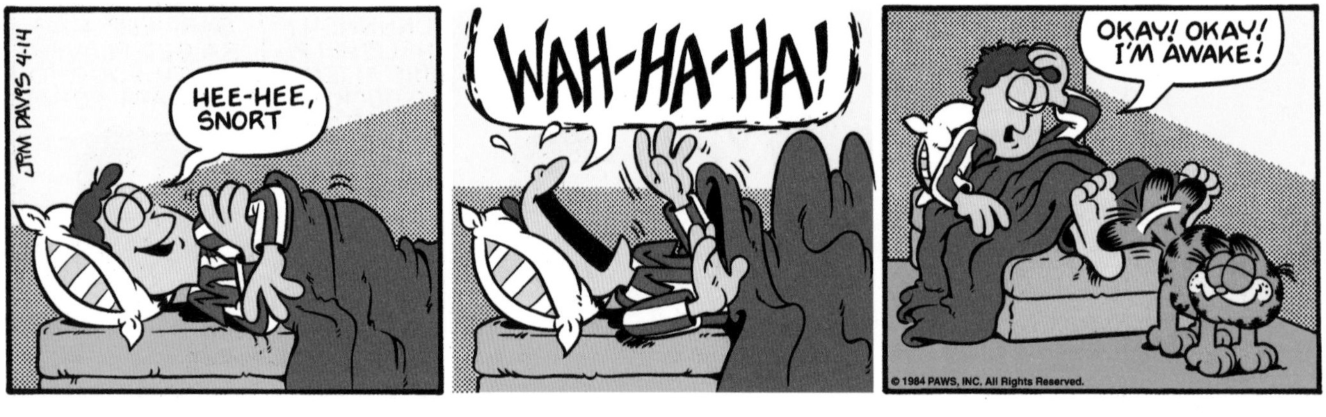
JIM DAVIS 4-14
HEE-HEE, SNORT
WAH-HA-HA!
OKAY! OKAY! I'M AWAKE!
© 1984 PAWS, INC. All Rights Reserved.

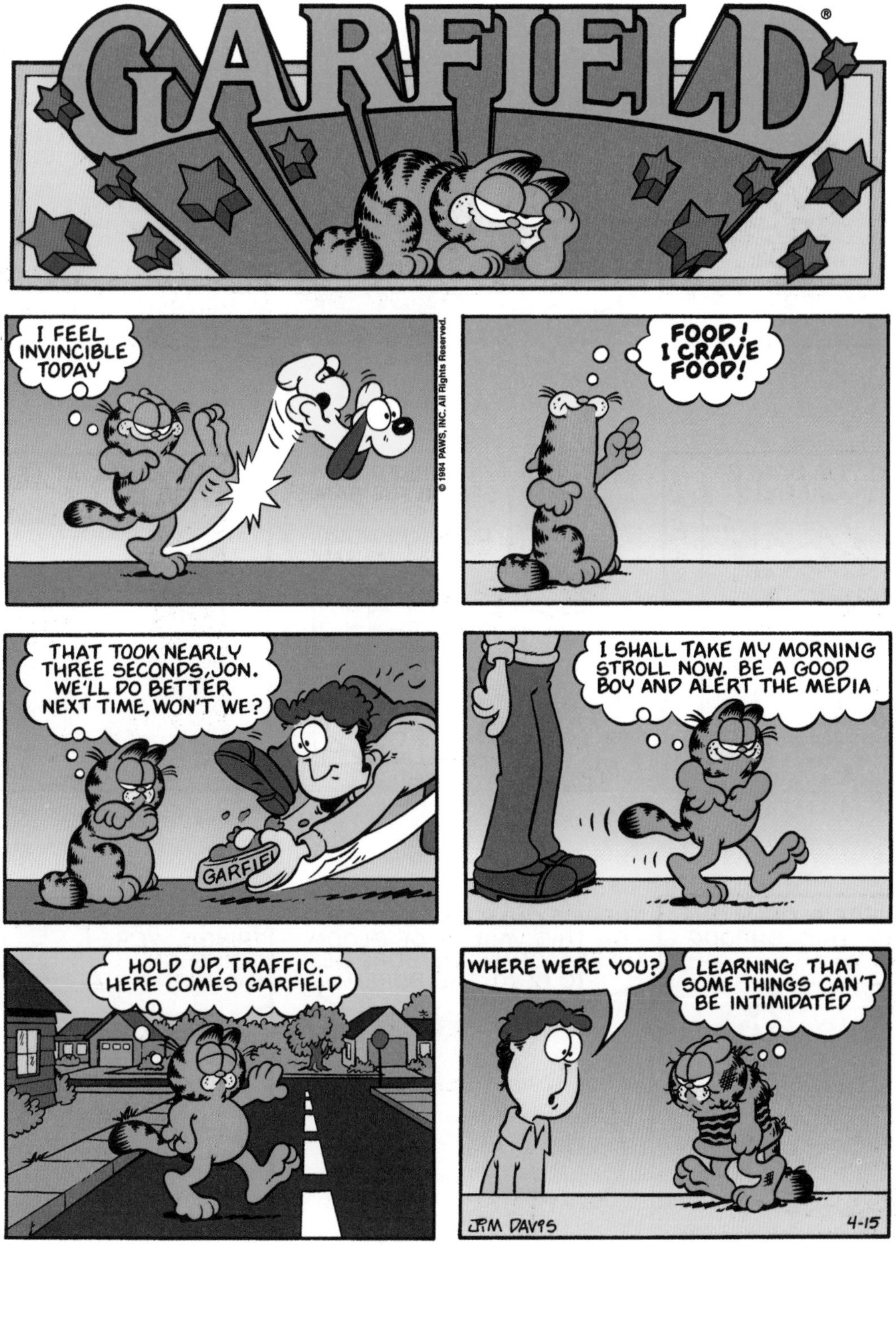
GARFIELD®
I FEEL INVINCIBLE TODAY
© 1984 PAWS, INC. All Rights Reserved.
FOOD! I CRAVE FOOD!
THAT TOOK NEARLY THREE SECONDS, JON. WE'LL DO BETTER NEXT TIME, WON'T WE?
GARFIEL
I SHALL TAKE MY MORNING STROLL NOW. BE A GOOD BOY AND ALERT THE MEDIA
HOLD UP, TRAFFIC. HERE COMES GARFIELD
WHERE WERE YOU?
LEARNING THAT SOME THINGS CAN'T BE INTIMIDATED
JPM DAVPS
4-15

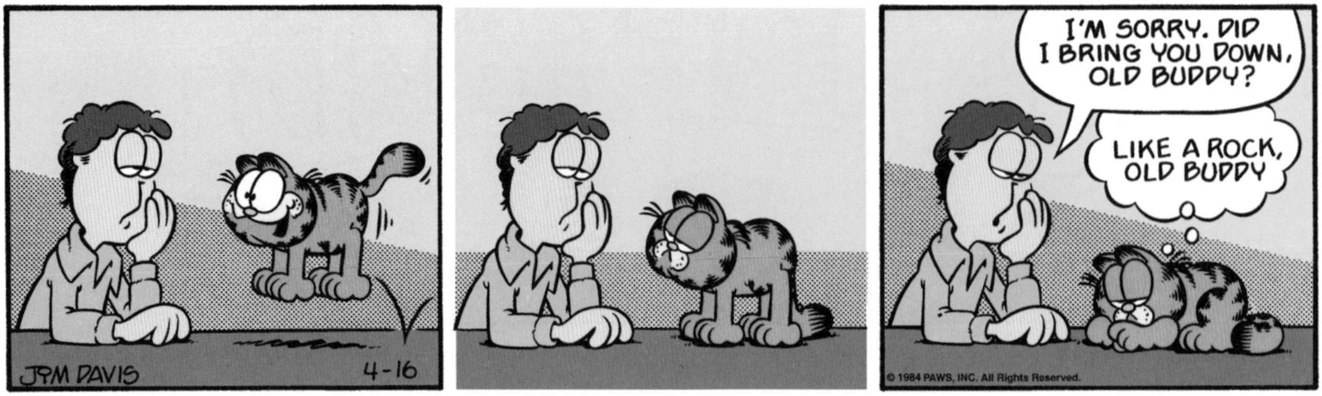
JIM DAVIS
4-16
I'M SORRY. DID I BRING YOU DOWN, OLD BUDDY?
LIKE A ROCK, OLD BUDDY
© 1984 PAWS, INC. All Rights Reserved.

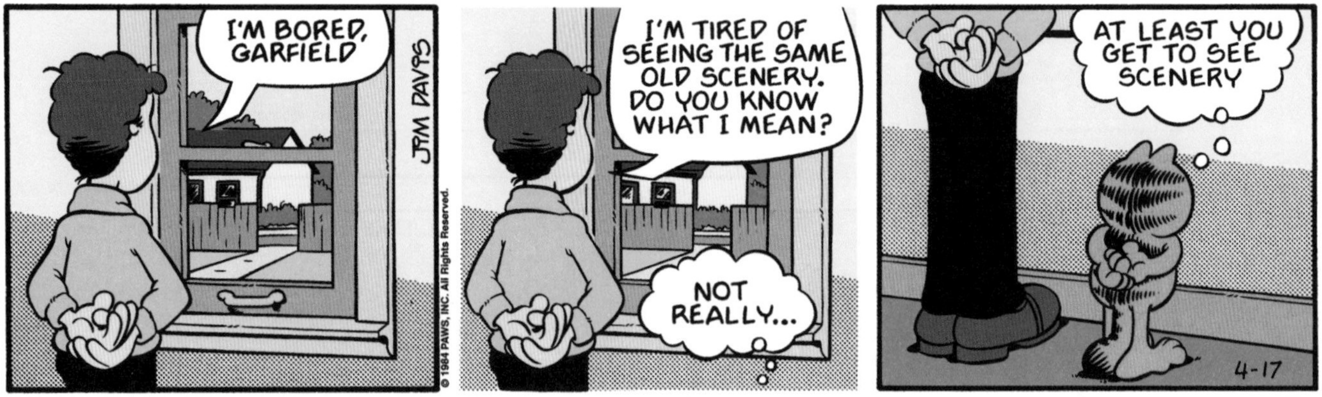
I'M BORED, GARFIELD
JIM DAVIS
© 1984 PAWS, INC. All Rights Reserved.
I'M TIRED OF SEEING THE SAME OLD SCENERY. DO YOU KNOW WHAT I MEAN?
NOT REALLY...
AT LEAST YOU GET TO SEE SCENERY
4-17

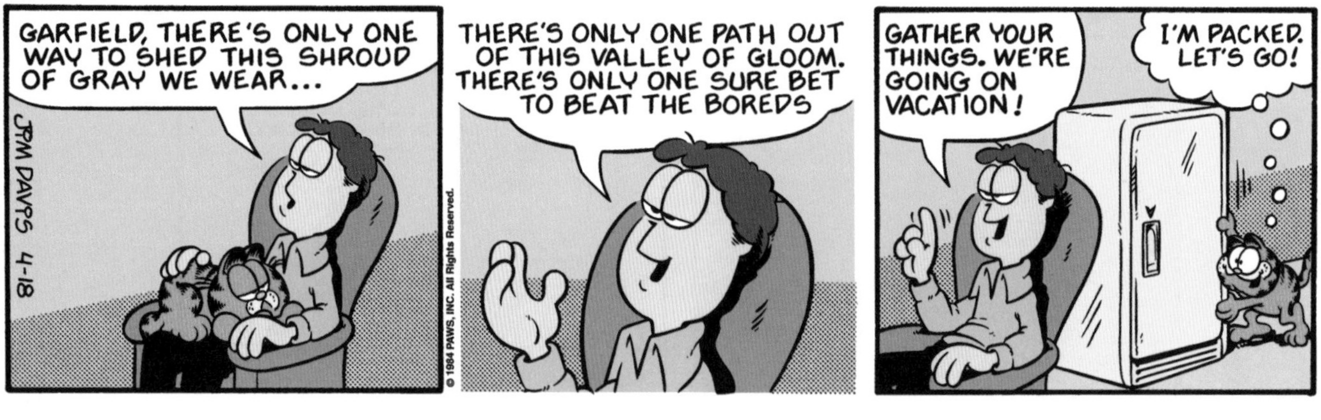
GARFIELD, THERE'S ONLY ONE WAY TO SHED THIS SHROUD OF GRAY WE WEAR...
JIM DAVIS 4-18
© 1984 PAWS, INC. All Rights Reserved.
THERE'S ONLY ONE PATH OUT OF THIS VALLEY OF GLOOM. THERE'S ONLY ONE SURE BET TO BEAT THE BOREDS
GATHER YOUR THINGS. WE'RE GOING ON VACATION!
I'M PACKED. LET'S GO!

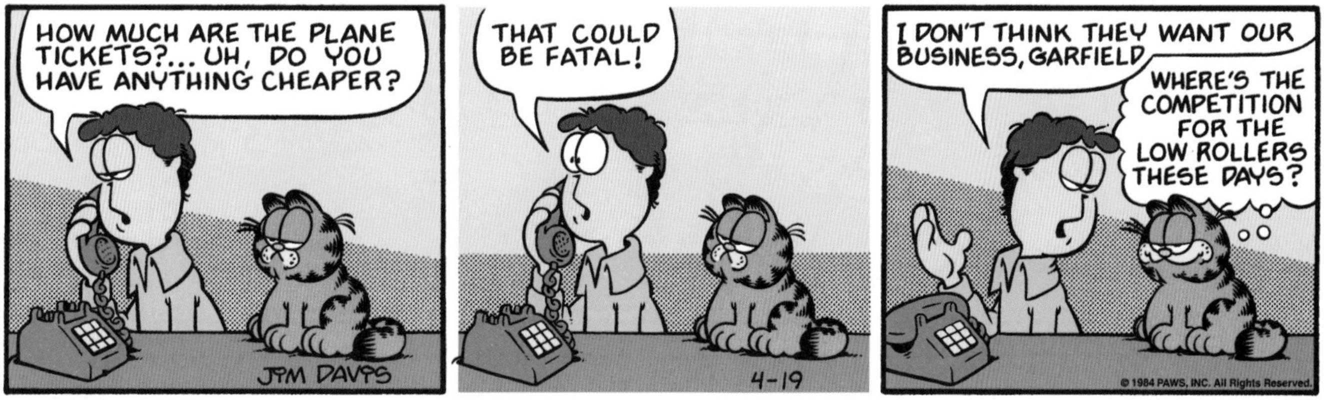
HOW MUCH ARE THE PLANE TICKETS?... UH, DO YOU HAVE ANYTHING CHEAPER?
JIM DAVIS
THAT COULD BE FATAL!
4-19
I DON'T THINK THEY WANT OUR BUSINESS, GARFIELD
WHERE'S THE COMPETITION FOR THE LOW ROLLERS THESE DAYS?
© 1984 PAWS, INC. All Rights Reserved.

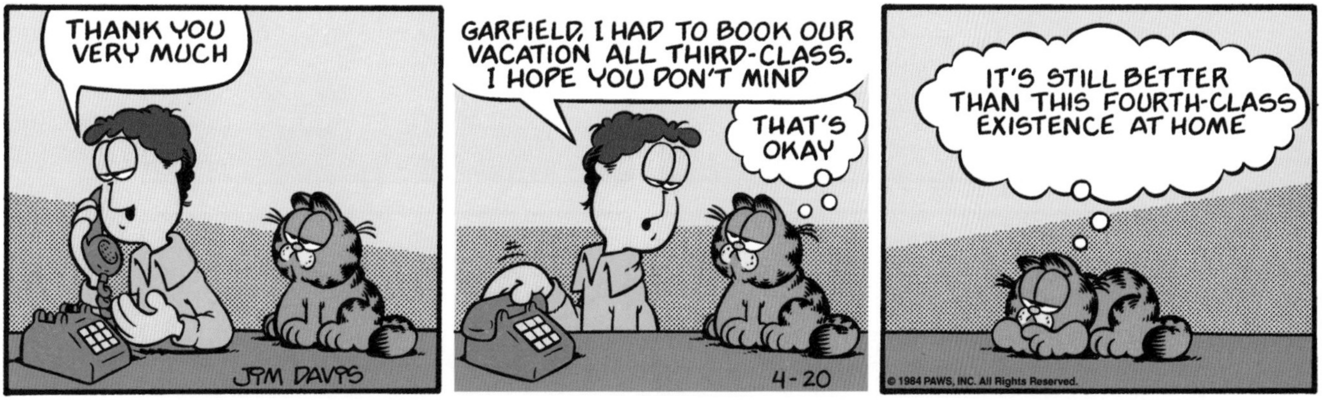
THANK YOU VERY MUCH
JIM DAVIS
GARFIELD, I HAD TO BOOK OUR VACATION ALL THIRD-CLASS. I HOPE YOU DON'T MIND
THAT'S OKAY
4-20
IT'S STILL BETTER THAN THIS FOURTH-CLASS EXISTENCE AT HOME
© 1984 PAWS, INC. All Rights Reserved.

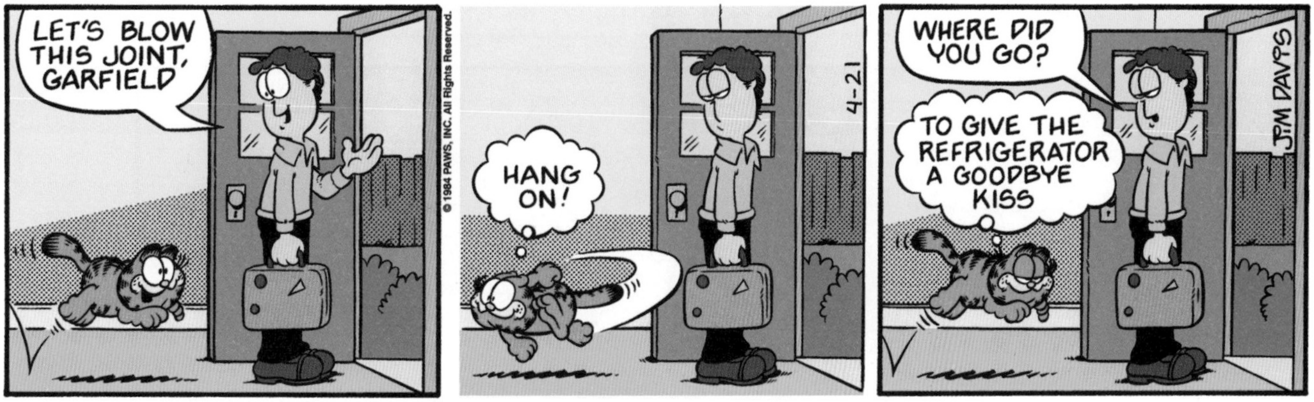
LET'S BLOW THIS JOINT, GARFIELD
© 1984 PAWS, INC. All Rights Reserved.
HANG ON!
4-21
WHERE DID YOU GO?
TO GIVE THE REFRIGERATOR A GOODBYE KISS
JIM DAVIS

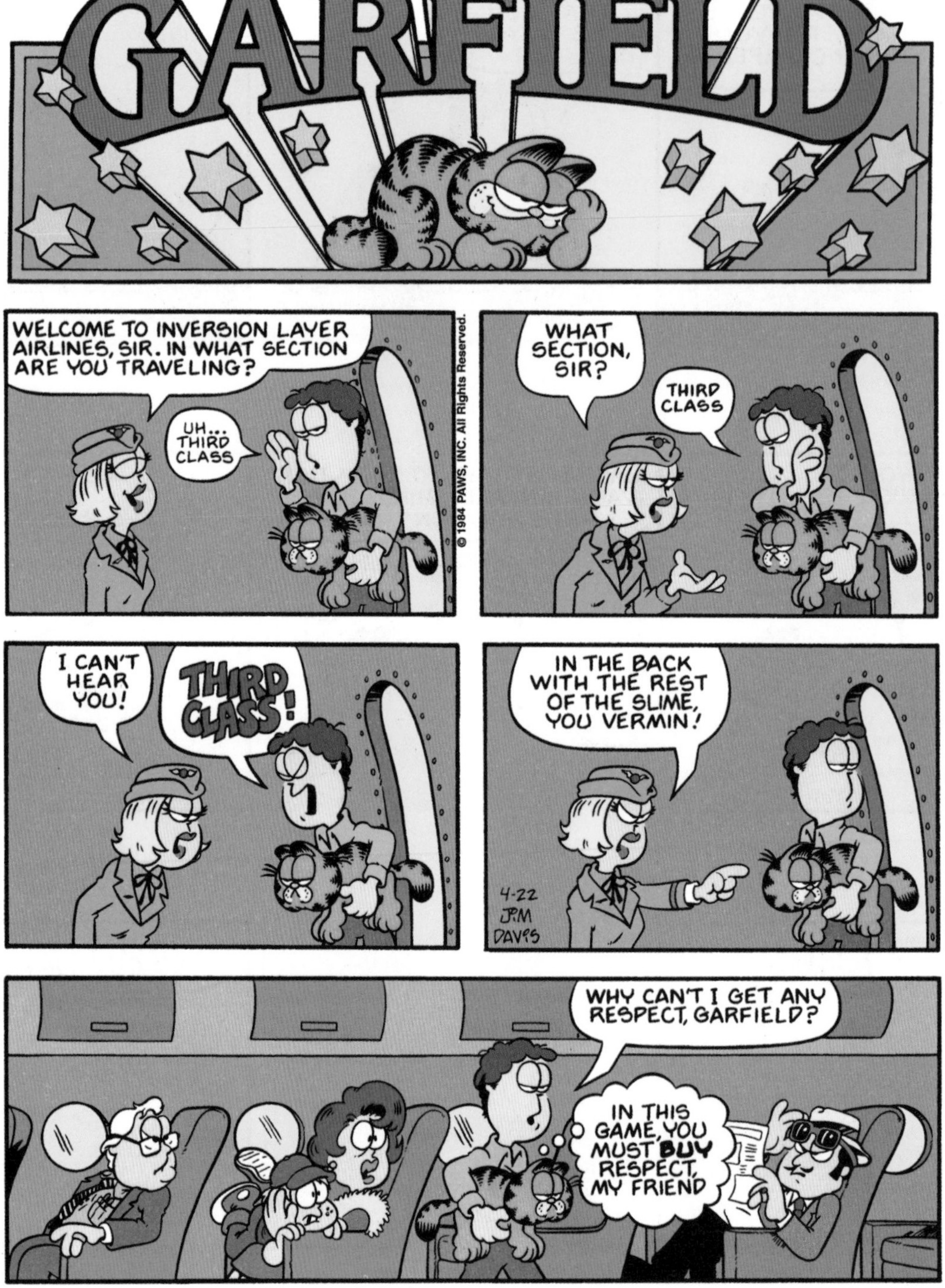
GARFIELD
WELCOME TO INVERSION LAYER AIRLINES, SIR. IN WHAT SECTION ARE YOU TRAVELING?
UH... THIRD CLASS
© 1984 PAWS, INC. All Rights Reserved.
WHAT SECTION, SIR?
THIRD CLASS
I CAN'T HEAR YOU!
THIRD CLASS!
IN THE BACK WITH THE REST OF THE SLIME, YOU VERMIN!
4-22 JIM DAVIS
WHY CAN'T I GET ANY RESPECT, GARFIELD?
IN THIS GAME, YOU MUST **BUY** RESPECT, MY FRIEND

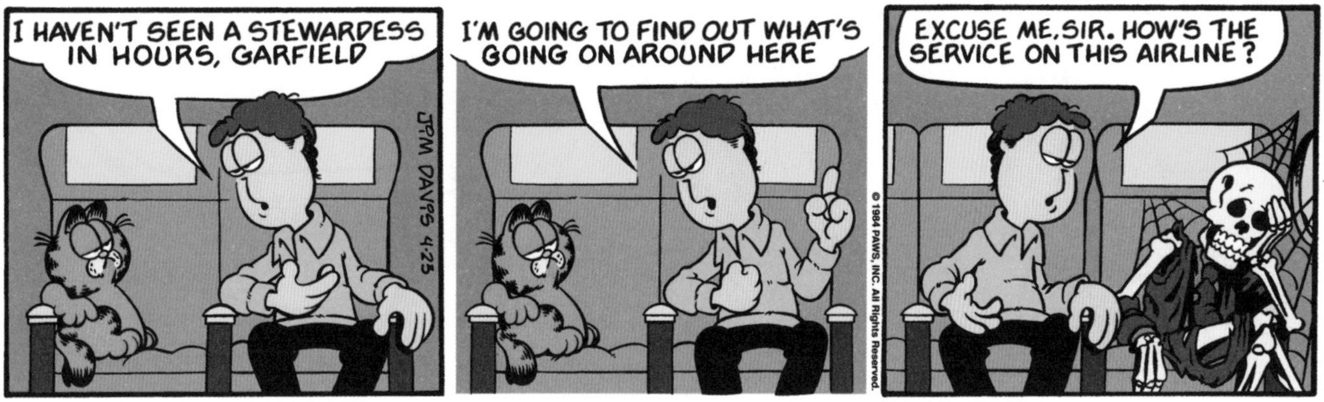
I HAVEN'T SEEN A STEWARDESS IN HOURS, GARFIELD
JIM DAVIS 4·23
I'M GOING TO FIND OUT WHAT'S GOING ON AROUND HERE
© 1984 PAWS, INC. All Rights Reserved.
EXCUSE ME, SIR. HOW'S THE SERVICE ON THIS AIRLINE?

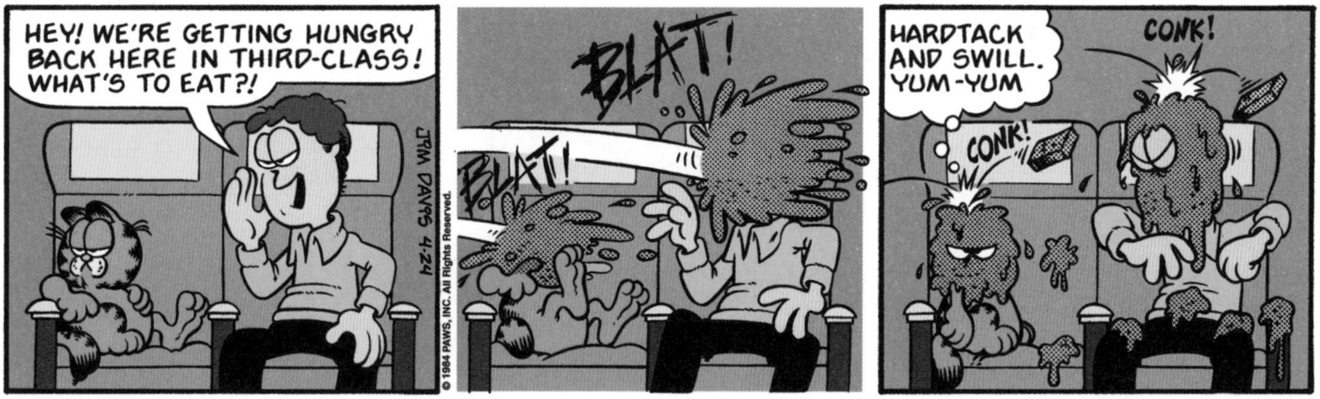
HEY! WE'RE GETTING HUNGRY BACK HERE IN THIRD-CLASS! WHAT'S TO EAT?!
JIM DAVIS 4·24
© 1984 PAWS, INC. All Rights Reserved.
BLAT!
BLAT!
HARDTACK AND SWILL. YUM-YUM
CONK!
CONK!

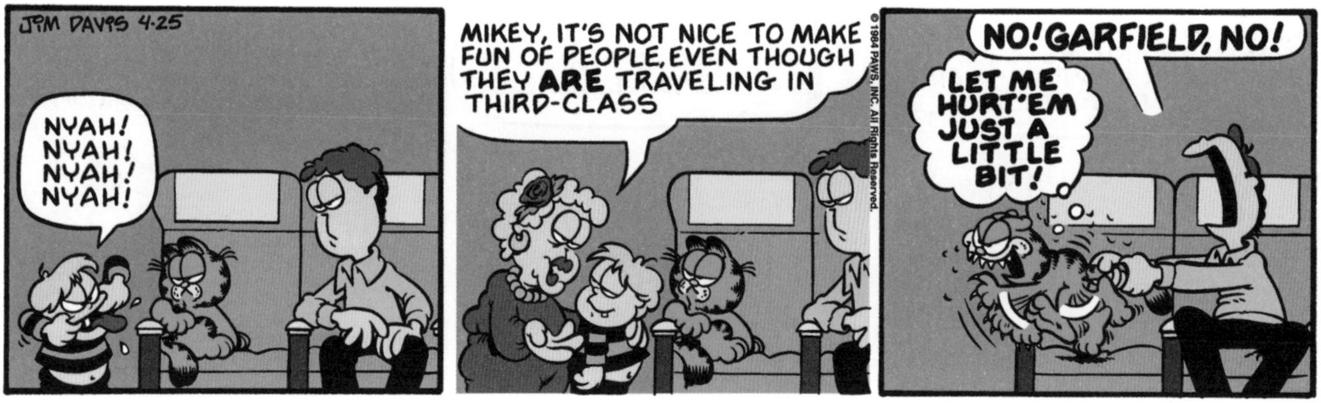
JIM DAVIS 4·25
NYAH! NYAH! NYAH! NYAH!
MIKEY, IT'S NOT NICE TO MAKE FUN OF PEOPLE, EVEN THOUGH THEY **ARE** TRAVELING IN THIRD-CLASS
© 1984 PAWS, INC. All Rights Reserved.
NO! GARFIELD, NO!
LET ME HURT'EM JUST A LITTLE BIT!

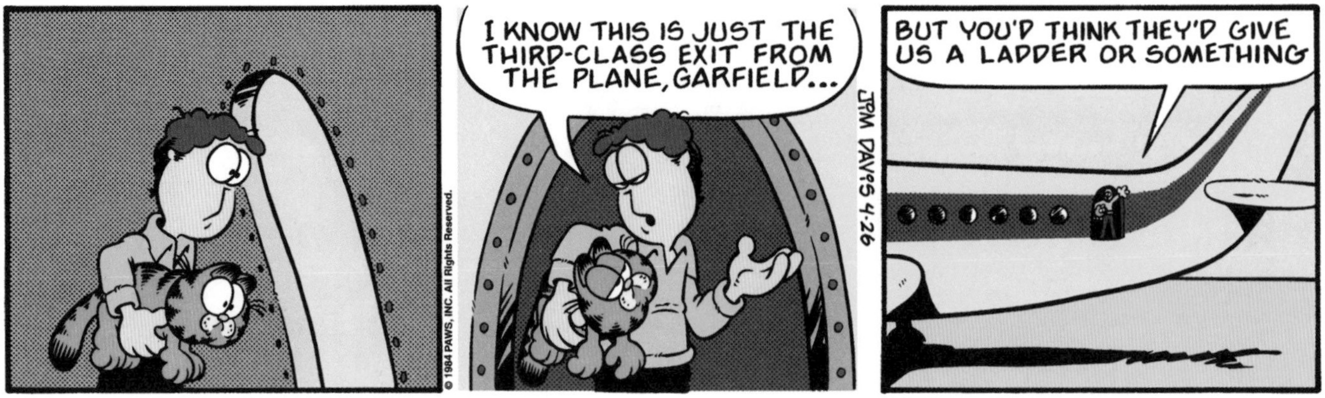

© 1984 PAWS, INC. All Rights Reserved.
I KNOW THIS IS JUST THE THIRD-CLASS EXIT FROM THE PLANE, GARFIELD...
JIM DAVIS 4-26
BUT YOU'D THINK THEY'D GIVE US A LADDER OR SOMETHING

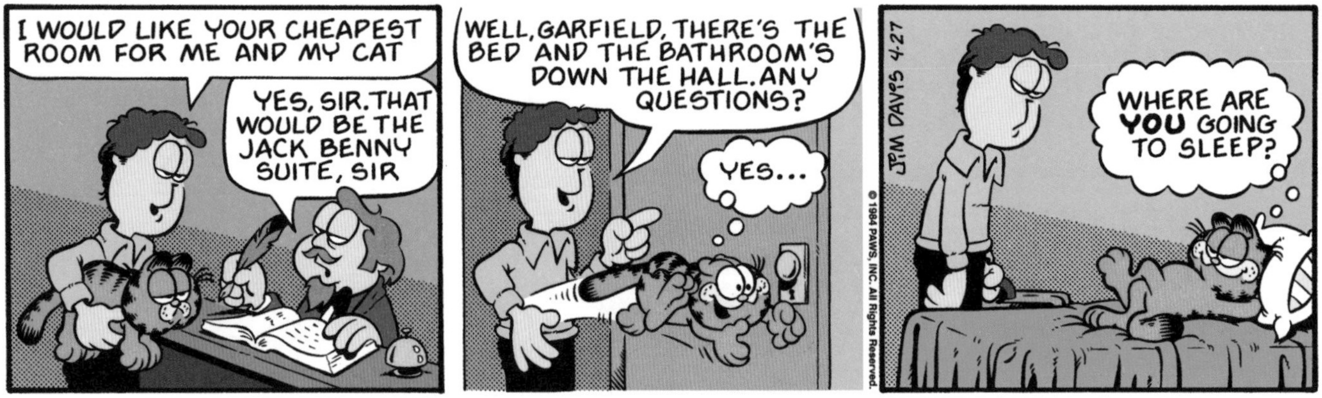

I WOULD LIKE YOUR CHEAPEST ROOM FOR ME AND MY CAT
YES, SIR. THAT WOULD BE THE JACK BENNY SUITE, SIR
WELL, GARFIELD, THERE'S THE BED AND THE BATHROOM'S DOWN THE HALL. ANY QUESTIONS?
YES...
© 1984 PAWS, INC. All Rights Reserved.
JIM DAVIS 4-27
WHERE ARE **YOU** GOING TO SLEEP?

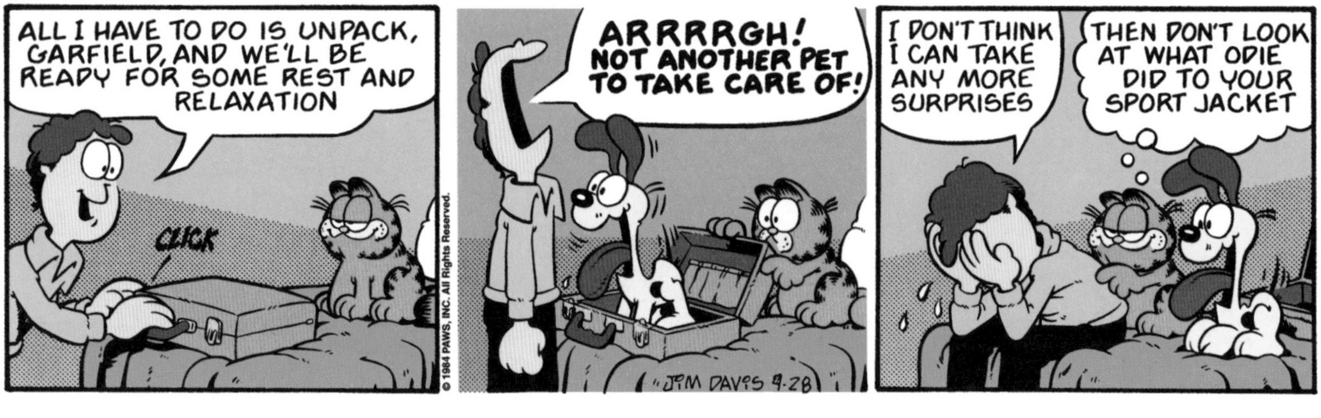

ALL I HAVE TO DO IS UNPACK, GARFIELD, AND WE'LL BE READY FOR SOME REST AND RELAXATION
CLICK
© 1984 PAWS, INC. All Rights Reserved.
ARRRRGH! NOT ANOTHER PET TO TAKE CARE OF!
JIM DAVIS 4-28
I DON'T THINK I CAN TAKE ANY MORE SURPRISES
THEN DON'T LOOK AT WHAT ODIE DID TO YOUR SPORT JACKET

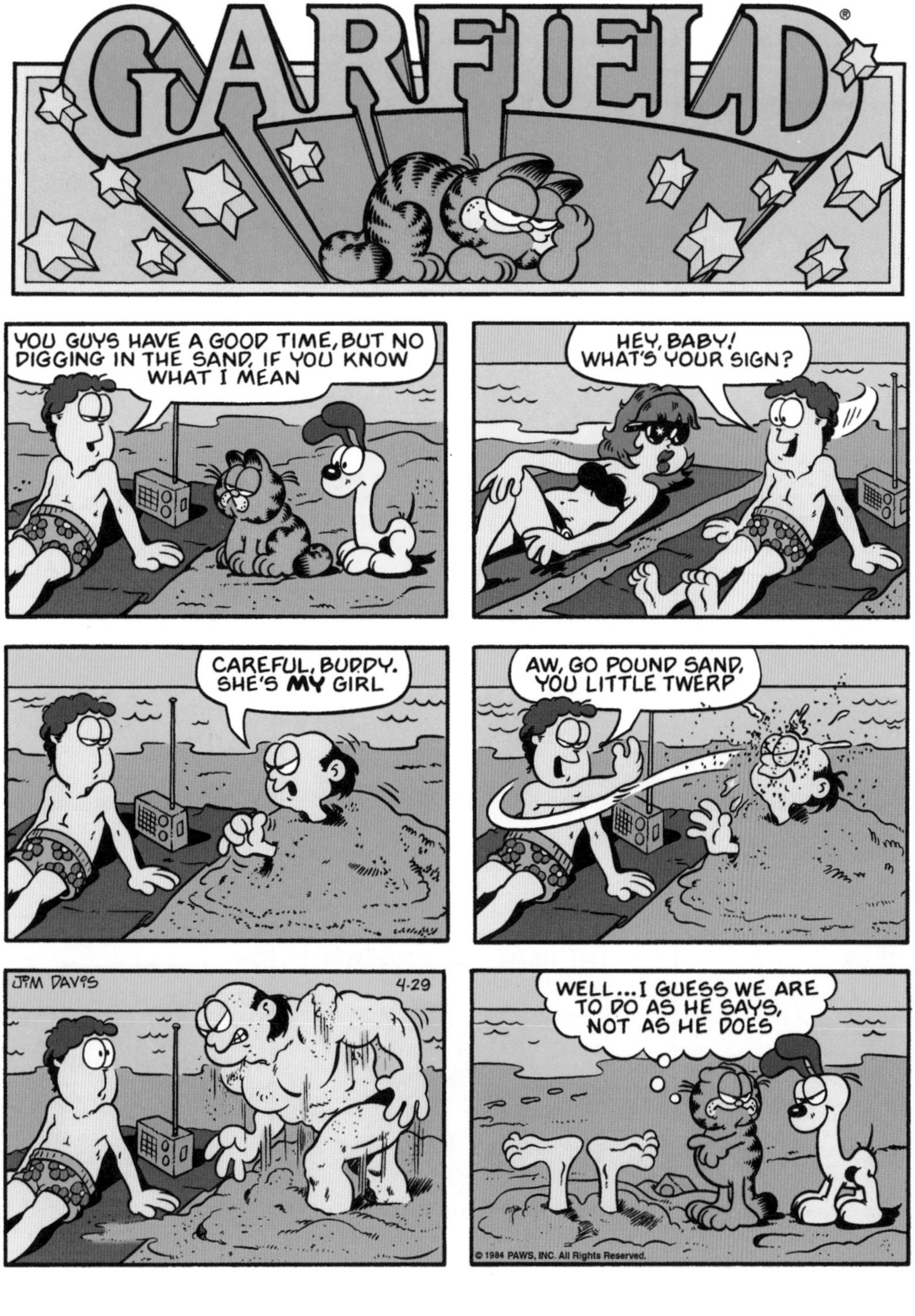
GARFIELD®
YOU GUYS HAVE A GOOD TIME, BUT NO DIGGING IN THE SAND, IF YOU KNOW WHAT I MEAN
HEY, BABY! WHAT'S YOUR SIGN?
CAREFUL, BUDDY. SHE'S **MY** GIRL
AW, GO POUND SAND, YOU LITTLE TWERP
JPM DAVPS
4-29
WELL...I GUESS WE ARE TO DO AS HE SAYS, NOT AS HE DOES
© 1984 PAWS, INC. All Rights Reserved.

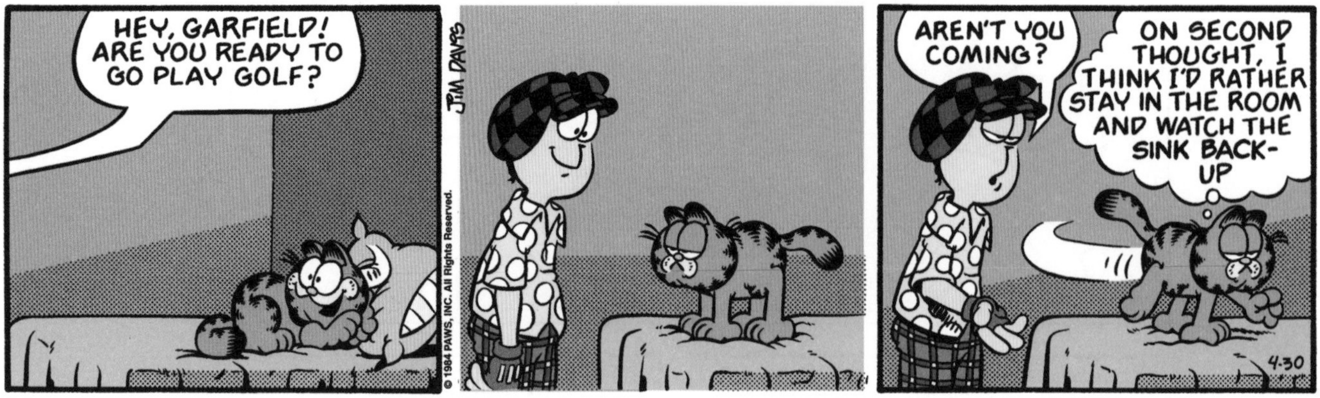
HEY, GARFIELD! ARE YOU READY TO GO PLAY GOLF?
JIM DAVIS
© 1984 PAWS, INC. All Rights Reserved.
AREN'T YOU COMING?
ON SECOND THOUGHT, I THINK I'D RATHER STAY IN THE ROOM AND WATCH THE SINK BACK-UP
4-30

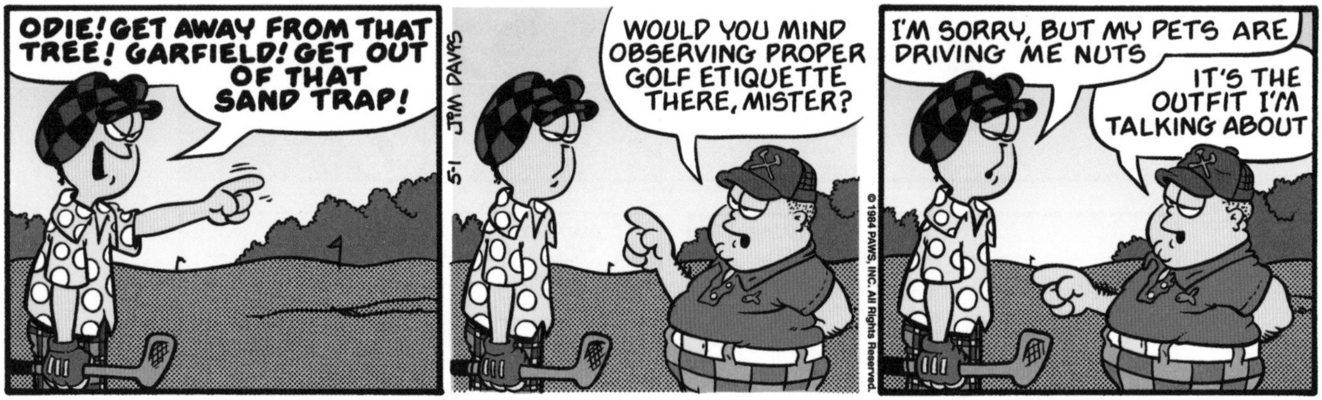
ODIE! GET AWAY FROM THAT TREE! GARFIELD! GET OUT OF THAT SAND TRAP!
JIM DAVIS
5-1
WOULD YOU MIND OBSERVING PROPER GOLF ETIQUETTE THERE, MISTER?
© 1984 PAWS, INC. All Rights Reserved.
I'M SORRY, BUT MY PETS ARE DRIVING ME NUTS
IT'S THE OUTFIT I'M TALKING ABOUT

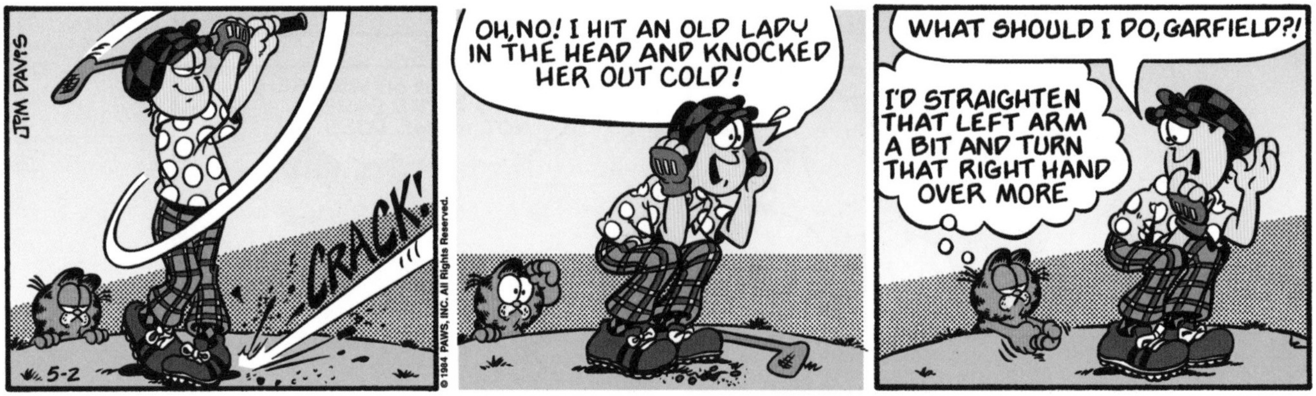
JIM DAVIS
CRACK!
5-2
© 1984 PAWS, INC. All Rights Reserved.
OH, NO! I HIT AN OLD LADY IN THE HEAD AND KNOCKED HER OUT COLD!
WHAT SHOULD I DO, GARFIELD?!
I'D STRAIGHTEN THAT LEFT ARM A BIT AND TURN THAT RIGHT HAND OVER MORE

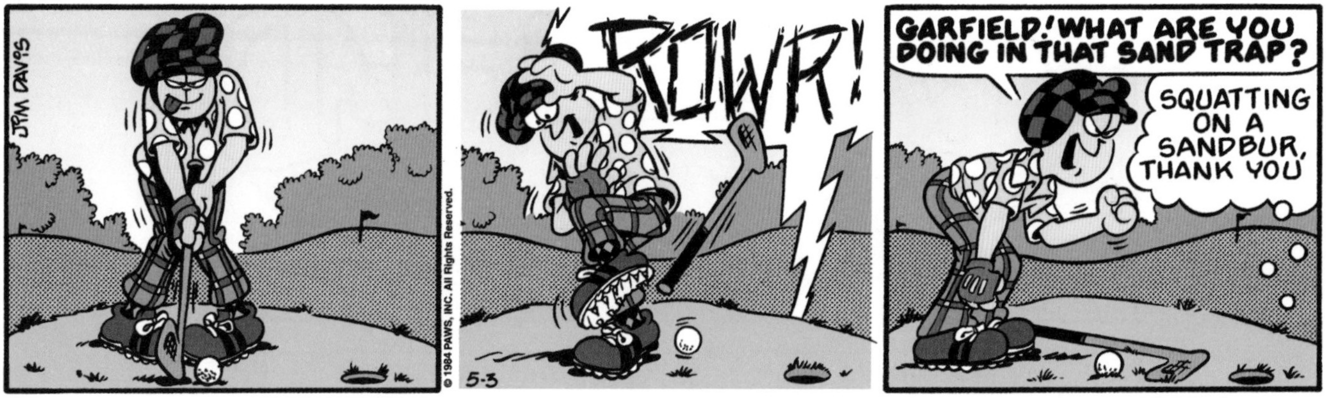
JIM DAVIS
ROWR!
5-3
© 1984 PAWS, INC. All Rights Reserved.
GARFIELD! WHAT ARE YOU DOING IN THAT SAND TRAP?
SQUATTING ON A SANDBUR, THANK YOU

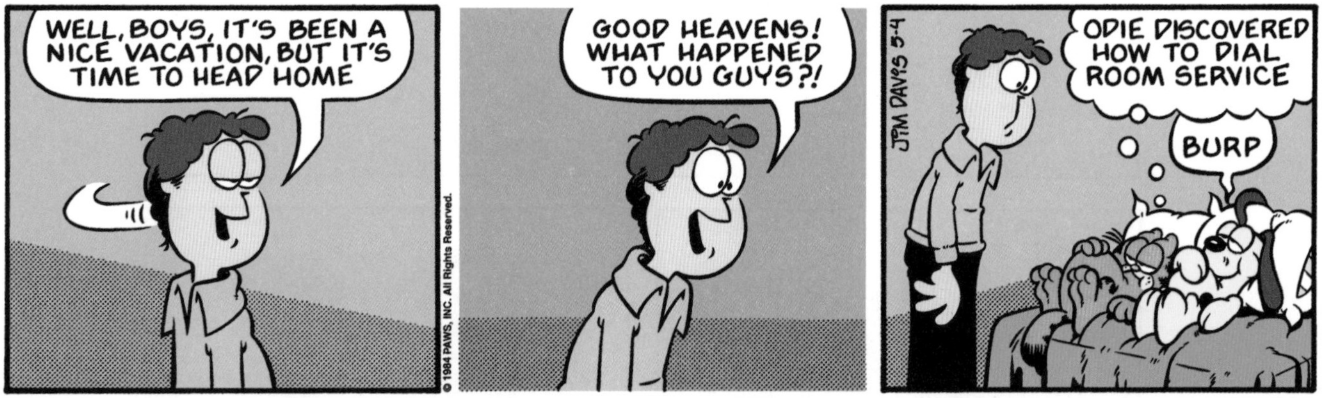
WELL, BOYS, IT'S BEEN A NICE VACATION, BUT IT'S TIME TO HEAD HOME
© 1984 PAWS, INC. All Rights Reserved.
GOOD HEAVENS! WHAT HAPPENED TO YOU GUYS?!
JIM DAVIS 5-4
ODIE DISCOVERED HOW TO DIAL ROOM SERVICE
BURP

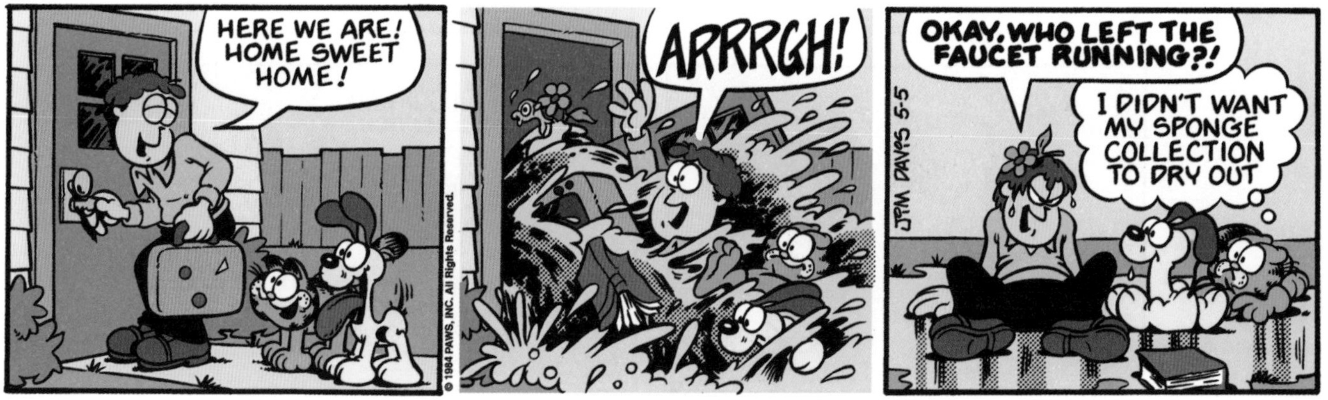
HERE WE ARE! HOME SWEET HOME!
© 1984 PAWS, INC. All Rights Reserved.
ARRRGH!
OKAY, WHO LEFT THE FAUCET RUNNING?!
JIM DAVIS 5-5
I DIDN'T WANT MY SPONGE COLLECTION TO DRY OUT

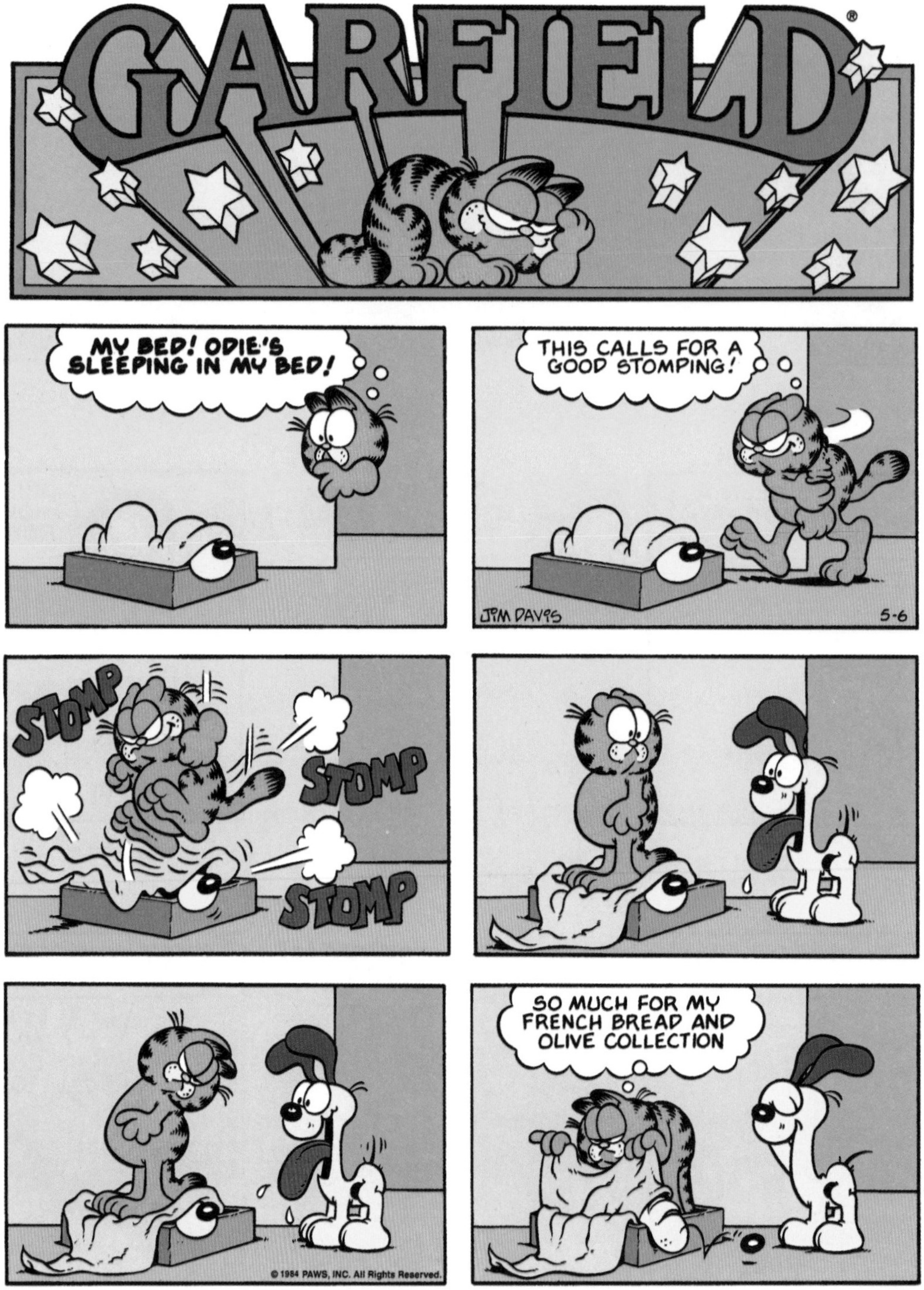
GARFIELD®
MY BED! ODIE'S SLEEPING IN MY BED!
THIS CALLS FOR A GOOD STOMPING!
JIM DAVIS
5-6
STOMP
STOMP
STOMP
© 1984 PAWS, INC. All Rights Reserved.
SO MUCH FOR MY FRENCH BREAD AND OLIVE COLLECTION

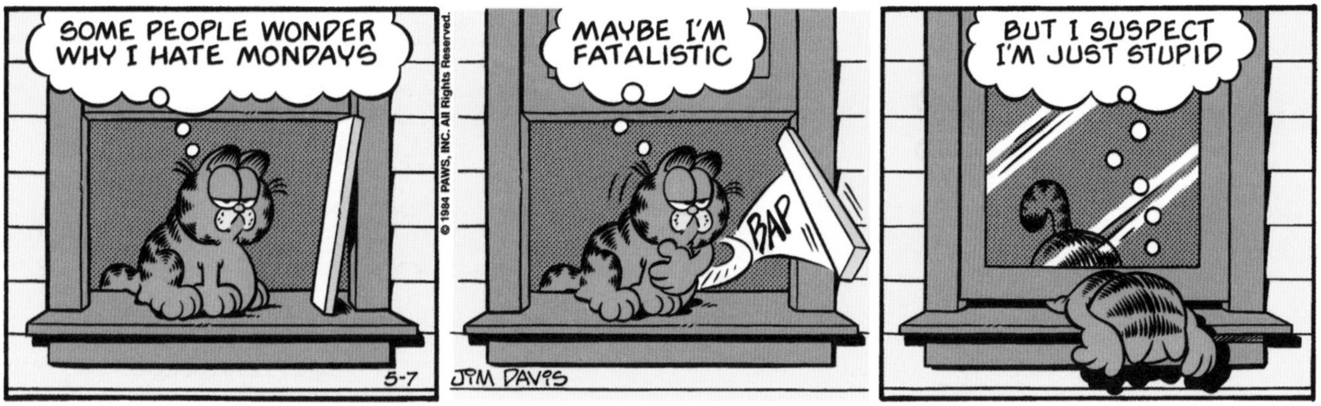
SOME PEOPLE WONDER WHY I HATE MONDAYS
5-7
© 1984 PAWS, INC. All Rights Reserved.
MAYBE I'M FATALISTIC
BAP
JIM DAVIS
BUT I SUSPECT I'M JUST STUPID

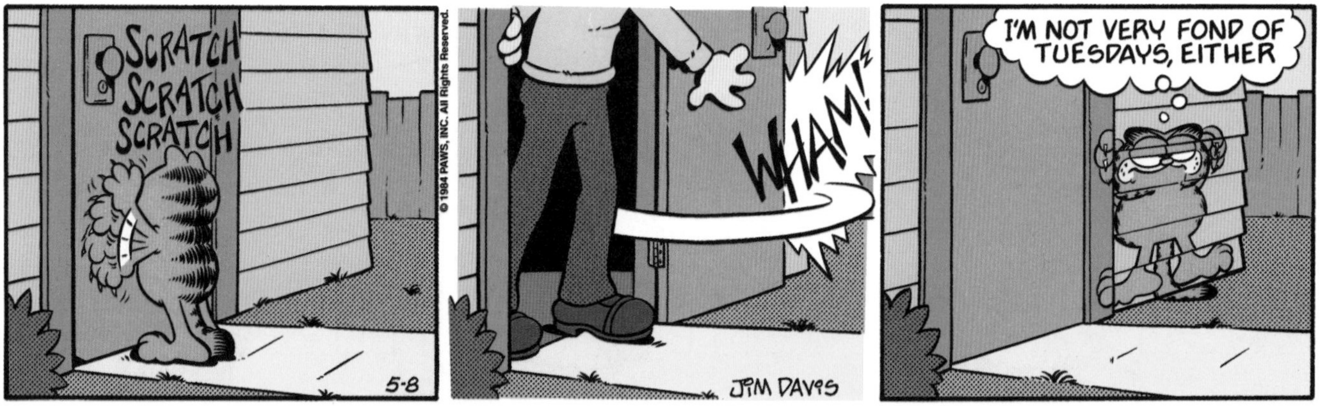
SCRATCH
SCRATCH
SCRATCH
5-8
© 1984 PAWS, INC. All Rights Reserved.
WHAM!
JIM DAVIS
I'M NOT VERY FOND OF TUESDAYS, EITHER

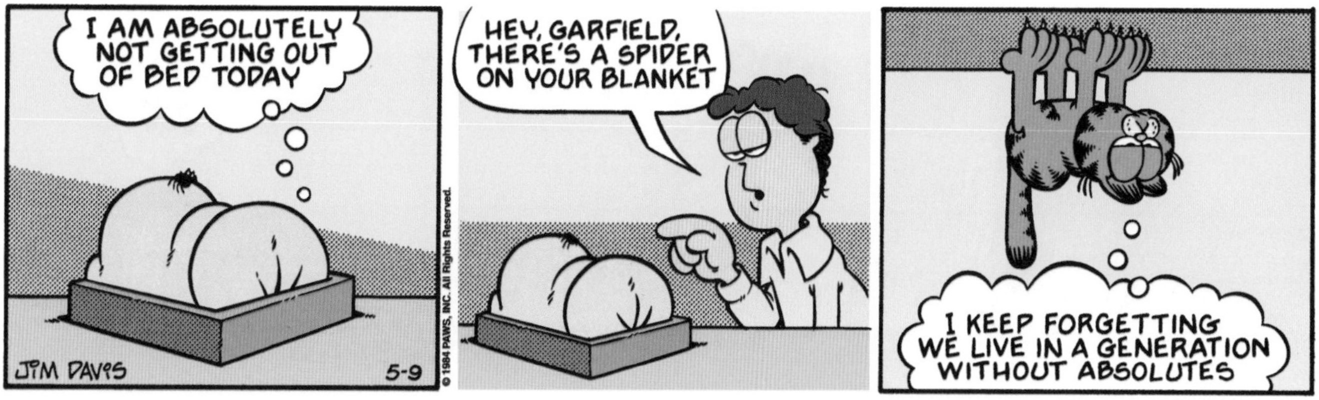
I AM ABSOLUTELY NOT GETTING OUT OF BED TODAY
JIM DAVIS
5-9
© 1984 PAWS, INC. All Rights Reserved.
HEY, GARFIELD, THERE'S A SPIDER ON YOUR BLANKET
I KEEP FORGETTING WE LIVE IN A GENERATION WITHOUT ABSOLUTES

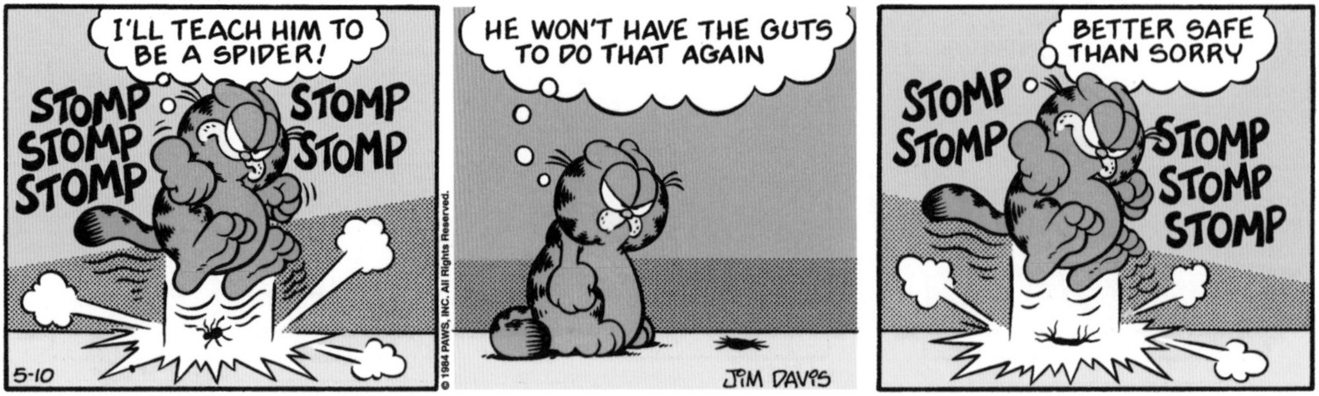
I'LL TEACH HIM TO BE A SPIDER!
STOMP STOMP STOMP
STOMP STOMP
5-10
© 1984 PAWS, INC. All Rights Reserved.
HE WON'T HAVE THE GUTS TO DO THAT AGAIN
JIM DAVIS
BETTER SAFE THAN SORRY
STOMP STOMP
STOMP STOMP STOMP

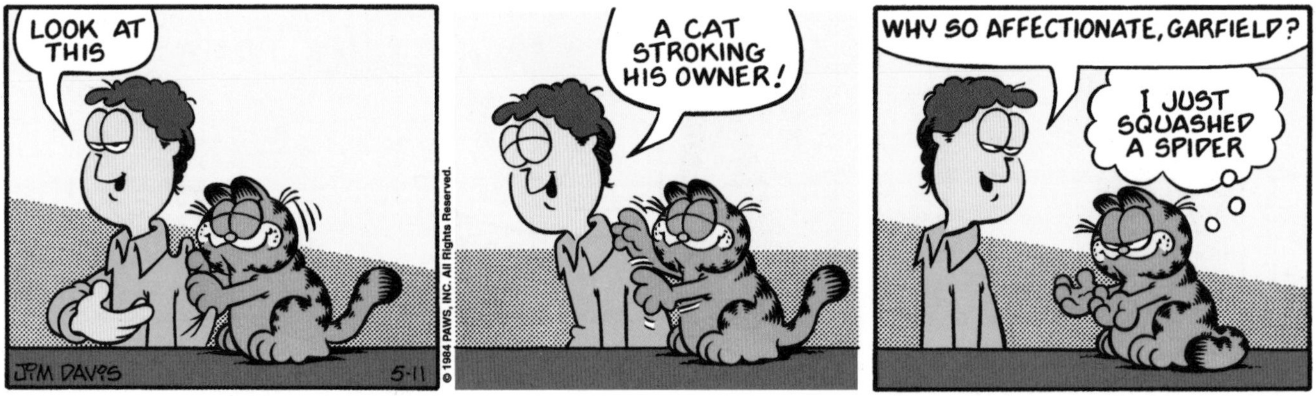
LOOK AT THIS
JIM DAVIS
5-11
© 1984 PAWS, INC. All Rights Reserved.
A CAT STROKING HIS OWNER!
WHY SO AFFECTIONATE, GARFIELD?
I JUST SQUASHED A SPIDER

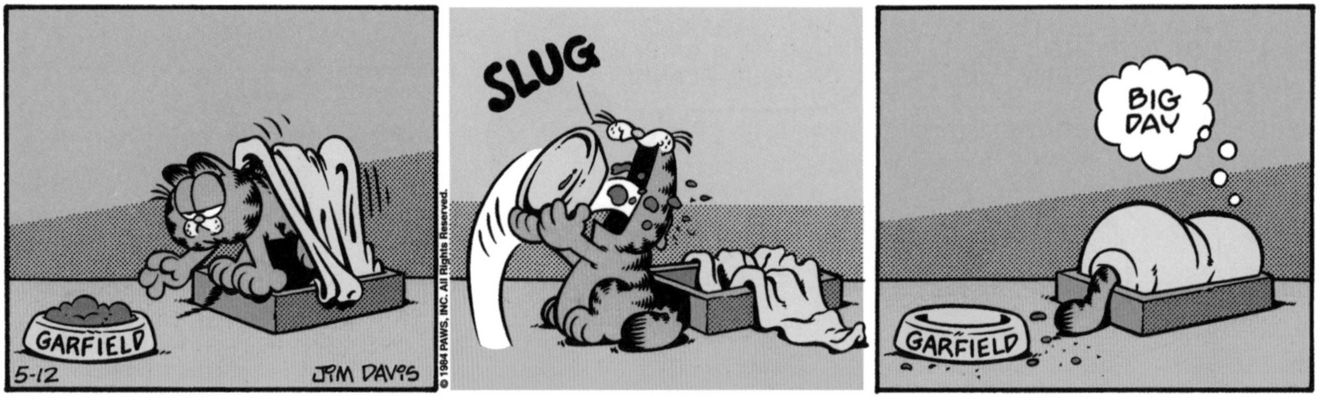
GARFIELD
5-12
JIM DAVIS
© 1984 PAWS, INC. All Rights Reserved.
SLUG
BIG DAY
GARFIELD

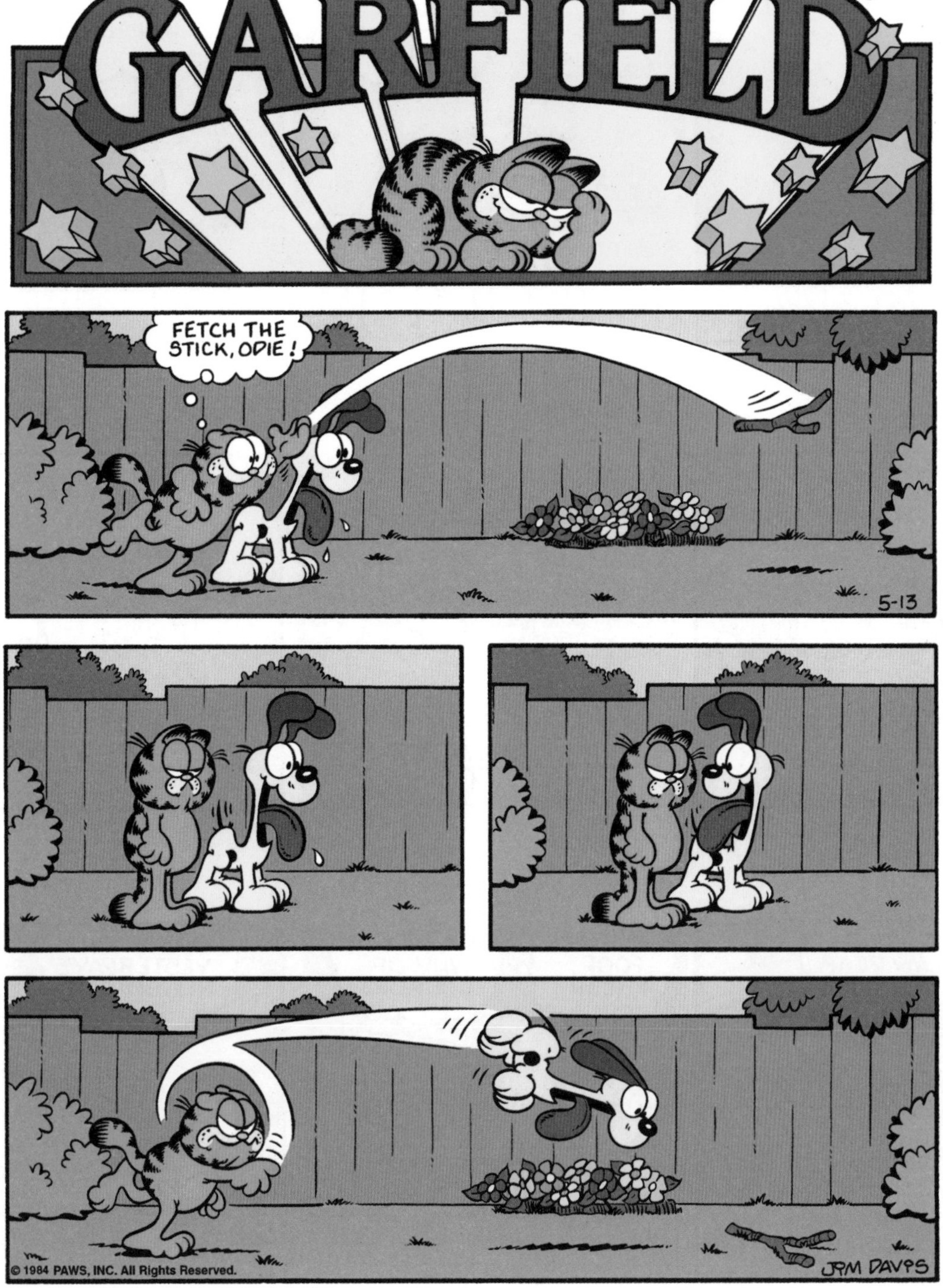
GARFIELD®
FETCH THE STICK, ODIE!
5-13
© 1984 PAWS, INC. All Rights Reserved.
JIM DAVIS

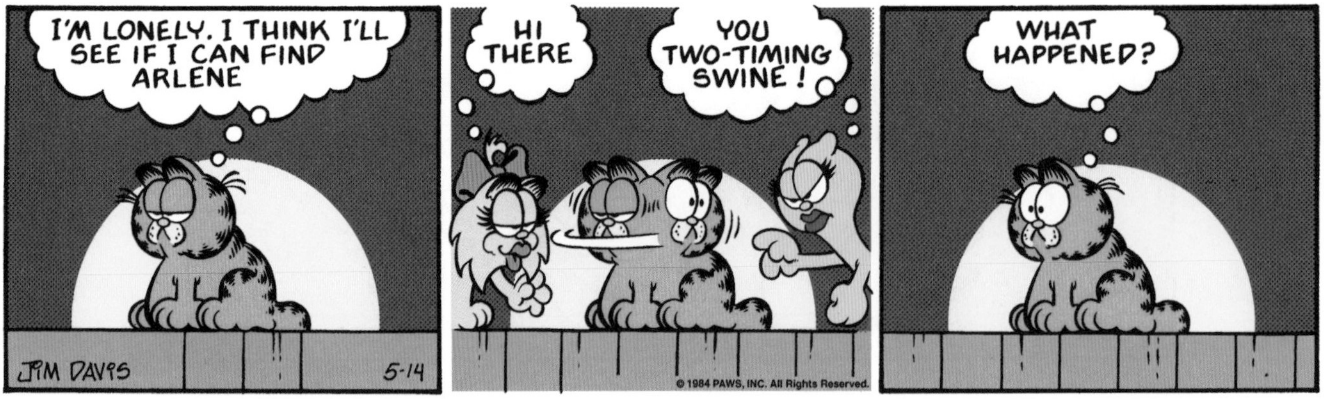
I'M LONELY. I THINK I'LL SEE IF I CAN FIND ARLENE
JIM DAVIS
5-14
HI THERE
YOU TWO-TIMING SWINE!
© 1984 PAWS, INC. All Rights Reserved.
WHAT HAPPENED?

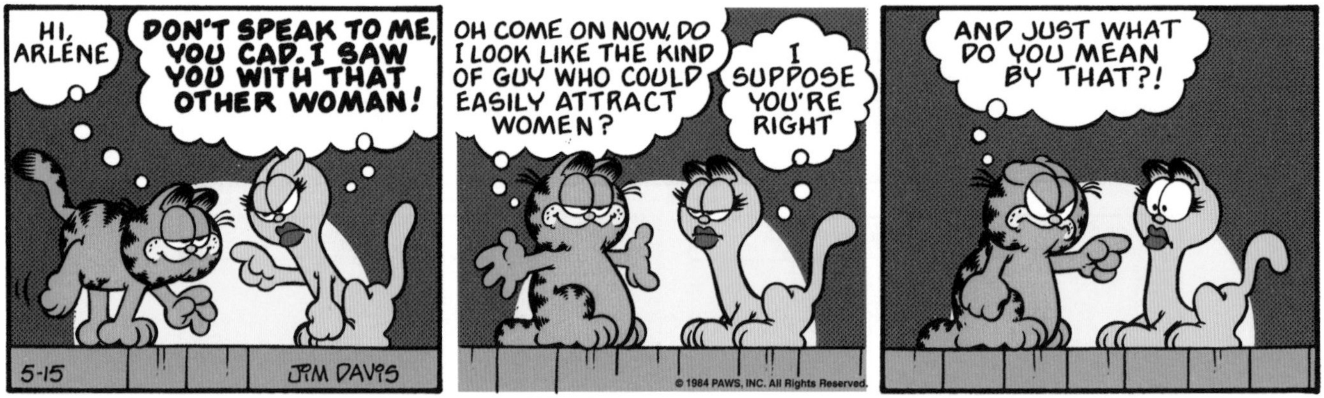
HI, ARLENE
DON'T SPEAK TO ME, YOU CAD. I SAW YOU WITH THAT OTHER WOMAN!
5-15
JIM DAVIS
OH COME ON NOW, DO I LOOK LIKE THE KIND OF GUY WHO COULD EASILY ATTRACT WOMEN?
I SUPPOSE YOU'RE RIGHT
© 1984 PAWS, INC. All Rights Reserved.
AND JUST WHAT DO YOU MEAN BY THAT?!

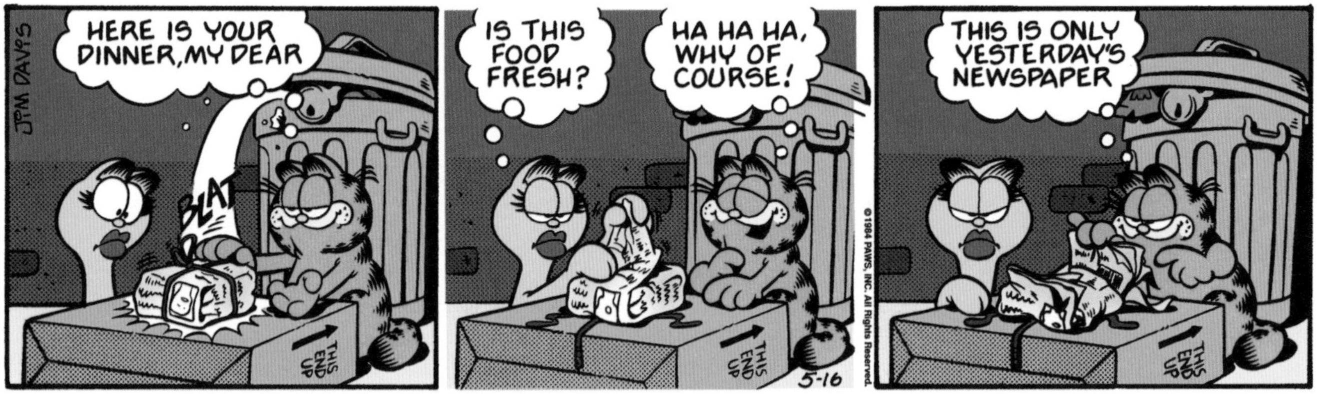
JIM DAVIS
HERE IS YOUR DINNER, MY DEAR
SPLAT
THIS END UP
IS THIS FOOD FRESH?
HA HA HA, WHY OF COURSE!
THIS END UP
5-16
© 1984 PAWS, INC. All Rights Reserved.
THIS IS ONLY YESTERDAY'S NEWSPAPER
THIS END UP

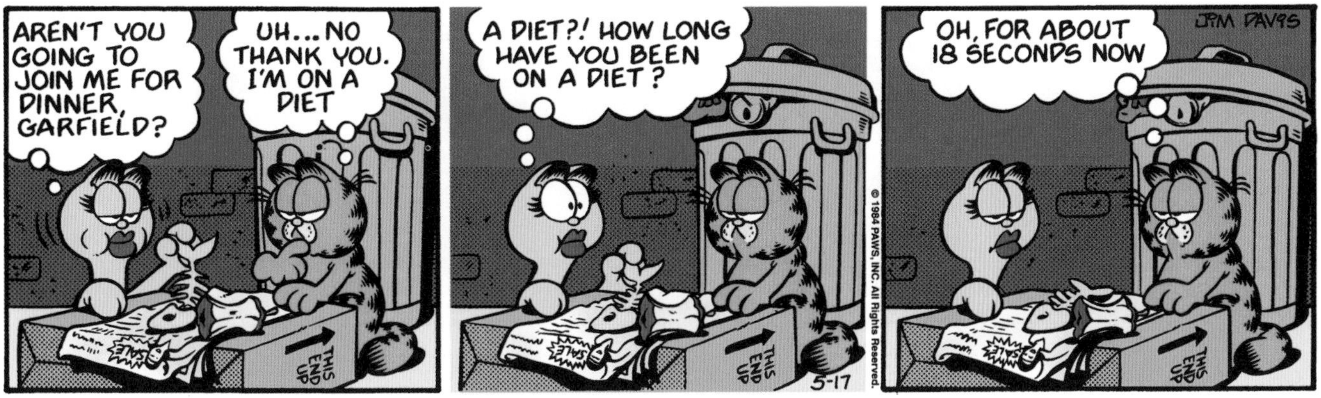
AREN'T YOU GOING TO JOIN ME FOR DINNER, GARFIELD?
UH... NO THANK YOU. I'M ON A DIET
A DIET?! HOW LONG HAVE YOU BEEN ON A DIET?
OH, FOR ABOUT 18 SECONDS NOW
JIM DAVIS
5-17
© 1984 PAWS, INC. All Rights Reserved.
THIS END UP
SALE

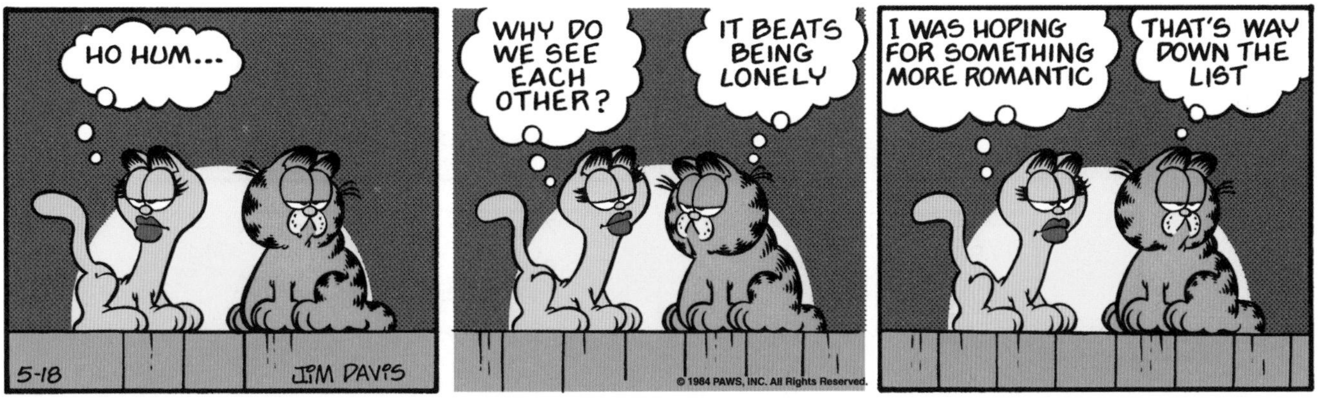
HO HUM...
WHY DO WE SEE EACH OTHER?
IT BEATS BEING LONELY
I WAS HOPING FOR SOMETHING MORE ROMANTIC
THAT'S WAY DOWN THE LIST
5-18
JIM DAVIS
© 1984 PAWS, INC. All Rights Reserved.

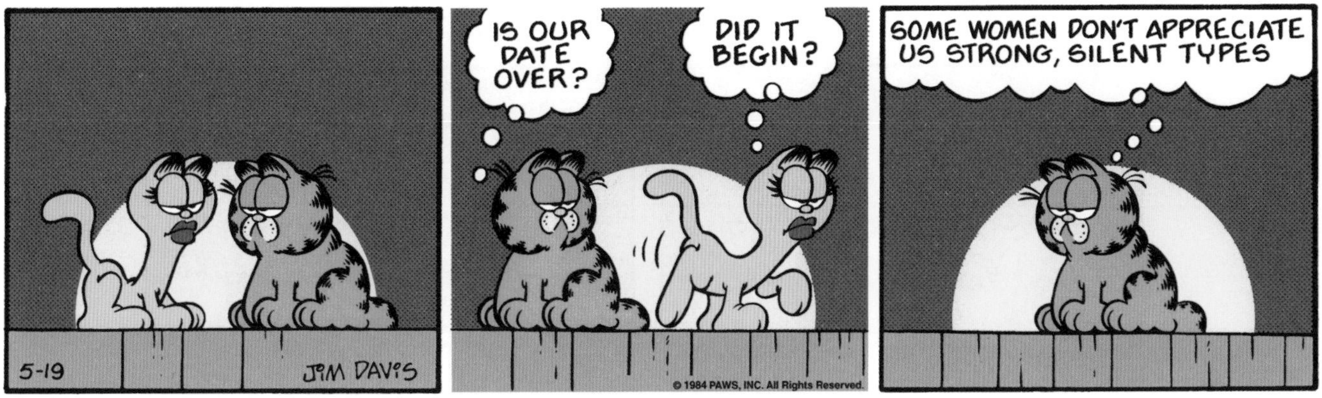
IS OUR DATE OVER?
DID IT BEGIN?
SOME WOMEN DON'T APPRECIATE US STRONG, SILENT TYPES
5-19
JIM DAVIS
© 1984 PAWS, INC. All Rights Reserved.

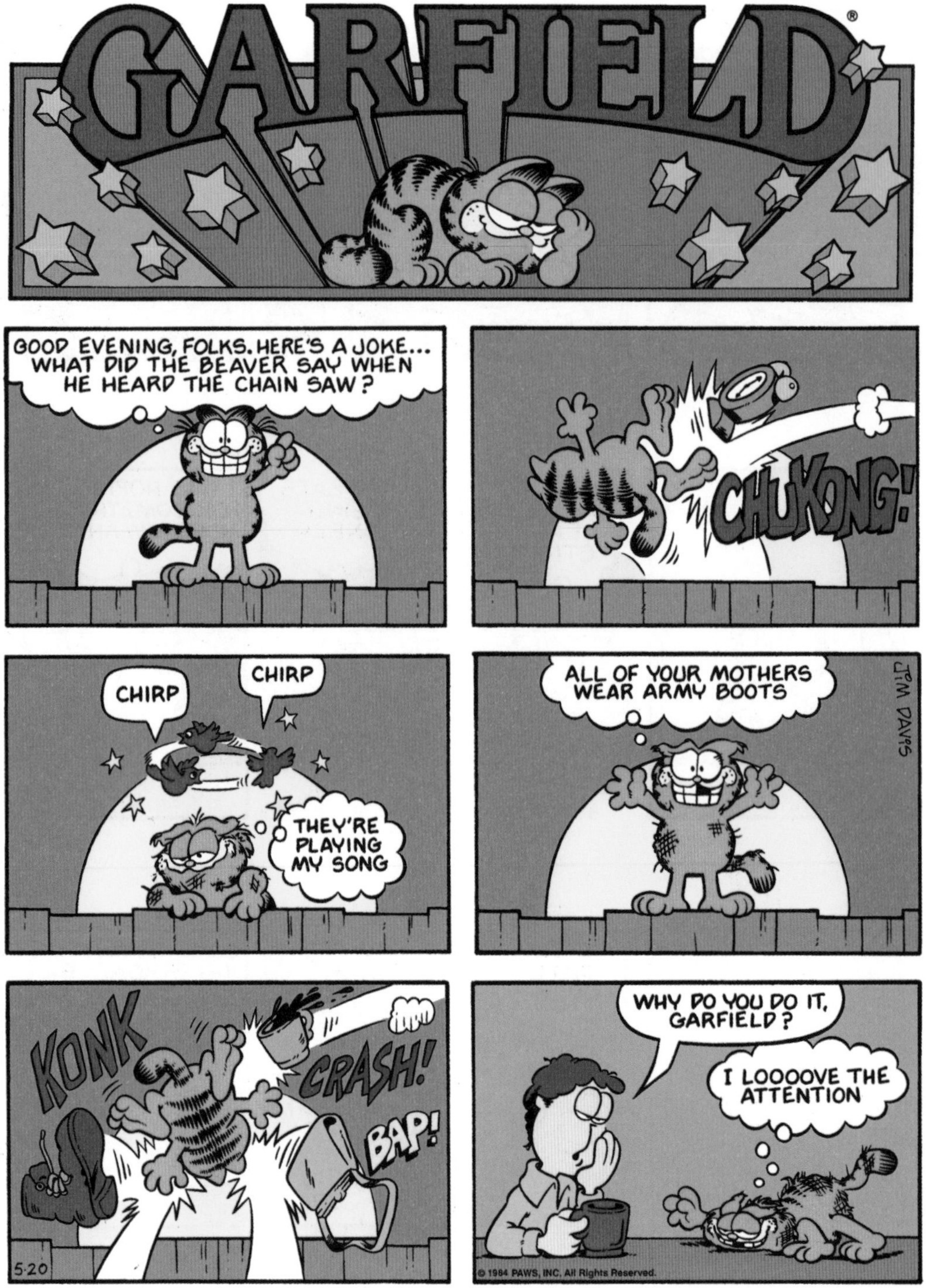
GARFIELD
GOOD EVENING, FOLKS. HERE'S A JOKE... WHAT DID THE BEAVER SAY WHEN HE HEARD THE CHAIN SAW?
CHUKONG!
CHIRP
CHIRP
THEY'RE PLAYING MY SONG
ALL OF YOUR MOTHERS WEAR ARMY BOOTS
JIM DAVIS
KONK
CRASH!
BAP!
5-20
WHY DO YOU DO IT, GARFIELD?
I LOOOOVE THE ATTENTION
© 1984 PAWS, INC. All Rights Reserved.

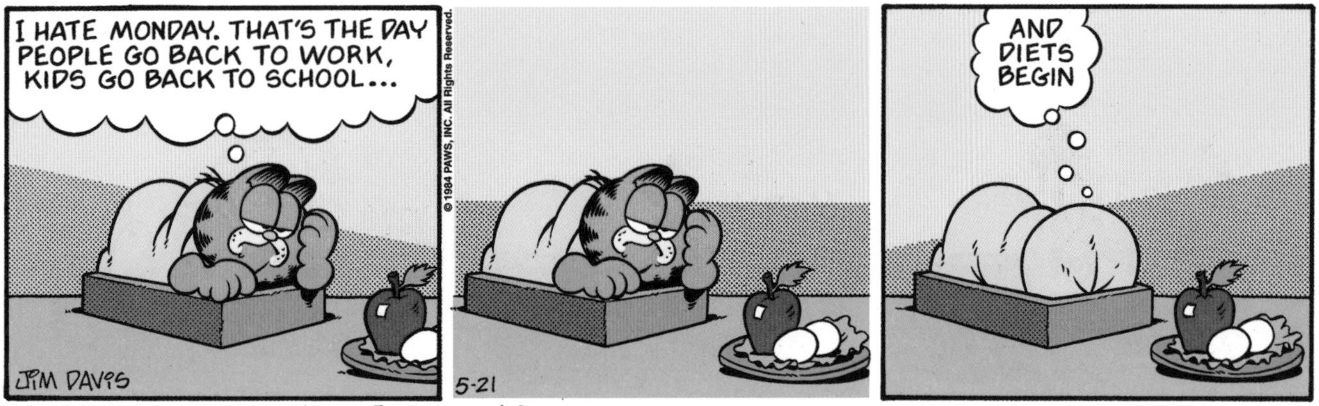

I HATE MONDAY. THAT'S THE DAY PEOPLE GO BACK TO WORK, KIDS GO BACK TO SCHOOL...
JIM DAVIS
© 1984 PAWS, INC. All Rights Reserved.
5-21
AND DIETS BEGIN

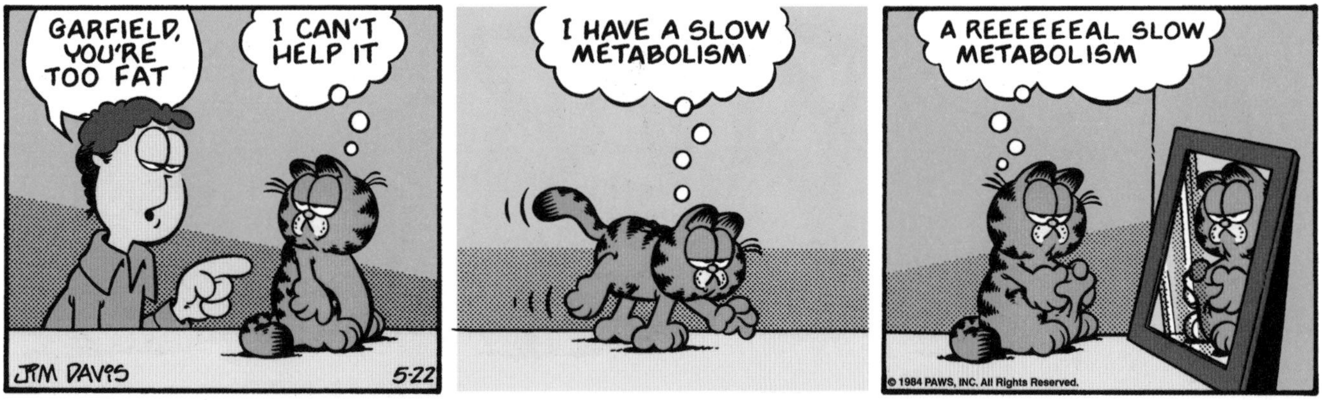

GARFIELD, YOU'RE TOO FAT
I CAN'T HELP IT
JIM DAVIS
5-22
I HAVE A SLOW METABOLISM
A REEEEEEAL SLOW METABOLISM
© 1984 PAWS, INC. All Rights Reserved.

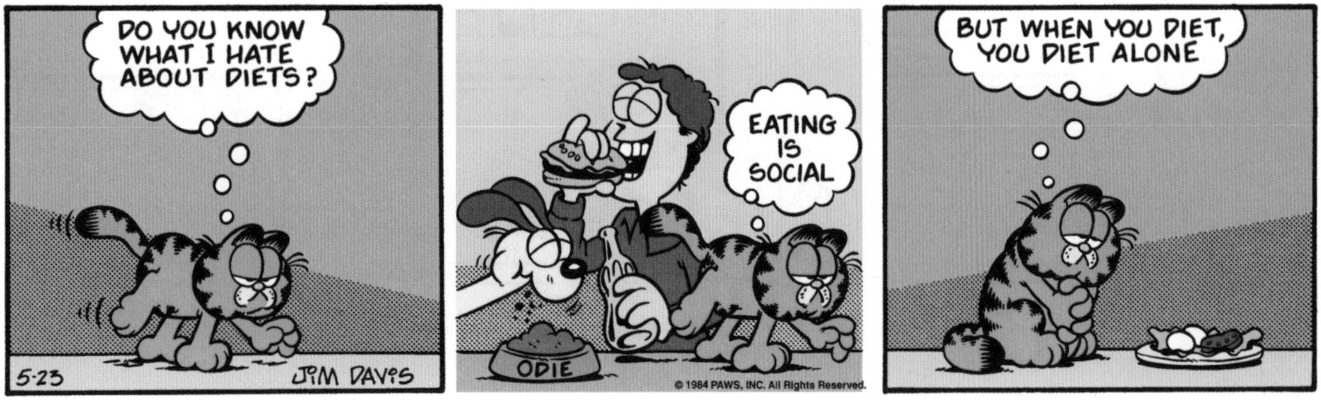

DO YOU KNOW WHAT I HATE ABOUT DIETS?
5-23
JIM DAVIS
EATING IS SOCIAL
ODIE
© 1984 PAWS, INC. All Rights Reserved.
BUT WHEN YOU DIET, YOU DIET ALONE

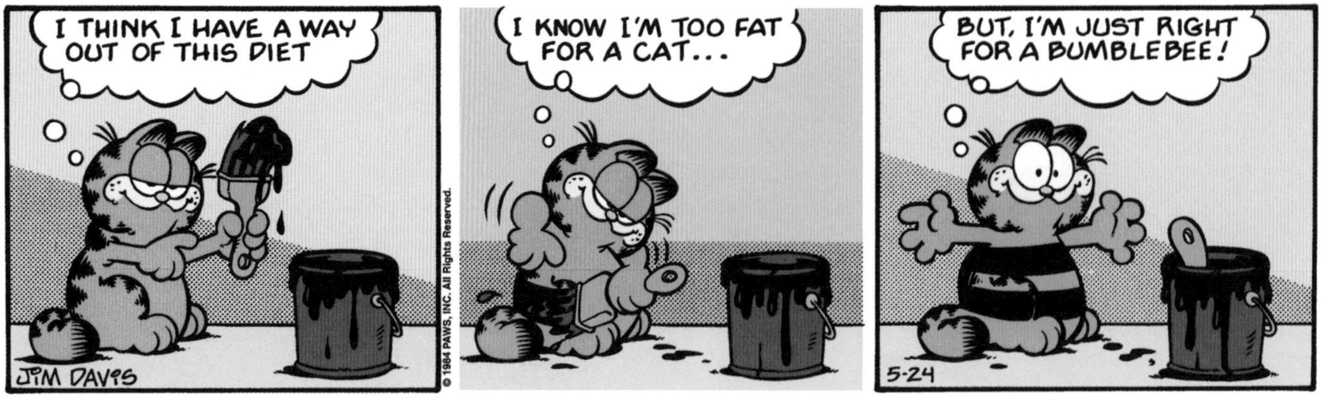
I THINK I HAVE A WAY OUT OF THIS DIET
JIM DAVIS
I KNOW I'M TOO FAT FOR A CAT...
© 1984 PAWS, INC. All Rights Reserved.
BUT, I'M JUST RIGHT FOR A BUMBLEBEE!
5-24

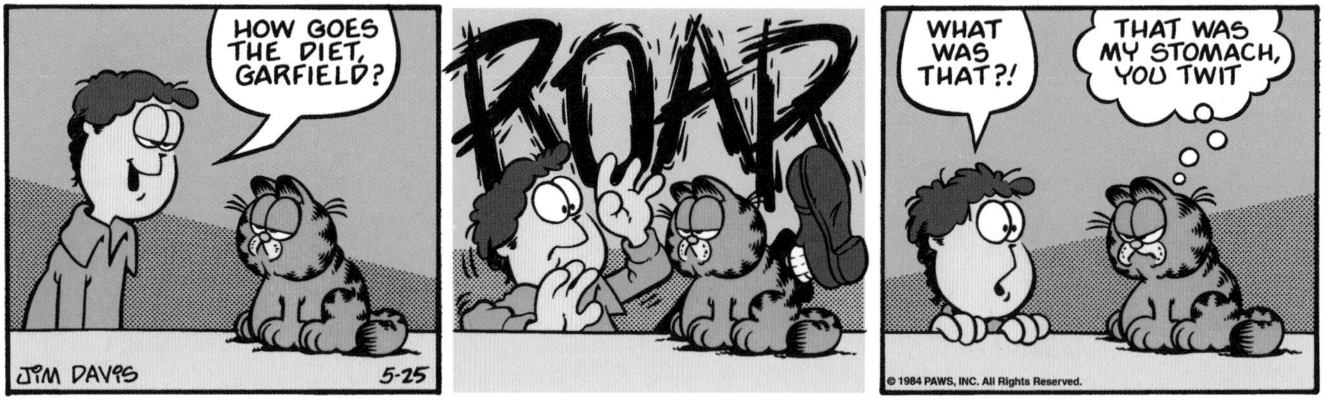
HOW GOES THE DIET, GARFIELD?
JIM DAVIS
5-25
ROAR
WHAT WAS THAT?!
THAT WAS MY STOMACH, YOU TWIT
© 1984 PAWS, INC. All Rights Reserved.

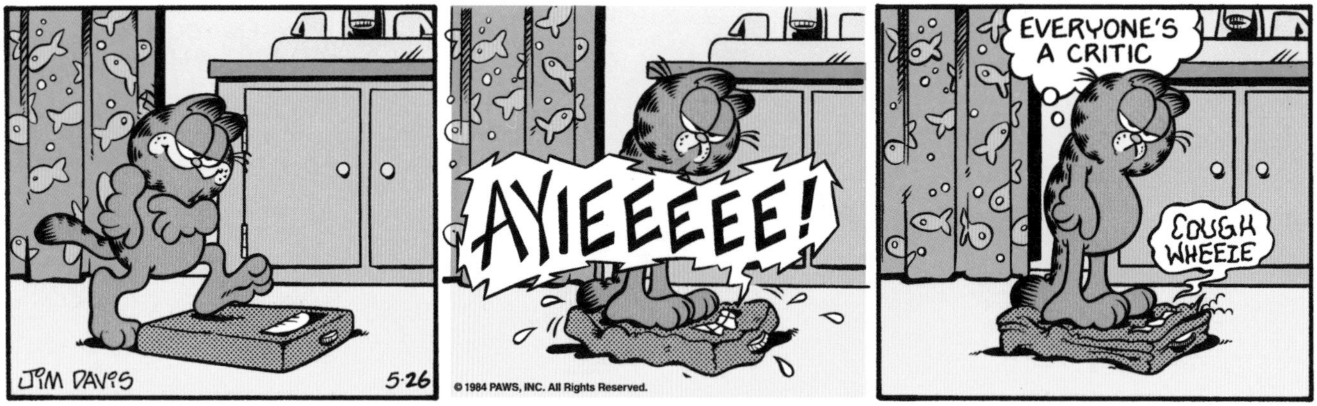
JIM DAVIS
5-26
AYIEEEEE!
© 1984 PAWS, INC. All Rights Reserved.
EVERYONE'S A CRITIC
COUGH WHEEZE

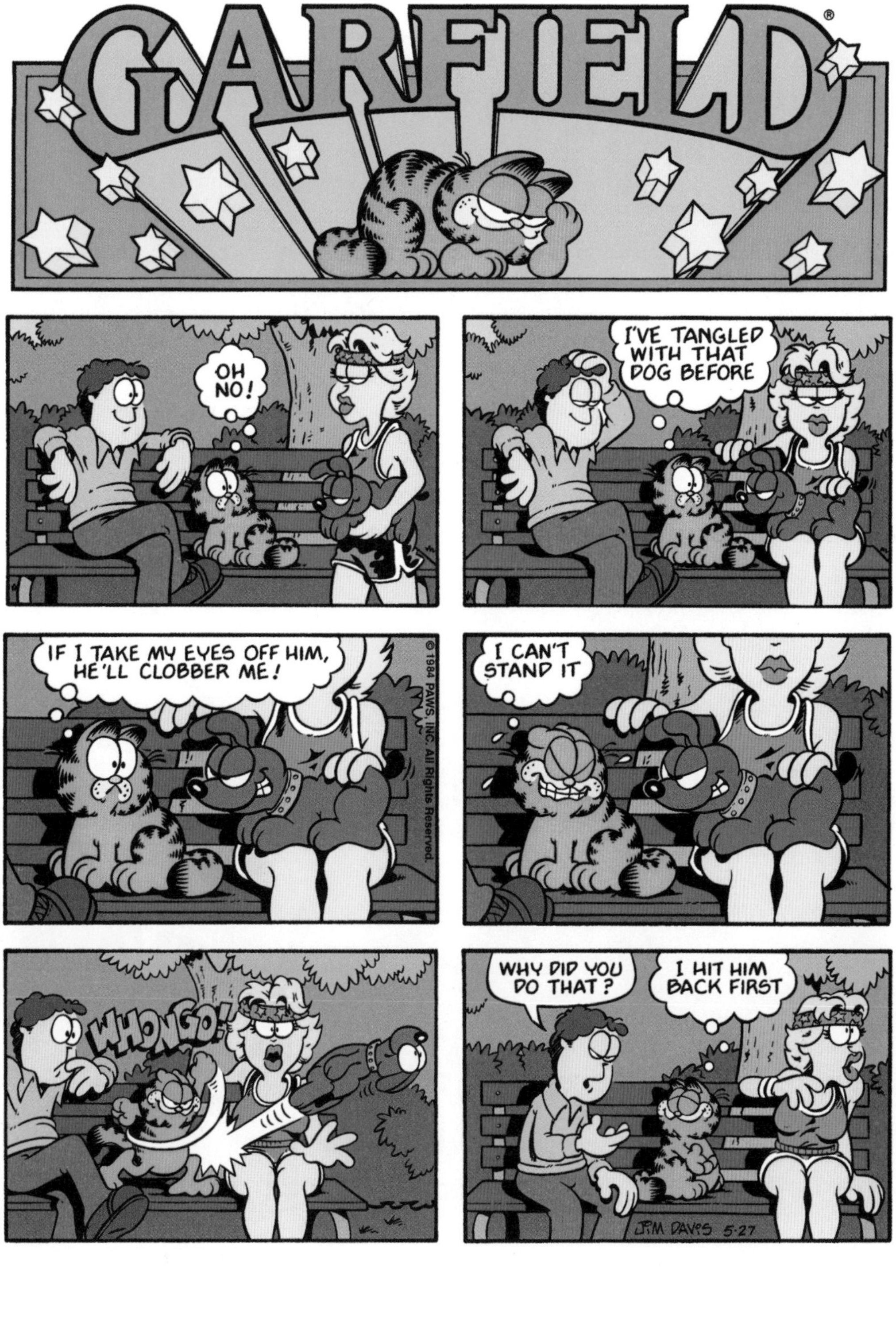
GARFIELD®
OH NO!
I'VE TANGLED WITH THAT DOG BEFORE
IF I TAKE MY EYES OFF HIM, HE'LL CLOBBER ME!
© 1984 PAWS, INC. All Rights Reserved.
I CAN'T STAND IT
WHONGO!
WHY DID YOU DO THAT?
I HIT HIM BACK FIRST
JIM DAVIS 5-27

TO THE PROSPECTIVE CARTOONIST

Al Capp once said, "You must have two qualities to be a successful cartoonist. First, it helps to have been dropped on your head as a small child. Second, you must have no desire, talent, or ability to do anything useful in life."

While his may seem a somewhat flippant observation, it nevertheless reflects how seriously cartoonists take themselves and their art. If I had only one piece of advice to give a prospective cartoonist, it would be: HAVE FUN WITH YOUR FEATURE!

If you have fun doing it, people have fun reading it. Your enthusiasm comes through.

Most hopeful cartoonists labor over their creations. An overworked, heavily laden cartoon strip or panel doesn't have the charm or witty appeal of a simply drawn, simply stated sentiment. All a cartoonist has to do is hold a mirror to life and show it back with a humorous twist. More often than not, when a reader laughs at a strip, it's not because it's funny but because it's true.

PREPARE YOURSELF . . .

HERE ARE SOME GENERAL RECOMMENDATIONS TO LAY THE GROUNDWORK FOR A CAREER IN CARTOONING . . .

1) GET A GOOD LIBERAL ARTS EDUCATION. Enroll in journalism courses, as well as art classes. DO A LOT OF READING. The better read you are, the more natural depth your writing will have. Learn to draw realistically. It helps any cartooning style.

2) SEEK AN ART OR JOURNALISM RELATED JOB. This affords you the luxury of having food to eat until you make a go of it in cartooning.

3) EXPERIMENT WITH ALL KINDS OF ART EQUIPMENT AND MATERIALS. I use India ink and a #2 Windsor-Newton sable brush. For lettering, I use a Speedball B-6 point. I work on Strathmore 3-ply bristol board, smooth surface.

4) STAY MOTIVATED. Try to get your work published in a school paper, local newspaper, or local publication. Many cartoonists give up the quest a year or two before they would have become marketable.

5) PREPARE NEAT, THOUGHTFUL SUBMISSIONS FOR THE SYNDICATE EDITORS. Send only your best work, and be prepared to submit it many times. I could wallpaper a bedroom with *my* rejection slips.

Again, don't forget to keep it simple and have fun. Oh, yes . . . a little luck along the way never hurts.

GOOD LUCK!

JIM DAViS

Garfield rolls on

BY JIM DAVIS

Ballantine Books • New York

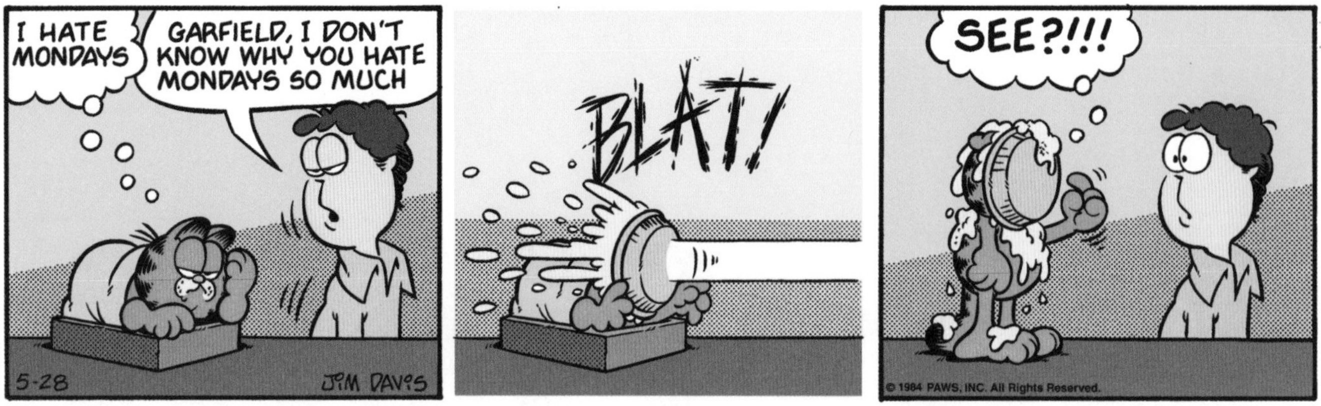
I HATE MONDAYS
GARFIELD, I DON'T KNOW WHY YOU HATE MONDAYS SO MUCH
5-28
JIM DAVIS
BLAT!
SEE?!!!
© 1984 PAWS, INC. All Rights Reserved.

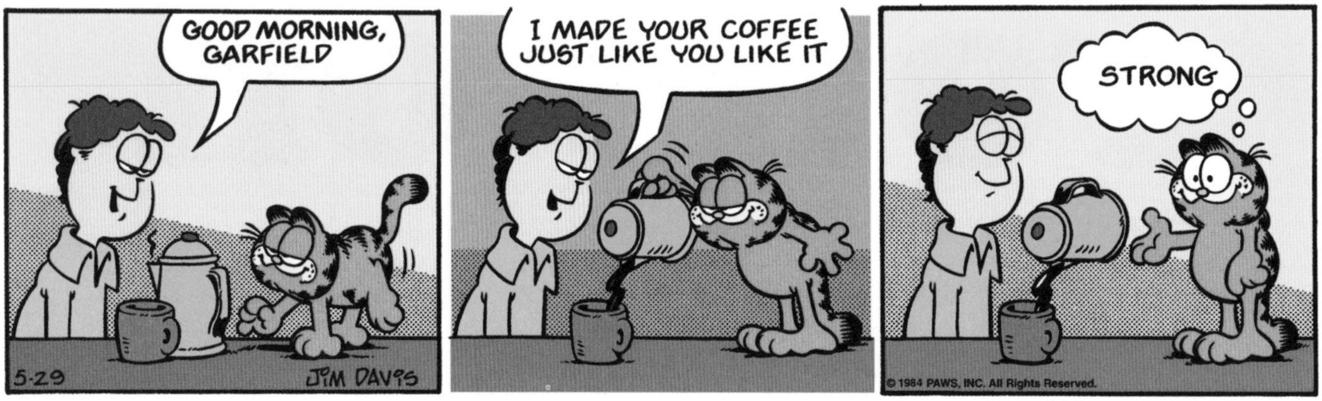
GOOD MORNING, GARFIELD
5-29
JIM DAVIS
I MADE YOUR COFFEE JUST LIKE YOU LIKE IT
STRONG
© 1984 PAWS, INC. All Rights Reserved.

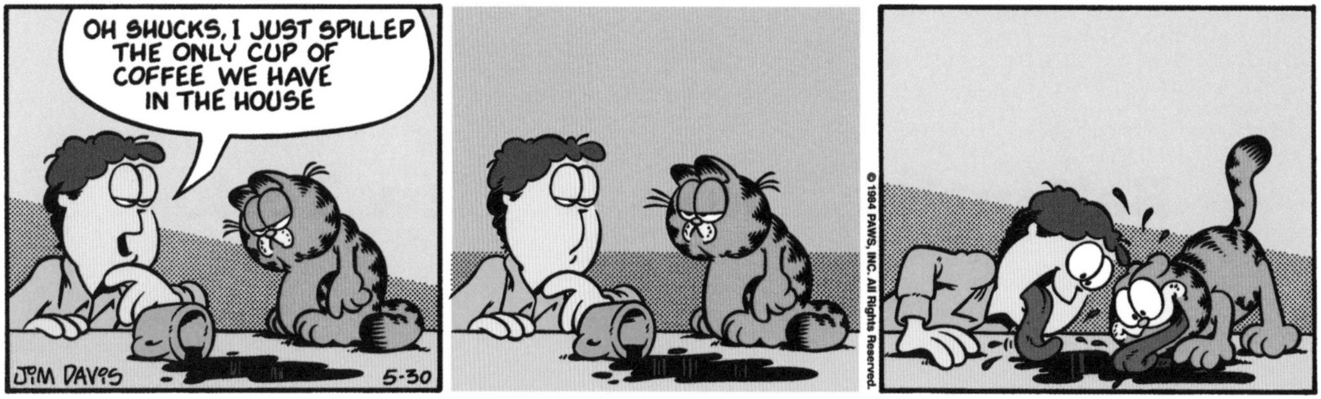
OH SHUCKS, I JUST SPILLED THE ONLY CUP OF COFFEE WE HAVE IN THE HOUSE
JIM DAVIS
5-30
© 1984 PAWS, INC. All Rights Reserved.

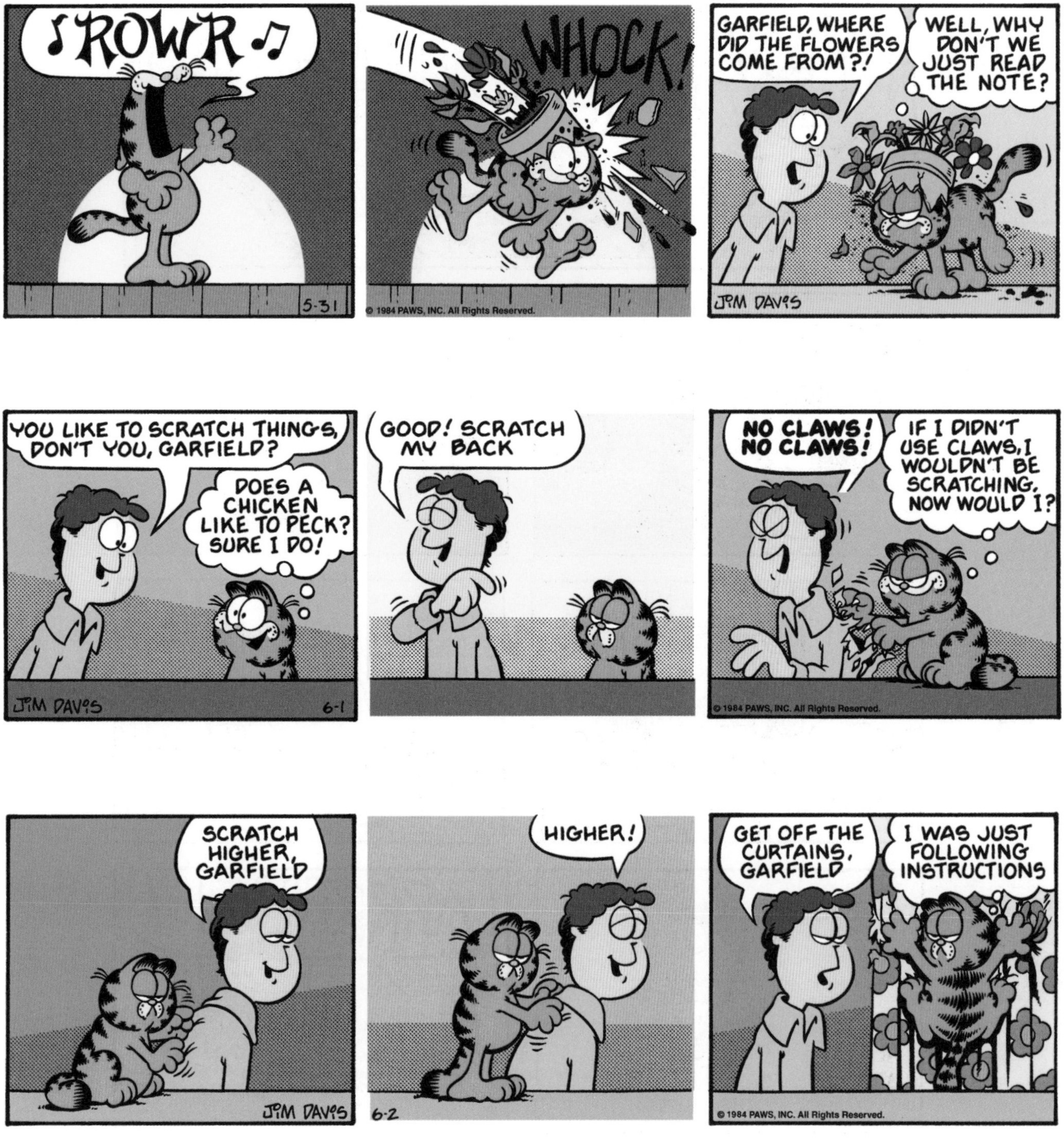
ROWR
WHOCK!
GARFIELD, WHERE DID THE FLOWERS COME FROM?!
WELL, WHY DON'T WE JUST READ THE NOTE?
JIM DAVIS
5-31
© 1984 PAWS, INC. All Rights Reserved.
YOU LIKE TO SCRATCH THINGS, DON'T YOU, GARFIELD?
DOES A CHICKEN LIKE TO PECK? SURE I DO!
JIM DAVIS
6-1
GOOD! SCRATCH MY BACK
NO CLAWS! NO CLAWS!
IF I DIDN'T USE CLAWS, I WOULDN'T BE SCRATCHING, NOW WOULD I?
© 1984 PAWS, INC. All Rights Reserved.
SCRATCH HIGHER, GARFIELD
JIM DAVIS
HIGHER!
6-2
GET OFF THE CURTAINS, GARFIELD
I WAS JUST FOLLOWING INSTRUCTIONS
© 1984 PAWS, INC. All Rights Reserved.

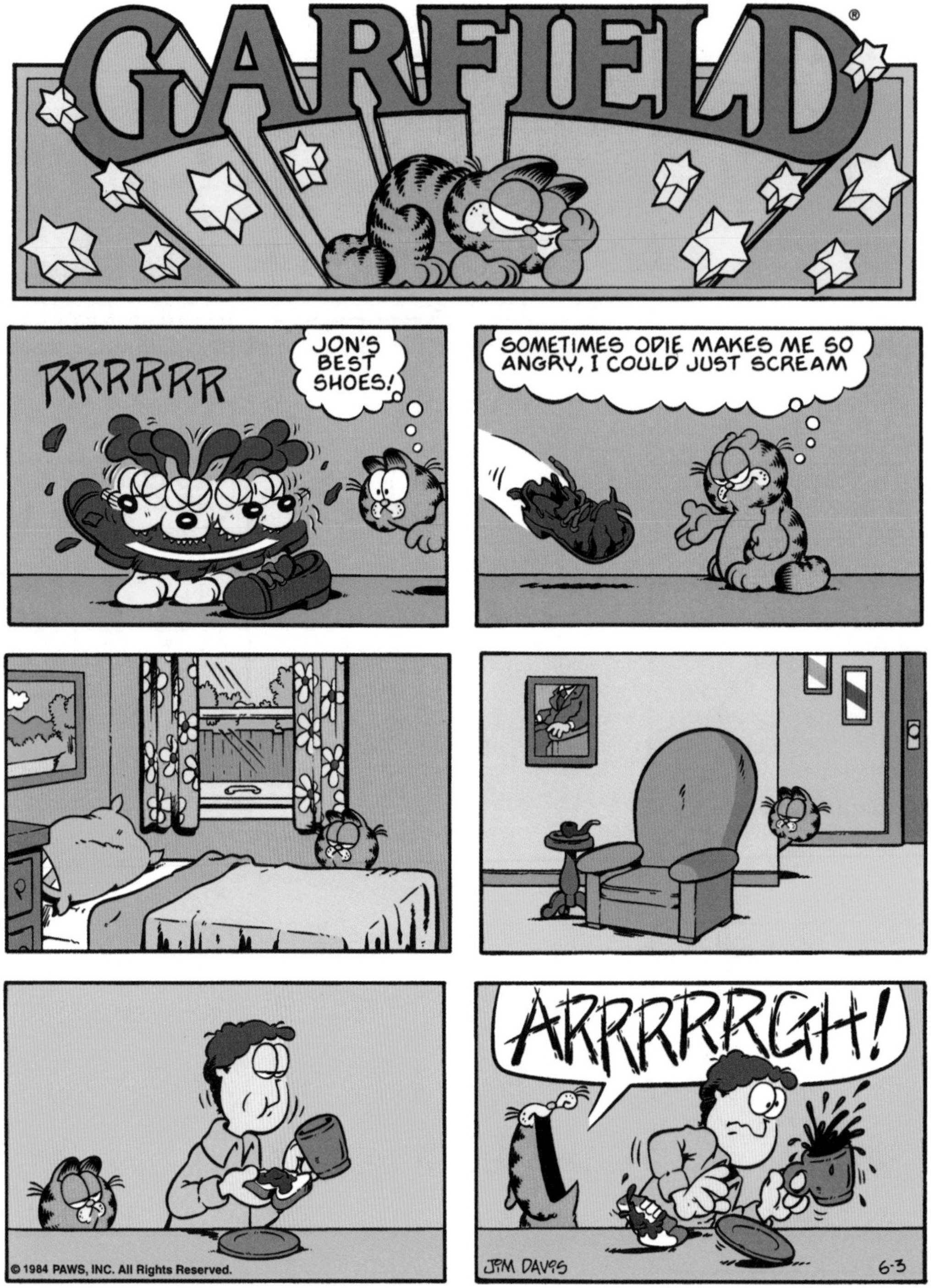
GARFIELD®
RRRRRR
JON'S BEST SHOES!
SOMETIMES ODIE MAKES ME SO ANGRY, I COULD JUST SCREAM
ARRRRRGH!
© 1984 PAWS, INC. All Rights Reserved.
JIM DAVIS
6-3

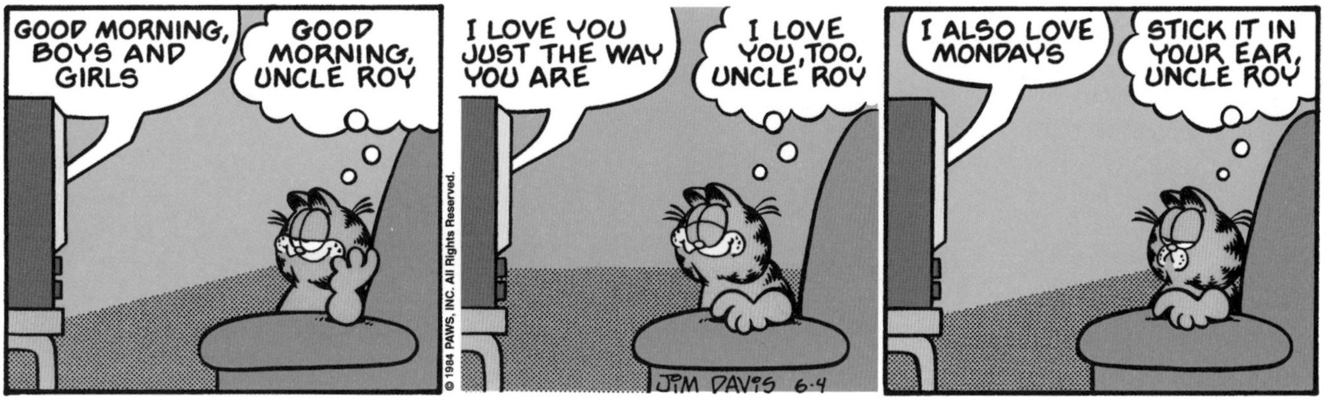
GOOD MORNING, BOYS AND GIRLS
GOOD MORNING, UNCLE ROY
© 1984 PAWS, INC. All Rights Reserved.
I LOVE YOU JUST THE WAY YOU ARE
I LOVE YOU, TOO, UNCLE ROY
JIM DAVIS 6-4
I ALSO LOVE MONDAYS
STICK IT IN YOUR EAR, UNCLE ROY

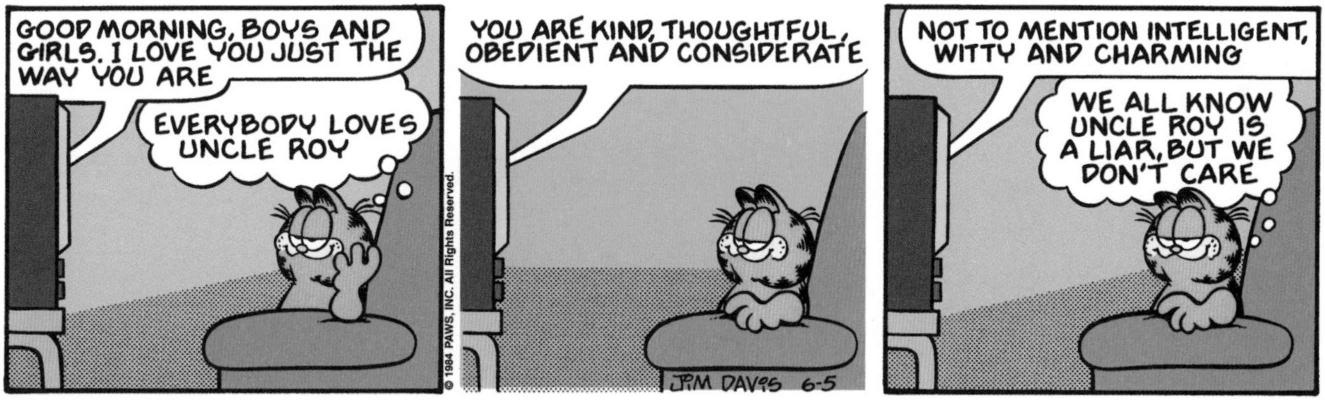
GOOD MORNING, BOYS AND GIRLS. I LOVE YOU JUST THE WAY YOU ARE
EVERYBODY LOVES UNCLE ROY
© 1984 PAWS, INC. All Rights Reserved.
YOU ARE KIND, THOUGHTFUL, OBEDIENT AND CONSIDERATE
JIM DAVIS 6-5
NOT TO MENTION INTELLIGENT, WITTY AND CHARMING
WE ALL KNOW UNCLE ROY IS A LIAR, BUT WE DON'T CARE

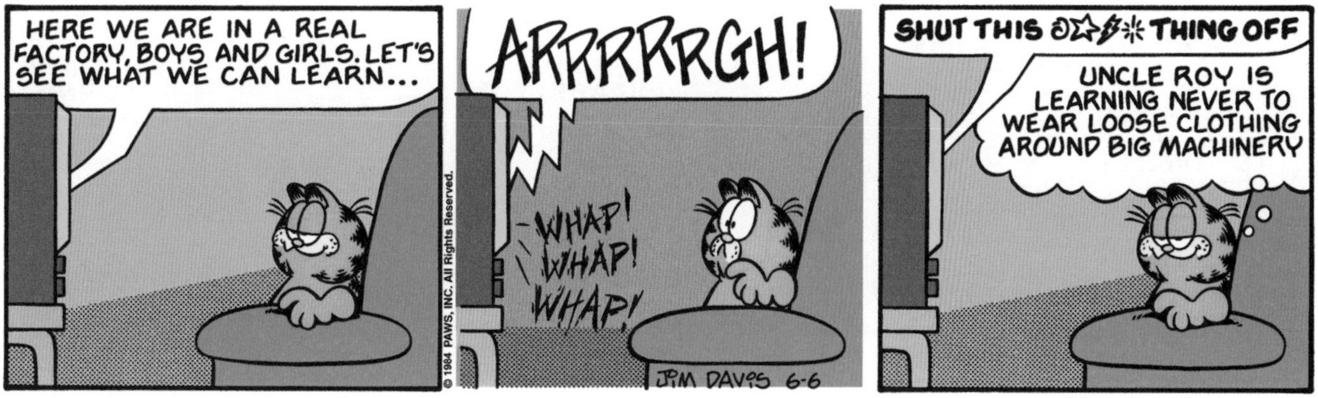
HERE WE ARE IN A REAL FACTORY, BOYS AND GIRLS. LET'S SEE WHAT WE CAN LEARN...
© 1984 PAWS, INC. All Rights Reserved.
ARRRRRGH!
WHAP! WHAP! WHAP!
JIM DAVIS 6-6
SHUT THIS @☆#* THING OFF
UNCLE ROY IS LEARNING NEVER TO WEAR LOOSE CLOTHING AROUND BIG MACHINERY

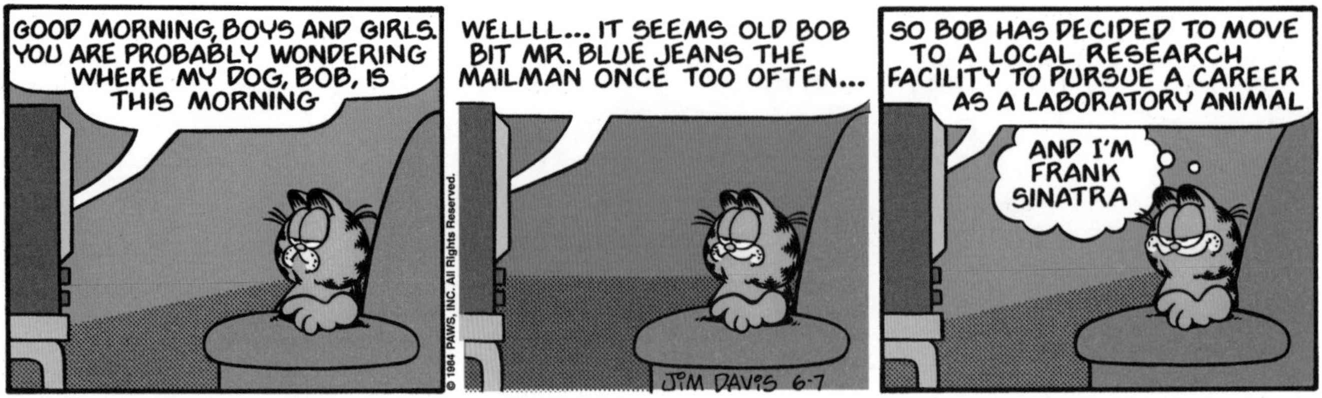
GOOD MORNING, BOYS AND GIRLS. YOU ARE PROBABLY WONDERING WHERE MY DOG, BOB, IS THIS MORNING
WELLLL... IT SEEMS OLD BOB BIT MR. BLUE JEANS THE MAILMAN ONCE TOO OFTEN...
SO BOB HAS DECIDED TO MOVE TO A LOCAL RESEARCH FACILITY TO PURSUE A CAREER AS A LABORATORY ANIMAL
AND I'M FRANK SINATRA
© 1984 PAWS, INC. All Rights Reserved.
JIM DAVIS 6-7

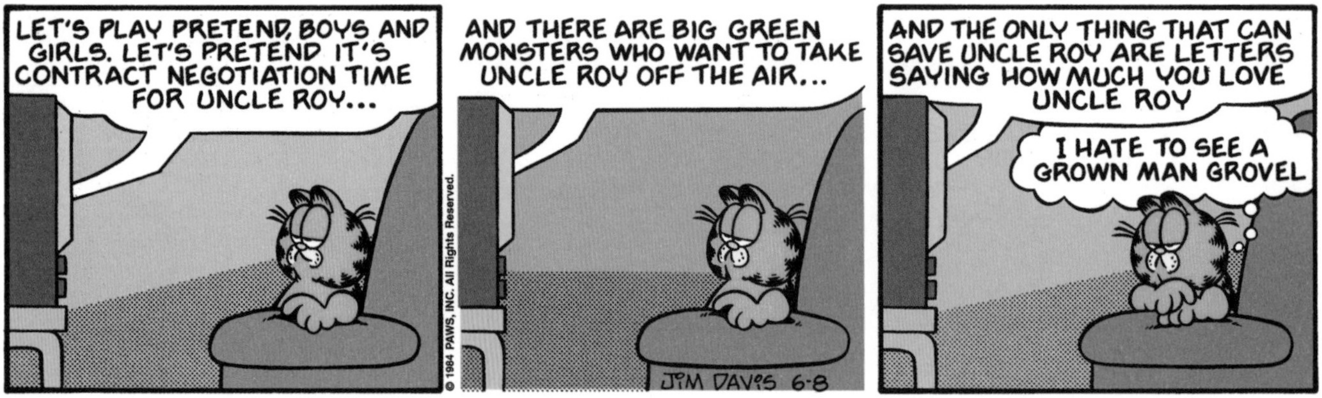
LET'S PLAY PRETEND, BOYS AND GIRLS. LET'S PRETEND IT'S CONTRACT NEGOTIATION TIME FOR UNCLE ROY...
AND THERE ARE BIG GREEN MONSTERS WHO WANT TO TAKE UNCLE ROY OFF THE AIR...
AND THE ONLY THING THAT CAN SAVE UNCLE ROY ARE LETTERS SAYING HOW MUCH YOU LOVE UNCLE ROY
I HATE TO SEE A GROWN MAN GROVEL
© 1984 PAWS, INC. All Rights Reserved.
JIM DAVIS 6-8

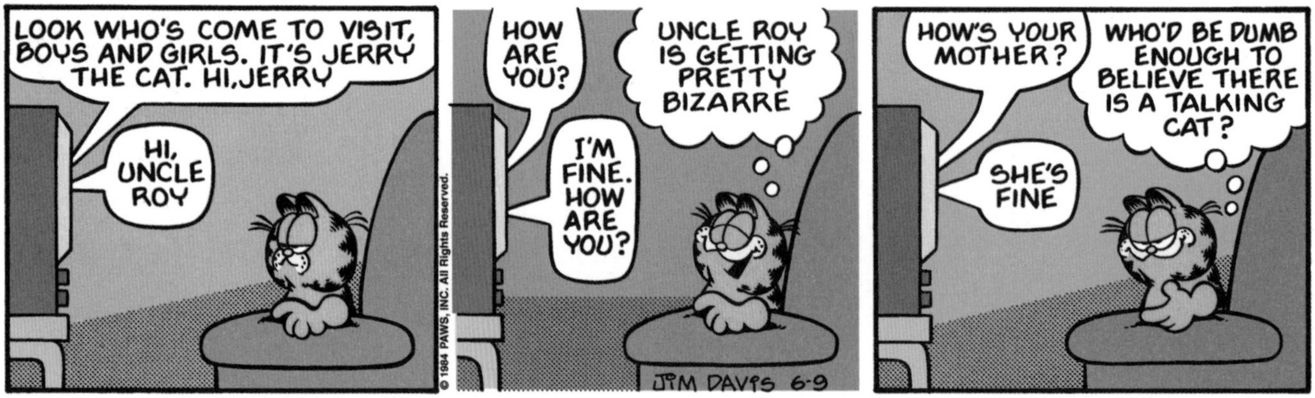
LOOK WHO'S COME TO VISIT, BOYS AND GIRLS. IT'S JERRY THE CAT. HI, JERRY
HI, UNCLE ROY
HOW ARE YOU?
UNCLE ROY IS GETTING PRETTY BIZARRE
I'M FINE. HOW ARE YOU?
HOW'S YOUR MOTHER?
WHO'D BE DUMB ENOUGH TO BELIEVE THERE IS A TALKING CAT?
SHE'S FINE
© 1984 PAWS, INC. All Rights Reserved.
JIM DAVIS 6-9

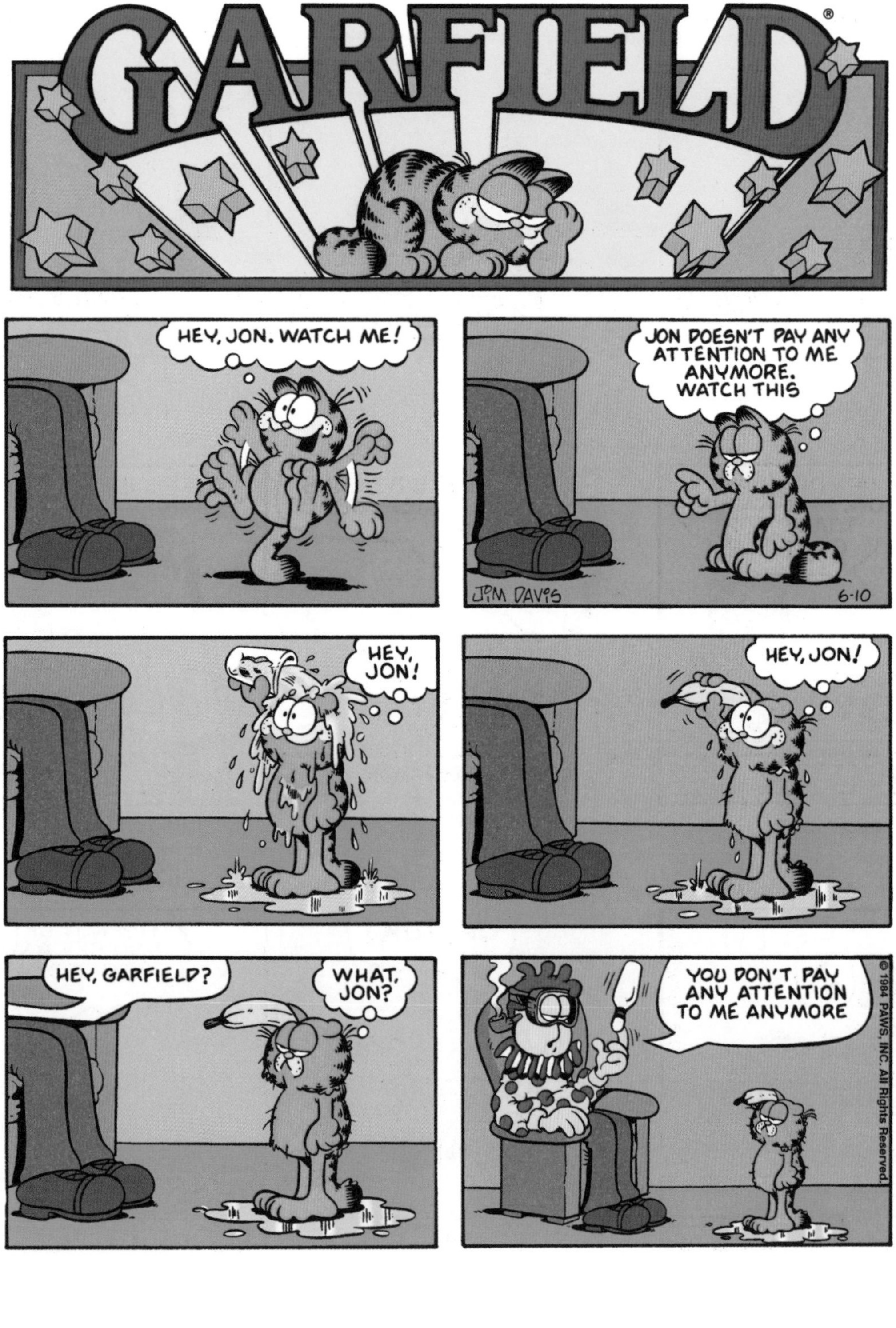
GARFIELD®
HEY, JON. WATCH ME!
JON DOESN'T PAY ANY ATTENTION TO ME ANYMORE. WATCH THIS
JIM DAVIS 6-10
HEY, JON!
HEY, JON!
HEY, GARFIELD?
WHAT, JON?
YOU DON'T PAY ANY ATTENTION TO ME ANYMORE
© 1984 PAWS, INC. All Rights Reserved.

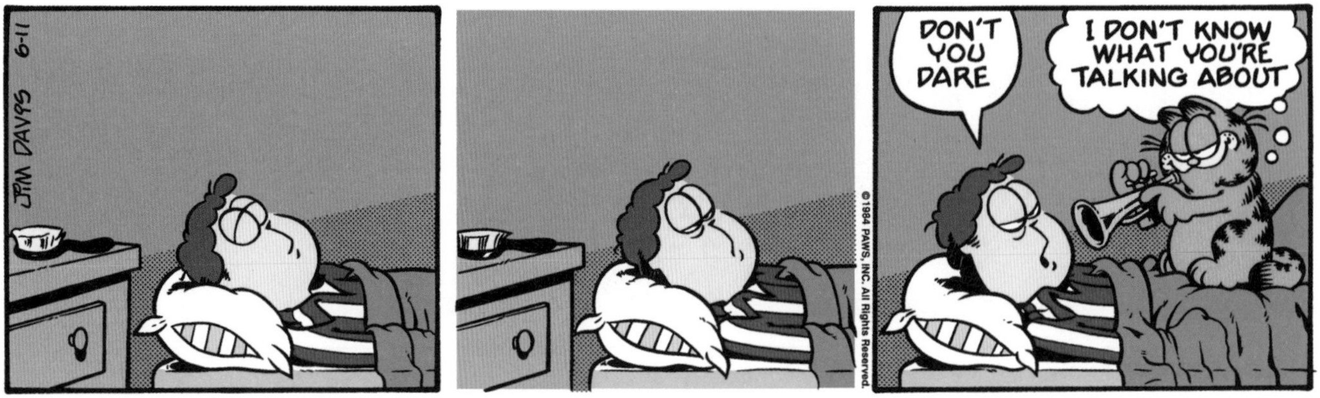
JIM DAVIS 6-11
© 1984 PAWS, INC. All Rights Reserved.
DON'T YOU DARE
I DON'T KNOW WHAT YOU'RE TALKING ABOUT

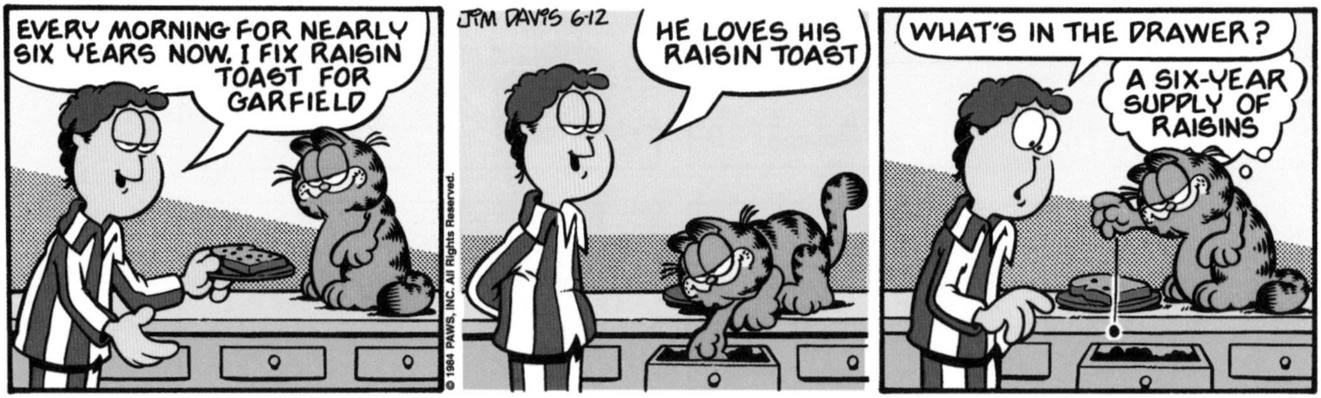
EVERY MORNING FOR NEARLY SIX YEARS NOW, I FIX RAISIN TOAST FOR GARFIELD
© 1984 PAWS, INC. All Rights Reserved.
JIM DAVIS 6-12
HE LOVES HIS RAISIN TOAST
WHAT'S IN THE DRAWER?
A SIX-YEAR SUPPLY OF RAISINS

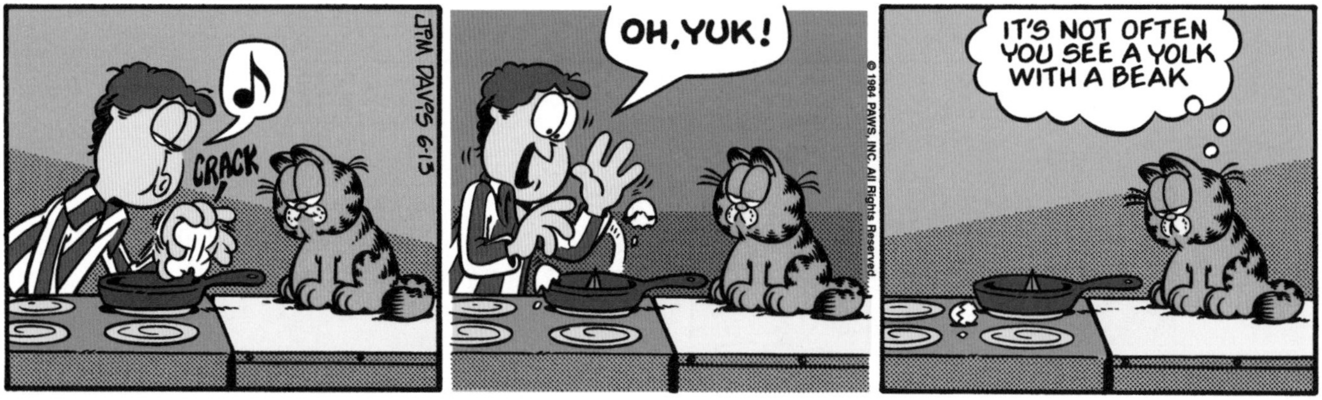
JIM DAVIS 6-13
♪
CRACK
OH, YUK!
© 1984 PAWS, INC. All Rights Reserved.
IT'S NOT OFTEN YOU SEE A YOLK WITH A BEAK

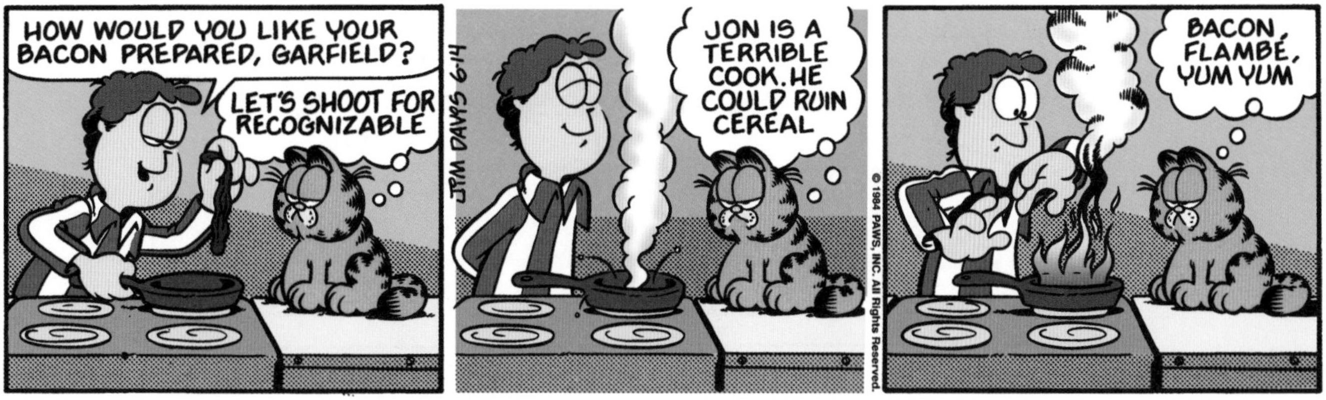
HOW WOULD YOU LIKE YOUR BACON PREPARED, GARFIELD?
LET'S SHOOT FOR RECOGNIZABLE
JIM DAVIS 6-14
JON IS A TERRIBLE COOK. HE COULD RUIN CEREAL
© 1984 PAWS, INC. All Rights Reserved.
BACON, FLAMBÉ, YUM YUM

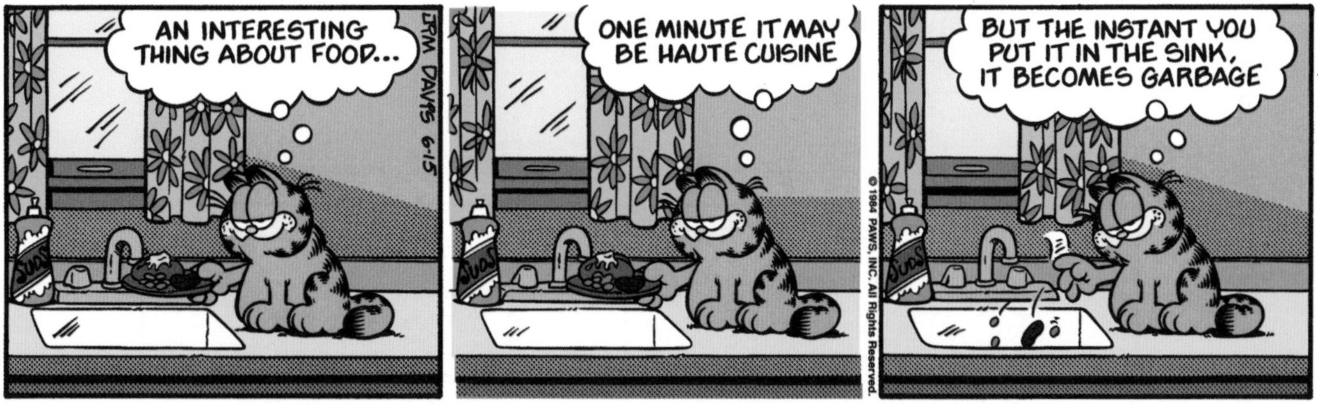
AN INTERESTING THING ABOUT FOOD...
JIM DAVIS 6-15
ONE MINUTE IT MAY BE HAUTE CUISINE
© 1984 PAWS, INC. All Rights Reserved.
BUT THE INSTANT YOU PUT IT IN THE SINK, IT BECOMES GARBAGE

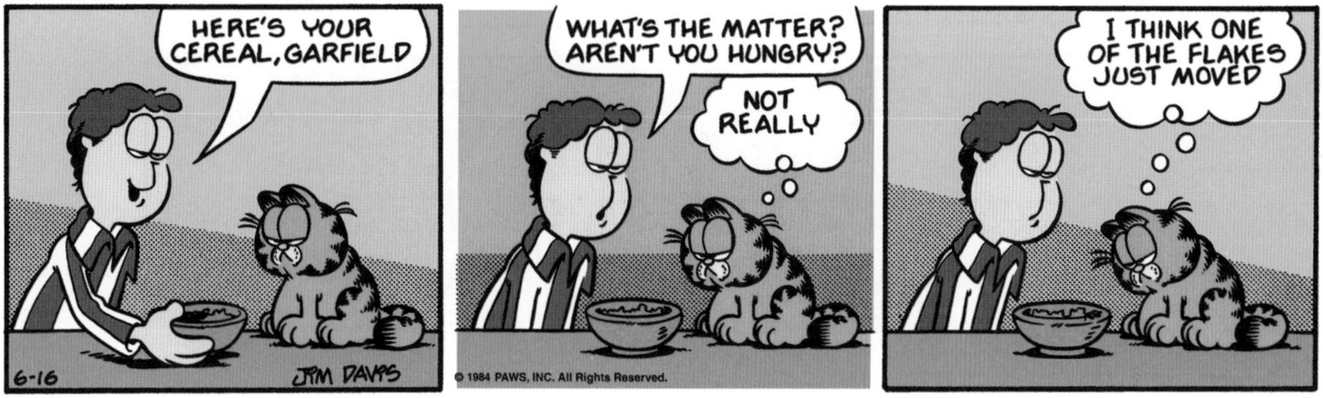
HERE'S YOUR CEREAL, GARFIELD
6-16
JIM DAVIS
WHAT'S THE MATTER? AREN'T YOU HUNGRY?
NOT REALLY
© 1984 PAWS, INC. All Rights Reserved.
I THINK ONE OF THE FLAKES JUST MOVED

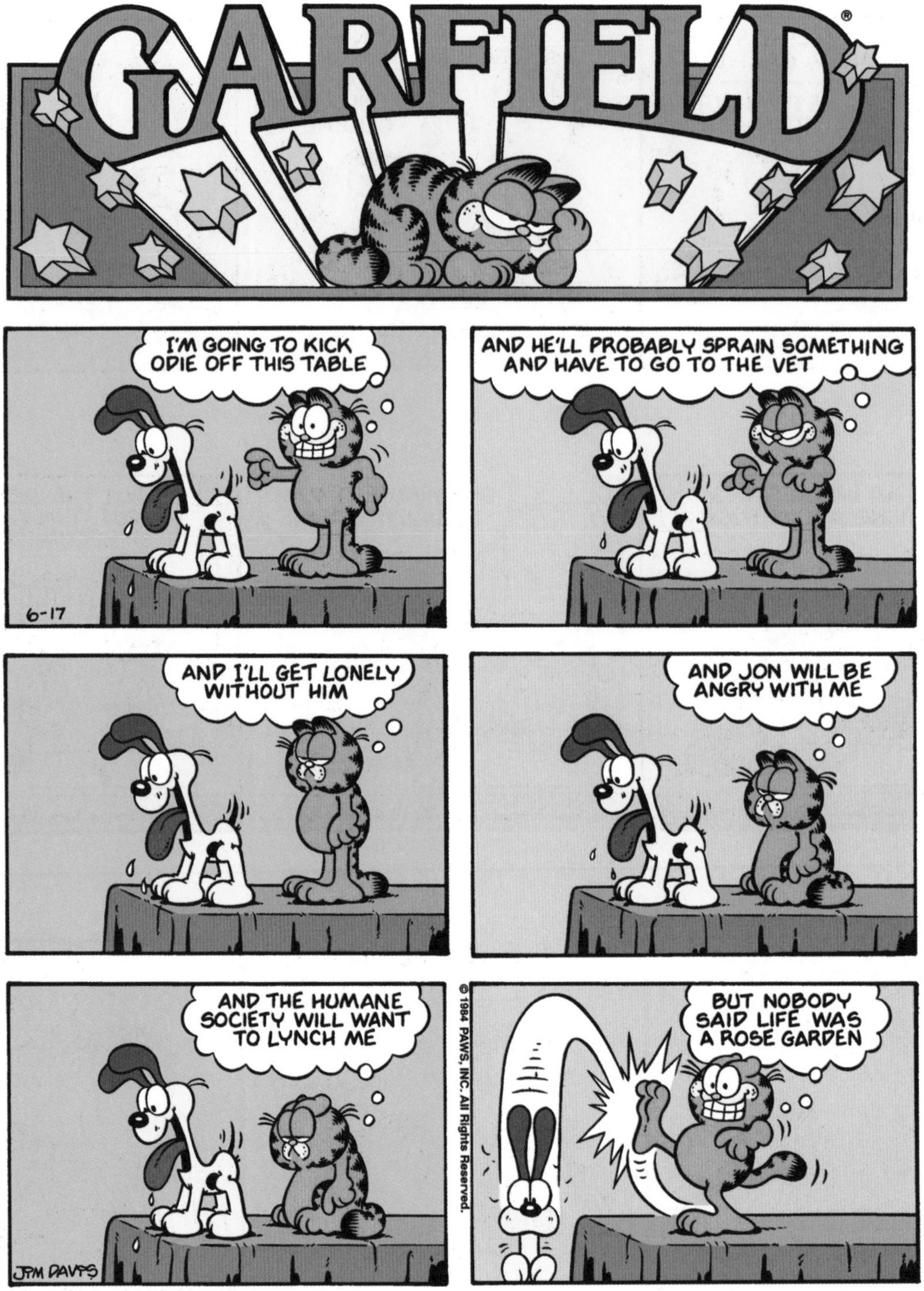
GARFIELD®
I'M GOING TO KICK ODIE OFF THIS TABLE
6-17
AND HE'LL PROBABLY SPRAIN SOMETHING AND HAVE TO GO TO THE VET
AND I'LL GET LONELY WITHOUT HIM
AND JON WILL BE ANGRY WITH ME
AND THE HUMANE SOCIETY WILL WANT TO LYNCH ME
JPM DAVPS
© 1984 PAWS, INC. All Rights Reserved.
BUT NOBODY SAID LIFE WAS A ROSE GARDEN

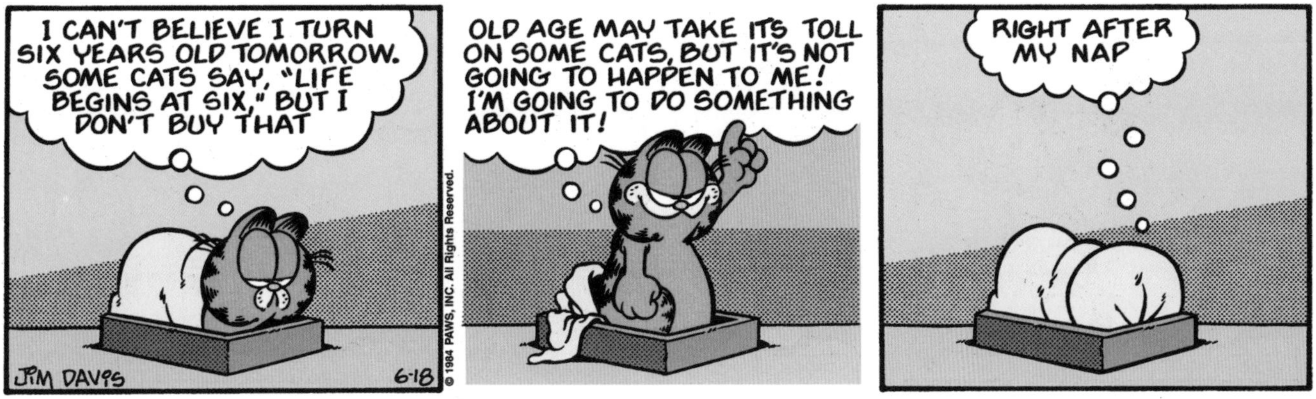
I CAN'T BELIEVE I TURN SIX YEARS OLD TOMORROW. SOME CATS SAY, "LIFE BEGINS AT SIX," BUT I DON'T BUY THAT
JIM DAVIS
6-18
© 1984 PAWS, INC. All Rights Reserved.
OLD AGE MAY TAKE ITS TOLL ON SOME CATS, BUT IT'S NOT GOING TO HAPPEN TO ME! I'M GOING TO DO SOMETHING ABOUT IT!
RIGHT AFTER MY NAP

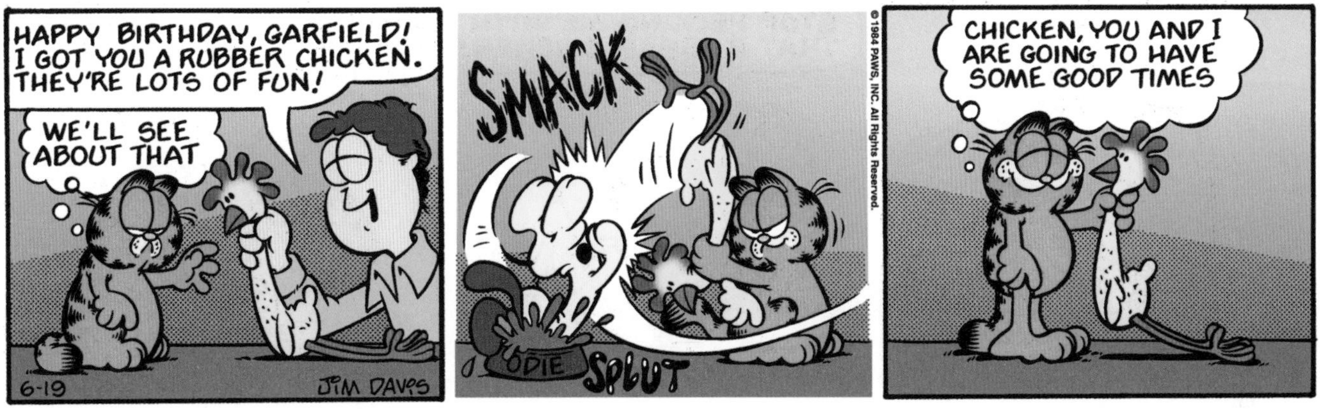
HAPPY BIRTHDAY, GARFIELD! I GOT YOU A RUBBER CHICKEN. THEY'RE LOTS OF FUN!
WE'LL SEE ABOUT THAT
6-19
JIM DAVIS
SMACK
ODIE
SPLUT
© 1984 PAWS, INC. All Rights Reserved.
CHICKEN, YOU AND I ARE GOING TO HAVE SOME GOOD TIMES

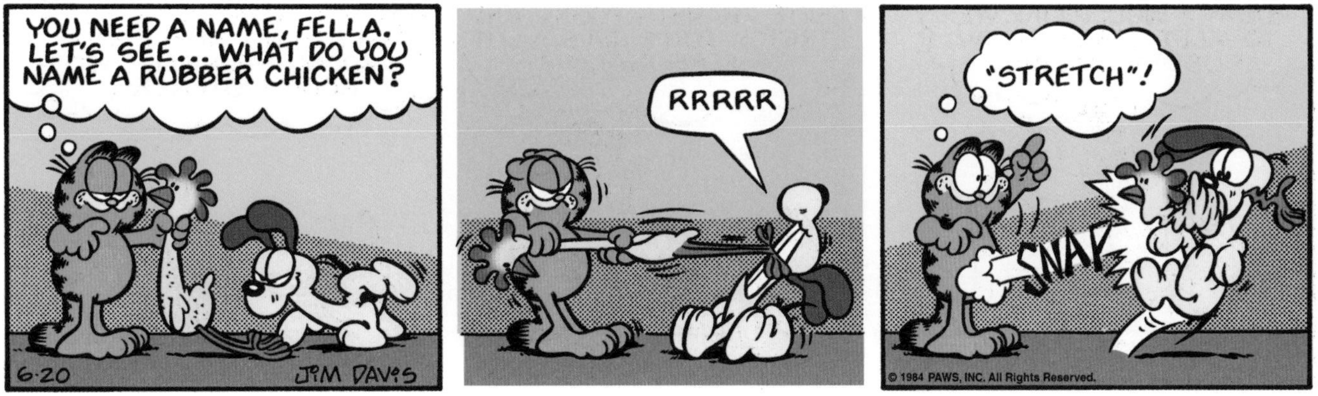
YOU NEED A NAME, FELLA. LET'S SEE... WHAT DO YOU NAME A RUBBER CHICKEN?
6-20
JIM DAVIS
RRRRR
"STRETCH"!
SNAP
© 1984 PAWS, INC. All Rights Reserved.

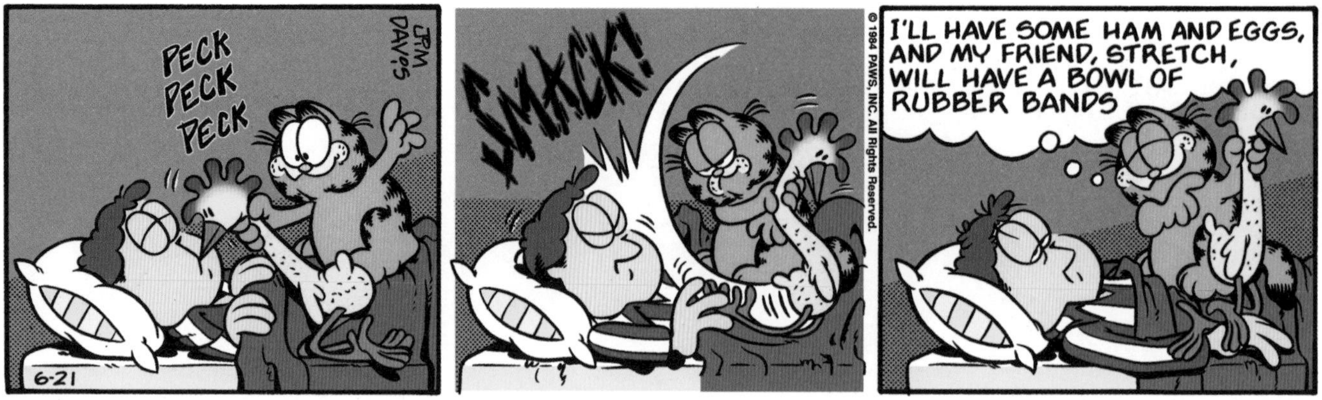
JIM DAVIS
PECK PECK PECK
6-21
SMACK!
© 1984 PAWS, INC. All Rights Reserved.
I'LL HAVE SOME HAM AND EGGS, AND MY FRIEND, STRETCH, WILL HAVE A BOWL OF RUBBER BANDS

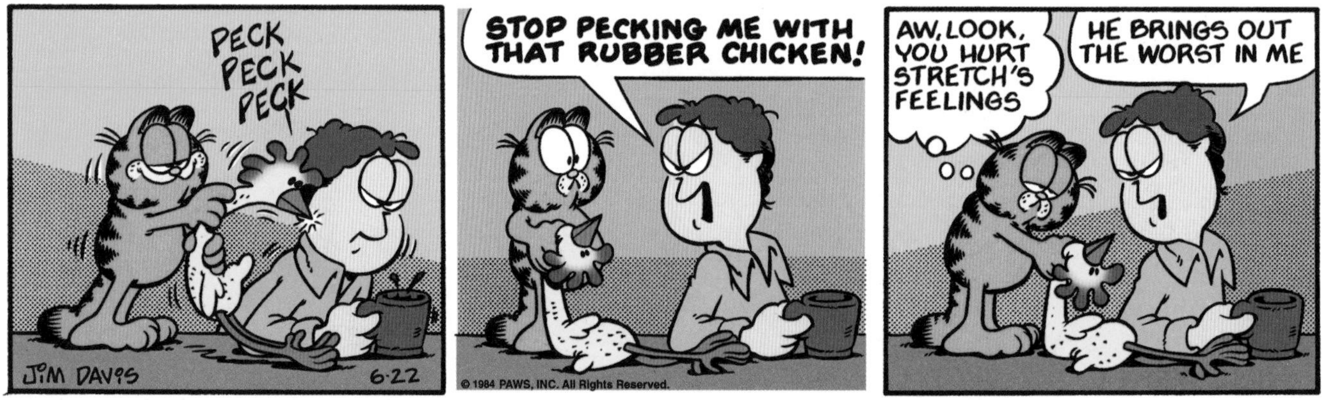
PECK PECK PECK
JIM DAVIS
6-22
STOP PECKING ME WITH THAT RUBBER CHICKEN!
© 1984 PAWS, INC. All Rights Reserved.
AW, LOOK, YOU HURT STRETCH'S FEELINGS
HE BRINGS OUT THE WORST IN ME

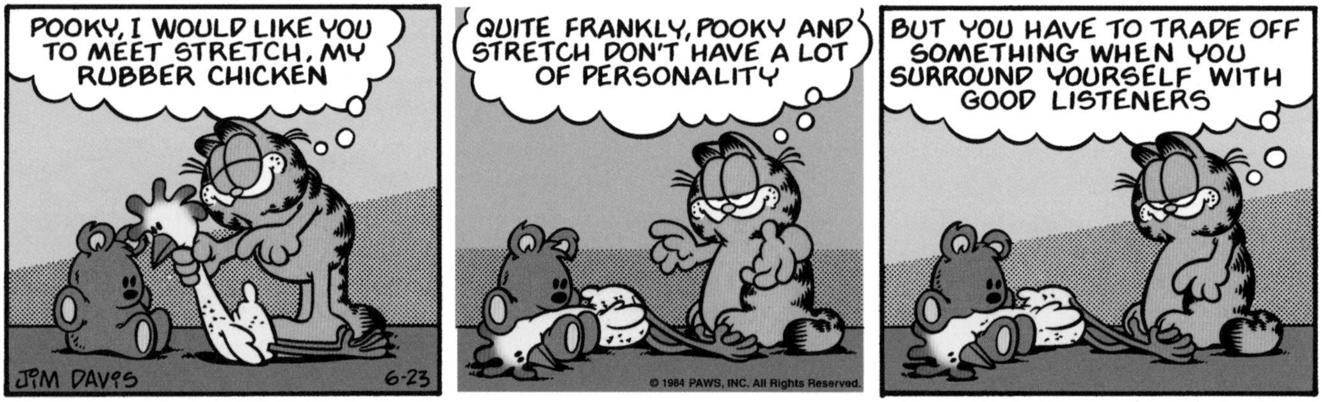
POOKY, I WOULD LIKE YOU TO MEET STRETCH, MY RUBBER CHICKEN
JIM DAVIS
6-23
QUITE FRANKLY, POOKY AND STRETCH DON'T HAVE A LOT OF PERSONALITY
© 1984 PAWS, INC. All Rights Reserved.
BUT YOU HAVE TO TRADE OFF SOMETHING WHEN YOU SURROUND YOURSELF WITH GOOD LISTENERS

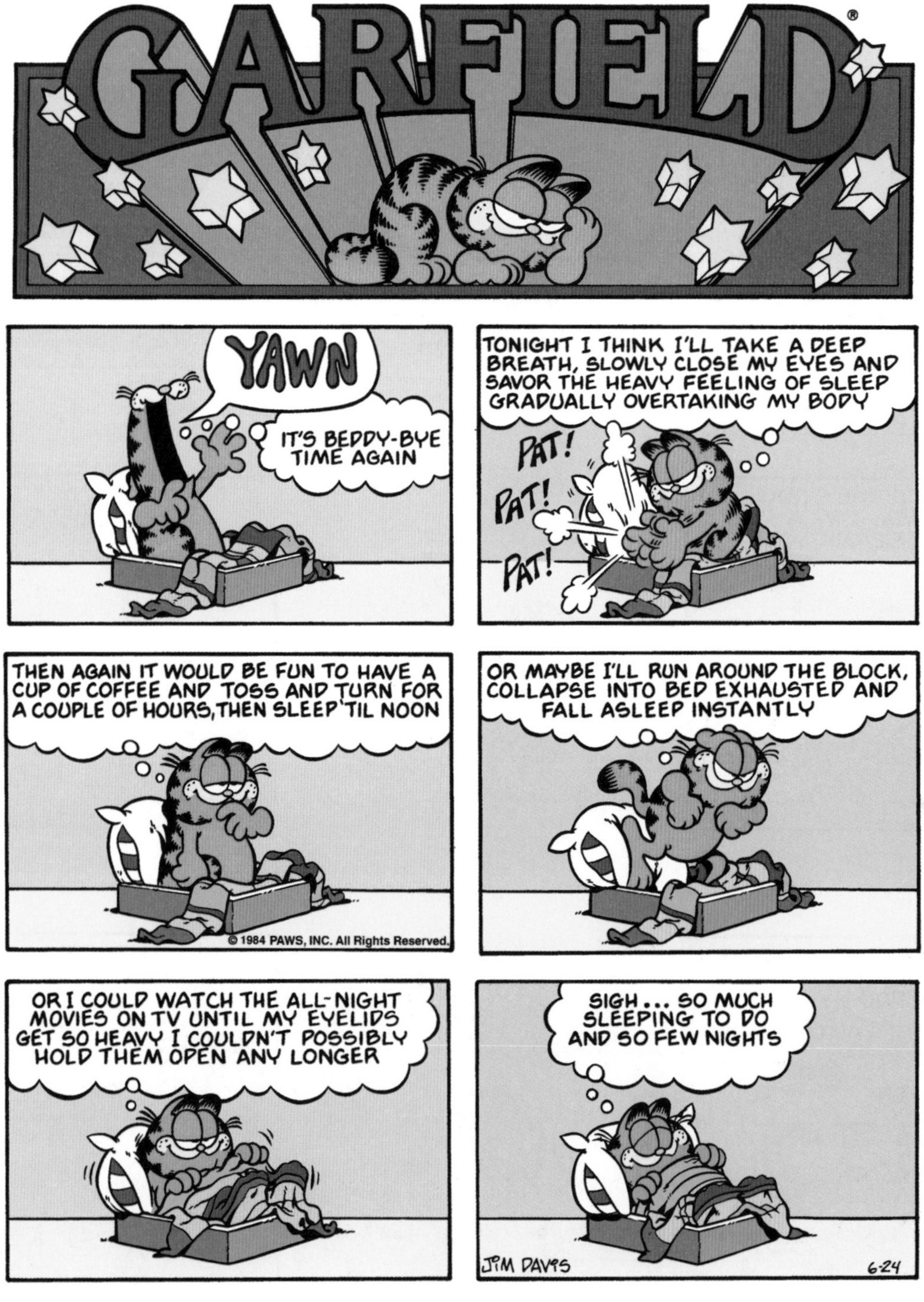
GARFIELD
YAWN
IT'S BEDDY-BYE TIME AGAIN
TONIGHT I THINK I'LL TAKE A DEEP BREATH, SLOWLY CLOSE MY EYES AND SAVOR THE HEAVY FEELING OF SLEEP GRADUALLY OVERTAKING MY BODY
PAT!
PAT!
PAT!
THEN AGAIN IT WOULD BE FUN TO HAVE A CUP OF COFFEE AND TOSS AND TURN FOR A COUPLE OF HOURS, THEN SLEEP 'TIL NOON
© 1984 PAWS, INC. All Rights Reserved.
OR MAYBE I'LL RUN AROUND THE BLOCK, COLLAPSE INTO BED EXHAUSTED AND FALL ASLEEP INSTANTLY
OR I COULD WATCH THE ALL-NIGHT MOVIES ON TV UNTIL MY EYELIDS GET SO HEAVY I COULDN'T POSSIBLY HOLD THEM OPEN ANY LONGER
SIGH ... SO MUCH SLEEPING TO DO AND SO FEW NIGHTS
JIM DAVIS
6-24

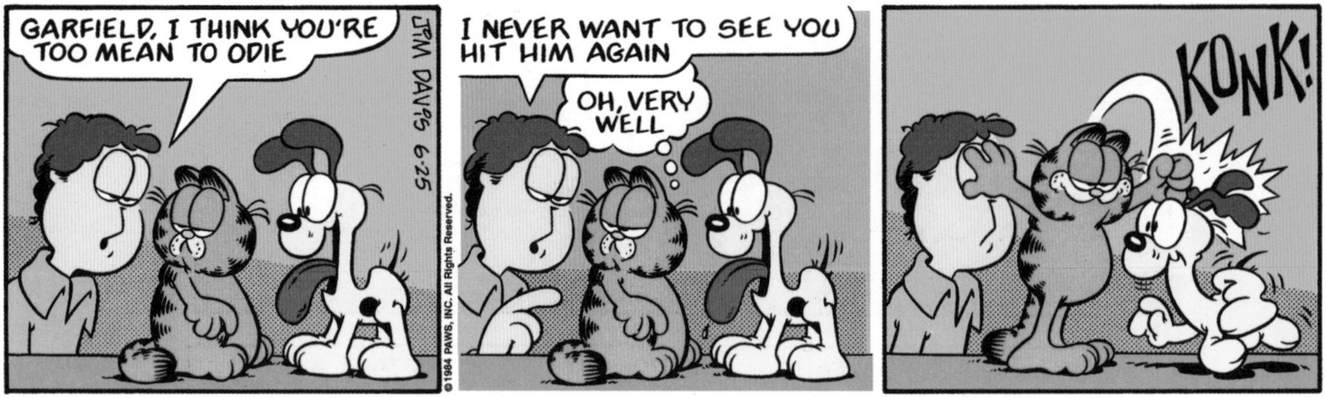
GARFIELD, I THINK YOU'RE TOO MEAN TO ODIE
JIM DAVIS 6-25
© 1984 PAWS, INC. All Rights Reserved.
I NEVER WANT TO SEE YOU HIT HIM AGAIN
OH, VERY WELL
KONK!

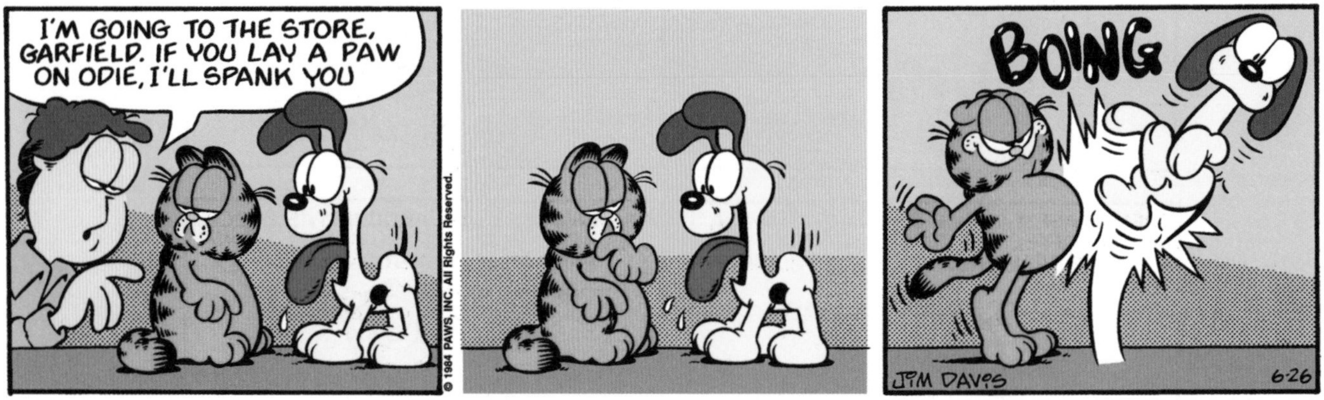
I'M GOING TO THE STORE, GARFIELD. IF YOU LAY A PAW ON ODIE, I'LL SPANK YOU
© 1984 PAWS, INC. All Rights Reserved.
BOING
JIM DAVIS
6-26

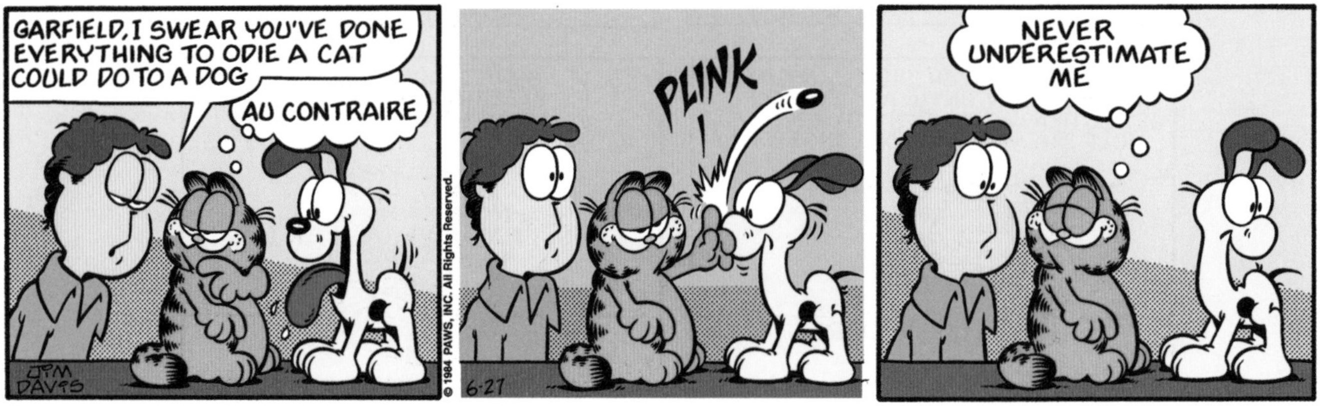
GARFIELD, I SWEAR YOU'VE DONE EVERYTHING TO ODIE A CAT COULD DO TO A DOG
AU CONTRAIRE
JIM DAVIS
© 1984 PAWS, INC. All Rights Reserved.
PLINK !
6-27
NEVER UNDERESTIMATE ME

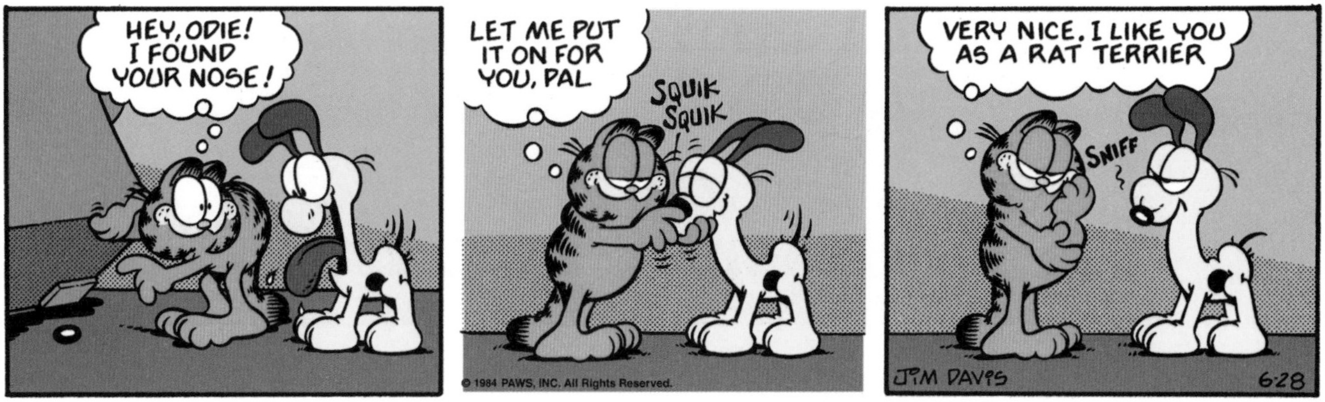
HEY, ODIE! I FOUND YOUR NOSE!
LET ME PUT IT ON FOR YOU, PAL
SQUIK SQUIK
© 1984 PAWS, INC. All Rights Reserved.
VERY NICE. I LIKE YOU AS A RAT TERRIER
SNIFF
JIM DAVIS
6-28

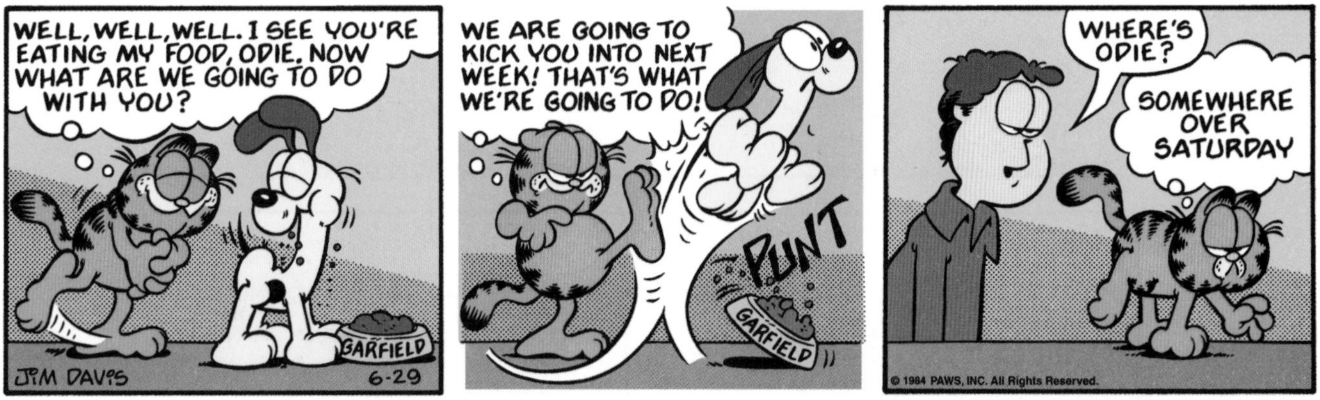
WELL, WELL, WELL. I SEE YOU'RE EATING MY FOOD, ODIE. NOW WHAT ARE WE GOING TO DO WITH YOU?
GARFIELD
JIM DAVIS
6-29
WE ARE GOING TO KICK YOU INTO NEXT WEEK! THAT'S WHAT WE'RE GOING TO DO!
PUNT
GARFIELD
WHERE'S ODIE?
SOMEWHERE OVER SATURDAY
© 1984 PAWS, INC. All Rights Reserved.

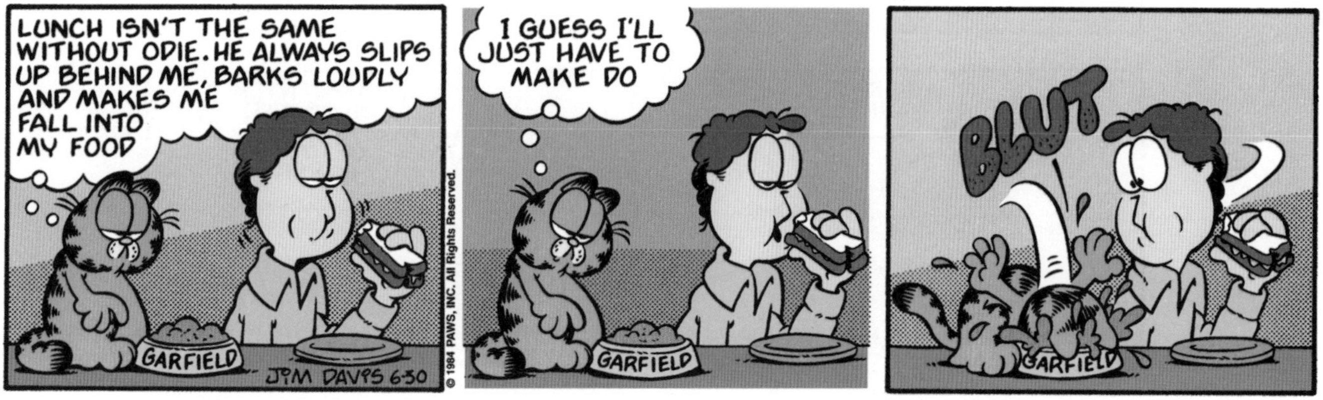
LUNCH ISN'T THE SAME WITHOUT ODIE. HE ALWAYS SLIPS UP BEHIND ME, BARKS LOUDLY AND MAKES ME FALL INTO MY FOOD
GARFIELD
JIM DAVIS 6-30
© 1984 PAWS, INC. All Rights Reserved.
I GUESS I'LL JUST HAVE TO MAKE DO
GARFIELD
BLUT
GARFIELD

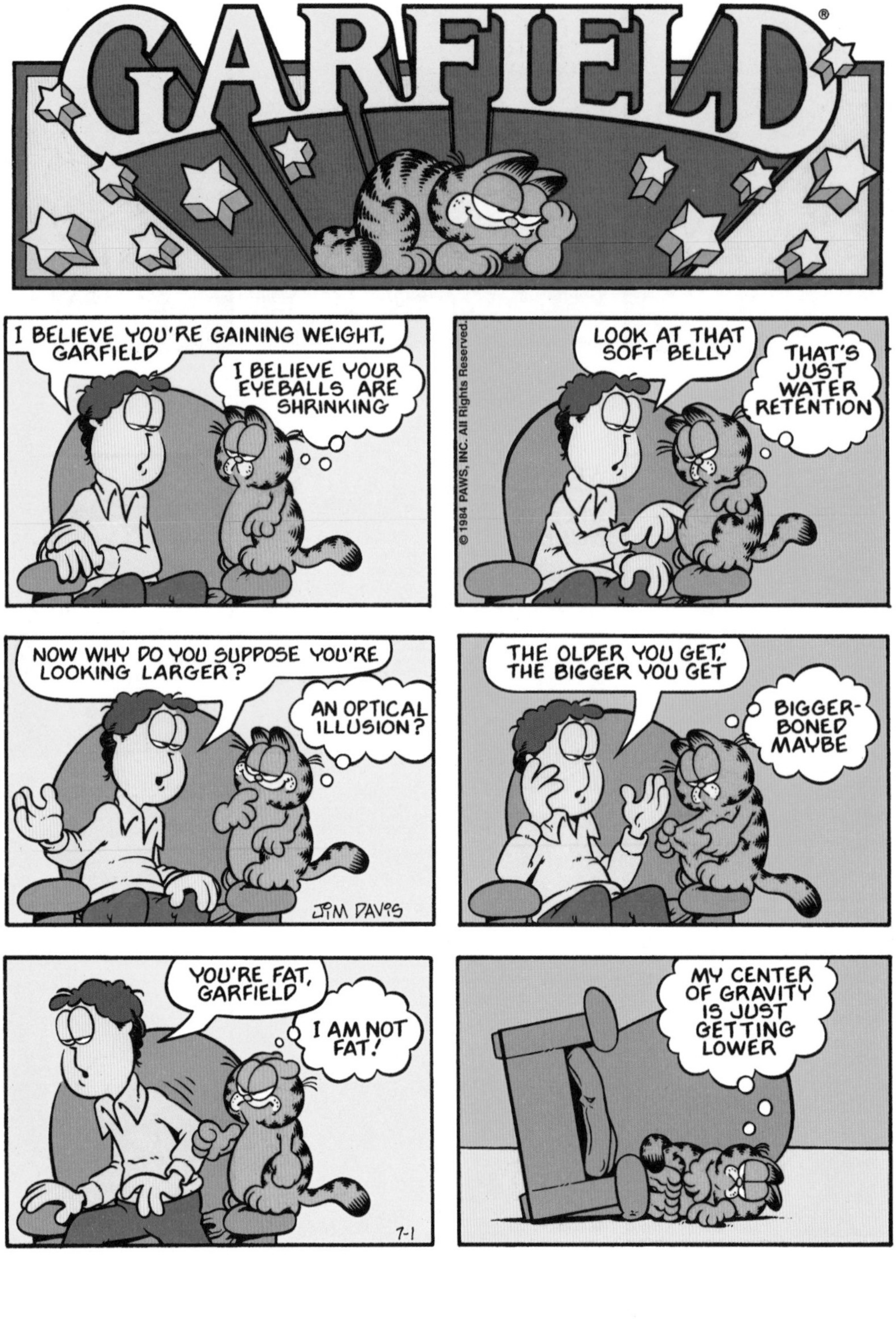
GARFIELD
© 1984 PAWS, INC. All Rights Reserved.
I BELIEVE YOU'RE GAINING WEIGHT, GARFIELD
I BELIEVE YOUR EYEBALLS ARE SHRINKING
LOOK AT THAT SOFT BELLY
THAT'S JUST WATER RETENTION
NOW WHY DO YOU SUPPOSE YOU'RE LOOKING LARGER?
AN OPTICAL ILLUSION?
JIM DAVIS
THE OLDER YOU GET, THE BIGGER YOU GET
BIGGER-BONED MAYBE
YOU'RE FAT, GARFIELD
I AM NOT FAT!
7-1
MY CENTER OF GRAVITY IS JUST GETTING LOWER

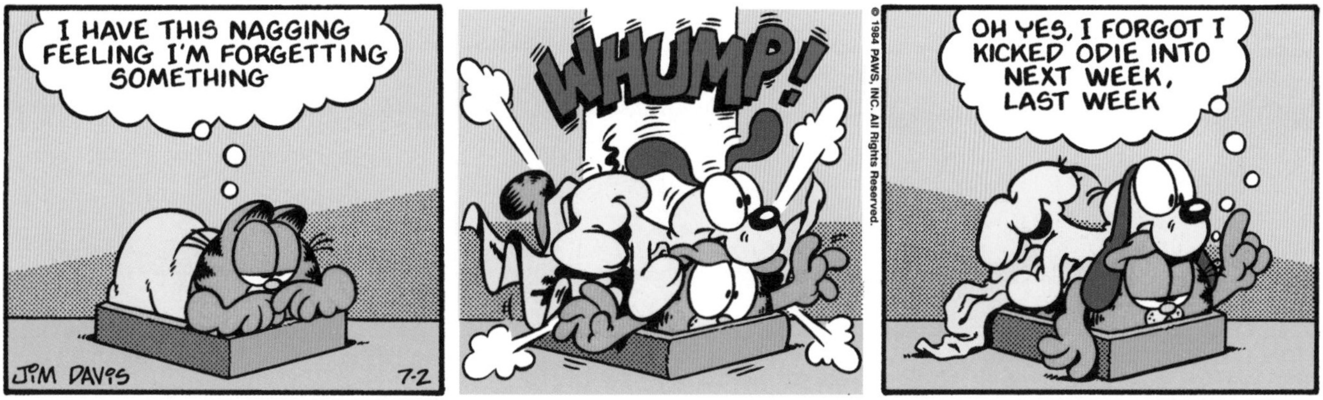
I HAVE THIS NAGGING FEELING I'M FORGETTING SOMETHING
JIM DAVIS 7-2
WHUMP!
© 1984 PAWS, INC. All Rights Reserved.
OH YES, I FORGOT I KICKED ODIE INTO NEXT WEEK, LAST WEEK

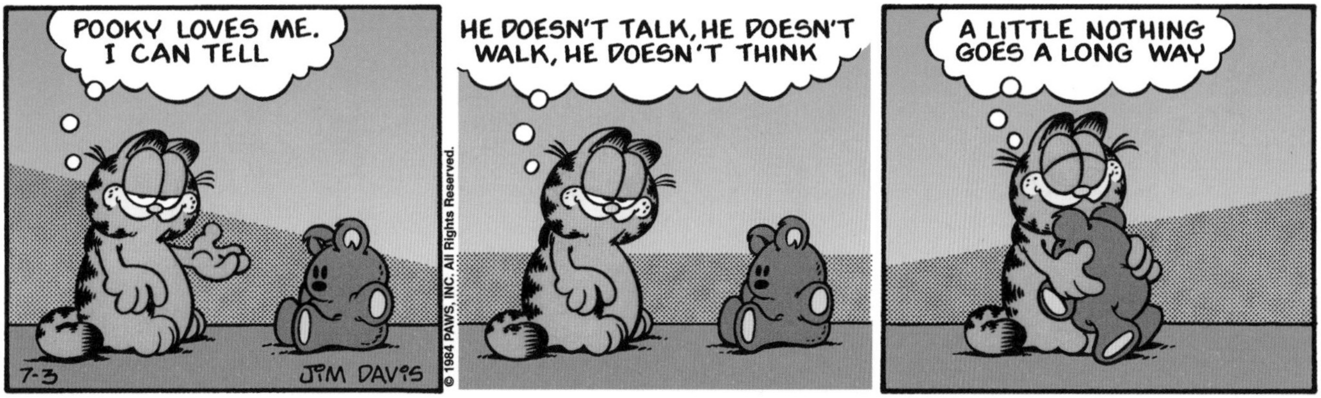
POOKY LOVES ME. I CAN TELL
7-3 JIM DAVIS
© 1984 PAWS, INC. All Rights Reserved.
HE DOESN'T TALK, HE DOESN'T WALK, HE DOESN'T THINK
A LITTLE NOTHING GOES A LONG WAY

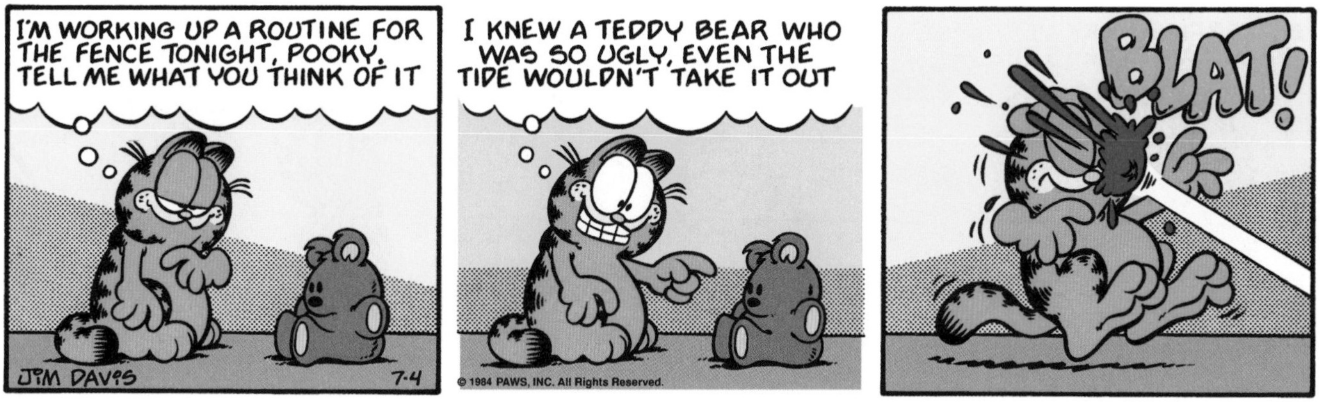
I'M WORKING UP A ROUTINE FOR THE FENCE TONIGHT, POOKY. TELL ME WHAT YOU THINK OF IT
JIM DAVIS 7-4
I KNEW A TEDDY BEAR WHO WAS SO UGLY, EVEN THE TIDE WOULDN'T TAKE IT OUT
© 1984 PAWS, INC. All Rights Reserved.
BLAT!

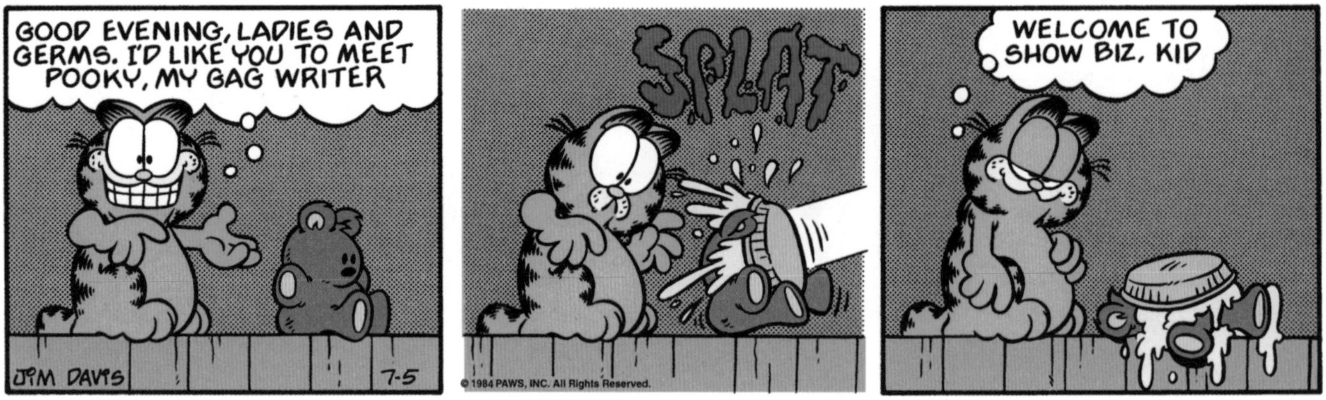
GOOD EVENING, LADIES AND GERMS. I'D LIKE YOU TO MEET POOKY, MY GAG WRITER
JIM DAVIS 7-5
SPLAT
© 1984 PAWS, INC. All Rights Reserved.
WELCOME TO SHOW BIZ, KID

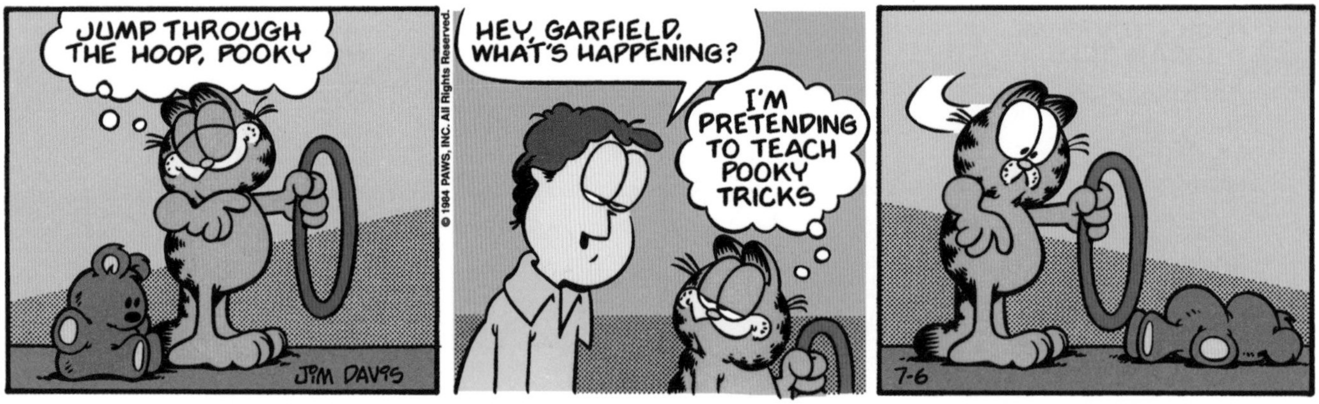
JUMP THROUGH THE HOOP, POOKY
JIM DAVIS
© 1984 PAWS, INC. All Rights Reserved.
HEY, GARFIELD, WHAT'S HAPPENING?
I'M PRETENDING TO TEACH POOKY TRICKS
7-6

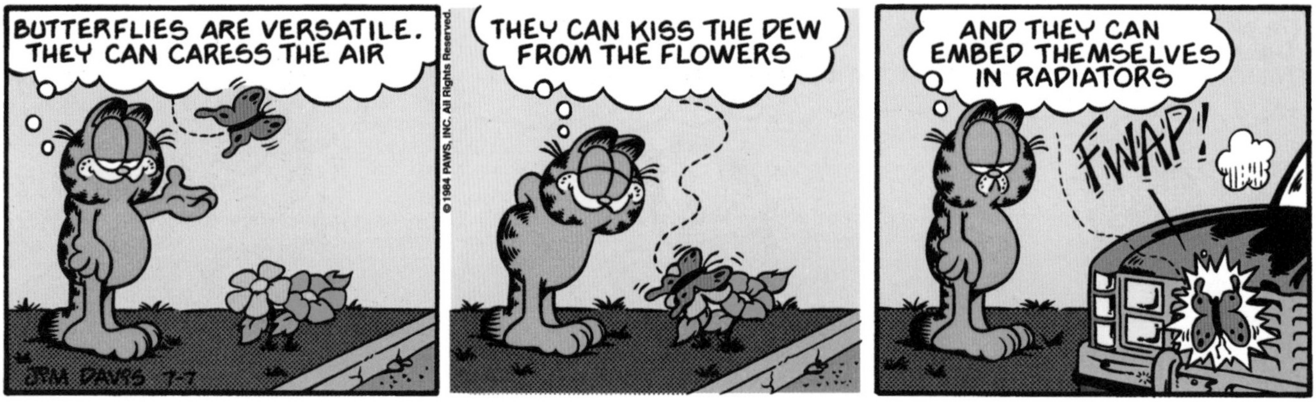
BUTTERFLIES ARE VERSATILE. THEY CAN CARESS THE AIR
JIM DAVIS 7-7
© 1984 PAWS, INC. All Rights Reserved.
THEY CAN KISS THE DEW FROM THE FLOWERS
AND THEY CAN EMBED THEMSELVES IN RADIATORS
FWAP!

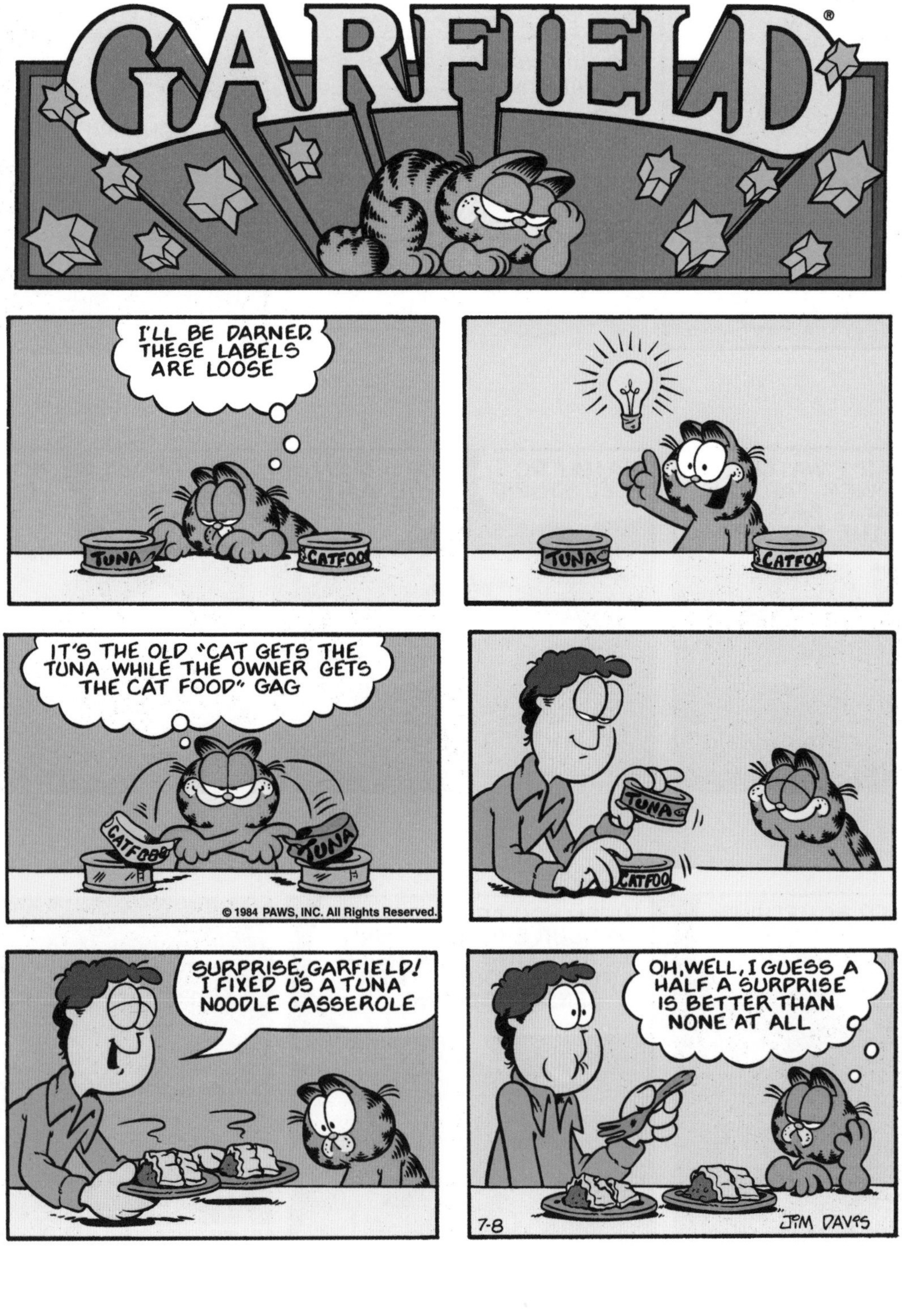
GARFIELD®
I'LL BE DARNED. THESE LABELS ARE LOOSE
TUNA
CATFOO
IT'S THE OLD "CAT GETS THE TUNA WHILE THE OWNER GETS THE CAT FOOD" GAG
CATFOOD
TUNA
© 1984 PAWS, INC. All Rights Reserved.
SURPRISE, GARFIELD! I FIXED US A TUNA NOODLE CASSEROLE
OH, WELL, I GUESS A HALF A SURPRISE IS BETTER THAN NONE AT ALL
7-8
JIM DAVIS

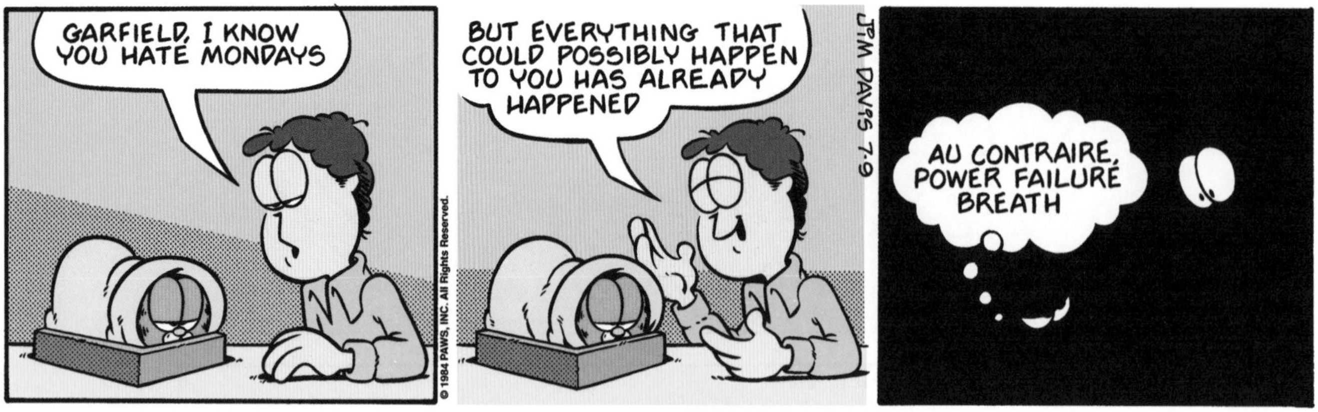
GARFIELD, I KNOW YOU HATE MONDAYS
BUT EVERYTHING THAT COULD POSSIBLY HAPPEN TO YOU HAS ALREADY HAPPENED
AU CONTRAIRE, POWER FAILURE BREATH
JPM DAVPS 7-9
© 1984 PAWS, INC. All Rights Reserved.

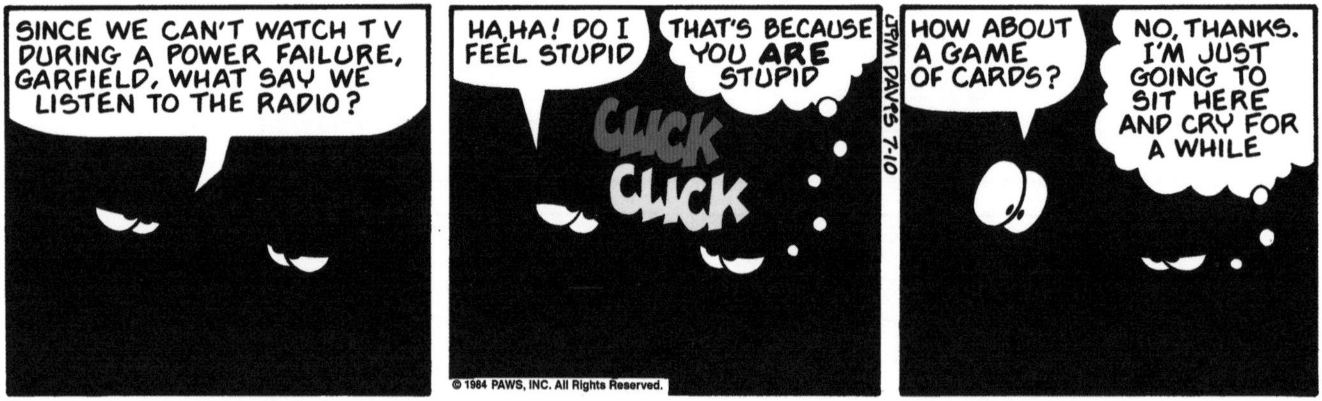
SINCE WE CAN'T WATCH T V DURING A POWER FAILURE, GARFIELD, WHAT SAY WE LISTEN TO THE RADIO?
HA,HA! DO I FEEL STUPID
CLICK
CLICK
THAT'S BECAUSE YOU **ARE** STUPID
HOW ABOUT A GAME OF CARDS?
NO, THANKS. I'M JUST GOING TO SIT HERE AND CRY FOR A WHILE
JPM DAVPS 7-10
© 1984 PAWS, INC. All Rights Reserved.

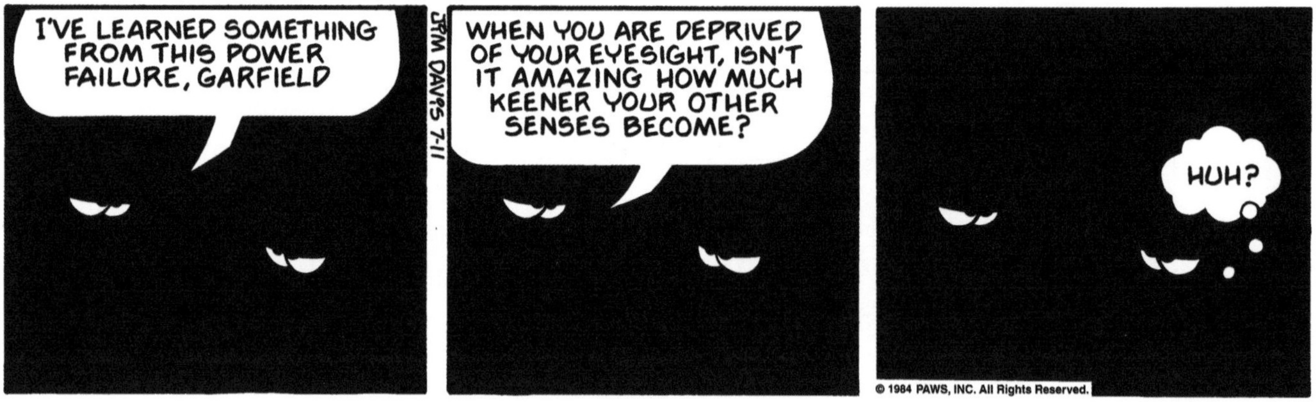
I'VE LEARNED SOMETHING FROM THIS POWER FAILURE, GARFIELD
WHEN YOU ARE DEPRIVED OF YOUR EYESIGHT, ISN'T IT AMAZING HOW MUCH KEENER YOUR OTHER SENSES BECOME?
HUH?
JPM DAVPS 7-11
© 1984 PAWS, INC. All Rights Reserved.

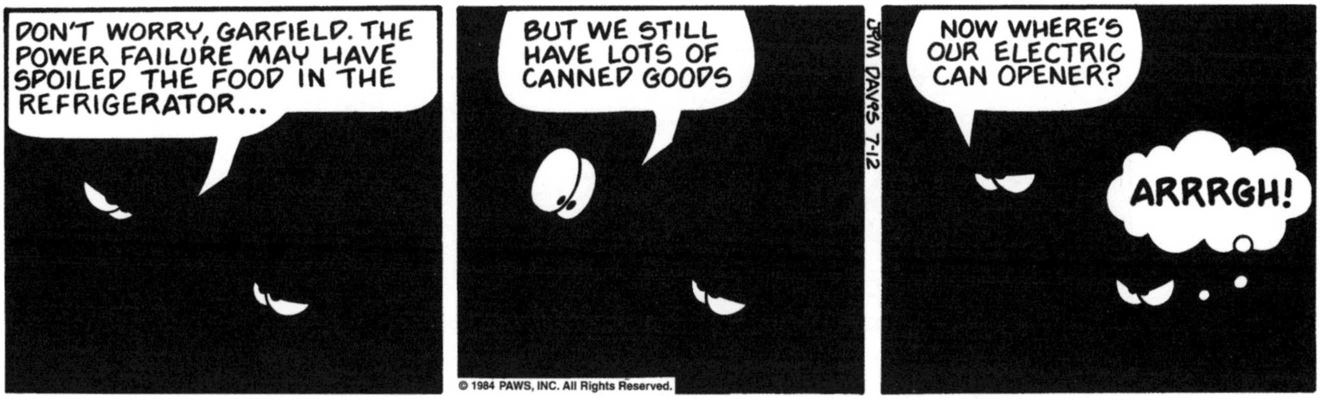
DON'T WORRY, GARFIELD. THE POWER FAILURE MAY HAVE SPOILED THE FOOD IN THE REFRIGERATOR...
BUT WE STILL HAVE LOTS OF CANNED GOODS
© 1984 PAWS, INC. All Rights Reserved.
JIM DAVIS 7-12
NOW WHERE'S OUR ELECTRIC CAN OPENER?
ARRRGH!

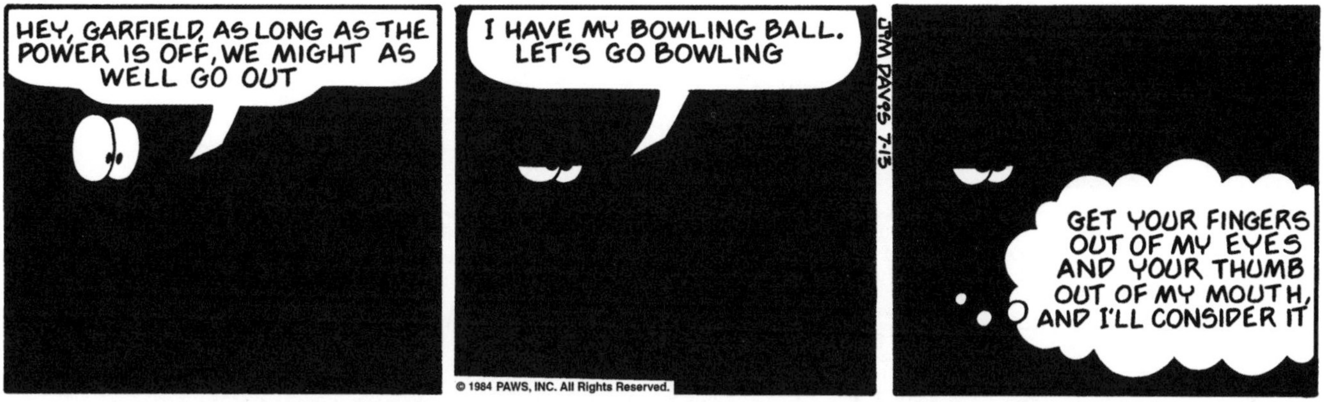
HEY, GARFIELD, AS LONG AS THE POWER IS OFF, WE MIGHT AS WELL GO OUT
I HAVE MY BOWLING BALL. LET'S GO BOWLING
© 1984 PAWS, INC. All Rights Reserved.
JIM DAVIS 7-13
GET YOUR FINGERS OUT OF MY EYES AND YOUR THUMB OUT OF MY MOUTH, AND I'LL CONSIDER IT

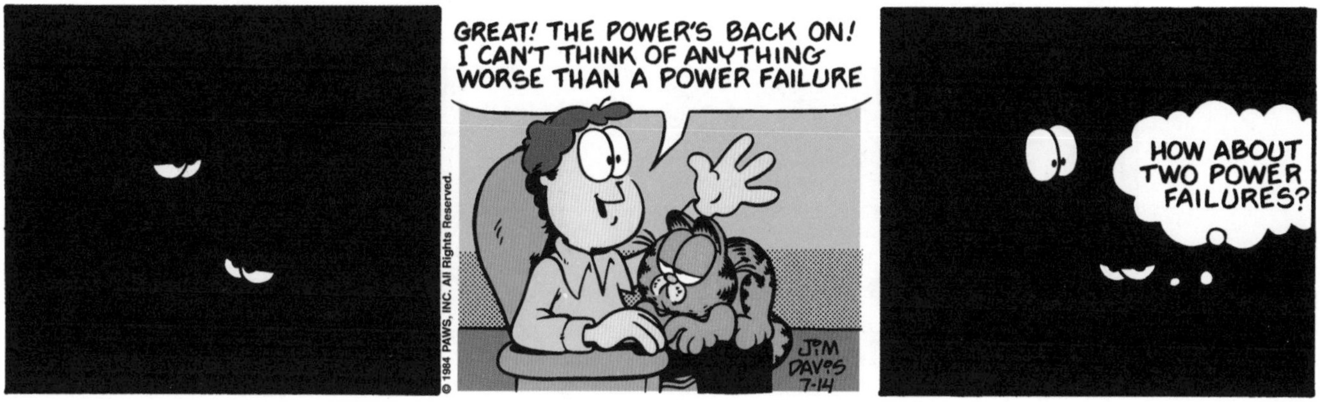
© 1984 PAWS, INC. All Rights Reserved.
GREAT! THE POWER'S BACK ON! I CAN'T THINK OF ANYTHING WORSE THAN A POWER FAILURE
JIM DAVIS 7-14
HOW ABOUT TWO POWER FAILURES?

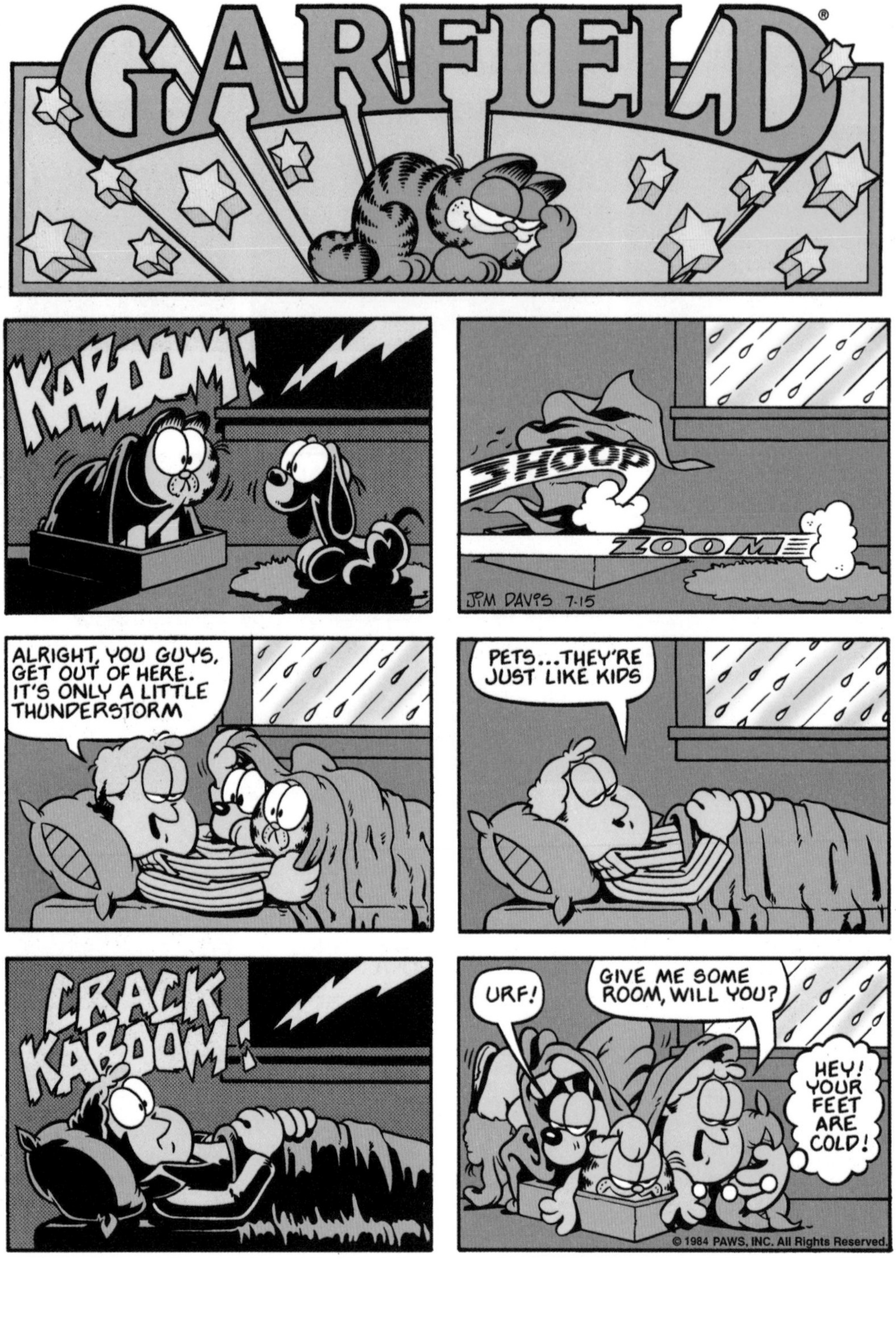
GARFIELD
KABOOM!
SHOOP
ZOOM
JIM DAVIS 7-15
ALRIGHT, YOU GUYS, GET OUT OF HERE. IT'S ONLY A LITTLE THUNDERSTORM
PETS...THEY'RE JUST LIKE KIDS
CRACK KABOOM!
URF!
GIVE ME SOME ROOM, WILL YOU?
HEY! YOUR FEET ARE COLD!
© 1984 PAWS, INC. All Rights Reserved.

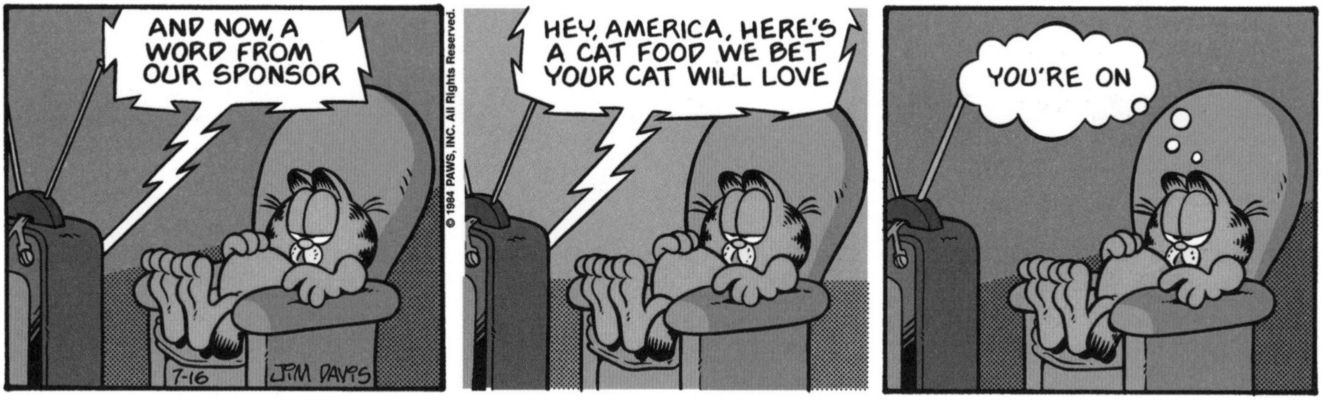
AND NOW, A WORD FROM OUR SPONSOR
© 1984 PAWS, INC. All Rights Reserved.
HEY, AMERICA, HERE'S A CAT FOOD WE BET YOUR CAT WILL LOVE
YOU'RE ON
7-16
JIM DAVIS

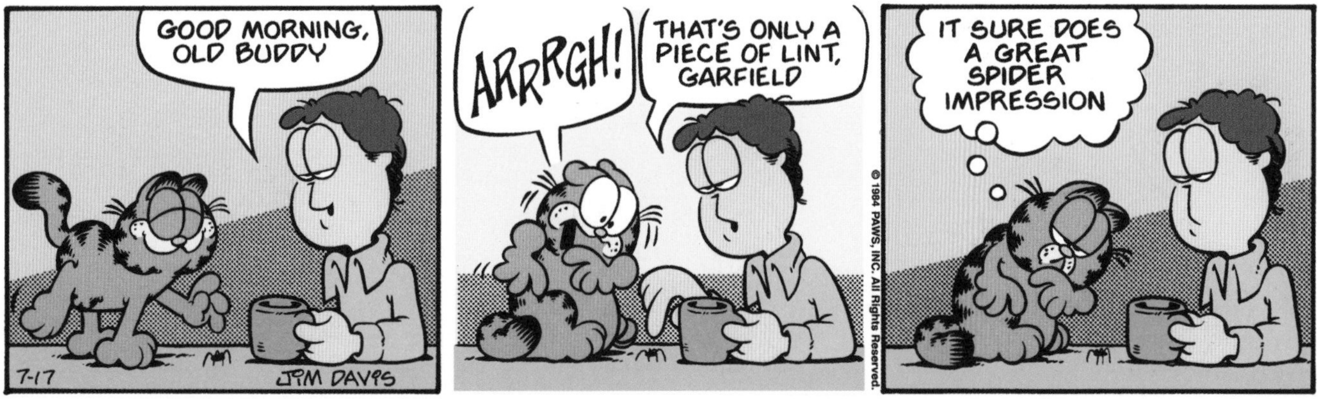
GOOD MORNING, OLD BUDDY
7-17
JIM DAVIS
ARRRGH!
THAT'S ONLY A PIECE OF LINT, GARFIELD
© 1984 PAWS, INC. All Rights Reserved.
IT SURE DOES A GREAT SPIDER IMPRESSION

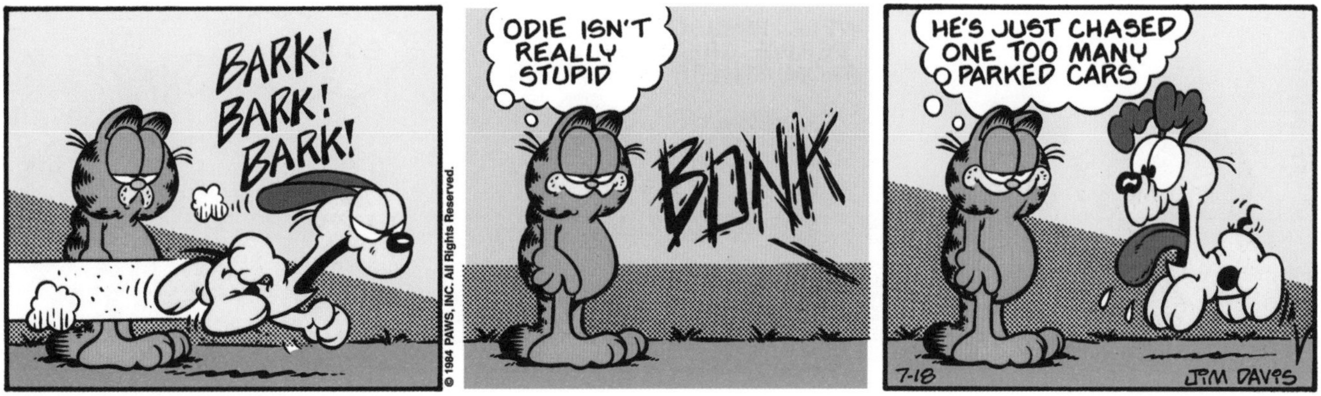
BARK! BARK! BARK!
© 1984 PAWS, INC. All Rights Reserved.
ODIE ISN'T REALLY STUPID
BONK
HE'S JUST CHASED ONE TOO MANY PARKED CARS
7-18
JIM DAVIS

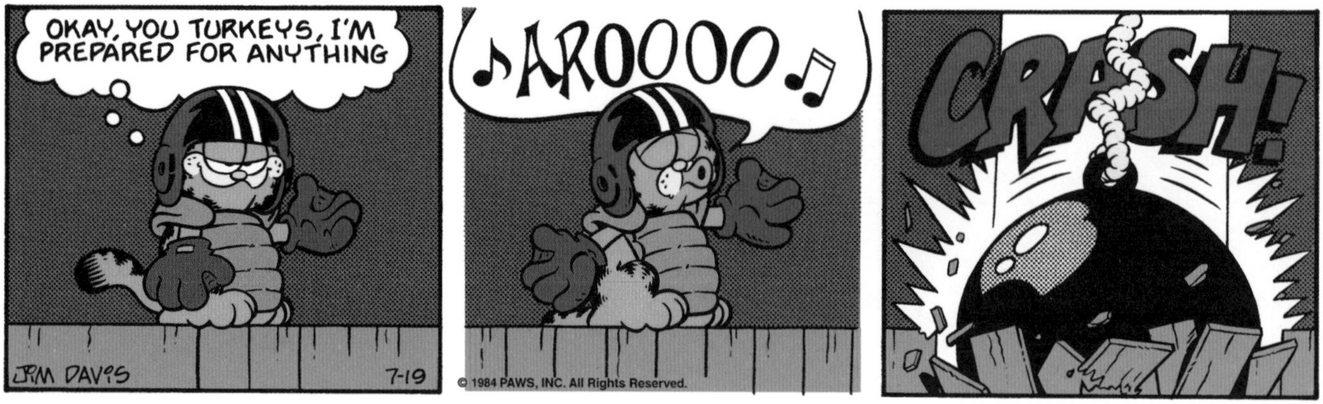
OKAY, YOU TURKEYS, I'M PREPARED FOR ANYTHING
JIM DAVIS 7-19
♪AROOOO♫
© 1984 PAWS, INC. All Rights Reserved.
CRASH!

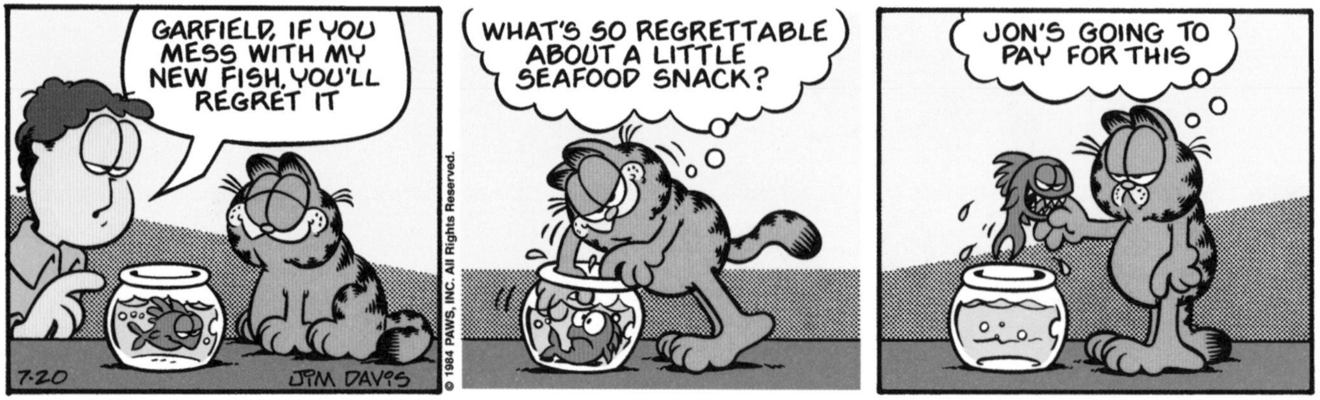
GARFIELD, IF YOU MESS WITH MY NEW FISH, YOU'LL REGRET IT
7-20 JIM DAVIS
© 1984 PAWS, INC. All Rights Reserved.
WHAT'S SO REGRETTABLE ABOUT A LITTLE SEAFOOD SNACK?
JON'S GOING TO PAY FOR THIS

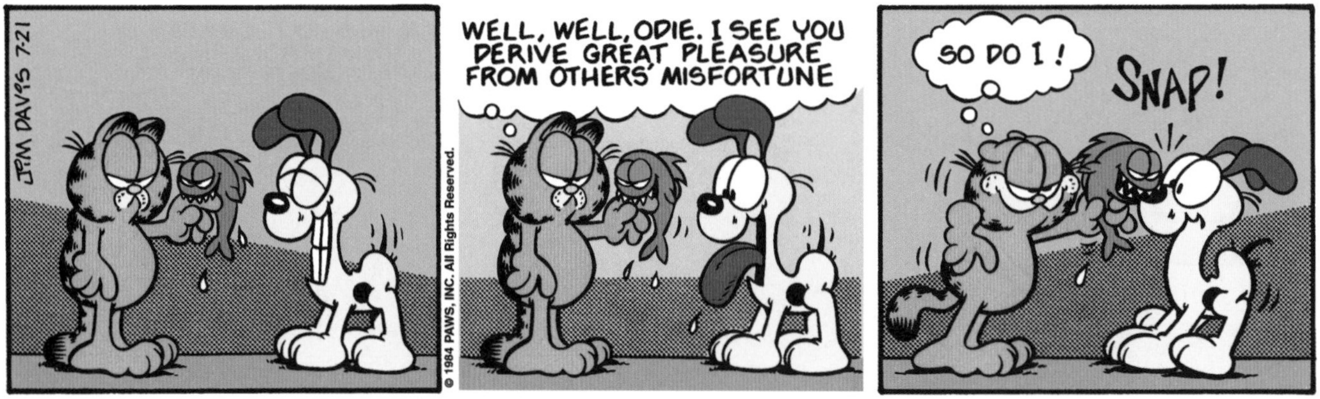
JIM DAVIS 7-21
© 1984 PAWS, INC. All Rights Reserved.
WELL, WELL, ODIE. I SEE YOU DERIVE GREAT PLEASURE FROM OTHERS' MISFORTUNE
SO DO I!
SNAP!

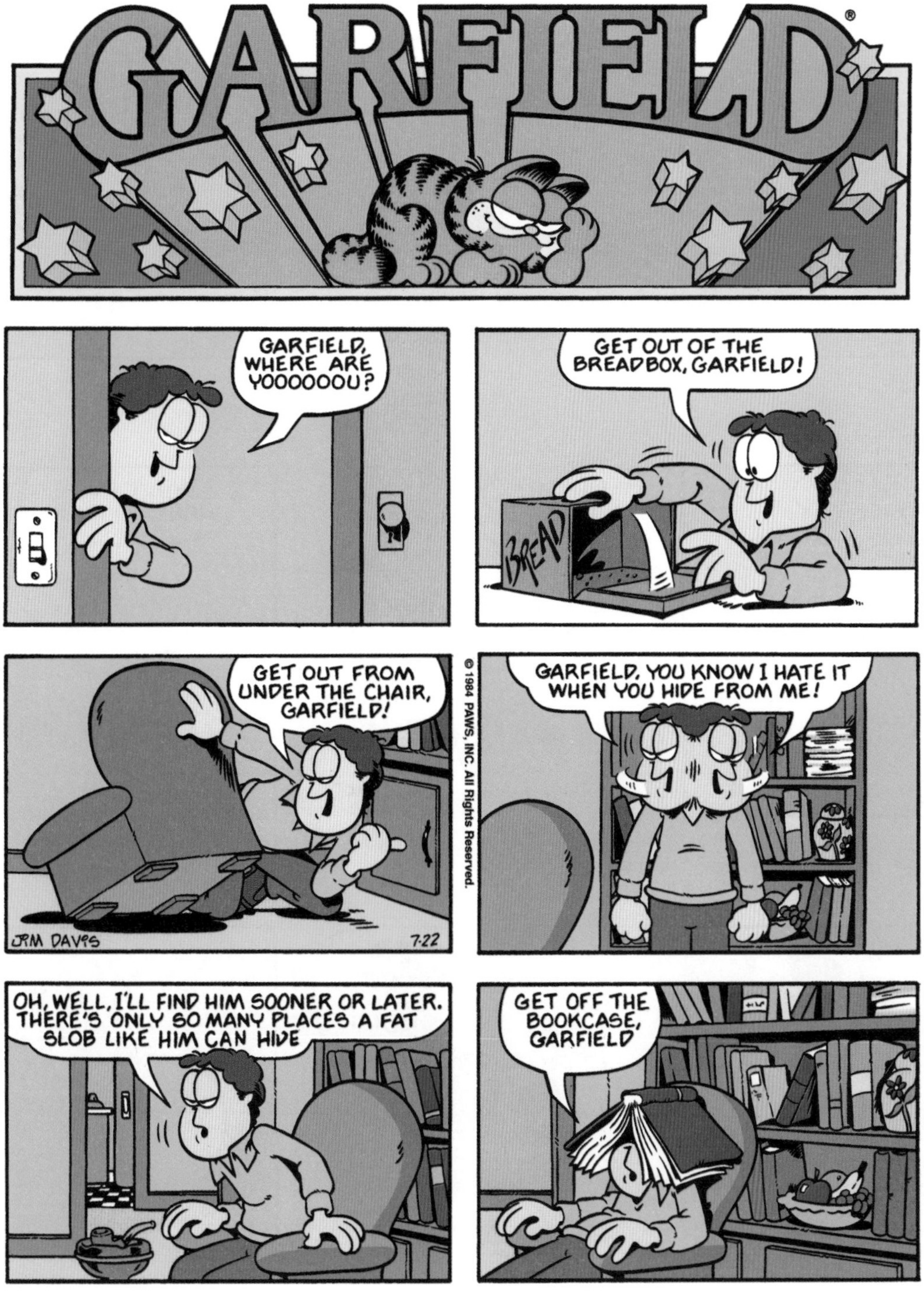
GARFIELD
GARFIELD, WHERE ARE YOOOOOOU?
GET OUT OF THE BREADBOX, GARFIELD!
BREAD
GET OUT FROM UNDER THE CHAIR, GARFIELD!
JIM DAVIS
7-22
© 1984 PAWS, INC. All Rights Reserved.
GARFIELD, YOU KNOW I HATE IT WHEN YOU HIDE FROM ME!
OH, WELL, I'LL FIND HIM SOONER OR LATER. THERE'S ONLY SO MANY PLACES A FAT SLOB LIKE HIM CAN HIDE
GET OFF THE BOOKCASE, GARFIELD

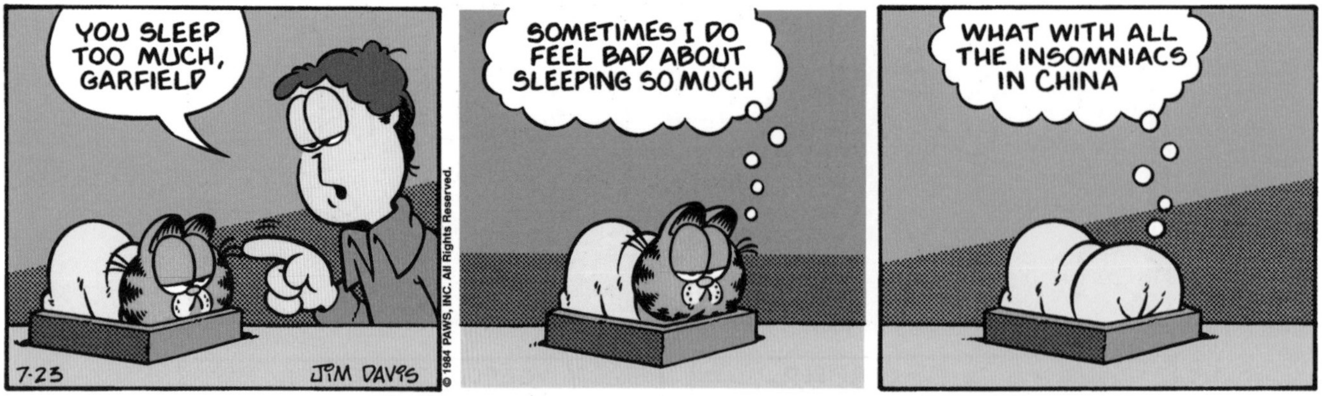
YOU SLEEP TOO MUCH, GARFIELD
SOMETIMES I DO FEEL BAD ABOUT SLEEPING SO MUCH
WHAT WITH ALL THE INSOMNIACS IN CHINA
7-23
JIM DAVIS
© 1984 PAWS, INC. All Rights Reserved.

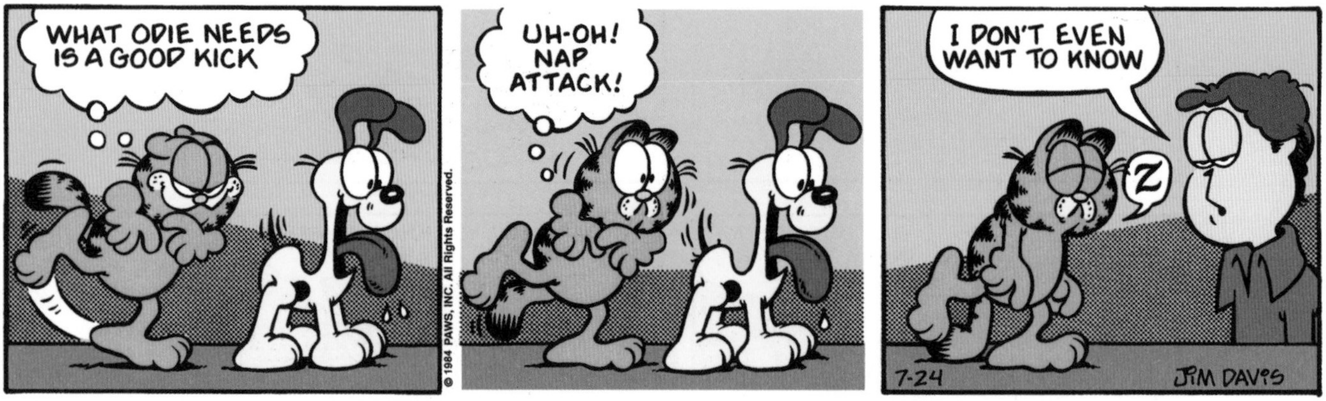
WHAT ODIE NEEDS IS A GOOD KICK
UH-OH! NAP ATTACK!
I DON'T EVEN WANT TO KNOW
Z
7-24
JIM DAVIS
© 1984 PAWS, INC. All Rights Reserved.

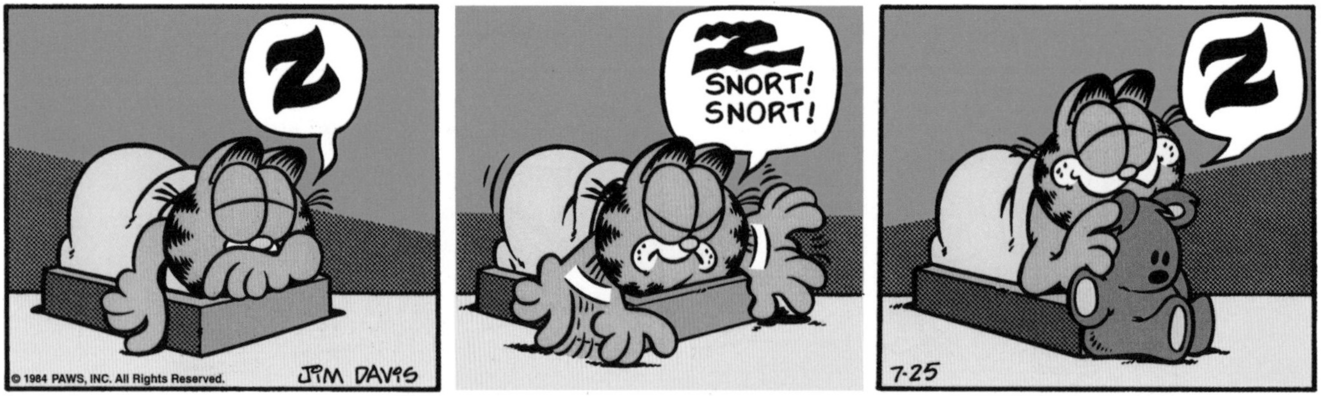
Z
Z
SNORT! SNORT!
Z
© 1984 PAWS, INC. All Rights Reserved.
JIM DAVIS
7-25

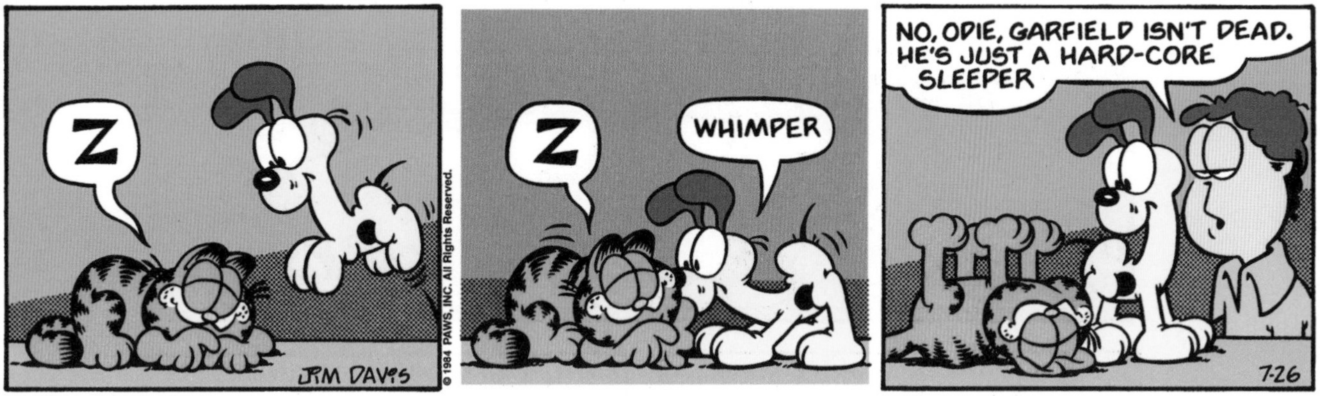
Z
JIM DAVIS
© 1984 PAWS, INC. All Rights Reserved.
Z
WHIMPER
NO, ODIE, GARFIELD ISN'T DEAD. HE'S JUST A HARD-CORE SLEEPER
7-26

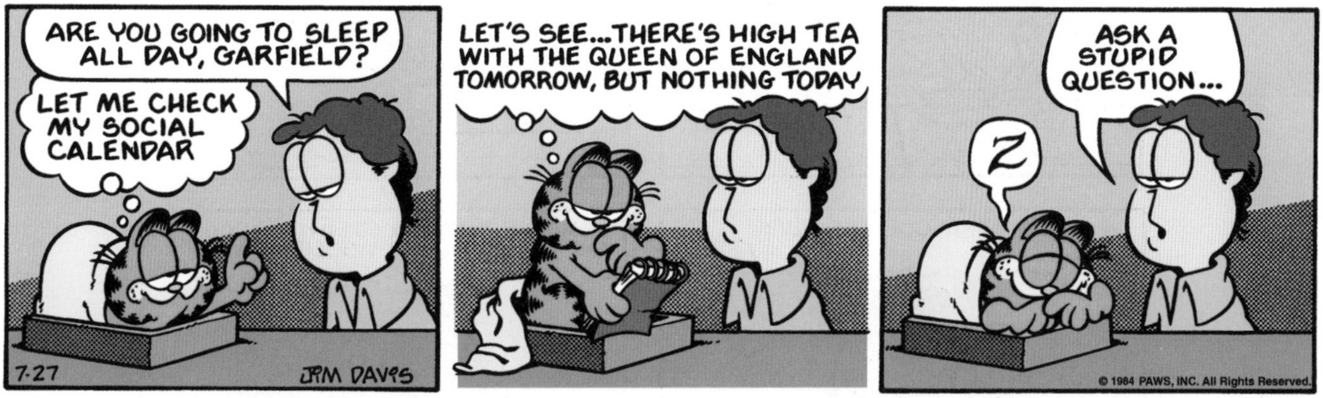
ARE YOU GOING TO SLEEP ALL DAY, GARFIELD?
LET ME CHECK MY SOCIAL CALENDAR
7-27
JIM DAVIS
LET'S SEE...THERE'S HIGH TEA WITH THE QUEEN OF ENGLAND TOMORROW, BUT NOTHING TODAY
Z
ASK A STUPID QUESTION...
© 1984 PAWS, INC. All Rights Reserved.

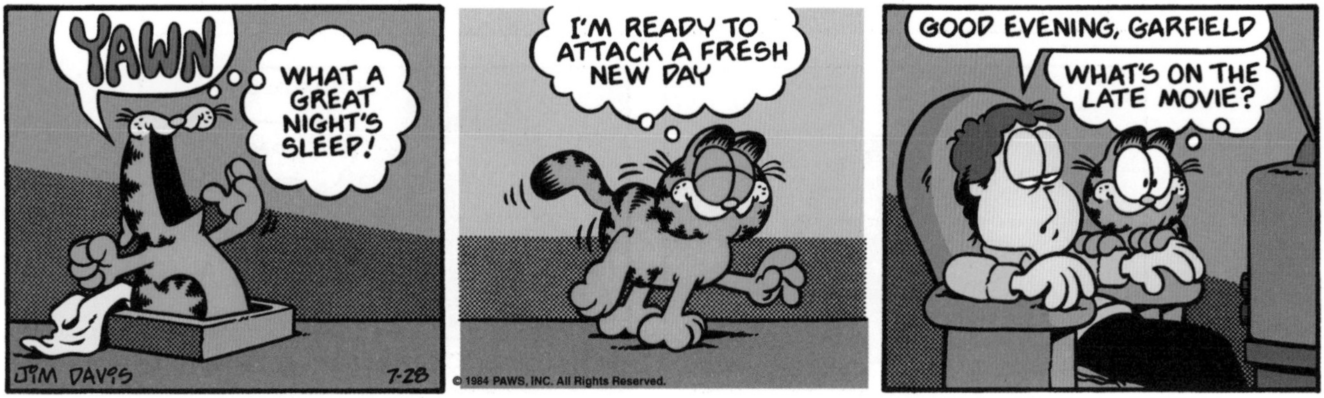
YAWN
WHAT A GREAT NIGHT'S SLEEP!
JIM DAVIS
7-28
© 1984 PAWS, INC. All Rights Reserved.
I'M READY TO ATTACK A FRESH NEW DAY
GOOD EVENING, GARFIELD
WHAT'S ON THE LATE MOVIE?

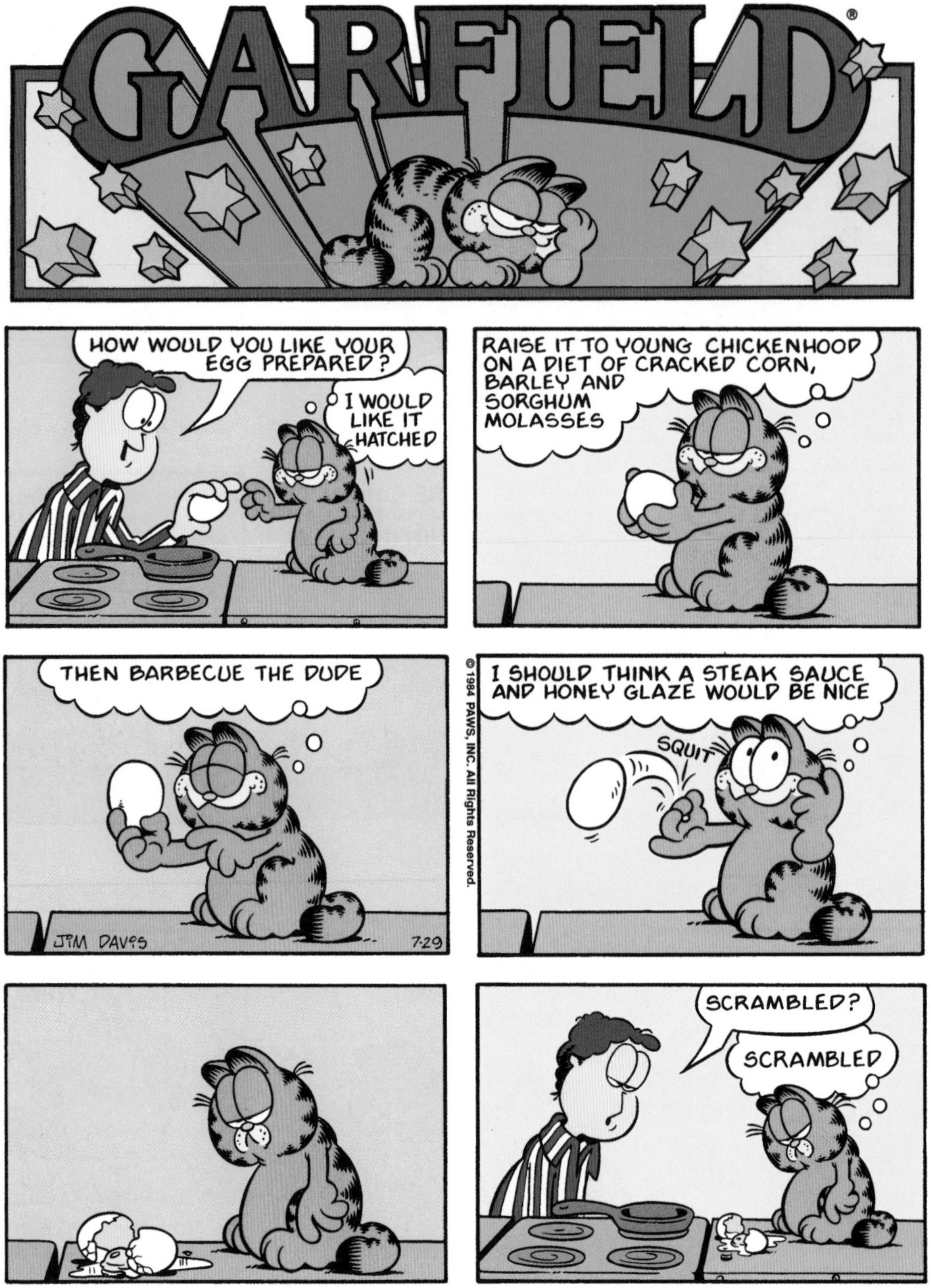
GARFIELD
HOW WOULD YOU LIKE YOUR EGG PREPARED?
I WOULD LIKE IT HATCHED
RAISE IT TO YOUNG CHICKENHOOD ON A DIET OF CRACKED CORN, BARLEY AND SORGHUM MOLASSES
THEN BARBECUE THE DUDE
JIM DAVIS
7-29
© 1984 PAWS, INC. All Rights Reserved.
I SHOULD THINK A STEAK SAUCE AND HONEY GLAZE WOULD BE NICE
SQUIT
SCRAMBLED?
SCRAMBLED

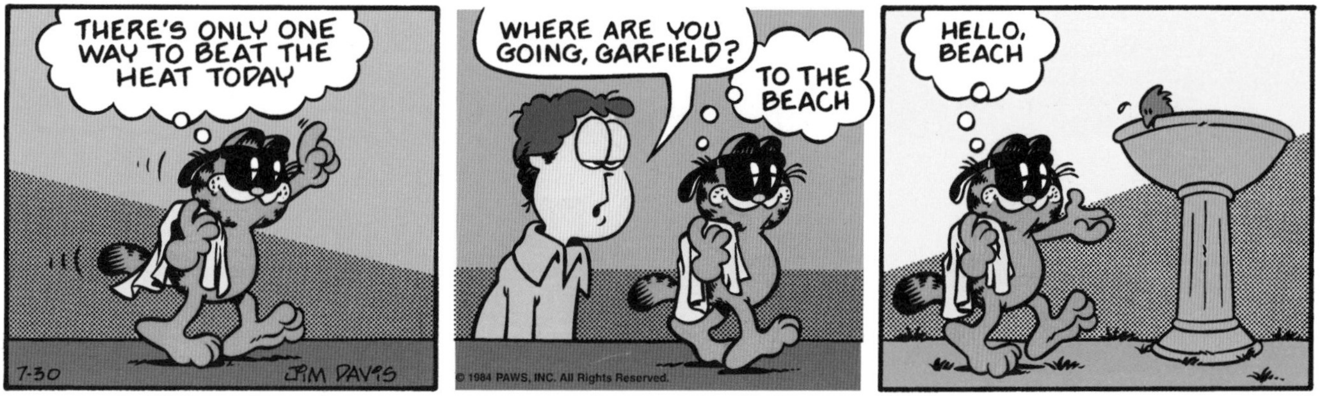
THERE'S ONLY ONE WAY TO BEAT THE HEAT TODAY
7-30
JIM DAVIS
WHERE ARE YOU GOING, GARFIELD?
TO THE BEACH
© 1984 PAWS, INC. All Rights Reserved.
HELLO, BEACH

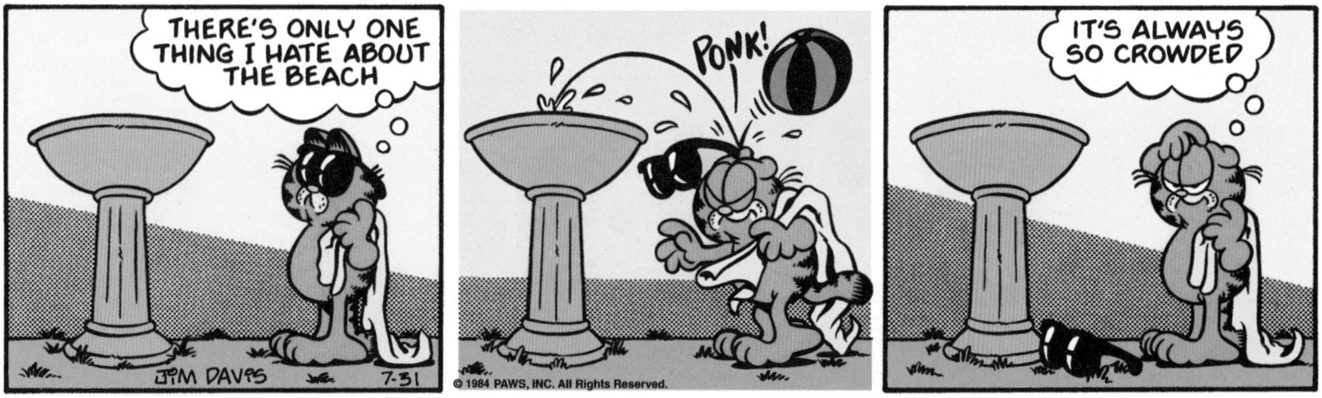
THERE'S ONLY ONE THING I HATE ABOUT THE BEACH
JIM DAVIS
7-31
PONK!
© 1984 PAWS, INC. All Rights Reserved.
IT'S ALWAYS SO CROWDED

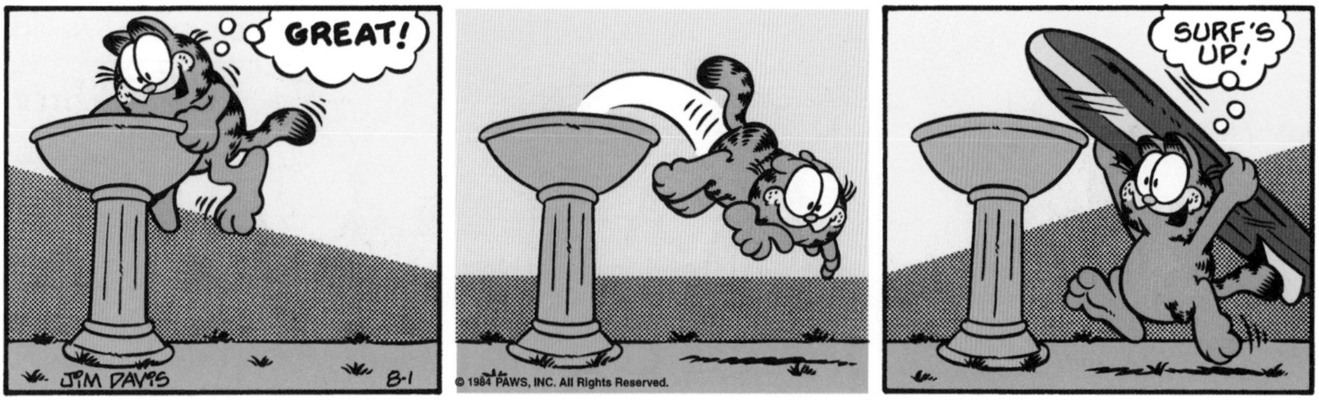
GREAT!
JIM DAVIS
8-1
© 1984 PAWS, INC. All Rights Reserved.
SURF'S UP!

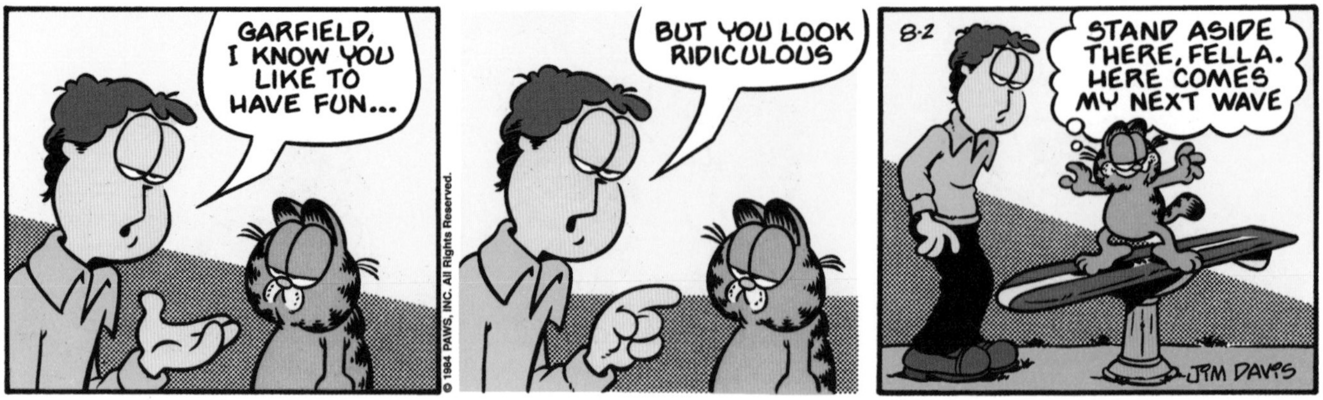
GARFIELD, I KNOW YOU LIKE TO HAVE FUN...
© 1984 PAWS, INC. All Rights Reserved.
BUT YOU LOOK RIDICULOUS
8-2
STAND ASIDE THERE, FELLA. HERE COMES MY NEXT WAVE
JIM DAVIS

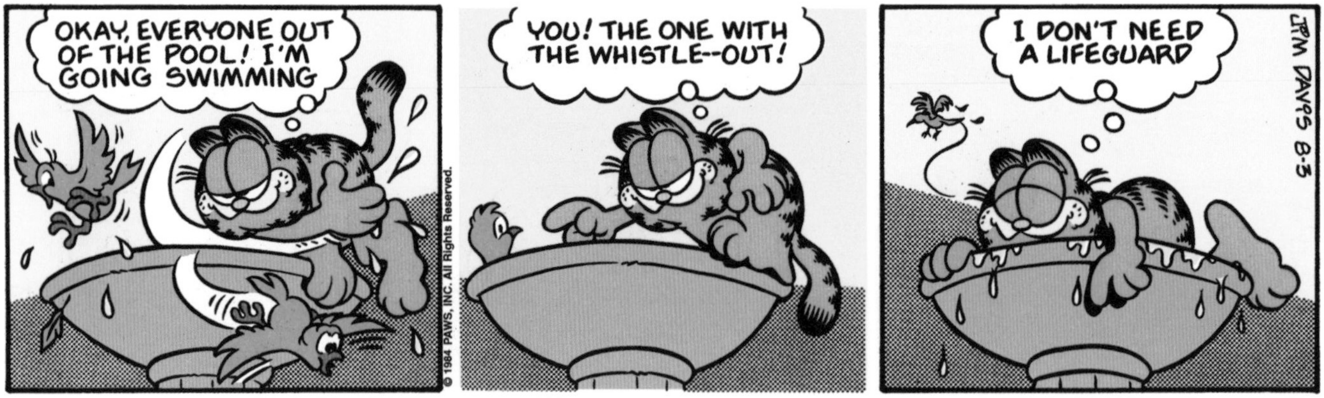
OKAY, EVERYONE OUT OF THE POOL! I'M GOING SWIMMING
© 1984 PAWS, INC. All Rights Reserved.
YOU! THE ONE WITH THE WHISTLE--OUT!
I DON'T NEED A LIFEGUARD
JIM DAVIS 8-3

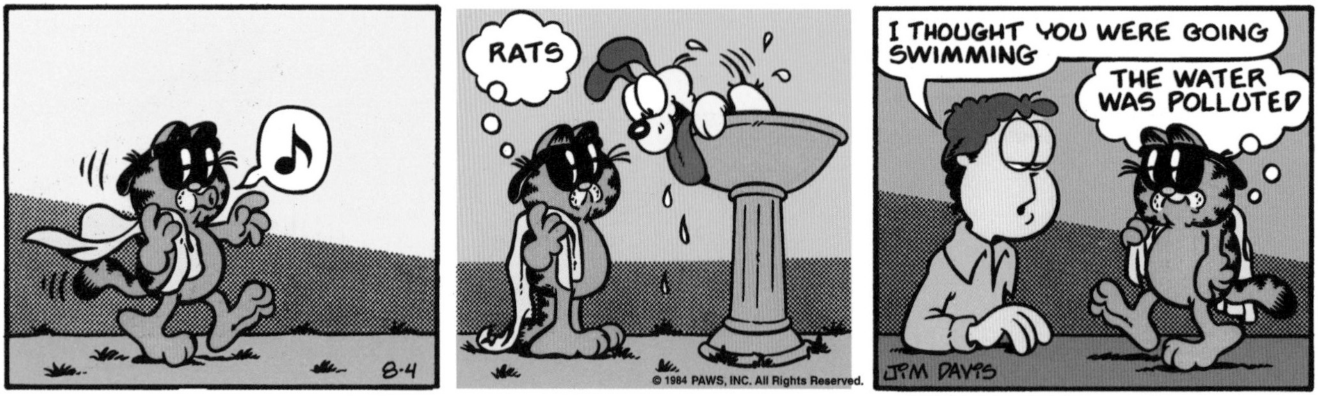
♪
8-4
RATS
© 1984 PAWS, INC. All Rights Reserved.
I THOUGHT YOU WERE GOING SWIMMING
THE WATER WAS POLLUTED
JIM DAVIS

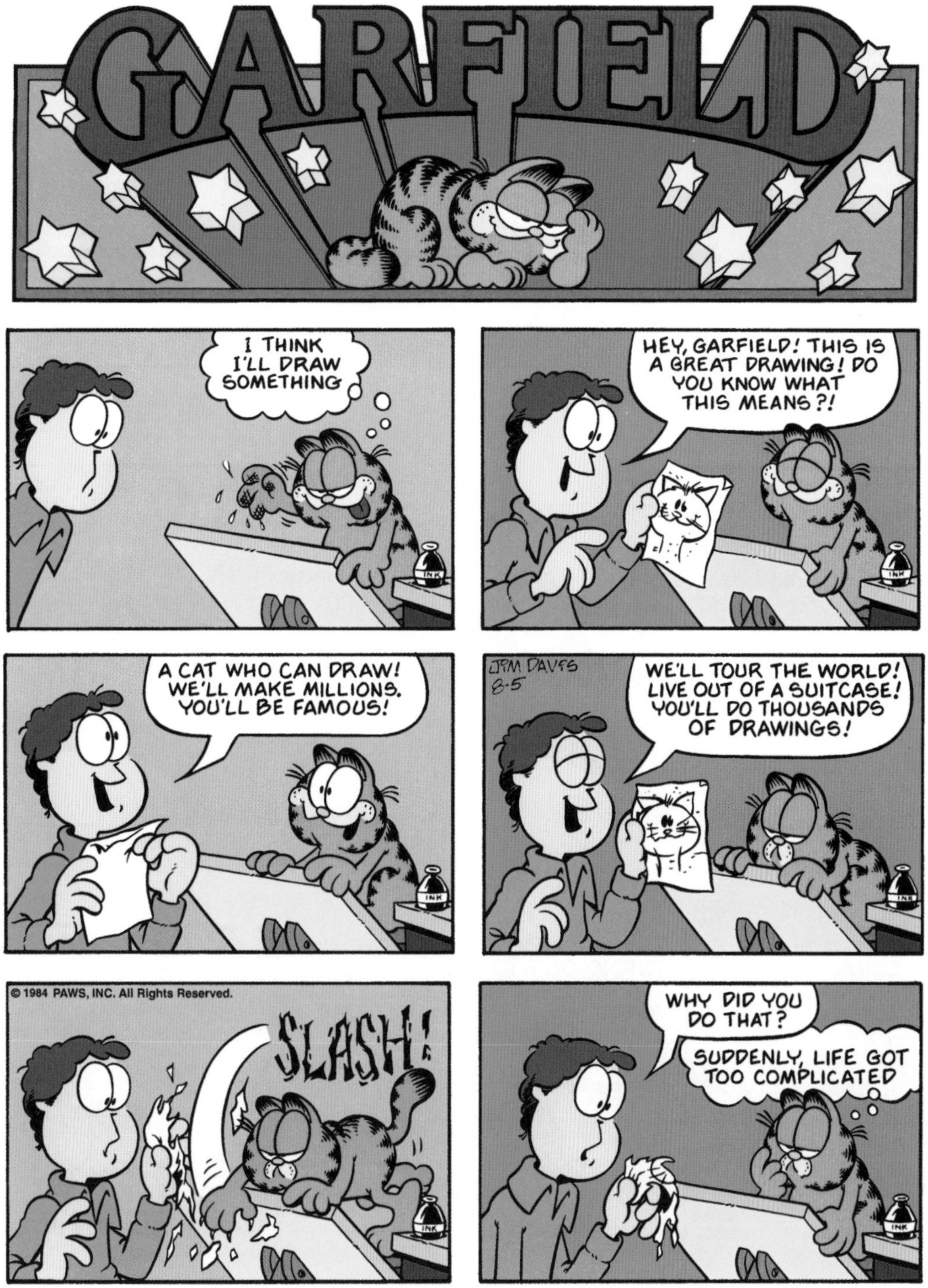
GARFIELD
I THINK I'LL DRAW SOMETHING
HEY, GARFIELD! THIS IS A GREAT DRAWING! DO YOU KNOW WHAT THIS MEANS?!
A CAT WHO CAN DRAW! WE'LL MAKE MILLIONS. YOU'LL BE FAMOUS!
JIM DAVIS 8-5
WE'LL TOUR THE WORLD! LIVE OUT OF A SUITCASE! YOU'LL DO THOUSANDS OF DRAWINGS!
SLASH!
WHY DID YOU DO THAT?
SUDDENLY, LIFE GOT TOO COMPLICATED

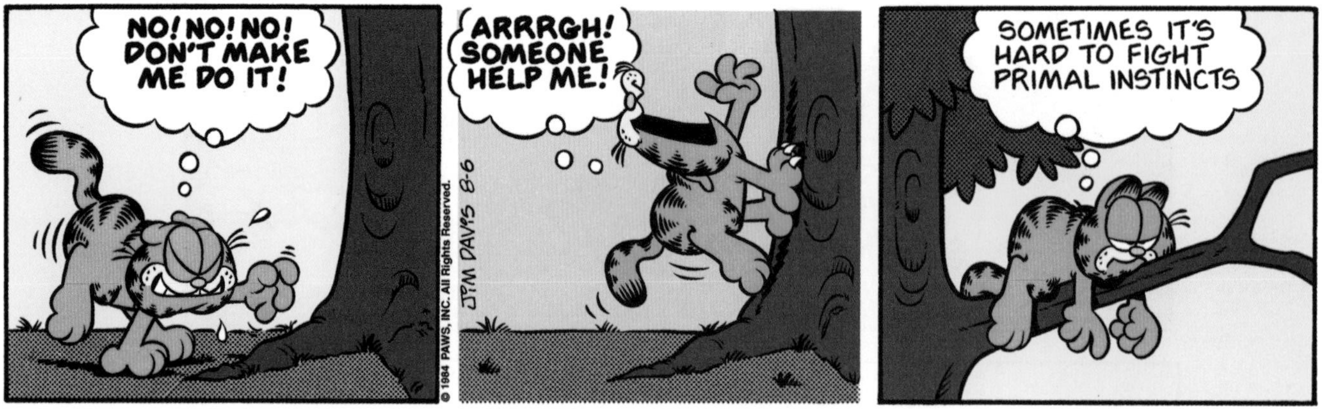
NO! NO! NO! DON'T MAKE ME DO IT!
ARRRGH! SOMEONE HELP ME!
© 1984 PAWS, INC. All Rights Reserved.
JIM DAVIS 8-6
SOMETIMES IT'S HARD TO FIGHT PRIMAL INSTINCTS

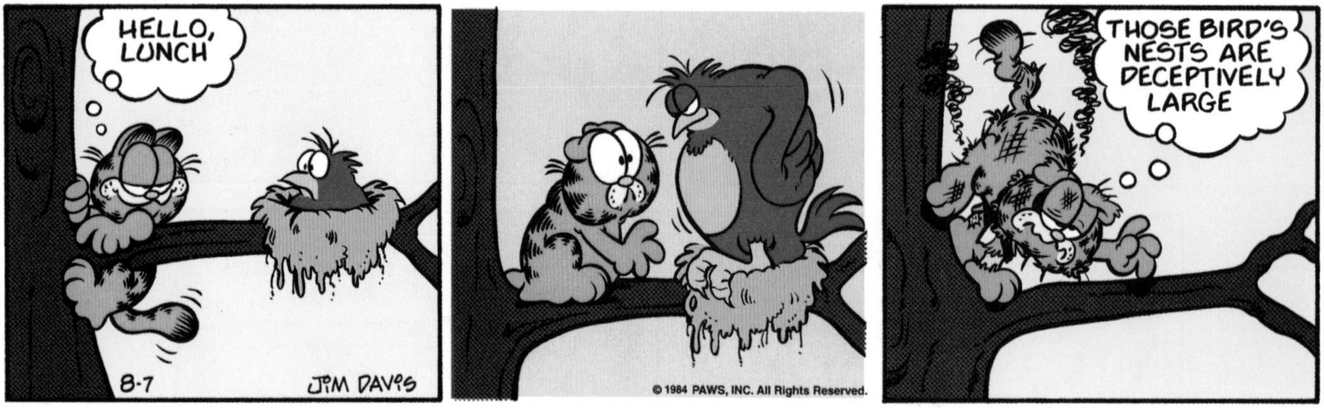
HELLO, LUNCH
8-7
JIM DAVIS
© 1984 PAWS, INC. All Rights Reserved.
THOSE BIRD'S NESTS ARE DECEPTIVELY LARGE

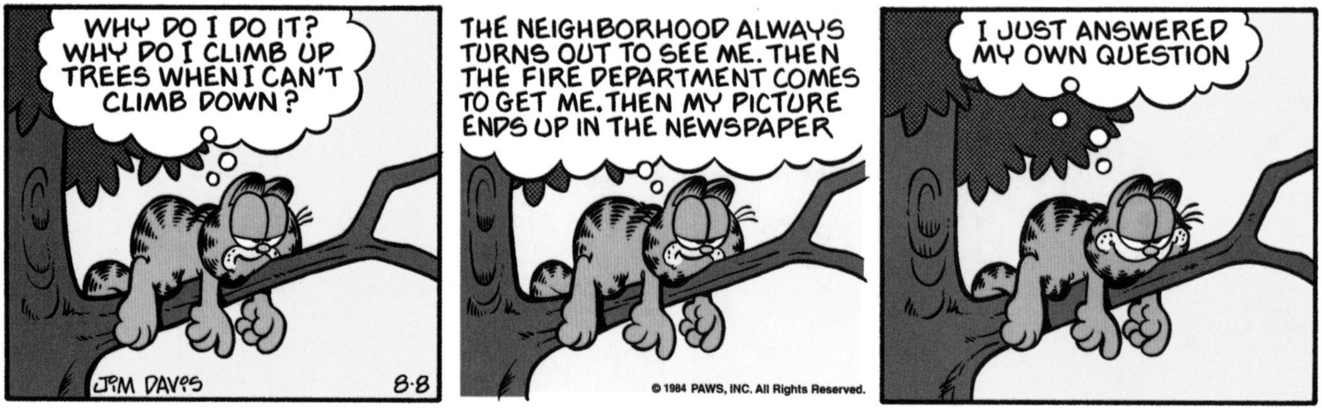
WHY DO I DO IT? WHY DO I CLIMB UP TREES WHEN I CAN'T CLIMB DOWN?
JIM DAVIS
8-8
THE NEIGHBORHOOD ALWAYS TURNS OUT TO SEE ME. THEN THE FIRE DEPARTMENT COMES TO GET ME. THEN MY PICTURE ENDS UP IN THE NEWSPAPER
© 1984 PAWS, INC. All Rights Reserved.
I JUST ANSWERED MY OWN QUESTION

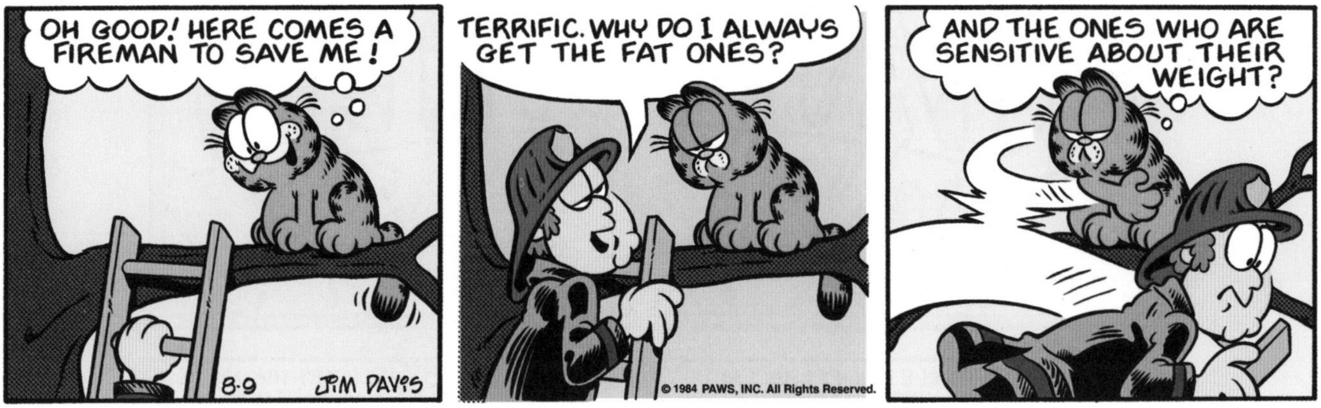
OH GOOD! HERE COMES A FIREMAN TO SAVE ME!
8-9
JIM DAVIS
TERRIFIC. WHY DO I ALWAYS GET THE FAT ONES?
© 1984 PAWS, INC. All Rights Reserved.
AND THE ONES WHO ARE SENSITIVE ABOUT THEIR WEIGHT?

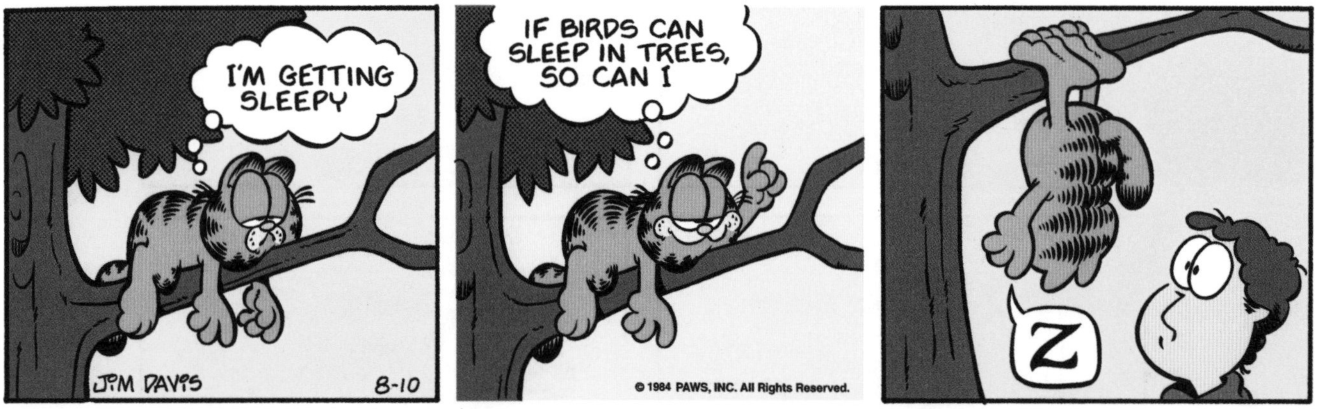
I'M GETTING SLEEPY
JIM DAVIS
8-10
IF BIRDS CAN SLEEP IN TREES, SO CAN I
© 1984 PAWS, INC. All Rights Reserved.
Z

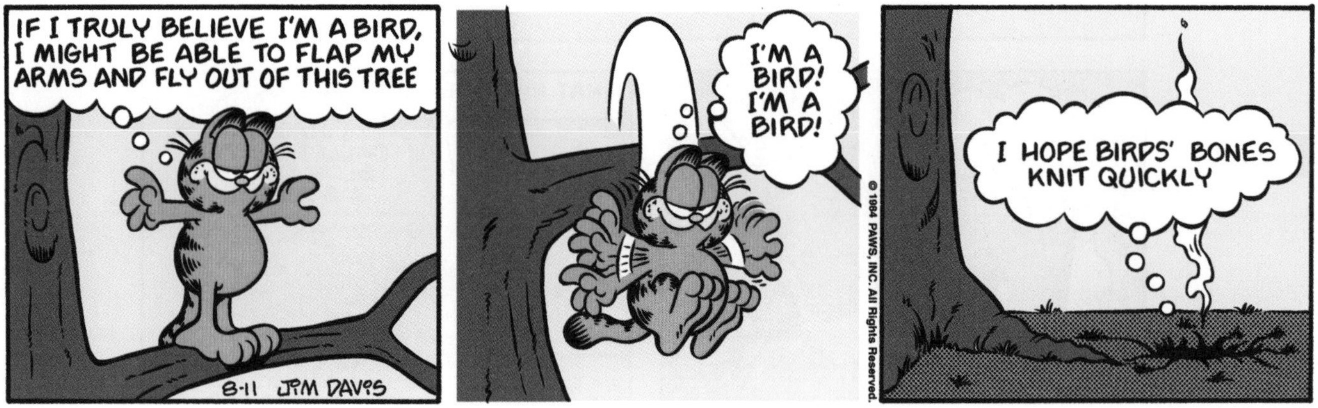
IF I TRULY BELIEVE I'M A BIRD, I MIGHT BE ABLE TO FLAP MY ARMS AND FLY OUT OF THIS TREE
8-11
JIM DAVIS
I'M A BIRD! I'M A BIRD!
© 1984 PAWS, INC. All Rights Reserved.
I HOPE BIRDS' BONES KNIT QUICKLY

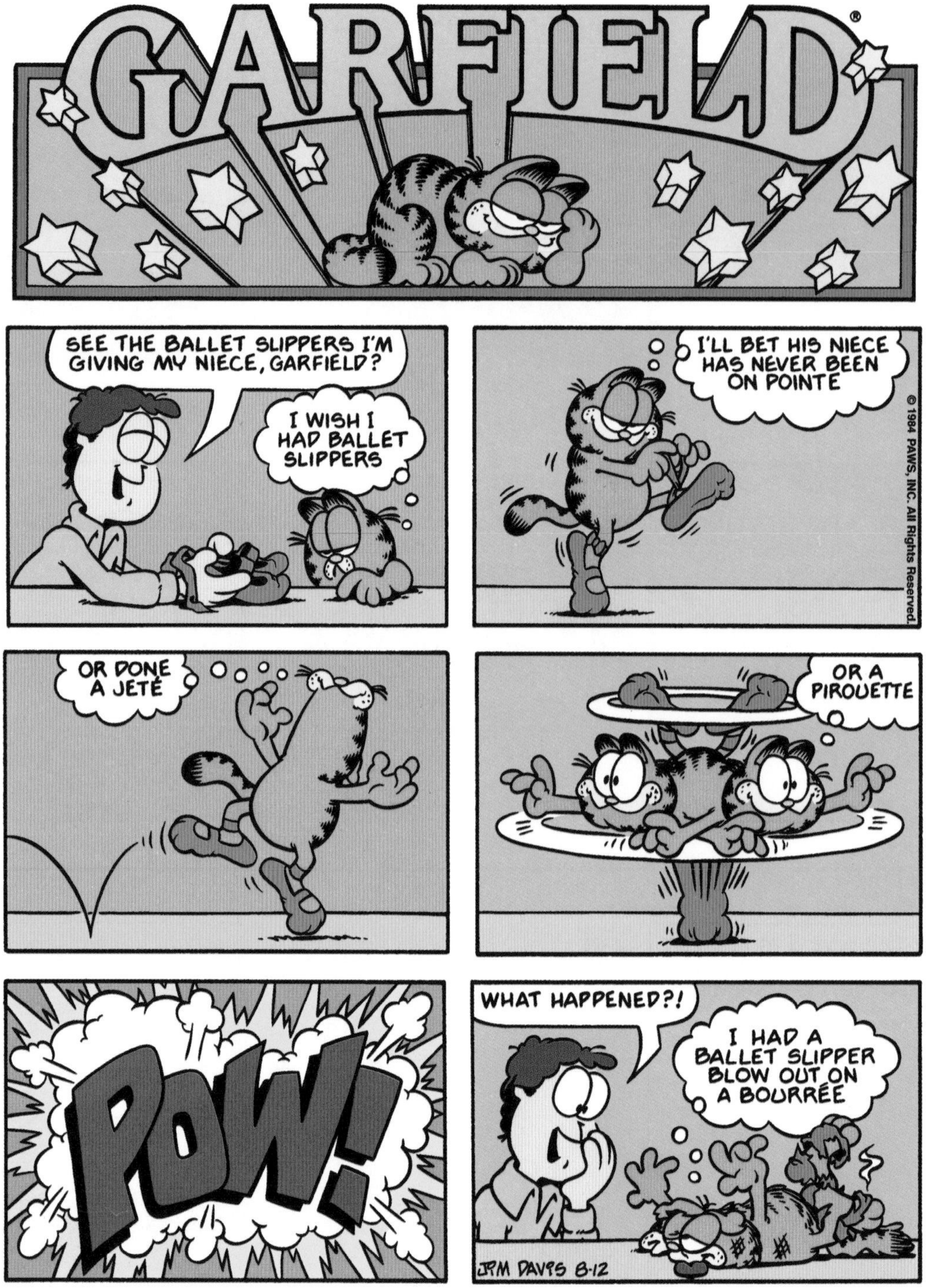
GARFIELD
SEE THE BALLET SLIPPERS I'M GIVING MY NIECE, GARFIELD?
I WISH I HAD BALLET SLIPPERS
I'LL BET HIS NIECE HAS NEVER BEEN ON POINTE
© 1984 PAWS, INC. All Rights Reserved.
OR DONE A JETÉ
OR A PIROUETTE
POW!
WHAT HAPPENED?!
I HAD A BALLET SLIPPER BLOW OUT ON A BOURRÉE
JPM DAVIS 8-12

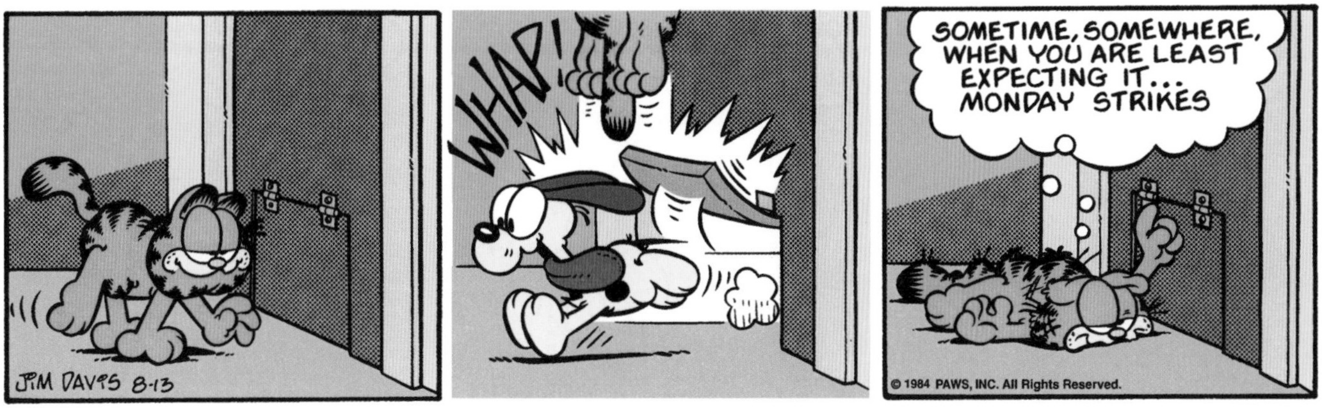
JIM DAVIS 8-13
WHAP!
SOMETIME, SOMEWHERE, WHEN YOU ARE LEAST EXPECTING IT... MONDAY STRIKES
© 1984 PAWS, INC. All Rights Reserved.

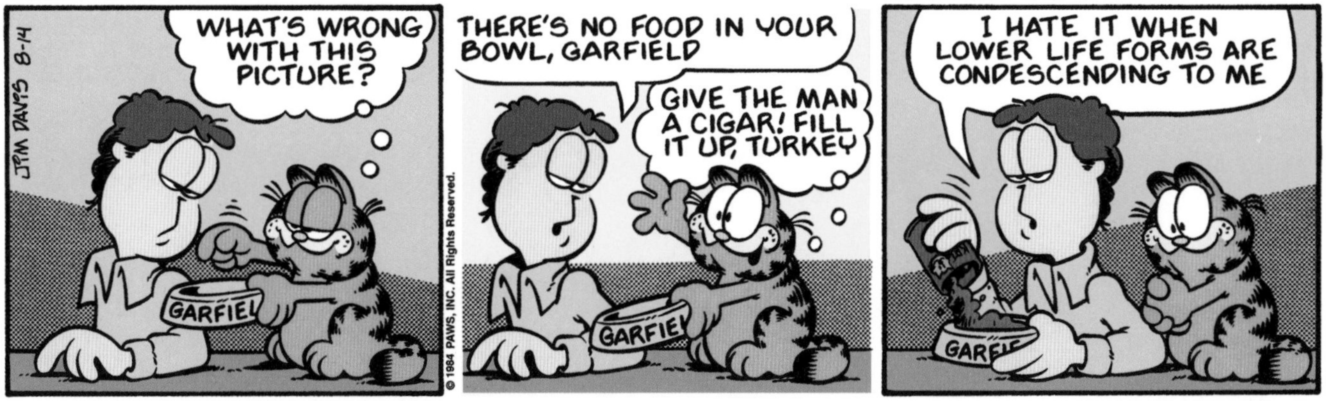
JIM DAVIS 8-14
WHAT'S WRONG WITH THIS PICTURE?
GARFIEL
© 1984 PAWS, INC. All Rights Reserved.
THERE'S NO FOOD IN YOUR BOWL, GARFIELD
GIVE THE MAN A CIGAR! FILL IT UP, TURKEY
GARFIE
I HATE IT WHEN LOWER LIFE FORMS ARE CONDESCENDING TO ME

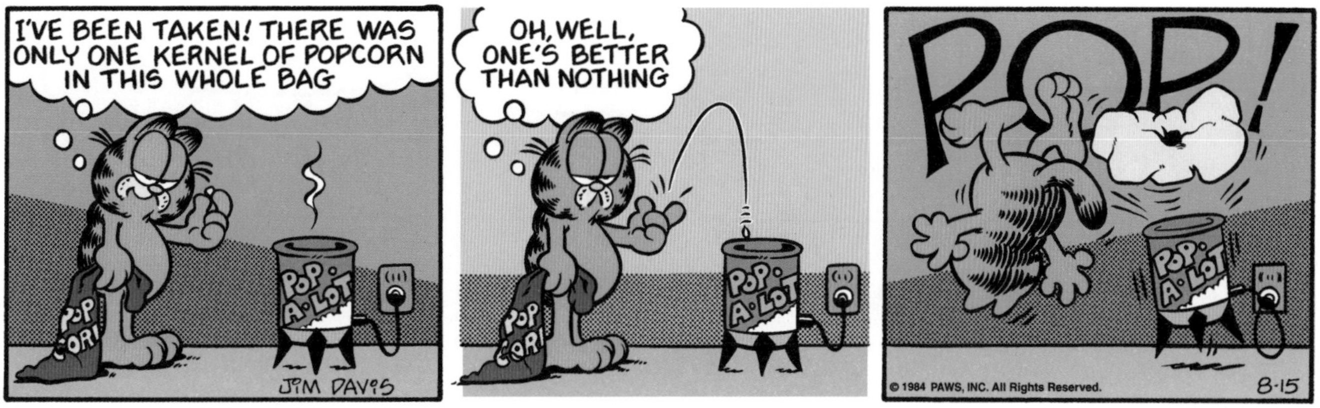
I'VE BEEN TAKEN! THERE WAS ONLY ONE KERNEL OF POPCORN IN THIS WHOLE BAG
POP-A-LOT
JIM DAVIS
OH, WELL, ONE'S BETTER THAN NOTHING
POP-A-LOT
POP!
POP-A-LOT
© 1984 PAWS, INC. All Rights Reserved.
8-15

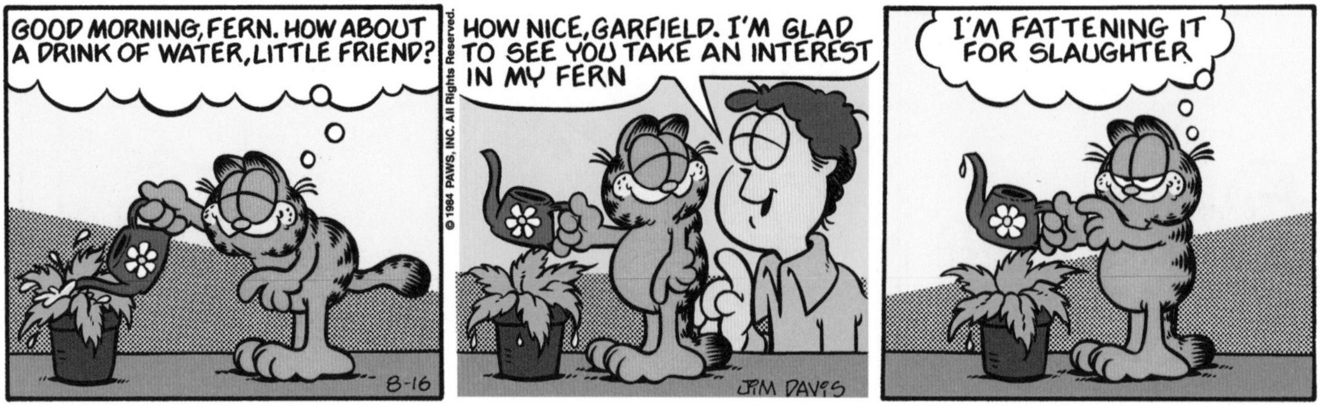
GOOD MORNING, FERN. HOW ABOUT A DRINK OF WATER, LITTLE FRIEND?
8-16
© 1984 PAWS, INC. All Rights Reserved.
HOW NICE, GARFIELD. I'M GLAD TO SEE YOU TAKE AN INTEREST IN MY FERN
JIM DAVIS
I'M FATTENING IT FOR SLAUGHTER

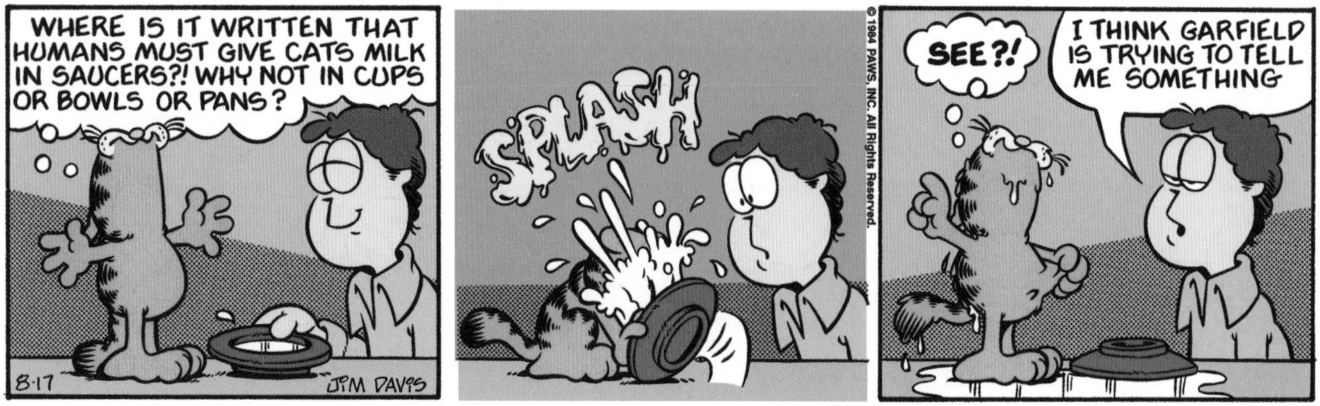
WHERE IS IT WRITTEN THAT HUMANS MUST GIVE CATS MILK IN SAUCERS?! WHY NOT IN CUPS OR BOWLS OR PANS?
8-17
JIM DAVIS
SPLASH
© 1984 PAWS, INC. All Rights Reserved.
SEE?!
I THINK GARFIELD IS TRYING TO TELL ME SOMETHING

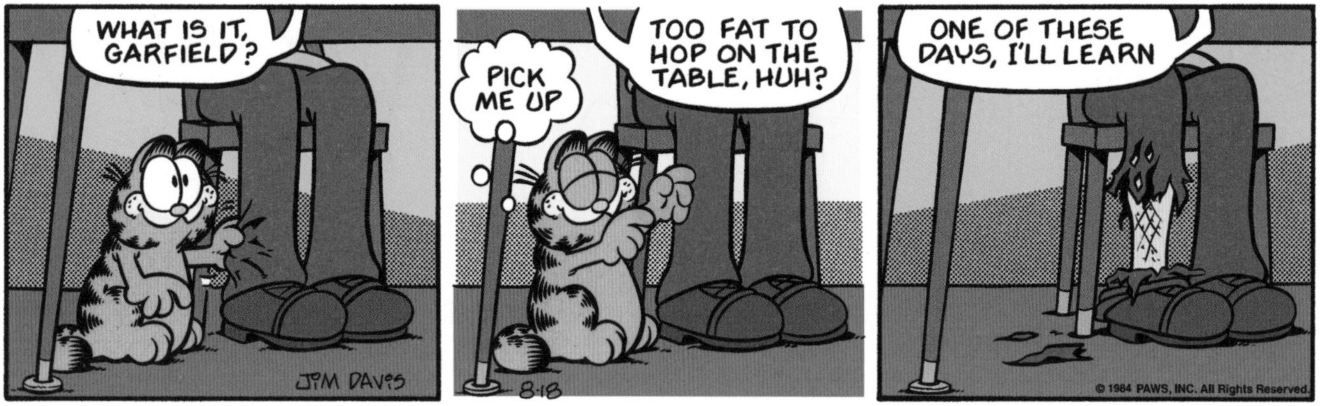
WHAT IS IT, GARFIELD?
JIM DAVIS
PICK ME UP
TOO FAT TO HOP ON THE TABLE, HUH?
8-18
ONE OF THESE DAYS, I'LL LEARN
© 1984 PAWS, INC. All Rights Reserved.

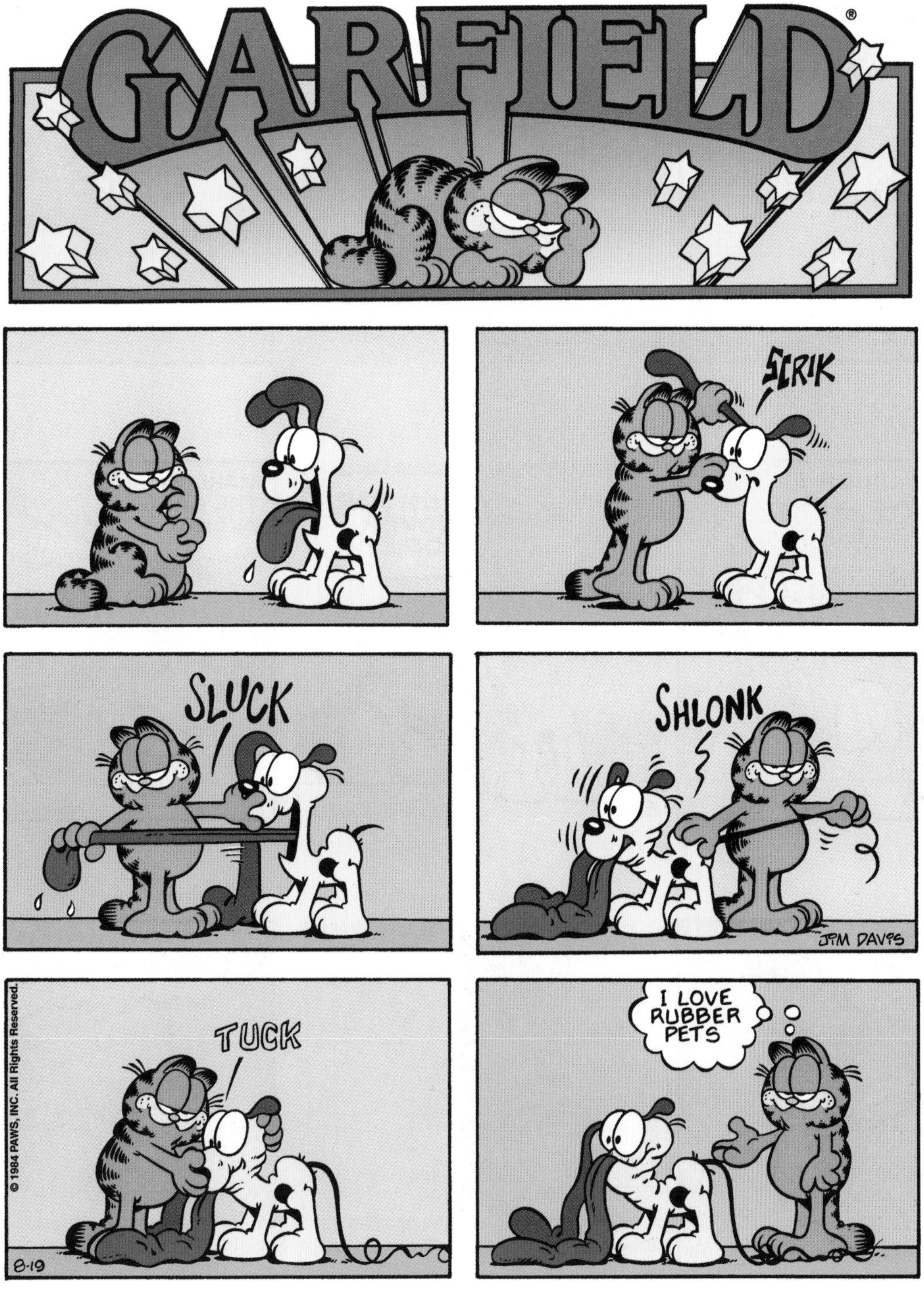
GARFIELD®
SCRIK
SLUCK
SHLONK
JIM DAVIS
© 1984 PAWS, INC. All Rights Reserved.
TUCK
8-19
I LOVE RUBBER PETS

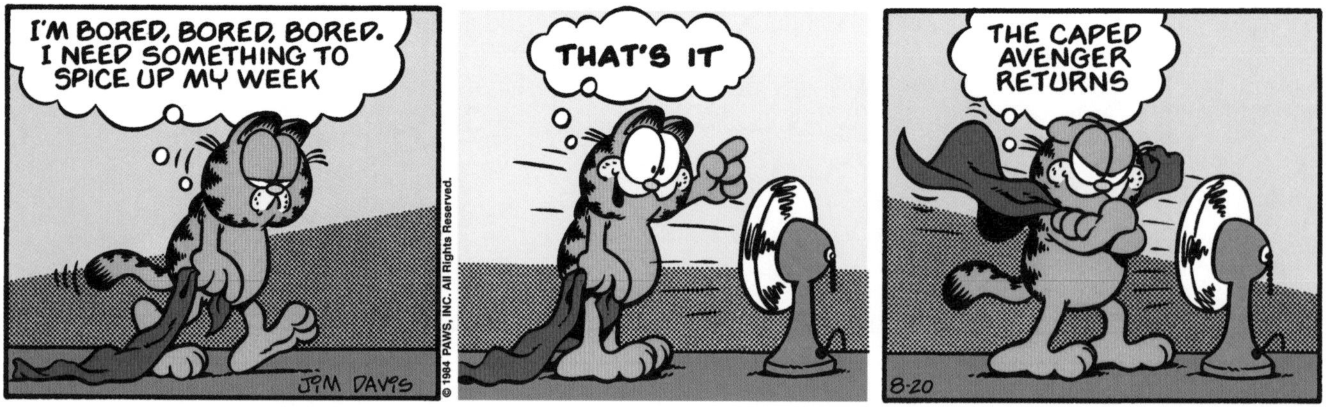
I'M BORED, BORED, BORED. I NEED SOMETHING TO SPICE UP MY WEEK
JIM DAVIS
© 1984 PAWS, INC. All Rights Reserved.
THAT'S IT
THE CAPED AVENGER RETURNS
8-20

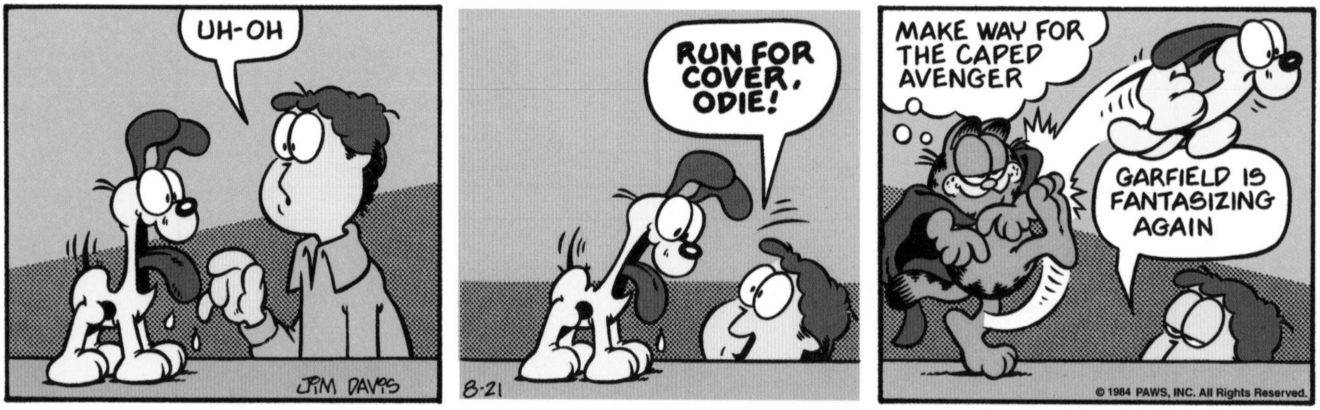
UH-OH
JIM DAVIS
RUN FOR COVER, ODIE!
8-21
MAKE WAY FOR THE CAPED AVENGER
GARFIELD IS FANTASIZING AGAIN
© 1984 PAWS, INC. All Rights Reserved.

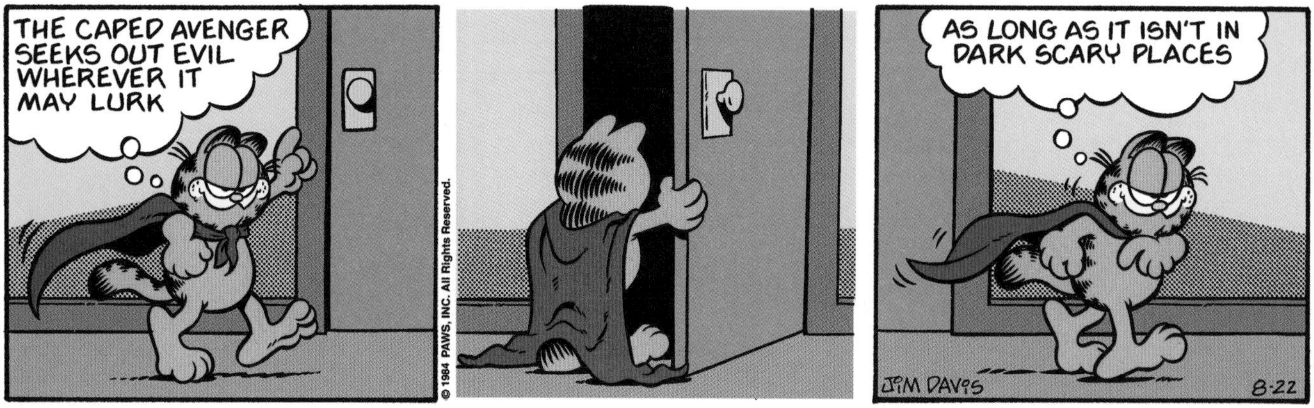
THE CAPED AVENGER SEEKS OUT EVIL WHEREVER IT MAY LURK
© 1984 PAWS, INC. All Rights Reserved.
AS LONG AS IT ISN'T IN DARK SCARY PLACES
JIM DAVIS
8-22

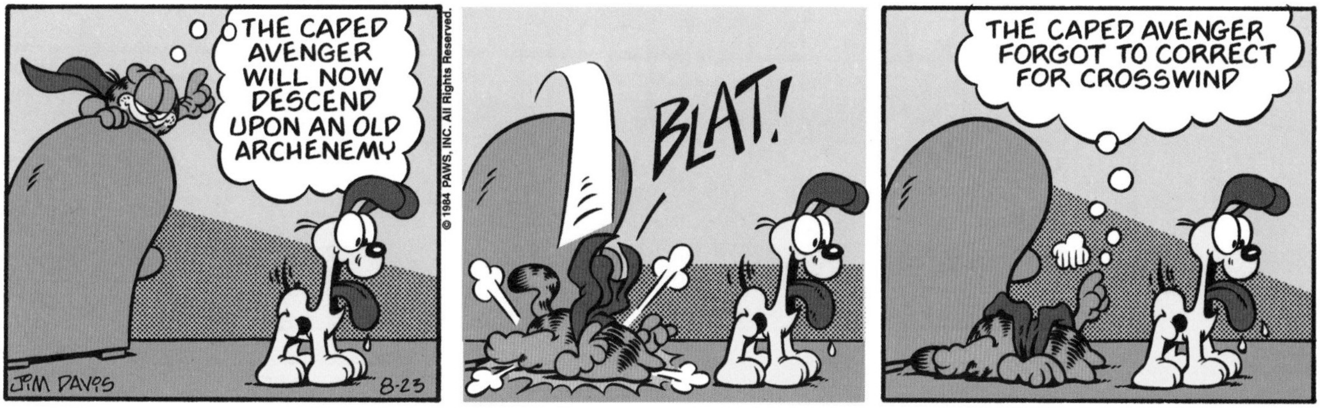
THE CAPED AVENGER WILL NOW DESCEND UPON AN OLD ARCHENEMY
JIM DAVIS
8-23
BLAT!
THE CAPED AVENGER FORGOT TO CORRECT FOR CROSSWIND
© 1984 PAWS, INC. All Rights Reserved.

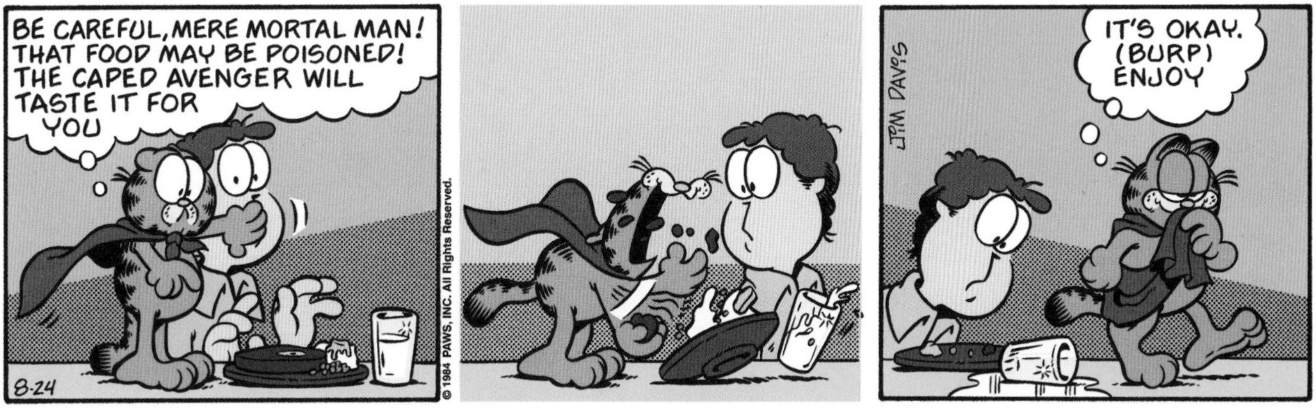
BE CAREFUL, MERE MORTAL MAN! THAT FOOD MAY BE POISONED! THE CAPED AVENGER WILL TASTE IT FOR YOU
8-24
JIM DAVIS
IT'S OKAY. (BURP) ENJOY
© 1984 PAWS, INC. All Rights Reserved.

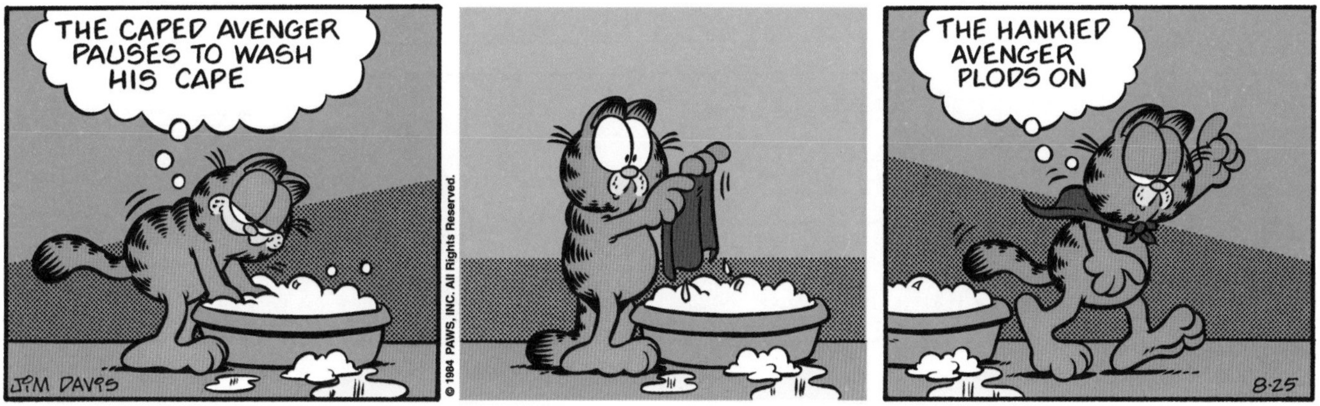
THE CAPED AVENGER PAUSES TO WASH HIS CAPE
JIM DAVIS
THE HANKIED AVENGER PLODS ON
8-25
© 1984 PAWS, INC. All Rights Reserved.

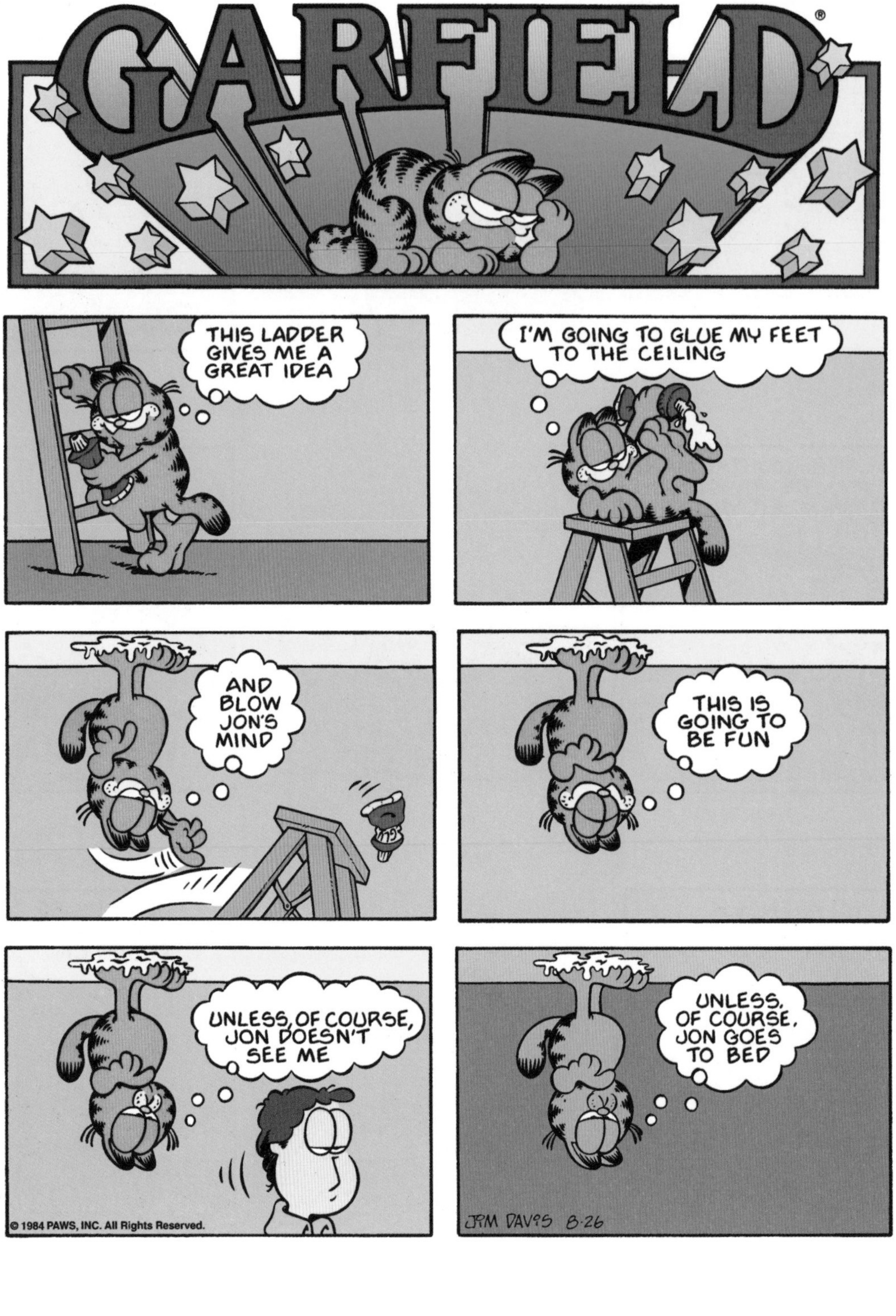
GARFIELD®
THIS LADDER GIVES ME A GREAT IDEA
I'M GOING TO GLUE MY FEET TO THE CEILING
AND BLOW JON'S MIND
THIS IS GOING TO BE FUN
UNLESS, OF COURSE, JON DOESN'T SEE ME
UNLESS, OF COURSE, JON GOES TO BED
JIM DAVIS 8-26

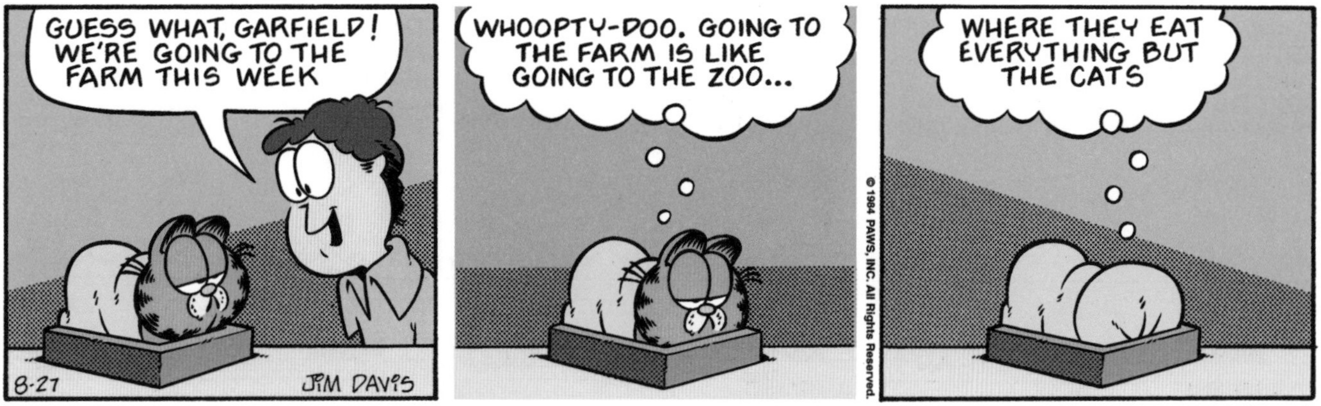
GUESS WHAT, GARFIELD! WE'RE GOING TO THE FARM THIS WEEK
8-27
JIM DAVIS
WHOOPTY-DOO. GOING TO THE FARM IS LIKE GOING TO THE ZOO...
© 1984 PAWS, INC. All Rights Reserved.
WHERE THEY EAT EVERYTHING BUT THE CATS

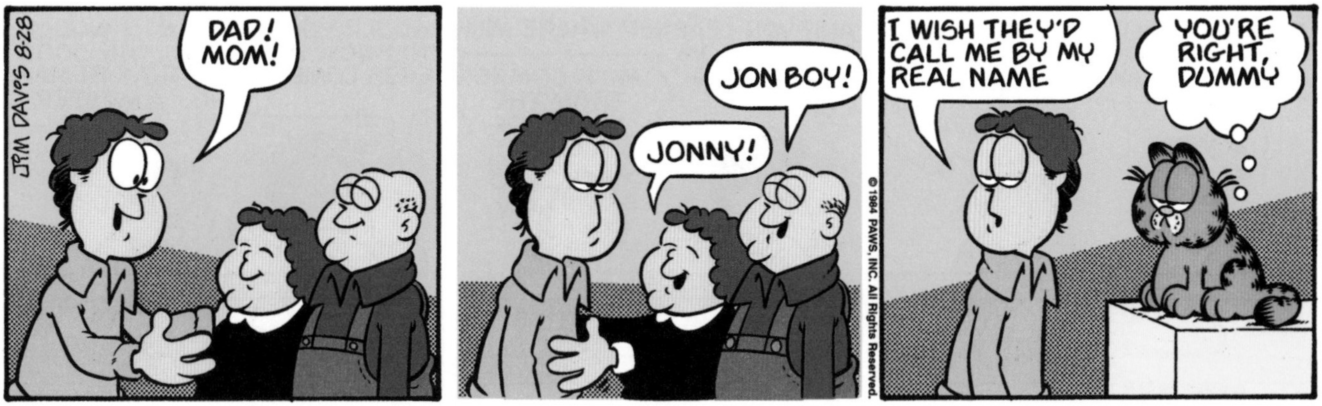
JIM DAVIS 8-28
DAD! MOM!
JON BOY!
JONNY!
© 1984 PAWS, INC. All Rights Reserved.
I WISH THEY'D CALL ME BY MY REAL NAME
YOU'RE RIGHT, DUMMY

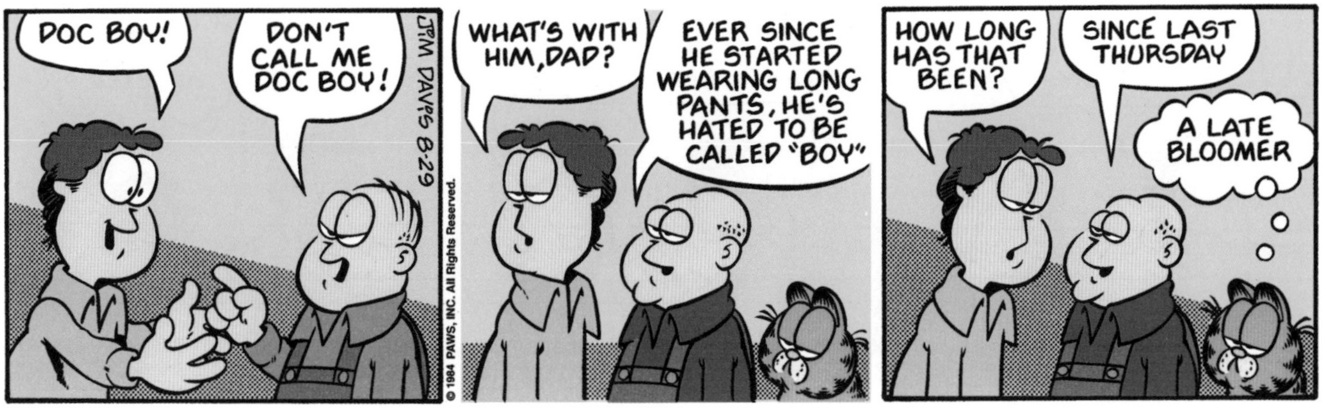
DOC BOY!
DON'T CALL ME DOC BOY!
JIM DAVIS 8-29
© 1984 PAWS, INC. All Rights Reserved.
WHAT'S WITH HIM, DAD?
EVER SINCE HE STARTED WEARING LONG PANTS, HE'S HATED TO BE CALLED "BOY"
HOW LONG HAS THAT BEEN?
SINCE LAST THURSDAY
A LATE BLOOMER

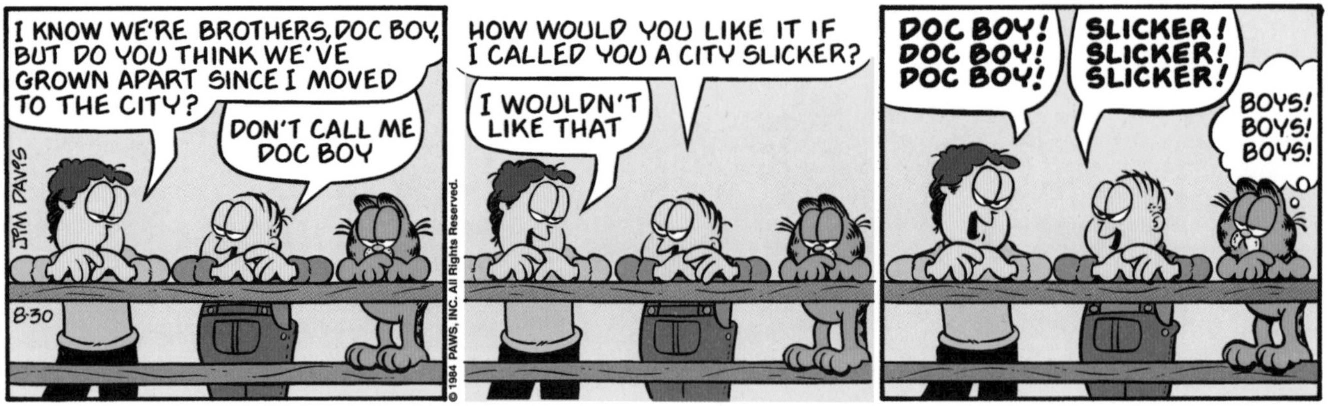
I KNOW WE'RE BROTHERS, DOC BOY, BUT DO YOU THINK WE'VE GROWN APART SINCE I MOVED TO THE CITY?
DON'T CALL ME DOC BOY
JIM DAVIS
8-30
HOW WOULD YOU LIKE IT IF I CALLED YOU A CITY SLICKER?
I WOULDN'T LIKE THAT
© 1984 PAWS, INC. All Rights Reserved.
DOC BOY! DOC BOY! DOC BOY!
SLICKER! SLICKER! SLICKER!
BOYS! BOYS! BOYS!

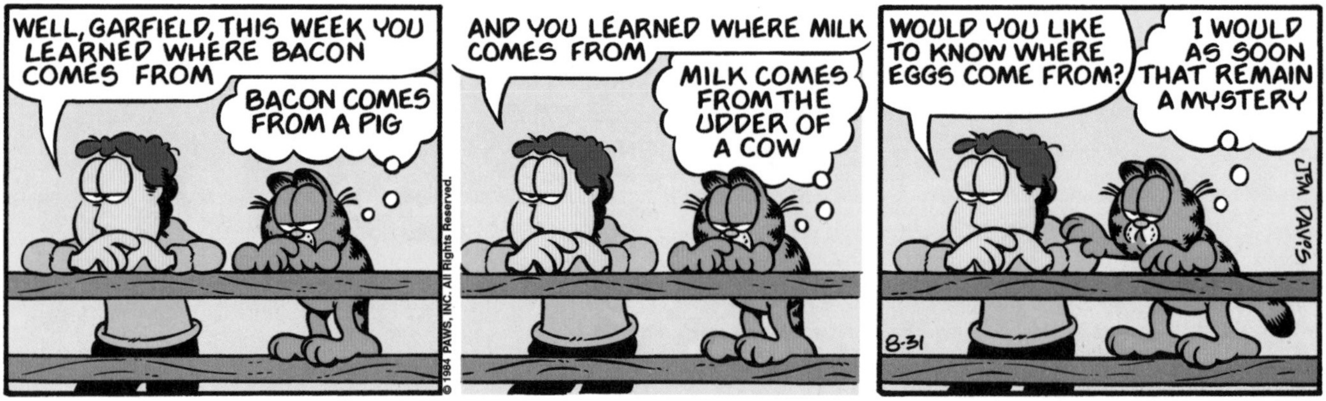
WELL, GARFIELD, THIS WEEK YOU LEARNED WHERE BACON COMES FROM
BACON COMES FROM A PIG
AND YOU LEARNED WHERE MILK COMES FROM
MILK COMES FROM THE UDDER OF A COW
© 1984 PAWS, INC. All Rights Reserved.
WOULD YOU LIKE TO KNOW WHERE EGGS COME FROM?
I WOULD AS SOON THAT REMAIN A MYSTERY
JIM DAVIS
8-31

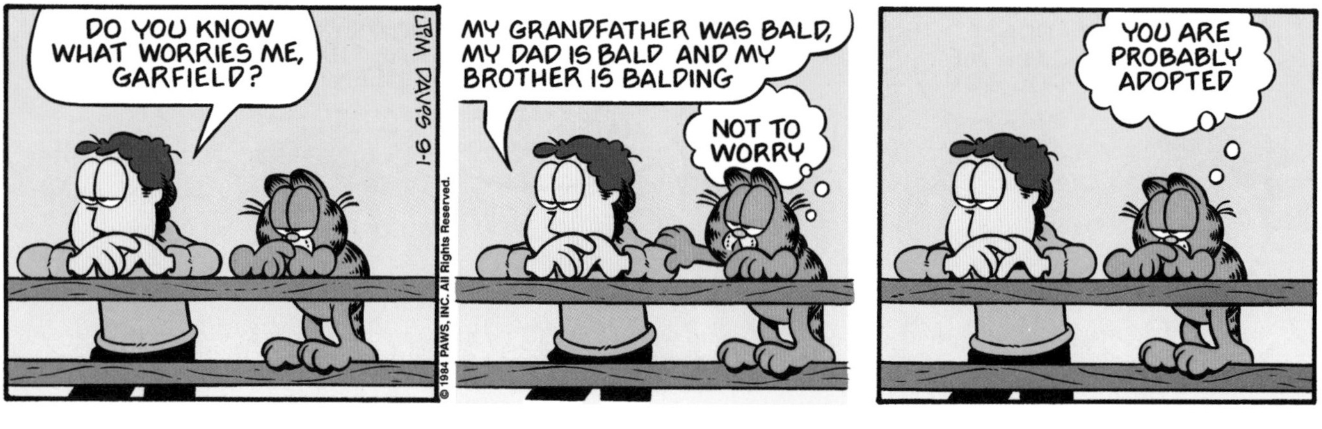
DO YOU KNOW WHAT WORRIES ME, GARFIELD?
JIM DAVIS 9-1
MY GRANDFATHER WAS BALD, MY DAD IS BALD AND MY BROTHER IS BALDING
NOT TO WORRY
© 1984 PAWS, INC. All Rights Reserved.
YOU ARE PROBABLY ADOPTED

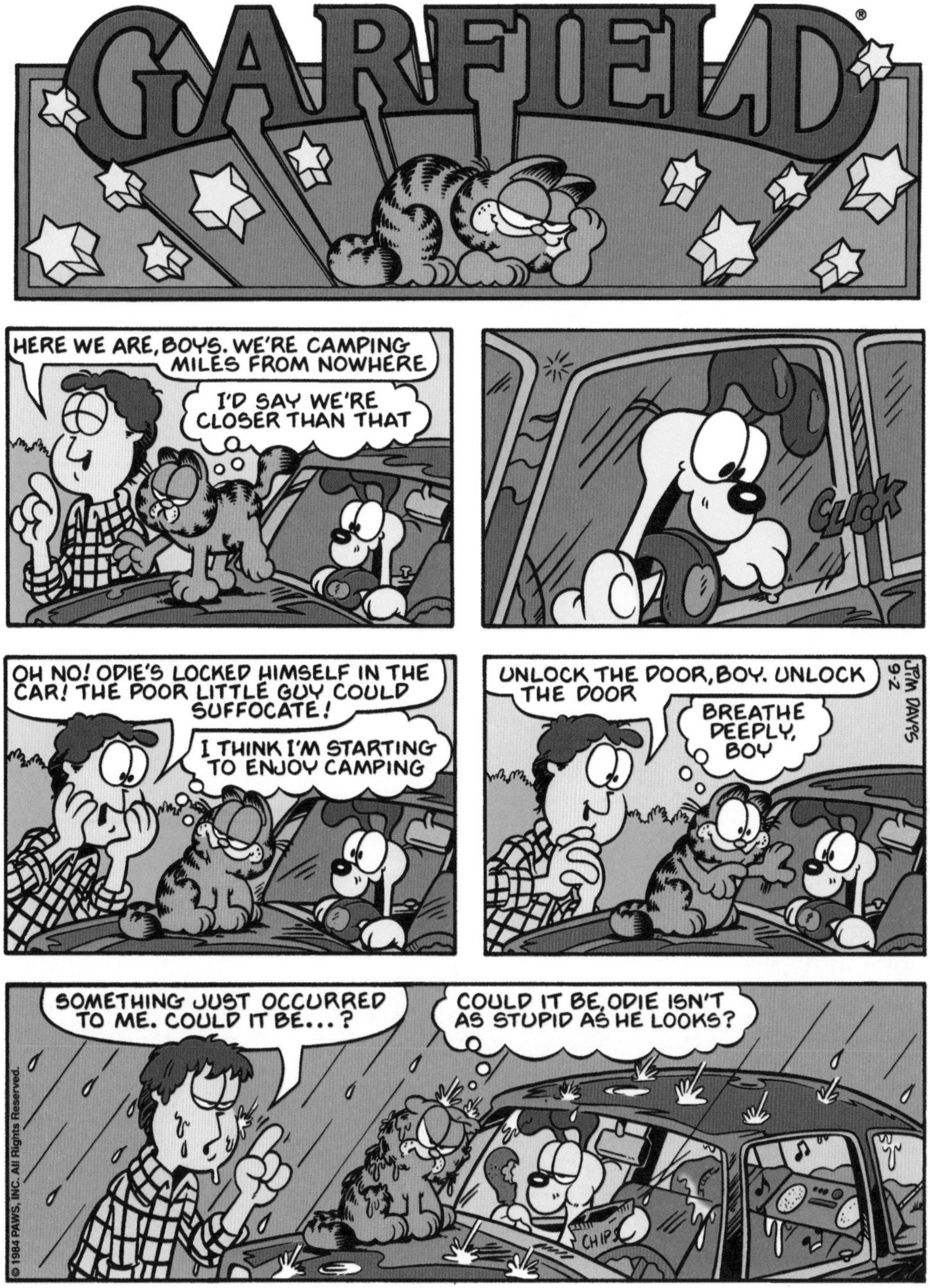
GARFIELD®
HERE WE ARE, BOYS. WE'RE CAMPING MILES FROM NOWHERE
I'D SAY WE'RE CLOSER THAN THAT
CLICK
OH NO! ODIE'S LOCKED HIMSELF IN THE CAR! THE POOR LITTLE GUY COULD SUFFOCATE!
I THINK I'M STARTING TO ENJOY CAMPING
UNLOCK THE DOOR, BOY. UNLOCK THE DOOR
BREATHE DEEPLY, BOY
JIM DAVIS 9-2
SOMETHING JUST OCCURRED TO ME. COULD IT BE...?
COULD IT BE, ODIE ISN'T AS STUPID AS HE LOOKS?
CHIPS
© 1984 PAWS, INC. All Rights Reserved.

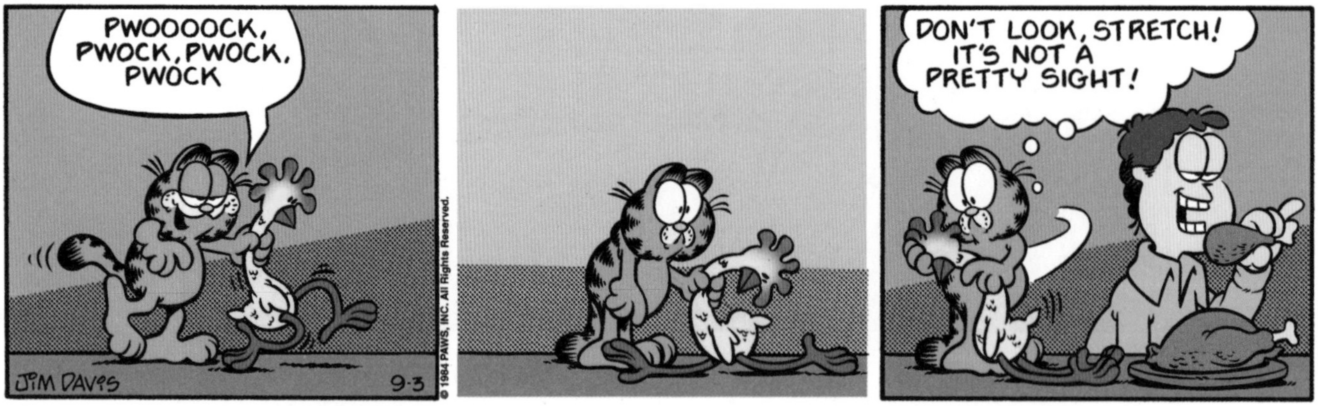
PWOOOOCK, PWOCK, PWOCK, PWOCK
JIM DAVIS 9-3
© 1984 PAWS, INC. All Rights Reserved.
DON'T LOOK, STRETCH! IT'S NOT A PRETTY SIGHT!

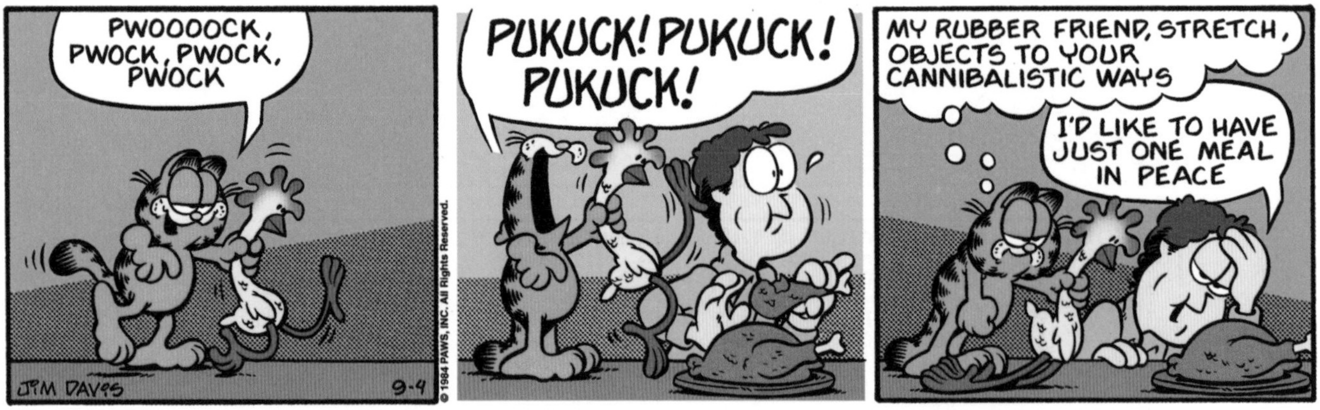
PWOOOOCK, PWOCK, PWOCK, PWOCK
JIM DAVIS 9-4
© 1984 PAWS, INC. All Rights Reserved.
PUKUCK! PUKUCK! PUKUCK!
MY RUBBER FRIEND, STRETCH, OBJECTS TO YOUR CANNIBALISTIC WAYS
I'D LIKE TO HAVE JUST ONE MEAL IN PEACE

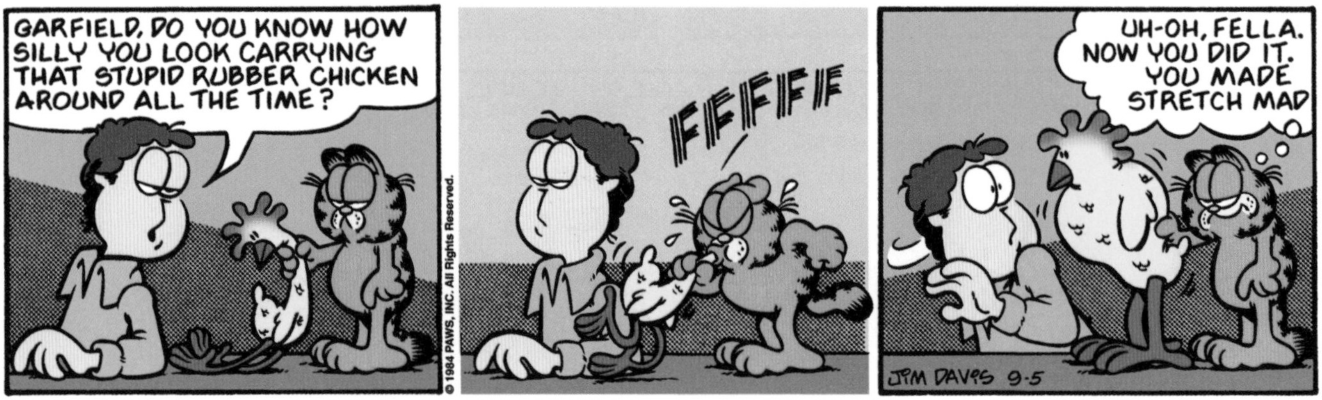
GARFIELD, DO YOU KNOW HOW SILLY YOU LOOK CARRYING THAT STUPID RUBBER CHICKEN AROUND ALL THE TIME?
© 1984 PAWS, INC. All Rights Reserved.
FFFFFF
UH-OH, FELLA. NOW YOU DID IT. YOU MADE STRETCH MAD
JIM DAVIS 9-5

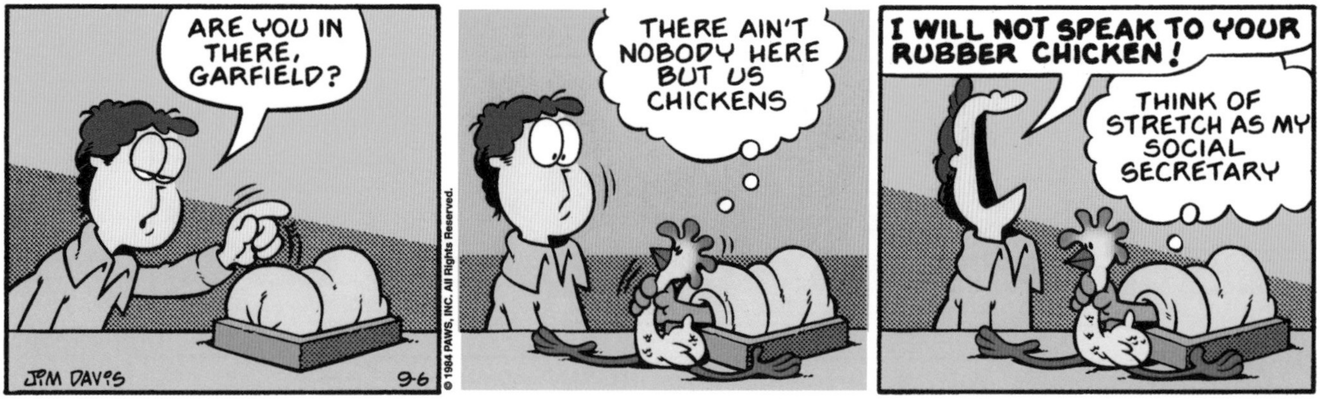
ARE YOU IN THERE, GARFIELD?
JIM DAVIS
9-6
© 1984 PAWS, INC. All Rights Reserved.
THERE AIN'T NOBODY HERE BUT US CHICKENS
I WILL NOT SPEAK TO YOUR RUBBER CHICKEN!
THINK OF STRETCH AS MY SOCIAL SECRETARY

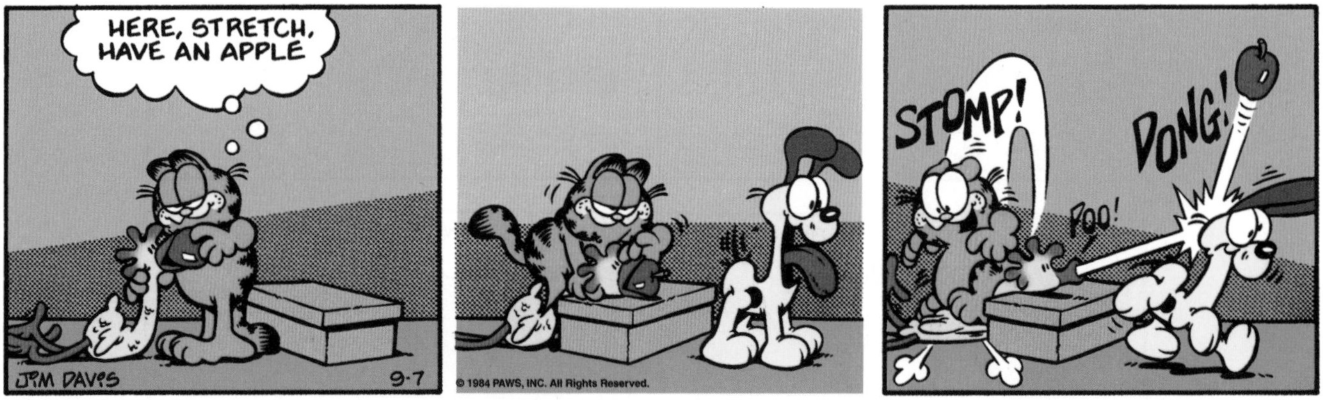
HERE, STRETCH, HAVE AN APPLE
JIM DAVIS
9-7
© 1984 PAWS, INC. All Rights Reserved.
STOMP!
POO!
DONG!

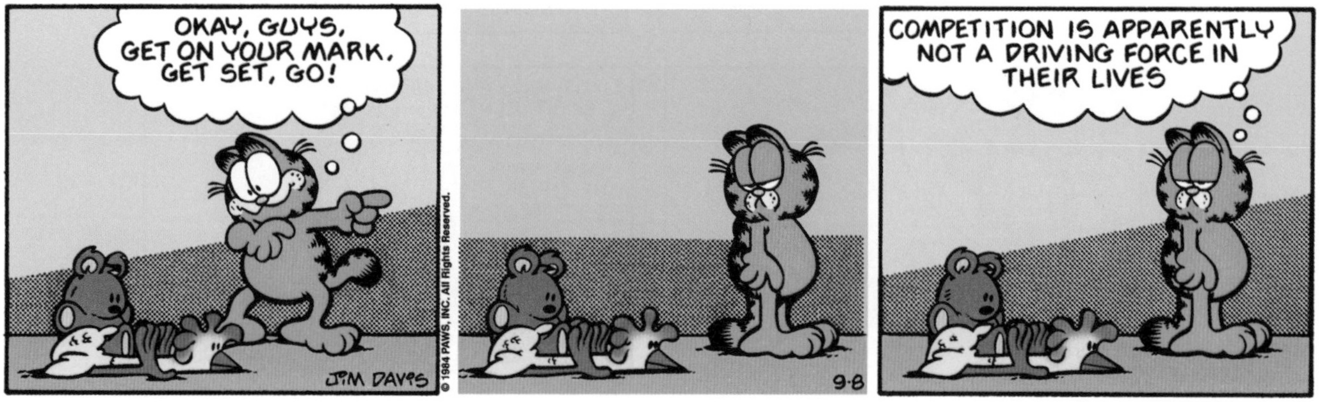
OKAY, GUYS, GET ON YOUR MARK, GET SET, GO!
JIM DAVIS
© 1984 PAWS, INC. All Rights Reserved.
9-8
COMPETITION IS APPARENTLY NOT A DRIVING FORCE IN THEIR LIVES

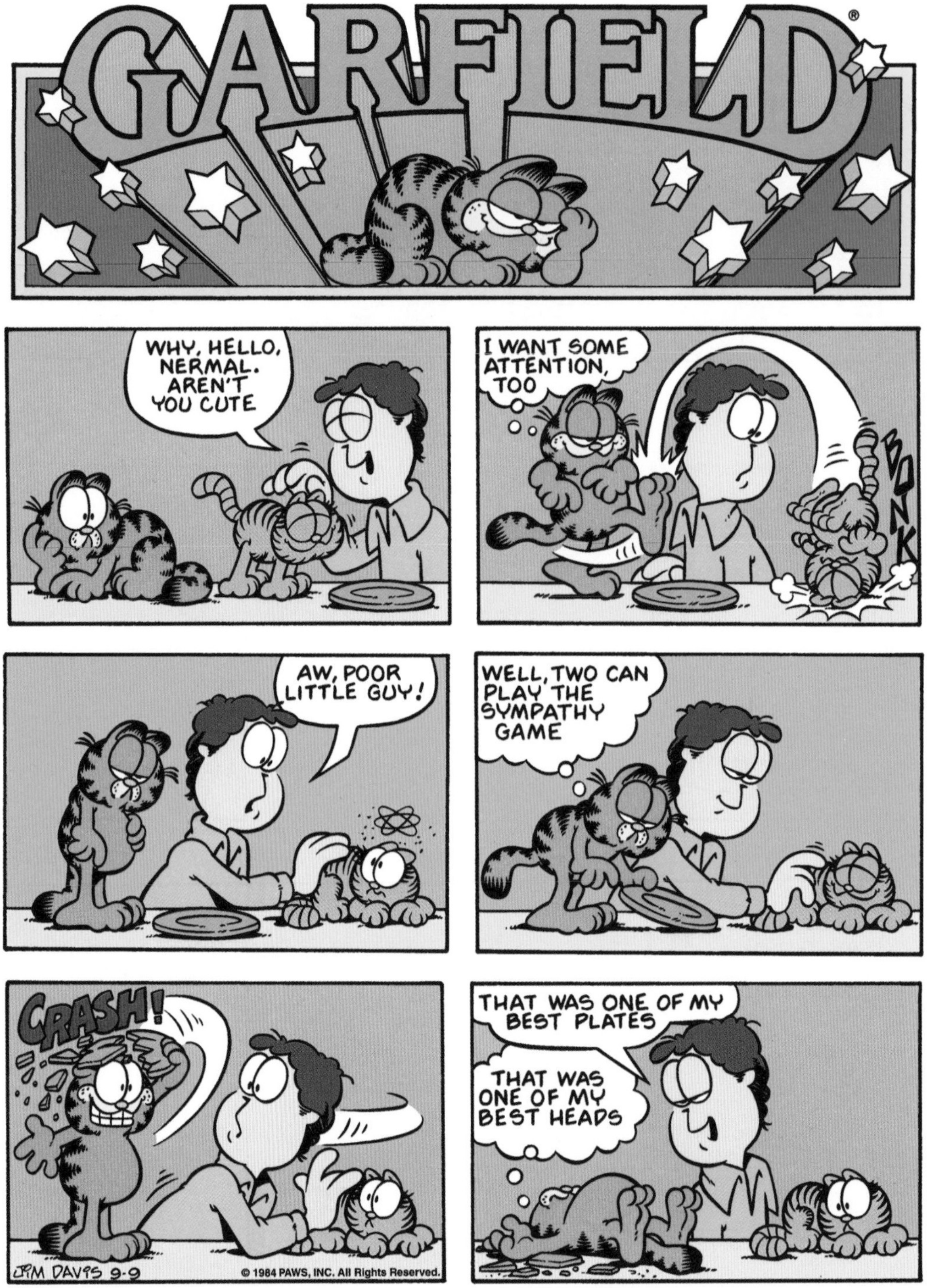
GARFIELD
WHY, HELLO, NERMAL. AREN'T YOU CUTE
I WANT SOME ATTENTION, TOO
BONK
AW, POOR LITTLE GUY!
WELL, TWO CAN PLAY THE SYMPATHY GAME
CRASH!
THAT WAS ONE OF MY BEST PLATES
THAT WAS ONE OF MY BEST HEADS
JIM DAVIS 9-9
© 1984 PAWS, INC. All Rights Reserved.

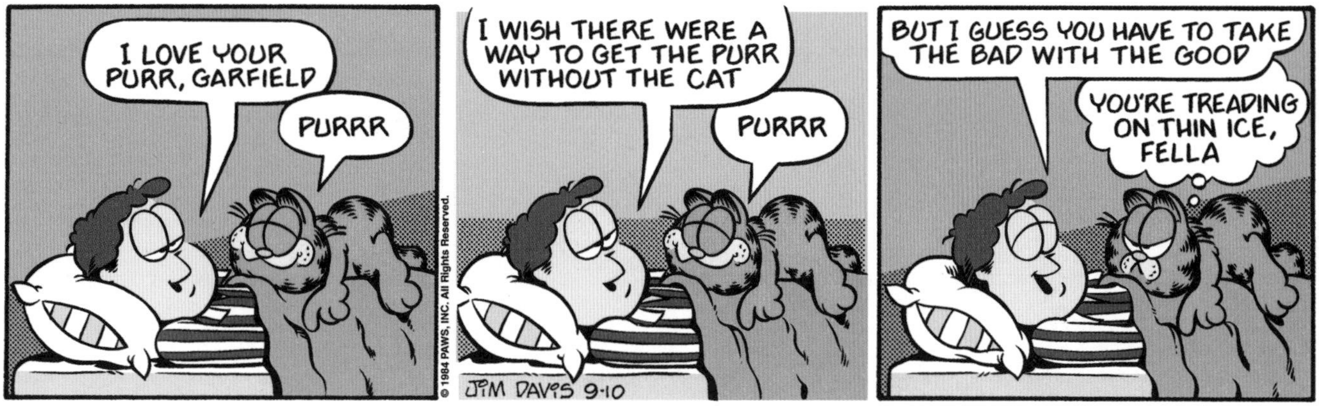
I LOVE YOUR PURR, GARFIELD
PURRR
I WISH THERE WERE A WAY TO GET THE PURR WITHOUT THE CAT
PURRR
BUT I GUESS YOU HAVE TO TAKE THE BAD WITH THE GOOD
YOU'RE TREADING ON THIN ICE, FELLA
JIM DAVIS 9-10
© 1984 PAWS, INC. All Rights Reserved.

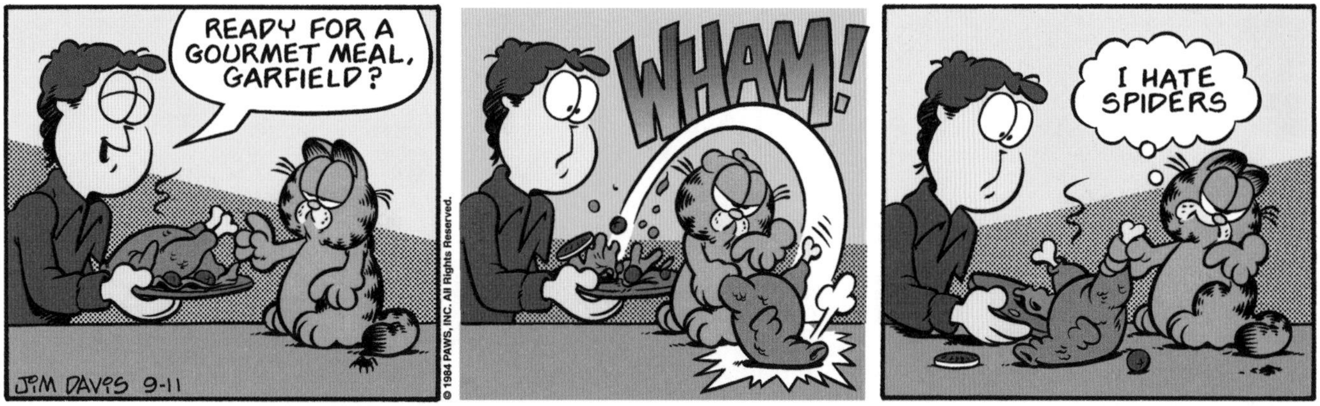
READY FOR A GOURMET MEAL, GARFIELD?
JIM DAVIS 9-11
WHAM!
I HATE SPIDERS
© 1984 PAWS, INC. All Rights Reserved.

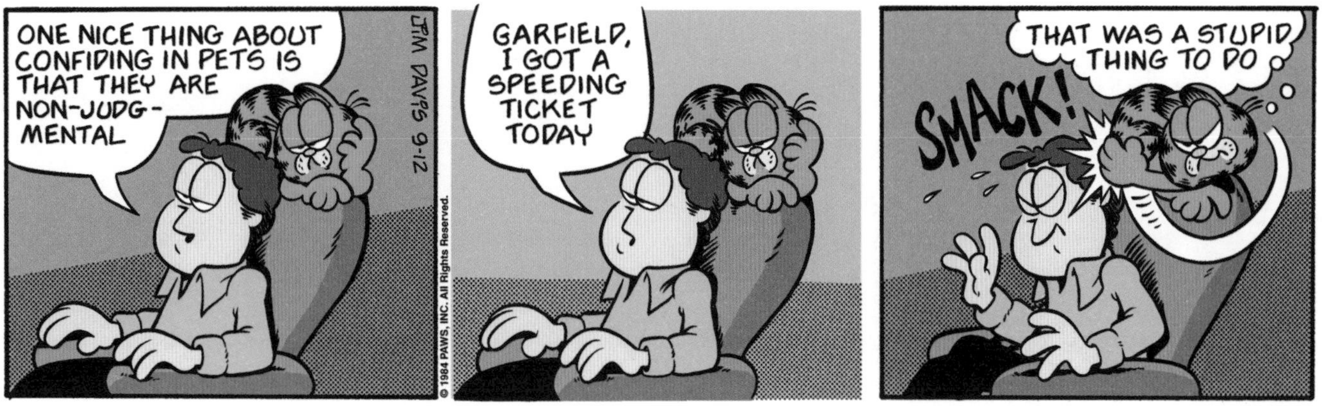
ONE NICE THING ABOUT CONFIDING IN PETS IS THAT THEY ARE NON-JUDG-MENTAL
JIM DAVIS 9-12
GARFIELD, I GOT A SPEEDING TICKET TODAY
SMACK!
THAT WAS A STUPID THING TO DO
© 1984 PAWS, INC. All Rights Reserved.

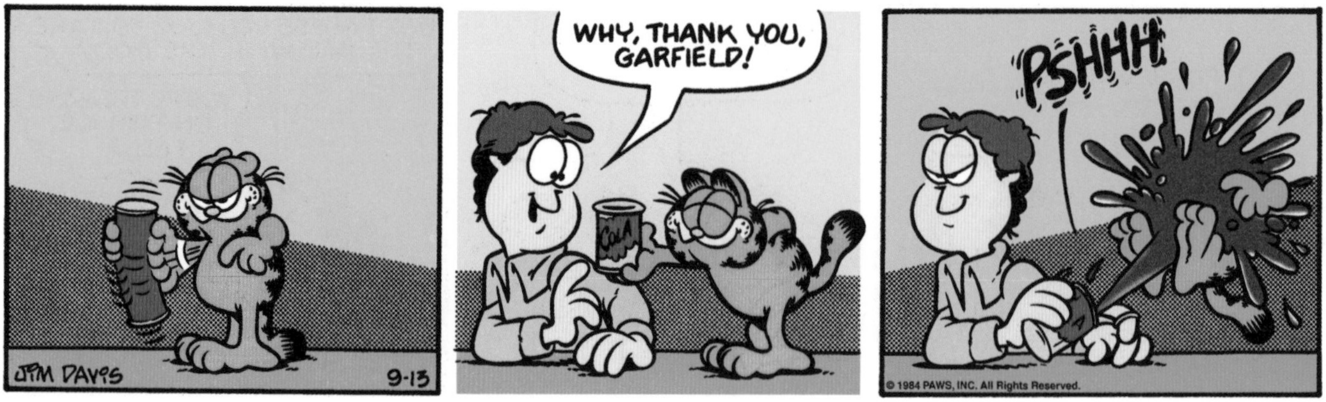
JIM DAVIS
9-13
WHY, THANK YOU, GARFIELD!
COLA
PSHHH
© 1984 PAWS, INC. All Rights Reserved.

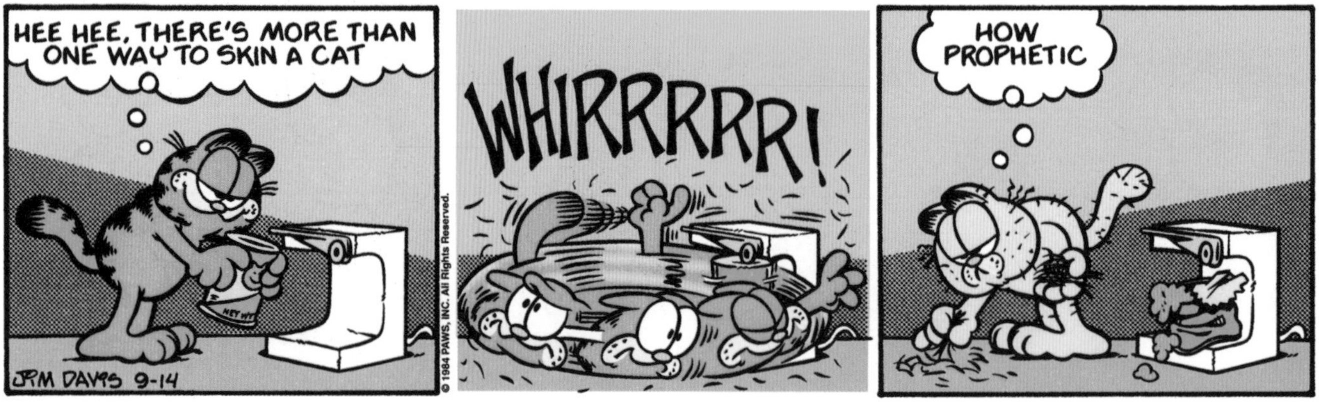
HEE HEE, THERE'S MORE THAN ONE WAY TO SKIN A CAT
JIM DAVIS 9-14
© 1984 PAWS, INC. All Rights Reserved.
WHIRRRRRR!
HOW PROPHETIC

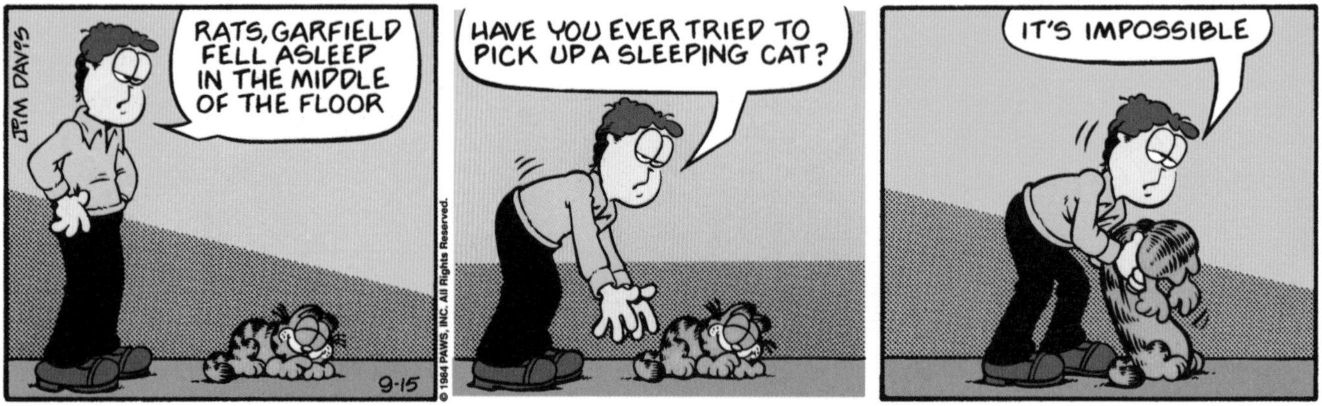
JIM DAVIS
RATS, GARFIELD FELL ASLEEP IN THE MIDDLE OF THE FLOOR
9-15
© 1984 PAWS, INC. All Rights Reserved.
HAVE YOU EVER TRIED TO PICK UP A SLEEPING CAT?
IT'S IMPOSSIBLE

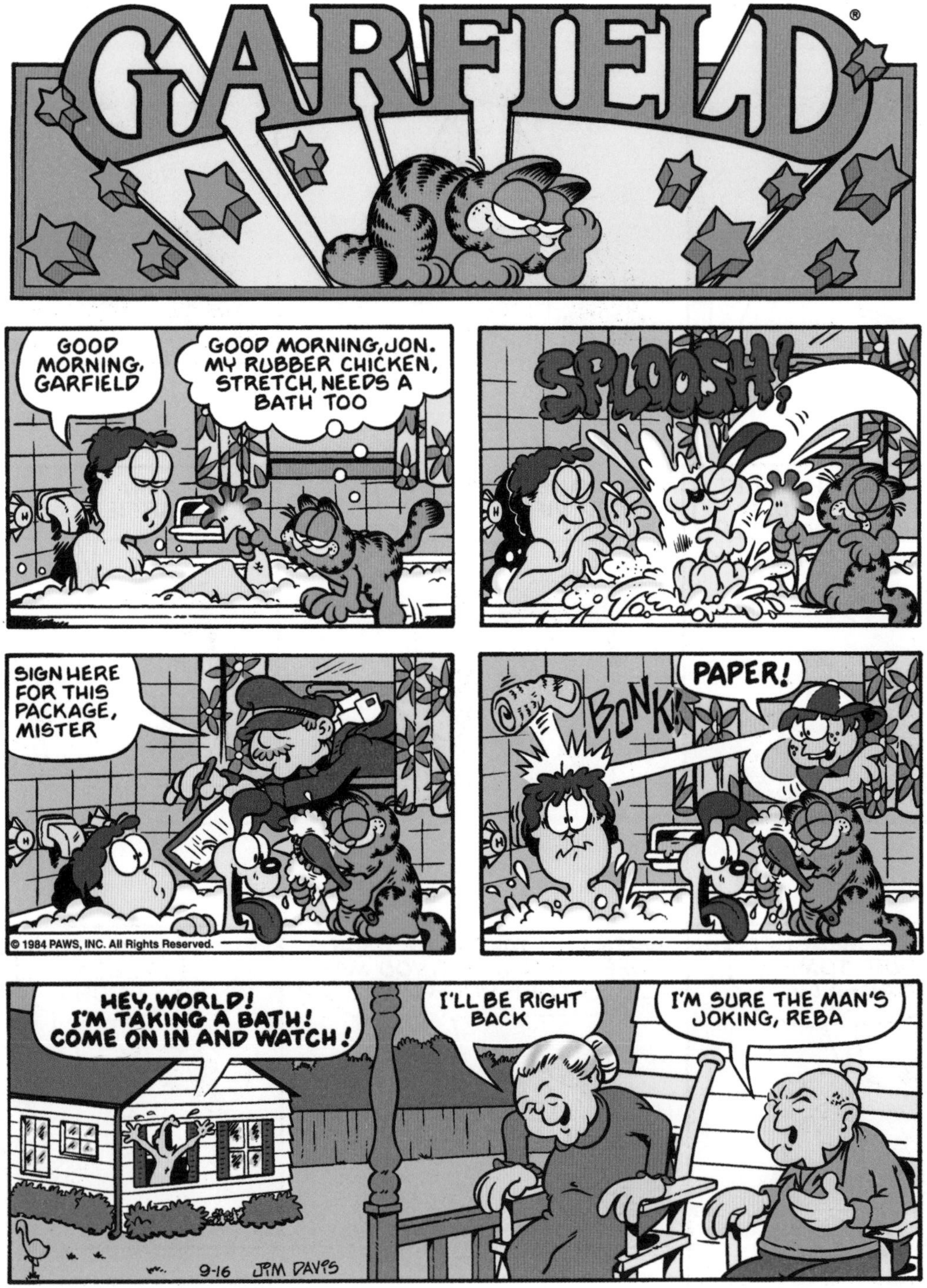

GARFIELD®
GOOD MORNING, GARFIELD
GOOD MORNING, JON. MY RUBBER CHICKEN, STRETCH, NEEDS A BATH TOO
SPLOOSH!
SIGN HERE FOR THIS PACKAGE, MISTER
© 1984 PAWS, INC. All Rights Reserved.
BONK!
PAPER!
HEY, WORLD! I'M TAKING A BATH! COME ON IN AND WATCH!
I'LL BE RIGHT BACK
I'M SURE THE MAN'S JOKING, REBA
9-16 JIM DAVIS

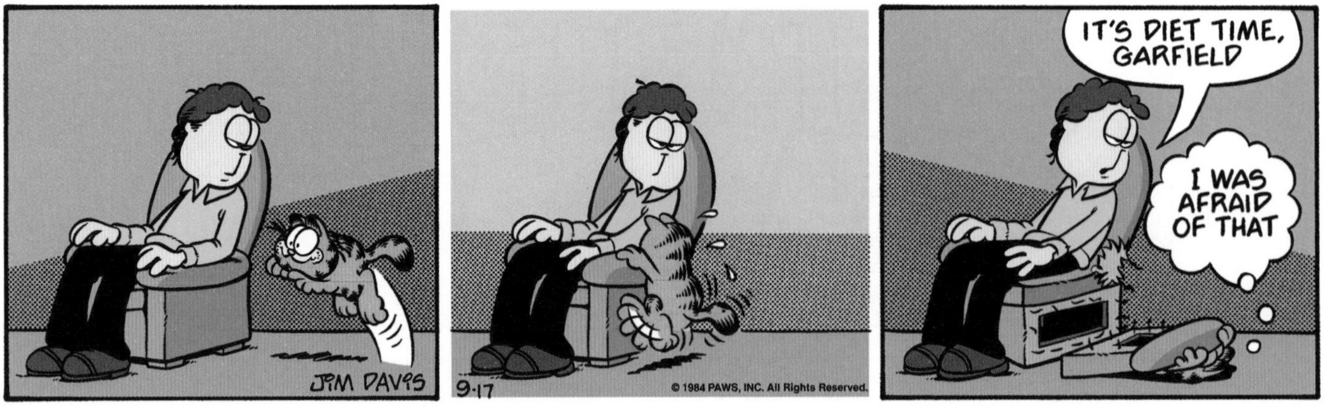
JIM DAVIS
9-17
© 1984 PAWS, INC. All Rights Reserved.
IT'S DIET TIME, GARFIELD
I WAS AFRAID OF THAT

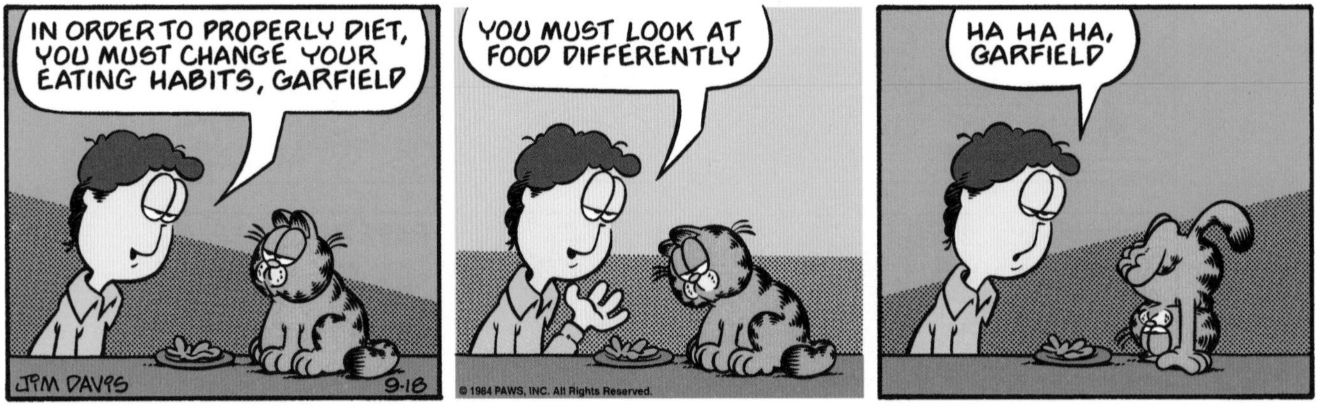
IN ORDER TO PROPERLY DIET, YOU MUST CHANGE YOUR EATING HABITS, GARFIELD
JIM DAVIS
9-18
YOU MUST LOOK AT FOOD DIFFERENTLY
© 1984 PAWS, INC. All Rights Reserved.
HA HA HA, GARFIELD

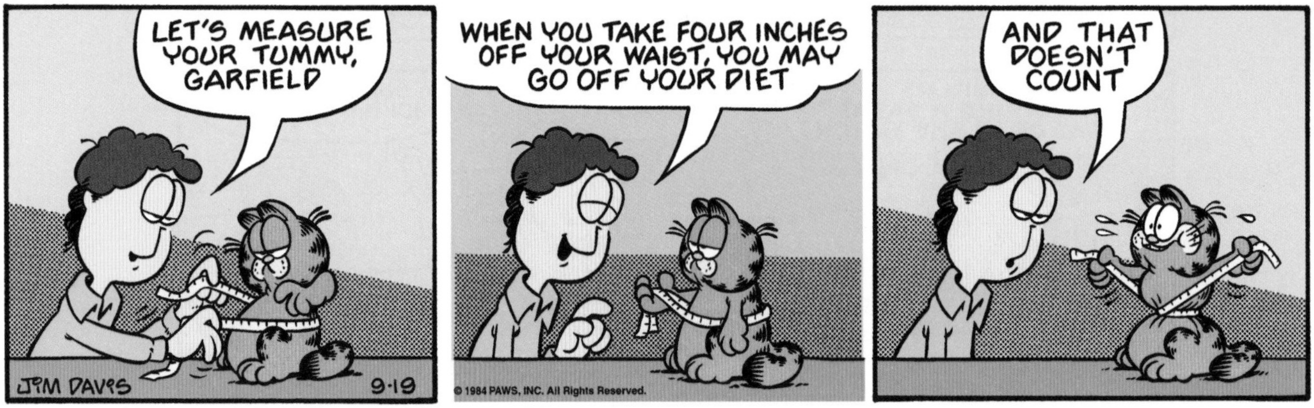
LET'S MEASURE YOUR TUMMY, GARFIELD
JIM DAVIS
9-19
WHEN YOU TAKE FOUR INCHES OFF YOUR WAIST, YOU MAY GO OFF YOUR DIET
© 1984 PAWS, INC. All Rights Reserved.
AND THAT DOESN'T COUNT

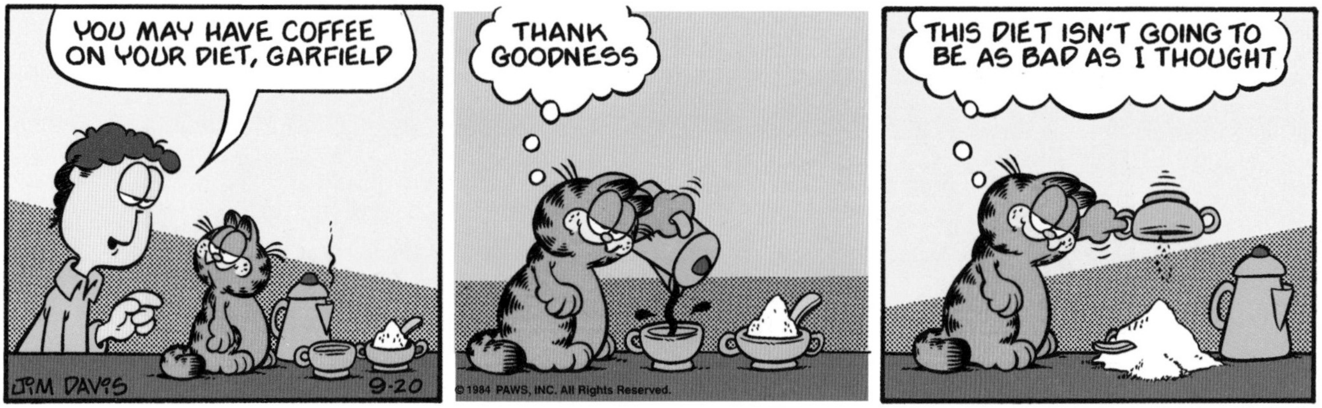
YOU MAY HAVE COFFEE ON YOUR DIET, GARFIELD
JIM DAVIS
9-20
THANK GOODNESS
© 1984 PAWS, INC. All Rights Reserved.
THIS DIET ISN'T GOING TO BE AS BAD AS I THOUGHT

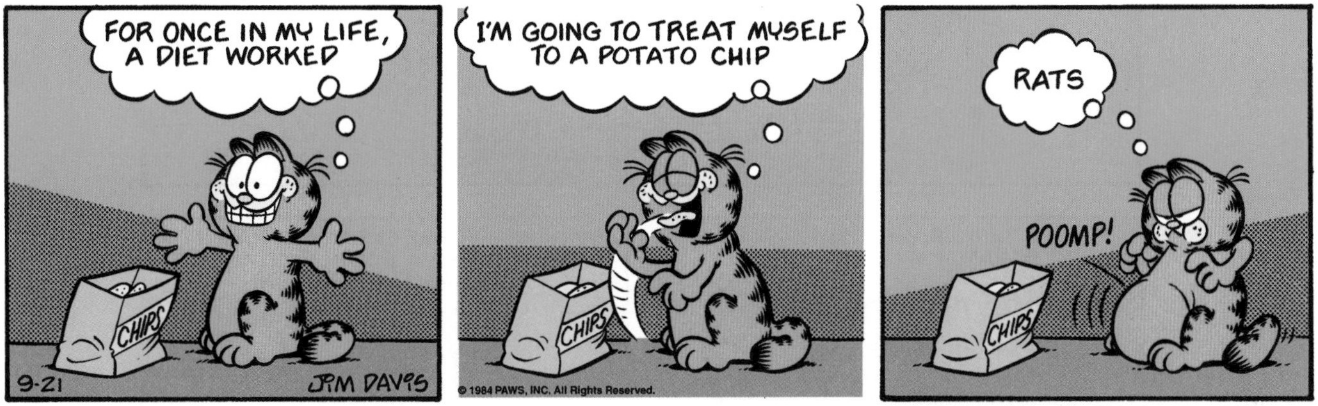
FOR ONCE IN MY LIFE, A DIET WORKED
CHIPS
9-21
JIM DAVIS
I'M GOING TO TREAT MYSELF TO A POTATO CHIP
CHIPS
© 1984 PAWS, INC. All Rights Reserved.
RATS
POOMP!
CHIPS

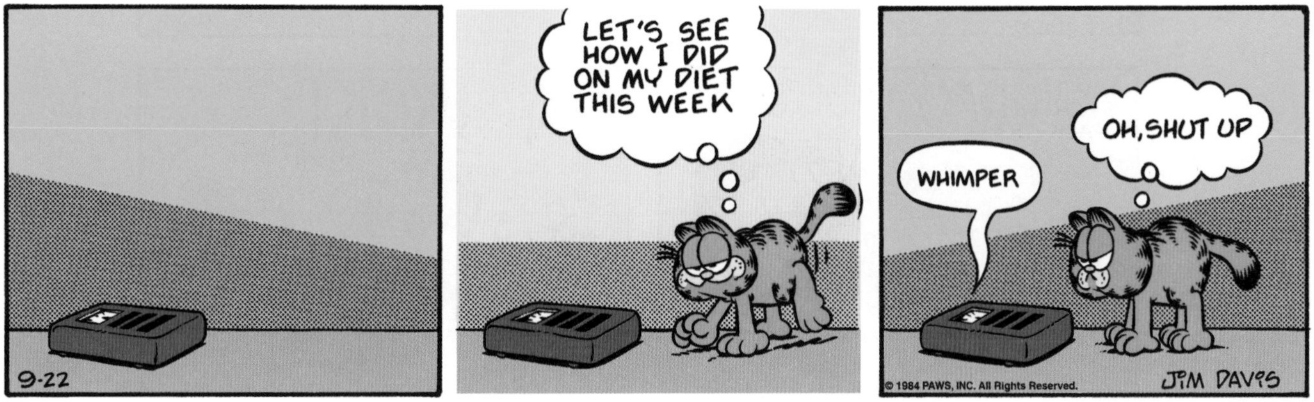
9-22
LET'S SEE HOW I DID ON MY DIET THIS WEEK
WHIMPER
OH, SHUT UP
© 1984 PAWS, INC. All Rights Reserved.
JIM DAVIS

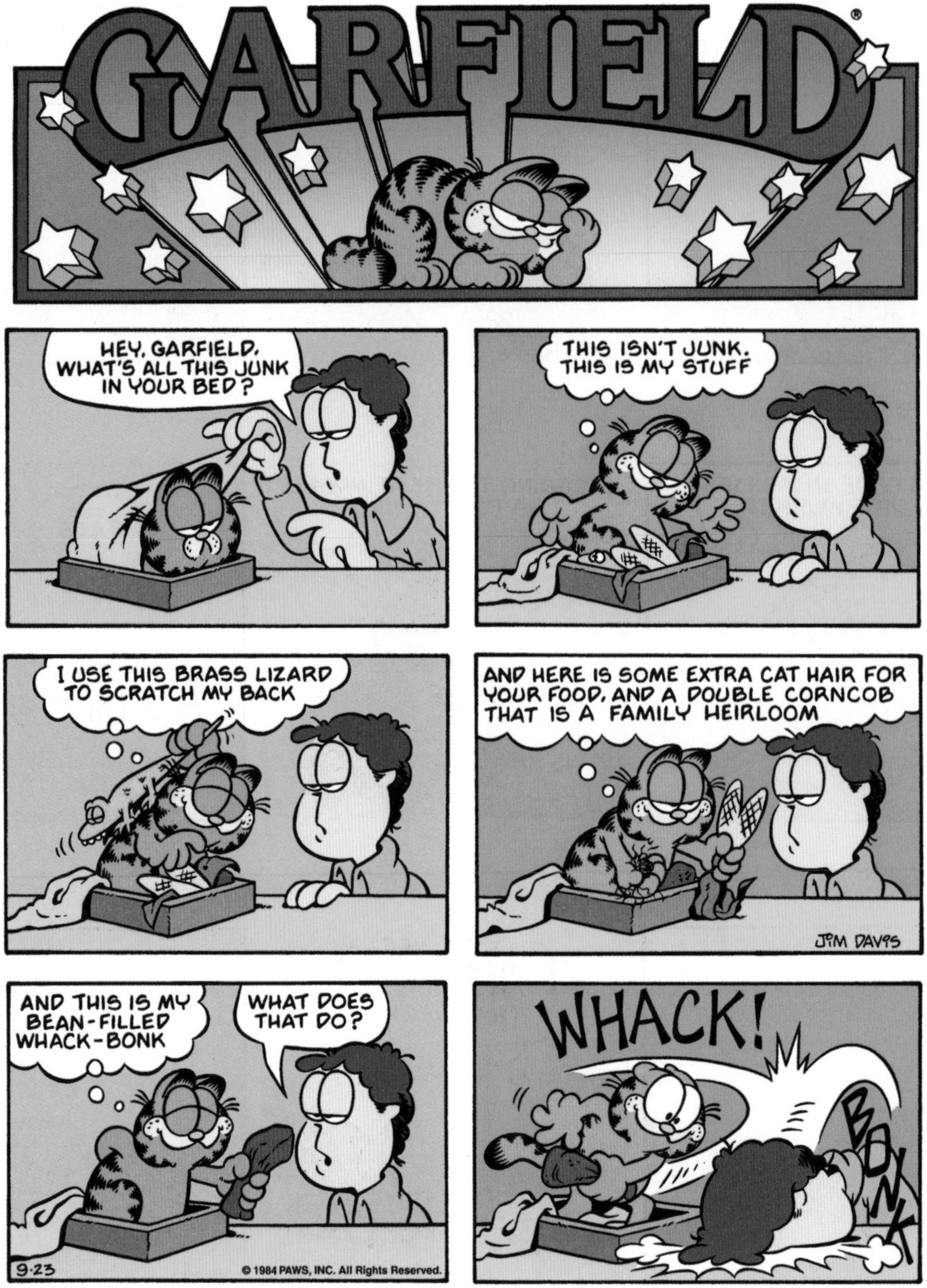
GARFIELD®
HEY, GARFIELD, WHAT'S ALL THIS JUNK IN YOUR BED?
THIS ISN'T JUNK. THIS IS MY STUFF
I USE THIS BRASS LIZARD TO SCRATCH MY BACK
AND HERE IS SOME EXTRA CAT HAIR FOR YOUR FOOD, AND A DOUBLE CORNCOB THAT IS A FAMILY HEIRLOOM
JIM DAVIS
AND THIS IS MY BEAN-FILLED WHACK-BONK
WHAT DOES THAT DO?
9·23
© 1984 PAWS, INC. All Rights Reserved.
WHACK!
BONK

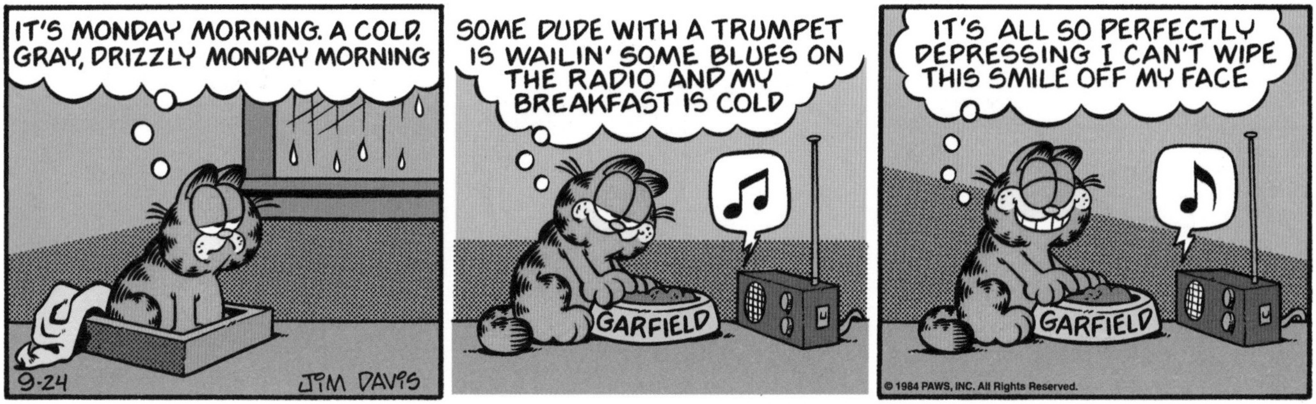
IT'S MONDAY MORNING. A COLD, GRAY, DRIZZLY MONDAY MORNING
9-24
JIM DAVIS
SOME DUDE WITH A TRUMPET IS WAILIN' SOME BLUES ON THE RADIO AND MY BREAKFAST IS COLD
GARFIELD
IT'S ALL SO PERFECTLY DEPRESSING I CAN'T WIPE THIS SMILE OFF MY FACE
GARFIELD
© 1984 PAWS, INC. All Rights Reserved.

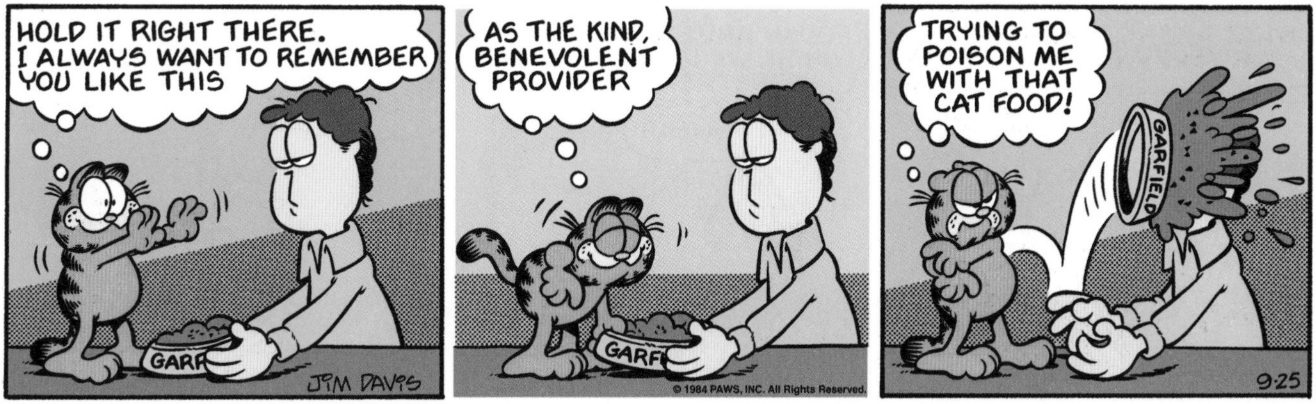
HOLD IT RIGHT THERE. I ALWAYS WANT TO REMEMBER YOU LIKE THIS
GARF
JIM DAVIS
AS THE KIND, BENEVOLENT PROVIDER
GARF
© 1984 PAWS, INC. All Rights Reserved.
TRYING TO POISON ME WITH THAT CAT FOOD!
GARFIELD
9-25

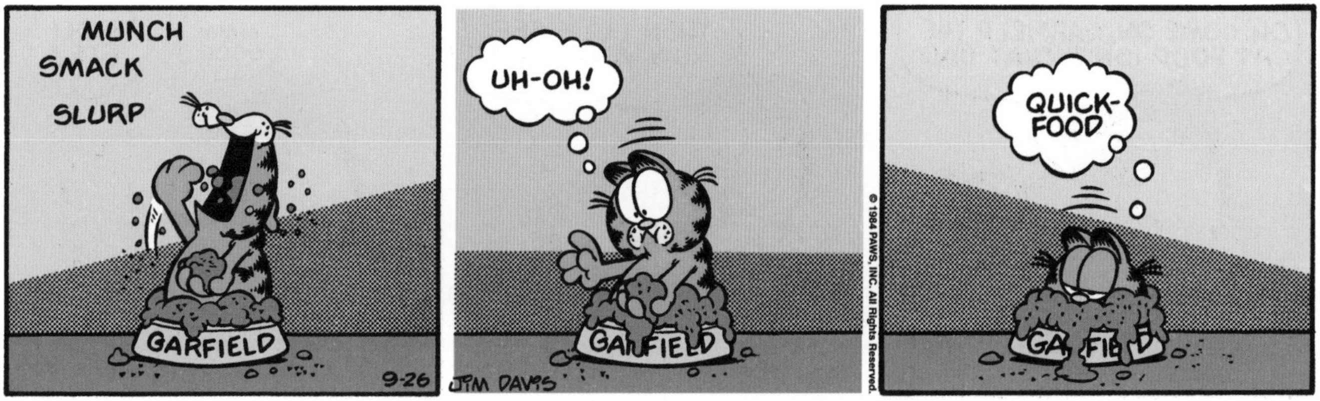
MUNCH
SMACK
SLURP
GARFIELD
9-26
UH-OH!
JIM DAVIS
© 1984 PAWS, INC. All Rights Reserved.
QUICK-FOOD

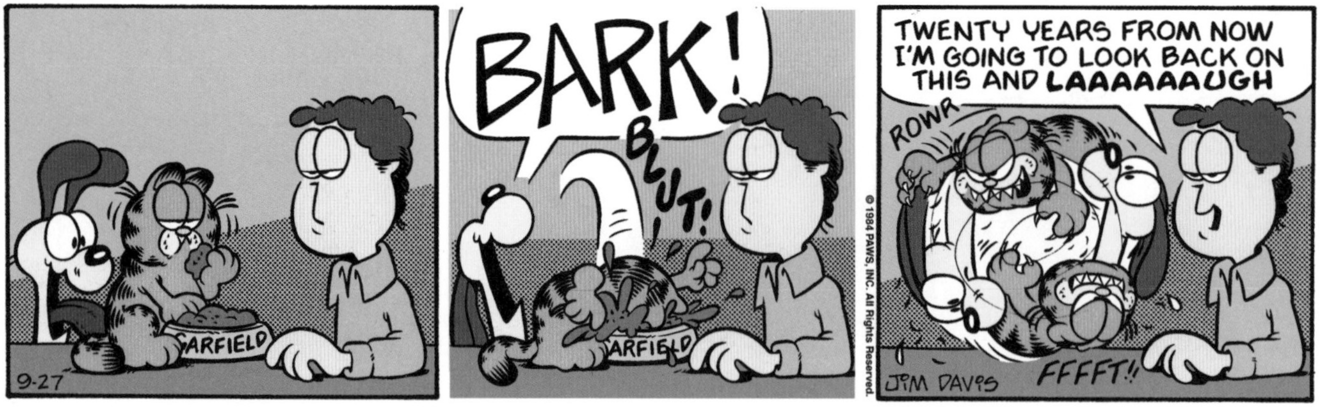
9-27
BARK!
BLUT!
© 1984 PAWS, INC. All Rights Reserved.
TWENTY YEARS FROM NOW I'M GOING TO LOOK BACK ON THIS AND LAAAAAAUGH
ROWR
FFFFT!!
JIM DAVIS

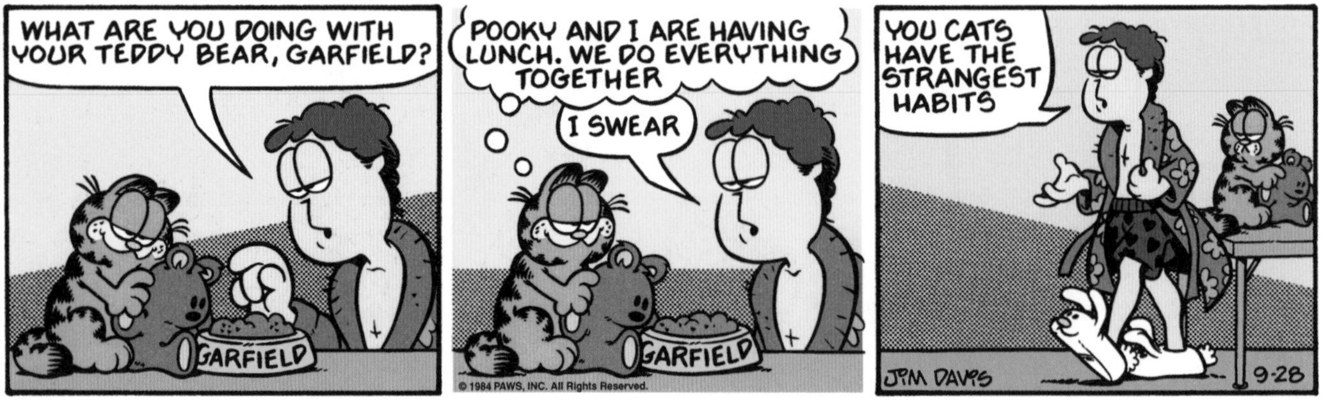
WHAT ARE YOU DOING WITH YOUR TEDDY BEAR, GARFIELD?
POOKY AND I ARE HAVING LUNCH. WE DO EVERYTHING TOGETHER
I SWEAR
© 1984 PAWS, INC. All Rights Reserved.
YOU CATS HAVE THE STRANGEST HABITS
JIM DAVIS
9-28

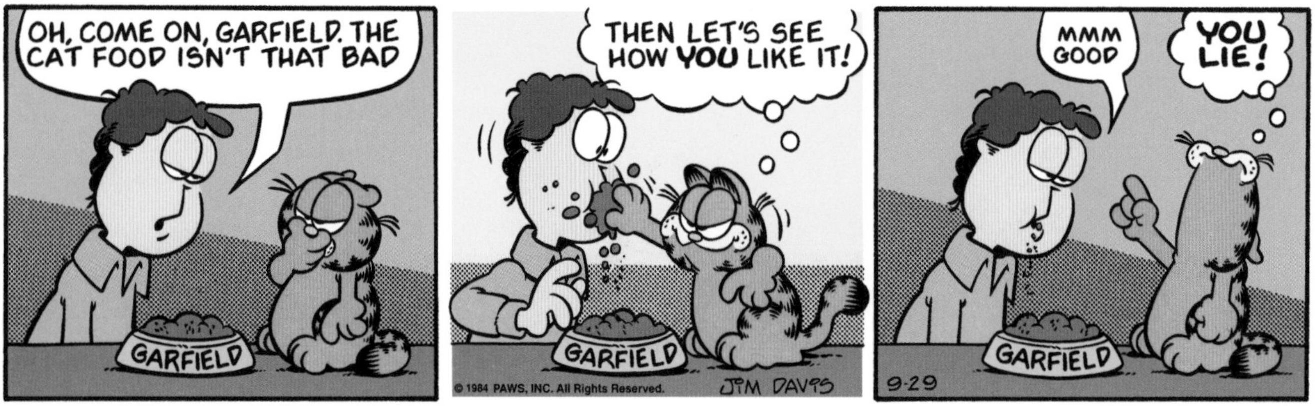
OH, COME ON, GARFIELD. THE CAT FOOD ISN'T THAT BAD
THEN LET'S SEE HOW **YOU** LIKE IT!
© 1984 PAWS, INC. All Rights Reserved.
JIM DAVIS
MMM GOOD
YOU LIE!
9-29

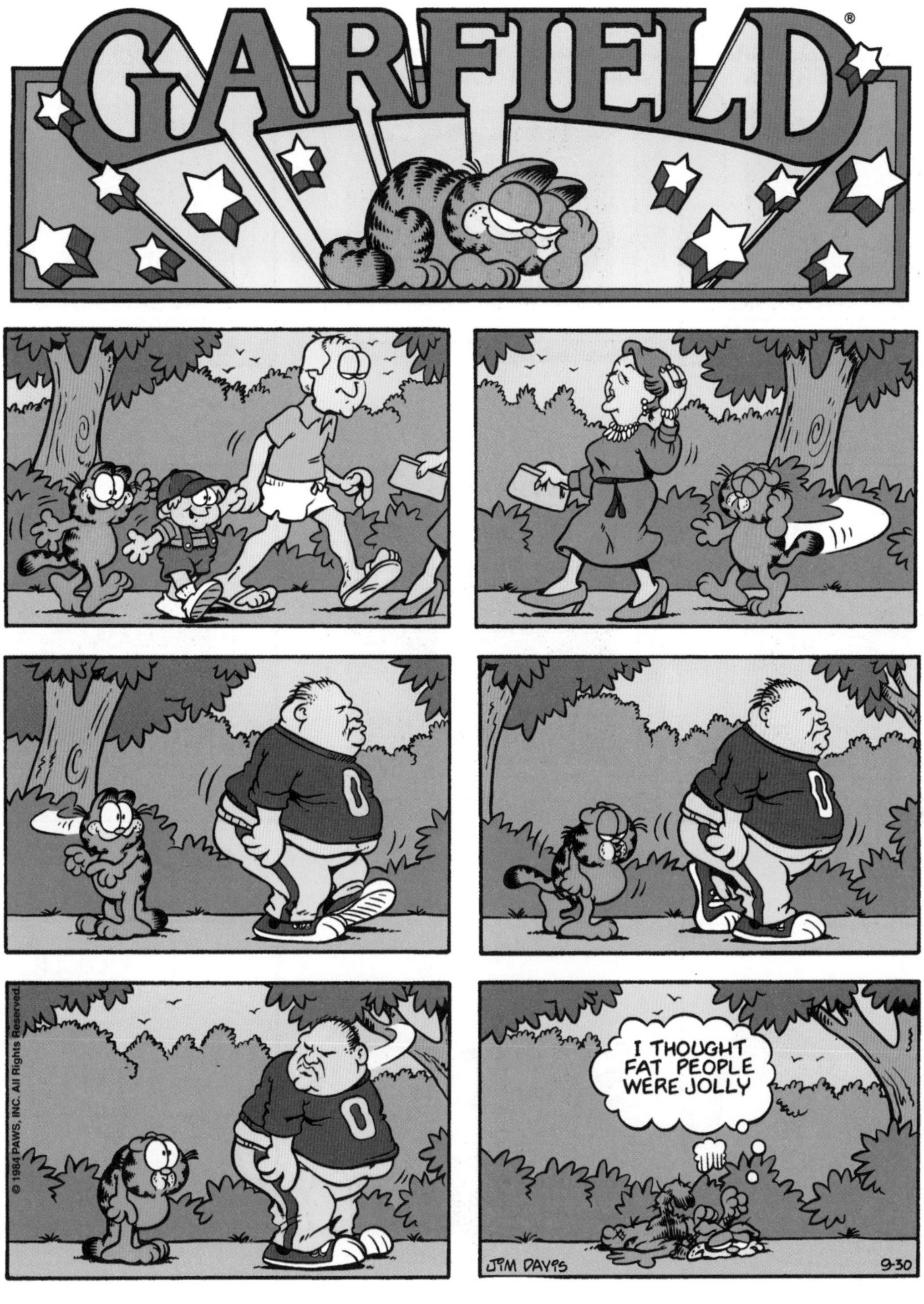
GARFIELD
© 1984 PAWS, INC. All Rights Reserved.
I THOUGHT FAT PEOPLE WERE JOLLY
JIM DAVIS
9-30

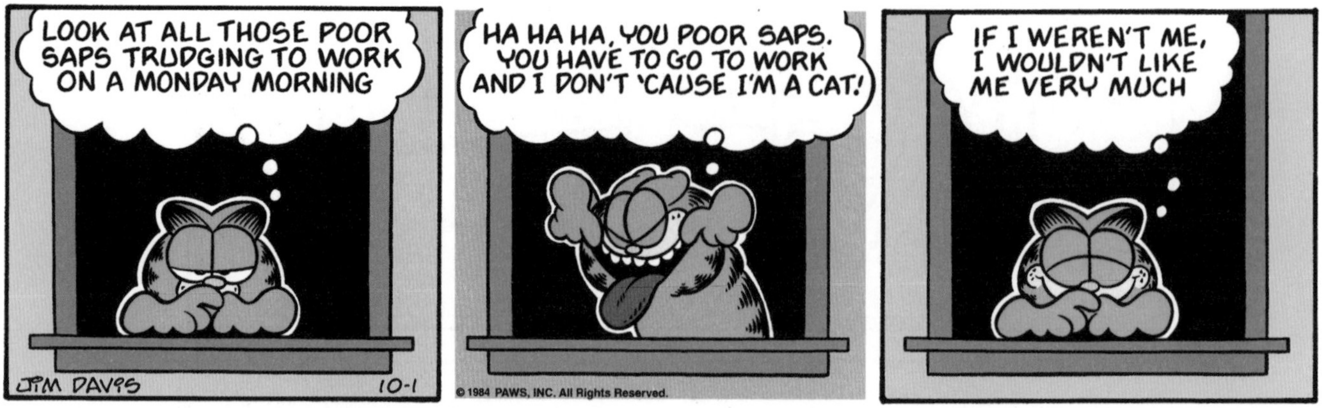
LOOK AT ALL THOSE POOR SAPS TRUDGING TO WORK ON A MONDAY MORNING
JIM DAVIS
10-1
HA HA HA, YOU POOR SAPS. YOU HAVE TO GO TO WORK AND I DON'T 'CAUSE I'M A CAT!
© 1984 PAWS, INC. All Rights Reserved.
IF I WEREN'T ME, I WOULDN'T LIKE ME VERY MUCH

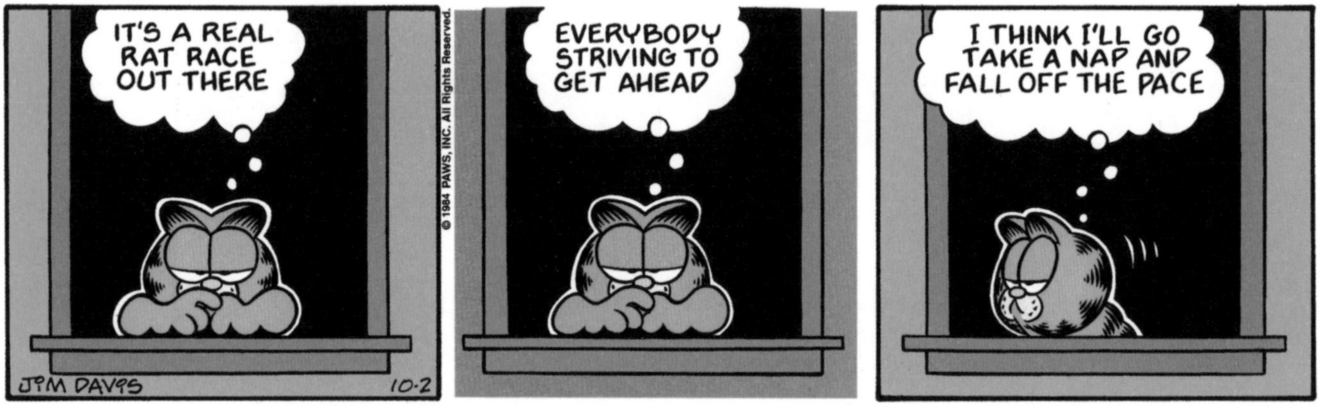
IT'S A REAL RAT RACE OUT THERE
JIM DAVIS
10-2
© 1984 PAWS, INC. All Rights Reserved.
EVERYBODY STRIVING TO GET AHEAD
I THINK I'LL GO TAKE A NAP AND FALL OFF THE PACE

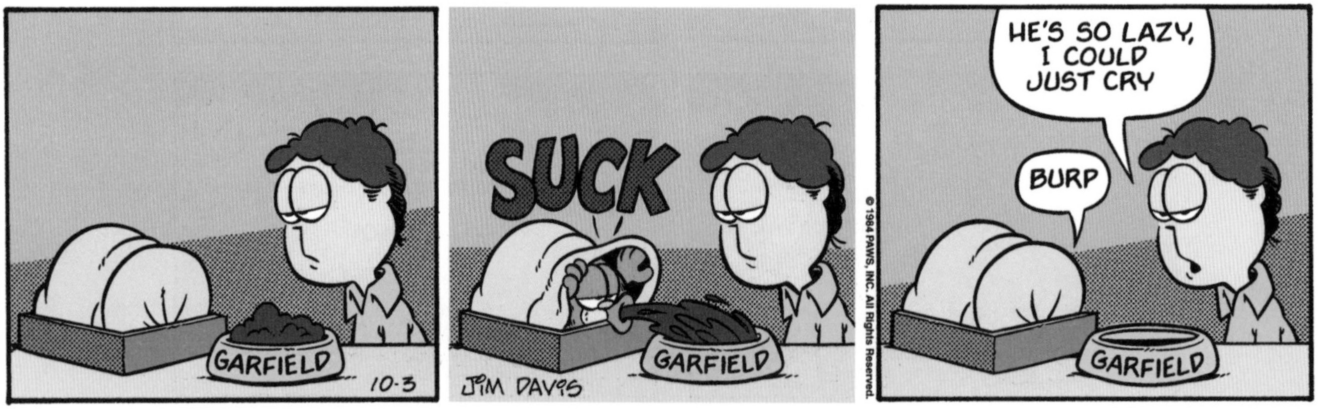
GARFIELD
10-3
SUCK
GARFIELD
JIM DAVIS
© 1984 PAWS, INC. All Rights Reserved.
HE'S SO LAZY, I COULD JUST CRY
BURP
GARFIELD

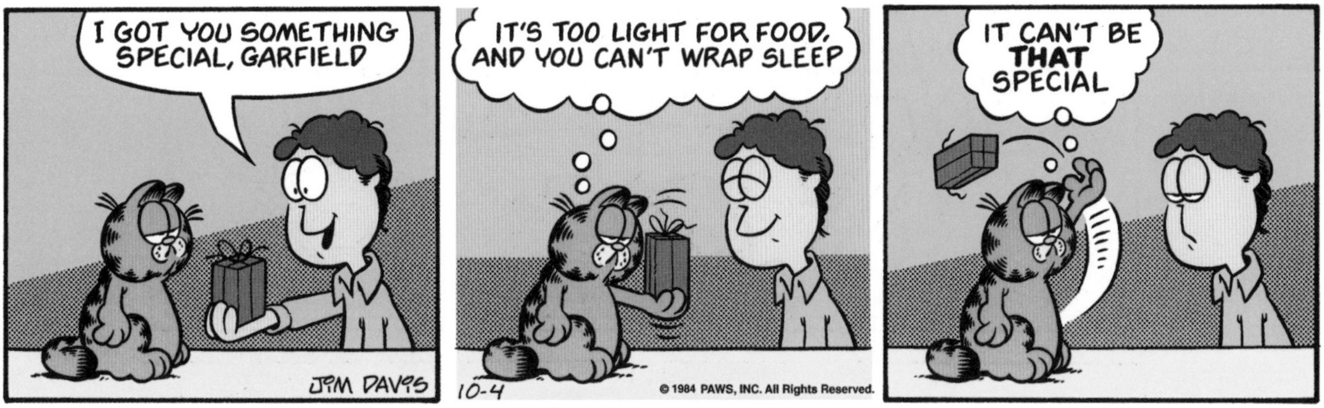
I GOT YOU SOMETHING SPECIAL, GARFIELD
JIM DAVIS
IT'S TOO LIGHT FOR FOOD, AND YOU CAN'T WRAP SLEEP
10-4
© 1984 PAWS, INC. All Rights Reserved.
IT CAN'T BE **THAT** SPECIAL

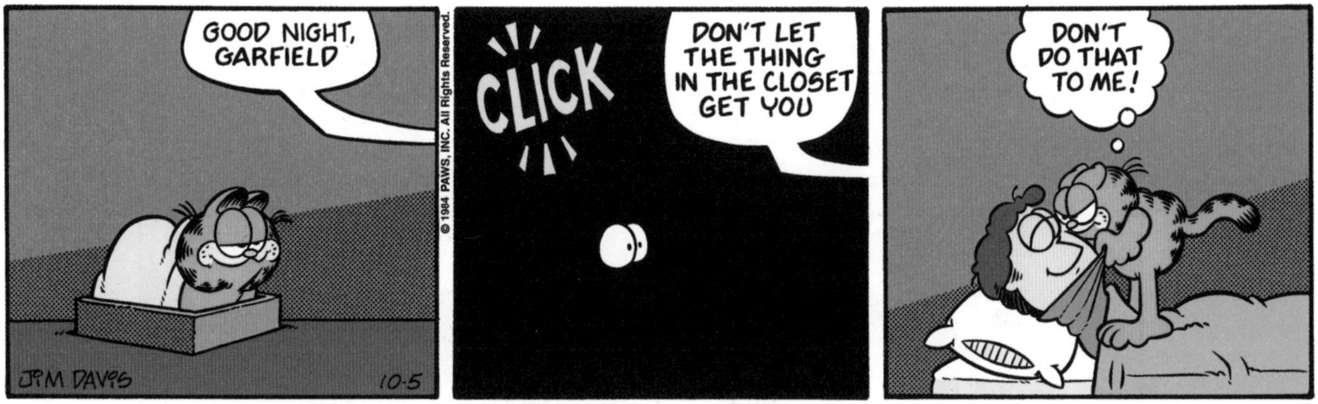
GOOD NIGHT, GARFIELD
JIM DAVIS
10-5
© 1984 PAWS, INC. All Rights Reserved.
CLICK
DON'T LET THE THING IN THE CLOSET GET YOU
DON'T DO THAT TO ME!

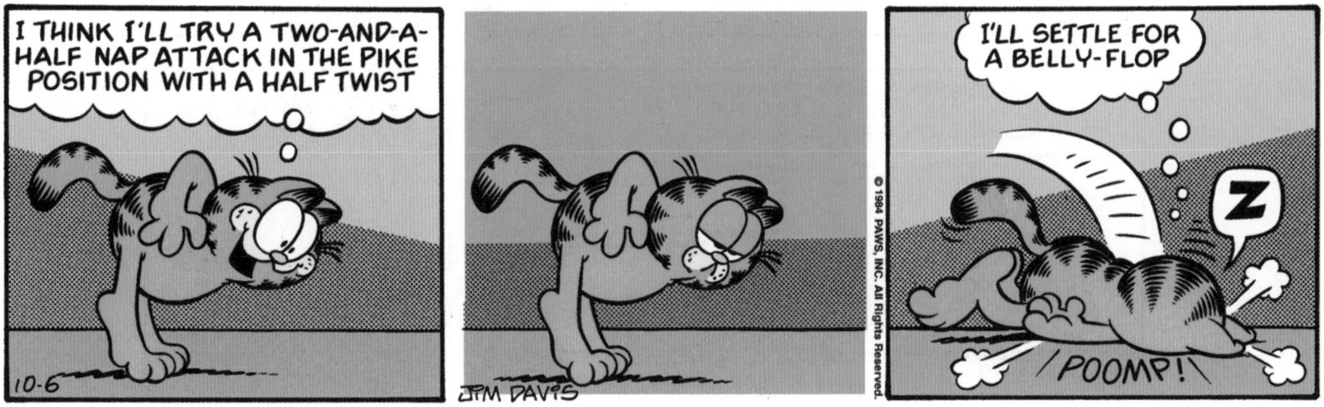
I THINK I'LL TRY A TWO-AND-A-HALF NAP ATTACK IN THE PIKE POSITION WITH A HALF TWIST
10-6
JIM DAVIS
© 1984 PAWS, INC. All Rights Reserved.
I'LL SETTLE FOR A BELLY-FLOP
Z
POOMP!

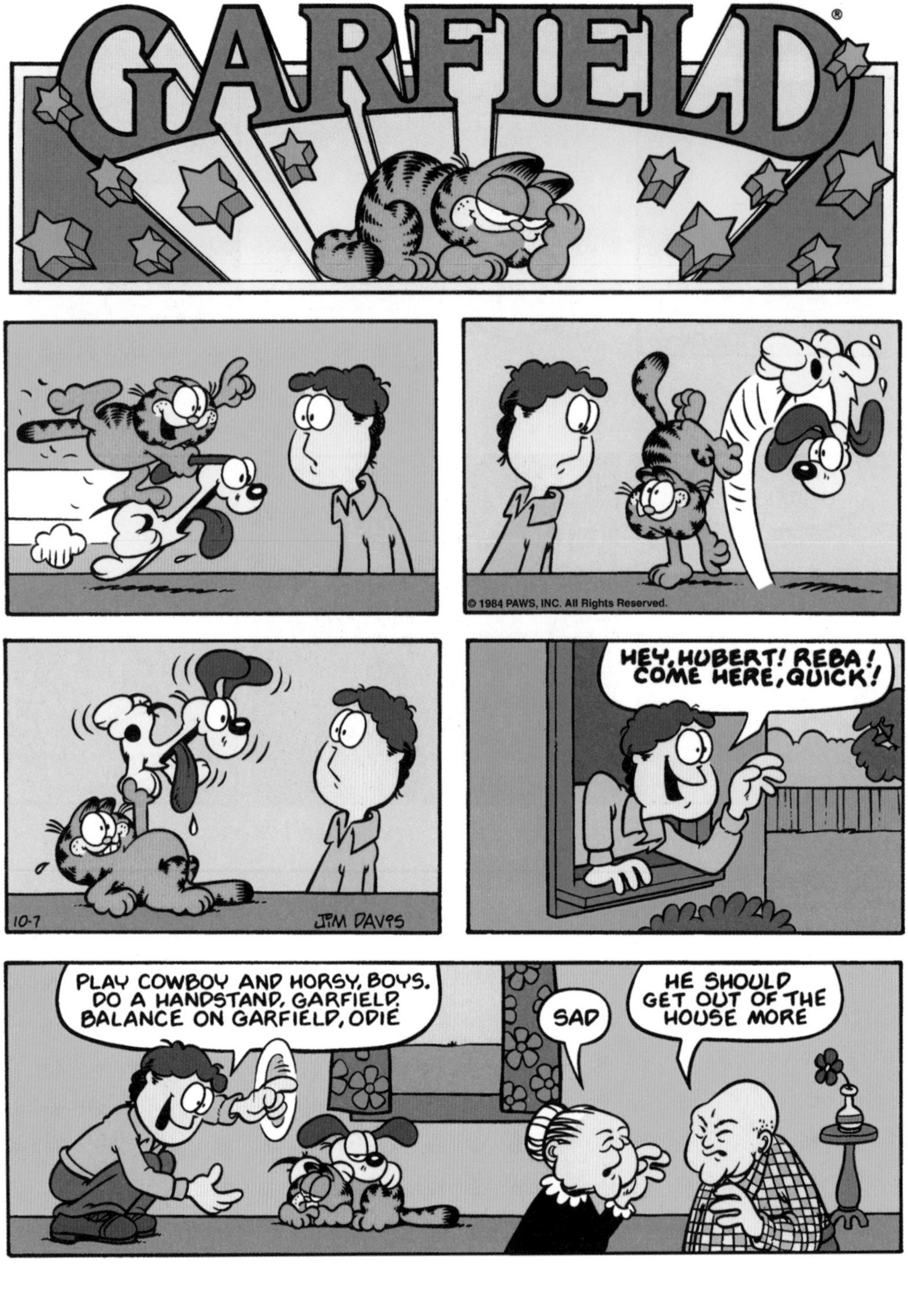
GARFIELD
© 1984 PAWS, INC. All Rights Reserved.
10-7
JIM DAVIS
HEY, HUBERT! REBA! COME HERE, QUICK!
PLAY COWBOY AND HORSY, BOYS. DO A HANDSTAND, GARFIELD. BALANCE ON GARFIELD, ODIE
SAD
HE SHOULD GET OUT OF THE HOUSE MORE

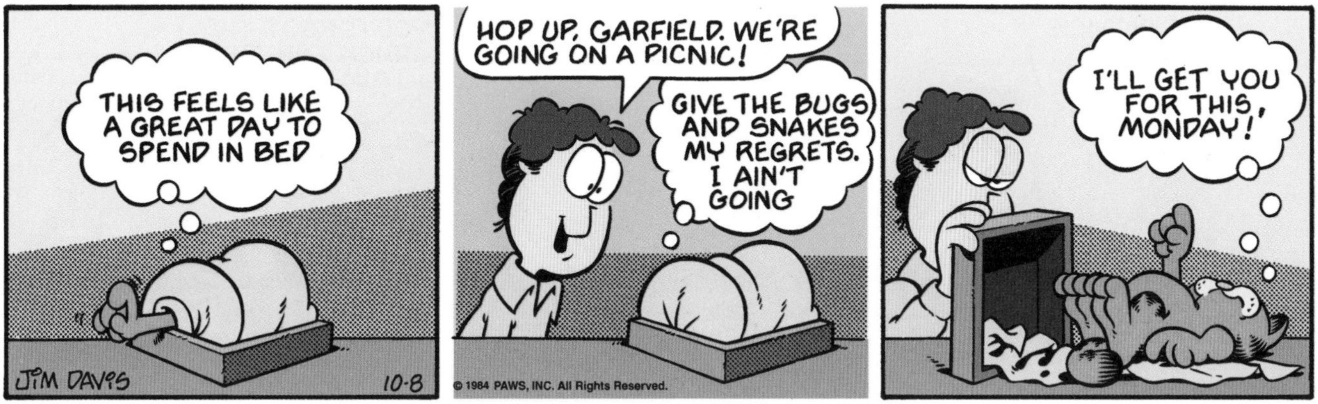
THIS FEELS LIKE A GREAT DAY TO SPEND IN BED
JIM DAVIS
10-8
HOP UP, GARFIELD. WE'RE GOING ON A PICNIC!
GIVE THE BUGS AND SNAKES MY REGRETS. I AIN'T GOING
© 1984 PAWS, INC. All Rights Reserved.
I'LL GET YOU FOR THIS, MONDAY!

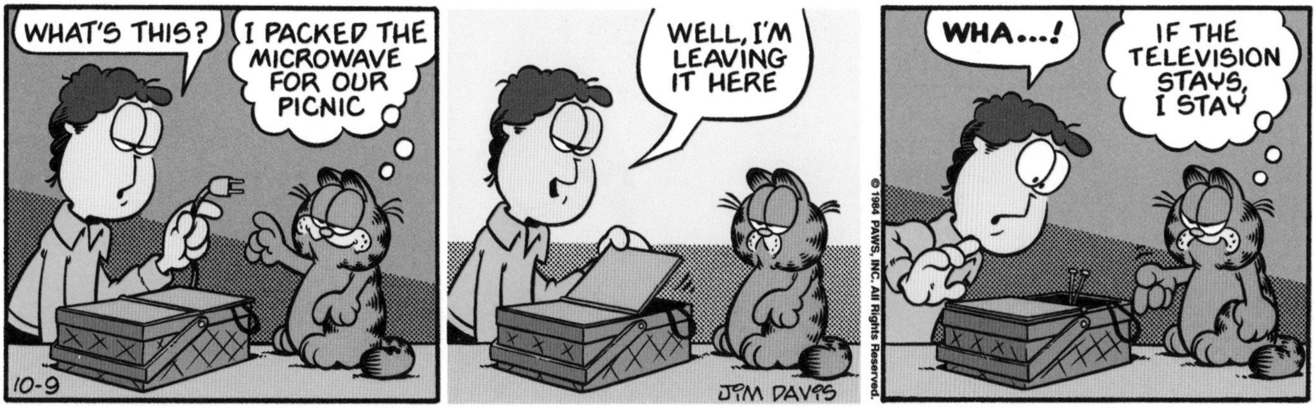
WHAT'S THIS?
I PACKED THE MICROWAVE FOR OUR PICNIC
10-9
WELL, I'M LEAVING IT HERE
JIM DAVIS
© 1984 PAWS, INC. All Rights Reserved.
WHA...!
IF THE TELEVISION STAYS, I STAY

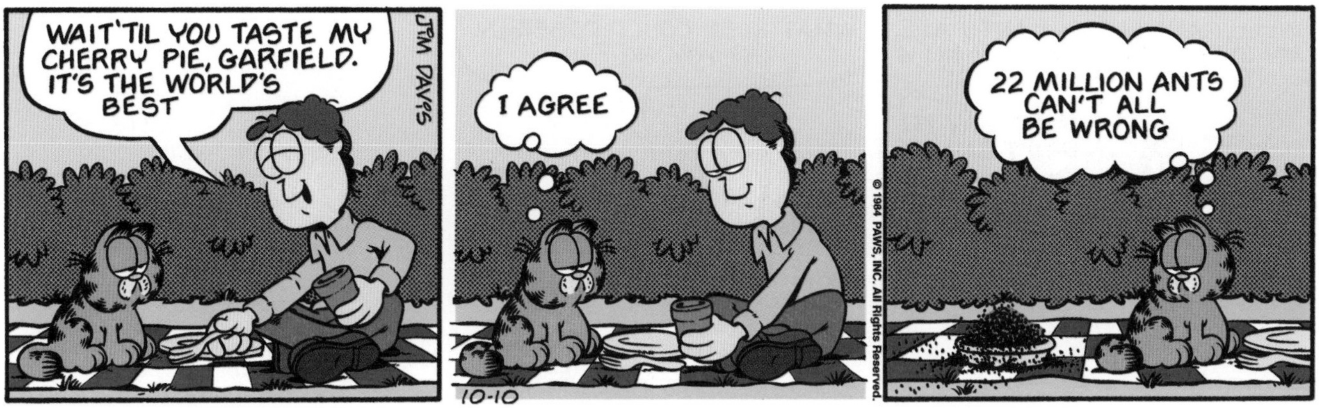
WAIT 'TIL YOU TASTE MY CHERRY PIE, GARFIELD. IT'S THE WORLD'S BEST
JIM DAVIS
I AGREE
10-10
© 1984 PAWS, INC. All Rights Reserved.
22 MILLION ANTS CAN'T ALL BE WRONG

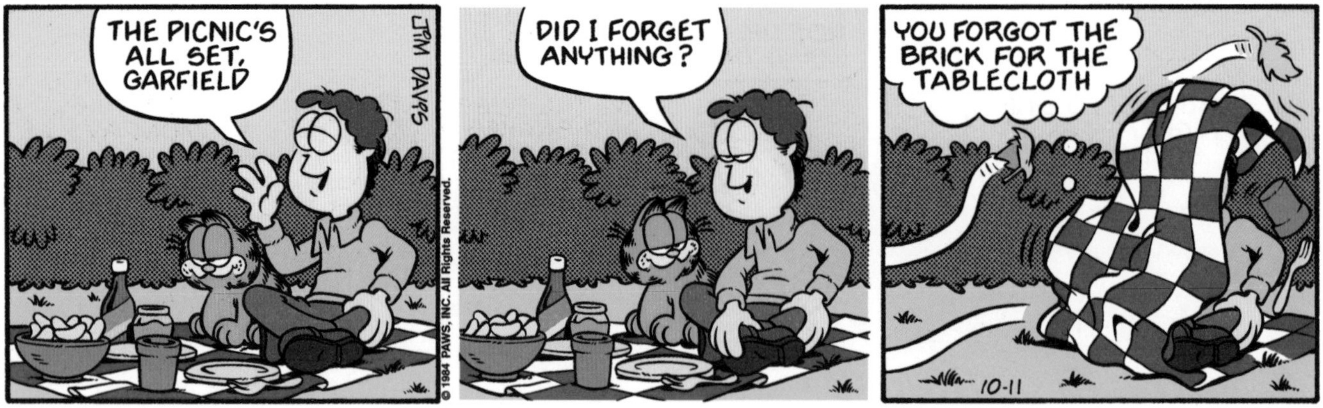
THE PICNIC'S ALL SET, GARFIELD
JIM DAVIS
© 1984 PAWS, INC. All Rights Reserved.
DID I FORGET ANYTHING?
YOU FORGOT THE BRICK FOR THE TABLECLOTH
10-11

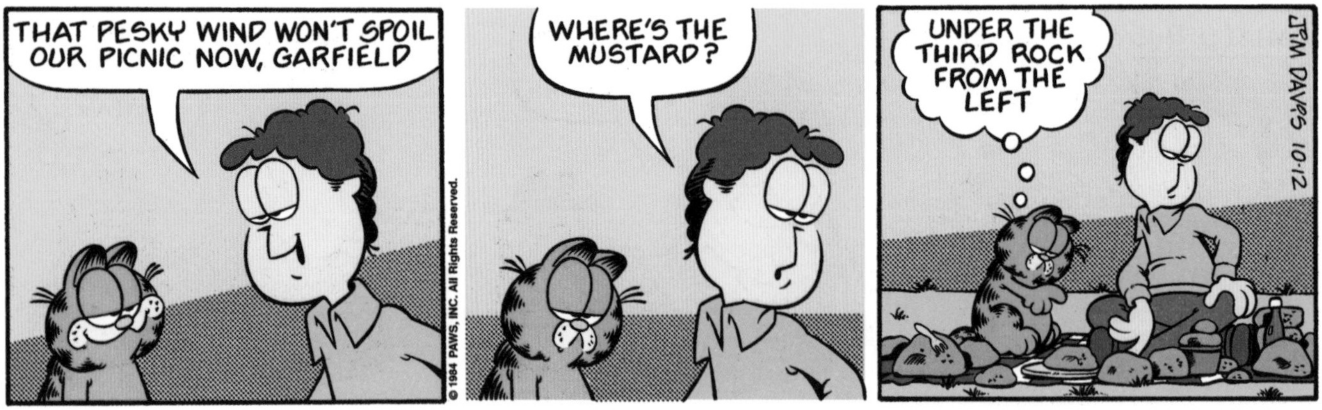
THAT PESKY WIND WON'T SPOIL OUR PICNIC NOW, GARFIELD
© 1984 PAWS, INC. All Rights Reserved.
WHERE'S THE MUSTARD?
UNDER THE THIRD ROCK FROM THE LEFT
JIM DAVIS 10-12

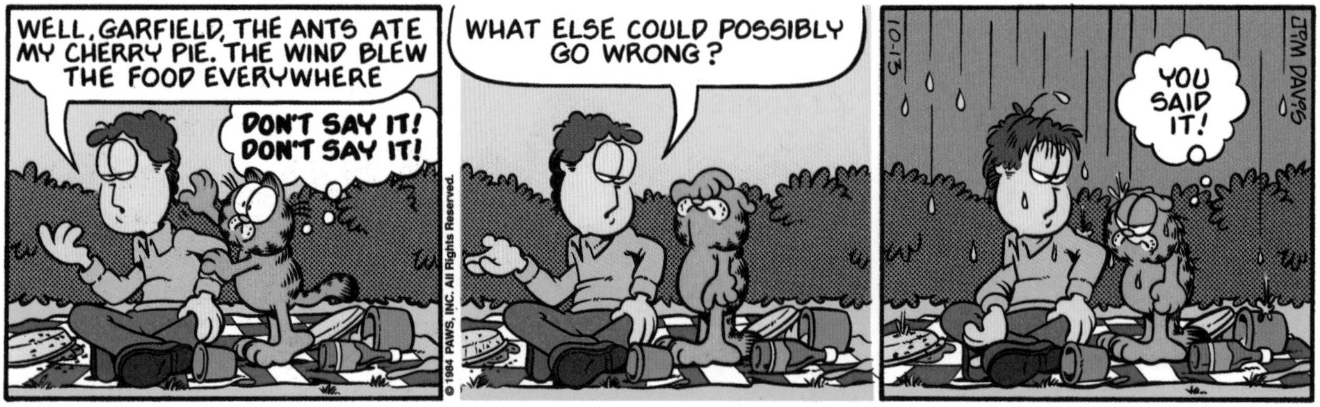
WELL, GARFIELD, THE ANTS ATE MY CHERRY PIE. THE WIND BLEW THE FOOD EVERYWHERE
DON'T SAY IT! DON'T SAY IT!
© 1984 PAWS, INC. All Rights Reserved.
WHAT ELSE COULD POSSIBLY GO WRONG?
10-13
JIM DAVIS
YOU SAID IT!

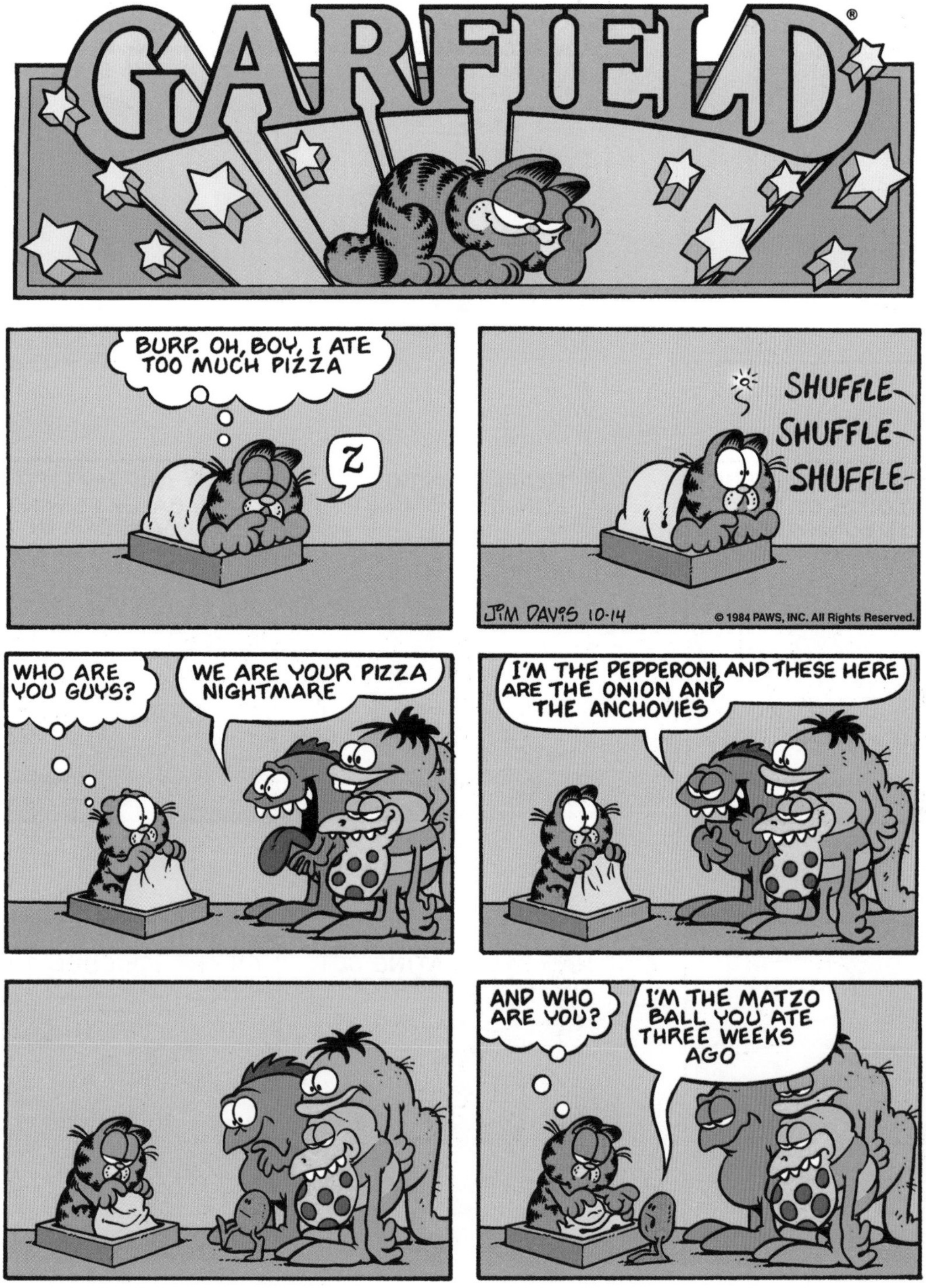
GARFIELD®
BURP. OH, BOY, I ATE TOO MUCH PIZZA
Z
SHUFFLE
SHUFFLE
SHUFFLE
JIM DAVIS 10-14
© 1984 PAWS, INC. All Rights Reserved.
WHO ARE YOU GUYS?
WE ARE YOUR PIZZA NIGHTMARE
I'M THE PEPPERONI, AND THESE HERE ARE THE ONION AND THE ANCHOVIES
AND WHO ARE YOU?
I'M THE MATZO BALL YOU ATE THREE WEEKS AGO

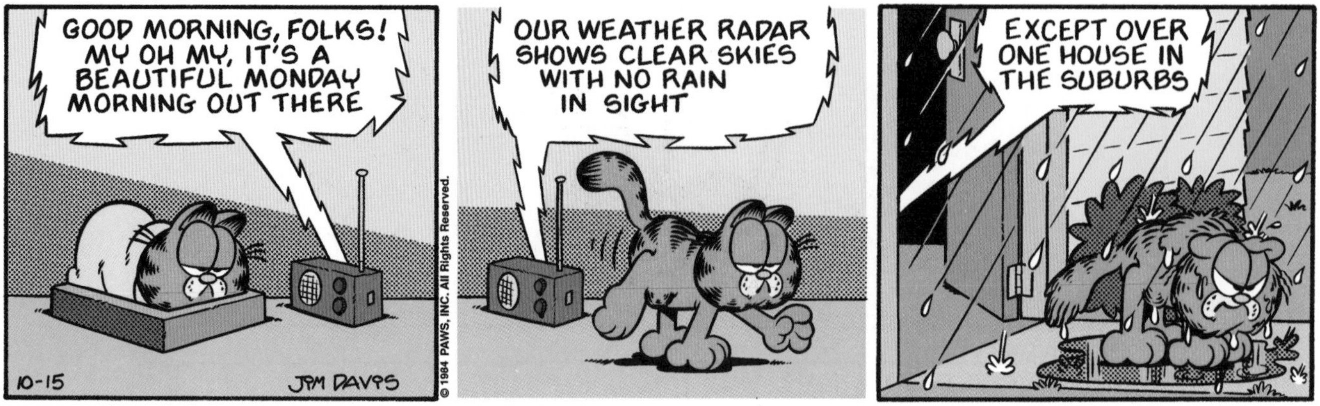
GOOD MORNING, FOLKS! MY OH MY, IT'S A BEAUTIFUL MONDAY MORNING OUT THERE
10-15
JIM DAVIS
© 1984 PAWS, INC. All Rights Reserved.
OUR WEATHER RADAR SHOWS CLEAR SKIES WITH NO RAIN IN SIGHT
EXCEPT OVER ONE HOUSE IN THE SUBURBS

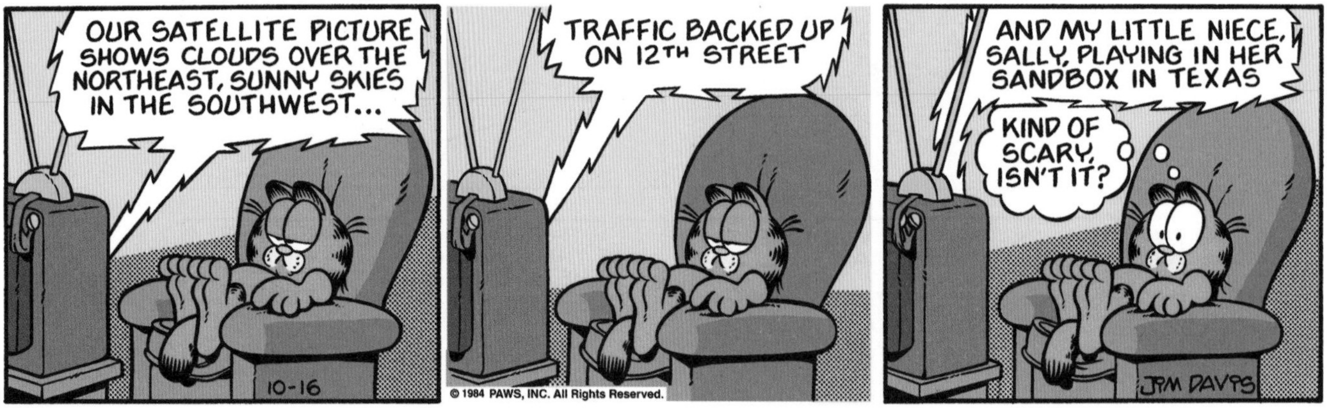
OUR SATELLITE PICTURE SHOWS CLOUDS OVER THE NORTHEAST, SUNNY SKIES IN THE SOUTHWEST...
10-16
TRAFFIC BACKED UP ON 12TH STREET
© 1984 PAWS, INC. All Rights Reserved.
AND MY LITTLE NIECE, SALLY, PLAYING IN HER SANDBOX IN TEXAS
KIND OF SCARY, ISN'T IT?
JIM DAVIS

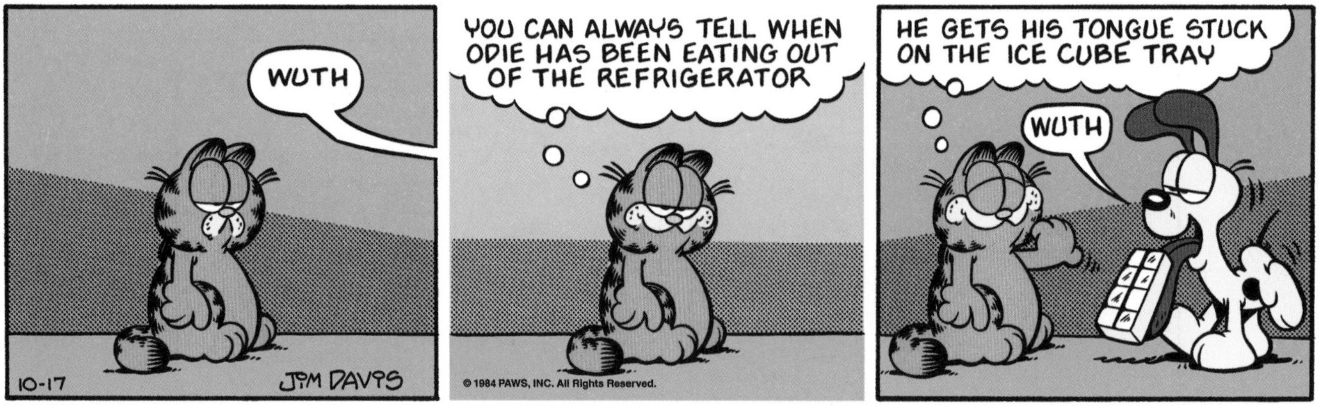
WUTH
10-17
JIM DAVIS
YOU CAN ALWAYS TELL WHEN ODIE HAS BEEN EATING OUT OF THE REFRIGERATOR
© 1984 PAWS, INC. All Rights Reserved.
HE GETS HIS TONGUE STUCK ON THE ICE CUBE TRAY
WUTH

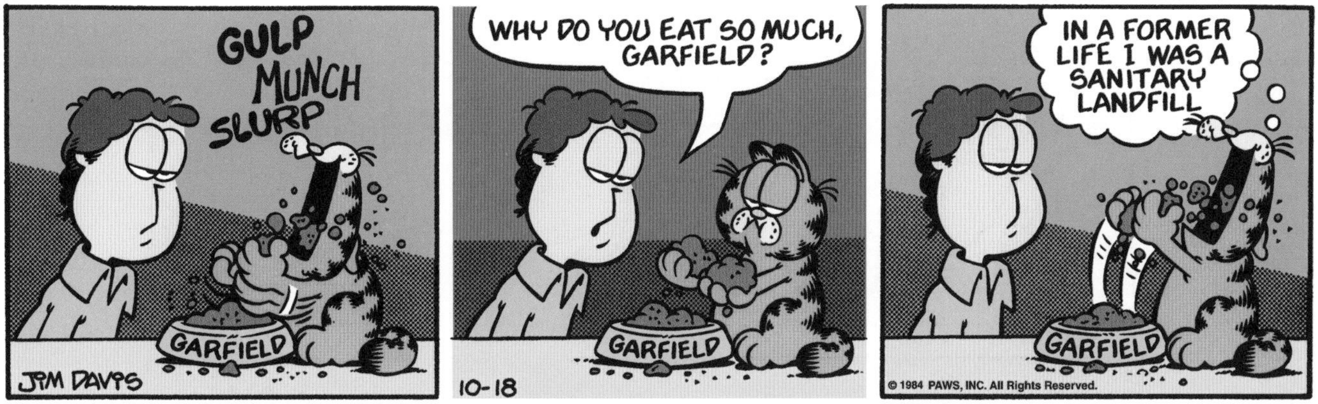
GULP
MUNCH
SLURP
GARFIELD
JIM DAVIS
WHY DO YOU EAT SO MUCH, GARFIELD?
GARFIELD
10-18
IN A FORMER LIFE I WAS A SANITARY LANDFILL
GARFIELD
© 1984 PAWS, INC. All Rights Reserved.

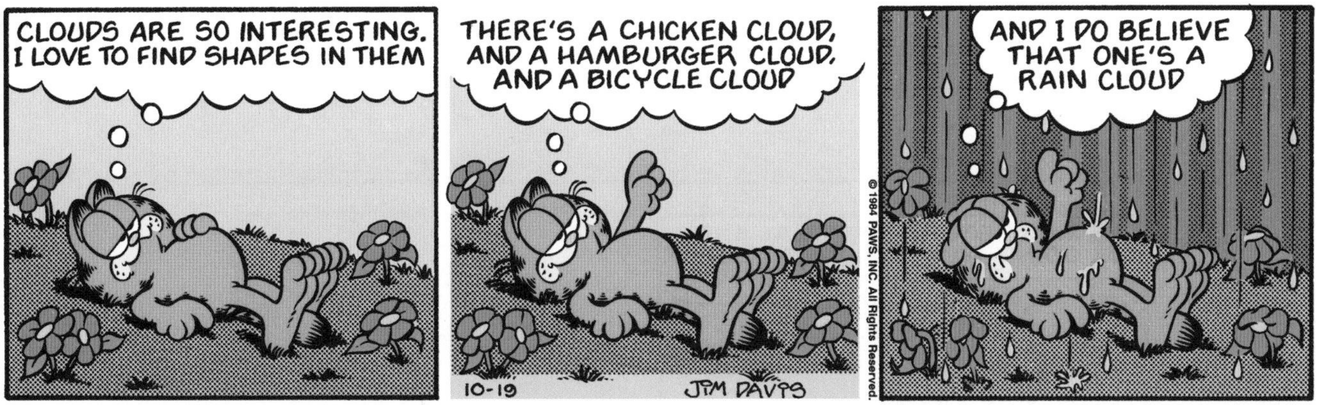
CLOUDS ARE SO INTERESTING. I LOVE TO FIND SHAPES IN THEM
THERE'S A CHICKEN CLOUD, AND A HAMBURGER CLOUD, AND A BICYCLE CLOUD
10-19
JIM DAVIS
© 1984 PAWS, INC. All Rights Reserved.
AND I DO BELIEVE THAT ONE'S A RAIN CLOUD

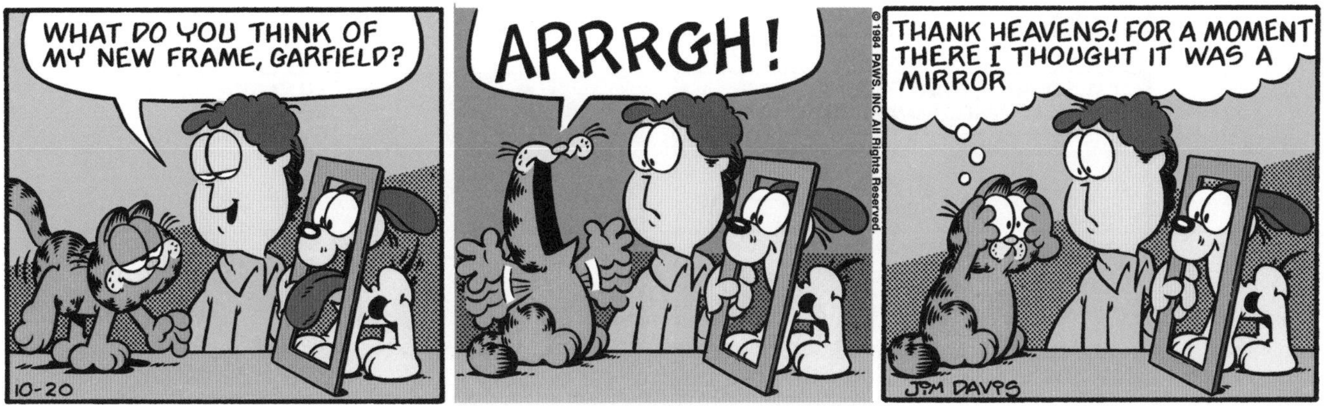
WHAT DO YOU THINK OF MY NEW FRAME, GARFIELD?
10-20
ARRRGH!
© 1984 PAWS, INC. All Rights Reserved.
THANK HEAVENS! FOR A MOMENT THERE I THOUGHT IT WAS A MIRROR
JIM DAVIS

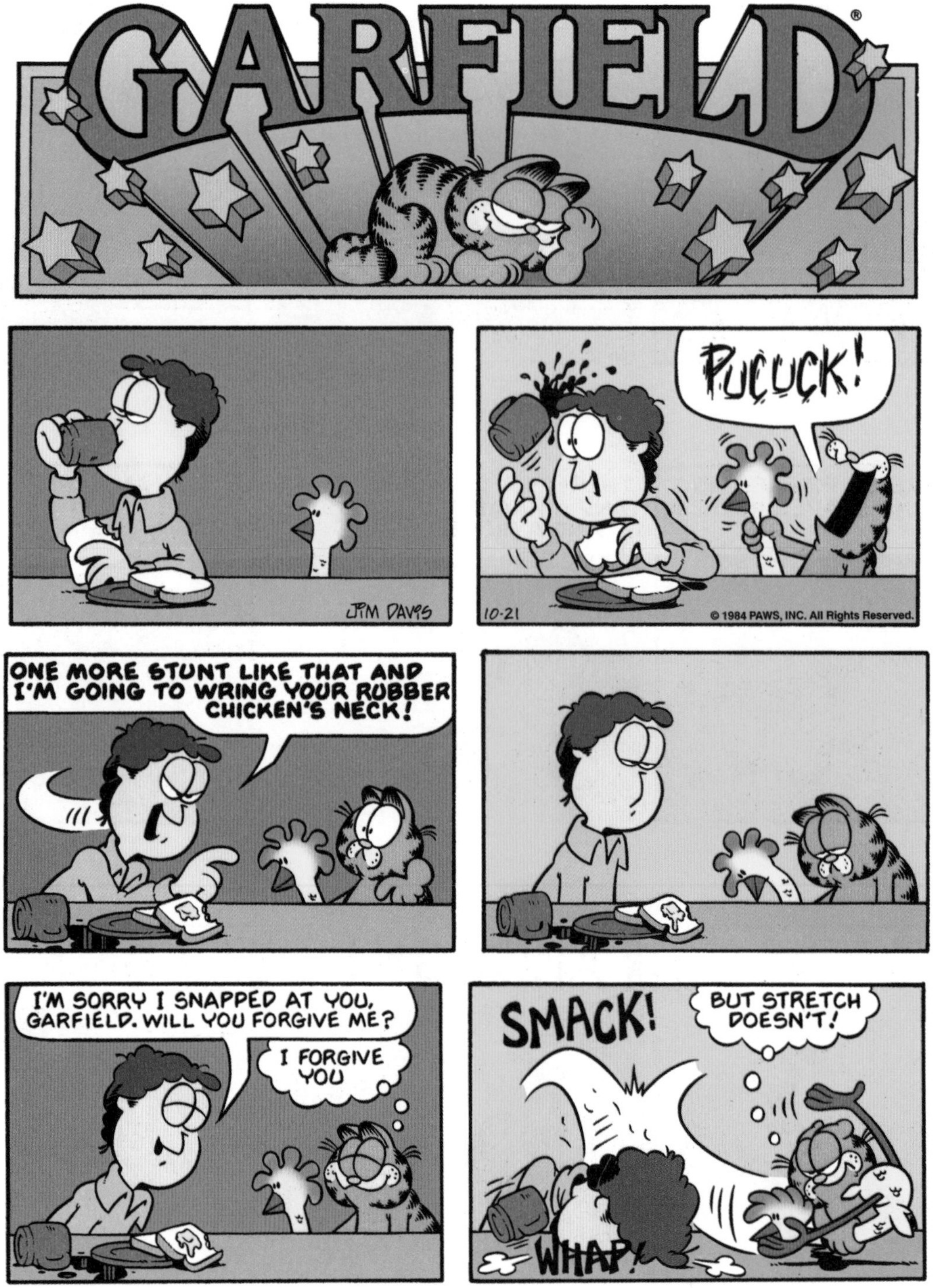
GARFIELD®
PUCUCK!
JIM DAVIS
10-21
© 1984 PAWS, INC. All Rights Reserved.
ONE MORE STUNT LIKE THAT AND I'M GOING TO WRING YOUR RUBBER CHICKEN'S NECK!
I'M SORRY I SNAPPED AT YOU, GARFIELD. WILL YOU FORGIVE ME?
I FORGIVE YOU
SMACK!
BUT STRETCH DOESN'T!
WHAP!

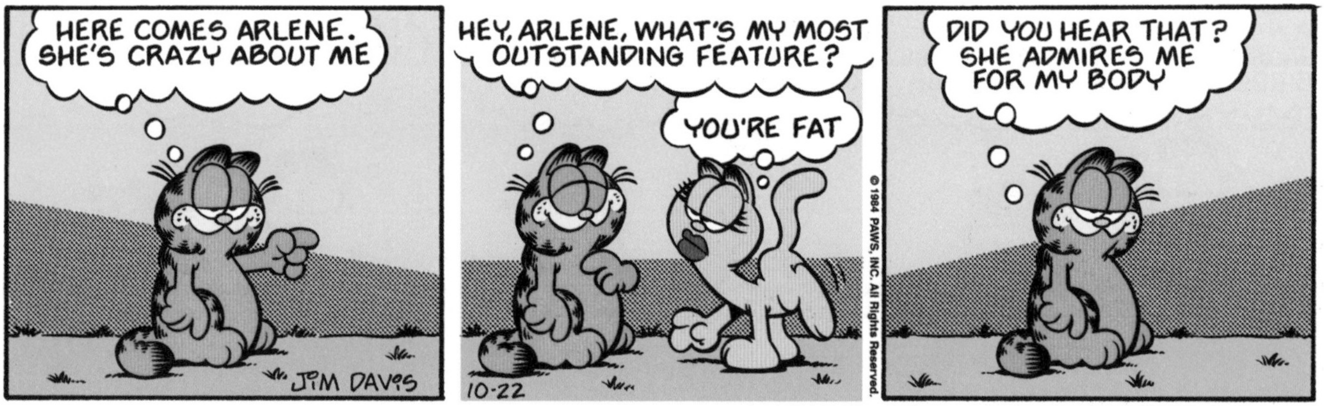
HERE COMES ARLENE. SHE'S CRAZY ABOUT ME
JIM DAVIS
HEY, ARLENE, WHAT'S MY MOST OUTSTANDING FEATURE?
YOU'RE FAT
10-22
© 1984 PAWS, INC. All Rights Reserved.
DID YOU HEAR THAT? SHE ADMIRES ME FOR MY BODY

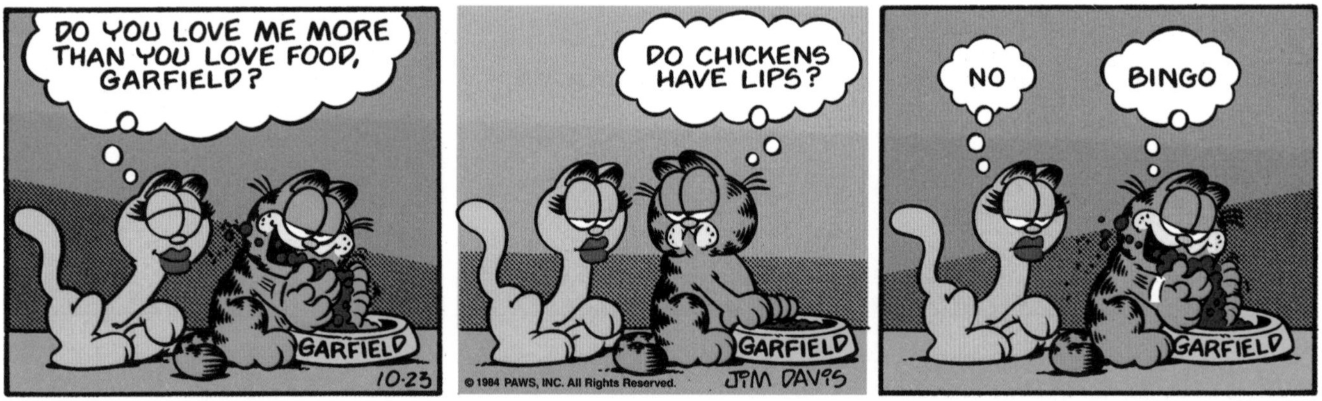
DO YOU LOVE ME MORE THAN YOU LOVE FOOD, GARFIELD?
GARFIELD
10-23
DO CHICKENS HAVE LIPS?
GARFIELD
© 1984 PAWS, INC. All Rights Reserved.
JIM DAVIS
NO
BINGO
GARFIELD

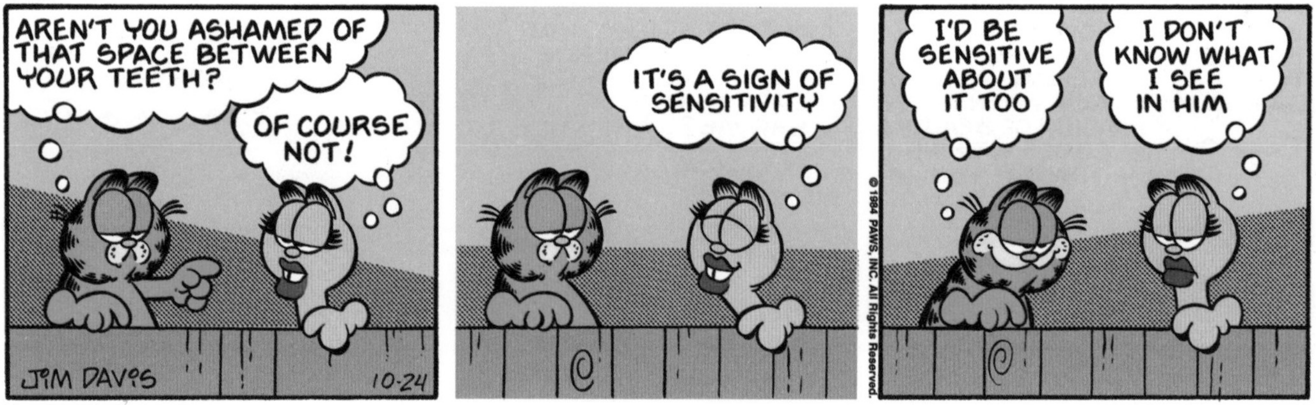
AREN'T YOU ASHAMED OF THAT SPACE BETWEEN YOUR TEETH?
OF COURSE NOT!
JIM DAVIS
10-24
IT'S A SIGN OF SENSITIVITY
© 1984 PAWS, INC. All Rights Reserved.
I'D BE SENSITIVE ABOUT IT TOO
I DON'T KNOW WHAT I SEE IN HIM

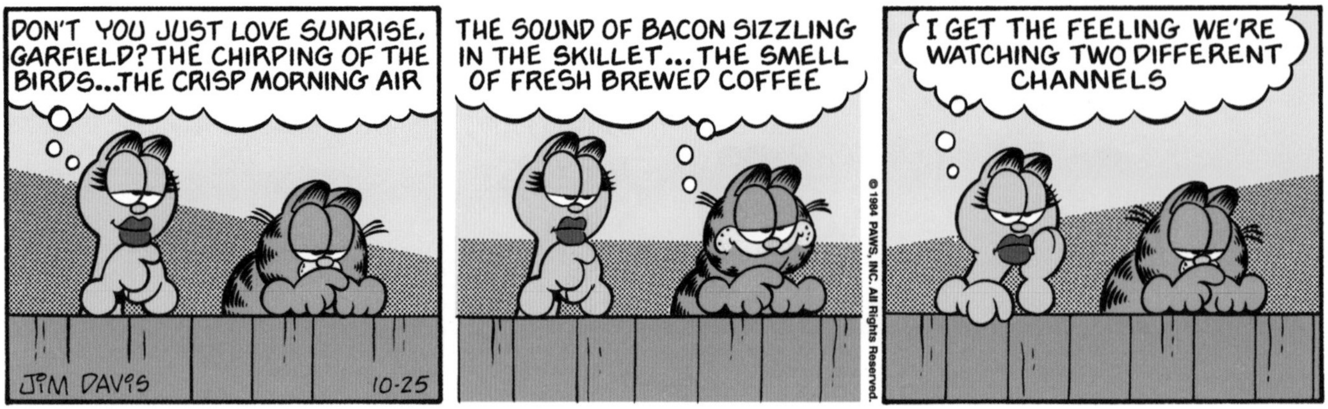
DON'T YOU JUST LOVE SUNRISE, GARFIELD? THE CHIRPING OF THE BIRDS...THE CRISP MORNING AIR
THE SOUND OF BACON SIZZLING IN THE SKILLET... THE SMELL OF FRESH BREWED COFFEE
I GET THE FEELING WE'RE WATCHING TWO DIFFERENT CHANNELS
JIM DAVIS
10-25
© 1984 PAWS, INC. All Rights Reserved.

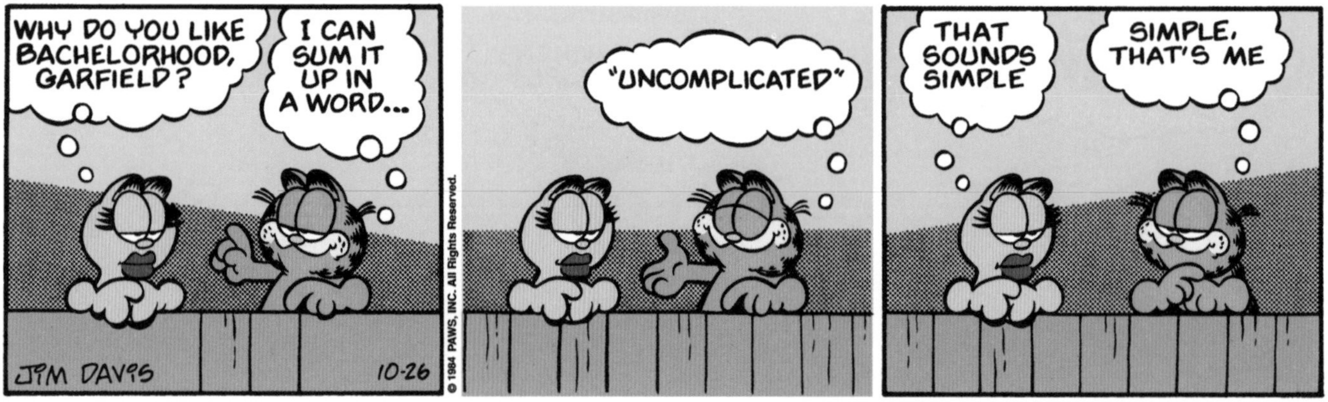
WHY DO YOU LIKE BACHELORHOOD, GARFIELD?
I CAN SUM IT UP IN A WORD...
"UNCOMPLICATED"
THAT SOUNDS SIMPLE
SIMPLE, THAT'S ME
JIM DAVIS
10-26
© 1984 PAWS, INC. All Rights Reserved.

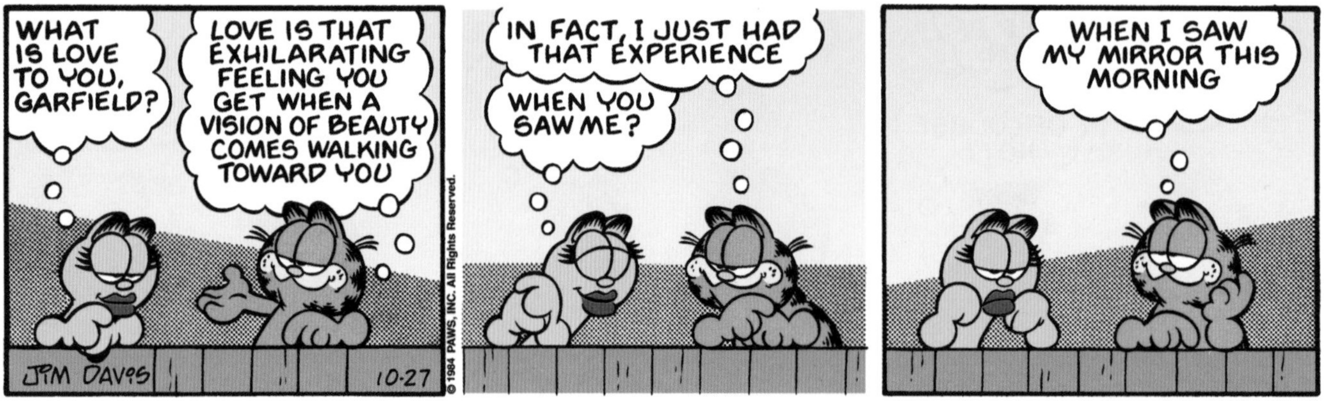
WHAT IS LOVE TO YOU, GARFIELD?
LOVE IS THAT EXHILARATING FEELING YOU GET WHEN A VISION OF BEAUTY COMES WALKING TOWARD YOU
IN FACT, I JUST HAD THAT EXPERIENCE
WHEN YOU SAW ME?
WHEN I SAW MY MIRROR THIS MORNING
JIM DAVIS
10-27
© 1984 PAWS, INC. All Rights Reserved.

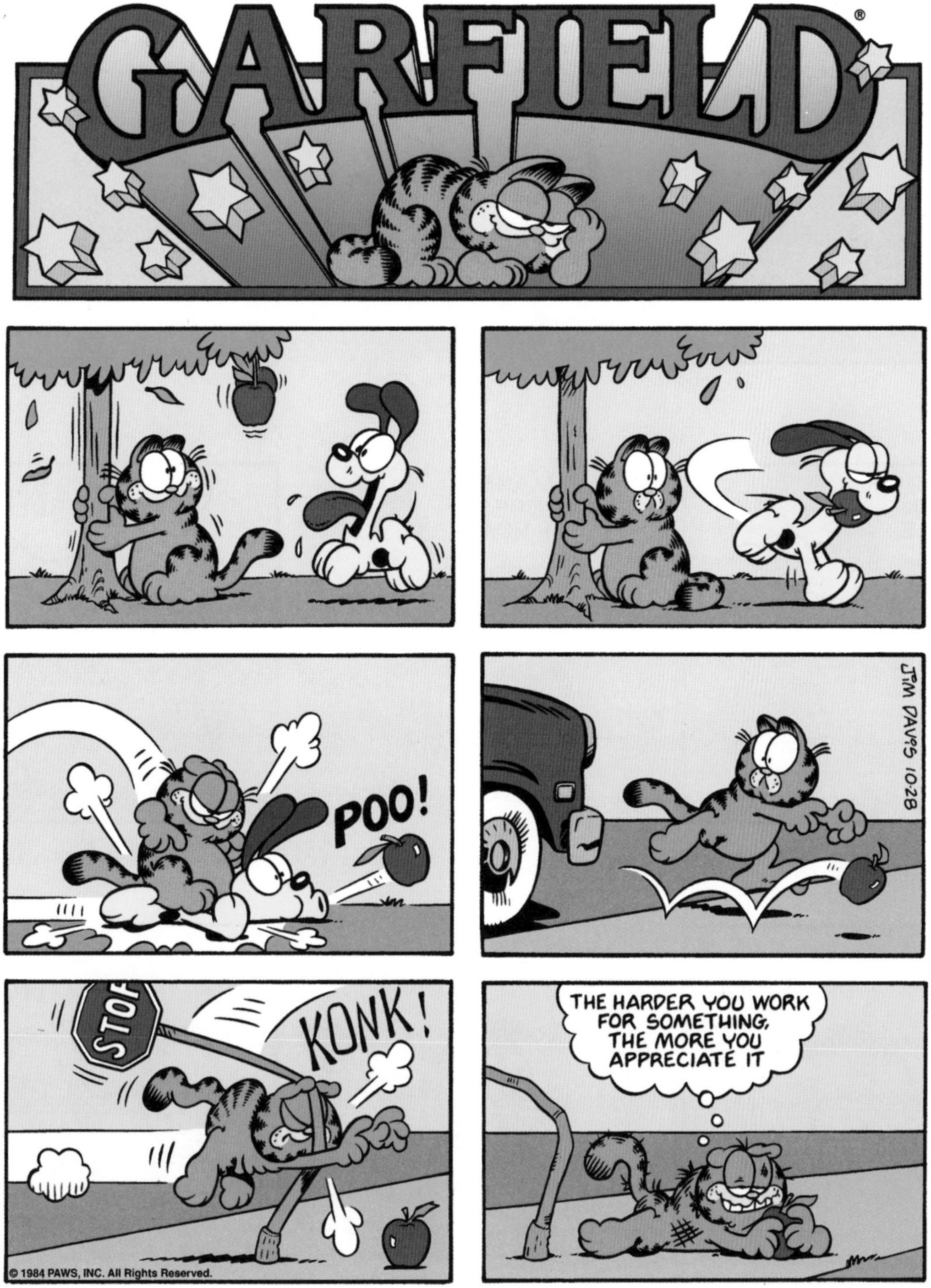
GARFIELD®
POO!
JIM DAVIS 10-28
STOP
KONK!
THE HARDER YOU WORK FOR SOMETHING, THE MORE YOU APPRECIATE IT
© 1984 PAWS, INC. All Rights Reserved.

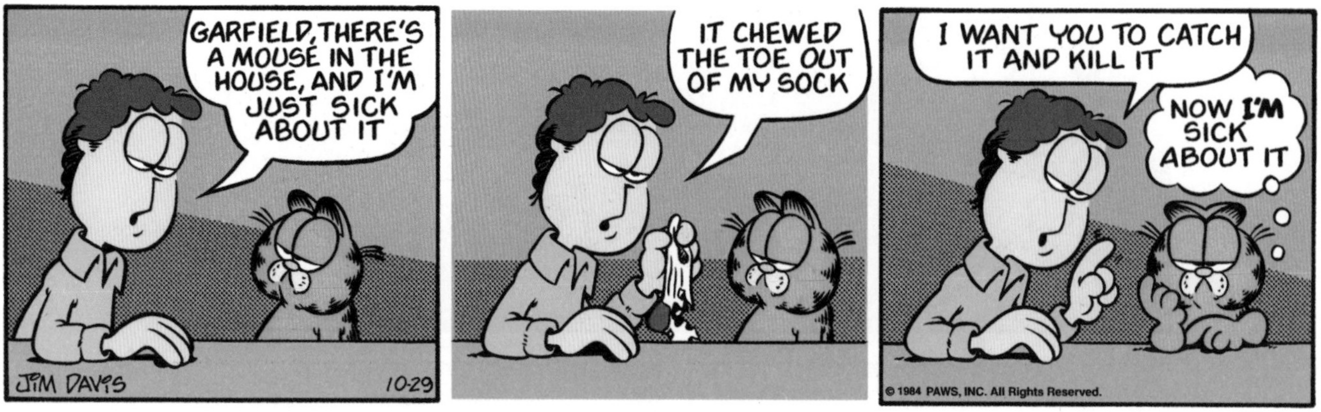
GARFIELD, THERE'S A MOUSE IN THE HOUSE, AND I'M JUST SICK ABOUT IT
JIM DAVIS 10-29
IT CHEWED THE TOE OUT OF MY SOCK
I WANT YOU TO CATCH IT AND KILL IT
NOW **I'M** SICK ABOUT IT
© 1984 PAWS, INC. All Rights Reserved.

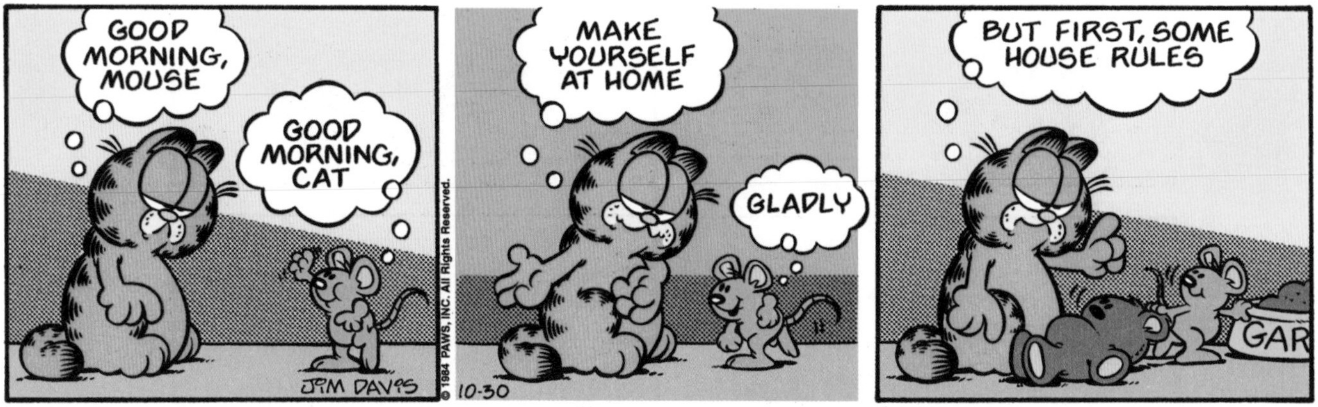
GOOD MORNING, MOUSE
GOOD MORNING, CAT
JIM DAVIS
© 1984 PAWS, INC. All Rights Reserved.
MAKE YOURSELF AT HOME
GLADLY
10-30
BUT FIRST, SOME HOUSE RULES
GAR

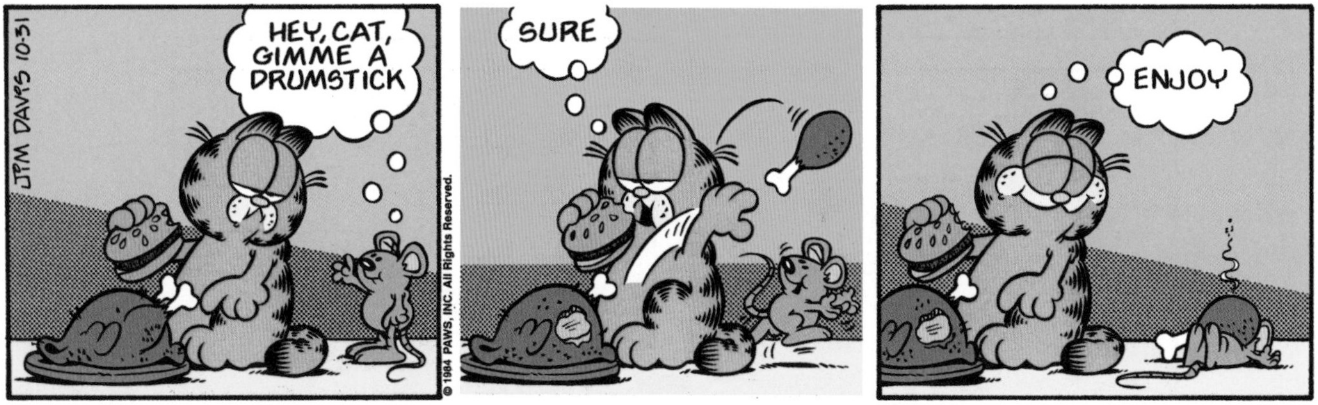
JIM DAVIS 10-31
HEY, CAT, GIMME A DRUMSTICK
© 1984 PAWS, INC. All Rights Reserved.
SURE
ENJOY

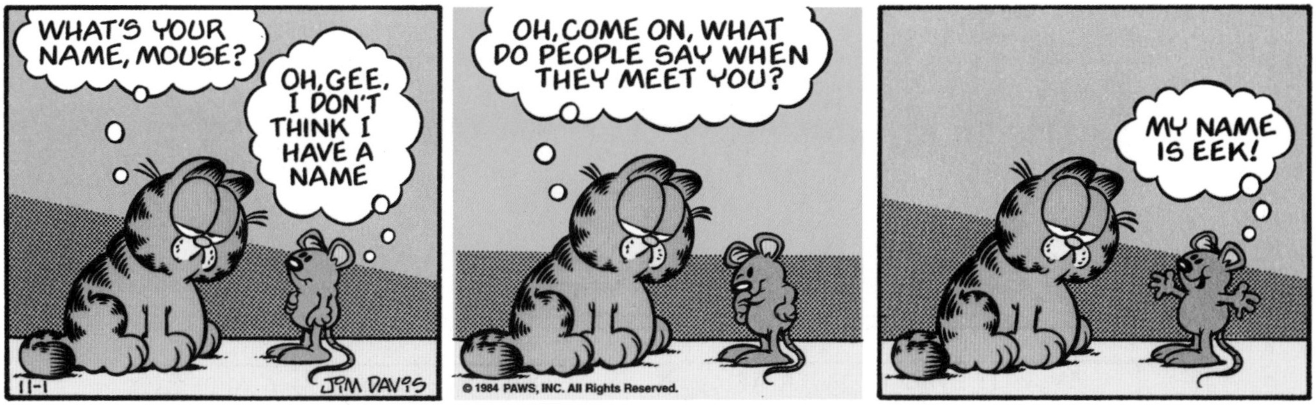
WHAT'S YOUR NAME, MOUSE?
OH, GEE, I DON'T THINK I HAVE A NAME
OH, COME ON, WHAT DO PEOPLE SAY WHEN THEY MEET YOU?
MY NAME IS EEK!
11-1
JIM DAVIS
© 1984 PAWS, INC. All Rights Reserved.

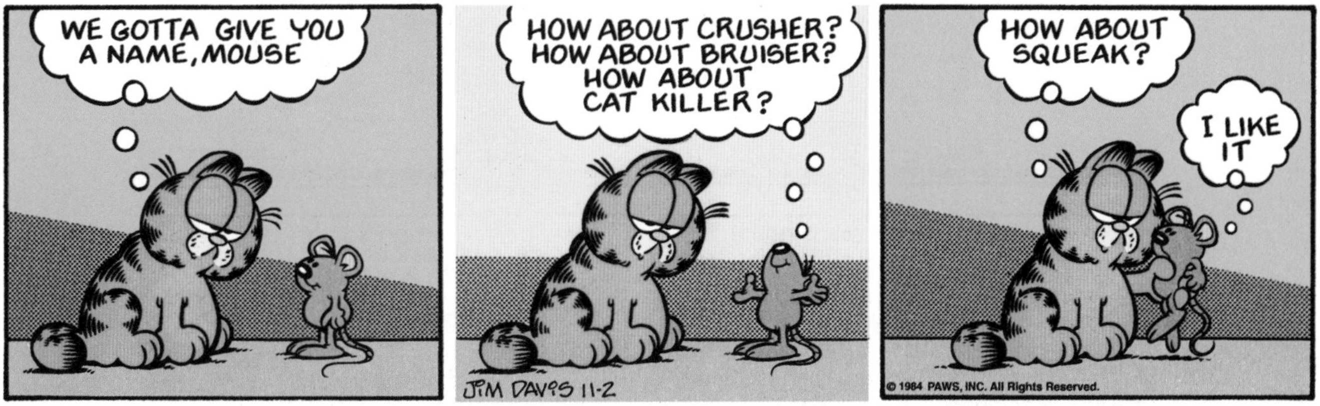
WE GOTTA GIVE YOU A NAME, MOUSE
HOW ABOUT CRUSHER? HOW ABOUT BRUISER? HOW ABOUT CAT KILLER?
HOW ABOUT SQUEAK?
I LIKE IT
JIM DAVIS 11-2
© 1984 PAWS, INC. All Rights Reserved.

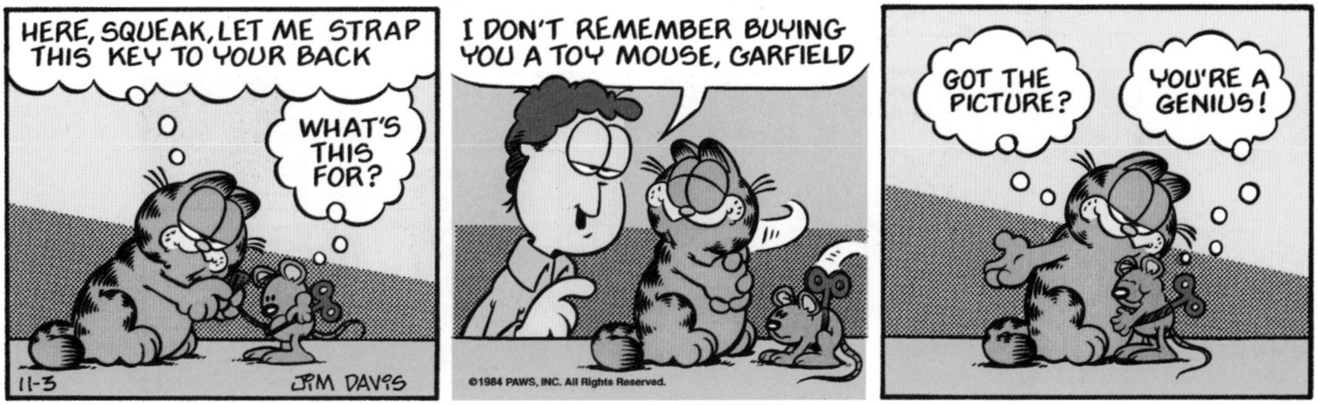
HERE, SQUEAK, LET ME STRAP THIS KEY TO YOUR BACK
WHAT'S THIS FOR?
I DON'T REMEMBER BUYING YOU A TOY MOUSE, GARFIELD
GOT THE PICTURE?
YOU'RE A GENIUS!
11-3
JIM DAVIS
©1984 PAWS, INC. All Rights Reserved.

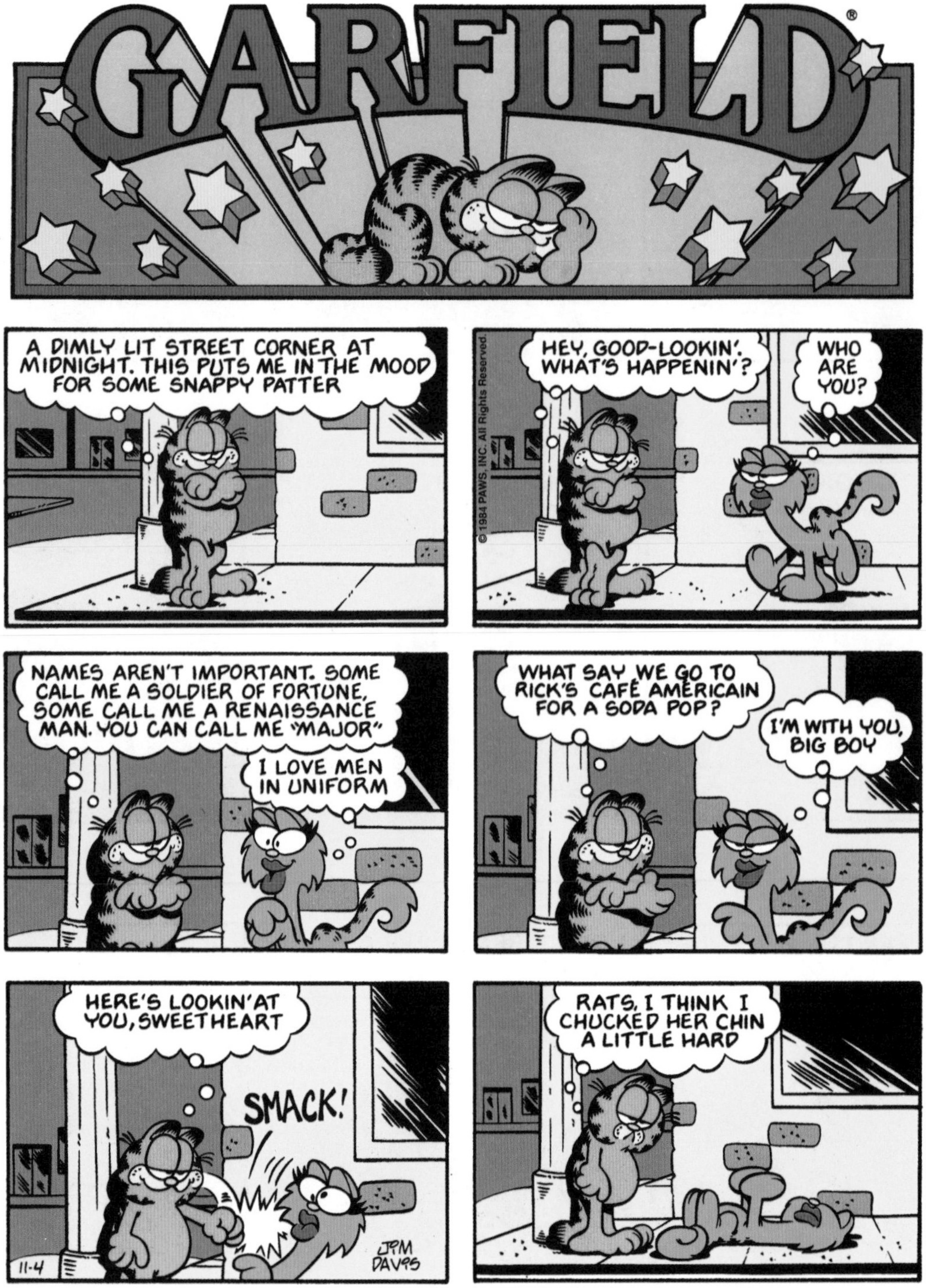
GARFIELD®
A DIMLY LIT STREET CORNER AT MIDNIGHT. THIS PUTS ME IN THE MOOD FOR SOME SNAPPY PATTER
HEY, GOOD-LOOKIN'. WHAT'S HAPPENIN'?
WHO ARE YOU?
© 1984 PAWS, INC. All Rights Reserved.
NAMES AREN'T IMPORTANT. SOME CALL ME A SOLDIER OF FORTUNE, SOME CALL ME A RENAISSANCE MAN. YOU CAN CALL ME "MAJOR"
I LOVE MEN IN UNIFORM
WHAT SAY WE GO TO RICK'S CAFÉ AMÉRICAIN FOR A SODA POP?
I'M WITH YOU, BIG BOY
HERE'S LOOKIN' AT YOU, SWEETHEART
SMACK!
11-4
JIM DAVIS
RATS, I THINK I CHUCKED HER CHIN A LITTLE HARD

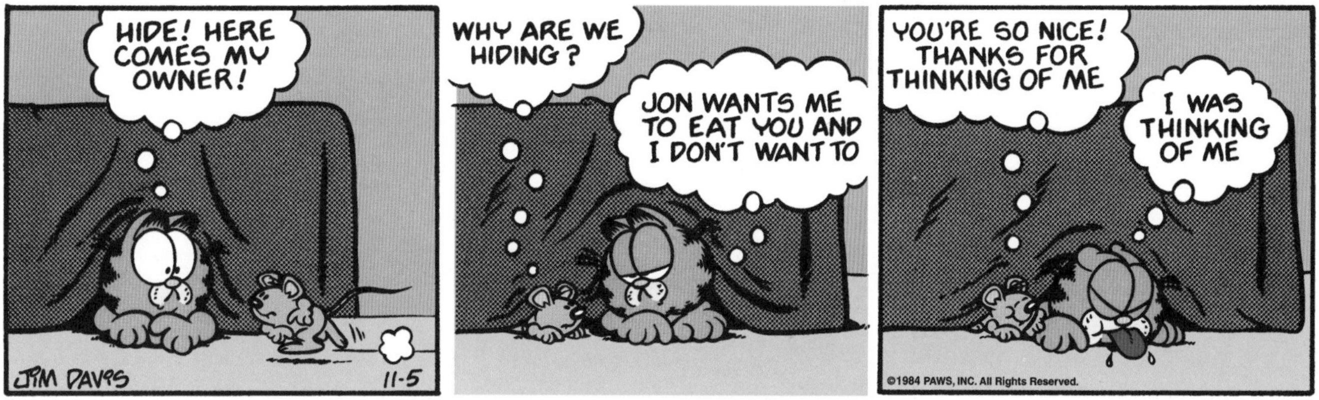
HIDE! HERE COMES MY OWNER!
JIM DAVIS
11-5
WHY ARE WE HIDING?
JON WANTS ME TO EAT YOU AND I DON'T WANT TO
YOU'RE SO NICE! THANKS FOR THINKING OF ME
I WAS THINKING OF ME
©1984 PAWS, INC. All Rights Reserved.

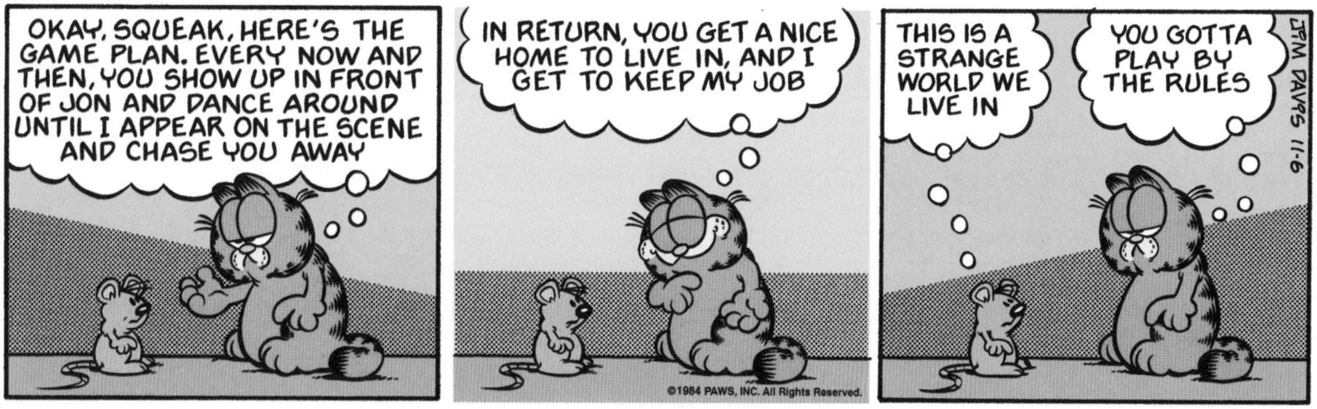
OKAY, SQUEAK, HERE'S THE GAME PLAN. EVERY NOW AND THEN, YOU SHOW UP IN FRONT OF JON AND DANCE AROUND UNTIL I APPEAR ON THE SCENE AND CHASE YOU AWAY
IN RETURN, YOU GET A NICE HOME TO LIVE IN, AND I GET TO KEEP MY JOB
©1984 PAWS, INC. All Rights Reserved.
THIS IS A STRANGE WORLD WE LIVE IN
YOU GOTTA PLAY BY THE RULES
JIM DAVIS 11-6

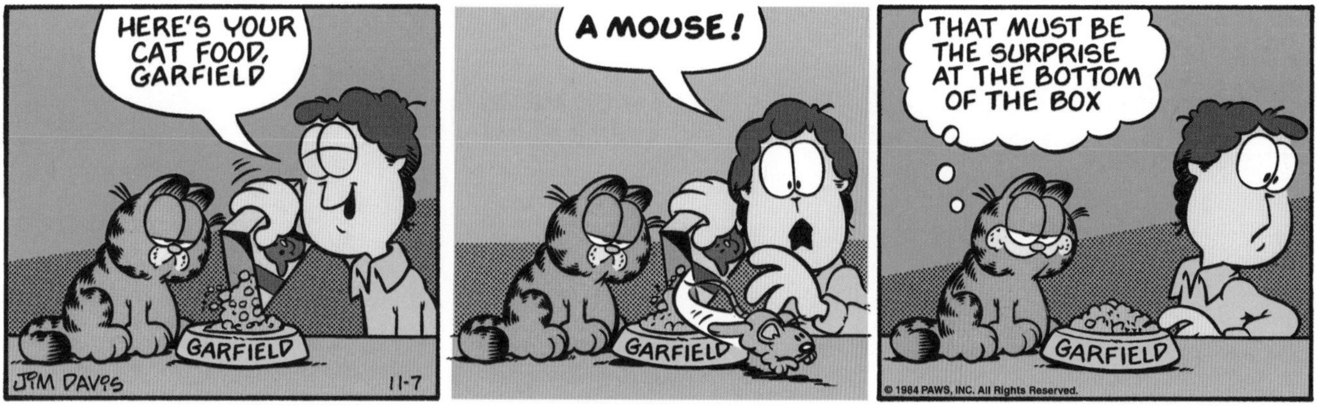
HERE'S YOUR CAT FOOD, GARFIELD
GARFIELD
JIM DAVIS
11-7
A MOUSE!
GARFIELD
THAT MUST BE THE SURPRISE AT THE BOTTOM OF THE BOX
GARFIELD
© 1984 PAWS, INC. All Rights Reserved.

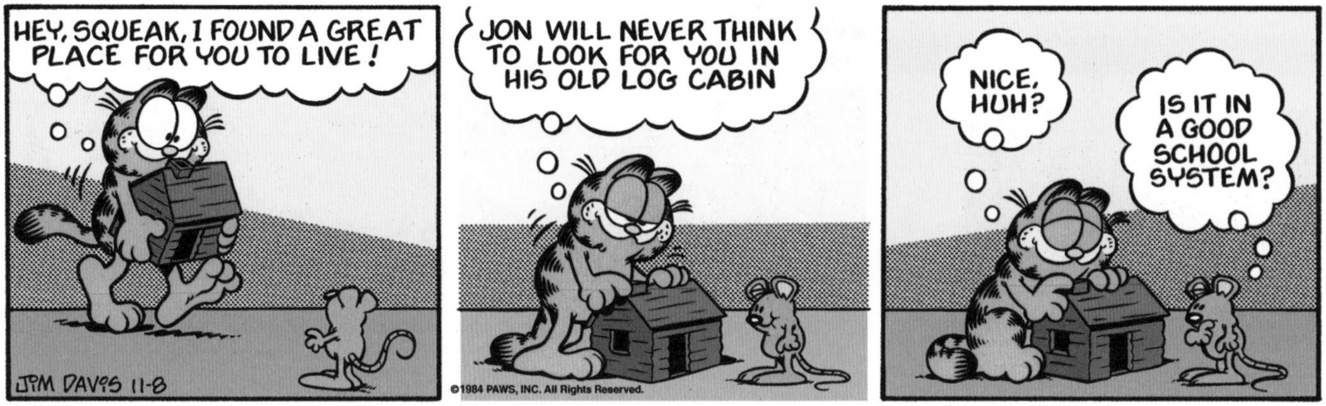
HEY, SQUEAK, I FOUND A GREAT PLACE FOR YOU TO LIVE!
JON WILL NEVER THINK TO LOOK FOR YOU IN HIS OLD LOG CABIN
NICE, HUH?
IS IT IN A GOOD SCHOOL SYSTEM?
JIM DAVIS 11-8
©1984 PAWS, INC. All Rights Reserved.

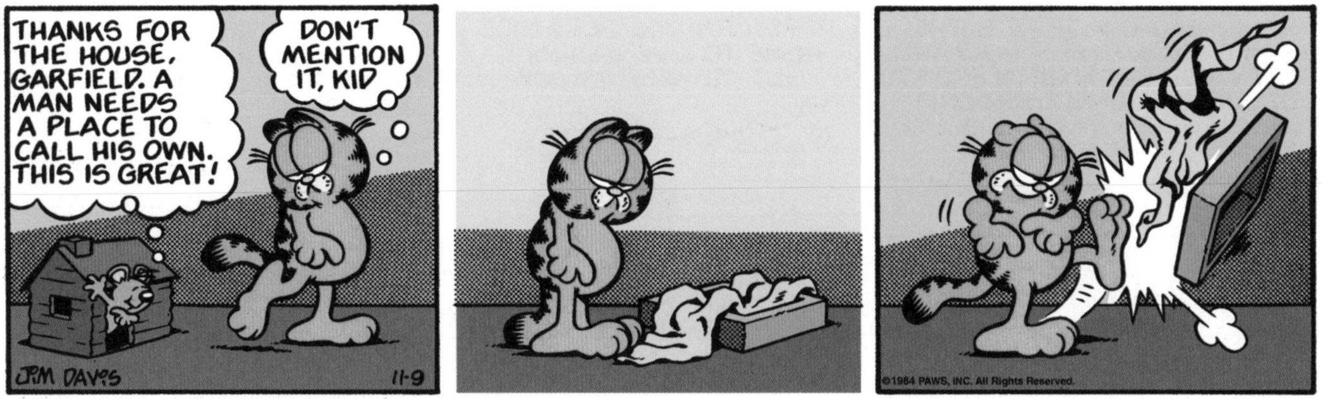
THANKS FOR THE HOUSE, GARFIELD. A MAN NEEDS A PLACE TO CALL HIS OWN. THIS IS GREAT!
DON'T MENTION IT, KID
JIM DAVIS 11-9
©1984 PAWS, INC. All Rights Reserved.

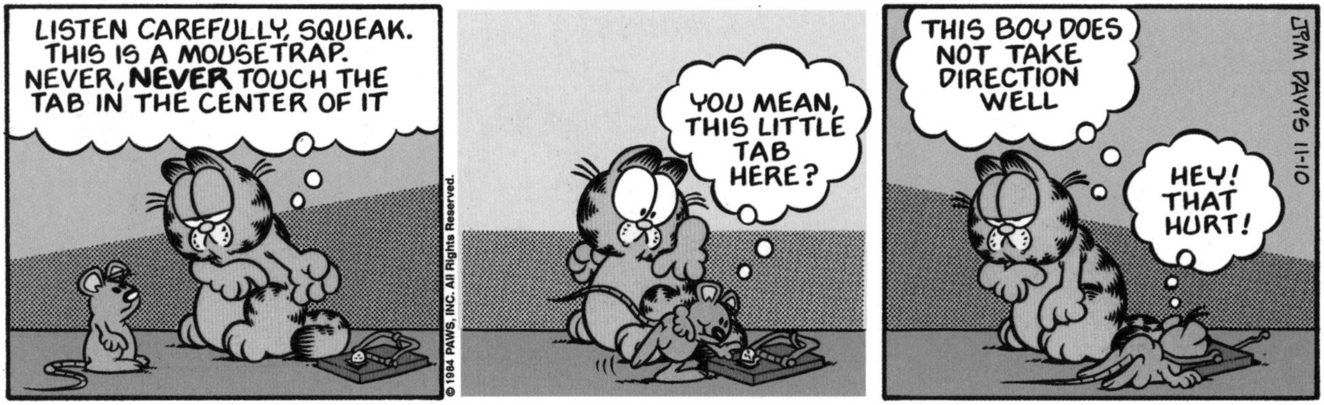
LISTEN CAREFULLY, SQUEAK. THIS IS A MOUSETRAP. NEVER, NEVER TOUCH THE TAB IN THE CENTER OF IT
YOU MEAN, THIS LITTLE TAB HERE?
THIS BOY DOES NOT TAKE DIRECTION WELL
HEY! THAT HURT!
JIM DAVIS 11-10
© 1984 PAWS, INC. All Rights Reserved.

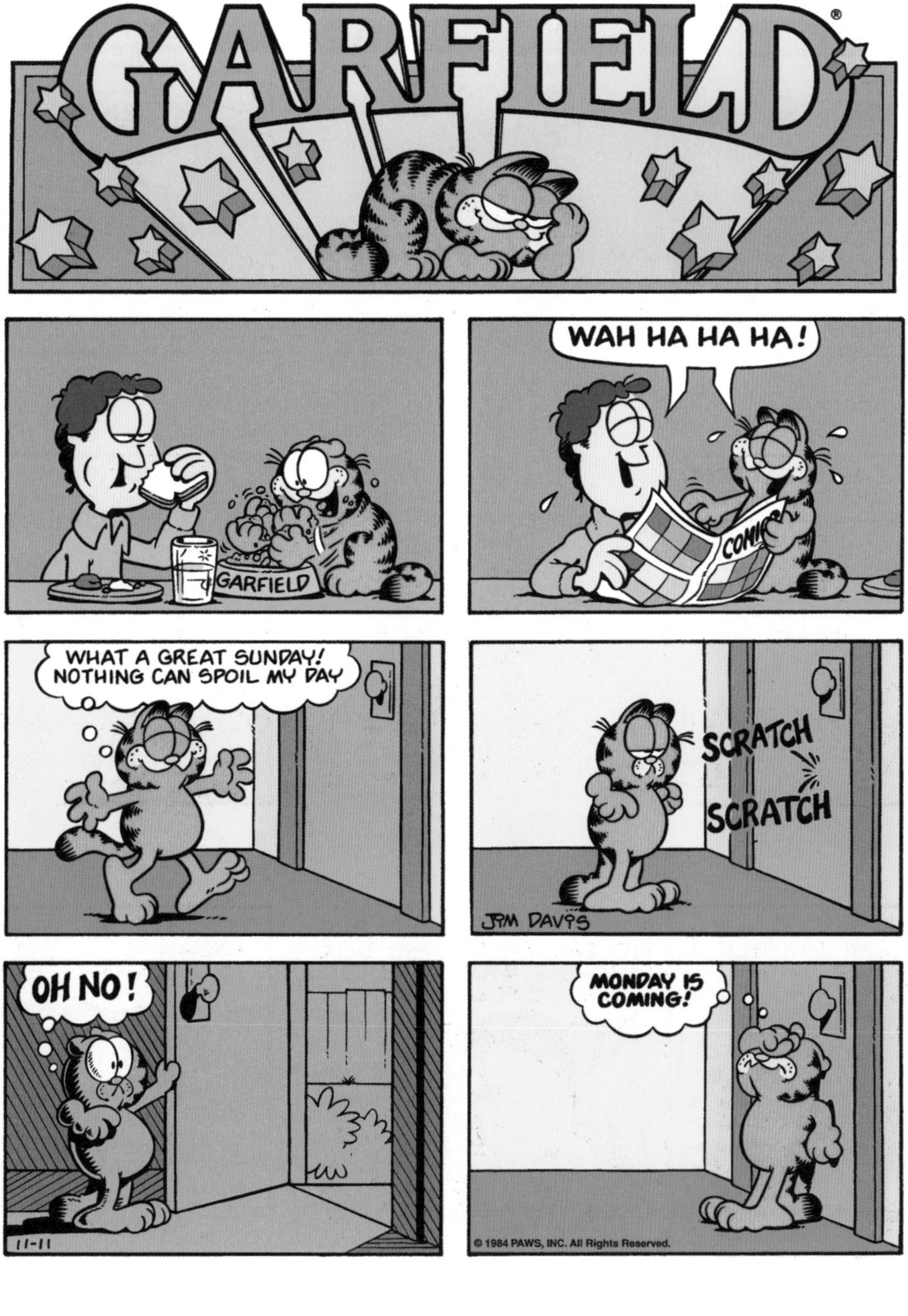
GARFIELD®
GARFIELD
WAH HA HA HA!
COMICS
WHAT A GREAT SUNDAY! NOTHING CAN SPOIL MY DAY
SCRATCH
SCRATCH
JIM DAVIS
OH NO!
MONDAY IS COMING!
11-11
© 1984 PAWS, INC. All Rights Reserved.

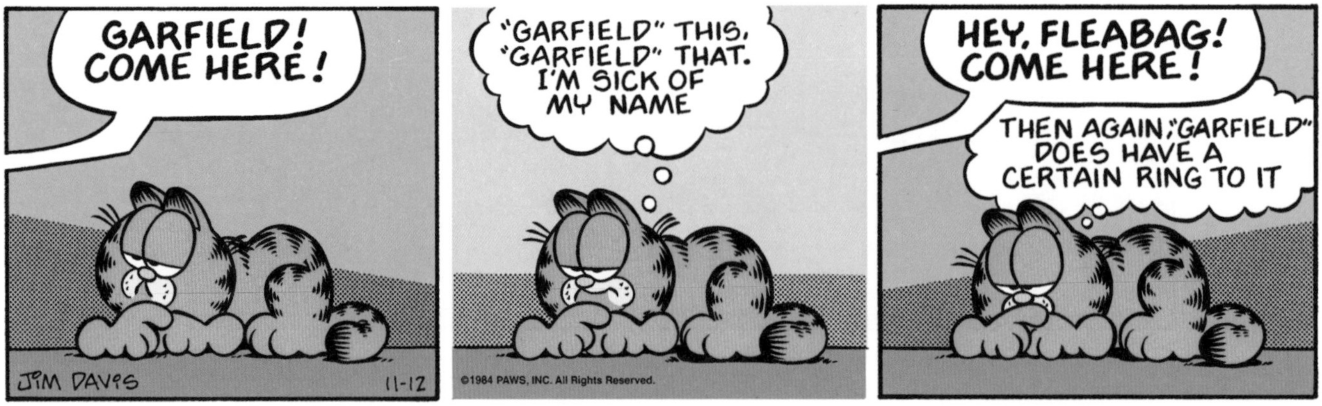
GARFIELD! COME HERE!
"GARFIELD" THIS, "GARFIELD" THAT. I'M SICK OF MY NAME
HEY, FLEABAG! COME HERE!
THEN AGAIN, "GARFIELD" DOES HAVE A CERTAIN RING TO IT
JIM DAVIS
11-12
©1984 PAWS, INC. All Rights Reserved.

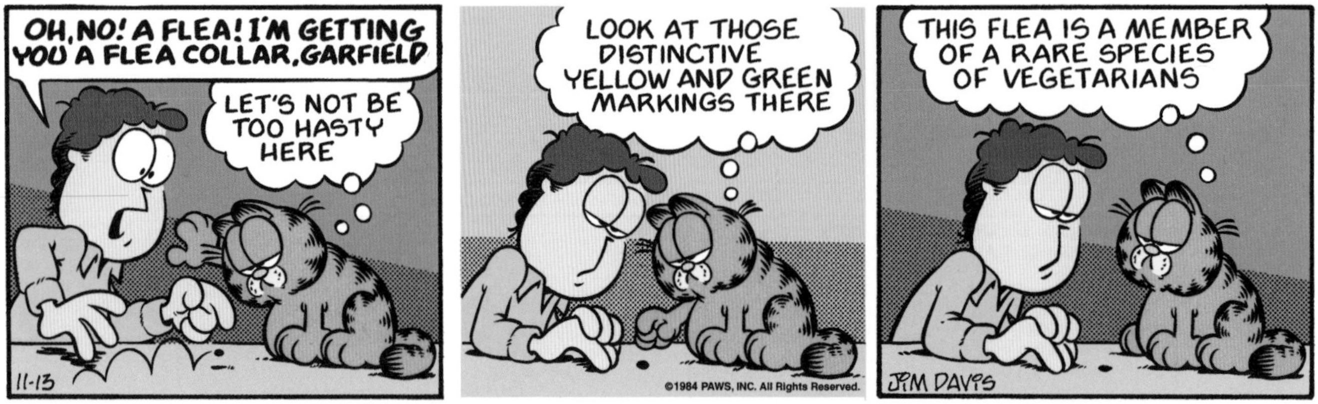
OH, NO! A FLEA! I'M GETTING YOU A FLEA COLLAR, GARFIELD
LET'S NOT BE TOO HASTY HERE
11-13
LOOK AT THOSE DISTINCTIVE YELLOW AND GREEN MARKINGS THERE
©1984 PAWS, INC. All Rights Reserved.
THIS FLEA IS A MEMBER OF A RARE SPECIES OF VEGETARIANS
JIM DAVIS

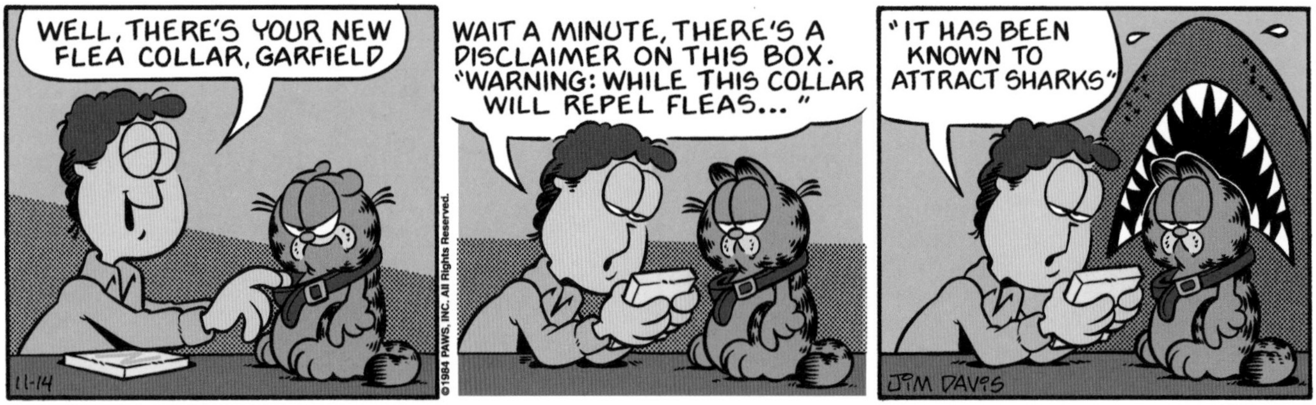
WELL, THERE'S YOUR NEW FLEA COLLAR, GARFIELD
11-14
©1984 PAWS, INC. All Rights Reserved.
WAIT A MINUTE, THERE'S A DISCLAIMER ON THIS BOX. "WARNING: WHILE THIS COLLAR WILL REPEL FLEAS..."
"IT HAS BEEN KNOWN TO ATTRACT SHARKS"
JIM DAVIS

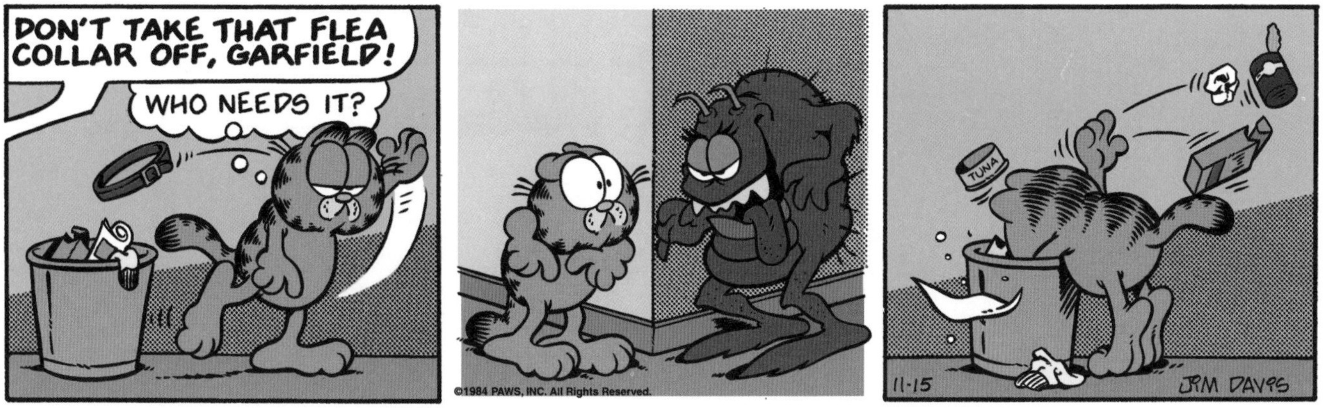
DON'T TAKE THAT FLEA COLLAR OFF, GARFIELD!
WHO NEEDS IT?
©1984 PAWS, INC. All Rights Reserved.
TUNA
11-15
JIM DAVIS

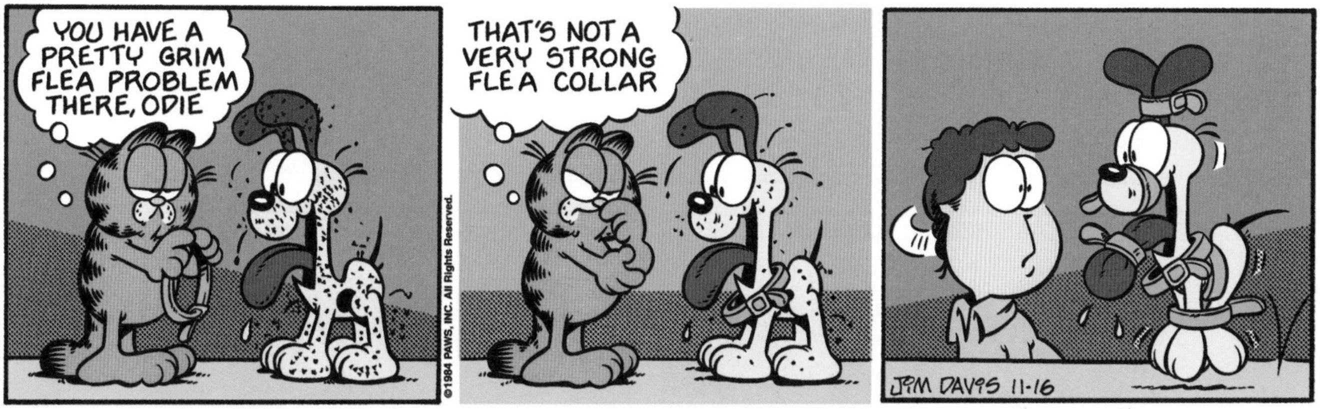
YOU HAVE A PRETTY GRIM FLEA PROBLEM THERE, ODIE
©1984 PAWS, INC. All Rights Reserved.
THAT'S NOT A VERY STRONG FLEA COLLAR
JIM DAVIS 11-16

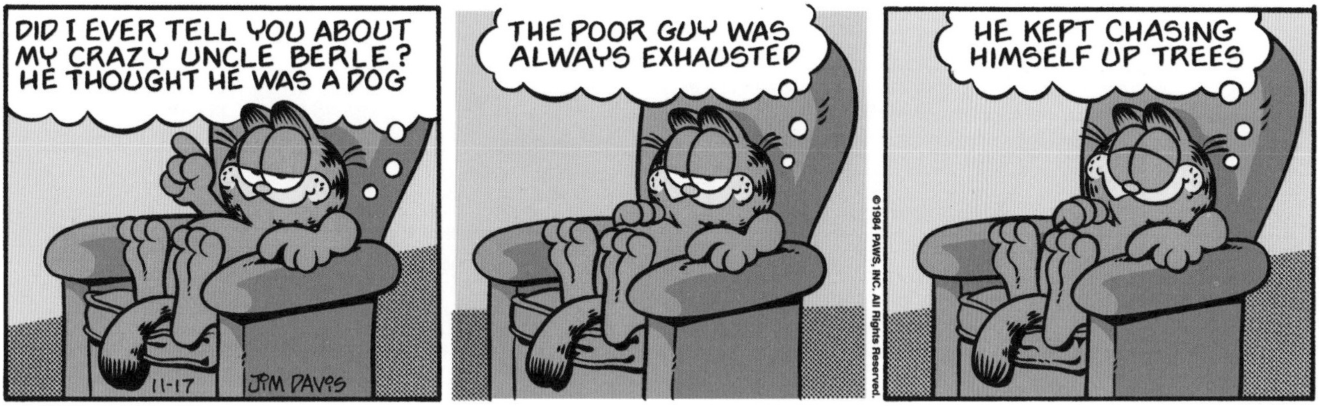
DID I EVER TELL YOU ABOUT MY CRAZY UNCLE BERLE? HE THOUGHT HE WAS A DOG
11-17
JIM DAVIS
THE POOR GUY WAS ALWAYS EXHAUSTED
©1984 PAWS, INC. All Rights Reserved.
HE KEPT CHASING HIMSELF UP TREES

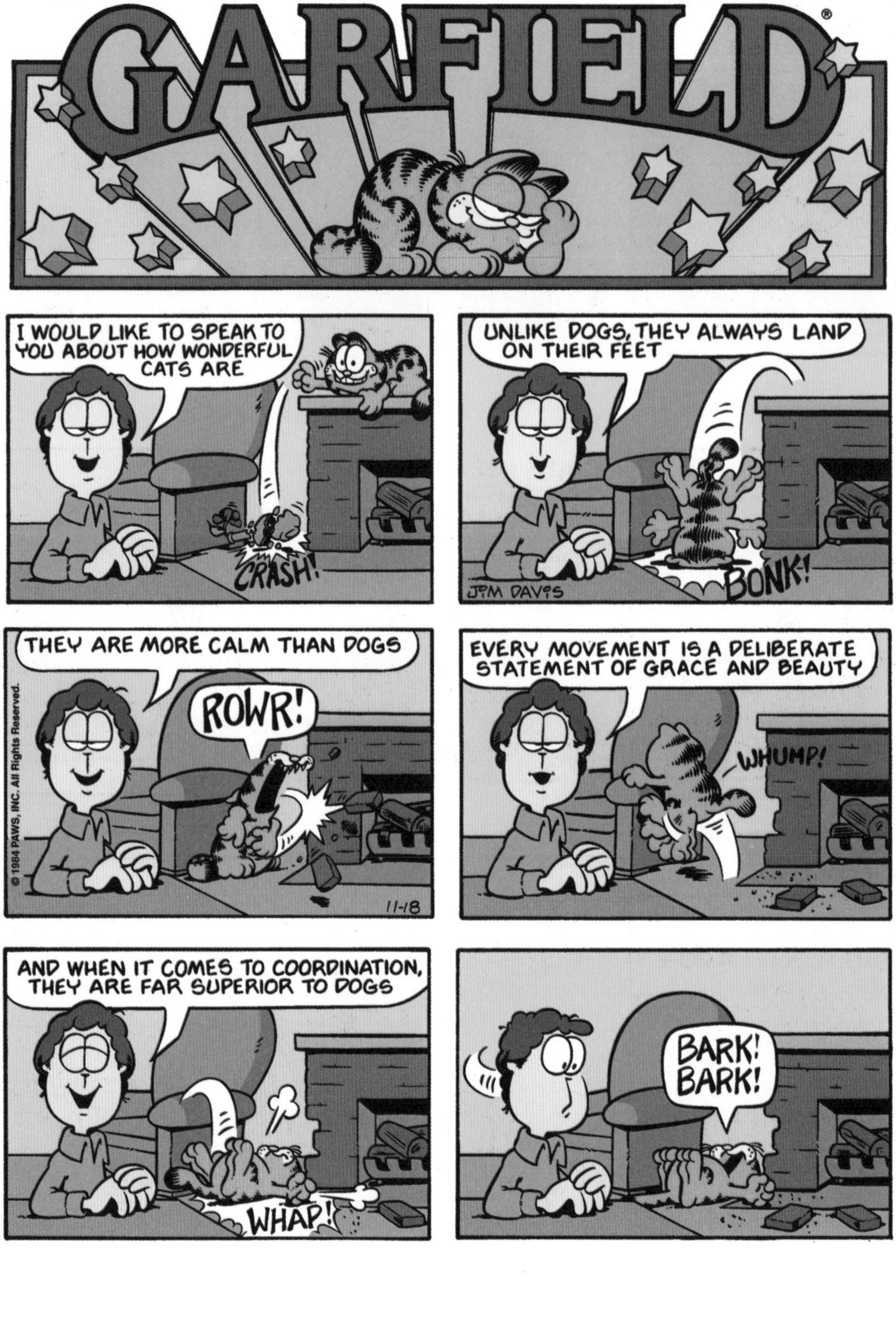
GARFIELD®
I WOULD LIKE TO SPEAK TO YOU ABOUT HOW WONDERFUL CATS ARE
CRASH!
UNLIKE DOGS, THEY ALWAYS LAND ON THEIR FEET
BONK!
JIM DAVIS
THEY ARE MORE CALM THAN DOGS
ROWR!
© 1984 PAWS, INC. All Rights Reserved.
11-18
EVERY MOVEMENT IS A DELIBERATE STATEMENT OF GRACE AND BEAUTY
WHUMP!
AND WHEN IT COMES TO COORDINATION, THEY ARE FAR SUPERIOR TO DOGS
WHAP!
BARK! BARK!

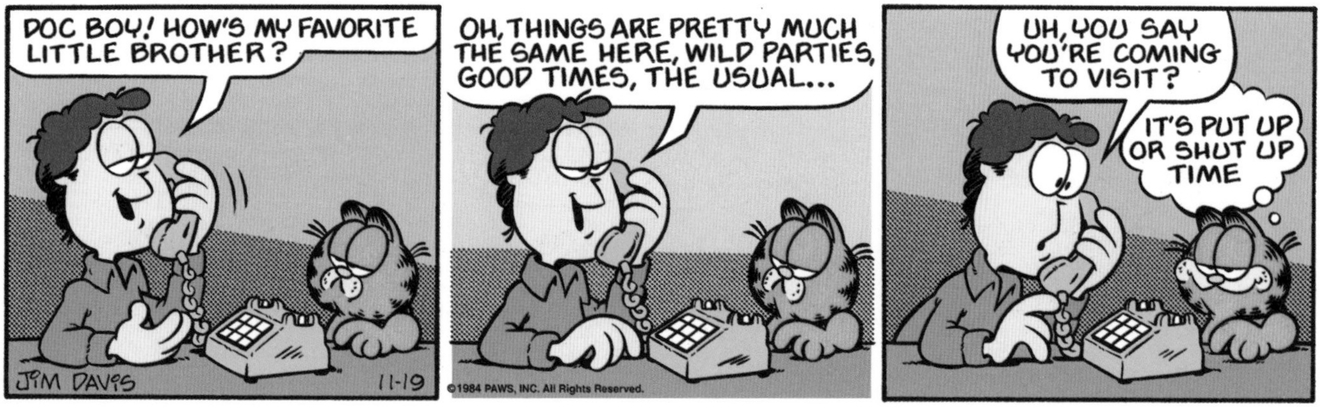
DOC BOY! HOW'S MY FAVORITE LITTLE BROTHER?
JIM DAVIS
11-19
OH, THINGS ARE PRETTY MUCH THE SAME HERE, WILD PARTIES, GOOD TIMES, THE USUAL...
©1984 PAWS, INC. All Rights Reserved.
UH, YOU SAY YOU'RE COMING TO VISIT?
IT'S PUT UP OR SHUT UP TIME

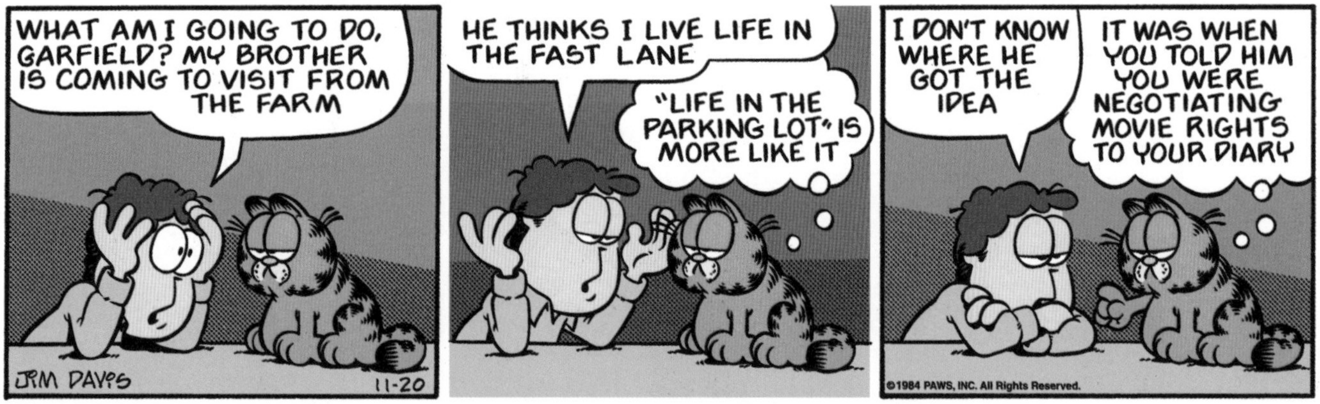
WHAT AM I GOING TO DO, GARFIELD? MY BROTHER IS COMING TO VISIT FROM THE FARM
JIM DAVIS
11-20
HE THINKS I LIVE LIFE IN THE FAST LANE
"LIFE IN THE PARKING LOT" IS MORE LIKE IT
I DON'T KNOW WHERE HE GOT THE IDEA
IT WAS WHEN YOU TOLD HIM YOU WERE NEGOTIATING MOVIE RIGHTS TO YOUR DIARY
©1984 PAWS, INC. All Rights Reserved.

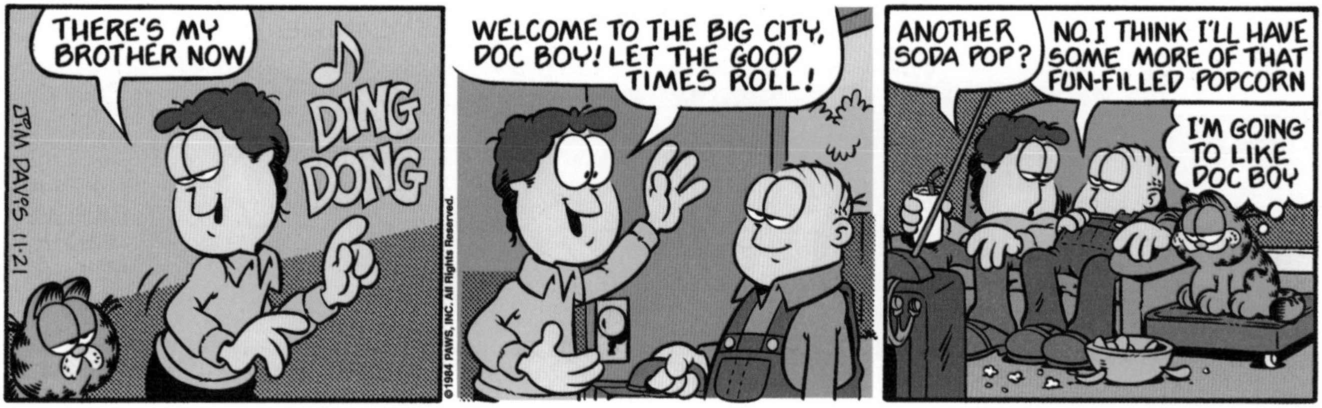
THERE'S MY BROTHER NOW
DING DONG
JIM DAVIS 11-21
WELCOME TO THE BIG CITY, DOC BOY! LET THE GOOD TIMES ROLL!
©1984 PAWS, INC. All Rights Reserved.
ANOTHER SODA POP?
NO. I THINK I'LL HAVE SOME MORE OF THAT FUN-FILLED POPCORN
I'M GOING TO LIKE DOC BOY

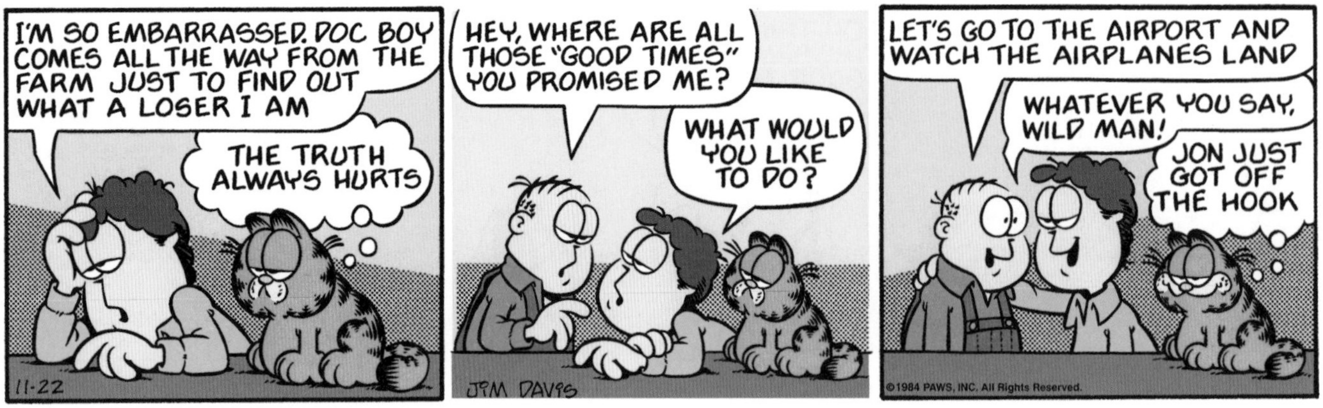
I'M SO EMBARRASSED. DOC BOY COMES ALL THE WAY FROM THE FARM JUST TO FIND OUT WHAT A LOSER I AM
THE TRUTH ALWAYS HURTS
11-22
HEY, WHERE ARE ALL THOSE "GOOD TIMES" YOU PROMISED ME?
WHAT WOULD YOU LIKE TO DO?
JIM DAVIS
LET'S GO TO THE AIRPORT AND WATCH THE AIRPLANES LAND
WHATEVER YOU SAY, WILD MAN!
JON JUST GOT OFF THE HOOK
©1984 PAWS, INC. All Rights Reserved.

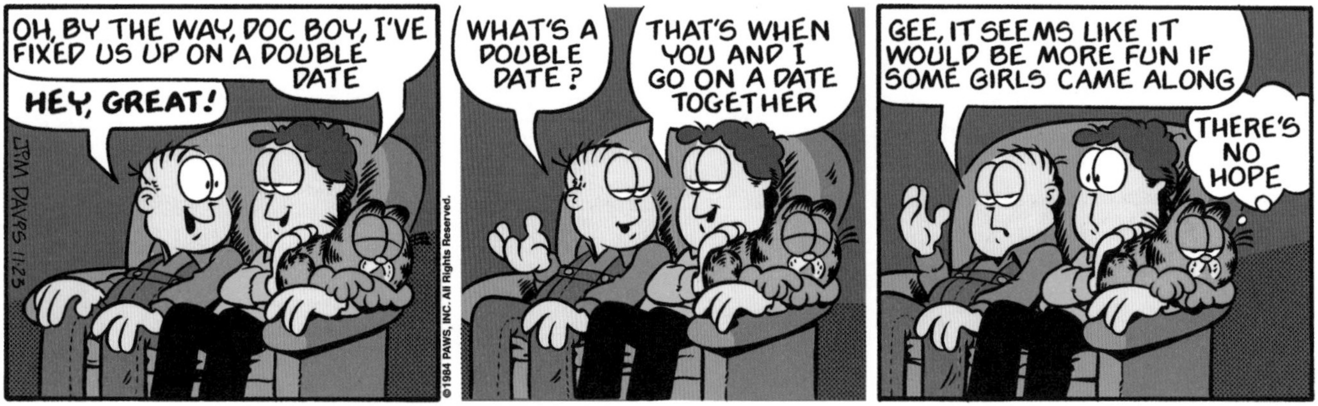
OH, BY THE WAY, DOC BOY, I'VE FIXED US UP ON A DOUBLE DATE
HEY, GREAT!
JIM DAVIS 11-23
©1984 PAWS, INC. All Rights Reserved.
WHAT'S A DOUBLE DATE?
THAT'S WHEN YOU AND I GO ON A DATE TOGETHER
GEE, IT SEEMS LIKE IT WOULD BE MORE FUN IF SOME GIRLS CAME ALONG
THERE'S NO HOPE

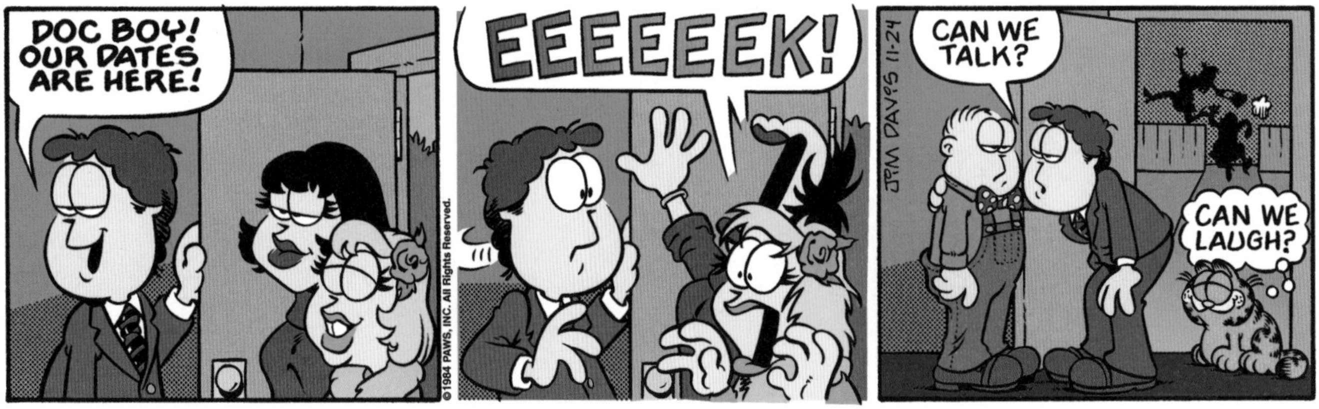
DOC BOY! OUR DATES ARE HERE!
©1984 PAWS, INC. All Rights Reserved.
EEEEEEK!
JIM DAVIS 11-24
CAN WE TALK?
CAN WE LAUGH?

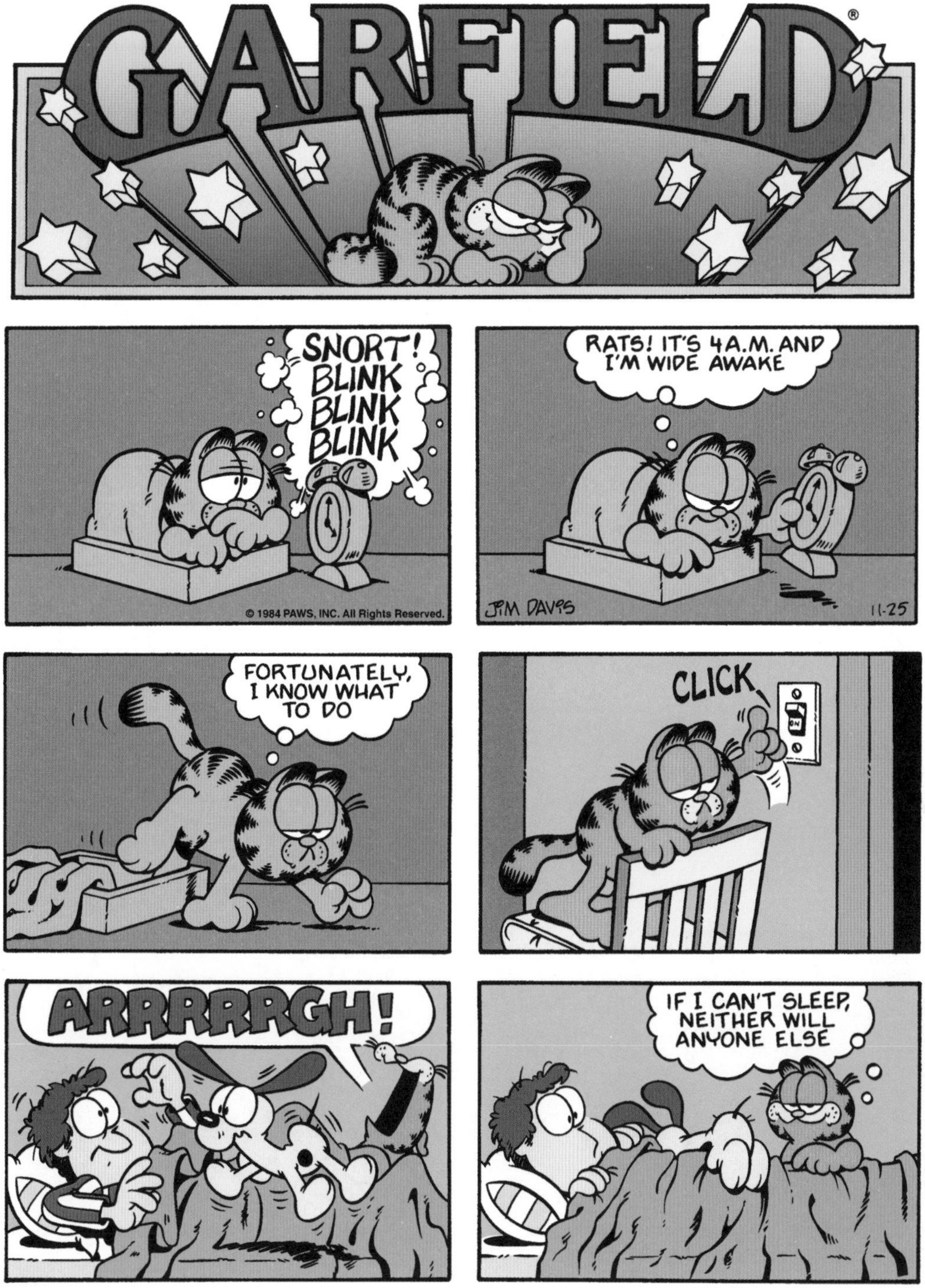
GARFIELD®
SNORT! BLINK BLINK BLINK
© 1984 PAWS, INC. All Rights Reserved.
RATS! IT'S 4 A.M. AND I'M WIDE AWAKE
JIM DAVIS
11-25
FORTUNATELY, I KNOW WHAT TO DO
CLICK
ON
ARRRRRGH!
IF I CAN'T SLEEP, NEITHER WILL ANYONE ELSE

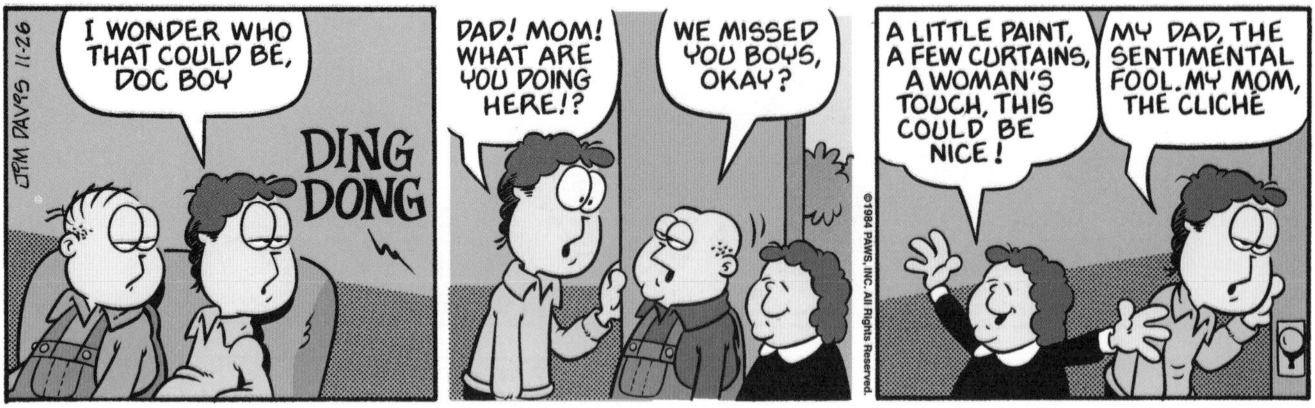
JIM DAVIS 11-26
I WONDER WHO THAT COULD BE, DOC BOY
DING DONG
DAD! MOM! WHAT ARE YOU DOING HERE!?
WE MISSED YOU BOYS, OKAY?
©1984 PAWS, INC. All Rights Reserved.
A LITTLE PAINT, A FEW CURTAINS, A WOMAN'S TOUCH, THIS COULD BE NICE!
MY DAD, THE SENTIMENTAL FOOL. MY MOM, THE CLICHÉ

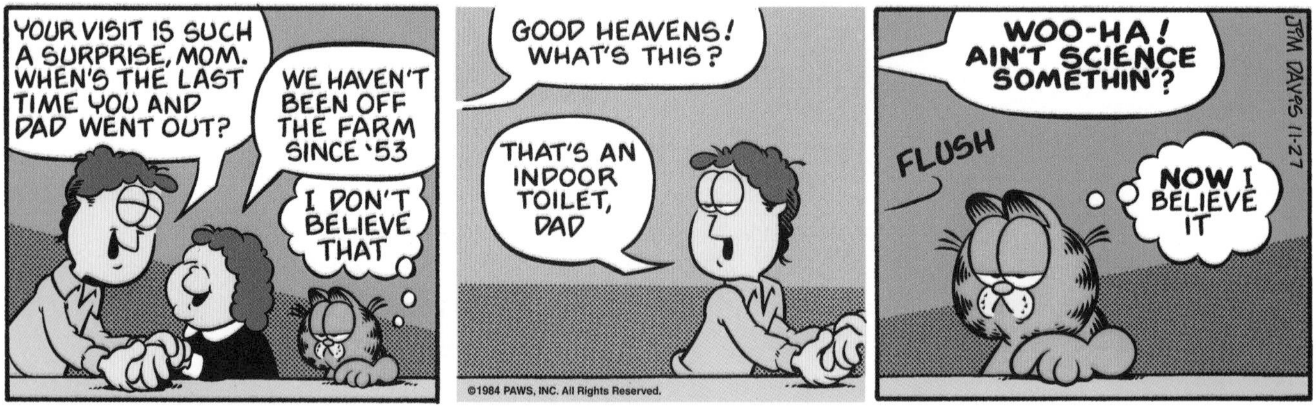
YOUR VISIT IS SUCH A SURPRISE, MOM. WHEN'S THE LAST TIME YOU AND DAD WENT OUT?
WE HAVEN'T BEEN OFF THE FARM SINCE '53
I DON'T BELIEVE THAT
GOOD HEAVENS! WHAT'S THIS?
THAT'S AN INDOOR TOILET, DAD
©1984 PAWS, INC. All Rights Reserved.
JIM DAVIS 11-27
WOO-HA! AIN'T SCIENCE SOMETHIN'?
FLUSH
NOW I BELIEVE IT

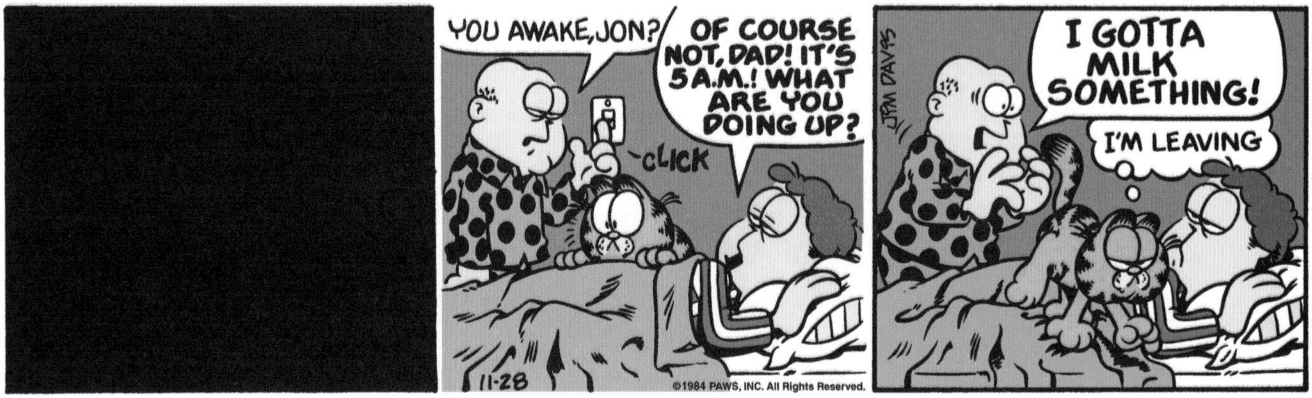
YOU AWAKE, JON?
OF COURSE NOT, DAD! IT'S 5 A.M.! WHAT ARE YOU DOING UP?
CLICK
11-28
©1984 PAWS, INC. All Rights Reserved.
JIM DAVIS
I GOTTA MILK SOMETHING!
I'M LEAVING

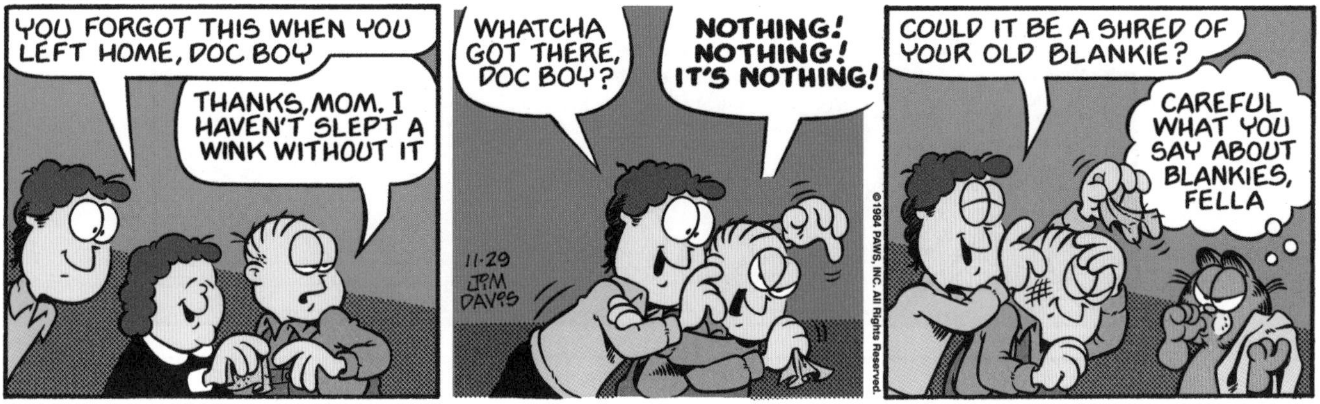
YOU FORGOT THIS WHEN YOU LEFT HOME, DOC BOY
THANKS, MOM. I HAVEN'T SLEPT A WINK WITHOUT IT
WHATCHA GOT THERE, DOC BOY?
NOTHING! NOTHING! IT'S NOTHING!
11-29 JIM DAVIS
COULD IT BE A SHRED OF YOUR OLD BLANKIE?
CAREFUL WHAT YOU SAY ABOUT BLANKIES, FELLA
©1984 PAWS, INC. All Rights Reserved.

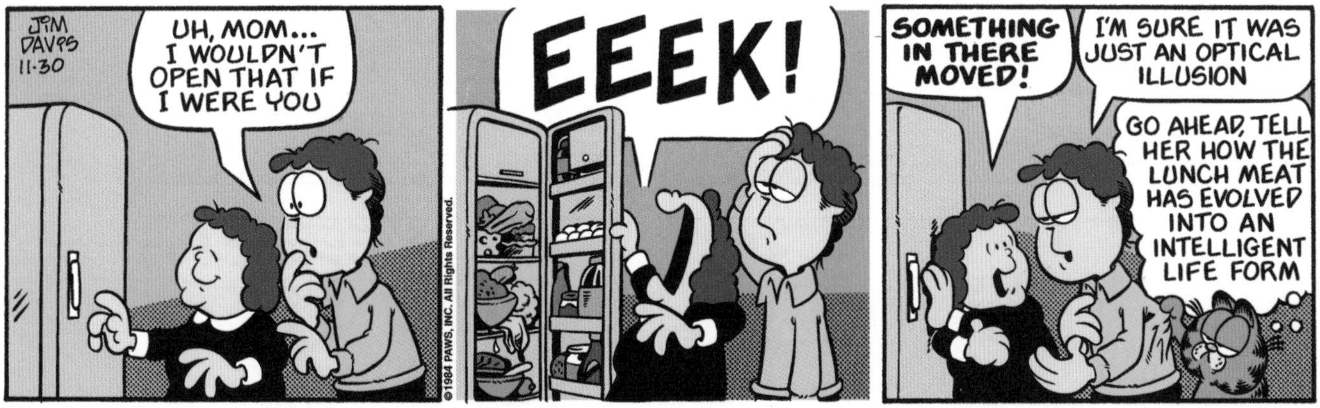
JIM DAVIS 11-30
UH, MOM... I WOULDN'T OPEN THAT IF I WERE YOU
©1984 PAWS, INC. All Rights Reserved.
EEEK!
SOMETHING IN THERE MOVED!
I'M SURE IT WAS JUST AN OPTICAL ILLUSION
GO AHEAD, TELL HER HOW THE LUNCH MEAT HAS EVOLVED INTO AN INTELLIGENT LIFE FORM

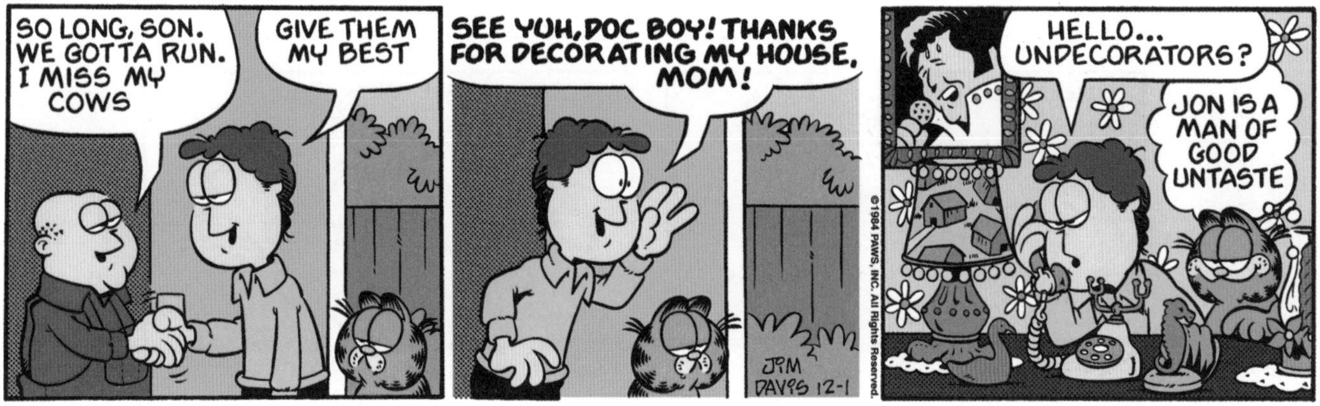
SO LONG, SON. WE GOTTA RUN. I MISS MY COWS
GIVE THEM MY BEST
SEE YUH, DOC BOY! THANKS FOR DECORATING MY HOUSE, MOM!
JIM DAVIS 12-1
HELLO... UNDECORATORS?
JON IS A MAN OF GOOD UNTASTE
©1984 PAWS, INC. All Rights Reserved.

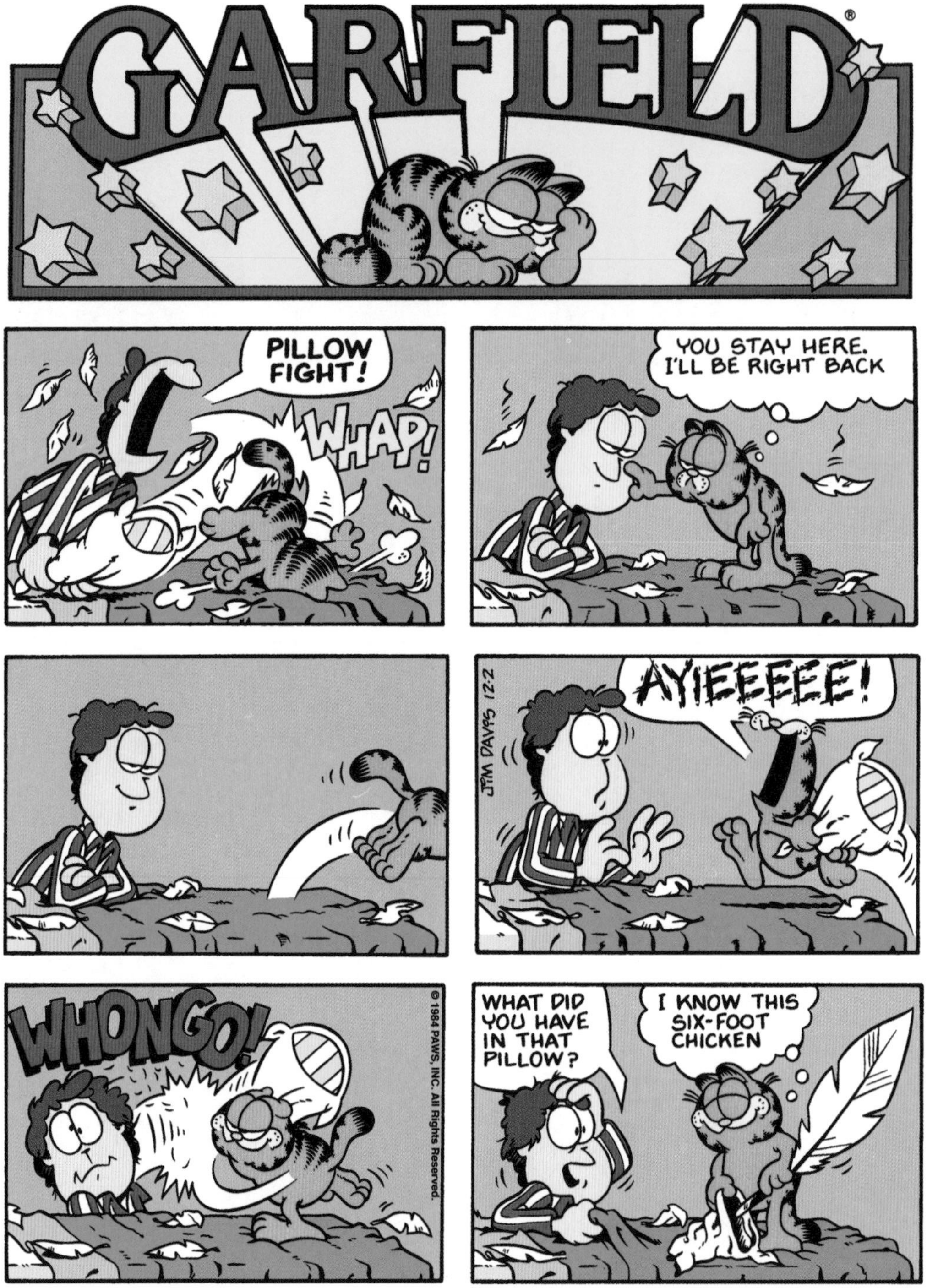
GARFIELD®
PILLOW FIGHT!
WHAP!
YOU STAY HERE. I'LL BE RIGHT BACK
JIM DAVIS 12-2
AYIEEEEEE!
WHONGO!
© 1984 PAWS, INC. All Rights Reserved.
WHAT DID YOU HAVE IN THAT PILLOW?
I KNOW THIS SIX-FOOT CHICKEN

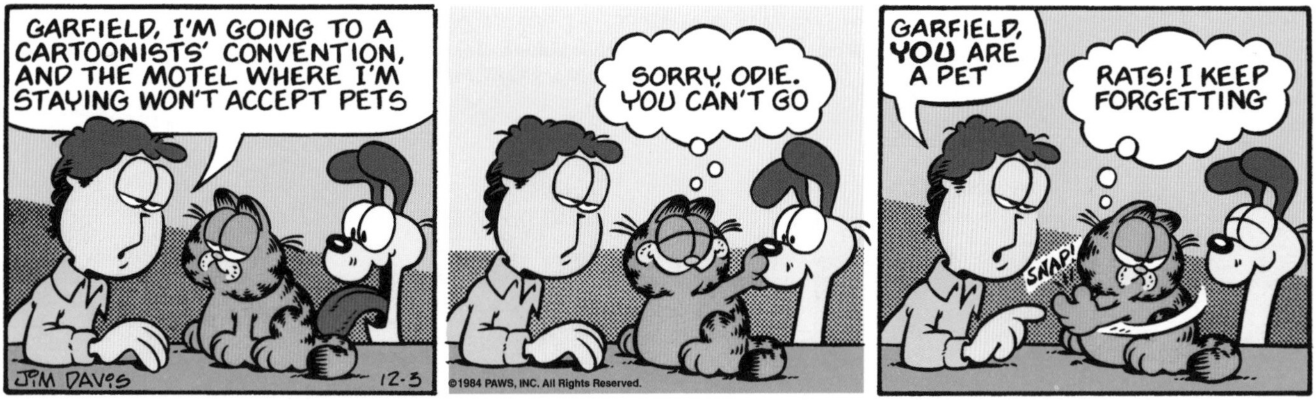
GARFIELD, I'M GOING TO A CARTOONISTS' CONVENTION, AND THE MOTEL WHERE I'M STAYING WON'T ACCEPT PETS
SORRY, ODIE. YOU CAN'T GO
GARFIELD, YOU ARE A PET
RATS! I KEEP FORGETTING
SNAP!
JIM DAVIS 12-3
©1984 PAWS, INC. All Rights Reserved.

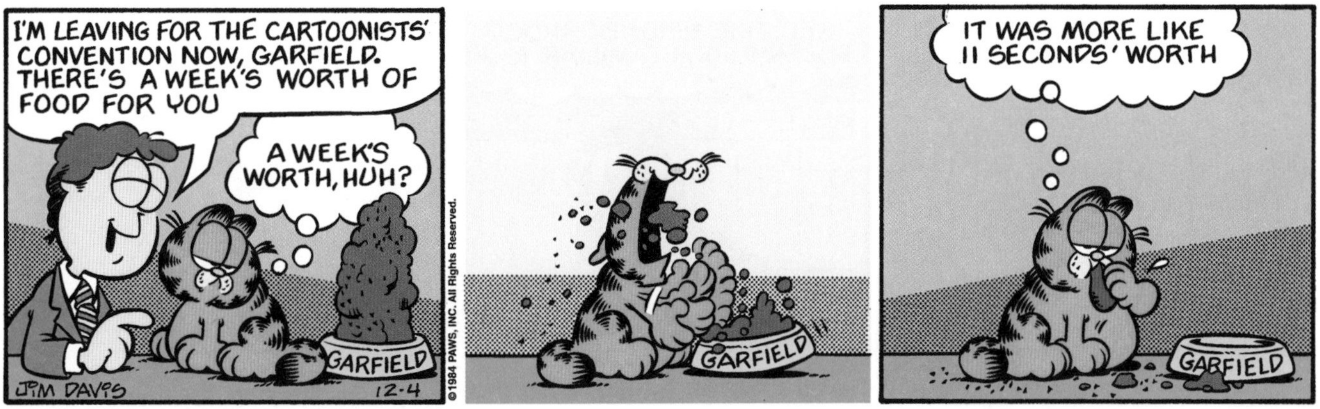
I'M LEAVING FOR THE CARTOONISTS' CONVENTION NOW, GARFIELD. THERE'S A WEEK'S WORTH OF FOOD FOR YOU
A WEEK'S WORTH, HUH?
GARFIELD
JIM DAVIS 12-4
©1984 PAWS, INC. All Rights Reserved.
GARFIELD
IT WAS MORE LIKE 11 SECONDS' WORTH
GARFIELD

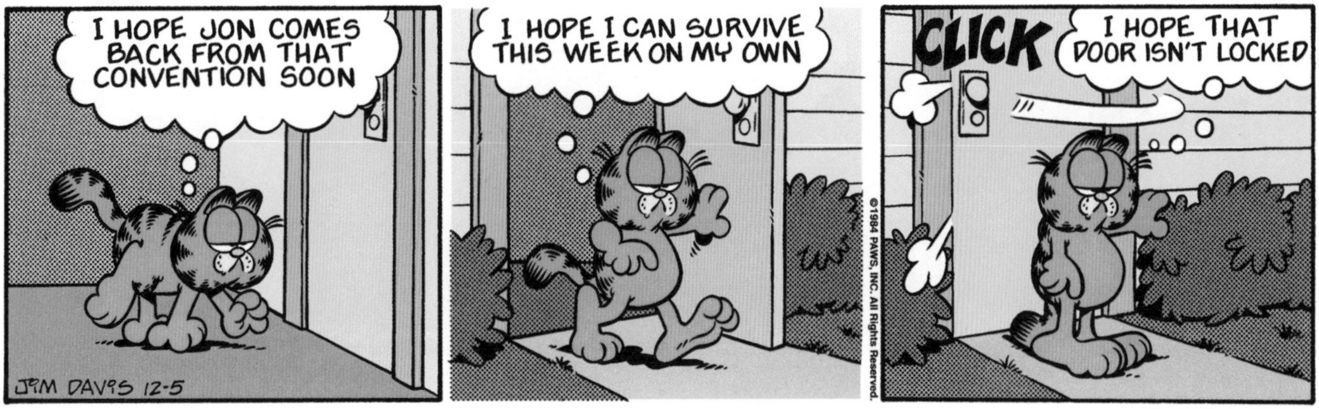
I HOPE JON COMES BACK FROM THAT CONVENTION SOON
JIM DAVIS 12-5
I HOPE I CAN SURVIVE THIS WEEK ON MY OWN
©1984 PAWS, INC. All Rights Reserved.
CLICK
I HOPE THAT DOOR ISN'T LOCKED

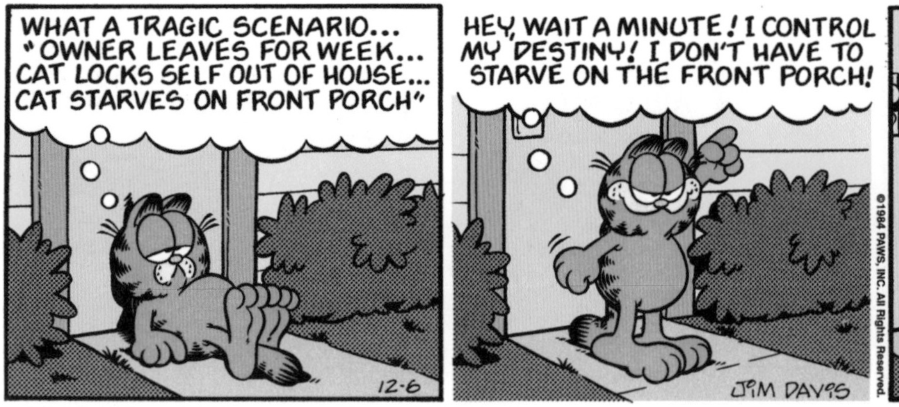
WHAT A TRAGIC SCENARIO... "OWNER LEAVES FOR WEEK... CAT LOCKS SELF OUT OF HOUSE... CAT STARVES ON FRONT PORCH"
12-6
HEY, WAIT A MINUTE! I CONTROL MY DESTINY! I DON'T HAVE TO STARVE ON THE FRONT PORCH!
JIM DAVIS
©1984 PAWS, INC. All Rights Reserved.
"CAT STARVES IN BUSHES"

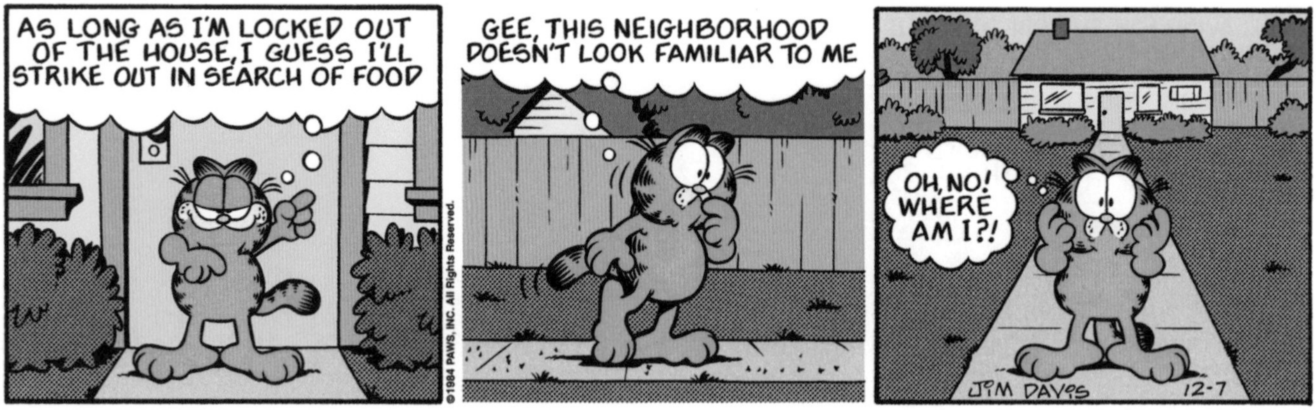
AS LONG AS I'M LOCKED OUT OF THE HOUSE, I GUESS I'LL STRIKE OUT IN SEARCH OF FOOD
©1984 PAWS, INC. All Rights Reserved.
GEE, THIS NEIGHBORHOOD DOESN'T LOOK FAMILIAR TO ME
OH, NO! WHERE AM I?!
JIM DAVIS
12-7

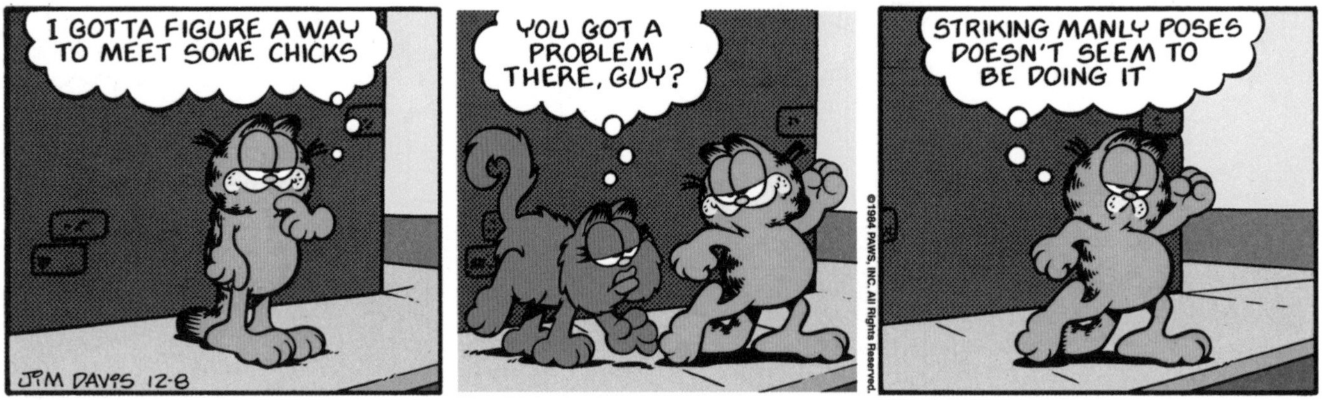
I GOTTA FIGURE A WAY TO MEET SOME CHICKS
JIM DAVIS 12-8
YOU GOT A PROBLEM THERE, GUY?
©1984 PAWS, INC. All Rights Reserved.
STRIKING MANLY POSES DOESN'T SEEM TO BE DOING IT

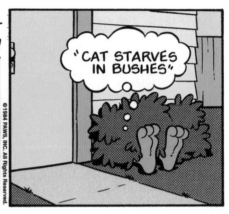

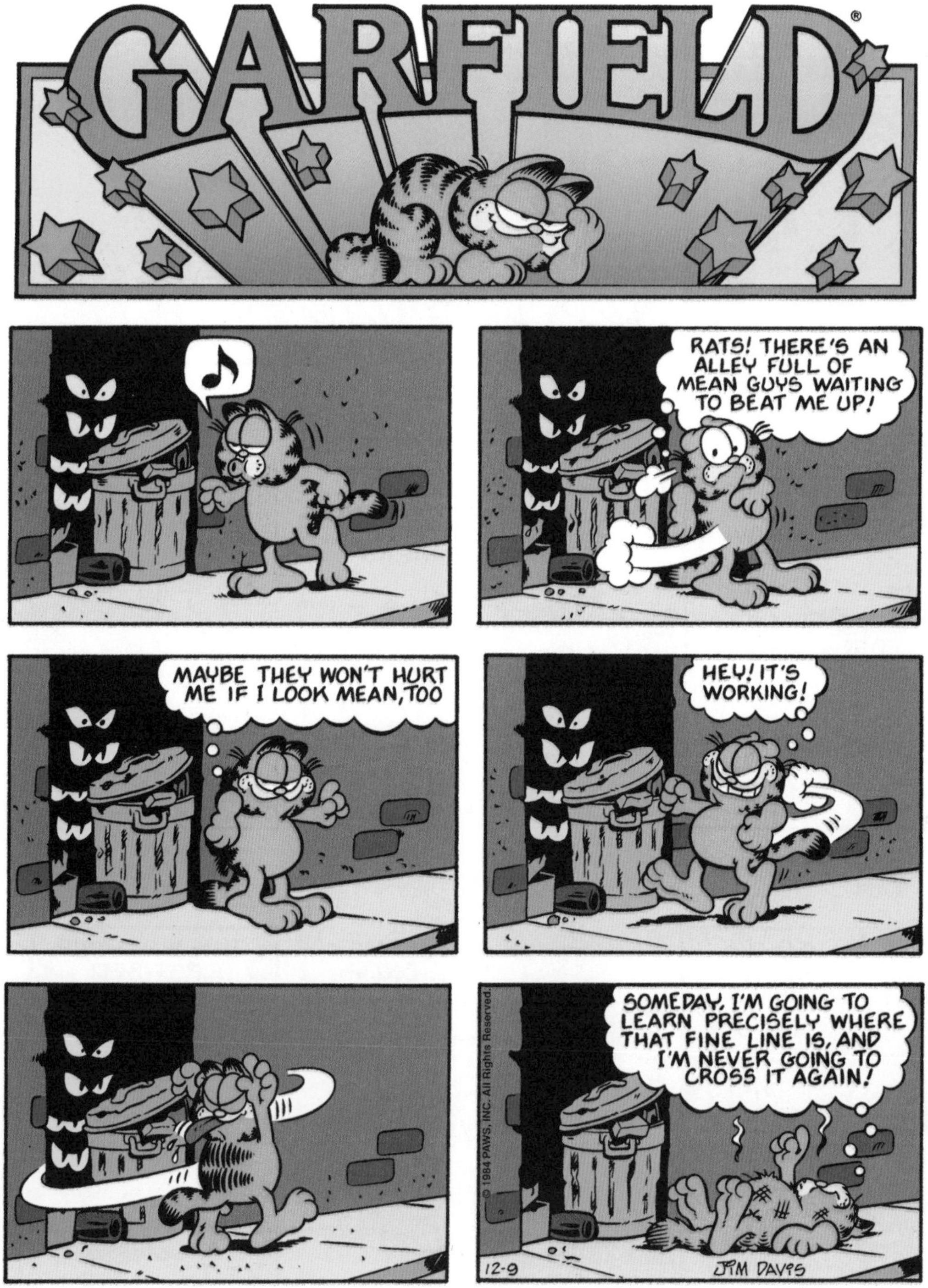
GARFIELD®
♪
RATS! THERE'S AN ALLEY FULL OF MEAN GUYS WAITING TO BEAT ME UP!
MAYBE THEY WON'T HURT ME IF I LOOK MEAN, TOO
HEY! IT'S WORKING!
SOMEDAY, I'M GOING TO LEARN PRECISELY WHERE THAT FINE LINE IS, AND I'M NEVER GOING TO CROSS IT AGAIN!
© 1984 PAWS, INC. All Rights Reserved.
12-9
JIM DAVIS

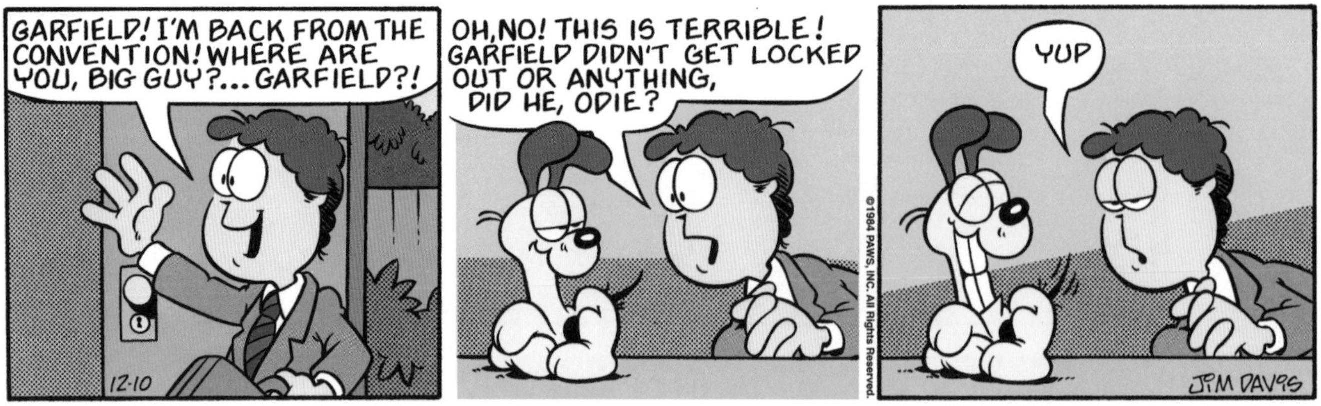
GARFIELD! I'M BACK FROM THE CONVENTION! WHERE ARE YOU, BIG GUY?... GARFIELD?!
12-10
OH, NO! THIS IS TERRIBLE! GARFIELD DIDN'T GET LOCKED OUT OR ANYTHING, DID HE, ODIE?
©1984 PAWS, INC. All Rights Reserved.
YUP
JIM DAVIS

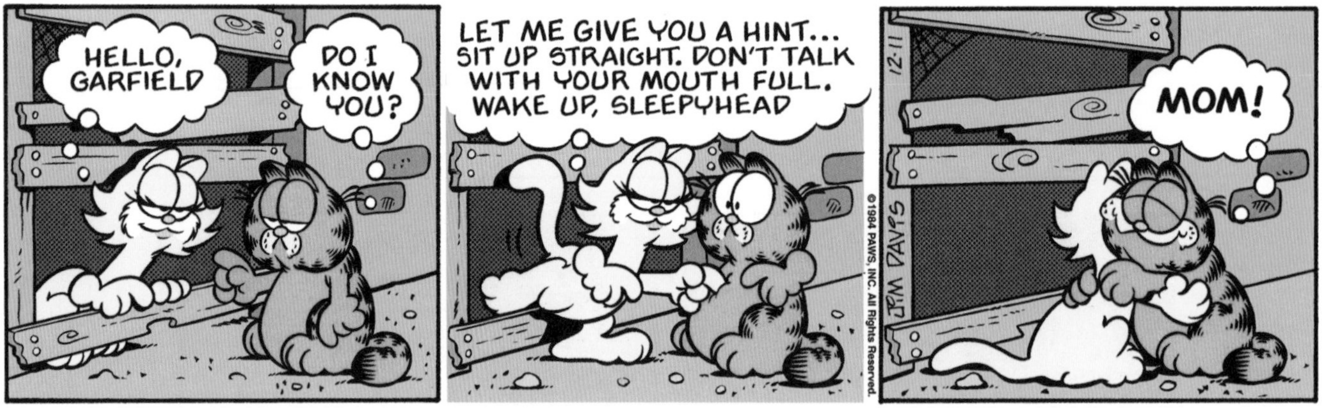
HELLO, GARFIELD
DO I KNOW YOU?
LET ME GIVE YOU A HINT... SIT UP STRAIGHT. DON'T TALK WITH YOUR MOUTH FULL. WAKE UP, SLEEPYHEAD
©1984 PAWS, INC. All Rights Reserved.
12-11
JIM DAVIS
MOM!

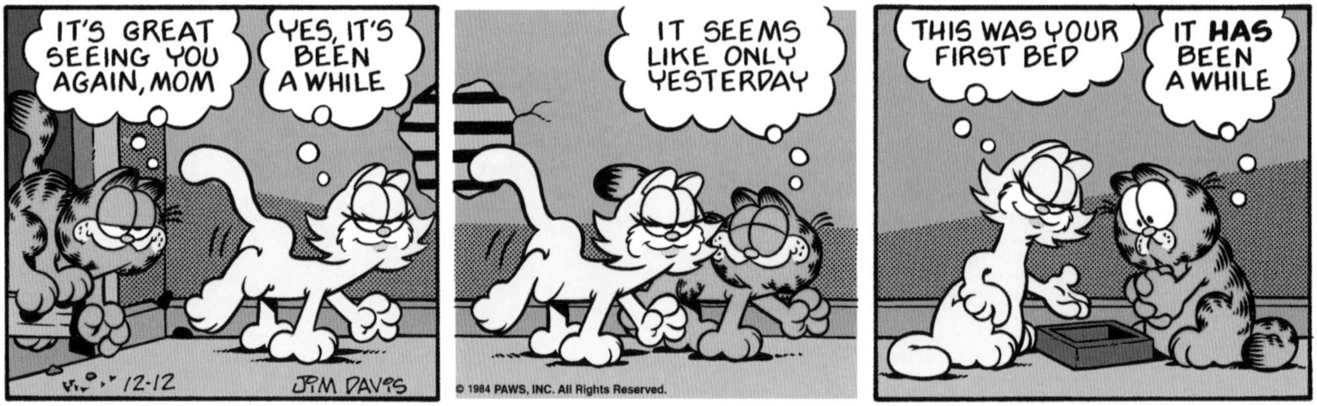
IT'S GREAT SEEING YOU AGAIN, MOM
YES, IT'S BEEN A WHILE
12-12
JIM DAVIS
IT SEEMS LIKE ONLY YESTERDAY
© 1984 PAWS, INC. All Rights Reserved.
THIS WAS YOUR FIRST BED
IT **HAS** BEEN A WHILE

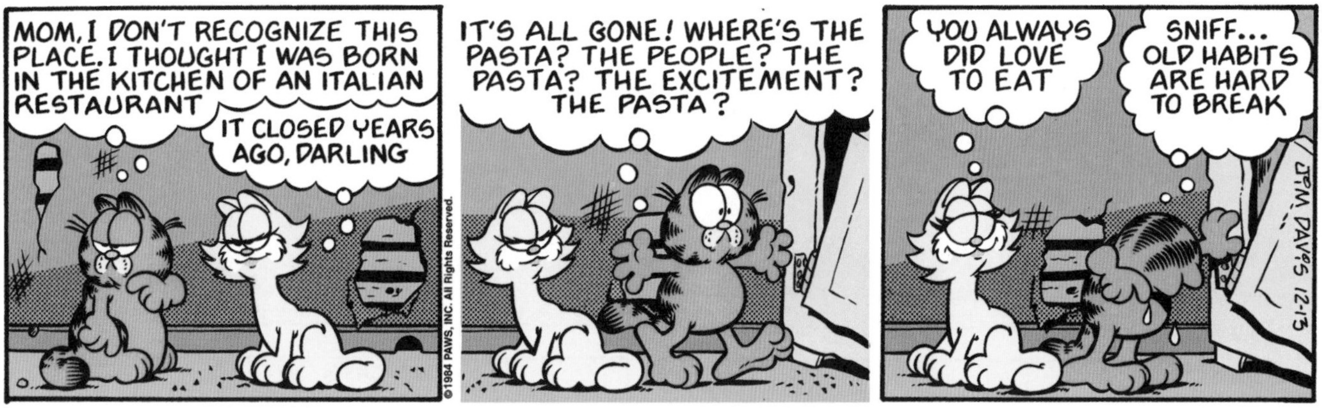
MOM, I DON'T RECOGNIZE THIS PLACE. I THOUGHT I WAS BORN IN THE KITCHEN OF AN ITALIAN RESTAURANT
IT CLOSED YEARS AGO, DARLING
©1984 PAWS, INC. All Rights Reserved.
IT'S ALL GONE! WHERE'S THE PASTA? THE PEOPLE? THE PASTA? THE EXCITEMENT? THE PASTA?
YOU ALWAYS DID LOVE TO EAT
SNIFF... OLD HABITS ARE HARD TO BREAK
JIM DAVIS 12-13

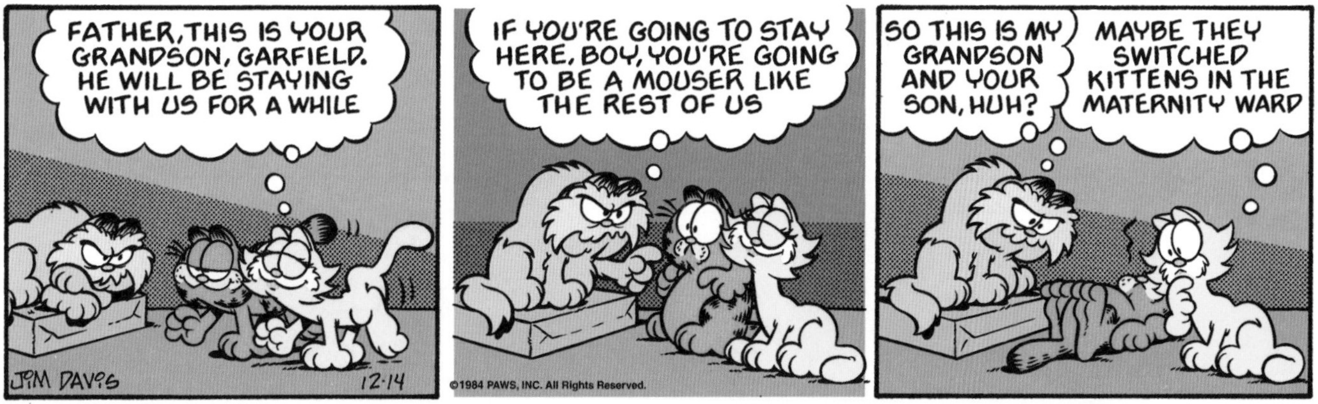
FATHER, THIS IS YOUR GRANDSON, GARFIELD. HE WILL BE STAYING WITH US FOR A WHILE
JIM DAVIS
12-14
IF YOU'RE GOING TO STAY HERE, BOY, YOU'RE GOING TO BE A MOUSER LIKE THE REST OF US
©1984 PAWS, INC. All Rights Reserved.
SO THIS IS MY GRANDSON AND YOUR SON, HUH?
MAYBE THEY SWITCHED KITTENS IN THE MATERNITY WARD

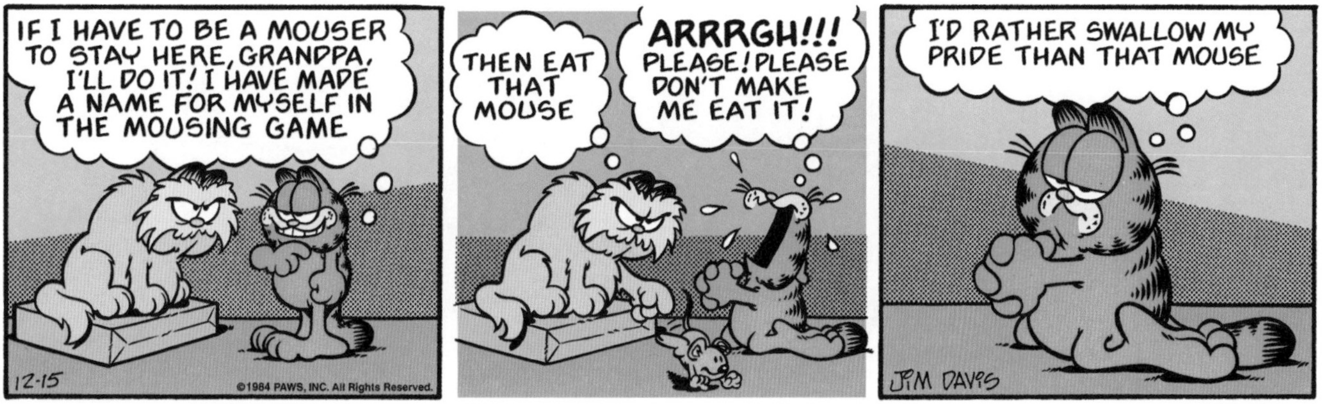
IF I HAVE TO BE A MOUSER TO STAY HERE, GRANDPA, I'LL DO IT! I HAVE MADE A NAME FOR MYSELF IN THE MOUSING GAME
12-15
©1984 PAWS, INC. All Rights Reserved.
THEN EAT THAT MOUSE
ARRRGH!!! PLEASE! PLEASE DON'T MAKE ME EAT IT!
I'D RATHER SWALLOW MY PRIDE THAN THAT MOUSE
JIM DAVIS

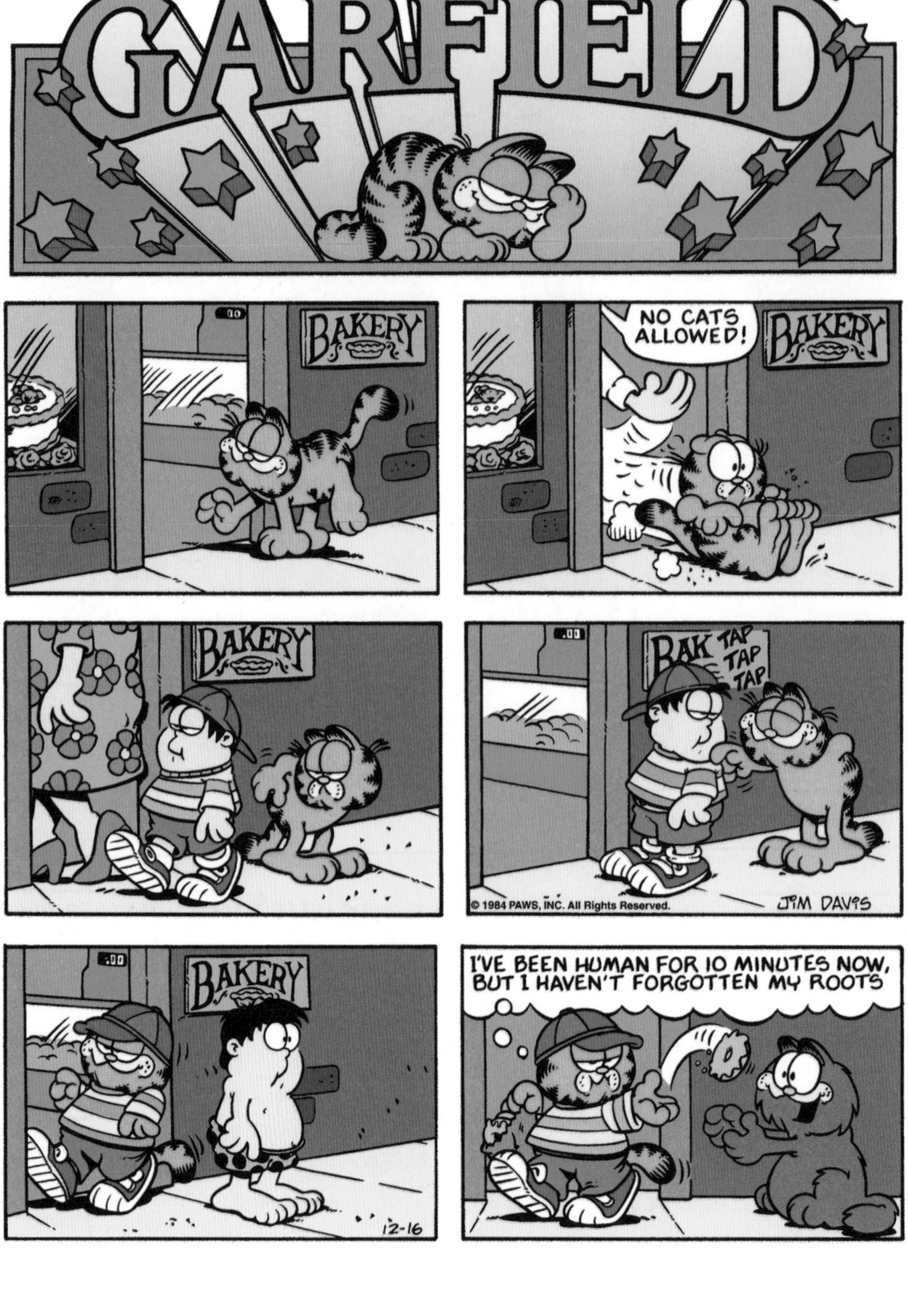
GARFIELD®
BAKERY
NO CATS ALLOWED!
BAKERY
BAKERY
BAK
TAP TAP TAP
© 1984 PAWS, INC. All Rights Reserved.
JIM DAVIS
BAKERY
12-16
I'VE BEEN HUMAN FOR 10 MINUTES NOW, BUT I HAVEN'T FORGOTTEN MY ROOTS

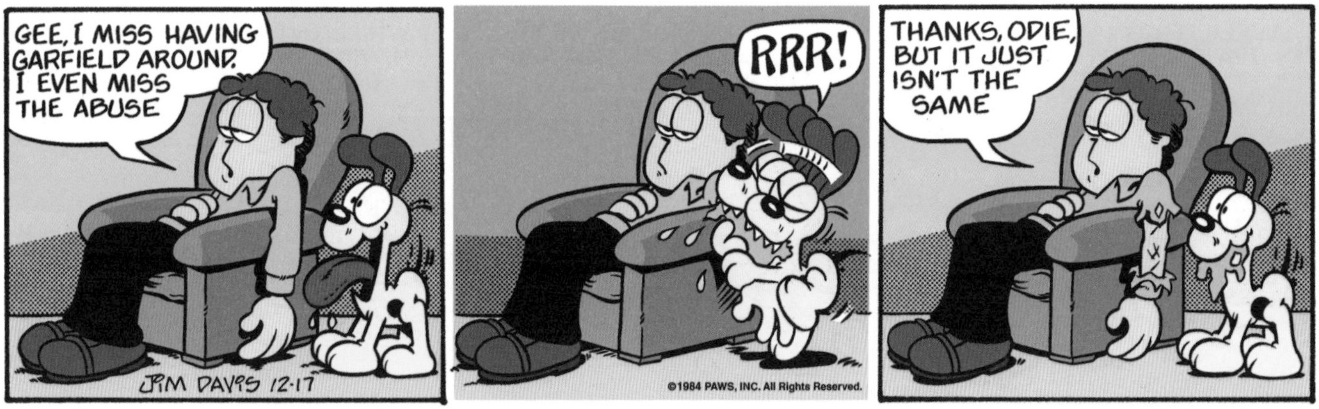
GEE, I MISS HAVING GARFIELD AROUND. I EVEN MISS THE ABUSE
JIM DAVIS 12-17
RRR!
©1984 PAWS, INC. All Rights Reserved.
THANKS, ODIE, BUT IT JUST ISN'T THE SAME

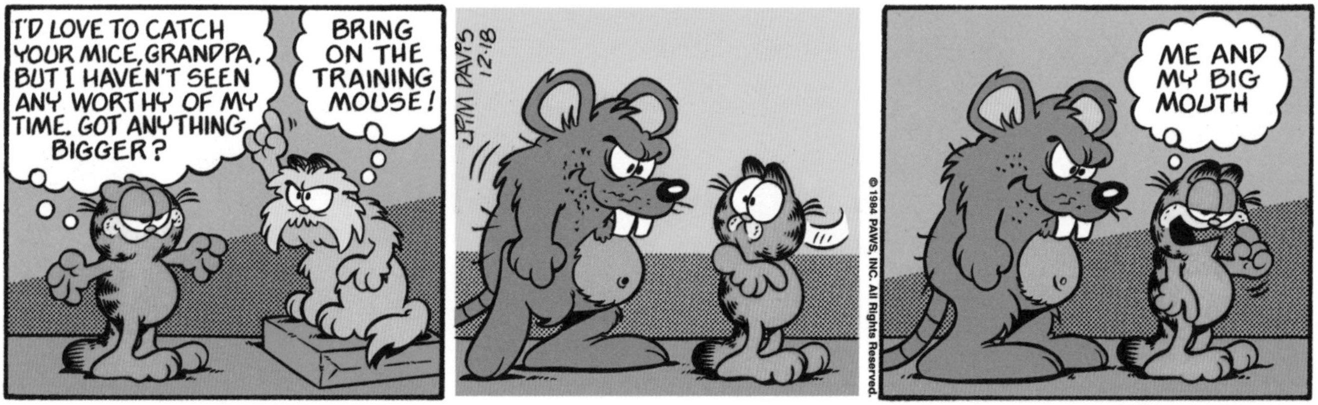
I'D LOVE TO CATCH YOUR MICE, GRANDPA, BUT I HAVEN'T SEEN ANY WORTHY OF MY TIME. GOT ANYTHING BIGGER?
BRING ON THE TRAINING MOUSE!
JIM DAVIS 12-18
©1984 PAWS, INC. All Rights Reserved.
ME AND MY BIG MOUTH

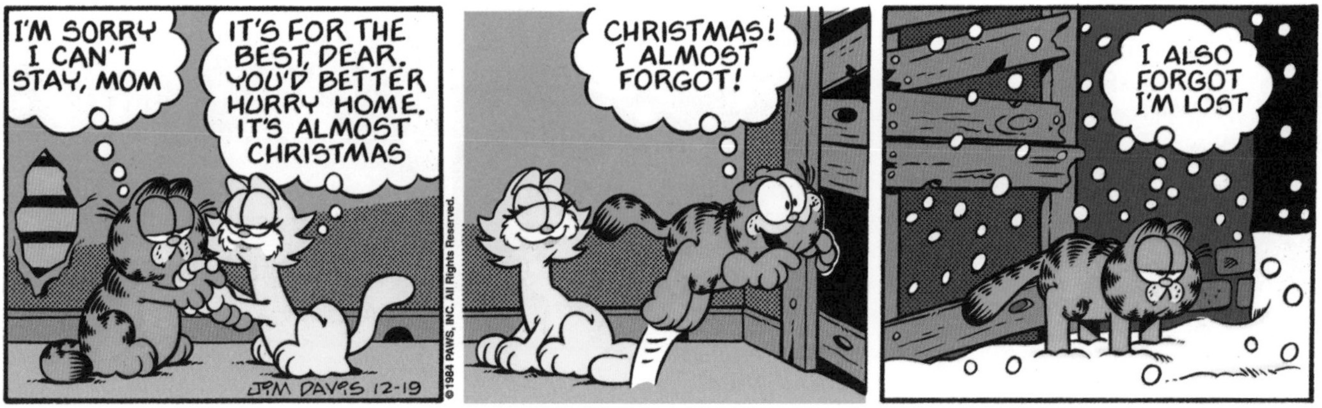
I'M SORRY I CAN'T STAY, MOM
IT'S FOR THE BEST, DEAR. YOU'D BETTER HURRY HOME. IT'S ALMOST CHRISTMAS
JIM DAVIS 12-19
©1984 PAWS, INC. All Rights Reserved.
CHRISTMAS! I ALMOST FORGOT!
I ALSO FORGOT I'M LOST

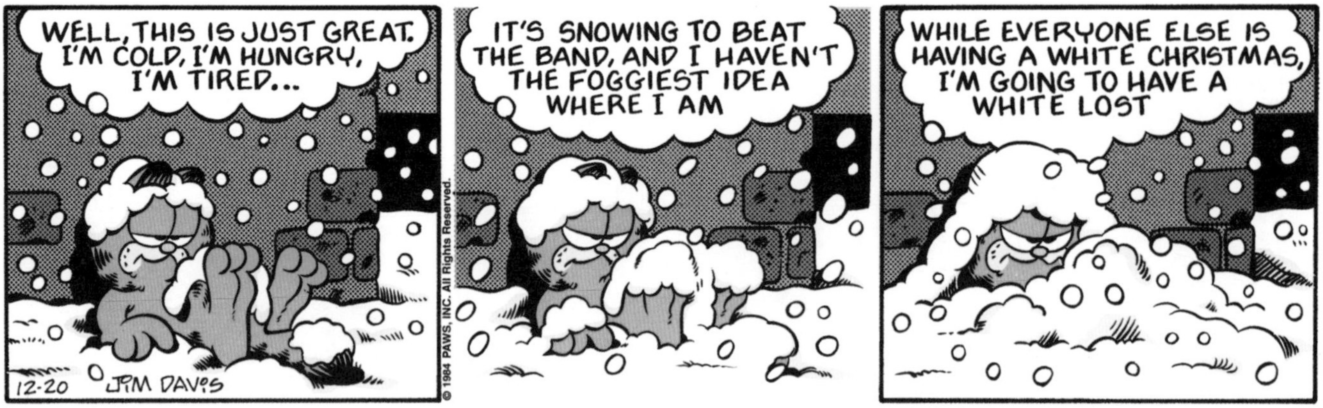
WELL, THIS IS JUST GREAT. I'M COLD, I'M HUNGRY, I'M TIRED...
12-20 JIM DAVIS
IT'S SNOWING TO BEAT THE BAND, AND I HAVEN'T THE FOGGIEST IDEA WHERE I AM
WHILE EVERYONE ELSE IS HAVING A WHITE CHRISTMAS, I'M GOING TO HAVE A WHITE LOST

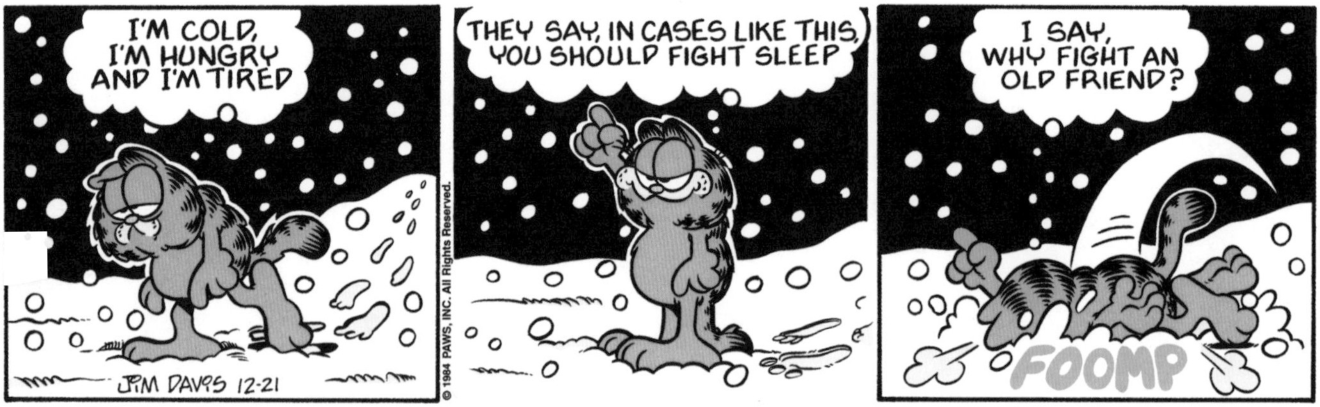
I'M COLD, I'M HUNGRY AND I'M TIRED
JIM DAVIS 12-21
THEY SAY, IN CASES LIKE THIS, YOU SHOULD FIGHT SLEEP
I SAY, WHY FIGHT AN OLD FRIEND?
FOOMP

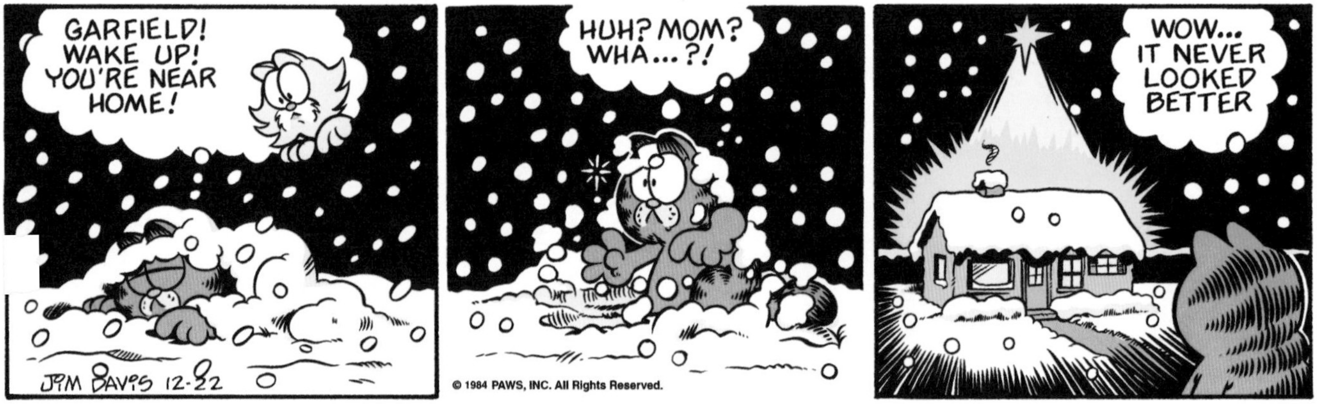
GARFIELD! WAKE UP! YOU'RE NEAR HOME!
JIM DAVIS 12-22
HUH? MOM? WHA...?!
WOW... IT NEVER LOOKED BETTER

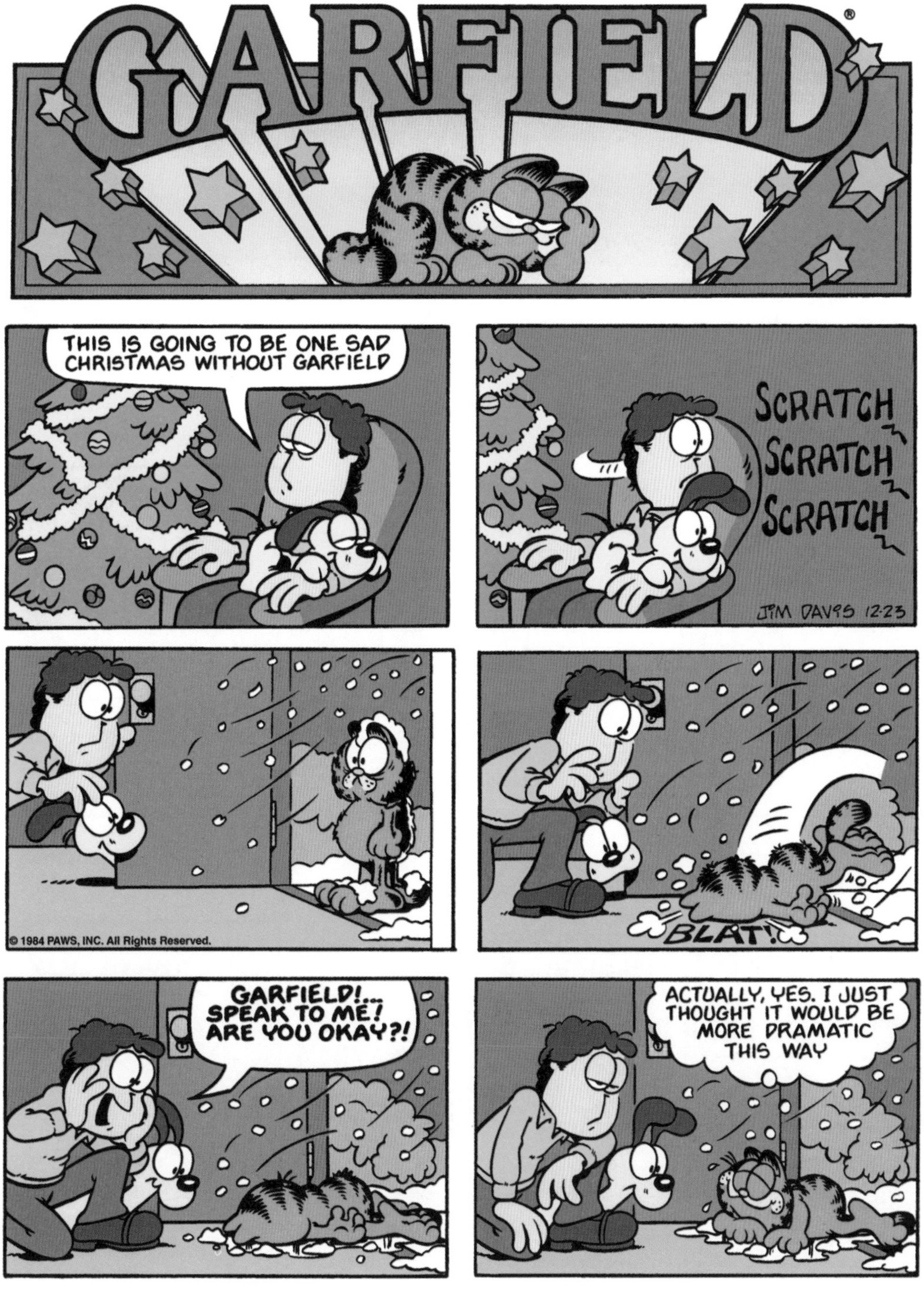
GARFIELD®
THIS IS GOING TO BE ONE SAD CHRISTMAS WITHOUT GARFIELD
SCRATCH SCRATCH SCRATCH
JIM DAVIS 12-23
© 1984 PAWS, INC. All Rights Reserved.
BLAT!
GARFIELD!... SPEAK TO ME! ARE YOU OKAY?!
ACTUALLY, YES. I JUST THOUGHT IT WOULD BE MORE DRAMATIC THIS WAY

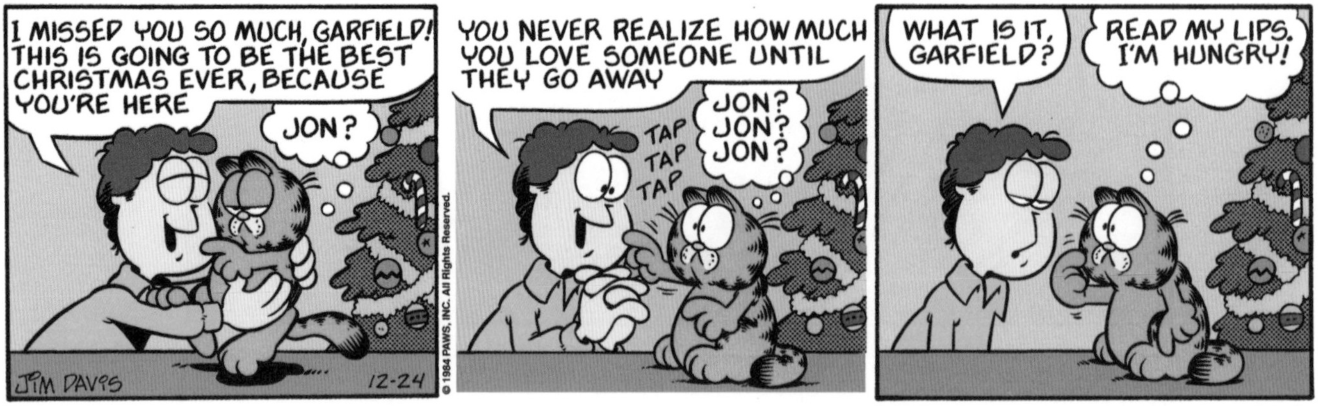
I MISSED YOU SO MUCH, GARFIELD! THIS IS GOING TO BE THE BEST CHRISTMAS EVER, BECAUSE YOU'RE HERE
JON?
JIM DAVIS 12-24
© 1984 PAWS, INC. All Rights Reserved.
YOU NEVER REALIZE HOW MUCH YOU LOVE SOMEONE UNTIL THEY GO AWAY
TAP TAP TAP
JON? JON? JON?
WHAT IS IT, GARFIELD?
READ MY LIPS. I'M HUNGRY!

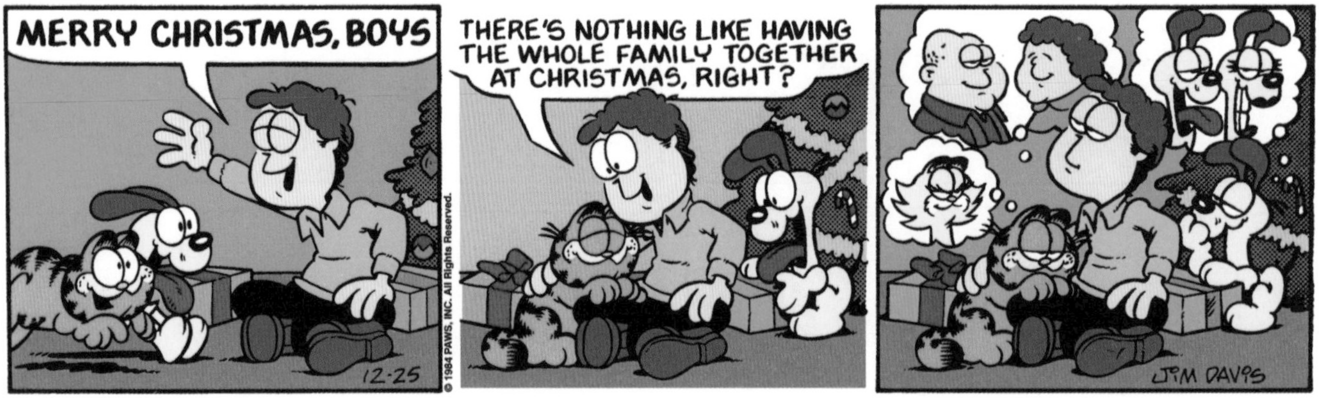
MERRY CHRISTMAS, BOYS
12-25
© 1984 PAWS, INC. All Rights Reserved.
THERE'S NOTHING LIKE HAVING THE WHOLE FAMILY TOGETHER AT CHRISTMAS, RIGHT?
JIM DAVIS

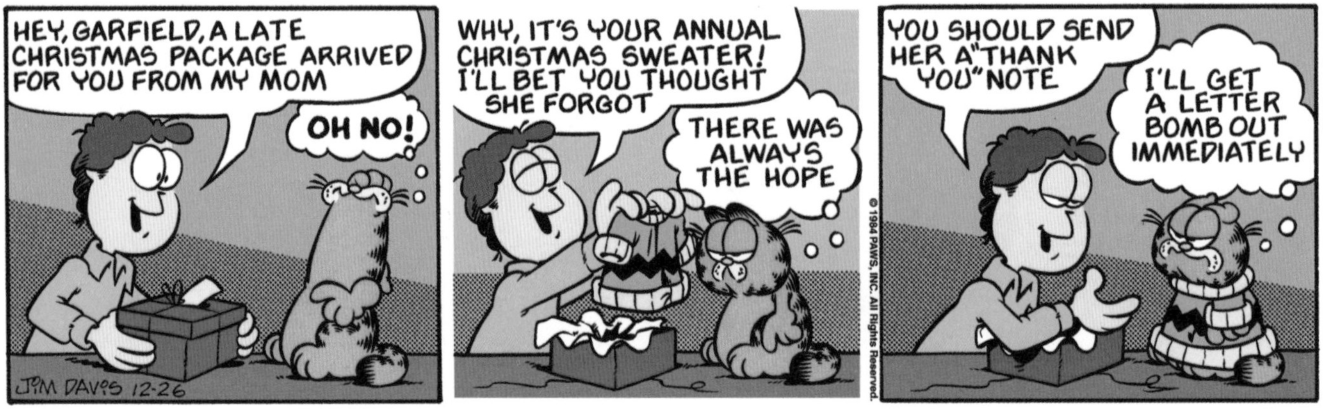
HEY, GARFIELD, A LATE CHRISTMAS PACKAGE ARRIVED FOR YOU FROM MY MOM
OH NO!
JIM DAVIS 12-26
WHY, IT'S YOUR ANNUAL CHRISTMAS SWEATER! I'LL BET YOU THOUGHT SHE FORGOT
THERE WAS ALWAYS THE HOPE
© 1984 PAWS, INC. All Rights Reserved.
YOU SHOULD SEND HER A "THANK YOU" NOTE
I'LL GET A LETTER BOMB OUT IMMEDIATELY

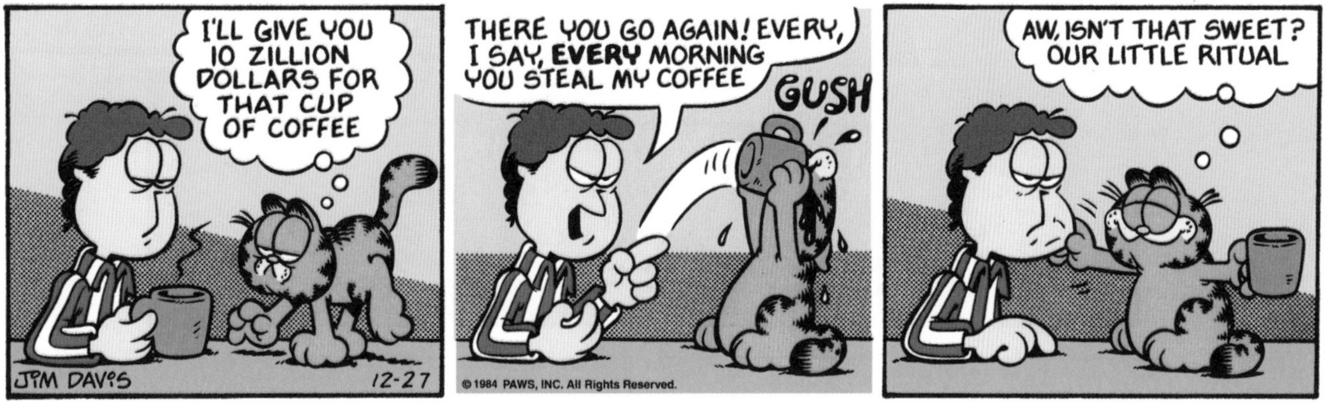
I'LL GIVE YOU 10 ZILLION DOLLARS FOR THAT CUP OF COFFEE
JIM DAVIS
12-27
THERE YOU GO AGAIN! EVERY, I SAY, **EVERY** MORNING YOU STEAL MY COFFEE
GUSH
© 1984 PAWS, INC. All Rights Reserved.
AW, ISN'T THAT SWEET? OUR LITTLE RITUAL

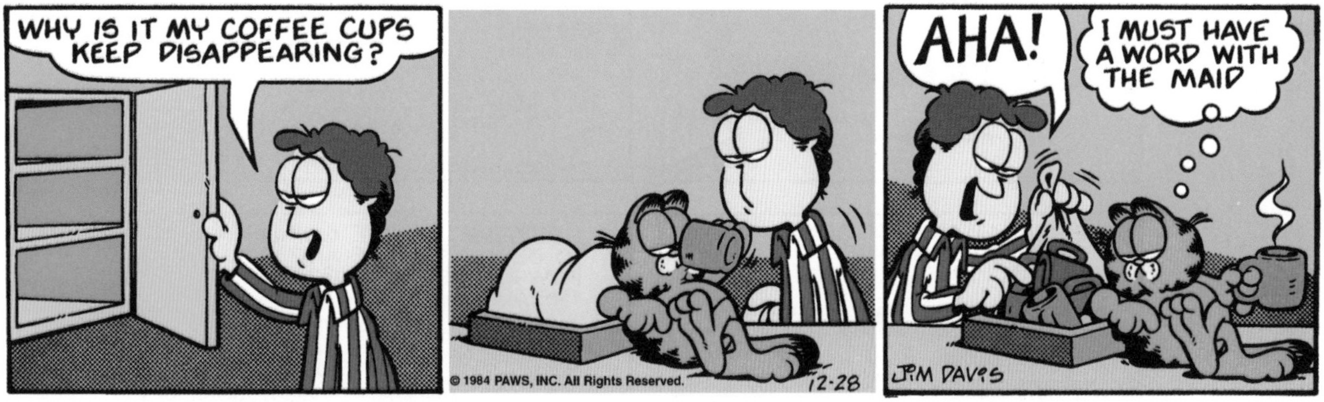
WHY IS IT MY COFFEE CUPS KEEP DISAPPEARING?
© 1984 PAWS, INC. All Rights Reserved.
12-28
AHA!
I MUST HAVE A WORD WITH THE MAID
JIM DAVIS

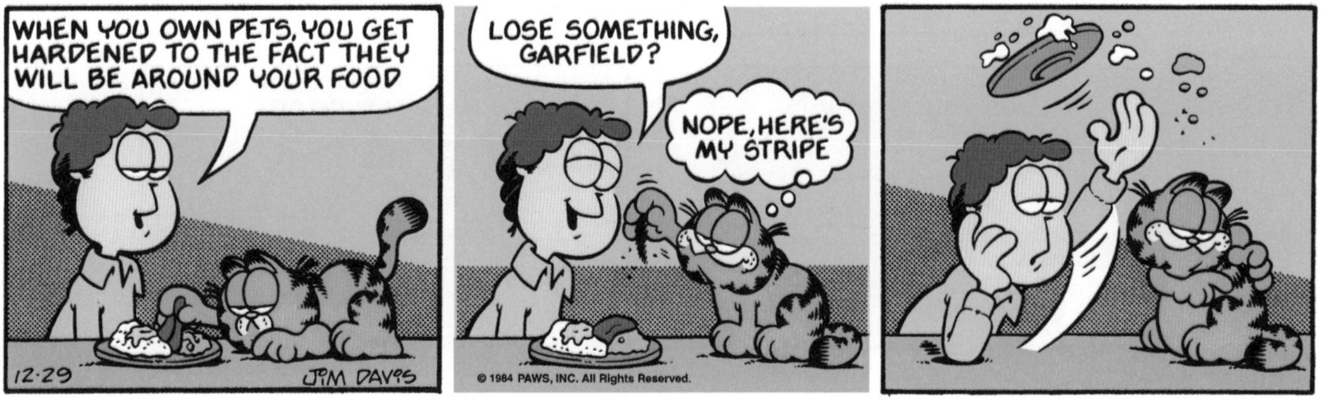
WHEN YOU OWN PETS, YOU GET HARDENED TO THE FACT THEY WILL BE AROUND YOUR FOOD
12-29
JIM DAVIS
LOSE SOMETHING, GARFIELD?
NOPE, HERE'S MY STRIPE
© 1984 PAWS, INC. All Rights Reserved.

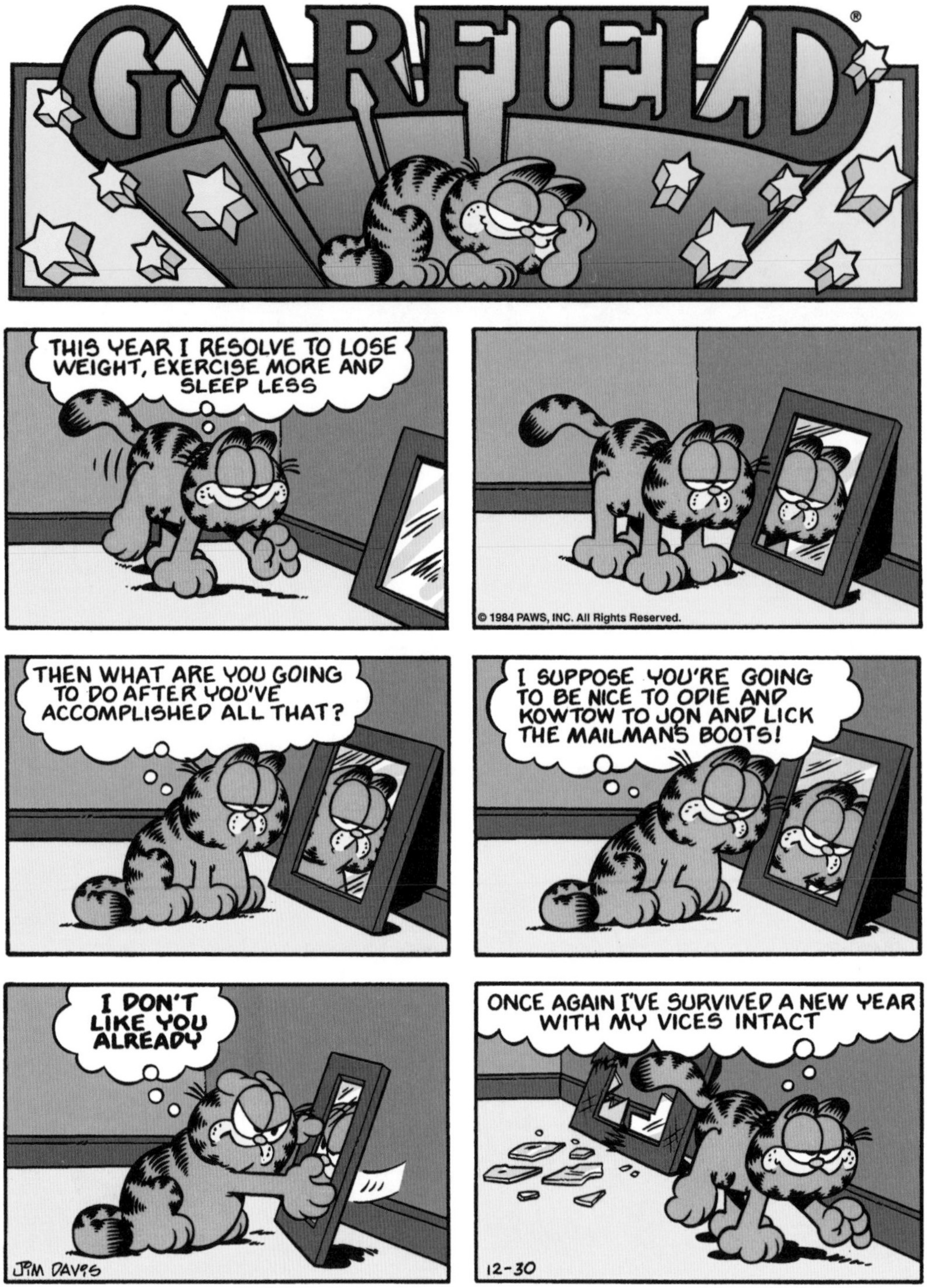
GARFIELD
THIS YEAR I RESOLVE TO LOSE WEIGHT, EXERCISE MORE AND SLEEP LESS
© 1984 PAWS, INC. All Rights Reserved.
THEN WHAT ARE YOU GOING TO DO AFTER YOU'VE ACCOMPLISHED ALL THAT?
I SUPPOSE YOU'RE GOING TO BE NICE TO ODIE AND KOWTOW TO JON AND LICK THE MAILMAN'S BOOTS!
I DON'T LIKE YOU ALREADY
JIM DAVIS
ONCE AGAIN I'VE SURVIVED A NEW YEAR WITH MY VICES INTACT
12-30

Garfield
out to lunch

BY JIM DAVIS

Ballantine Books • New York

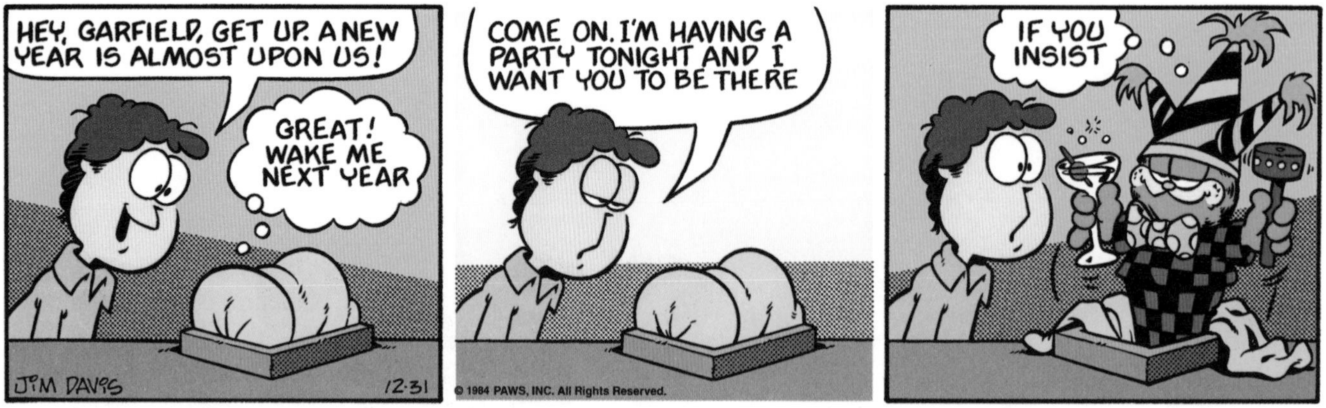
HEY, GARFIELD, GET UP. A NEW YEAR IS ALMOST UPON US!
GREAT! WAKE ME NEXT YEAR
JIM DAVIS
12-31
COME ON. I'M HAVING A PARTY TONIGHT AND I WANT YOU TO BE THERE
© 1984 PAWS, INC. All Rights Reserved.
IF YOU INSIST

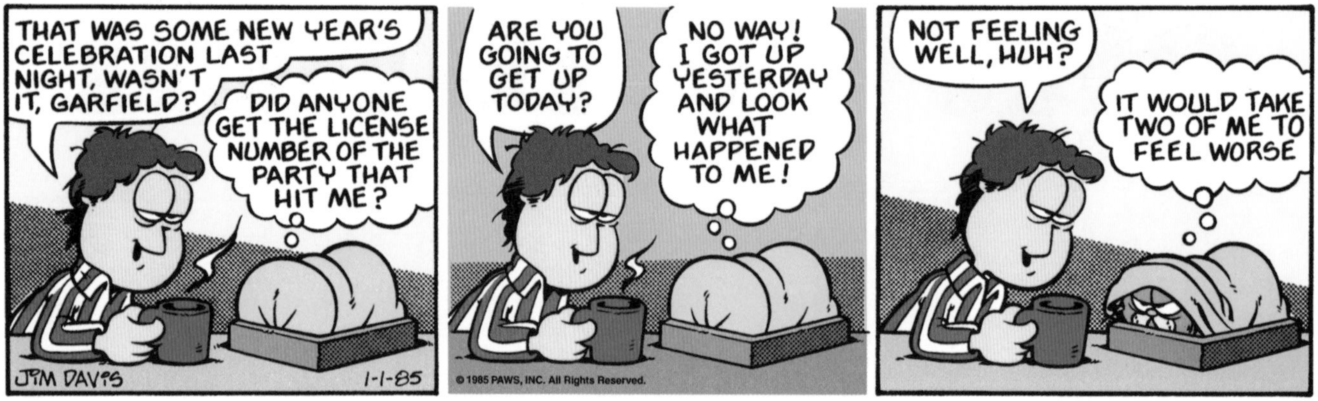
THAT WAS SOME NEW YEAR'S CELEBRATION LAST NIGHT, WASN'T IT, GARFIELD?
DID ANYONE GET THE LICENSE NUMBER OF THE PARTY THAT HIT ME?
JIM DAVIS
1-1-85
ARE YOU GOING TO GET UP TODAY?
NO WAY! I GOT UP YESTERDAY AND LOOK WHAT HAPPENED TO ME!
© 1985 PAWS, INC. All Rights Reserved.
NOT FEELING WELL, HUH?
IT WOULD TAKE TWO OF ME TO FEEL WORSE

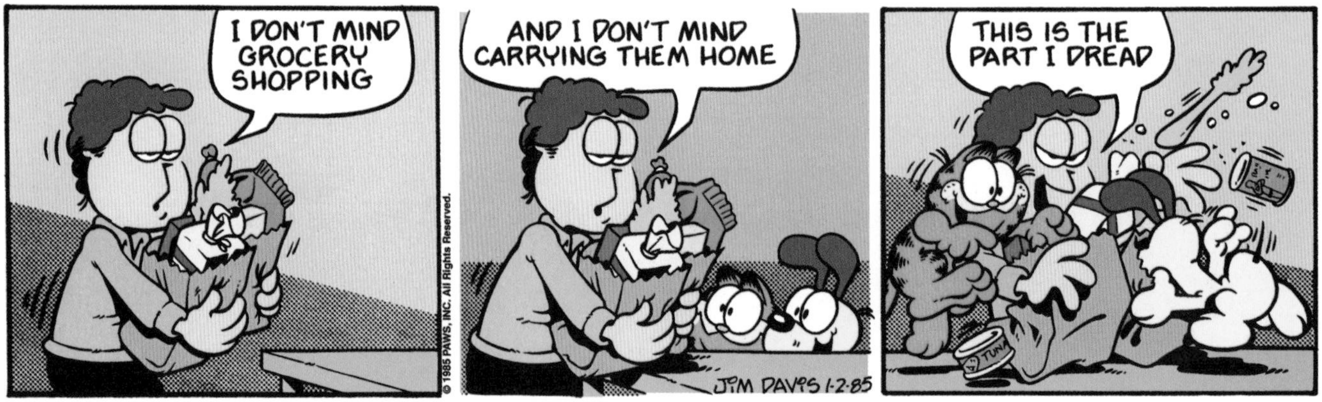
I DON'T MIND GROCERY SHOPPING
© 1985 PAWS, INC. All Rights Reserved.
AND I DON'T MIND CARRYING THEM HOME
JIM DAVIS 1-2-85
THIS IS THE PART I DREAD
TUNA

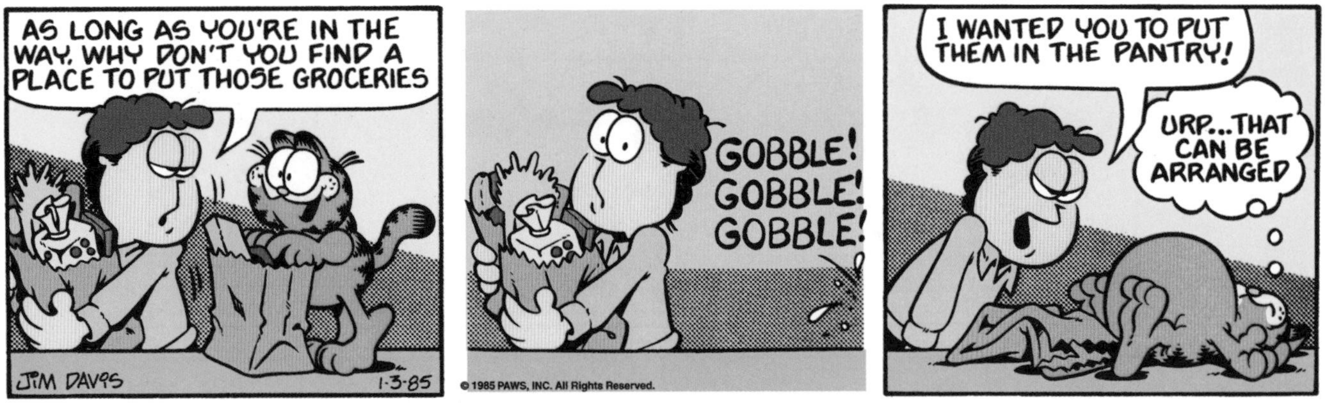
AS LONG AS YOU'RE IN THE WAY, WHY DON'T YOU FIND A PLACE TO PUT THOSE GROCERIES
JIM DAVIS
1-3-85
GOBBLE! GOBBLE! GOBBLE!
© 1985 PAWS, INC. All Rights Reserved.
I WANTED YOU TO PUT THEM IN THE PANTRY!
URP...THAT CAN BE ARRANGED

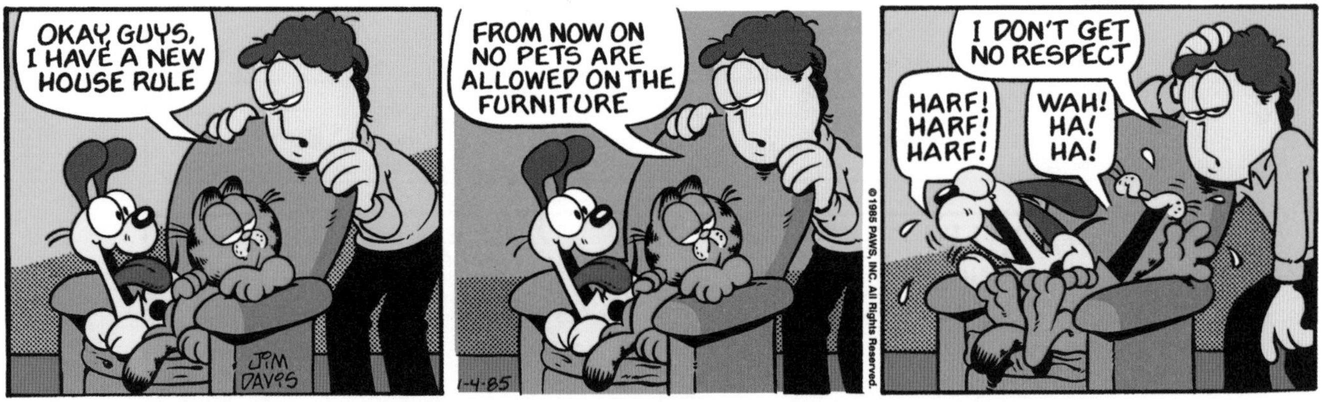
OKAY, GUYS, I HAVE A NEW HOUSE RULE
JIM DAVIS
FROM NOW ON NO PETS ARE ALLOWED ON THE FURNITURE
1-4-85
© 1985 PAWS, INC. All Rights Reserved.
I DON'T GET NO RESPECT
HARF! HARF! HARF!
WAH! HA! HA!

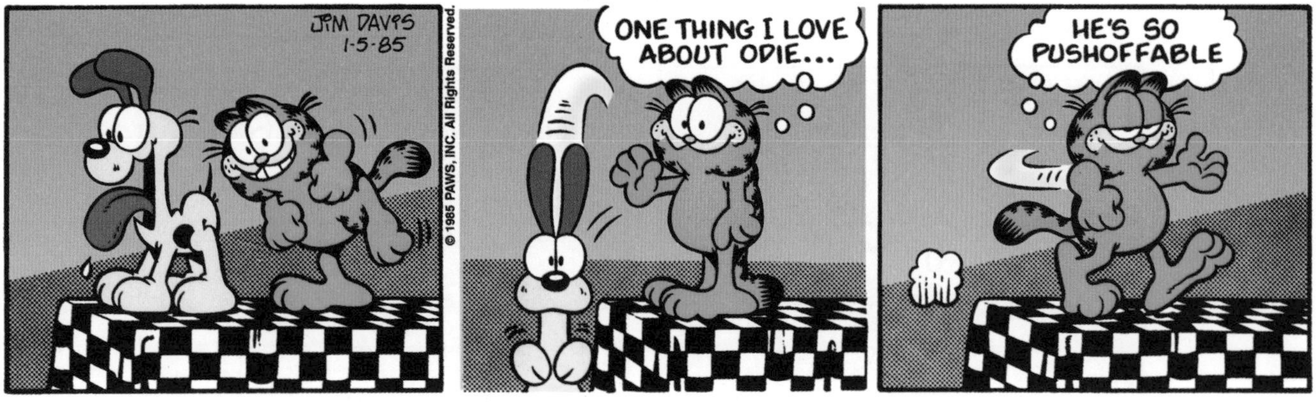
JIM DAVIS
1-5-85
© 1985 PAWS, INC. All Rights Reserved.
ONE THING I LOVE ABOUT ODIE...
HE'S SO PUSHOFFABLE

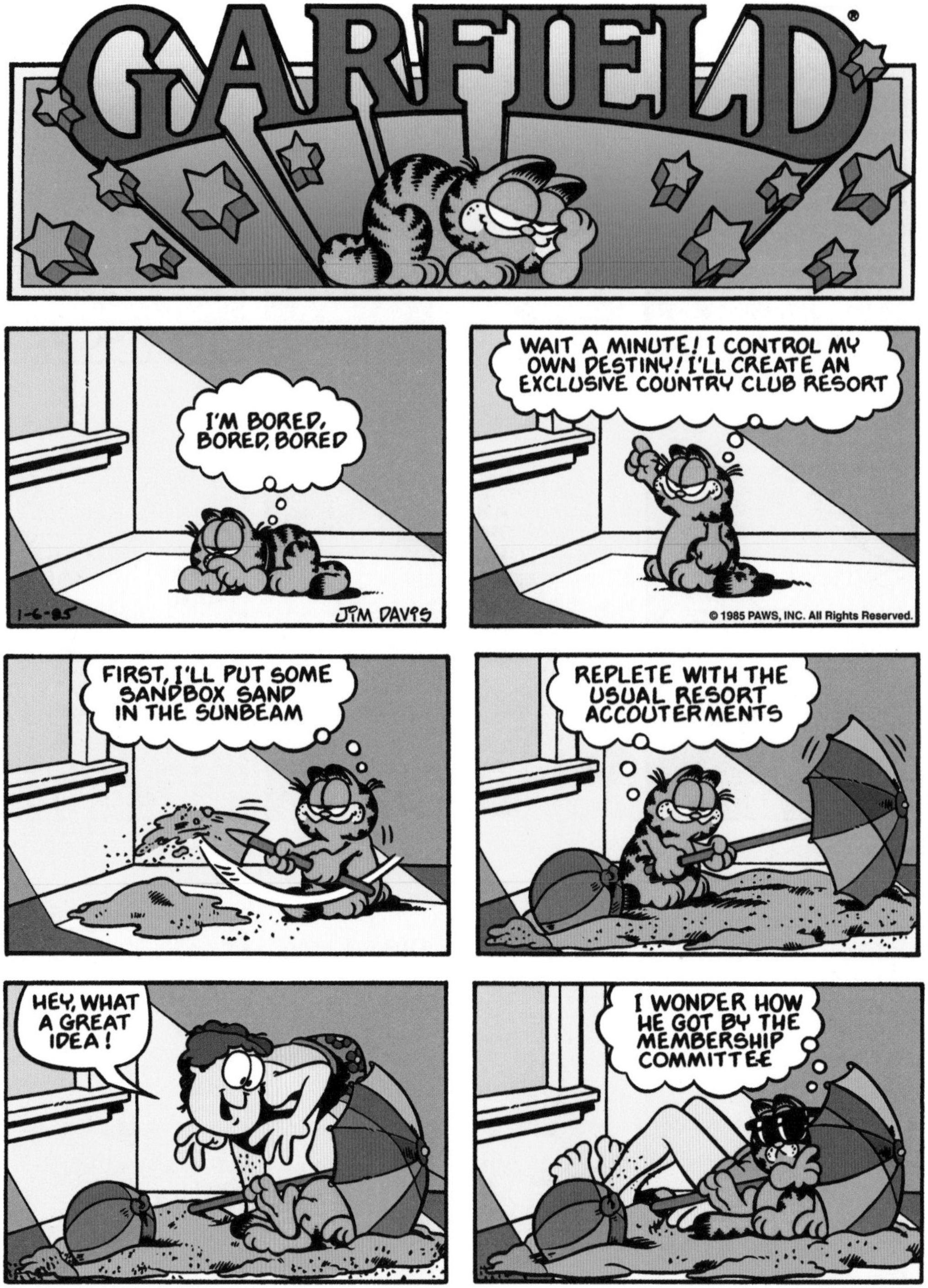
GARFIELD®
I'M BORED, BORED, BORED
1-6-85
JIM DAVIS
WAIT A MINUTE! I CONTROL MY OWN DESTINY! I'LL CREATE AN EXCLUSIVE COUNTRY CLUB RESORT
© 1985 PAWS, INC. All Rights Reserved.
FIRST, I'LL PUT SOME SANDBOX SAND IN THE SUNBEAM
REPLETE WITH THE USUAL RESORT ACCOUTERMENTS
HEY, WHAT A GREAT IDEA!
I WONDER HOW HE GOT BY THE MEMBERSHIP COMMITTEE

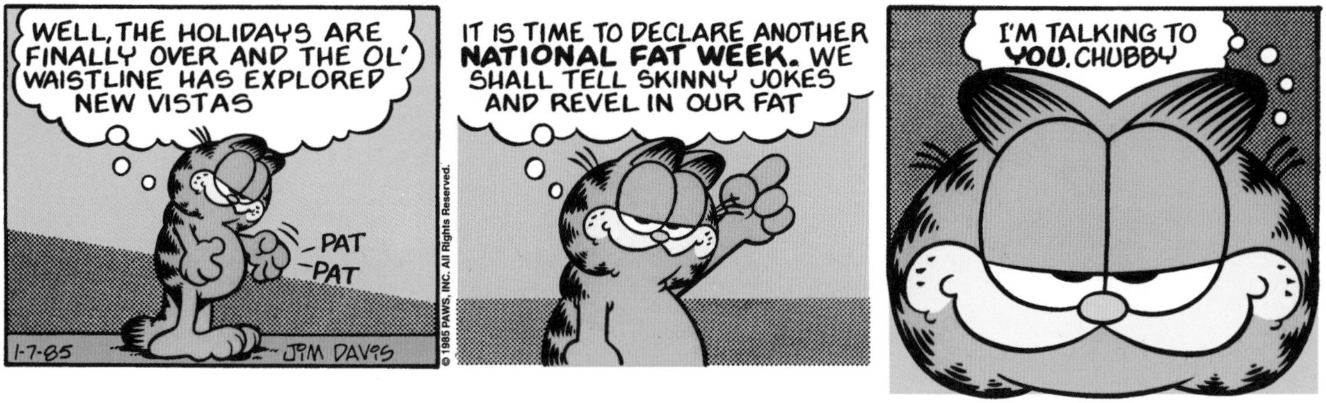
WELL, THE HOLIDAYS ARE FINALLY OVER AND THE OL' WAISTLINE HAS EXPLORED NEW VISTAS
PAT PAT
1-7-85
JIM DAVIS
© 1985 PAWS, INC. All Rights Reserved.
IT IS TIME TO DECLARE ANOTHER **NATIONAL FAT WEEK.** WE SHALL TELL SKINNY JOKES AND REVEL IN OUR FAT
I'M TALKING TO **YOU**, CHUBBY

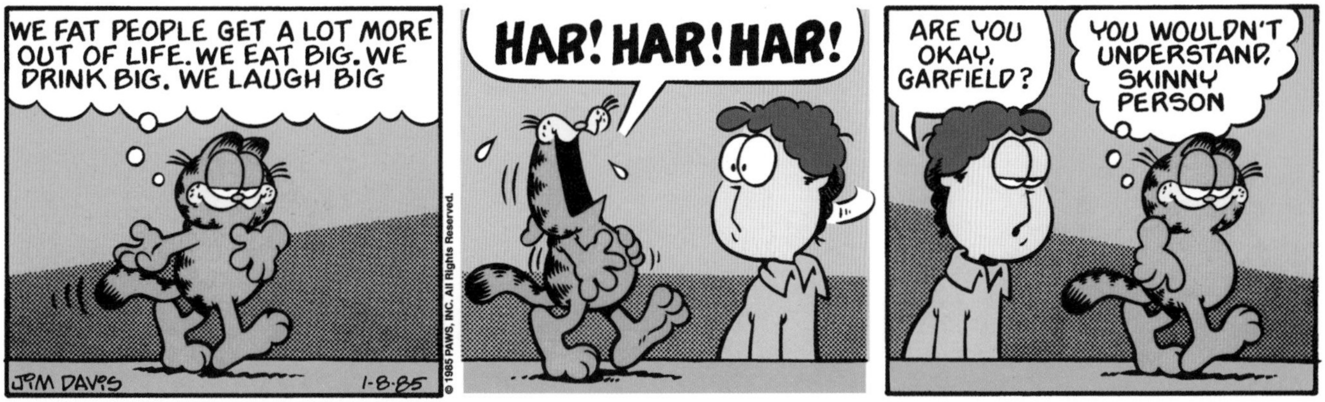
WE FAT PEOPLE GET A LOT MORE OUT OF LIFE. WE EAT BIG. WE DRINK BIG. WE LAUGH BIG
JIM DAVIS
1-8-85
© 1985 PAWS, INC. All Rights Reserved.
HAR! HAR! HAR!
ARE YOU OKAY, GARFIELD?
YOU WOULDN'T UNDERSTAND, SKINNY PERSON

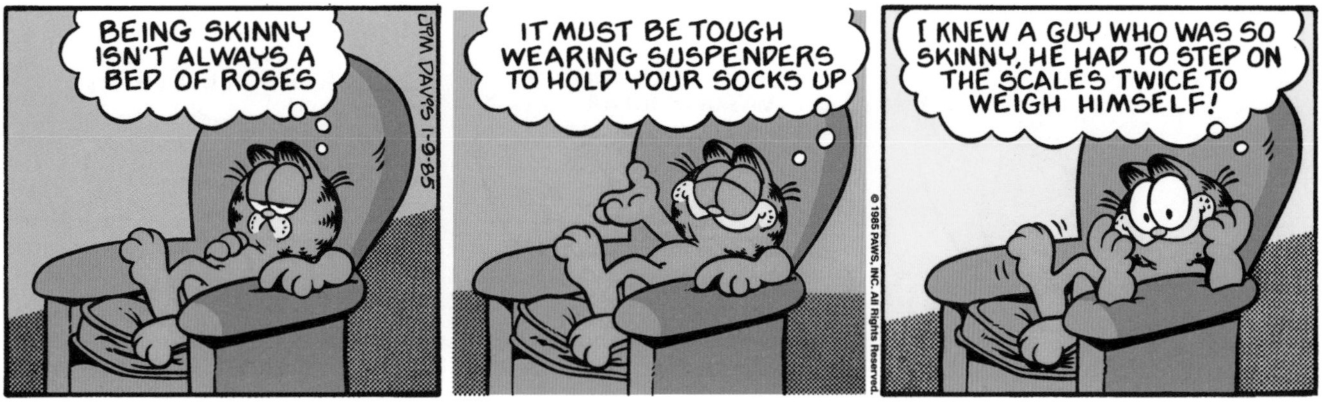
BEING SKINNY ISN'T ALWAYS A BED OF ROSES
JIM DAVIS 1-9-85
IT MUST BE TOUGH WEARING SUSPENDERS TO HOLD YOUR SOCKS UP
© 1985 PAWS, INC. All Rights Reserved.
I KNEW A GUY WHO WAS SO SKINNY, HE HAD TO STEP ON THE SCALES TWICE TO WEIGH HIMSELF!

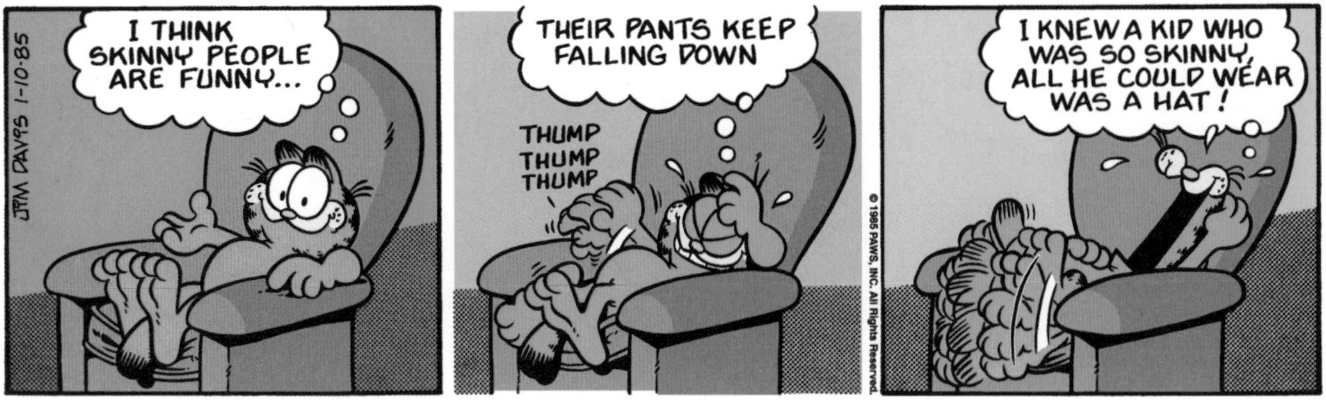
JPM DAVPS 1-10-85
I THINK SKINNY PEOPLE ARE FUNNY...
THEIR PANTS KEEP FALLING DOWN
THUMP THUMP THUMP
I KNEW A KID WHO WAS SO SKINNY, ALL HE COULD WEAR WAS A HAT!
© 1985 PAWS, INC. All Rights Reserved.

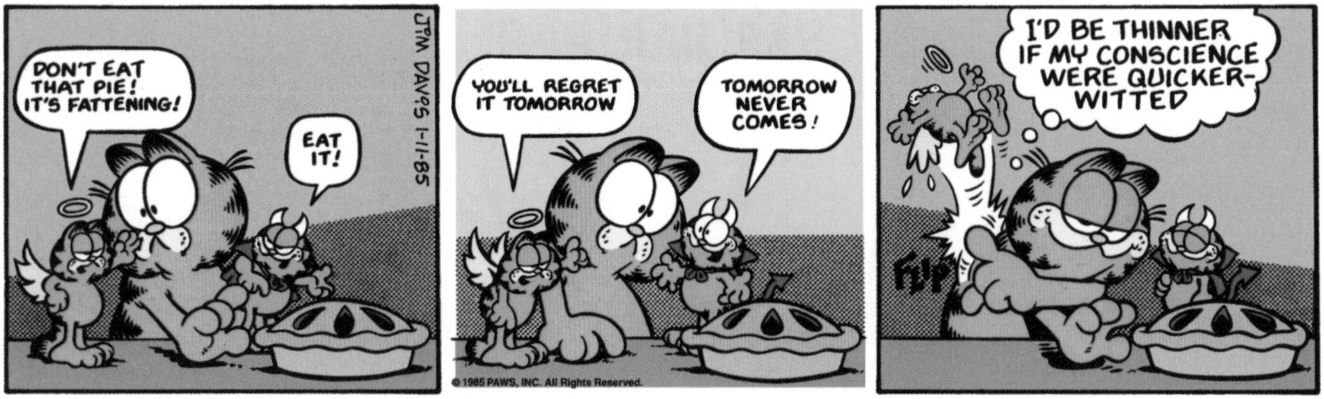
DON'T EAT THAT PIE! IT'S FATTENING!
EAT IT!
JPM DAVPS 1-11-85
YOU'LL REGRET IT TOMORROW
TOMORROW NEVER COMES!
© 1985 PAWS, INC. All Rights Reserved.
I'D BE THINNER IF MY CONSCIENCE WERE QUICKER-WITTED
FLIP

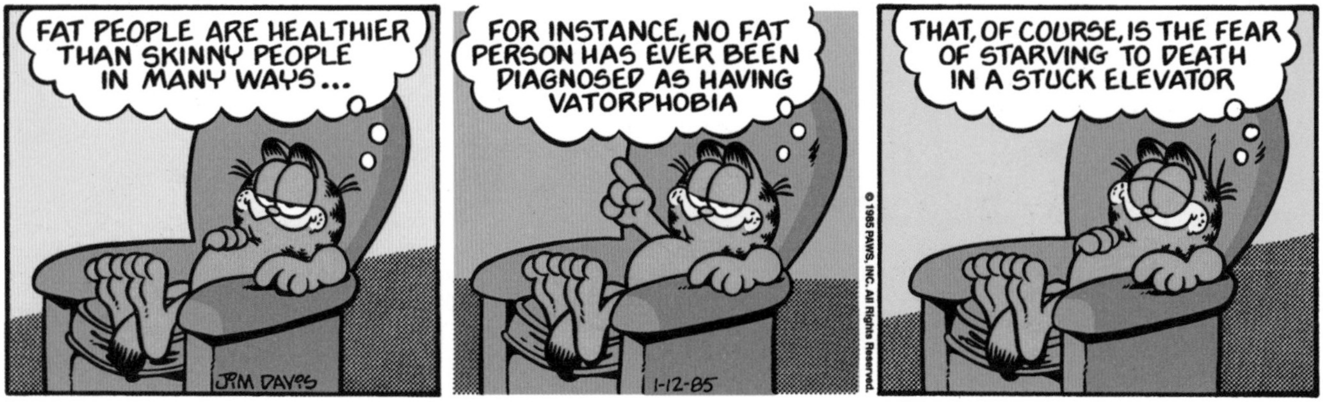
FAT PEOPLE ARE HEALTHIER THAN SKINNY PEOPLE IN MANY WAYS...
JPM DAVPS
FOR INSTANCE, NO FAT PERSON HAS EVER BEEN DIAGNOSED AS HAVING VATORPHOBIA
1-12-85
© 1985 PAWS, INC. All Rights Reserved.
THAT, OF COURSE, IS THE FEAR OF STARVING TO DEATH IN A STUCK ELEVATOR

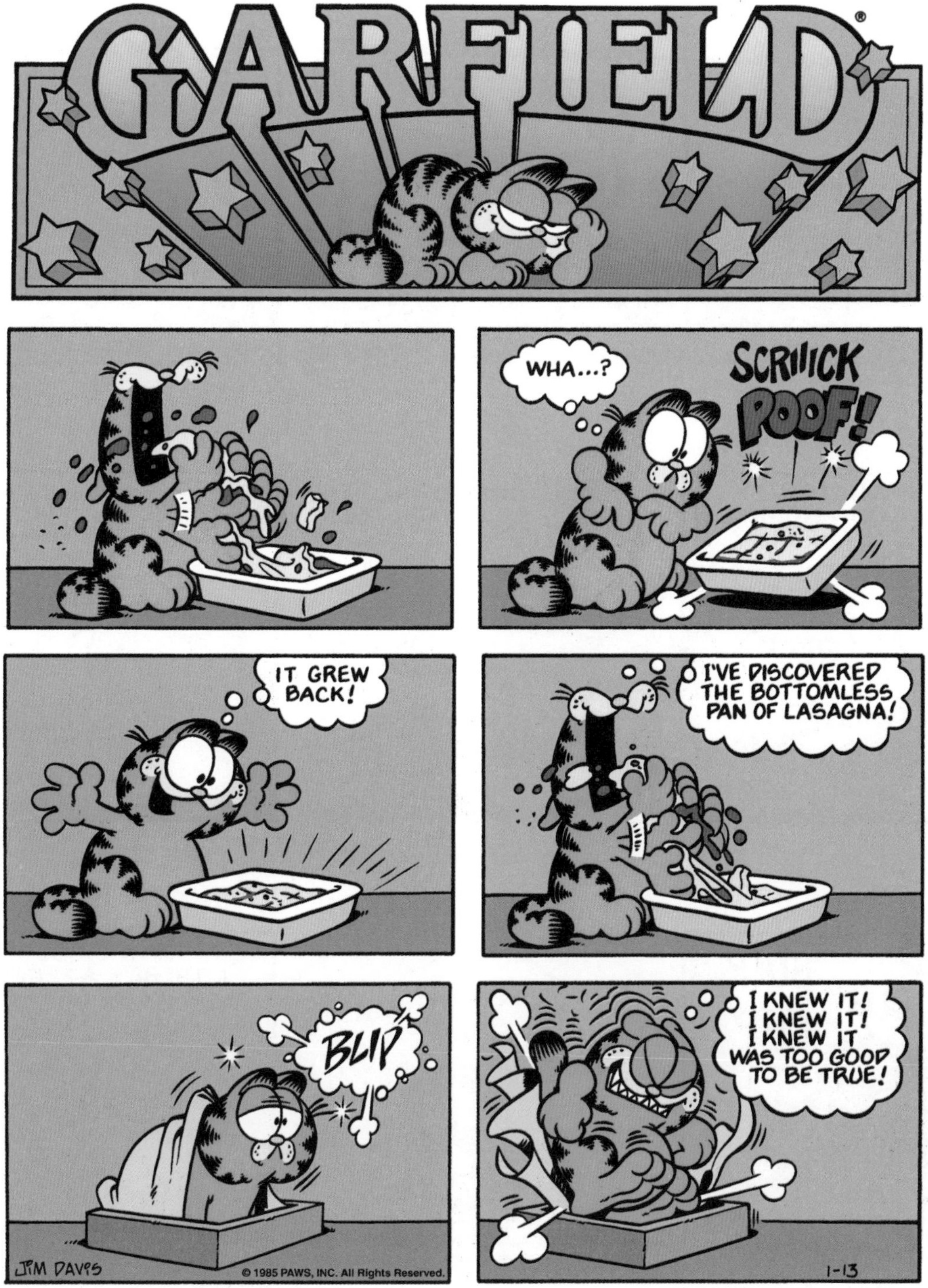
GARFIELD
WHA...?
SCRIIICK
POOF!
IT GREW BACK!
I'VE DISCOVERED THE BOTTOMLESS PAN OF LASAGNA!
BLIP
I KNEW IT! I KNEW IT! I KNEW IT WAS TOO GOOD TO BE TRUE!
JIM DAVIS
© 1985 PAWS, INC. All Rights Reserved.
1-13

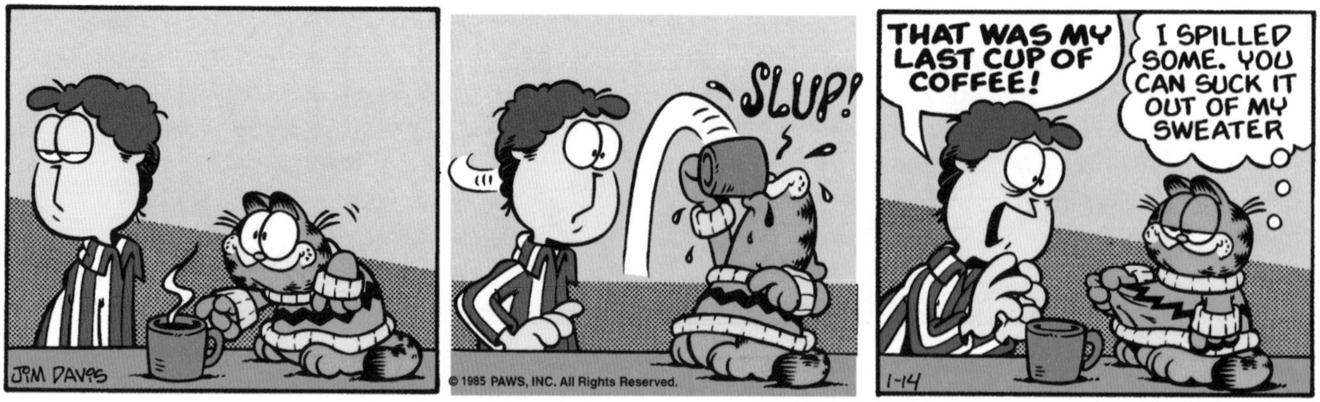
JIM DAVIS
© 1985 PAWS, INC. All Rights Reserved.
SLUP!
THAT WAS MY LAST CUP OF COFFEE!
I SPILLED SOME. YOU CAN SUCK IT OUT OF MY SWEATER
1-14

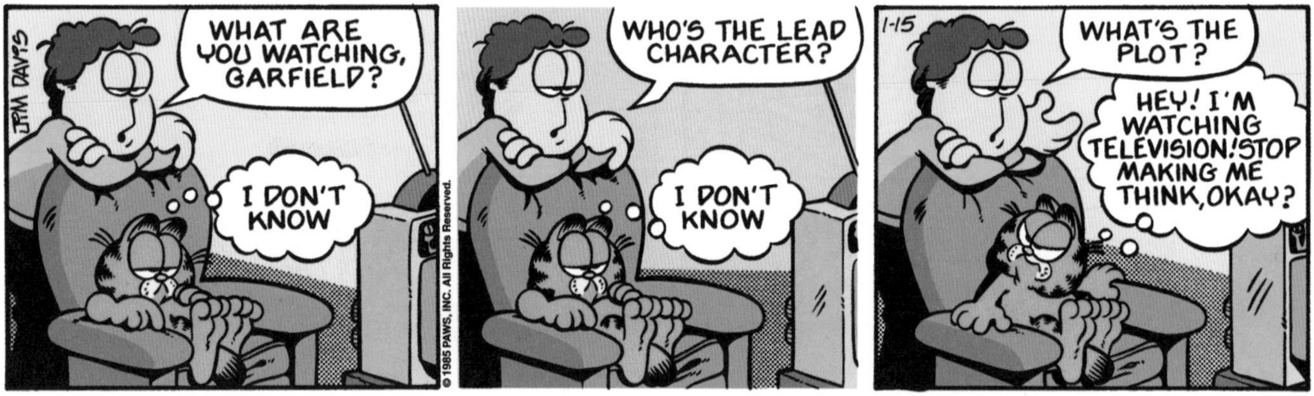
JIM DAVIS
WHAT ARE YOU WATCHING, GARFIELD?
I DON'T KNOW
© 1985 PAWS, INC. All Rights Reserved.
WHO'S THE LEAD CHARACTER?
I DON'T KNOW
1-15
WHAT'S THE PLOT?
HEY! I'M WATCHING TELEVISION! STOP MAKING ME THINK, OKAY?

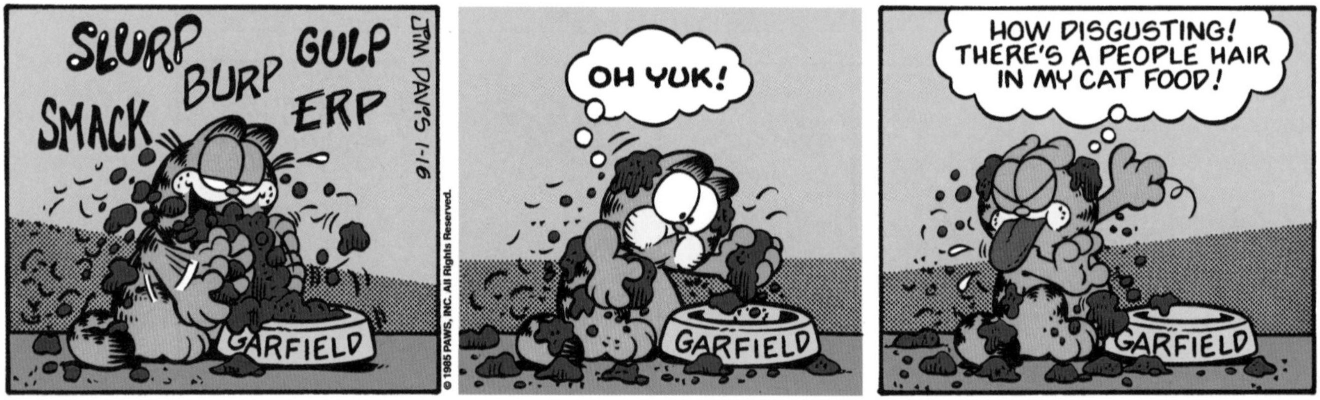
SLURP
BURP
GULP
SMACK
ERP
JIM DAVIS 1-16
GARFIELD
© 1985 PAWS, INC. All Rights Reserved.
OH YUK!
GARFIELD
HOW DISGUSTING! THERE'S A PEOPLE HAIR IN MY CAT FOOD!
GARFIELD

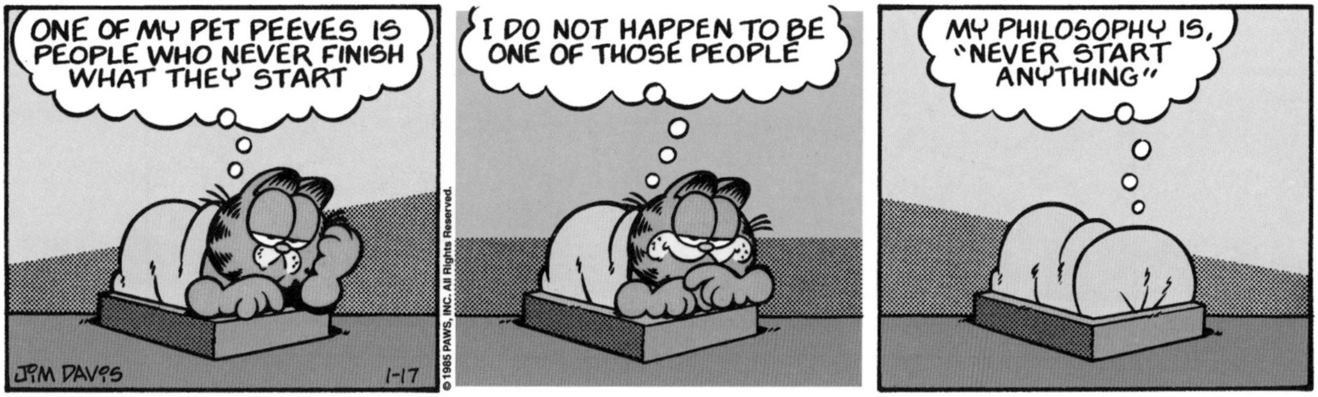
ONE OF MY PET PEEVES IS PEOPLE WHO NEVER FINISH WHAT THEY START
JIM DAVIS
1-17
I DO NOT HAPPEN TO BE ONE OF THOSE PEOPLE
© 1985 PAWS, INC. All Rights Reserved.
MY PHILOSOPHY IS, "NEVER START ANYTHING"

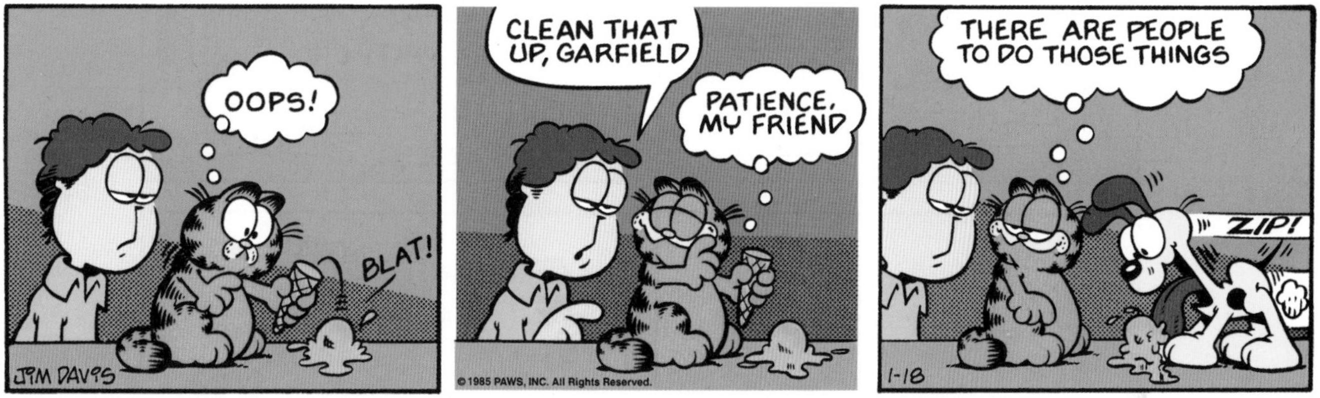
OOPS!
BLAT!
JIM DAVIS
CLEAN THAT UP, GARFIELD
PATIENCE, MY FRIEND
© 1985 PAWS, INC. All Rights Reserved.
THERE ARE PEOPLE TO DO THOSE THINGS
ZIP!
1-18

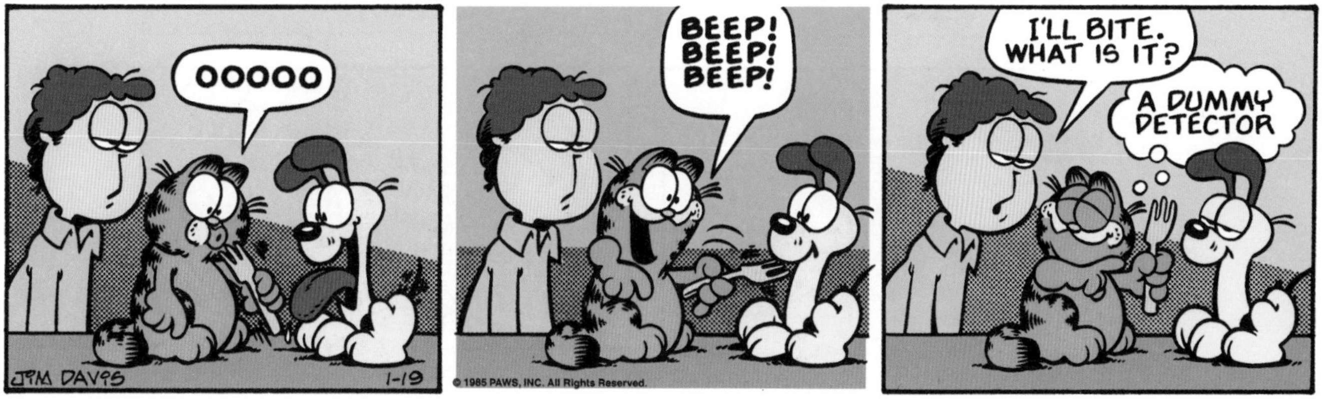
OOOOO
JIM DAVIS
1-19
BEEP! BEEP! BEEP!
© 1985 PAWS, INC. All Rights Reserved.
I'LL BITE. WHAT IS IT?
A DUMMY DETECTOR

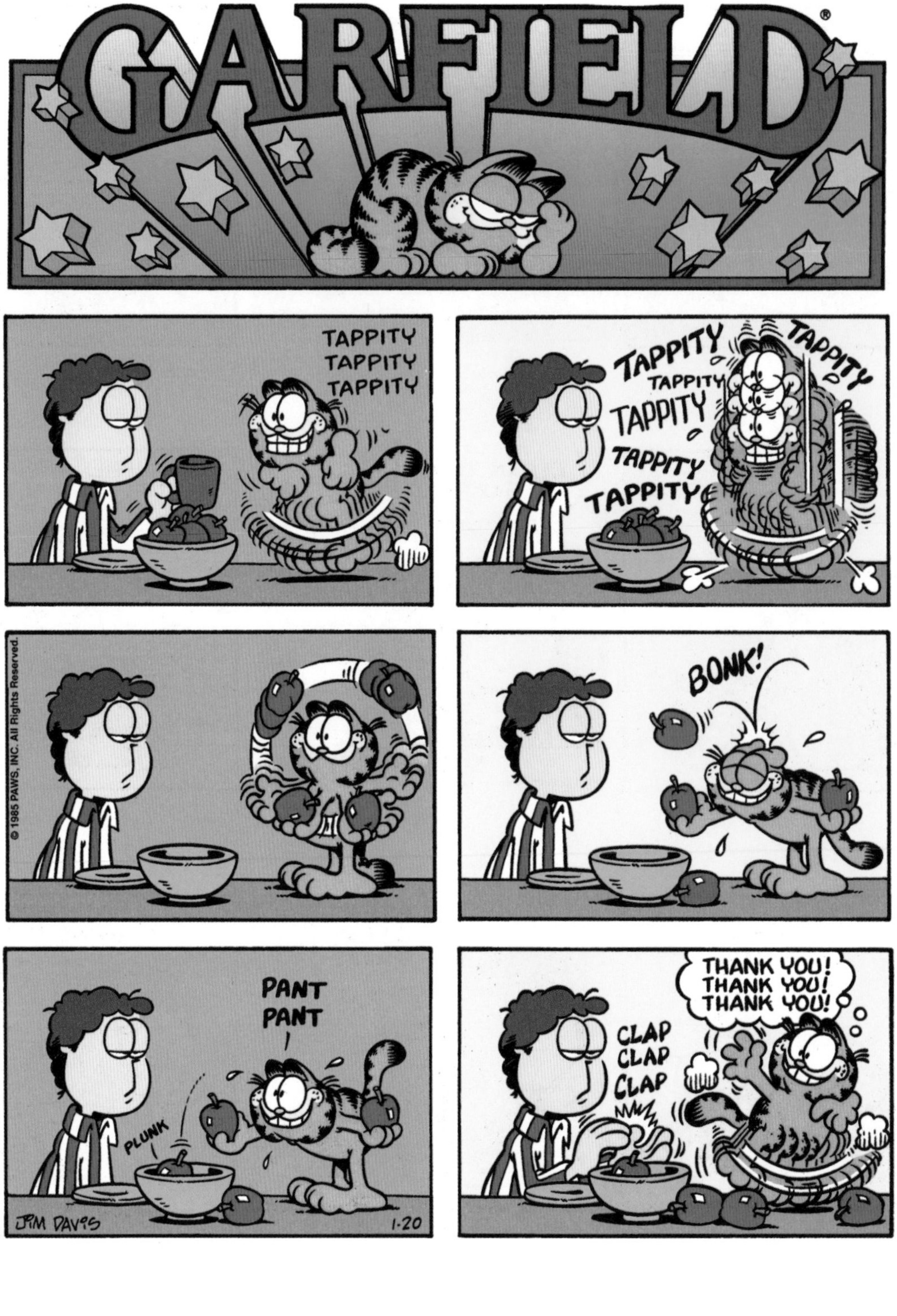
GARFIELD
TAPPITY TAPPITY TAPPITY
TAPPITY TAPPITY TAPPITY TAPPITY TAPPITY TAPPITY
BONK!
PANT PANT
PLUNK
JIM DAVIS
1-20
CLAP CLAP CLAP
THANK YOU! THANK YOU! THANK YOU!

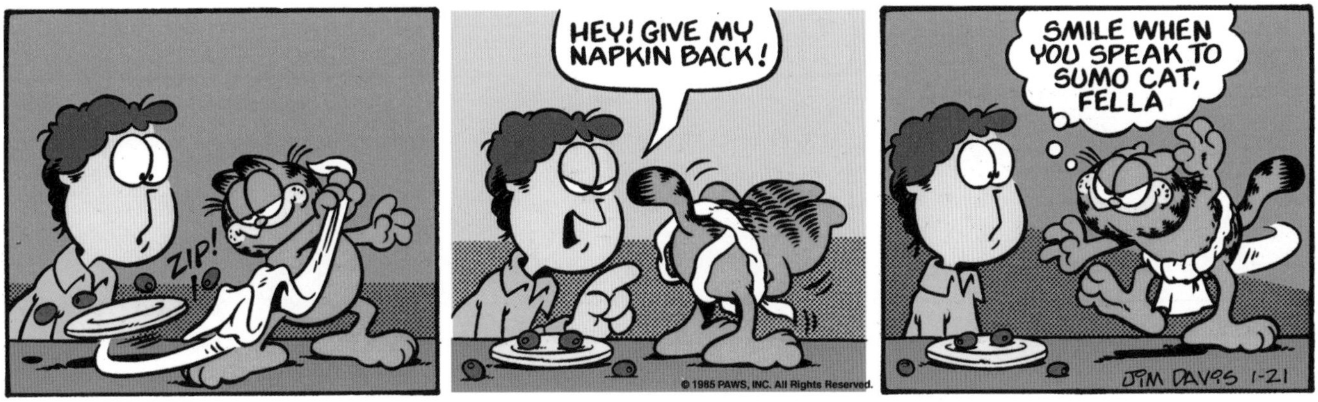
ZIP!
HEY! GIVE MY NAPKIN BACK!
© 1985 PAWS, INC. All Rights Reserved.
SMILE WHEN YOU SPEAK TO SUMO CAT, FELLA
JIM DAVIS 1-21

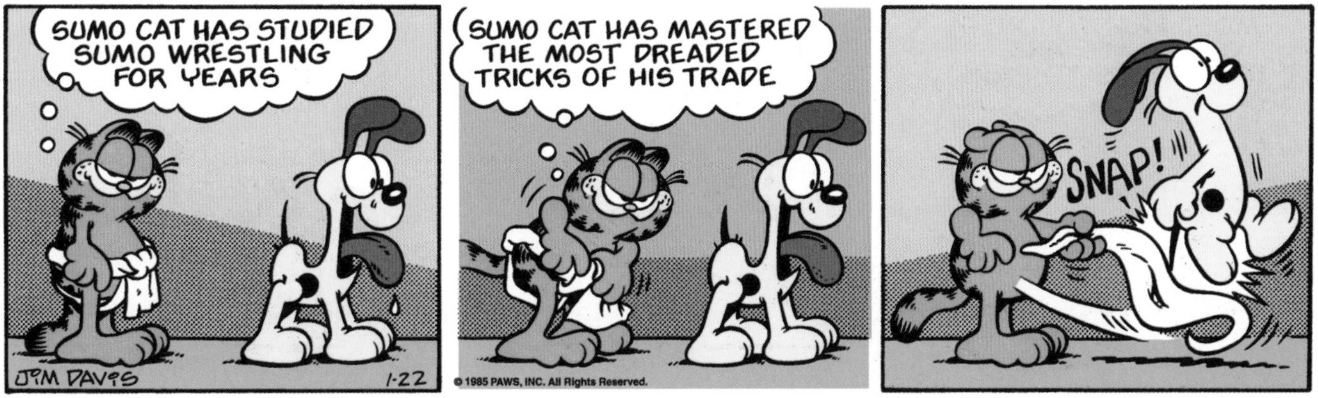
SUMO CAT HAS STUDIED SUMO WRESTLING FOR YEARS
JIM DAVIS 1-22
SUMO CAT HAS MASTERED THE MOST DREADED TRICKS OF HIS TRADE
© 1985 PAWS, INC. All Rights Reserved.
SNAP!

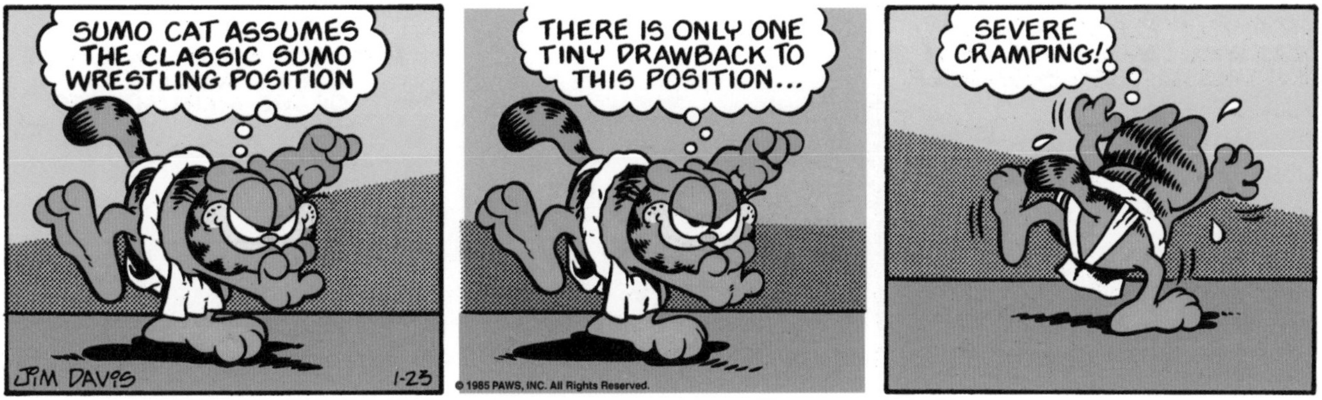
SUMO CAT ASSUMES THE CLASSIC SUMO WRESTLING POSITION
JIM DAVIS 1-23
THERE IS ONLY ONE TINY DRAWBACK TO THIS POSITION...
© 1985 PAWS, INC. All Rights Reserved.
SEVERE CRAMPING!

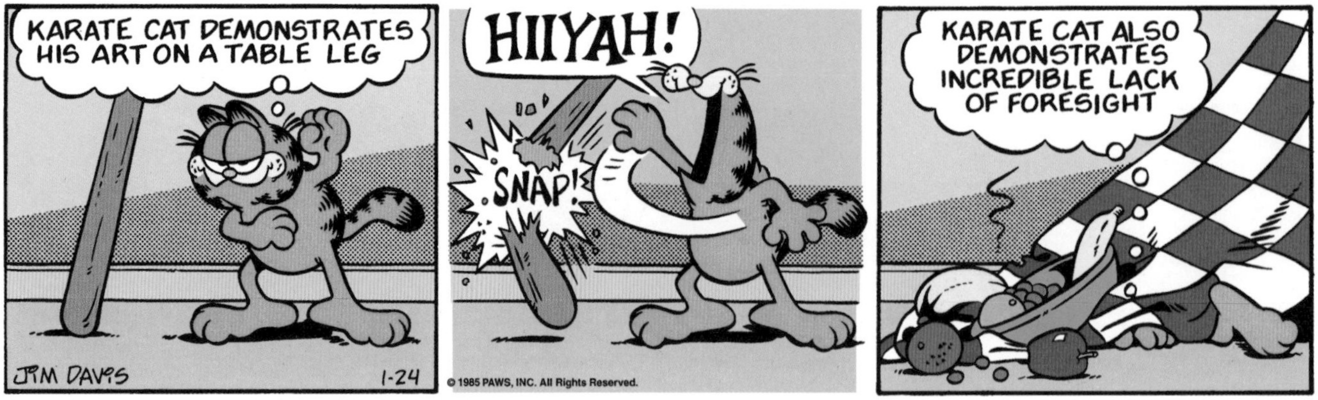
KARATE CAT DEMONSTRATES HIS ART ON A TABLE LEG
JIM DAVIS
1-24
HIIYAH!
SNAP!
© 1985 PAWS, INC. All Rights Reserved.
KARATE CAT ALSO DEMONSTRATES INCREDIBLE LACK OF FORESIGHT

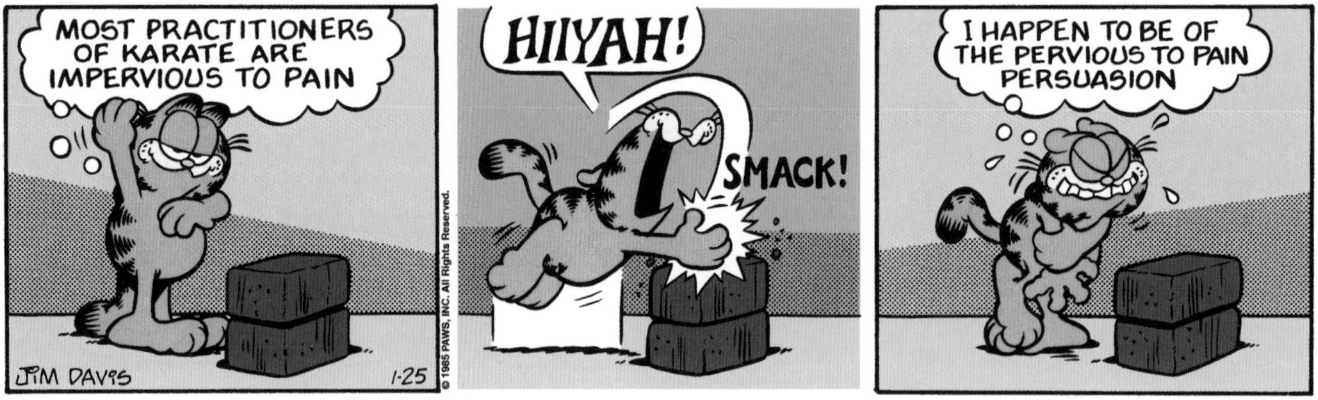
MOST PRACTITIONERS OF KARATE ARE IMPERVIOUS TO PAIN
JIM DAVIS
1-25
© 1985 PAWS, INC. All Rights Reserved.
HIIYAH!
SMACK!
I HAPPEN TO BE OF THE PERVIOUS TO PAIN PERSUASION

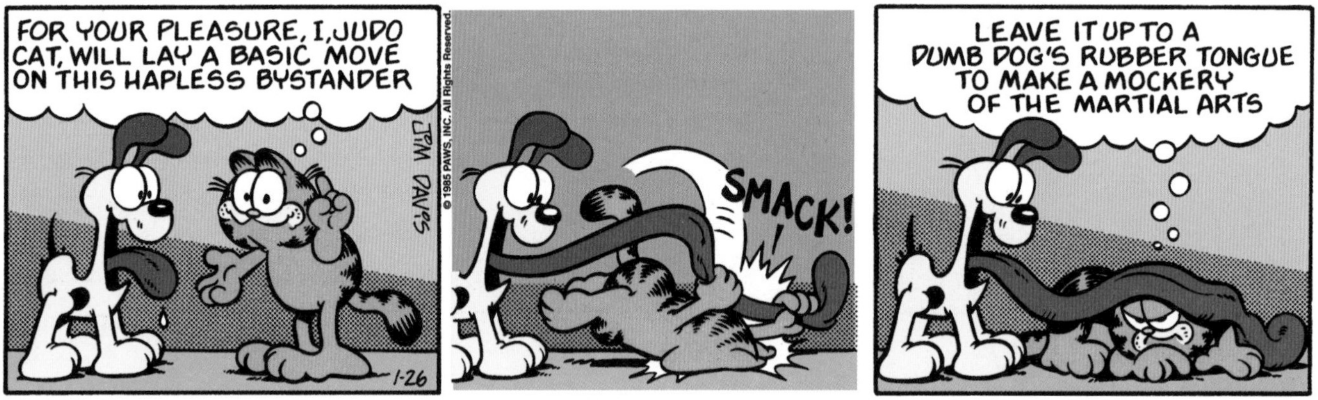
FOR YOUR PLEASURE, I, JUDO CAT, WILL LAY A BASIC MOVE ON THIS HAPLESS BYSTANDER
JIM DAVIS
1-26
© 1985 PAWS, INC. All Rights Reserved.
SMACK!
LEAVE IT UP TO A DUMB DOG'S RUBBER TONGUE TO MAKE A MOCKERY OF THE MARTIAL ARTS

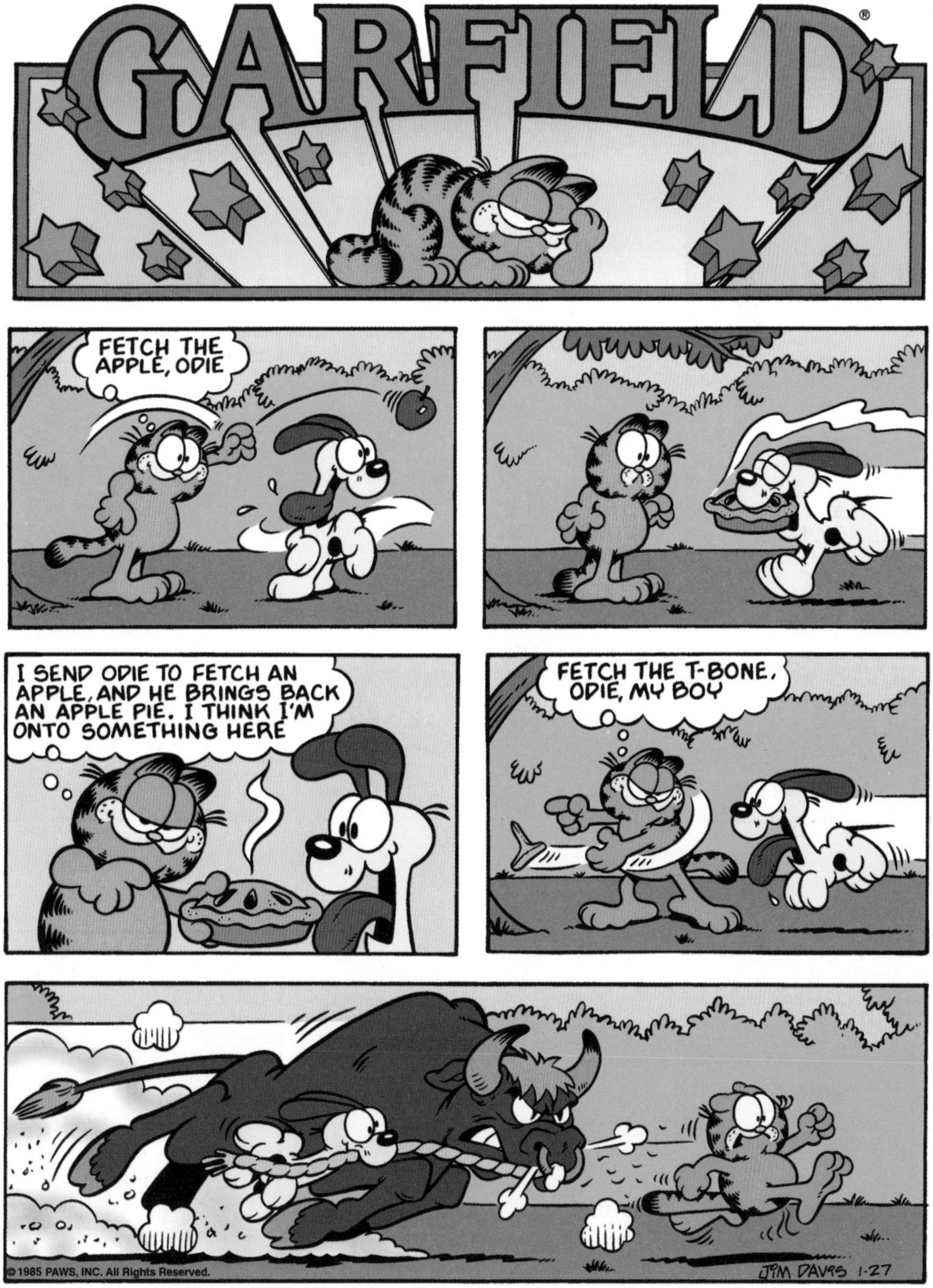
GARFIELD
FETCH THE APPLE, ODIE
I SEND ODIE TO FETCH AN APPLE, AND HE BRINGS BACK AN APPLE PIE. I THINK I'M ONTO SOMETHING HERE
FETCH THE T-BONE, ODIE, MY BOY
JIM DAVIS 1-27

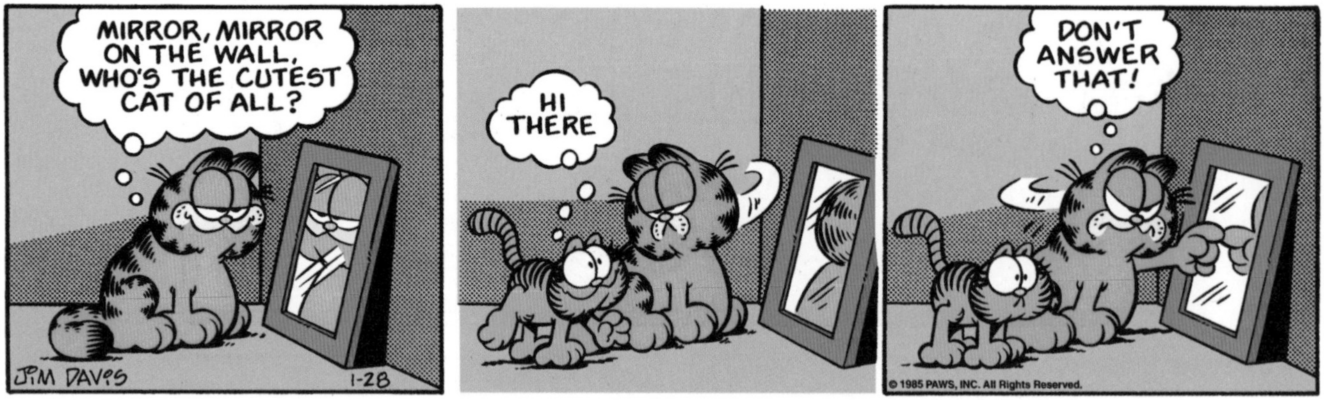
MIRROR, MIRROR ON THE WALL, WHO'S THE CUTEST CAT OF ALL?
JIM DAVIS
1-28
HI THERE
DON'T ANSWER THAT!
© 1985 PAWS, INC. All Rights Reserved.

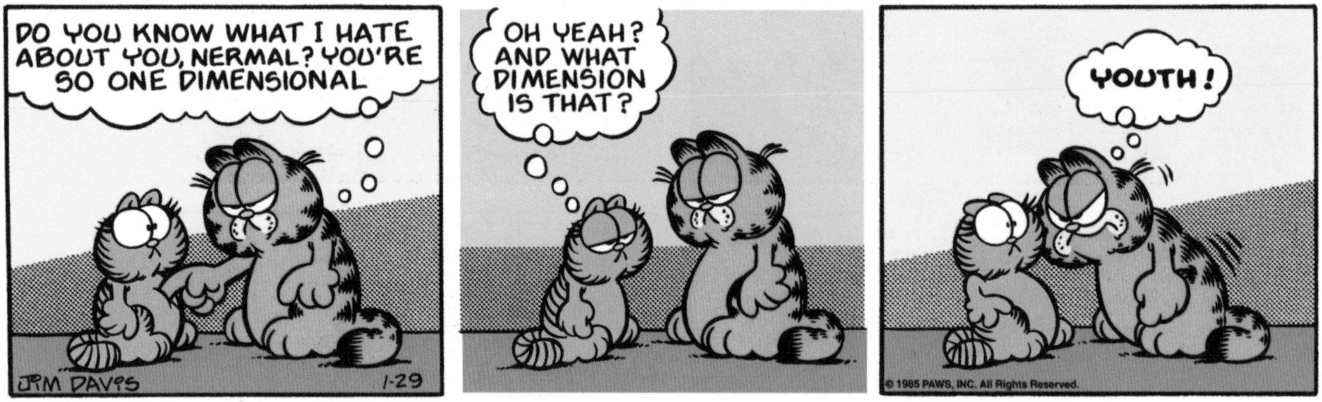
DO YOU KNOW WHAT I HATE ABOUT YOU, NERMAL? YOU'RE SO ONE DIMENSIONAL
JIM DAVIS
1-29
OH YEAH? AND WHAT DIMENSION IS THAT?
YOUTH!
© 1985 PAWS, INC. All Rights Reserved.

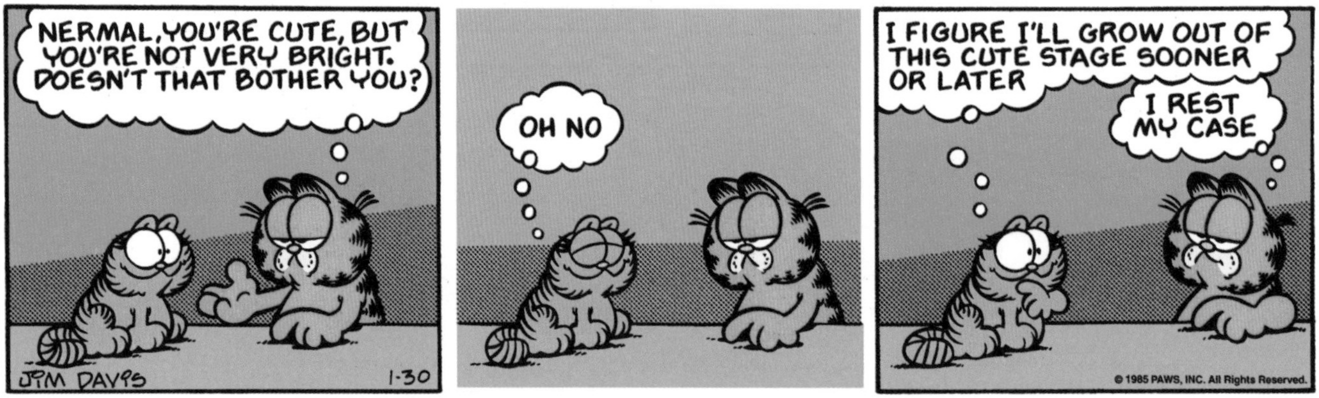
NERMAL, YOU'RE CUTE, BUT YOU'RE NOT VERY BRIGHT. DOESN'T THAT BOTHER YOU?
JIM DAVIS
1-30
OH NO
I FIGURE I'LL GROW OUT OF THIS CUTE STAGE SOONER OR LATER
I REST MY CASE
© 1985 PAWS, INC. All Rights Reserved.

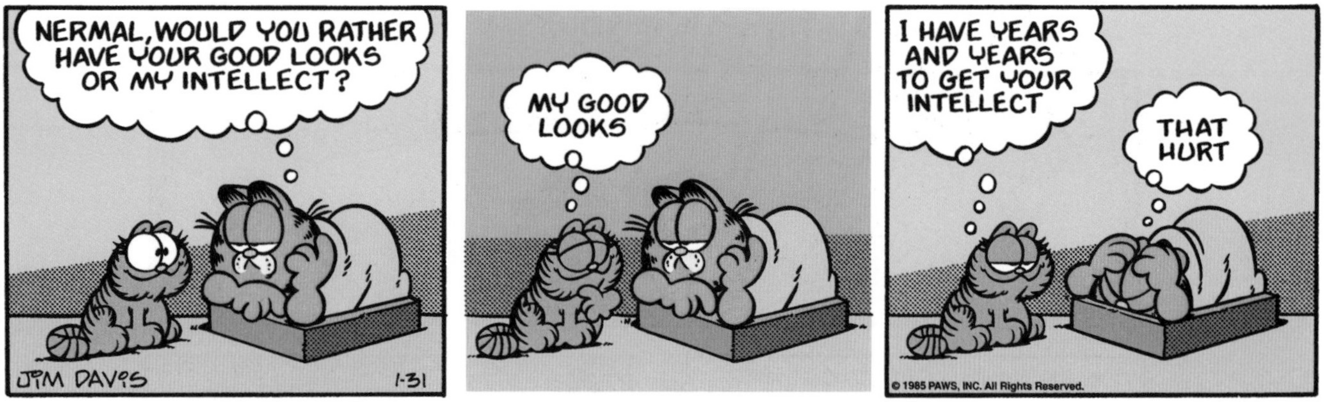
NERMAL, WOULD YOU RATHER HAVE YOUR GOOD LOOKS OR MY INTELLECT?
JIM DAVIS
1-31
MY GOOD LOOKS
I HAVE YEARS AND YEARS TO GET YOUR INTELLECT
THAT HURT
© 1985 PAWS, INC. All Rights Reserved.

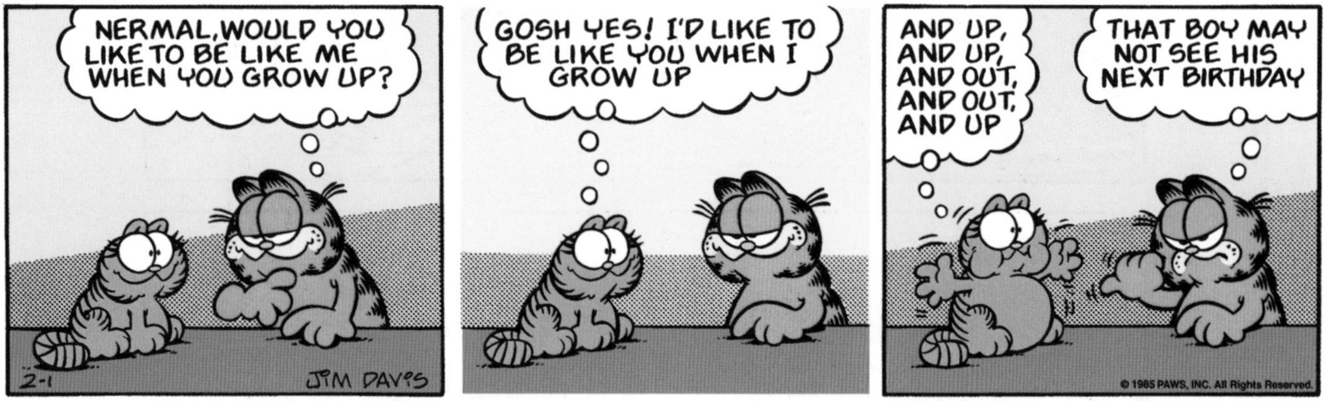
NERMAL, WOULD YOU LIKE TO BE LIKE ME WHEN YOU GROW UP?
2-1
JIM DAVIS
GOSH YES! I'D LIKE TO BE LIKE YOU WHEN I GROW UP
AND UP, AND UP, AND OUT, AND OUT, AND UP
THAT BOY MAY NOT SEE HIS NEXT BIRTHDAY
© 1985 PAWS, INC. All Rights Reserved.

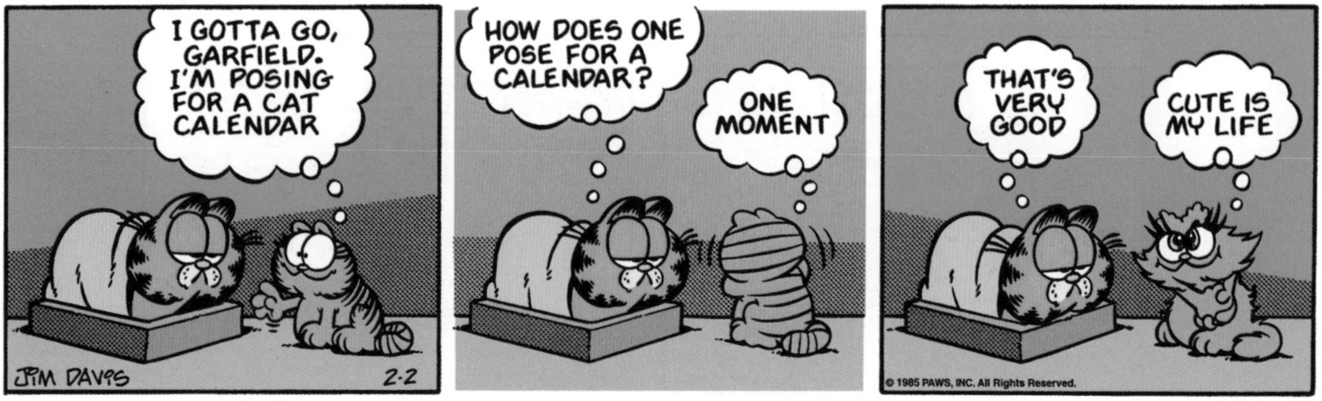
I GOTTA GO, GARFIELD. I'M POSING FOR A CAT CALENDAR
JIM DAVIS
2-2
HOW DOES ONE POSE FOR A CALENDAR?
ONE MOMENT
THAT'S VERY GOOD
CUTE IS MY LIFE
© 1985 PAWS, INC. All Rights Reserved.

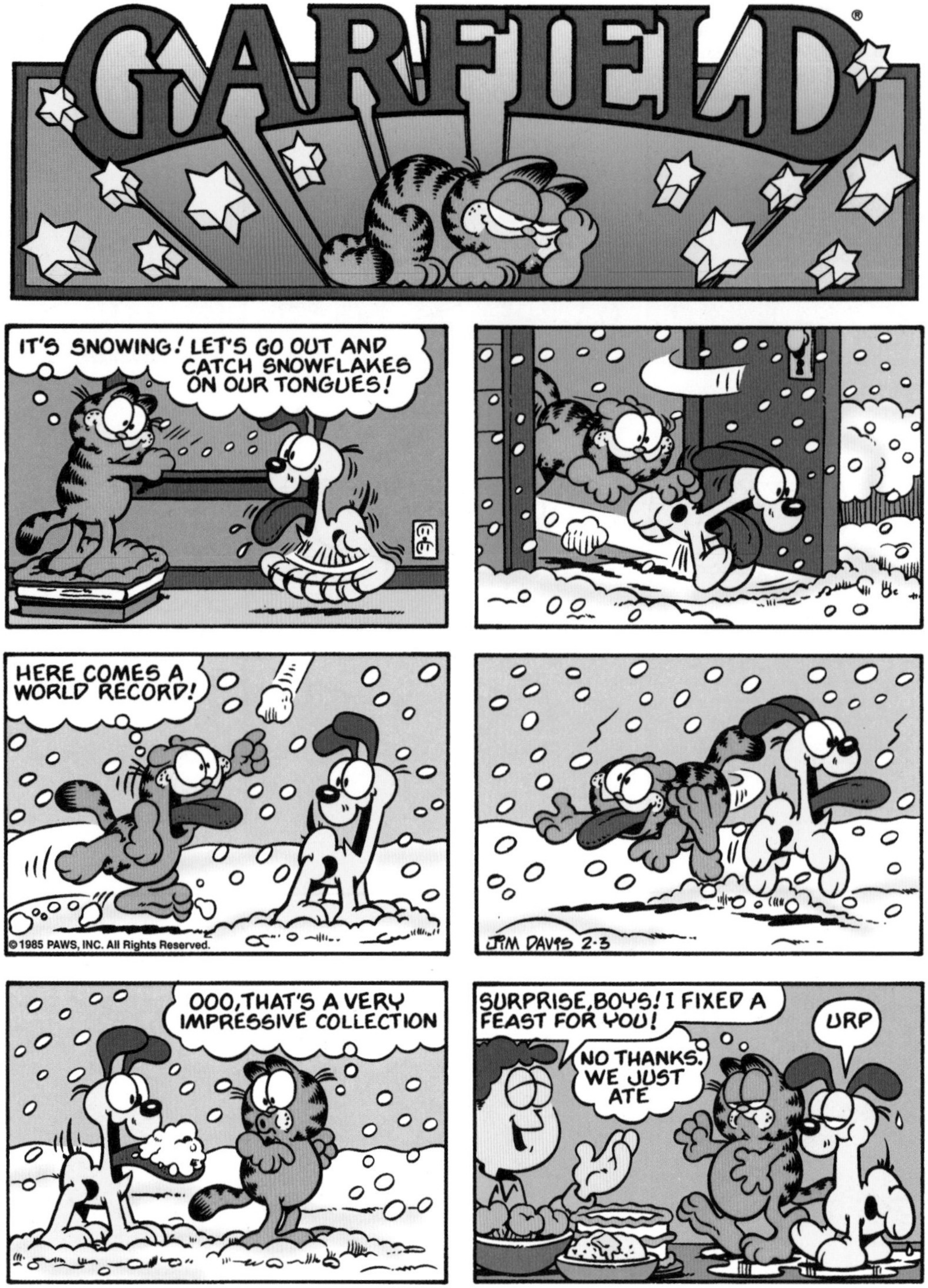
GARFIELD®
IT'S SNOWING! LET'S GO OUT AND CATCH SNOWFLAKES ON OUR TONGUES!
HERE COMES A WORLD RECORD!
© 1985 PAWS, INC. All Rights Reserved.
JIM DAVIS 2-3
OOO, THAT'S A VERY IMPRESSIVE COLLECTION
SURPRISE, BOYS! I FIXED A FEAST FOR YOU!
NO THANKS. WE JUST ATE
URP

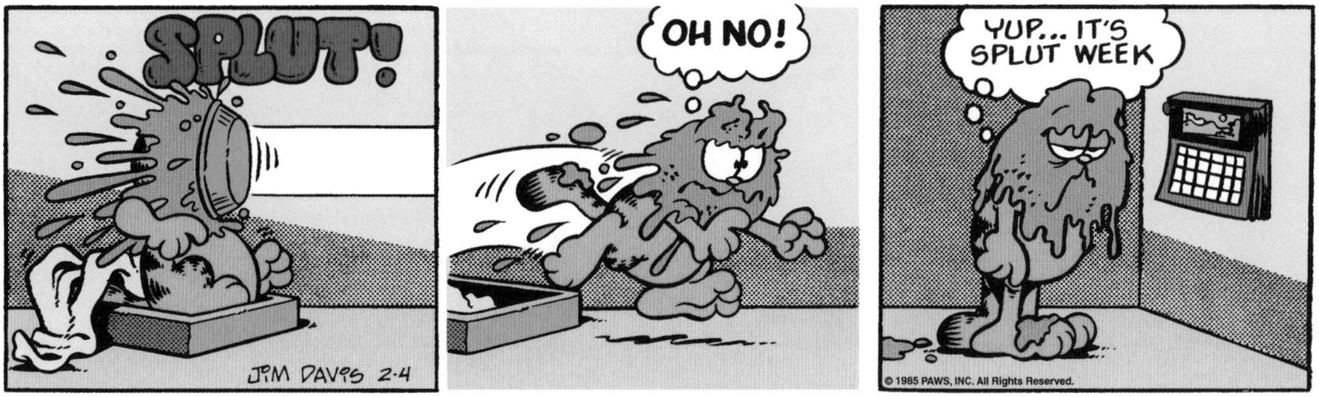
SPLUT!
OH NO!
YUP... IT'S SPLUT WEEK
JIM DAVIS 2-4
© 1985 PAWS, INC. All Rights Reserved.

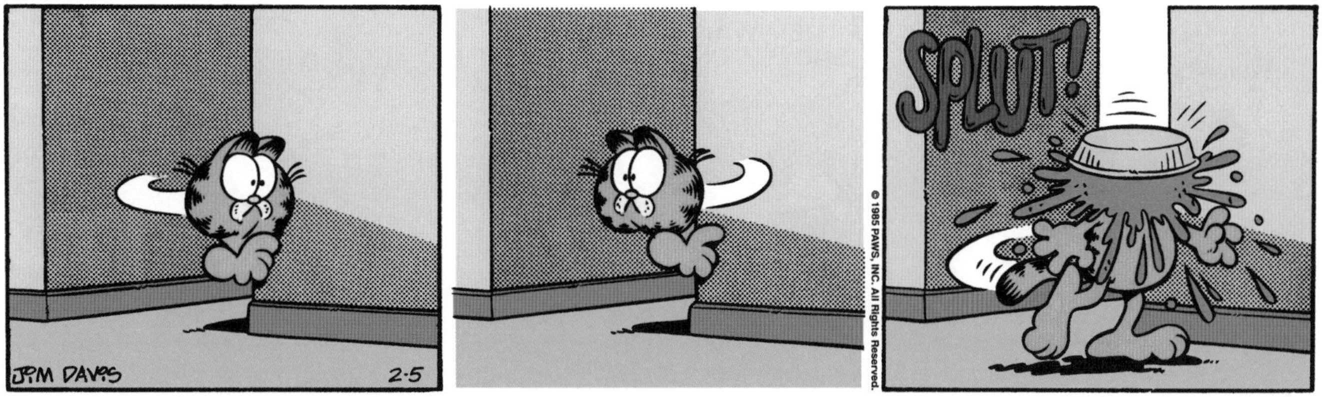
JIM DAVIS 2-5
© 1985 PAWS, INC. All Rights Reserved.
SPLUT!

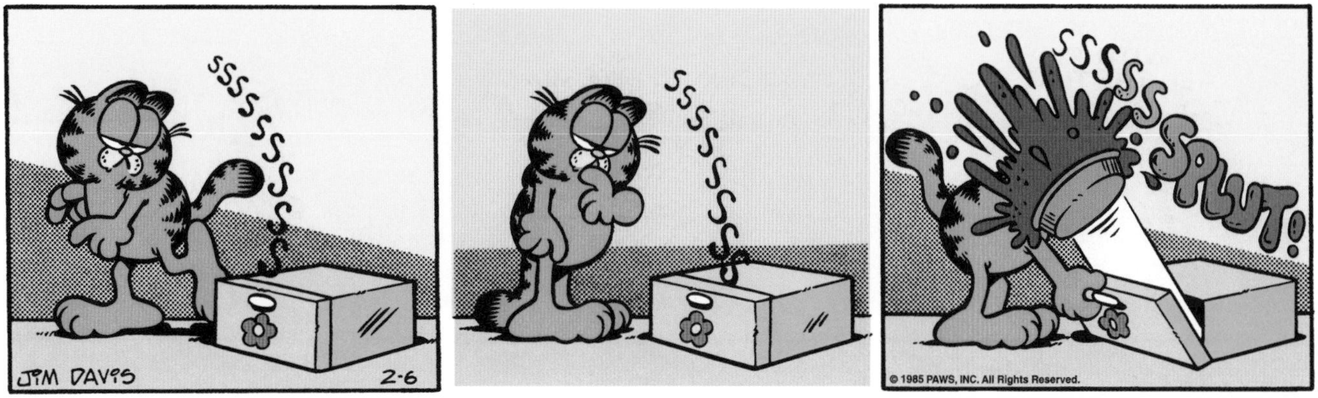
SSSSSSSS
JIM DAVIS 2-6
SSSSSSS
SSSSS
SPLUT!
© 1985 PAWS, INC. All Rights Reserved.

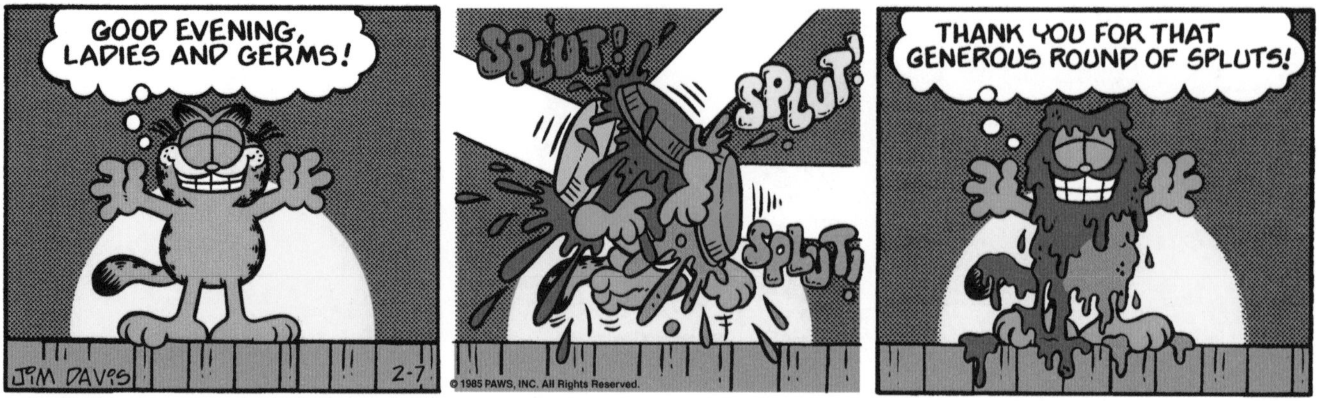
GOOD EVENING, LADIES AND GERMS!
JIM DAVIS
2-7
SPLUT!
SPLUT!
SPLUT!
© 1985 PAWS, INC. All Rights Reserved.
THANK YOU FOR THAT GENEROUS ROUND OF SPLUTS!

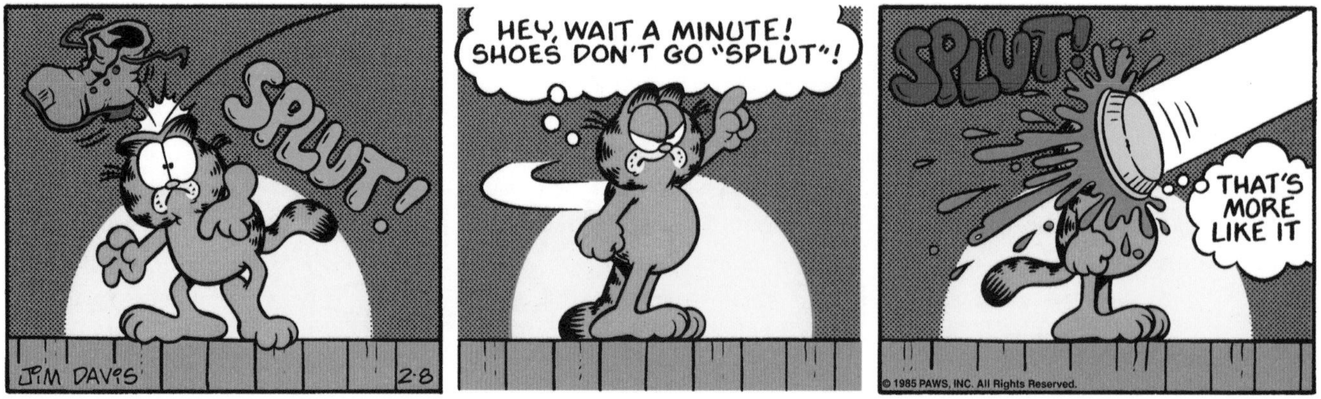
SPLUT!
JIM DAVIS
2-8
HEY, WAIT A MINUTE! SHOES DON'T GO "SPLUT"!
SPLUT!
THAT'S MORE LIKE IT
© 1985 PAWS, INC. All Rights Reserved.

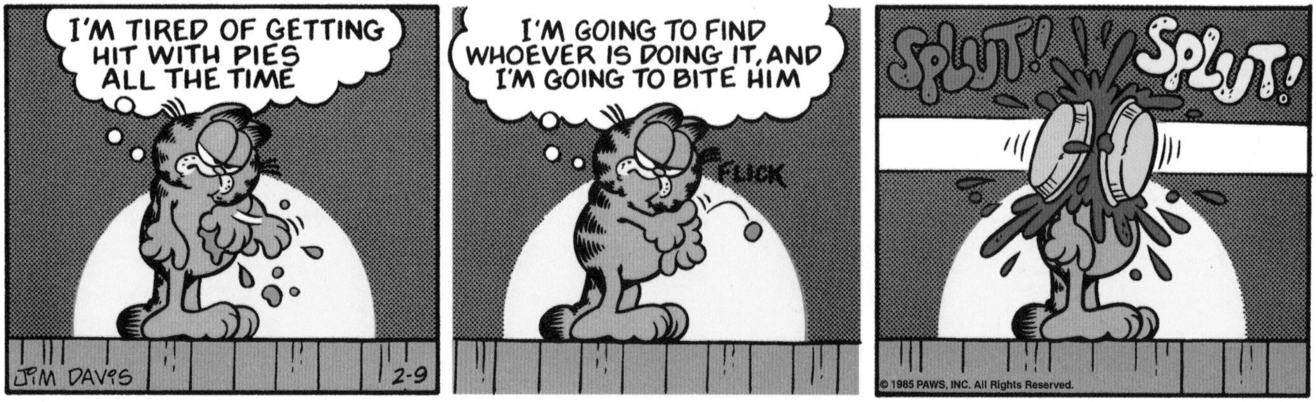
I'M TIRED OF GETTING HIT WITH PIES ALL THE TIME
JIM DAVIS
2-9
I'M GOING TO FIND WHOEVER IS DOING IT, AND I'M GOING TO BITE HIM
FLICK
SPLUT!
SPLUT!
© 1985 PAWS, INC. All Rights Reserved.

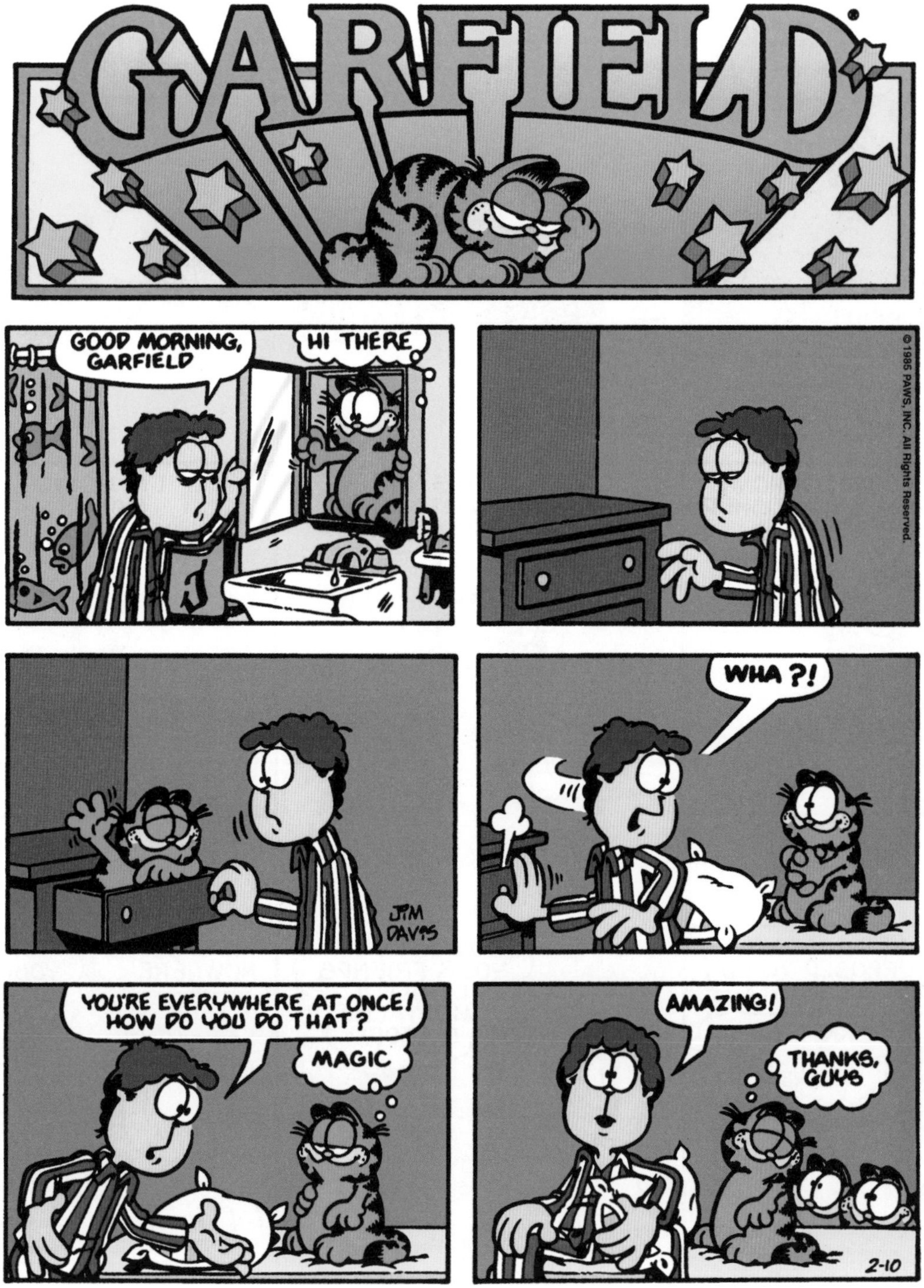

GARFIELD
GOOD MORNING, GARFIELD
HI THERE
© 1985 PAWS, INC. All Rights Reserved.
JIM DAVIS
WHA ?!
YOU'RE EVERYWHERE AT ONCE! HOW DO YOU DO THAT?
MAGIC
AMAZING!
THANKS, GUYS
2-10

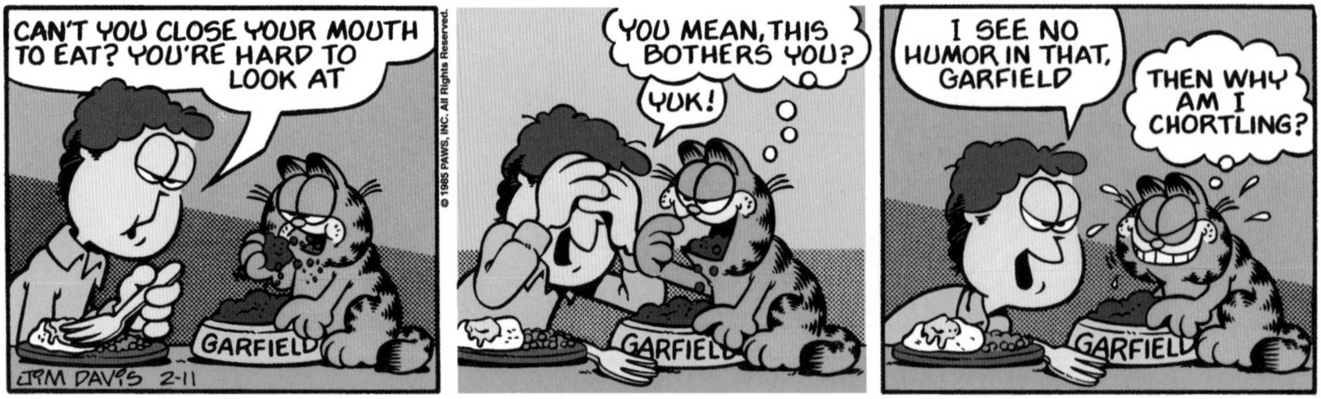
CAN'T YOU CLOSE YOUR MOUTH TO EAT? YOU'RE HARD TO LOOK AT
GARFIELD
JIM DAVIS 2-11
© 1985 PAWS, INC. All Rights Reserved.
YOU MEAN, THIS BOTHERS YOU?
YUK!
GARFIELD
I SEE NO HUMOR IN THAT, GARFIELD
THEN WHY AM I CHORTLING?
GARFIELD

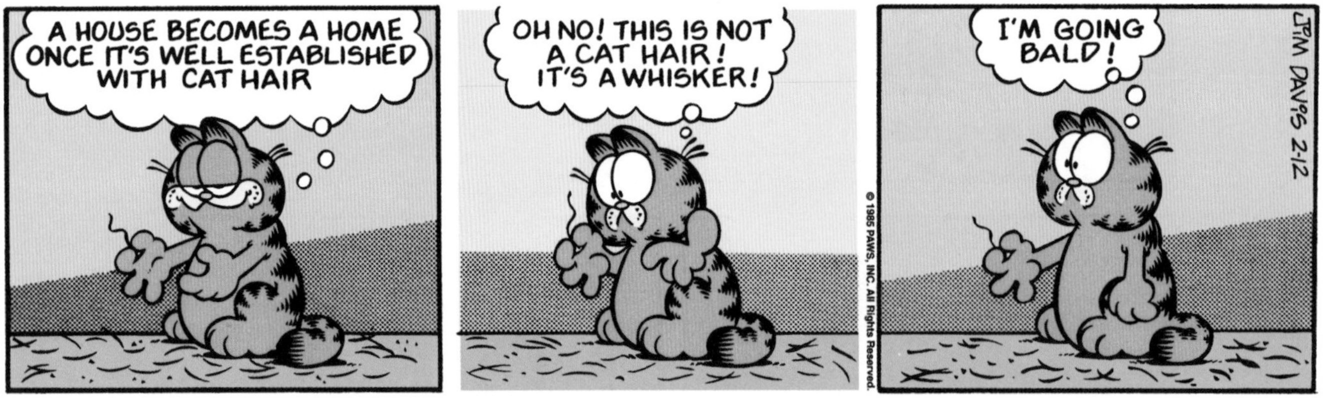
A HOUSE BECOMES A HOME ONCE IT'S WELL ESTABLISHED WITH CAT HAIR
OH NO! THIS IS NOT A CAT HAIR! IT'S A WHISKER!
© 1985 PAWS, INC. All Rights Reserved.
I'M GOING BALD!
JIM DAVIS 2-12

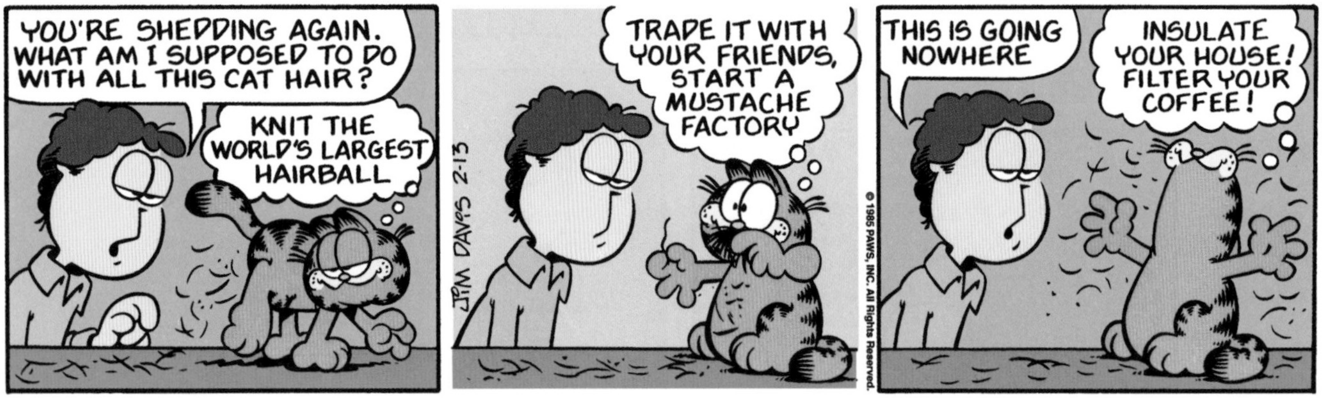
YOU'RE SHEDDING AGAIN. WHAT AM I SUPPOSED TO DO WITH ALL THIS CAT HAIR?
KNIT THE WORLD'S LARGEST HAIRBALL
JIM DAVIS 2-13
TRADE IT WITH YOUR FRIENDS, START A MUSTACHE FACTORY
© 1985 PAWS, INC. All Rights Reserved.
THIS IS GOING NOWHERE
INSULATE YOUR HOUSE! FILTER YOUR COFFEE!

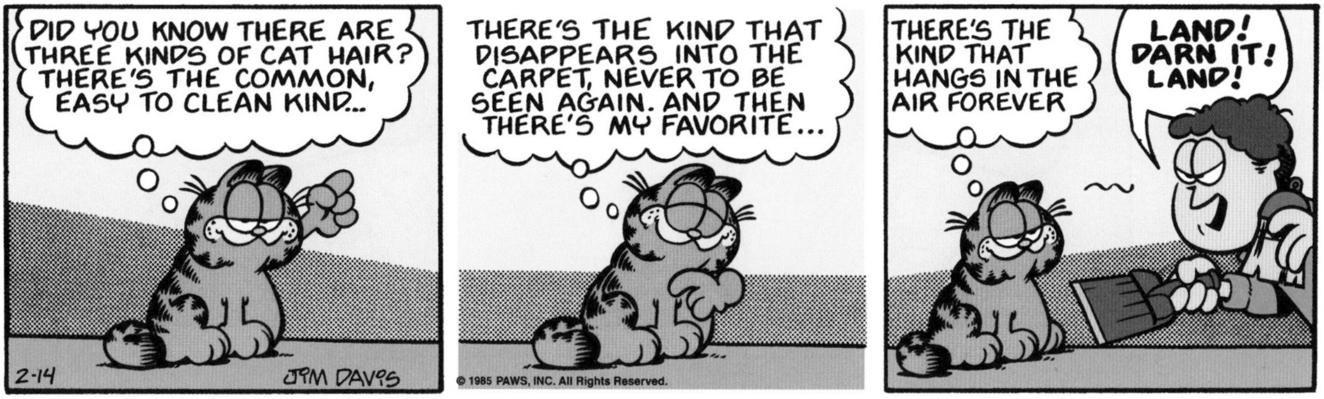
DID YOU KNOW THERE ARE THREE KINDS OF CAT HAIR? THERE'S THE COMMON, EASY TO CLEAN KIND...
2-14
JIM DAVIS
THERE'S THE KIND THAT DISAPPEARS INTO THE CARPET, NEVER TO BE SEEN AGAIN. AND THEN THERE'S MY FAVORITE...
© 1985 PAWS, INC. All Rights Reserved.
THERE'S THE KIND THAT HANGS IN THE AIR FOREVER
LAND! DARN IT! LAND!

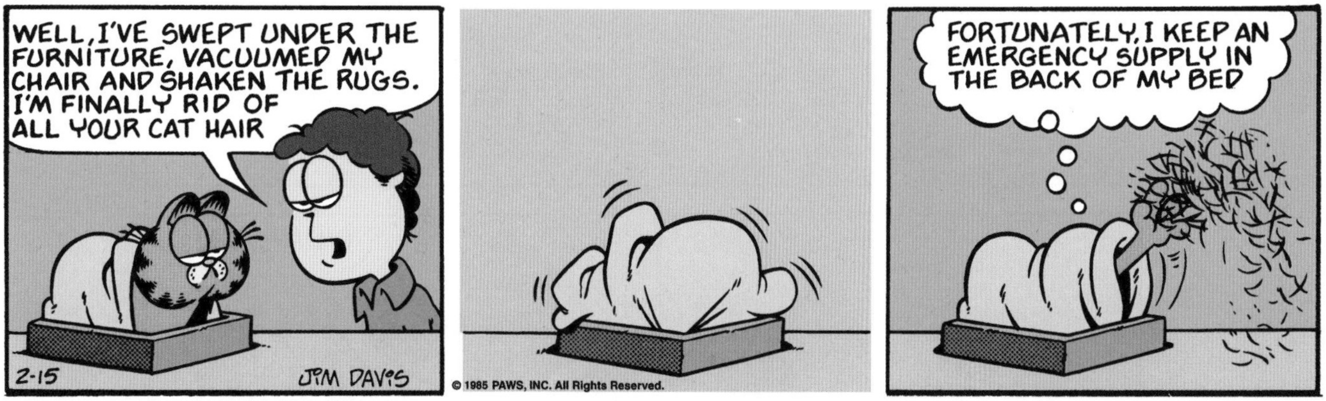
WELL, I'VE SWEPT UNDER THE FURNITURE, VACUUMED MY CHAIR AND SHAKEN THE RUGS. I'M FINALLY RID OF ALL YOUR CAT HAIR
2-15
JIM DAVIS
© 1985 PAWS, INC. All Rights Reserved.
FORTUNATELY, I KEEP AN EMERGENCY SUPPLY IN THE BACK OF MY BED

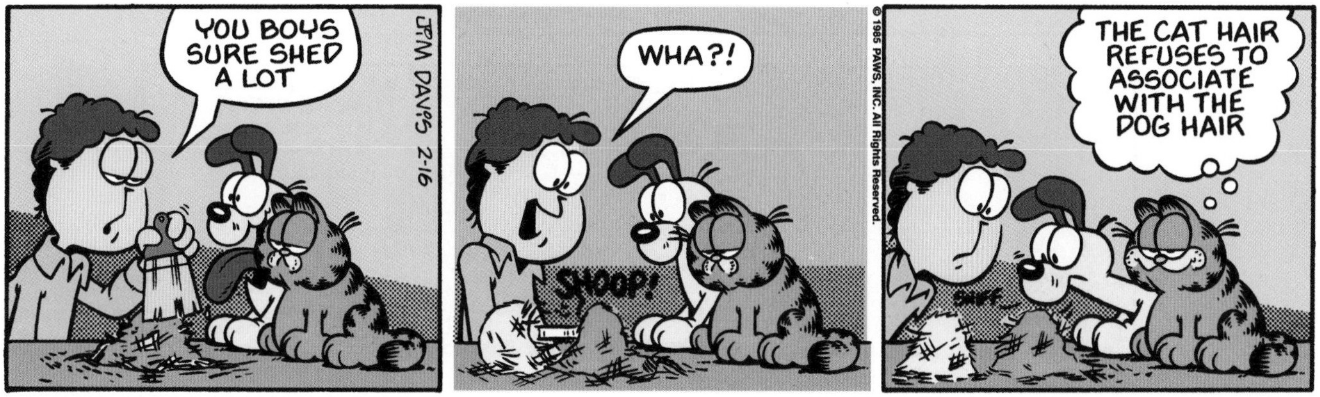
YOU BOYS SURE SHED A LOT
JIM DAVIS 2-16
WHA?!
SHOOP!
© 1985 PAWS, INC. All Rights Reserved.
THE CAT HAIR REFUSES TO ASSOCIATE WITH THE DOG HAIR
SNIFF

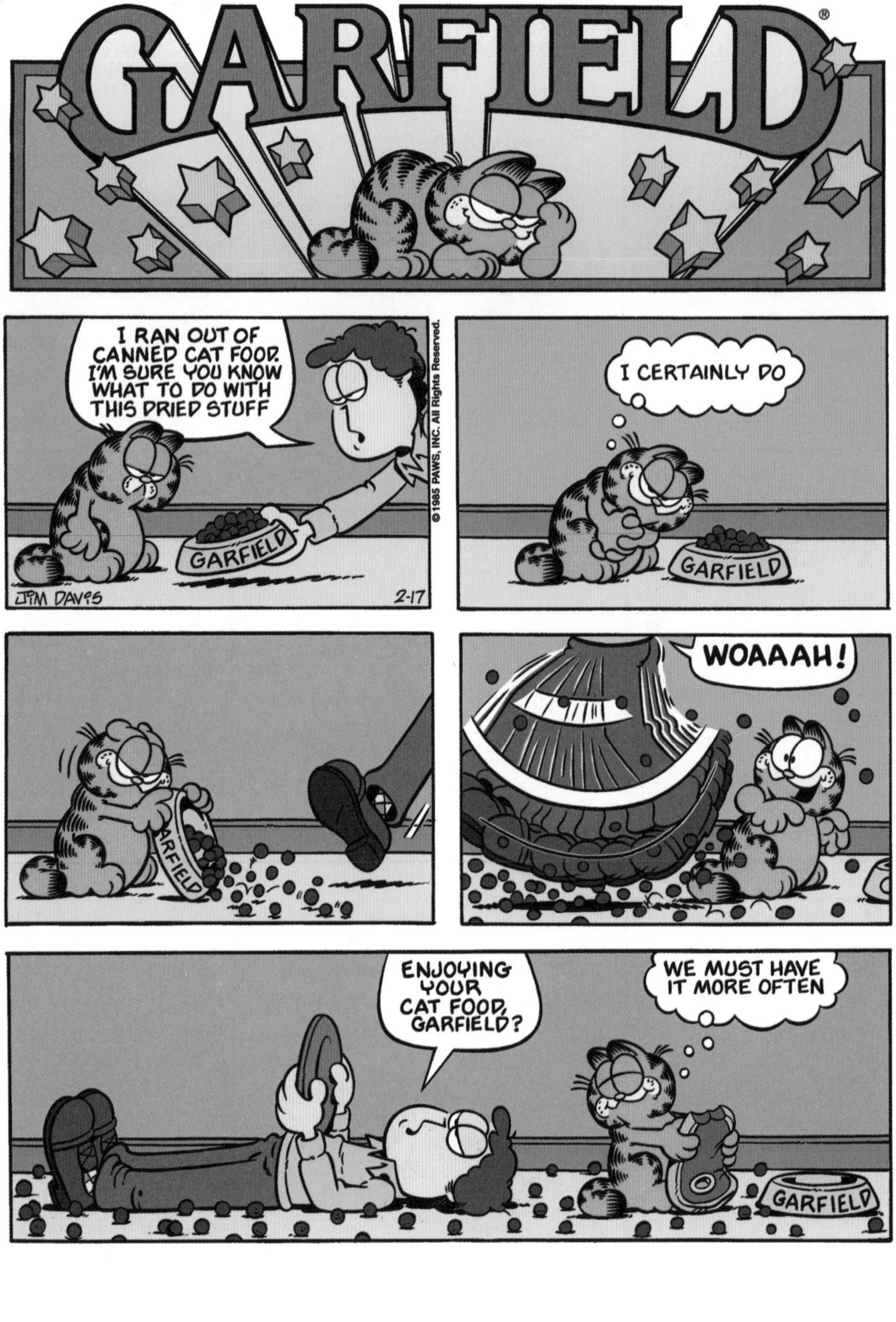
GARFIELD®
I RAN OUT OF CANNED CAT FOOD. I'M SURE YOU KNOW WHAT TO DO WITH THIS DRIED STUFF
GARFIELD
JIM DAVIS
2-17
© 1985 PAWS, INC. All Rights Reserved.
I CERTAINLY DO
GARFIELD
WOAAAH!
ENJOYING YOUR CAT FOOD, GARFIELD?
WE MUST HAVE IT MORE OFTEN
GARFIELD

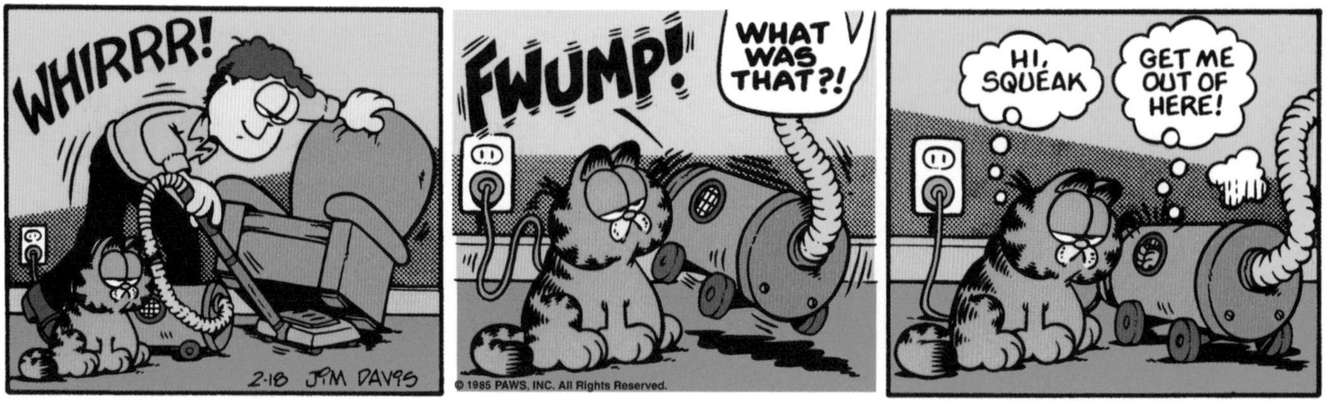
WHIRRR!
2-18 JIM DAVIS
FWUMP!
WHAT WAS THAT?!
© 1985 PAWS, INC. All Rights Reserved.
HI, SQUEAK
GET ME OUT OF HERE!

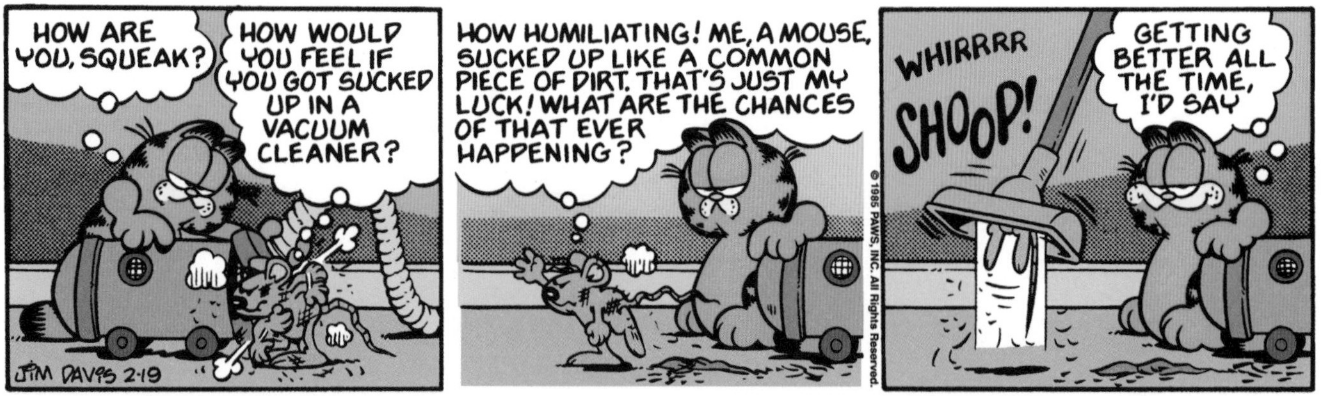
HOW ARE YOU, SQUEAK?
HOW WOULD YOU FEEL IF YOU GOT SUCKED UP IN A VACUUM CLEANER?
JIM DAVIS 2-19
HOW HUMILIATING! ME, A MOUSE, SUCKED UP LIKE A COMMON PIECE OF DIRT. THAT'S JUST MY LUCK! WHAT ARE THE CHANCES OF THAT EVER HAPPENING?
© 1985 PAWS, INC. All Rights Reserved.
WHIRRRR
SHOOP!
GETTING BETTER ALL THE TIME, I'D SAY

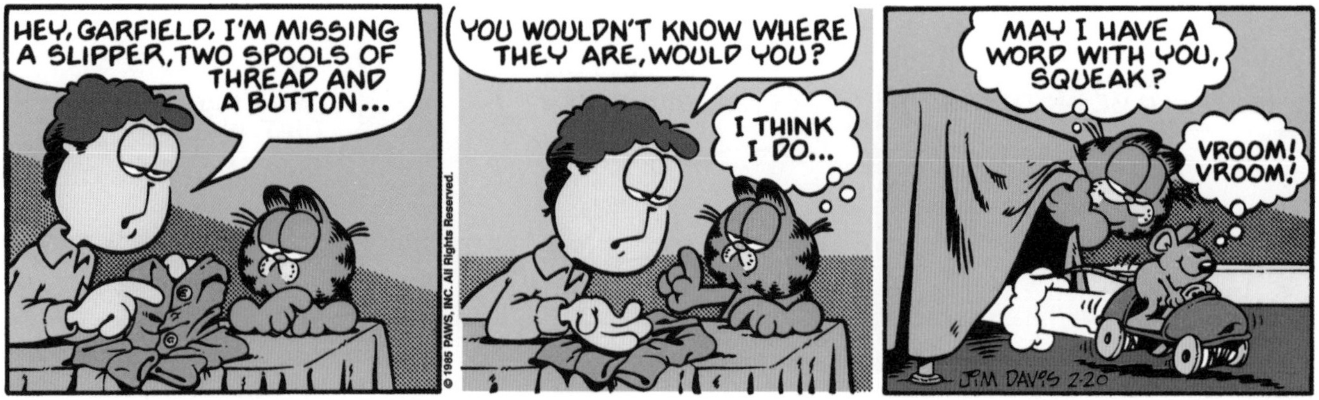
HEY, GARFIELD. I'M MISSING A SLIPPER, TWO SPOOLS OF THREAD AND A BUTTON...
© 1985 PAWS, INC. All Rights Reserved.
YOU WOULDN'T KNOW WHERE THEY ARE, WOULD YOU?
I THINK I DO...
MAY I HAVE A WORD WITH YOU, SQUEAK?
VROOM! VROOM!
JIM DAVIS 2-20

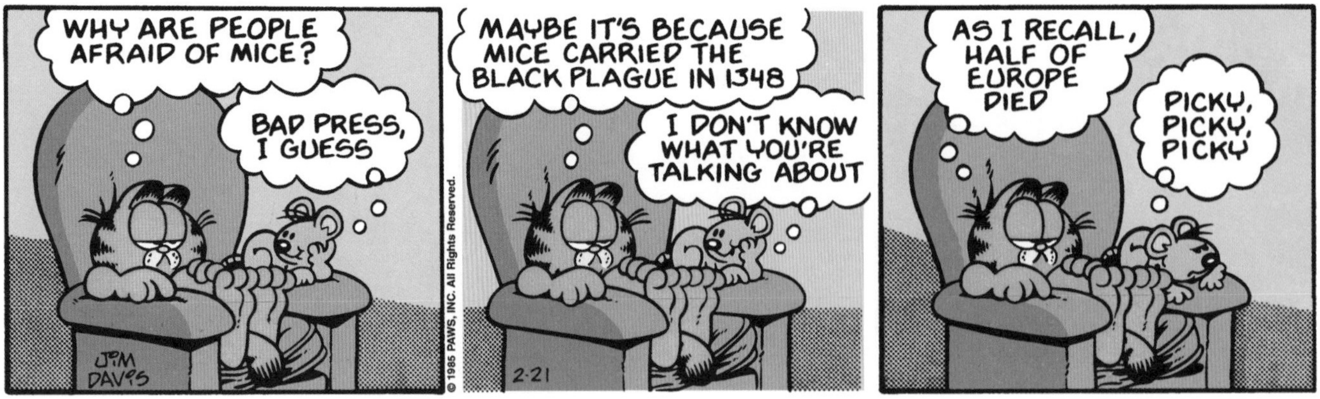
WHY ARE PEOPLE AFRAID OF MICE?
BAD PRESS, I GUESS
JIM DAVIS
© 1985 PAWS, INC. All Rights Reserved.
MAYBE IT'S BECAUSE MICE CARRIED THE BLACK PLAGUE IN 1348
I DON'T KNOW WHAT YOU'RE TALKING ABOUT
2-21
AS I RECALL, HALF OF EUROPE DIED
PICKY, PICKY, PICKY

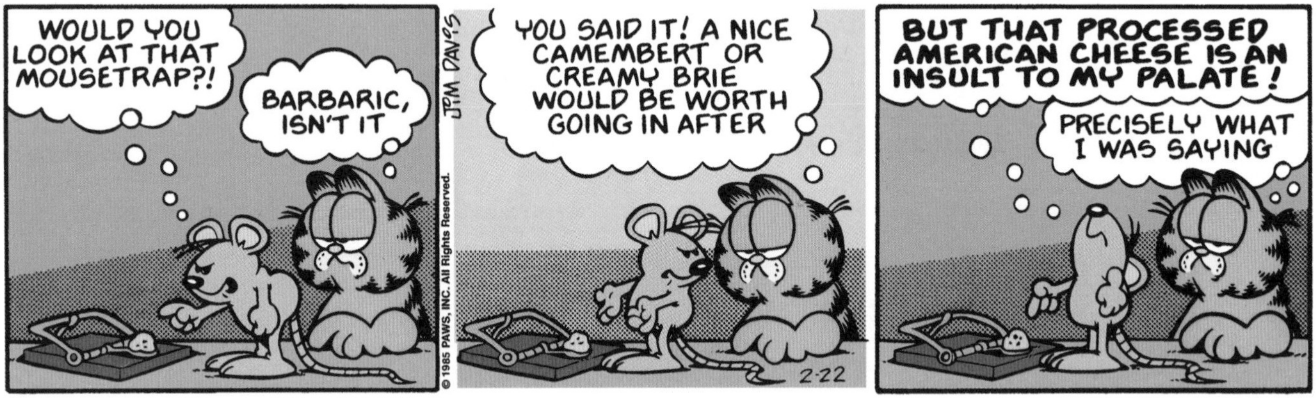
WOULD YOU LOOK AT THAT MOUSETRAP?!
BARBARIC, ISN'T IT
JIM DAVIS
© 1985 PAWS, INC. All Rights Reserved.
YOU SAID IT! A NICE CAMEMBERT OR CREAMY BRIE WOULD BE WORTH GOING IN AFTER
2-22
BUT THAT PROCESSED AMERICAN CHEESE IS AN INSULT TO MY PALATE!
PRECISELY WHAT I WAS SAYING

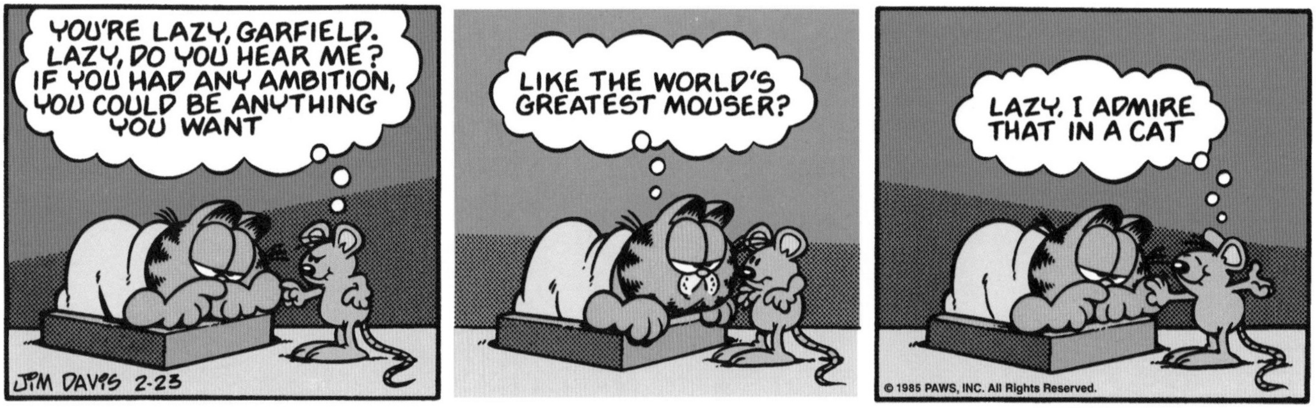
YOU'RE LAZY, GARFIELD. LAZY, DO YOU HEAR ME? IF YOU HAD ANY AMBITION, YOU COULD BE ANYTHING YOU WANT
JIM DAVIS 2-23
LIKE THE WORLD'S GREATEST MOUSER?
LAZY, I ADMIRE THAT IN A CAT
© 1985 PAWS, INC. All Rights Reserved.

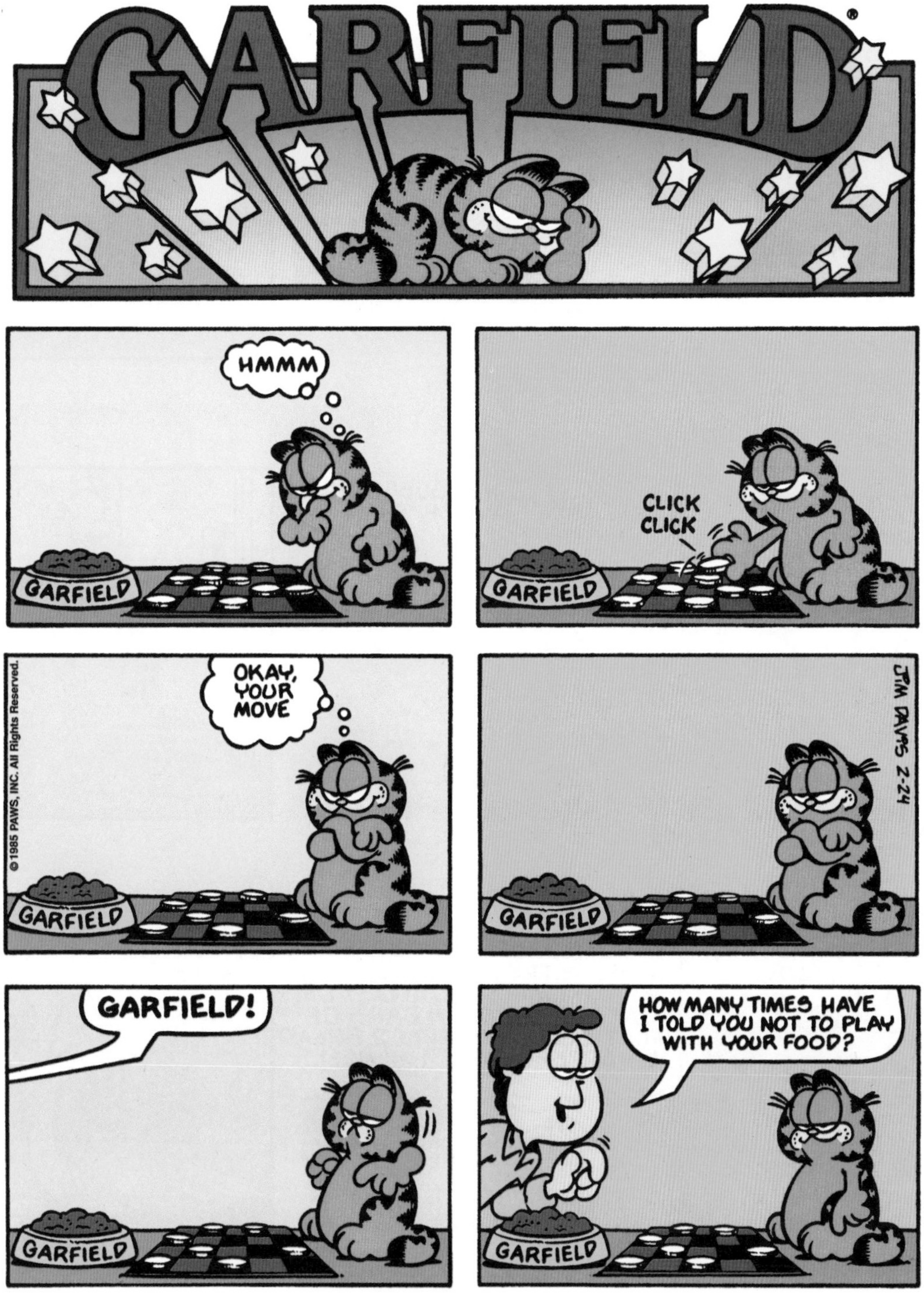
GARFIELD
HMMM
CLICK CLICK
GARFIELD
OKAY, YOUR MOVE
JIM DAVIS 2-24
GARFIELD!
HOW MANY TIMES HAVE I TOLD YOU NOT TO PLAY WITH YOUR FOOD?

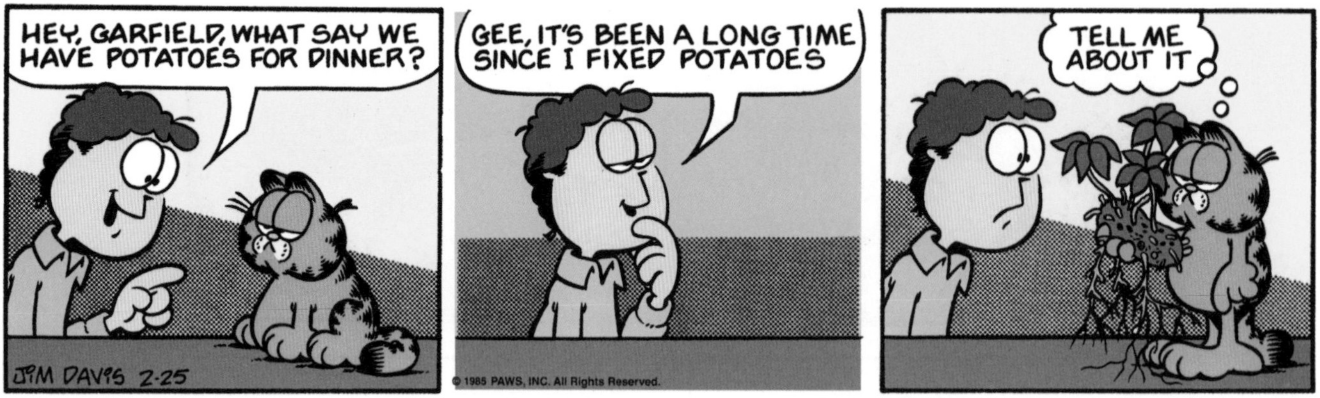
HEY, GARFIELD, WHAT SAY WE HAVE POTATOES FOR DINNER?
JIM DAVIS 2-25
GEE, IT'S BEEN A LONG TIME SINCE I FIXED POTATOES
© 1985 PAWS, INC. All Rights Reserved.
TELL ME ABOUT IT

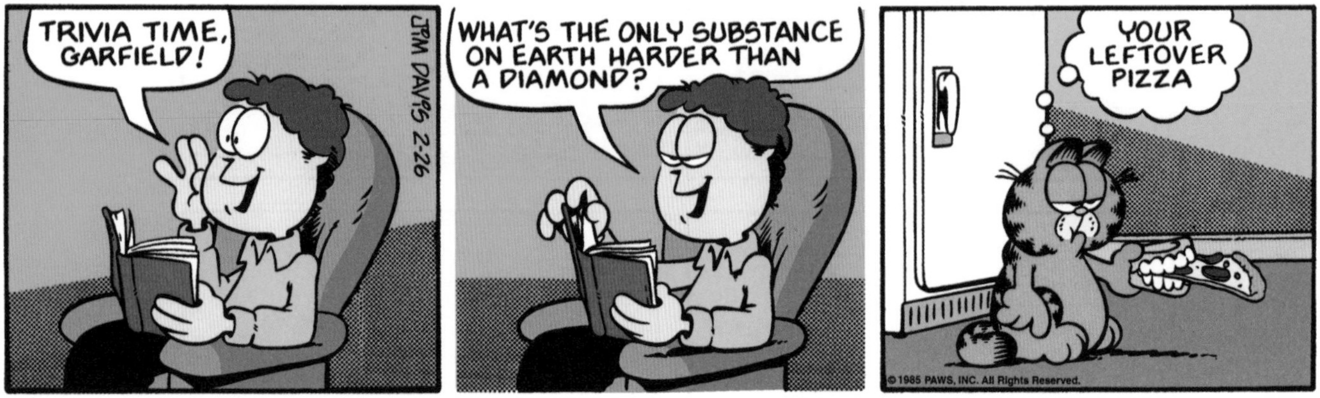
TRIVIA TIME, GARFIELD!
JIM DAVIS 2-26
WHAT'S THE ONLY SUBSTANCE ON EARTH HARDER THAN A DIAMOND?
YOUR LEFTOVER PIZZA
© 1985 PAWS, INC. All Rights Reserved.

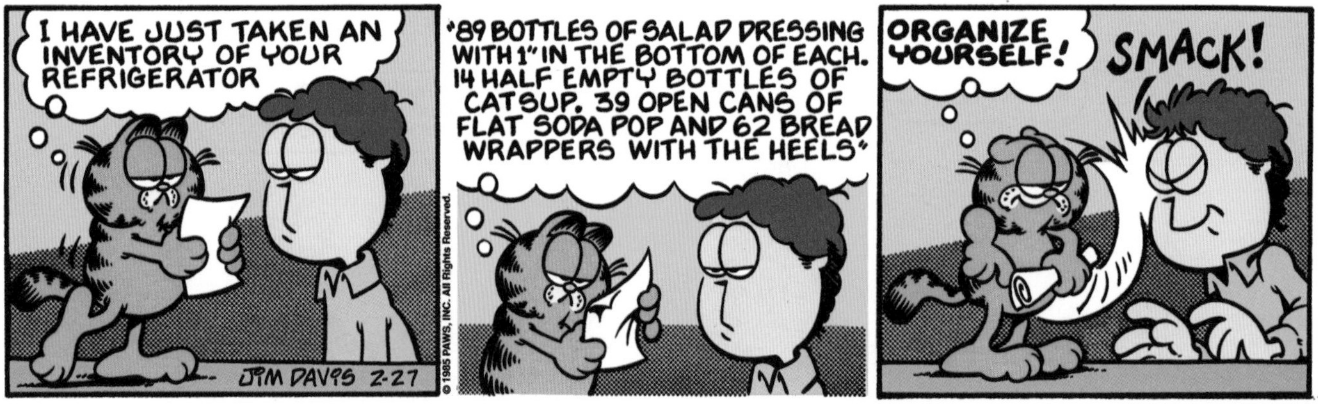
I HAVE JUST TAKEN AN INVENTORY OF YOUR REFRIGERATOR
JIM DAVIS 2-27
© 1985 PAWS, INC. All Rights Reserved.
"89 BOTTLES OF SALAD DRESSING WITH 1" IN THE BOTTOM OF EACH. 14 HALF EMPTY BOTTLES OF CATSUP. 39 OPEN CANS OF FLAT SODA POP AND 62 BREAD WRAPPERS WITH THE HEELS"
ORGANIZE YOURSELF!
SMACK!

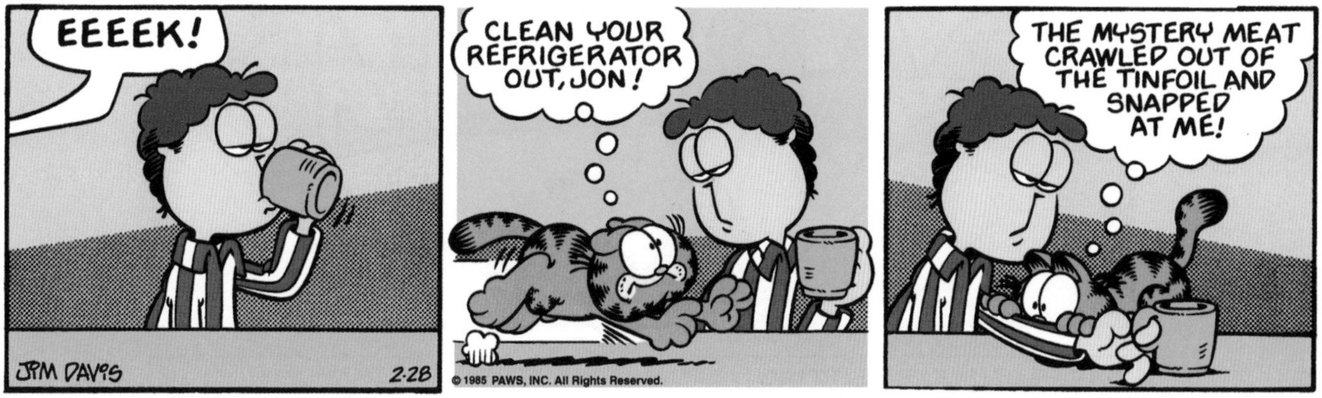
EEEEK!
JIM DAVIS 2-28
CLEAN YOUR REFRIGERATOR OUT, JON!
© 1985 PAWS, INC. All Rights Reserved.
THE MYSTERY MEAT CRAWLED OUT OF THE TINFOIL AND SNAPPED AT ME!

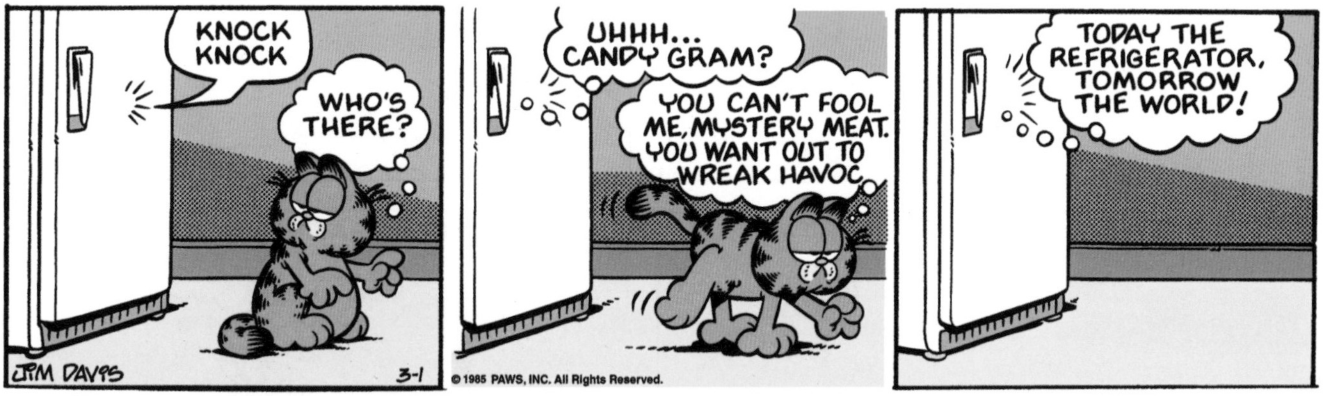
KNOCK KNOCK
WHO'S THERE?
JIM DAVIS 3-1
UHHH... CANDY GRAM?
YOU CAN'T FOOL ME, MYSTERY MEAT. YOU WANT OUT TO WREAK HAVOC
© 1985 PAWS, INC. All Rights Reserved.
TODAY THE REFRIGERATOR, TOMORROW THE WORLD!

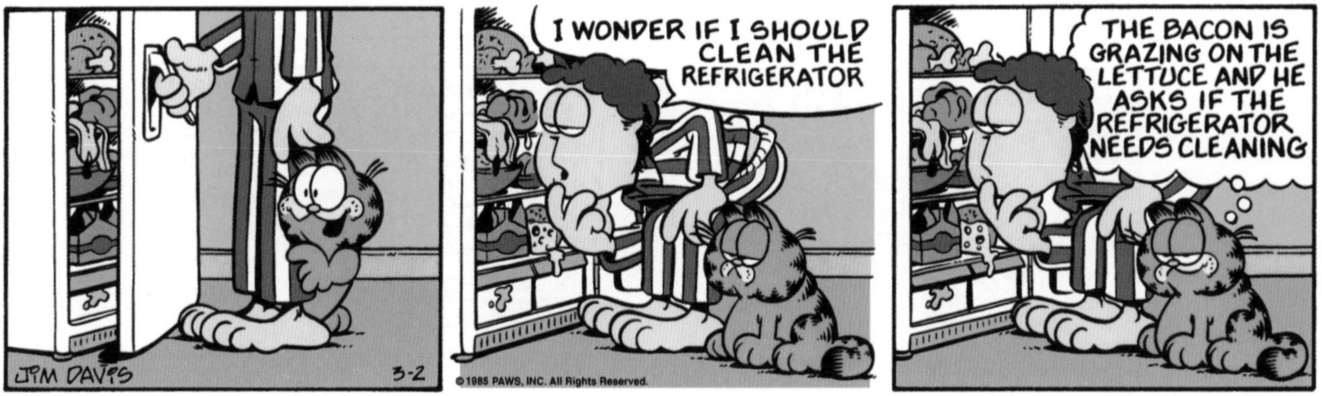
JIM DAVIS 3-2
I WONDER IF I SHOULD CLEAN THE REFRIGERATOR
© 1985 PAWS, INC. All Rights Reserved.
THE BACON IS GRAZING ON THE LETTUCE AND HE ASKS IF THE REFRIGERATOR NEEDS CLEANING

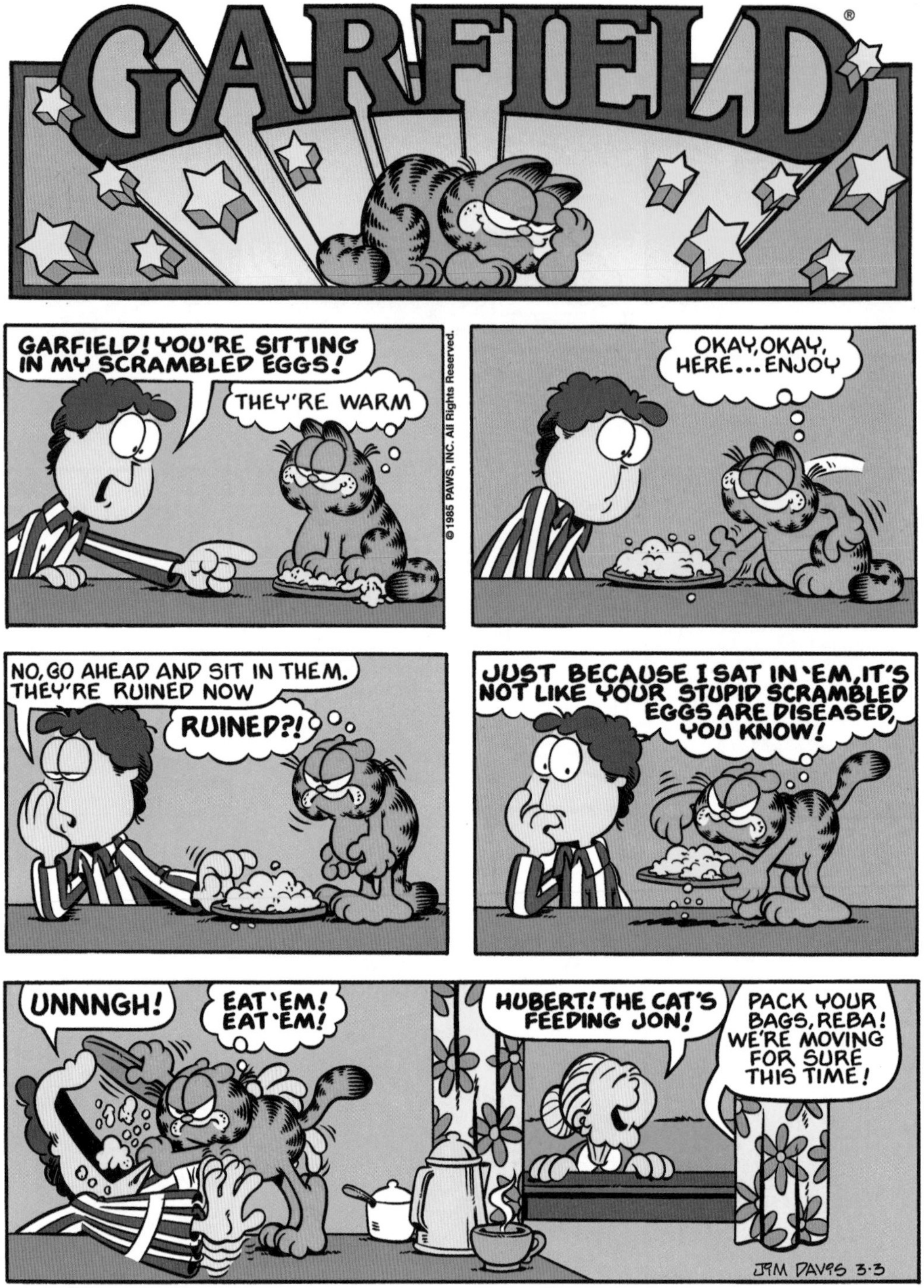
GARFIELD®
© 1985 PAWS, INC. All Rights Reserved.
GARFIELD! YOU'RE SITTING IN MY SCRAMBLED EGGS!
THEY'RE WARM
OKAY, OKAY, HERE... ENJOY
NO, GO AHEAD AND SIT IN THEM. THEY'RE RUINED NOW
RUINED?!
JUST BECAUSE I SAT IN 'EM, IT'S NOT LIKE YOUR STUPID SCRAMBLED EGGS ARE DISEASED, YOU KNOW!
UNNNGH!
EAT 'EM! EAT 'EM!
HUBERT! THE CAT'S FEEDING JON!
PACK YOUR BAGS, REBA! WE'RE MOVING FOR SURE THIS TIME!
JIM DAVIS 3·3

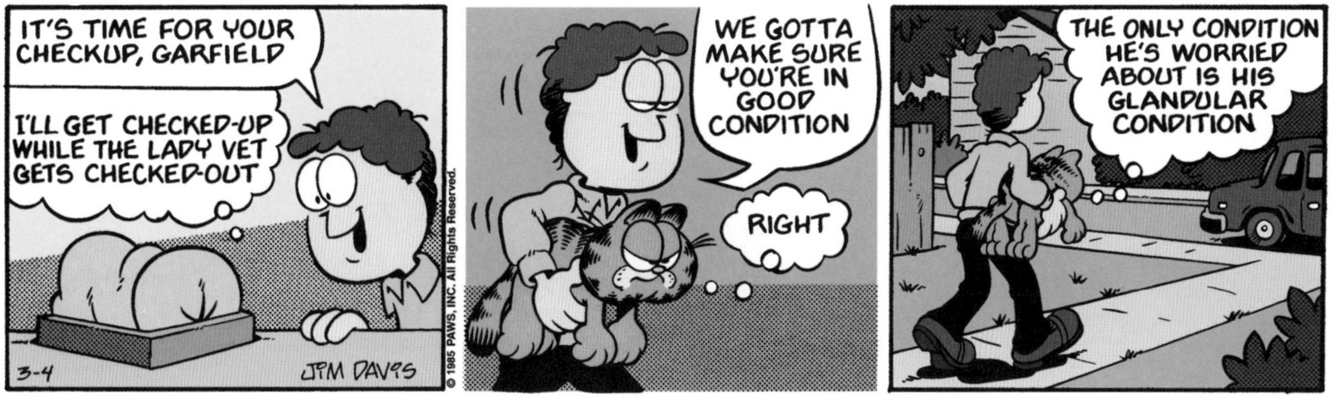
IT'S TIME FOR YOUR CHECKUP, GARFIELD
I'LL GET CHECKED-UP WHILE THE LADY VET GETS CHECKED-OUT
3-4
JIM DAVIS
© 1985 PAWS, INC. All Rights Reserved.
WE GOTTA MAKE SURE YOU'RE IN GOOD CONDITION
RIGHT
THE ONLY CONDITION HE'S WORRIED ABOUT IS HIS GLANDULAR CONDITION

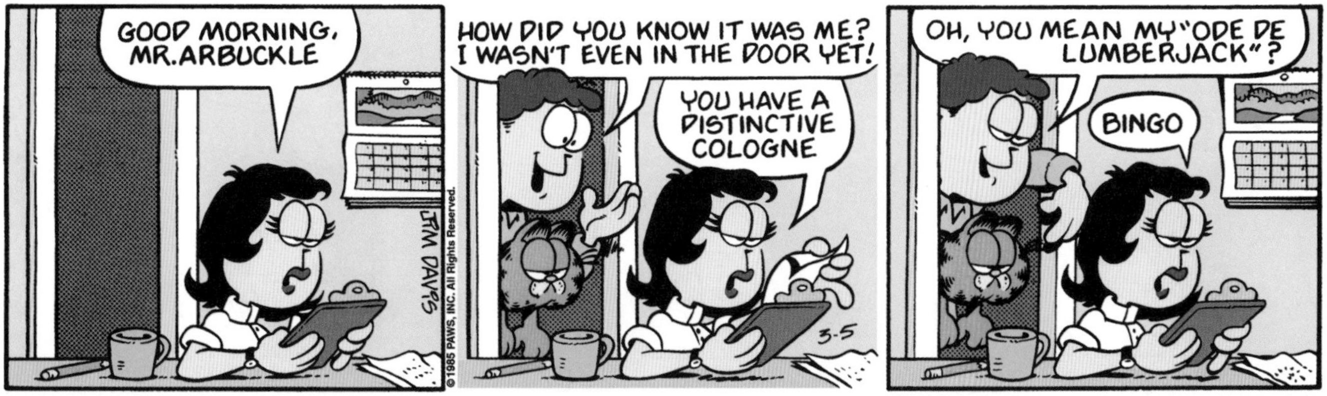
GOOD MORNING, MR. ARBUCKLE
JIM DAVIS
© 1985 PAWS, INC. All Rights Reserved.
HOW DID YOU KNOW IT WAS ME? I WASN'T EVEN IN THE DOOR YET!
YOU HAVE A DISTINCTIVE COLOGNE
3-5
OH, YOU MEAN MY "ODE DE LUMBERJACK"?
BINGO

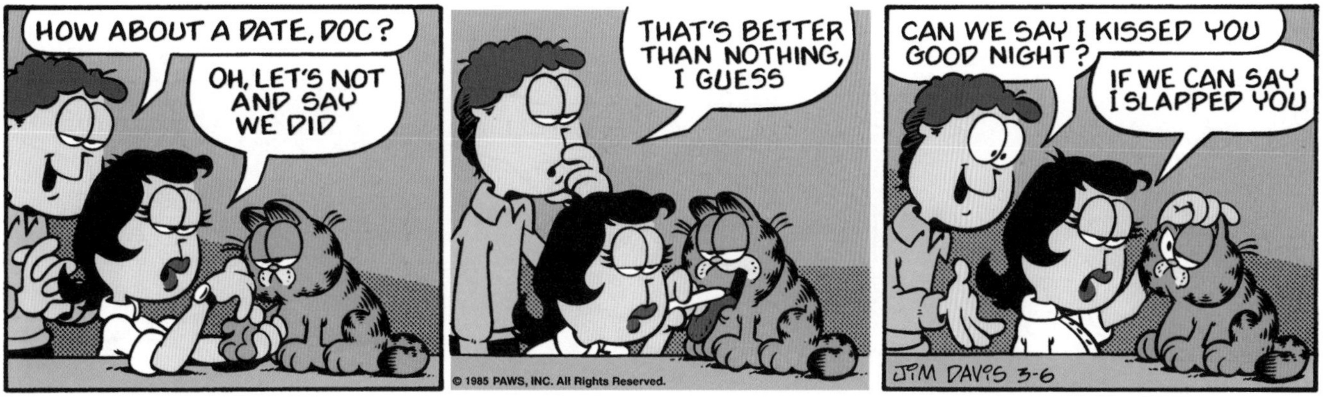
HOW ABOUT A DATE, DOC?
OH, LET'S NOT AND SAY WE DID
THAT'S BETTER THAN NOTHING, I GUESS
© 1985 PAWS, INC. All Rights Reserved.
CAN WE SAY I KISSED YOU GOOD NIGHT?
IF WE CAN SAY I SLAPPED YOU
JIM DAVIS 3-6

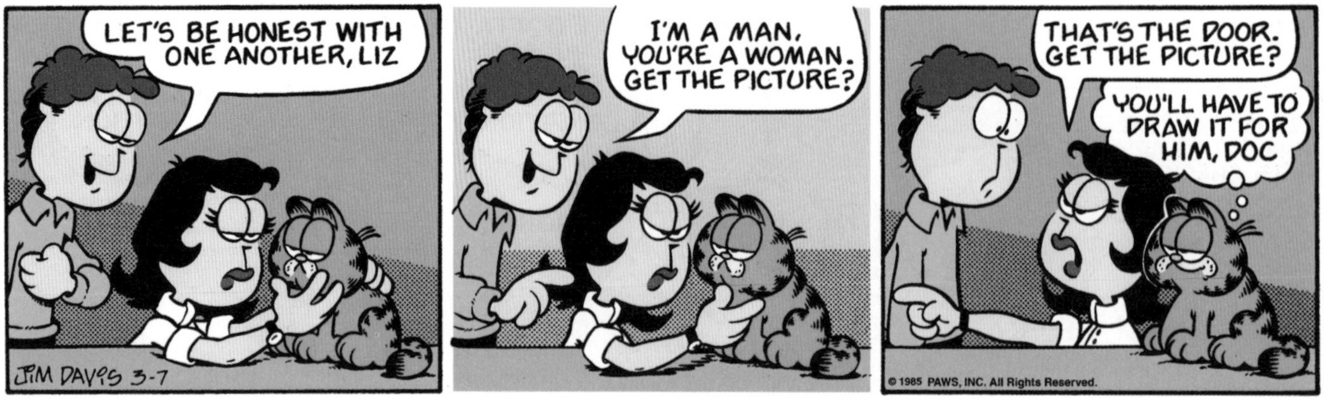
LET'S BE HONEST WITH ONE ANOTHER, LIZ
JIM DAVIS 3-7
I'M A MAN, YOU'RE A WOMAN. GET THE PICTURE?
THAT'S THE DOOR. GET THE PICTURE?
YOU'LL HAVE TO DRAW IT FOR HIM, DOC
© 1985 PAWS, INC. All Rights Reserved.

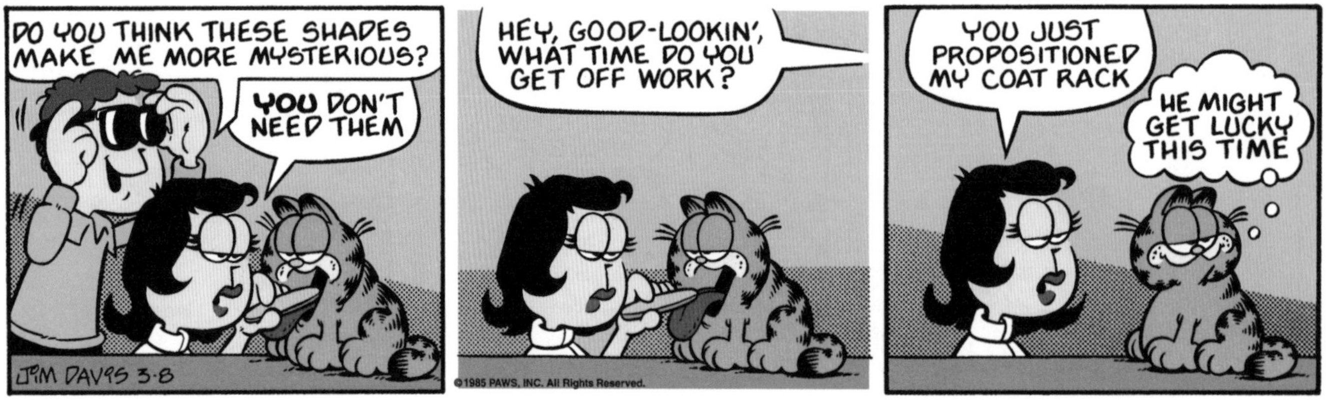
DO YOU THINK THESE SHADES MAKE ME MORE MYSTERIOUS?
YOU DON'T NEED THEM
JIM DAVIS 3-8
HEY, GOOD-LOOKIN', WHAT TIME DO YOU GET OFF WORK?
© 1985 PAWS, INC. All Rights Reserved.
YOU JUST PROPOSITIONED MY COAT RACK
HE MIGHT GET LUCKY THIS TIME

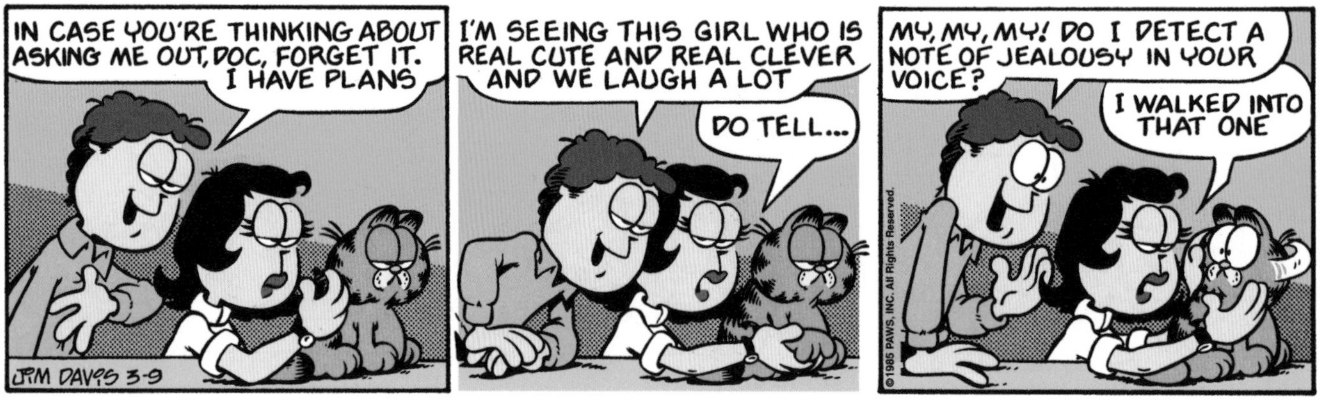
IN CASE YOU'RE THINKING ABOUT ASKING ME OUT, DOC, FORGET IT. I HAVE PLANS
JIM DAVIS 3-9
I'M SEEING THIS GIRL WHO IS REAL CUTE AND REAL CLEVER AND WE LAUGH A LOT
DO TELL...
© 1985 PAWS, INC. All Rights Reserved.
MY, MY, MY! DO I DETECT A NOTE OF JEALOUSY IN YOUR VOICE?
I WALKED INTO THAT ONE

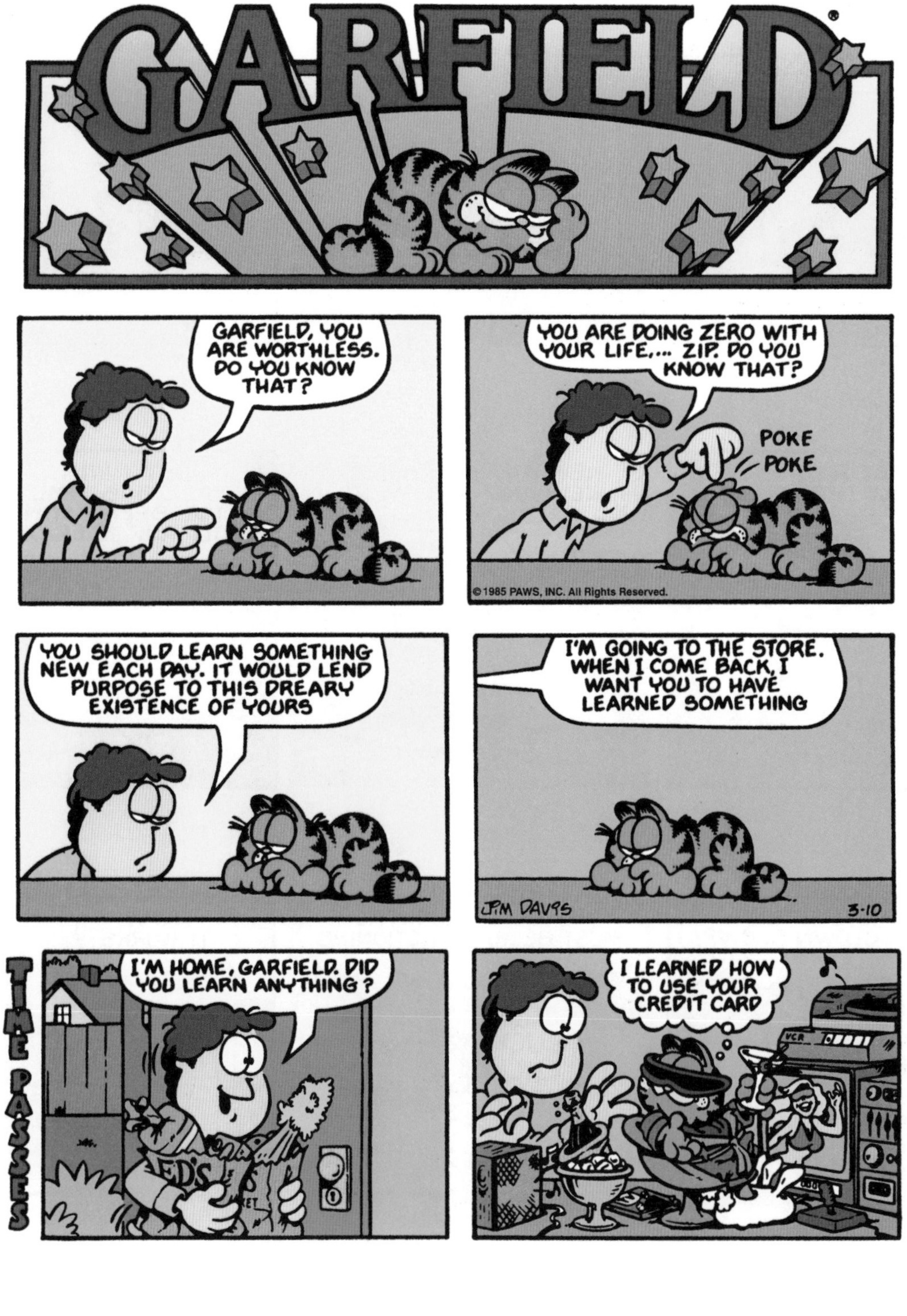
GARFIELD
GARFIELD, YOU ARE WORTHLESS. DO YOU KNOW THAT?
YOU ARE DOING ZERO WITH YOUR LIFE,... ZIP. DO YOU KNOW THAT?
POKE POKE
©1985 PAWS, INC. All Rights Reserved.
YOU SHOULD LEARN SOMETHING NEW EACH DAY. IT WOULD LEND PURPOSE TO THIS DREARY EXISTENCE OF YOURS
I'M GOING TO THE STORE. WHEN I COME BACK, I WANT YOU TO HAVE LEARNED SOMETHING
JIM DAVIS
3-10
TIME PASSES
I'M HOME, GARFIELD. DID YOU LEARN ANYTHING?
ED'S
I LEARNED HOW TO USE YOUR CREDIT CARD
VCR

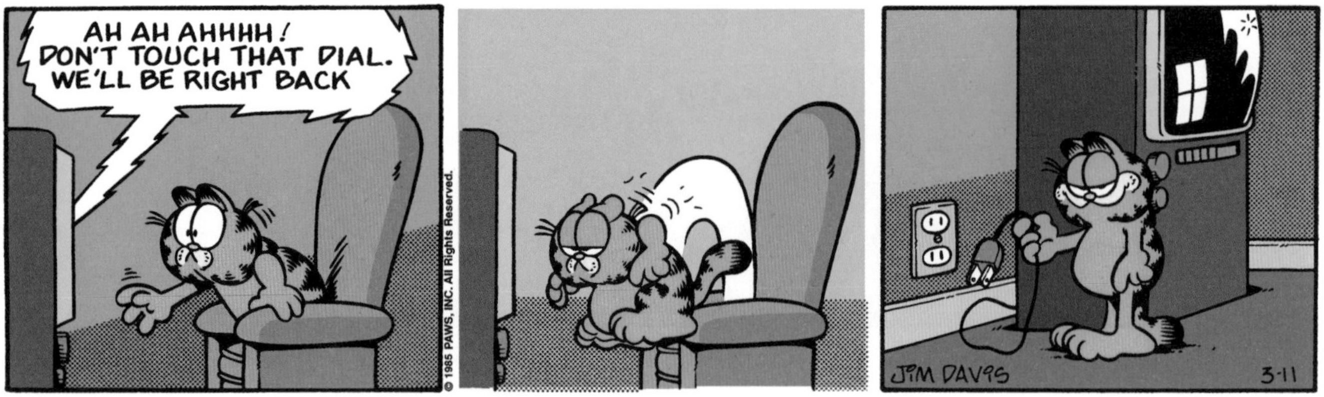
AH AH AHHHH! DON'T TOUCH THAT DIAL. WE'LL BE RIGHT BACK
© 1985 PAWS, INC. All Rights Reserved.
JIM DAVIS
3-11

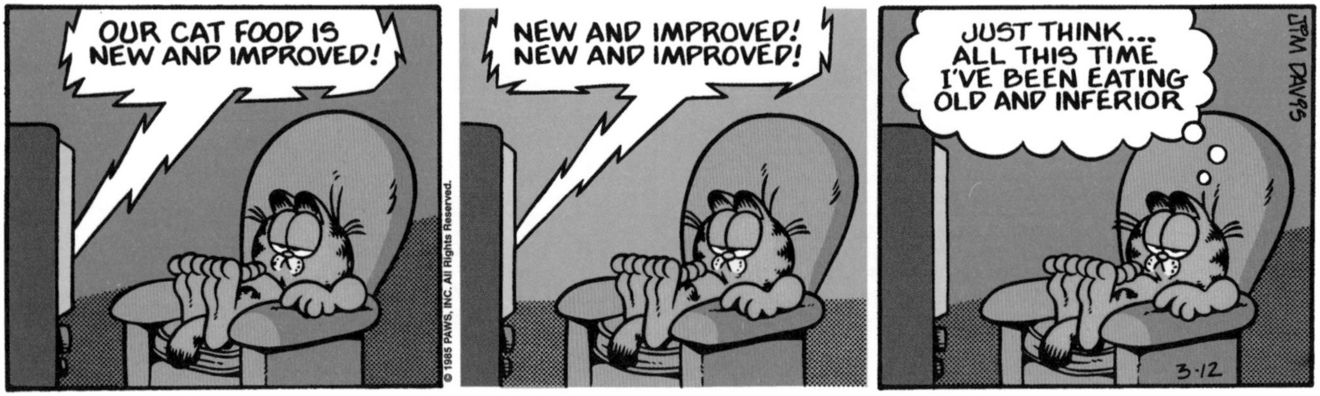
OUR CAT FOOD IS NEW AND IMPROVED!
© 1985 PAWS, INC. All Rights Reserved.
NEW AND IMPROVED! NEW AND IMPROVED!
JUST THINK... ALL THIS TIME I'VE BEEN EATING OLD AND INFERIOR
JIM DAVIS
3-12

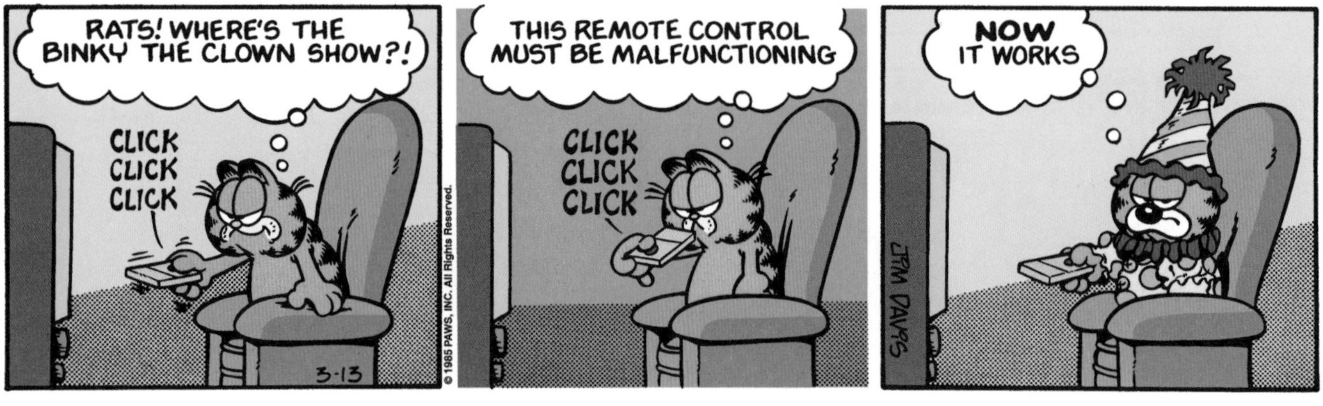
RATS! WHERE'S THE BINKY THE CLOWN SHOW?!
CLICK CLICK CLICK
3-13
© 1985 PAWS, INC. All Rights Reserved.
THIS REMOTE CONTROL MUST BE MALFUNCTIONING
CLICK CLICK CLICK
NOW IT WORKS
JIM DAVIS

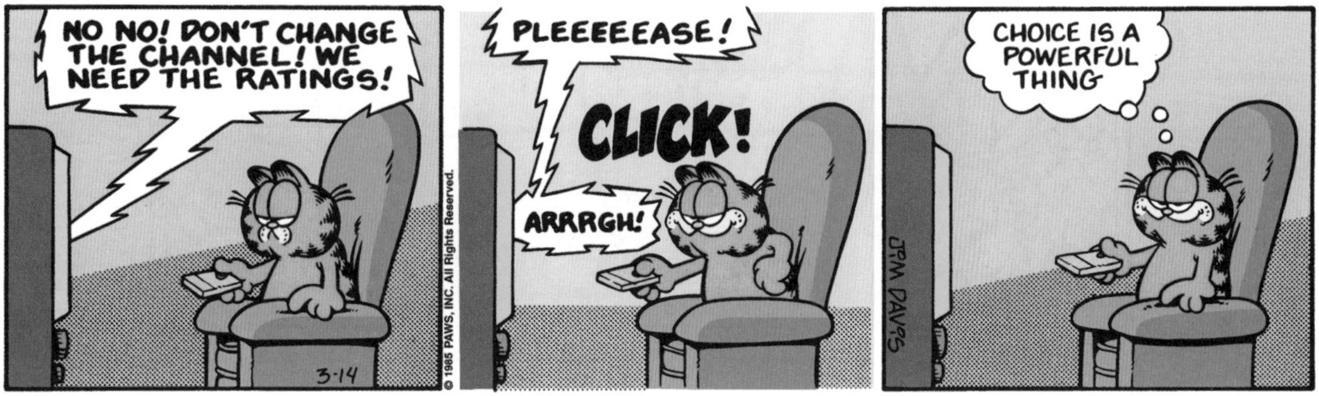
NO NO! DON'T CHANGE THE CHANNEL! WE NEED THE RATINGS!
3-14
© 1985 PAWS, INC. All Rights Reserved.
PLEEEEEASE!
CLICK!
ARRRGH!
JIM DAVIS
CHOICE IS A POWERFUL THING

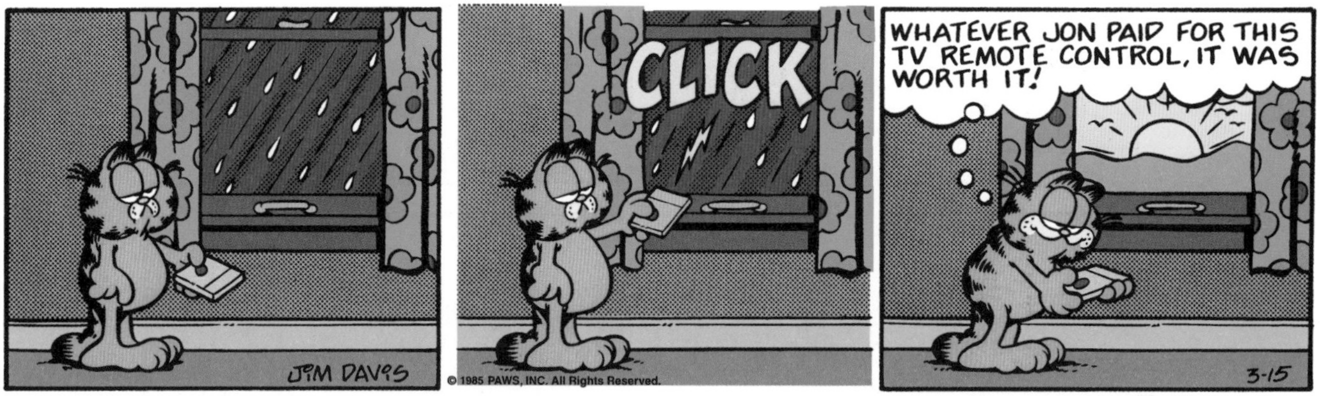
JIM DAVIS
CLICK
© 1985 PAWS, INC. All Rights Reserved.
WHATEVER JON PAID FOR THIS TV REMOTE CONTROL, IT WAS WORTH IT!
3-15

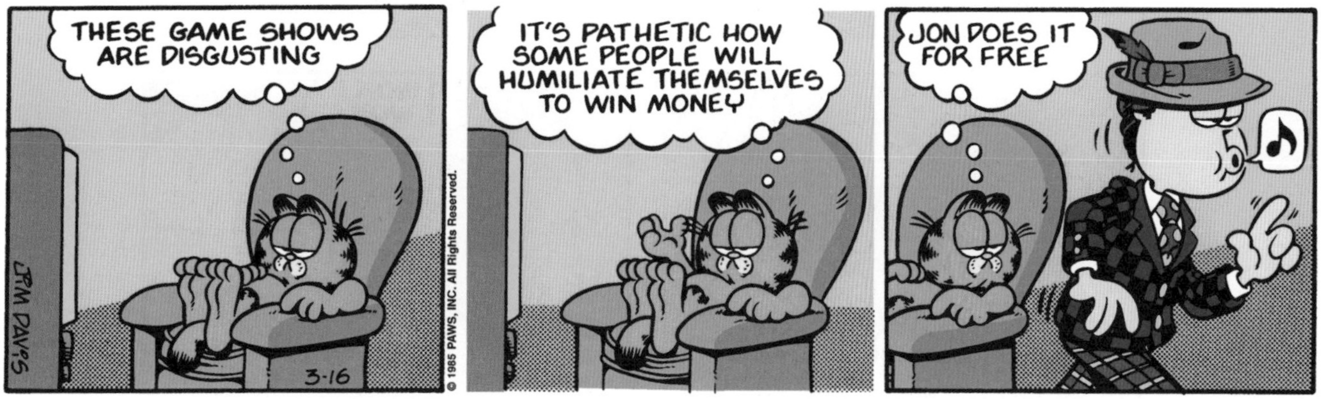
THESE GAME SHOWS ARE DISGUSTING
JIM DAVIS
3-16
© 1985 PAWS, INC. All Rights Reserved.
IT'S PATHETIC HOW SOME PEOPLE WILL HUMILIATE THEMSELVES TO WIN MONEY
JON DOES IT FOR FREE

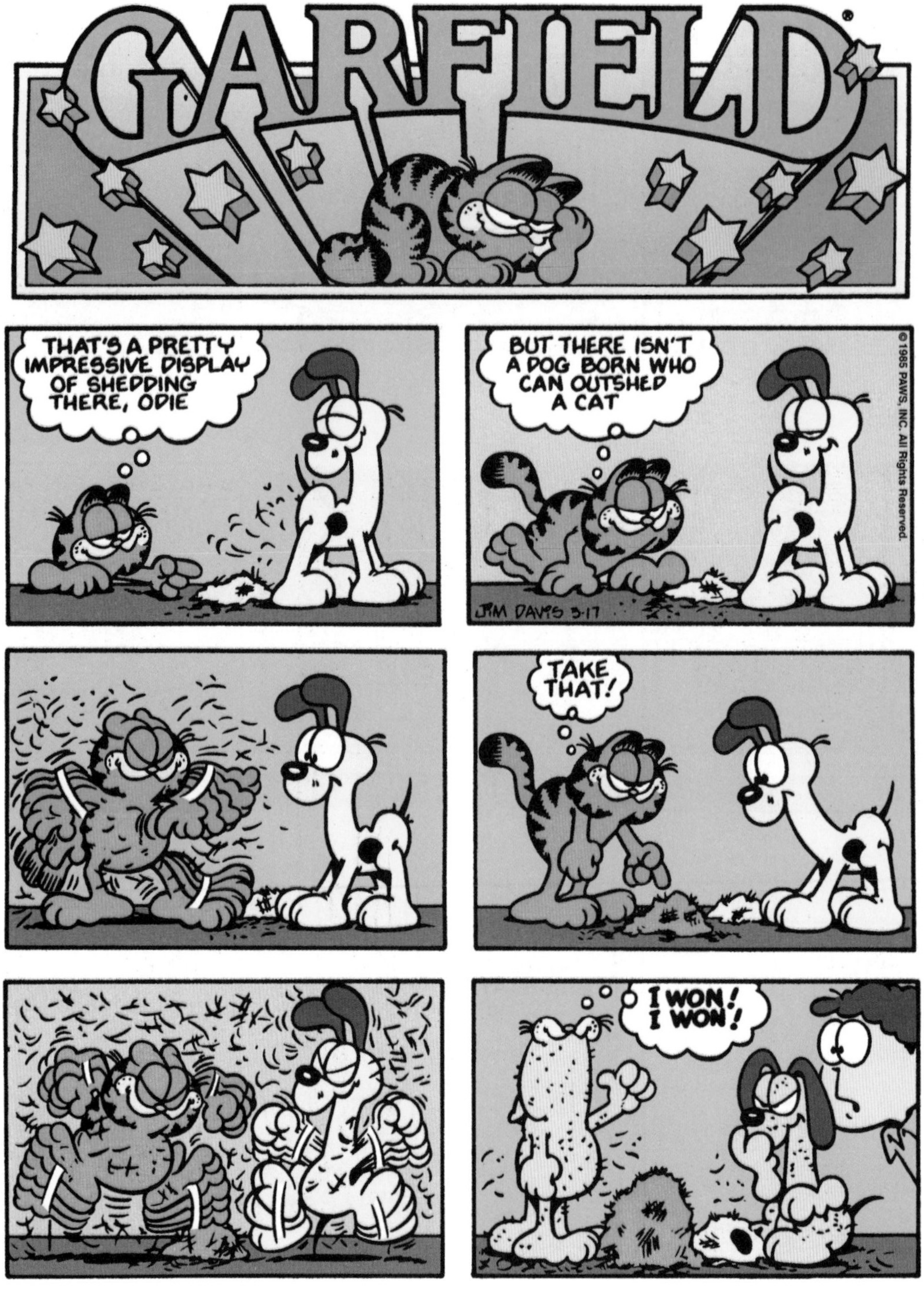
GARFIELD
THAT'S A PRETTY IMPRESSIVE DISPLAY OF SHEDDING THERE, ODIE
BUT THERE ISN'T A DOG BORN WHO CAN OUTSHED A CAT
© 1985 PAWS, INC. All Rights Reserved.
JIM DAVIS 3-17
TAKE THAT!
I WON! I WON!

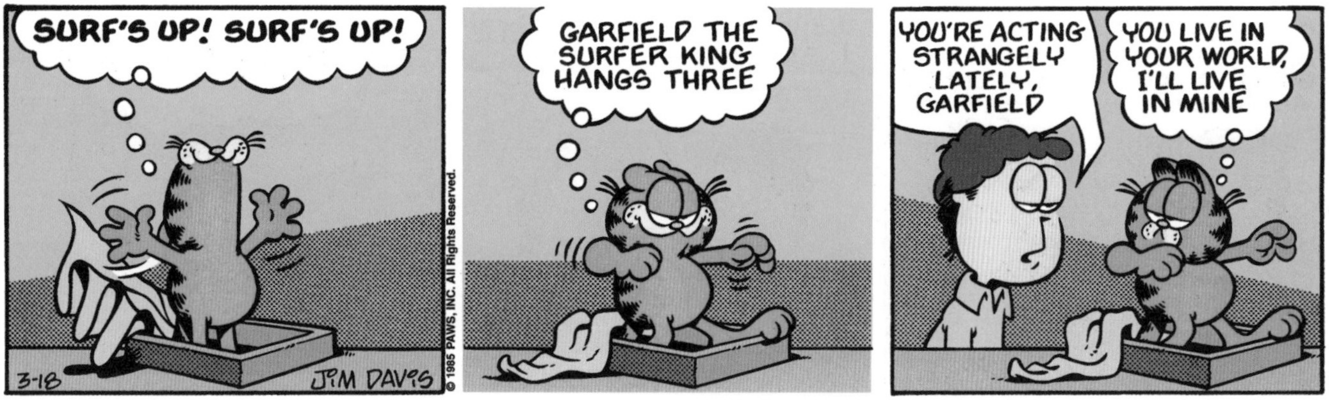
SURF'S UP! SURF'S UP!
3-18
JIM DAVIS
© 1985 PAWS, INC. All Rights Reserved.
GARFIELD THE SURFER KING HANGS THREE
YOU'RE ACTING STRANGELY LATELY, GARFIELD
YOU LIVE IN YOUR WORLD, I'LL LIVE IN MINE

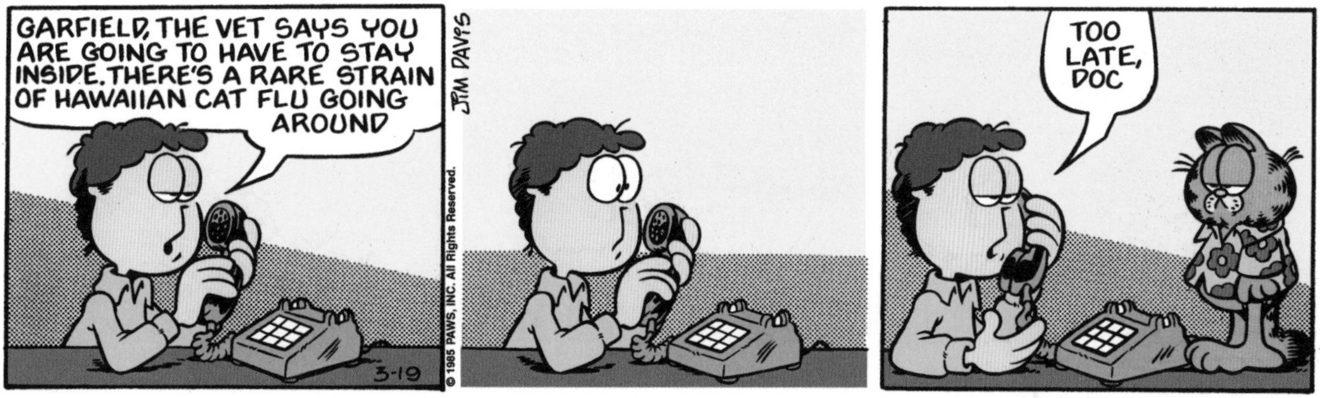
GARFIELD, THE VET SAYS YOU ARE GOING TO HAVE TO STAY INSIDE. THERE'S A RARE STRAIN OF HAWAIIAN CAT FLU GOING AROUND
3-19
© 1985 PAWS, INC. All Rights Reserved.
JIM DAVIS
TOO LATE, DOC

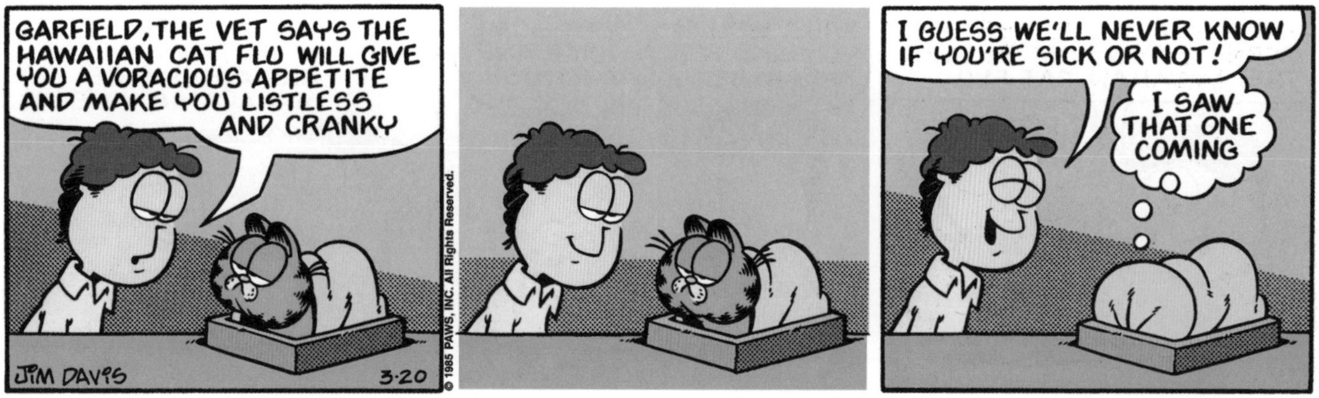
GARFIELD, THE VET SAYS THE HAWAIIAN CAT FLU WILL GIVE YOU A VORACIOUS APPETITE AND MAKE YOU LISTLESS AND CRANKY
JIM DAVIS
3-20
© 1985 PAWS, INC. All Rights Reserved.
I GUESS WE'LL NEVER KNOW IF YOU'RE SICK OR NOT!
I SAW THAT ONE COMING

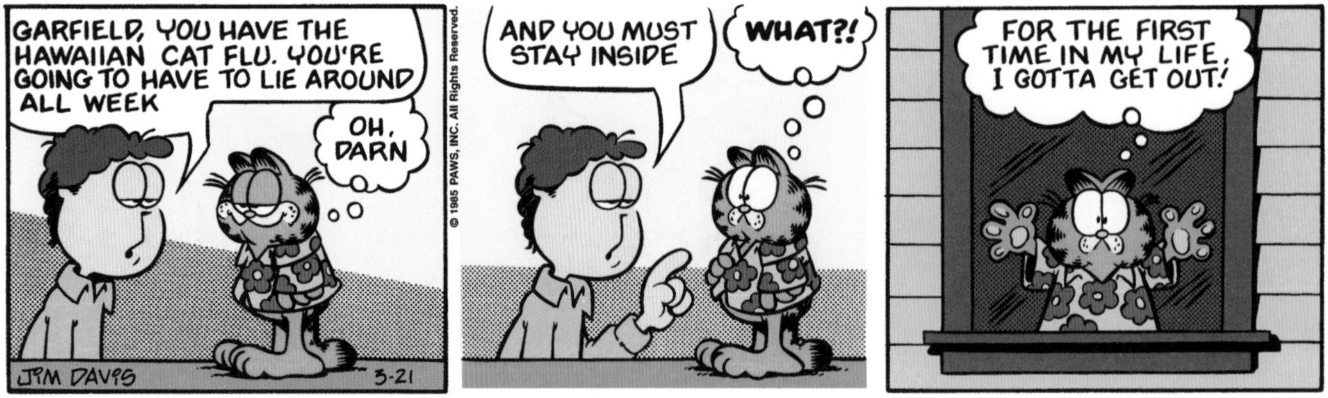
GARFIELD, YOU HAVE THE HAWAIIAN CAT FLU. YOU'RE GOING TO HAVE TO LIE AROUND ALL WEEK
OH, DARN
JIM DAVIS 3-21
© 1985 PAWS, INC. All Rights Reserved.
AND YOU MUST STAY INSIDE
WHAT?!
FOR THE FIRST TIME IN MY LIFE, I GOTTA GET OUT!

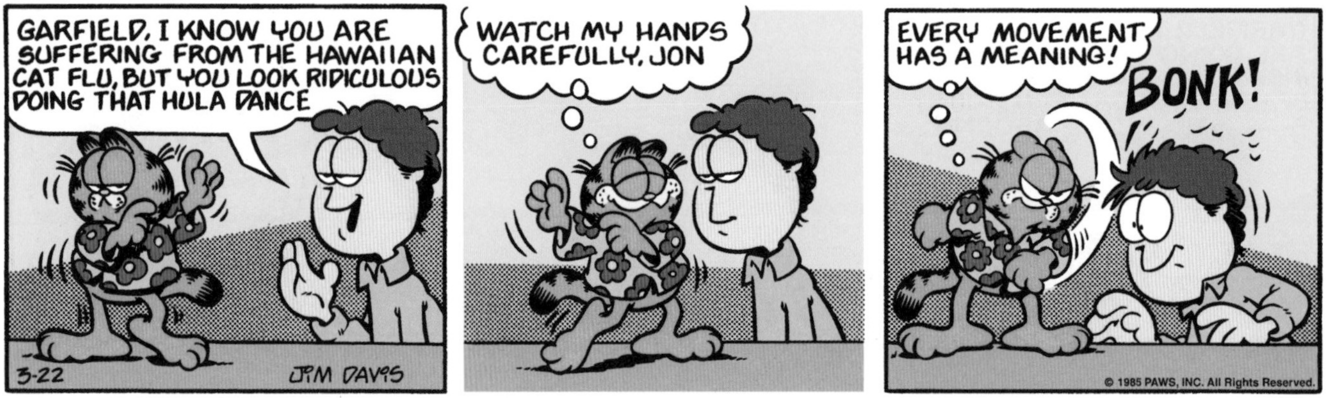
GARFIELD, I KNOW YOU ARE SUFFERING FROM THE HAWAIIAN CAT FLU, BUT YOU LOOK RIDICULOUS DOING THAT HULA DANCE
3-22 JIM DAVIS
WATCH MY HANDS CAREFULLY, JON
EVERY MOVEMENT HAS A MEANING!
BONK!
© 1985 PAWS, INC. All Rights Reserved.

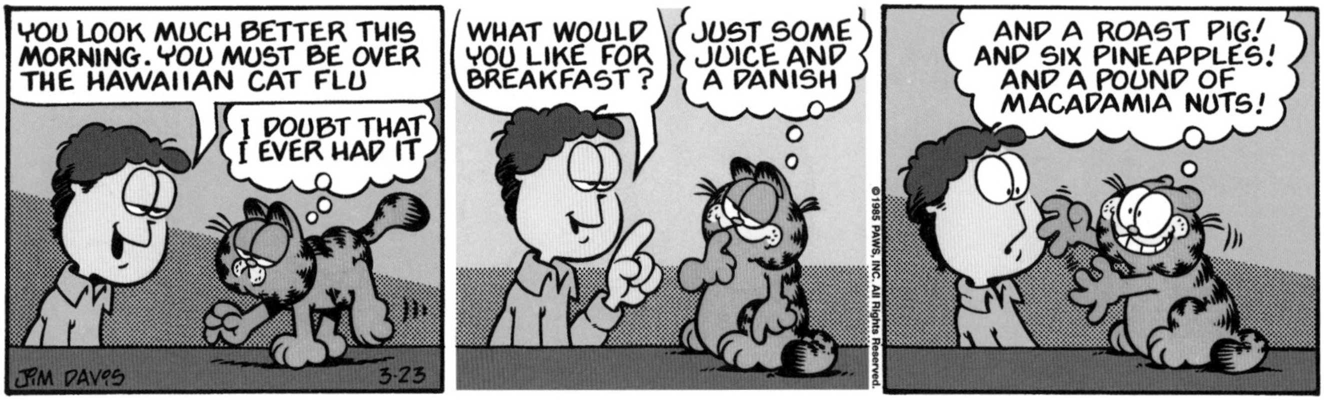
YOU LOOK MUCH BETTER THIS MORNING. YOU MUST BE OVER THE HAWAIIAN CAT FLU
I DOUBT THAT I EVER HAD IT
JIM DAVIS 3-23
WHAT WOULD YOU LIKE FOR BREAKFAST?
JUST SOME JUICE AND A DANISH
©1985 PAWS, INC. All Rights Reserved.
AND A ROAST PIG! AND SIX PINEAPPLES! AND A POUND OF MACADAMIA NUTS!

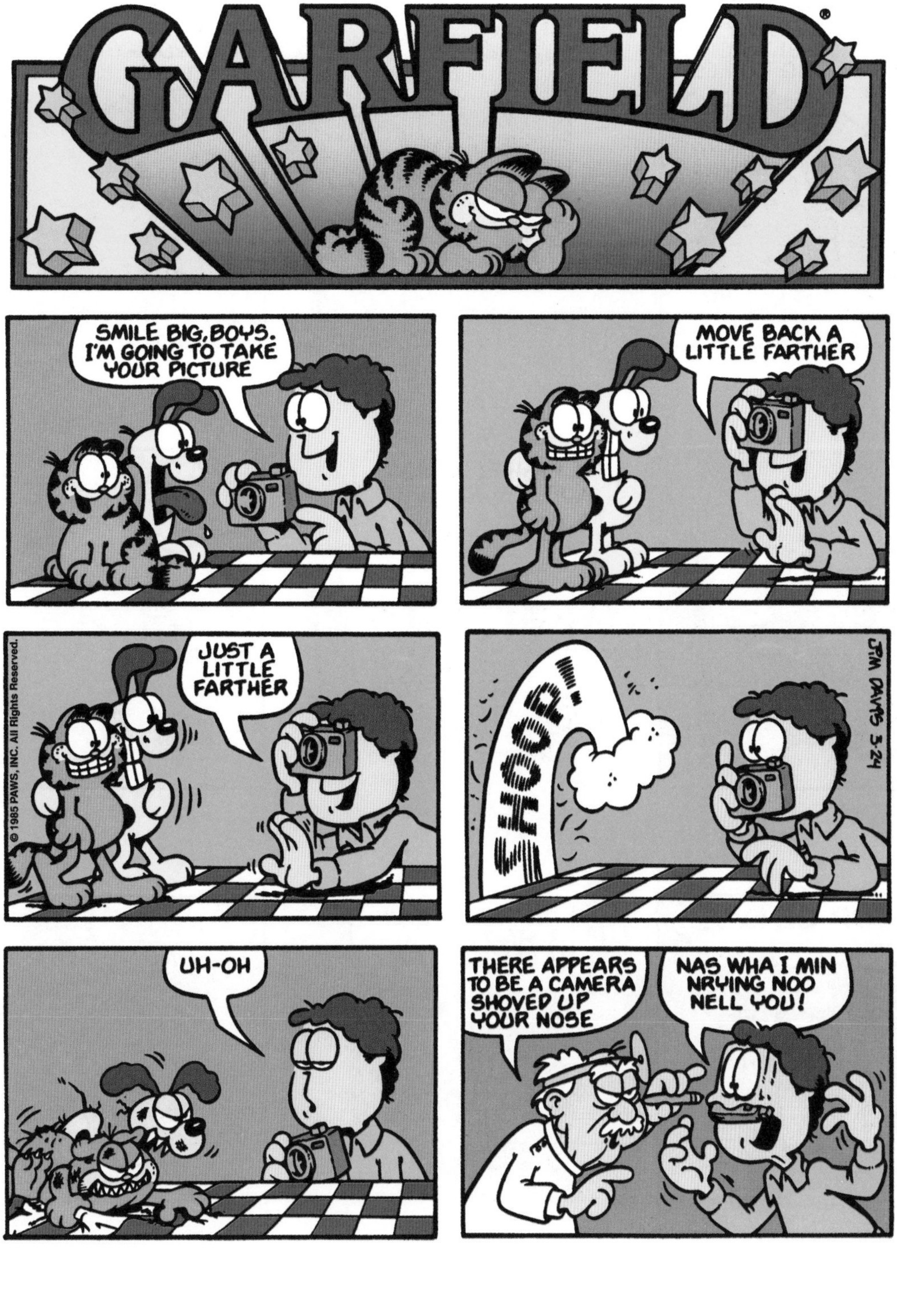
GARFIELD
SMILE BIG, BOYS. I'M GOING TO TAKE YOUR PICTURE
MOVE BACK A LITTLE FARTHER
JUST A LITTLE FARTHER
© 1985 PAWS, INC. All Rights Reserved.
WHOOP!!!
JIM DAVIS 3-24
UH-OH
THERE APPEARS TO BE A CAMERA SHOVED UP YOUR NOSE
NAS WHA I MIN NRYING NOO NELL YOU!

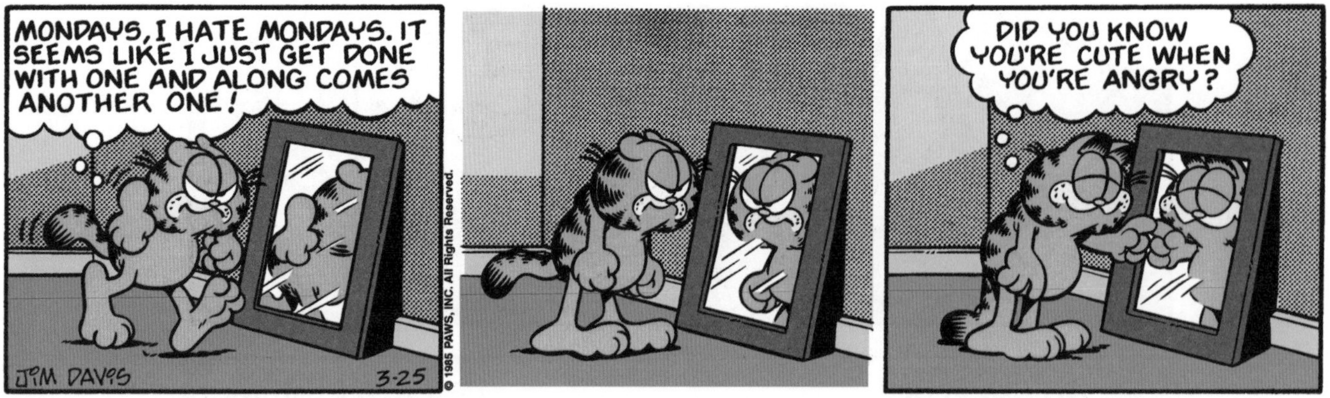
MONDAYS, I HATE MONDAYS. IT SEEMS LIKE I JUST GET DONE WITH ONE AND ALONG COMES ANOTHER ONE!
JIM DAVIS
3-25
© 1985 PAWS, INC. All Rights Reserved.
DID YOU KNOW YOU'RE CUTE WHEN YOU'RE ANGRY?

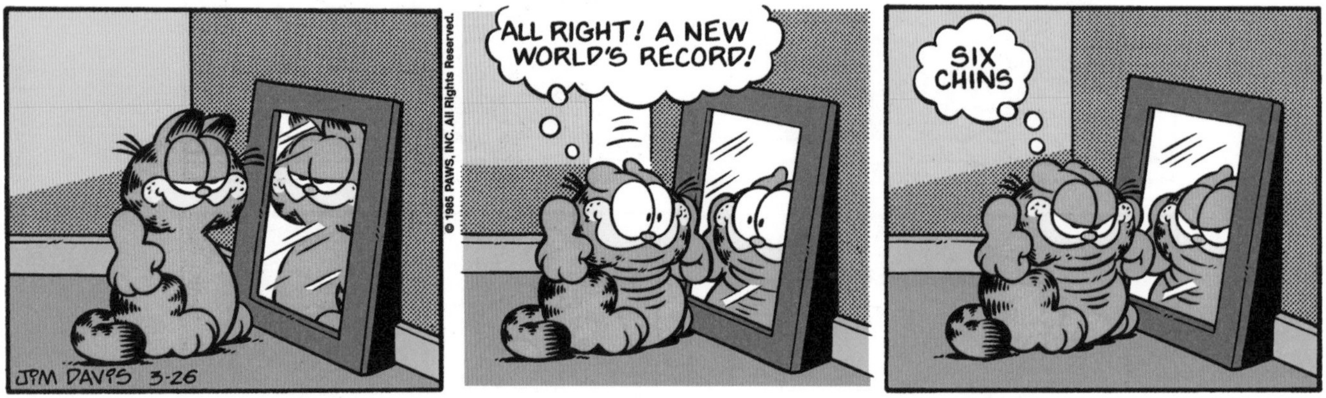
JIM DAVIS 3-26
© 1985 PAWS, INC. All Rights Reserved.
ALL RIGHT! A NEW WORLD'S RECORD!
SIX CHINS

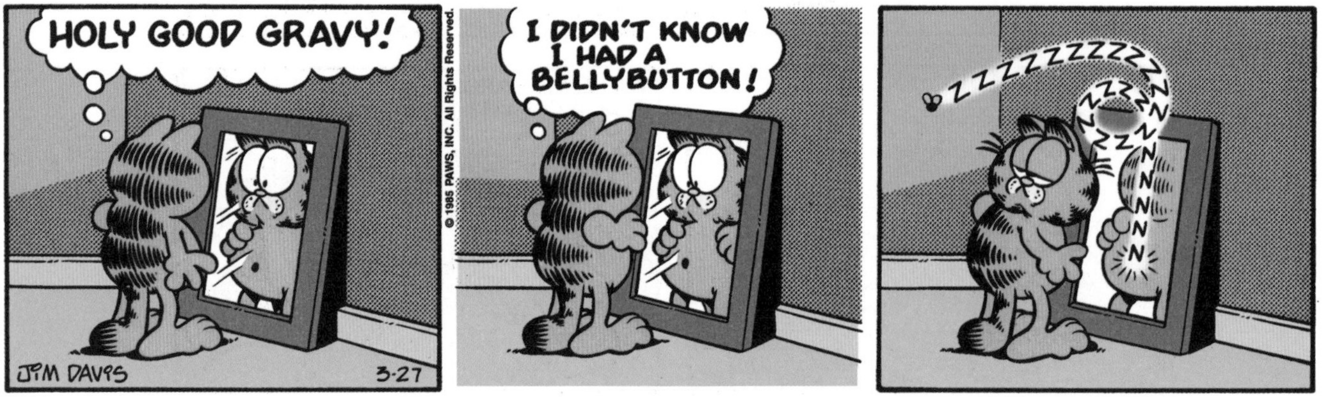
HOLY GOOD GRAVY!
JIM DAVIS
3-27
© 1985 PAWS, INC. All Rights Reserved.
I DIDN'T KNOW I HAD A BELLYBUTTON!
ZZZZZZZZZZZZZZZZZZNNNNNNN

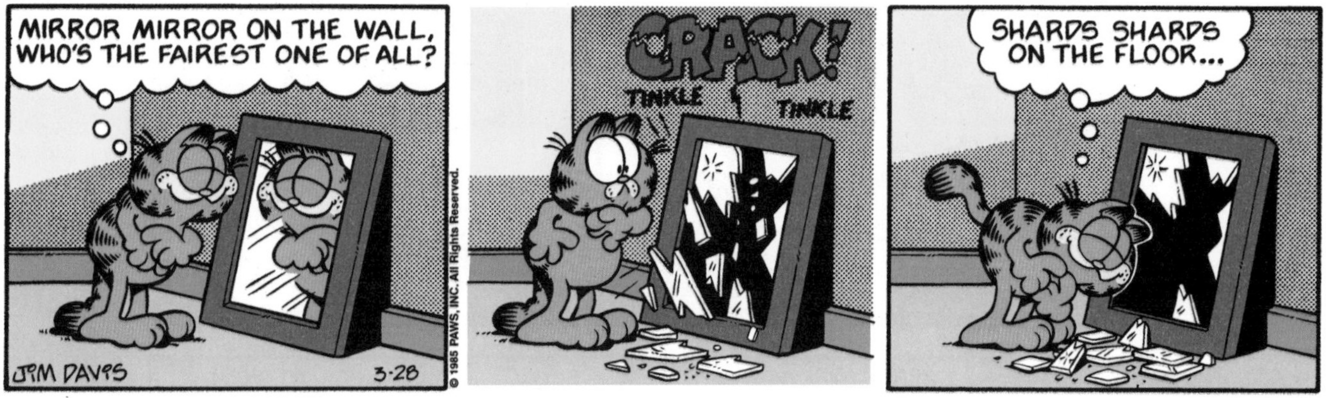
MIRROR MIRROR ON THE WALL, WHO'S THE FAIREST ONE OF ALL?
JIM DAVIS
3-28
© 1985 PAWS, INC. All Rights Reserved.
CRACK!
TINKLE
TINKLE
SHARDS SHARDS ON THE FLOOR...

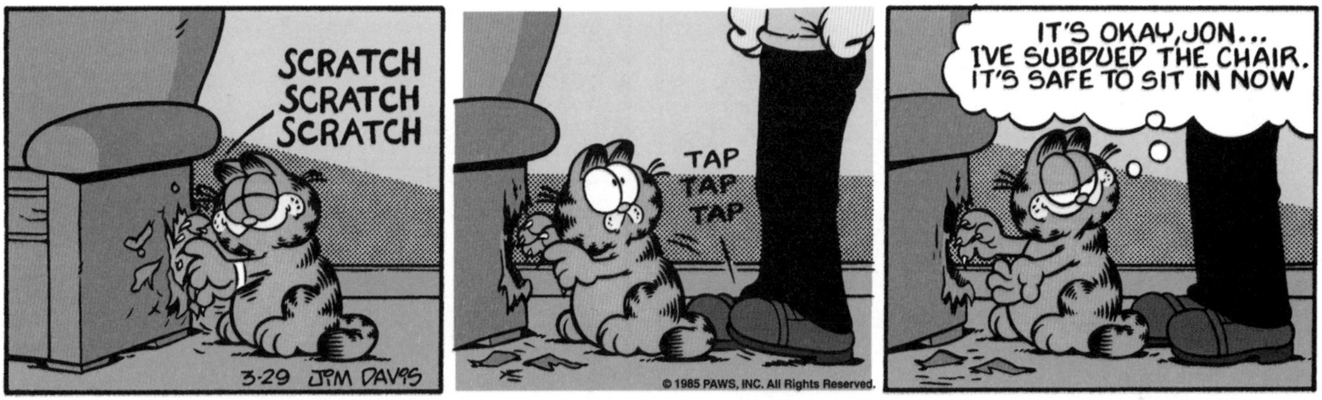
SCRATCH
SCRATCH
SCRATCH
3-29 JIM DAVIS
TAP
TAP
TAP
© 1985 PAWS, INC. All Rights Reserved.
IT'S OKAY, JON... I'VE SUBDUED THE CHAIR. IT'S SAFE TO SIT IN NOW

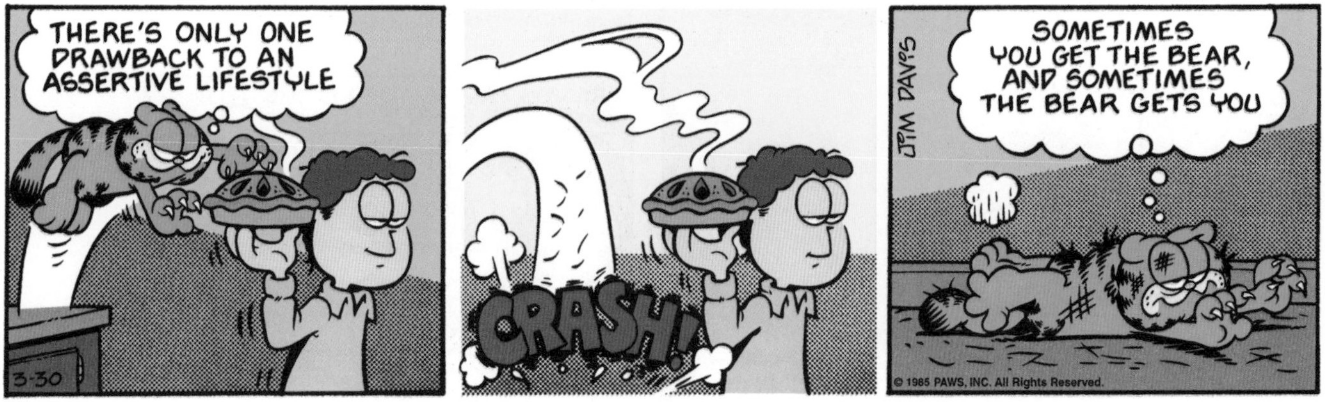
THERE'S ONLY ONE DRAWBACK TO AN ASSERTIVE LIFESTYLE
3-30
CRASH!
JIM DAVIS
SOMETIMES YOU GET THE BEAR, AND SOMETIMES THE BEAR GETS YOU
© 1985 PAWS, INC. All Rights Reserved.

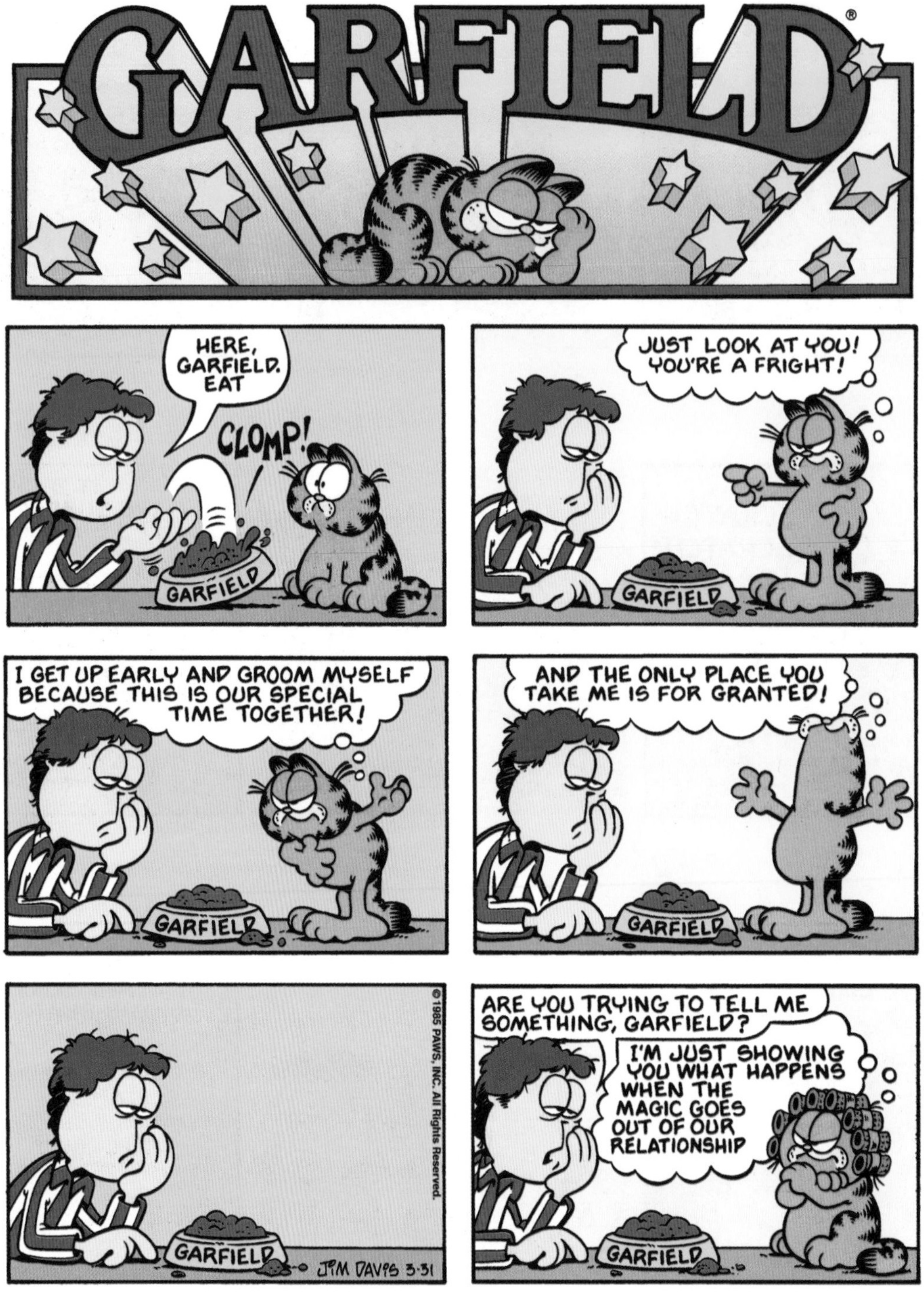
GARFIELD®
HERE, GARFIELD. EAT
CLOMP!
GARFIELD
JUST LOOK AT YOU! YOU'RE A FRIGHT!
GARFIELD
I GET UP EARLY AND GROOM MYSELF BECAUSE THIS IS OUR SPECIAL TIME TOGETHER!
GARFIELD
AND THE ONLY PLACE YOU TAKE ME IS FOR GRANTED!
GARFIELD
GARFIELD
© 1985 PAWS, INC. All Rights Reserved.
JIM DAVIS 3-31
ARE YOU TRYING TO TELL ME SOMETHING, GARFIELD?
I'M JUST SHOWING YOU WHAT HAPPENS WHEN THE MAGIC GOES OUT OF OUR RELATIONSHIP
GARFIELD

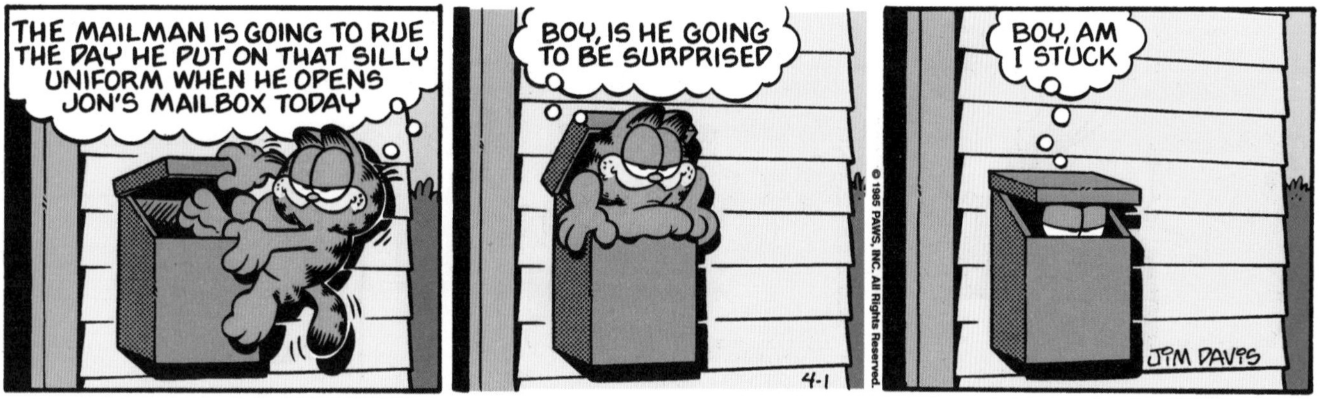
THE MAILMAN IS GOING TO RUE THE DAY HE PUT ON THAT SILLY UNIFORM WHEN HE OPENS JON'S MAILBOX TODAY
BOY, IS HE GOING TO BE SURPRISED
BOY, AM I STUCK
JIM DAVIS
4-1
© 1985 PAWS, INC. All Rights Reserved.

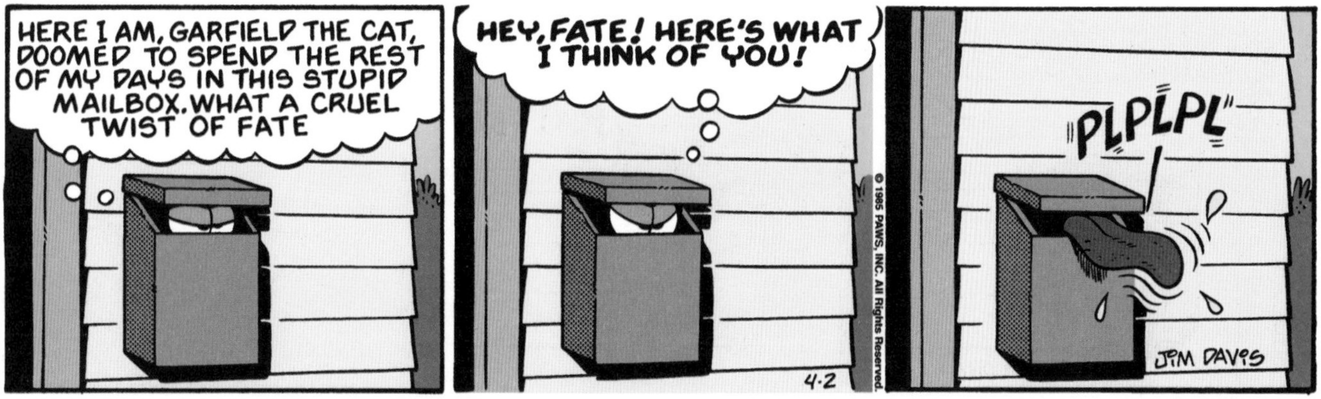
HERE I AM, GARFIELD THE CAT, DOOMED TO SPEND THE REST OF MY DAYS IN THIS STUPID MAILBOX. WHAT A CRUEL TWIST OF FATE
HEY, FATE! HERE'S WHAT I THINK OF YOU!
PLPLPL
JIM DAVIS
4-2
© 1985 PAWS, INC. All Rights Reserved.

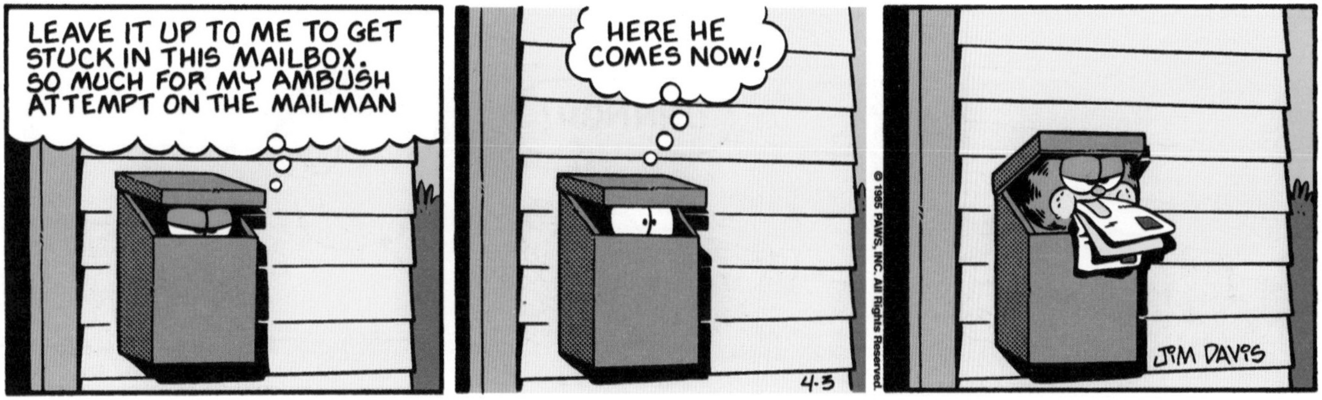
LEAVE IT UP TO ME TO GET STUCK IN THIS MAILBOX. SO MUCH FOR MY AMBUSH ATTEMPT ON THE MAILMAN
HERE HE COMES NOW!
JIM DAVIS
4-3
© 1985 PAWS, INC. All Rights Reserved.

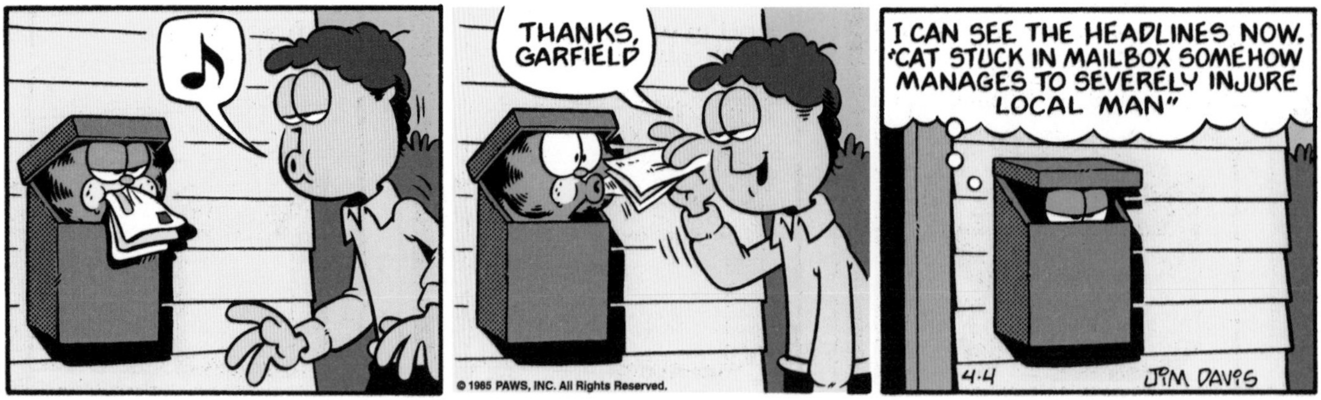
♪
THANKS, GARFIELD
I CAN SEE THE HEADLINES NOW. "CAT STUCK IN MAILBOX SOMEHOW MANAGES TO SEVERELY INJURE LOCAL MAN"
© 1985 PAWS, INC. All Rights Reserved.
4-4
JIM DAVIS

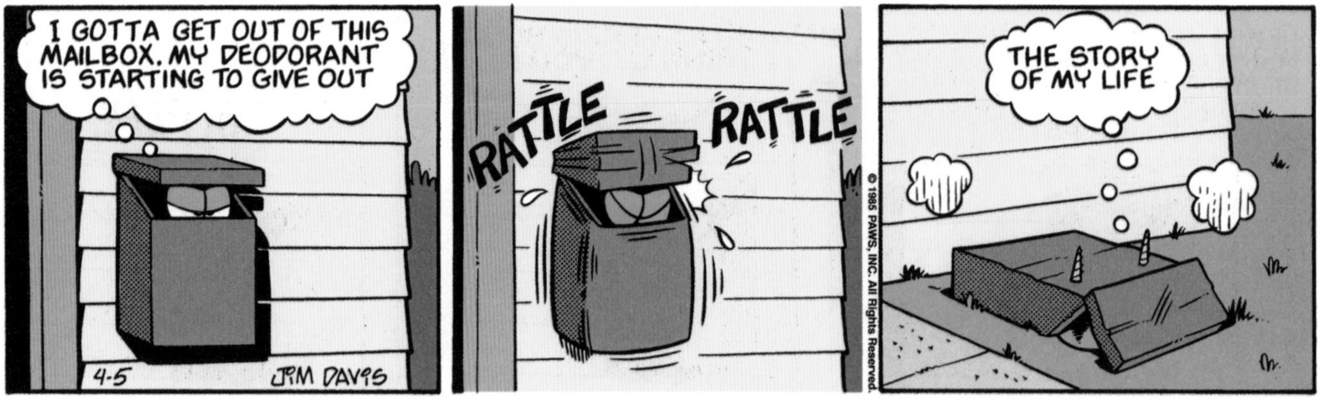
I GOTTA GET OUT OF THIS MAILBOX. MY DEODORANT IS STARTING TO GIVE OUT
4-5
JIM DAVIS
RATTLE
RATTLE
© 1985 PAWS, INC. All Rights Reserved.
THE STORY OF MY LIFE

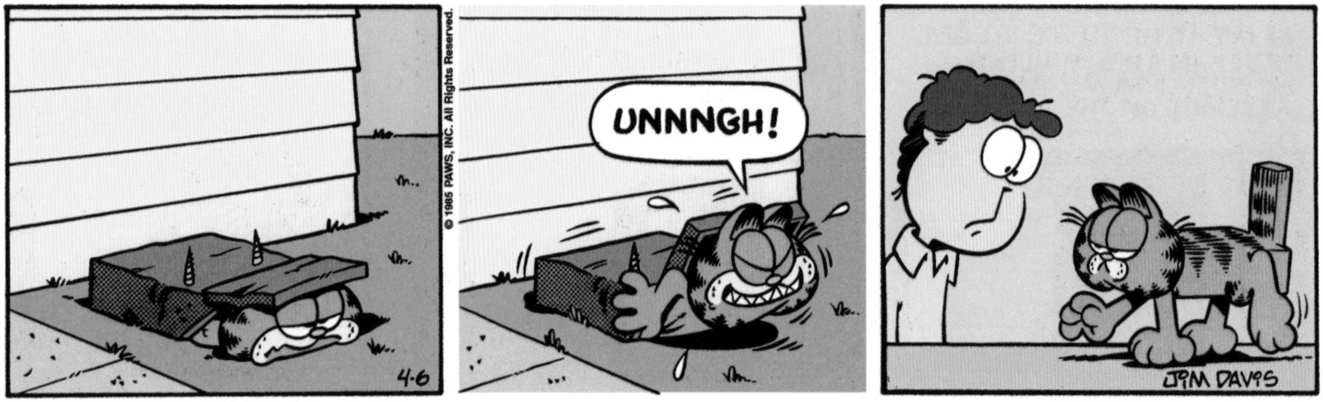
4-6
© 1985 PAWS, INC. All Rights Reserved.
UNNNGH!
JIM DAVIS

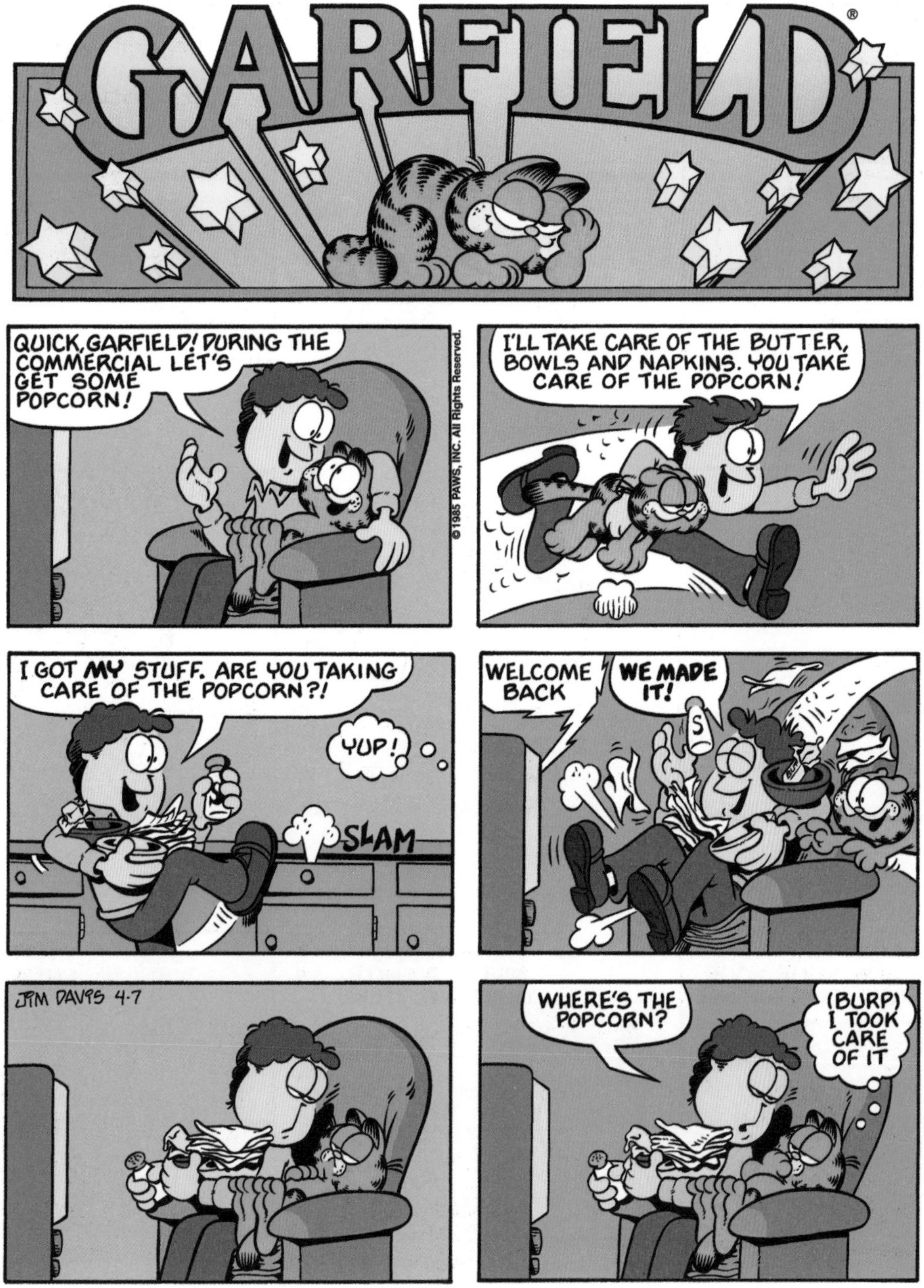
GARFIELD®
QUICK, GARFIELD! DURING THE COMMERCIAL LET'S GET SOME POPCORN!
I'LL TAKE CARE OF THE BUTTER, BOWLS AND NAPKINS. YOU TAKE CARE OF THE POPCORN!
I GOT MY STUFF. ARE YOU TAKING CARE OF THE POPCORN?!
YUP!
SLAM
WELCOME BACK
WE MADE IT!
S
JIM DAVIS 4-7
WHERE'S THE POPCORN?
(BURP) I TOOK CARE OF IT

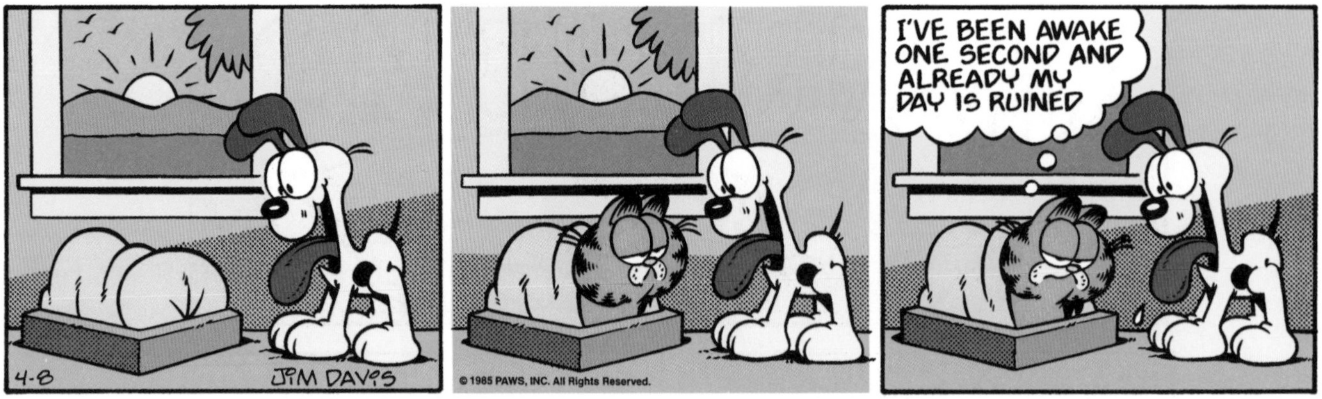
4-8
JIM DAVIS
© 1985 PAWS, INC. All Rights Reserved.
I'VE BEEN AWAKE ONE SECOND AND ALREADY MY DAY IS RUINED

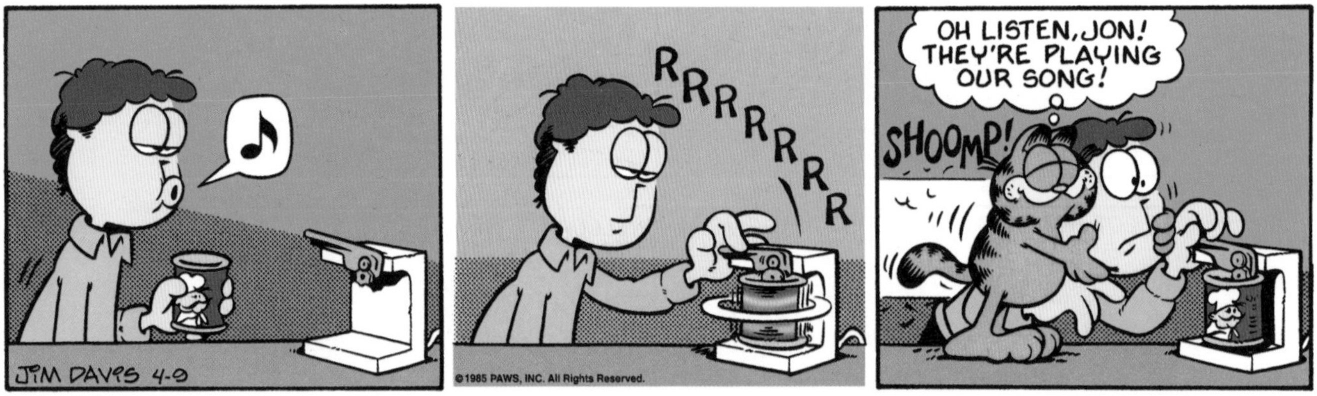
JIM DAVIS 4-9
♪
RRRRRRRR
© 1985 PAWS, INC. All Rights Reserved.
OH LISTEN, JON! THEY'RE PLAYING OUR SONG!
SHOOMP!

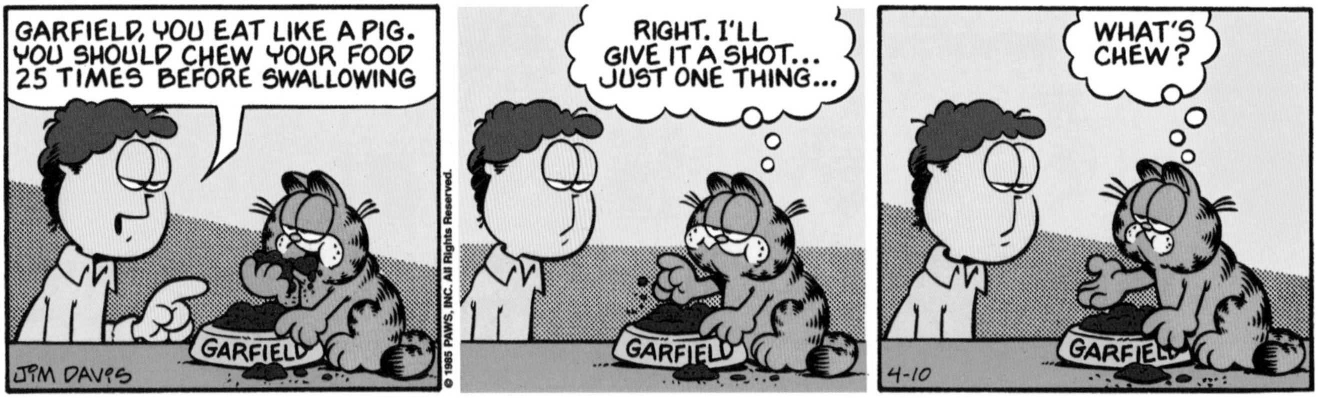
GARFIELD, YOU EAT LIKE A PIG. YOU SHOULD CHEW YOUR FOOD 25 TIMES BEFORE SWALLOWING
GARFIELD
JIM DAVIS
© 1985 PAWS, INC. All Rights Reserved.
RIGHT. I'LL GIVE IT A SHOT... JUST ONE THING...
GARFIELD
WHAT'S CHEW?
GARFIELD
4-10

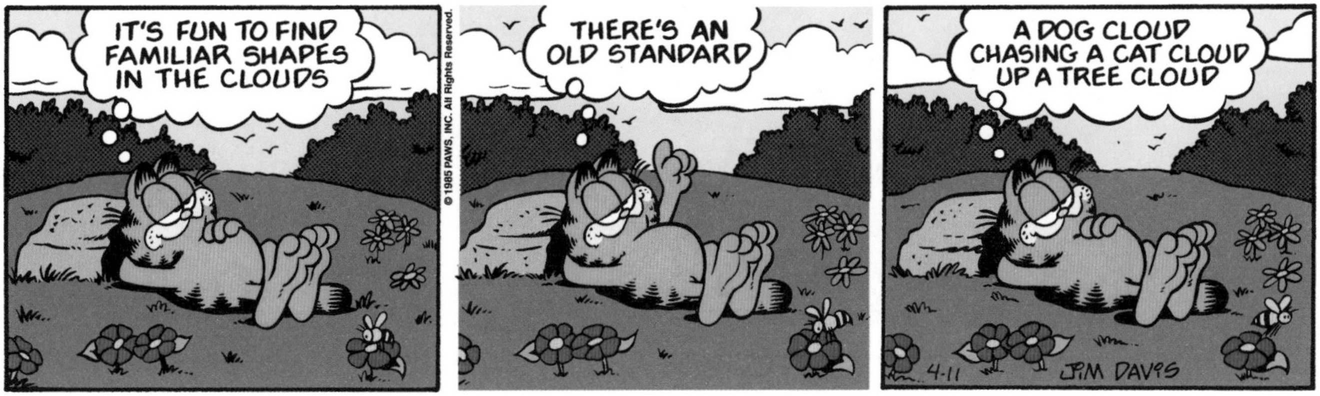
IT'S FUN TO FIND FAMILIAR SHAPES IN THE CLOUDS
© 1985 PAWS, INC. All Rights Reserved.
THERE'S AN OLD STANDARD
A DOG CLOUD CHASING A CAT CLOUD UP A TREE CLOUD
4-11
JIM DAVIS

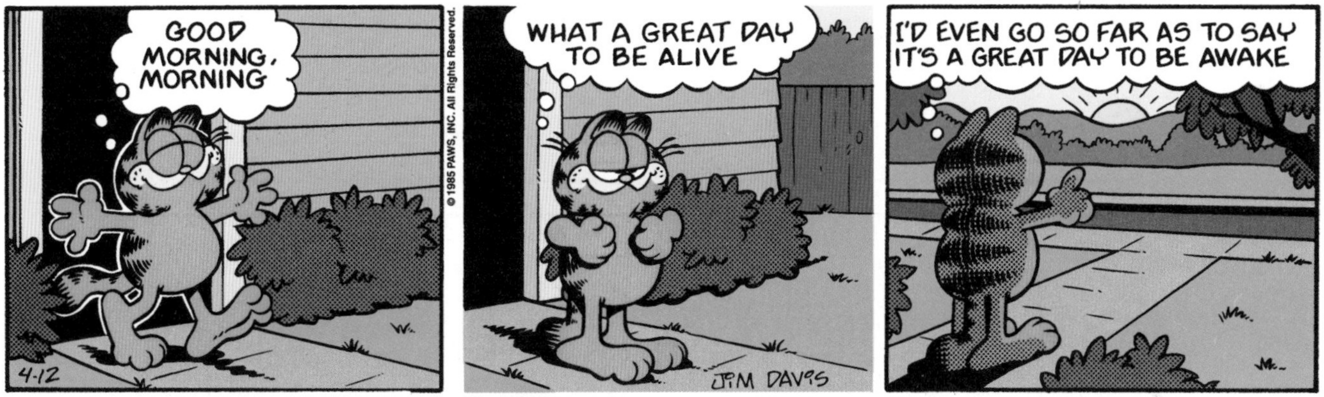
GOOD MORNING, MORNING
4-12
© 1985 PAWS, INC. All Rights Reserved.
WHAT A GREAT DAY TO BE ALIVE
JIM DAVIS
I'D EVEN GO SO FAR AS TO SAY IT'S A GREAT DAY TO BE AWAKE

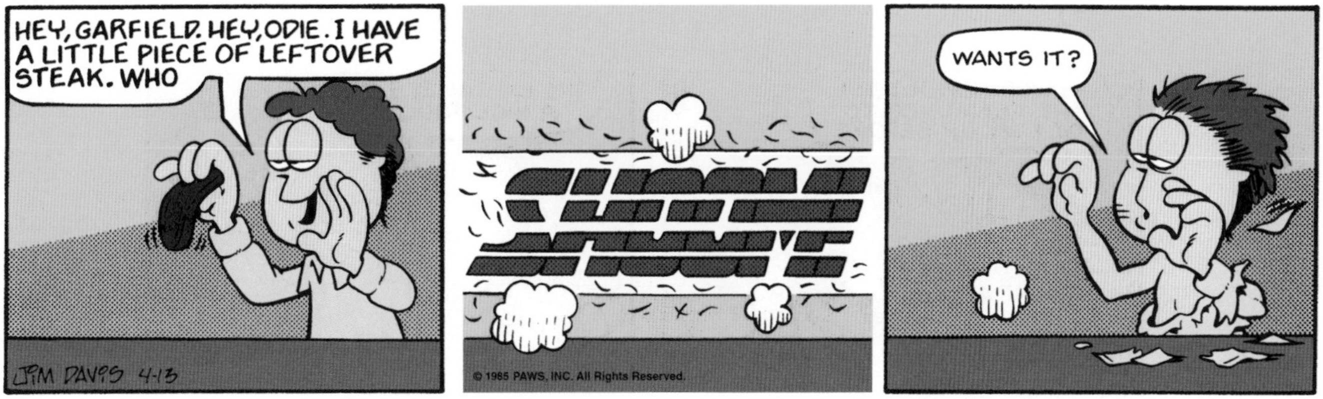
HEY, GARFIELD. HEY, ODIE. I HAVE A LITTLE PIECE OF LEFTOVER STEAK. WHO
JIM DAVIS 4-13
© 1985 PAWS, INC. All Rights Reserved.
WANTS IT?

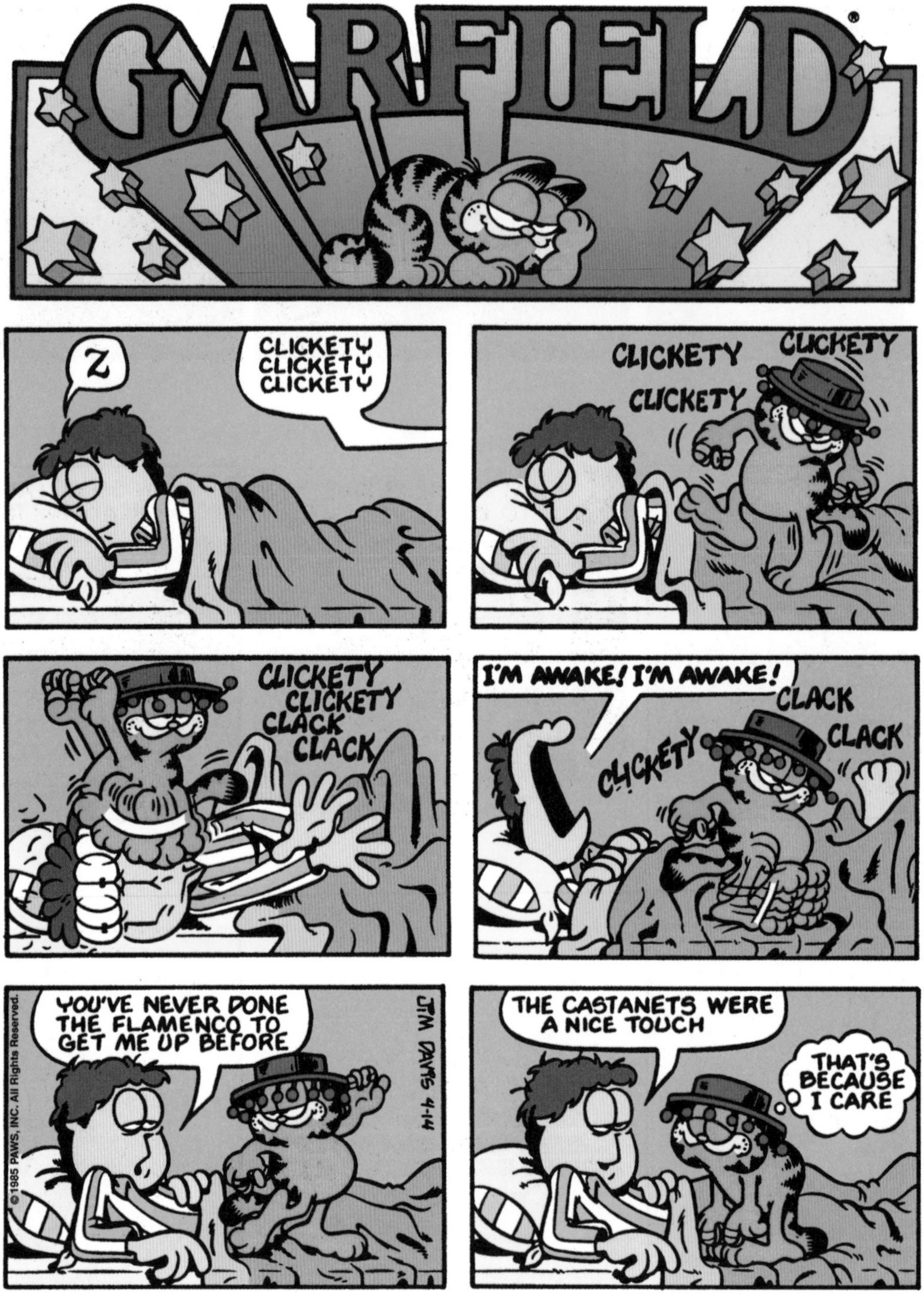

GARFIELD®
Z
CLICKETY CLICKETY CLICKETY
CLICKETY
CLICKETY
CLICKETY
CLICKETY
CLICKETY
CLACK
CLACK
I'M AWAKE! I'M AWAKE!
CLICKETY
CLACK
CLACK
YOU'VE NEVER DONE THE FLAMENCO TO GET ME UP BEFORE
JIM DAVIS 4-14
THE CASTANETS WERE A NICE TOUCH
THAT'S BECAUSE I CARE

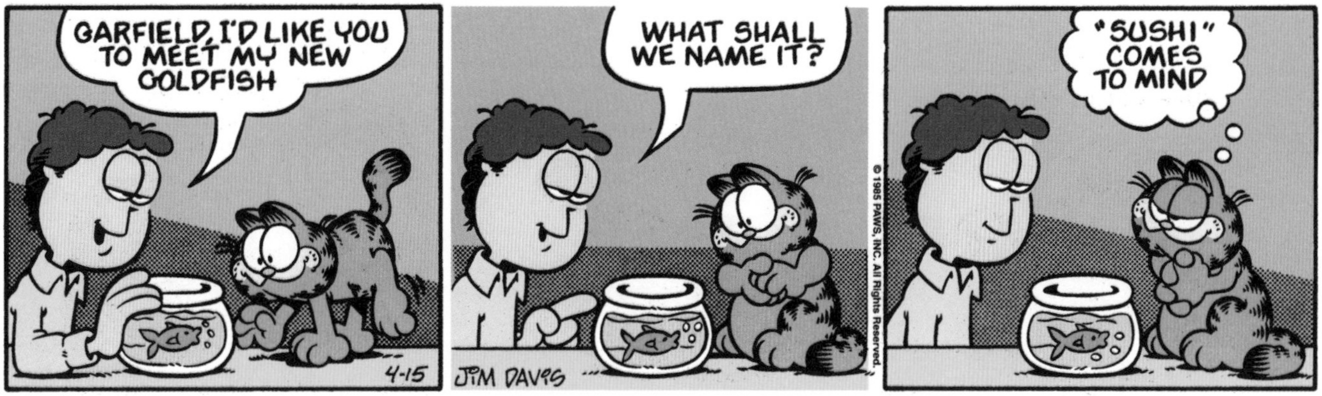
GARFIELD, I'D LIKE YOU TO MEET MY NEW GOLDFISH
4-15
WHAT SHALL WE NAME IT?
JIM DAVIS
© 1985 PAWS, INC. All Rights Reserved.
"SUSHI" COMES TO MIND

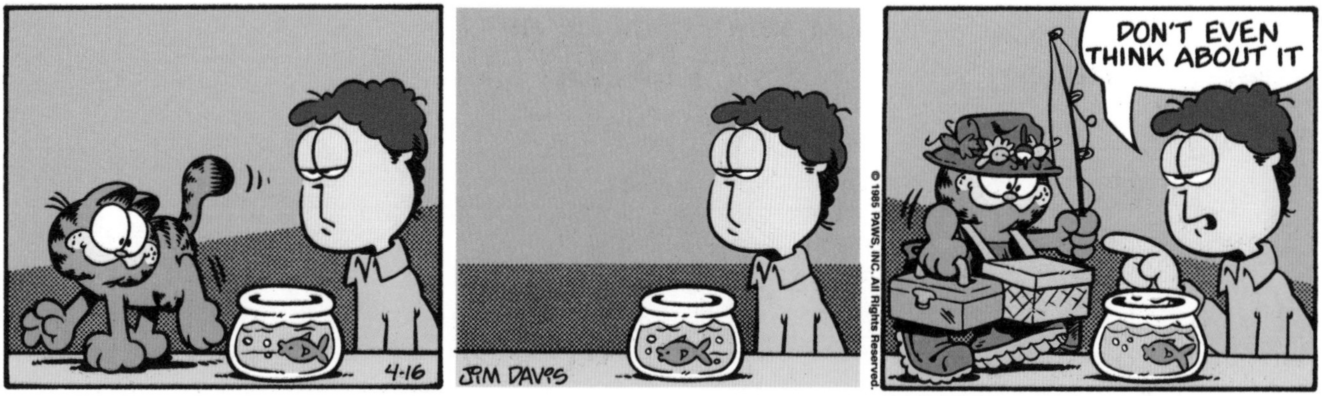
4-16
JIM DAVIS
© 1985 PAWS, INC. All Rights Reserved.
DON'T EVEN THINK ABOUT IT

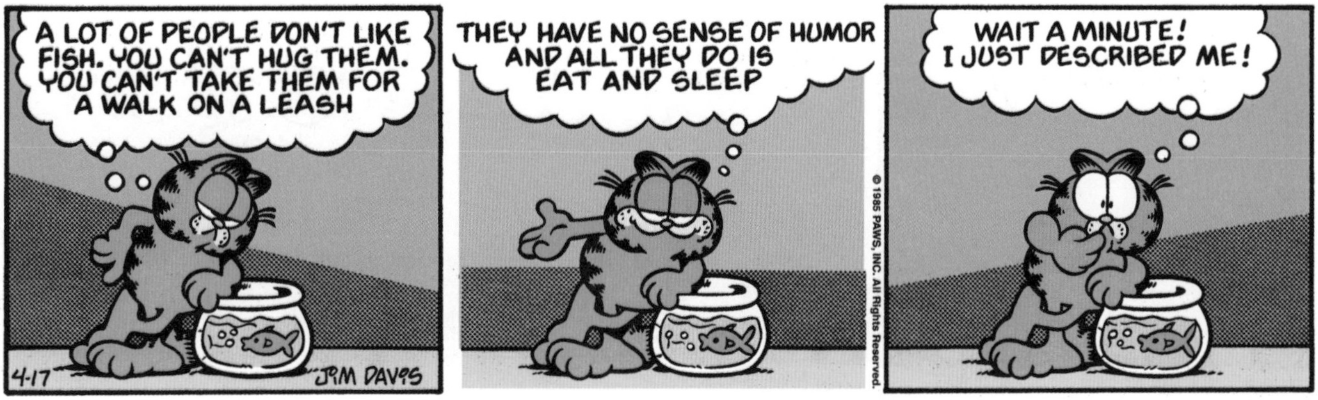
A LOT OF PEOPLE DON'T LIKE FISH. YOU CAN'T HUG THEM. YOU CAN'T TAKE THEM FOR A WALK ON A LEASH
4-17
JIM DAVIS
THEY HAVE NO SENSE OF HUMOR AND ALL THEY DO IS EAT AND SLEEP
© 1985 PAWS, INC. All Rights Reserved.
WAIT A MINUTE! I JUST DESCRIBED ME!

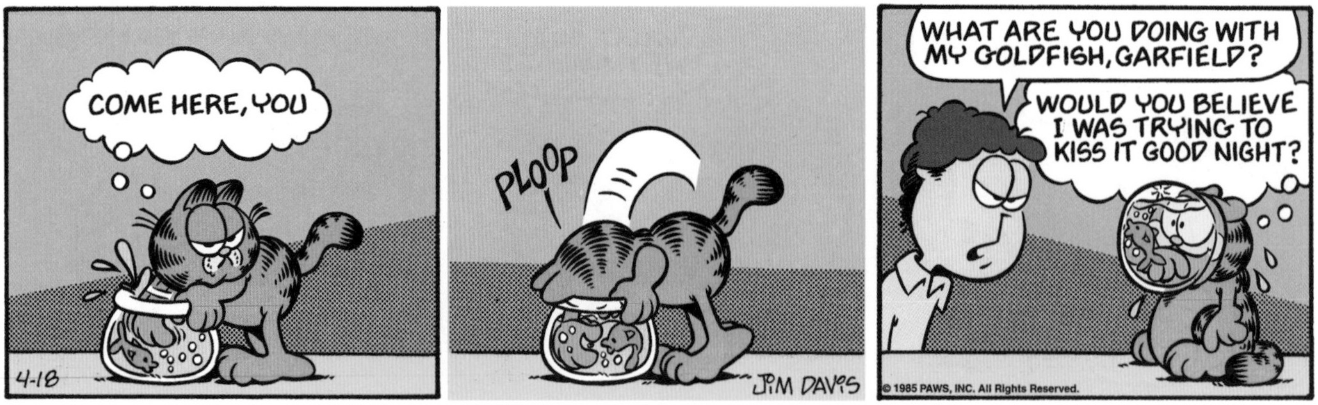
COME HERE, YOU
4-18
PLOOP
JIM DAVIS
WHAT ARE YOU DOING WITH MY GOLDFISH, GARFIELD?
WOULD YOU BELIEVE I WAS TRYING TO KISS IT GOOD NIGHT?
© 1985 PAWS, INC. All Rights Reserved.

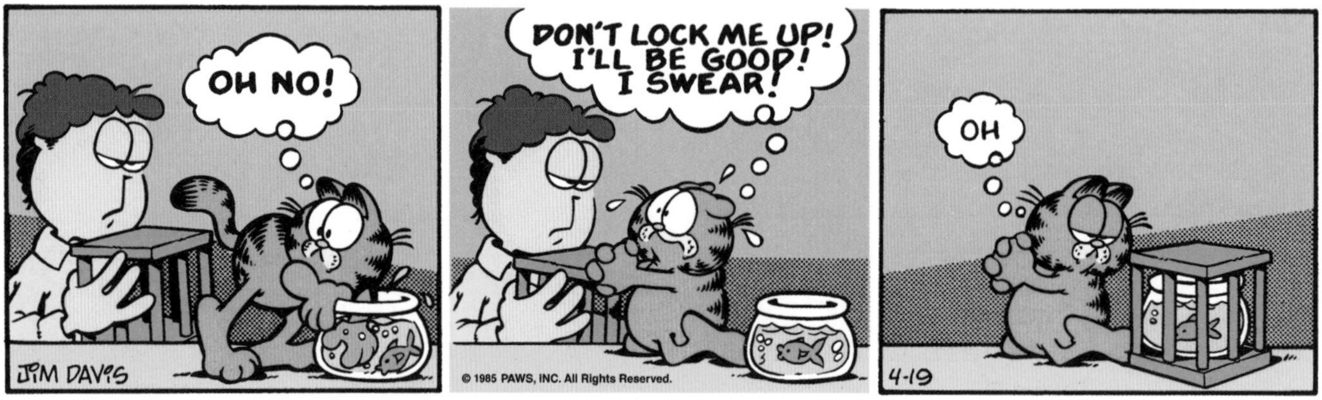
OH NO!
JIM DAVIS
DON'T LOCK ME UP! I'LL BE GOOD! I SWEAR!
© 1985 PAWS, INC. All Rights Reserved.
OH
4-19

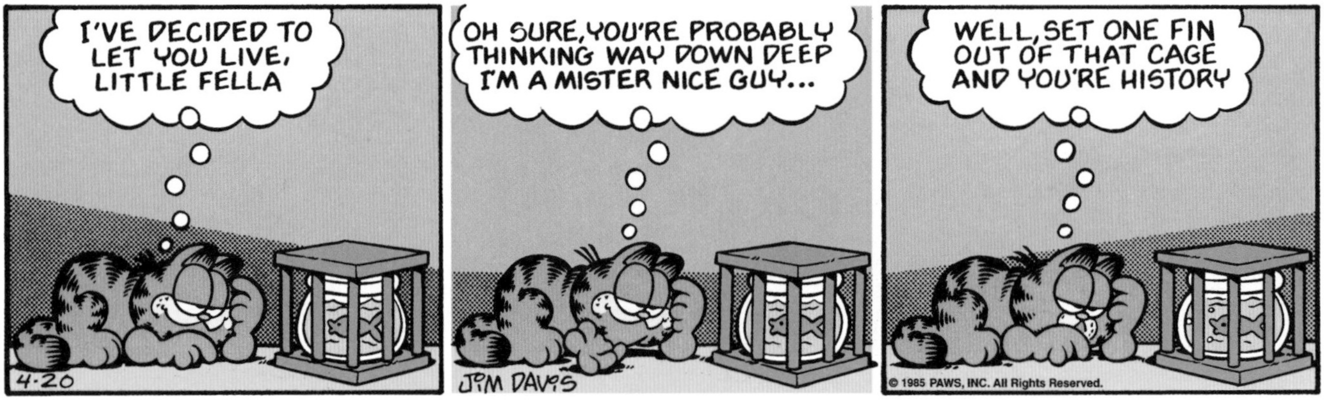
I'VE DECIDED TO LET YOU LIVE, LITTLE FELLA
4-20
OH SURE, YOU'RE PROBABLY THINKING WAY DOWN DEEP I'M A MISTER NICE GUY...
JIM DAVIS
WELL, SET ONE FIN OUT OF THAT CAGE AND YOU'RE HISTORY
© 1985 PAWS, INC. All Rights Reserved.

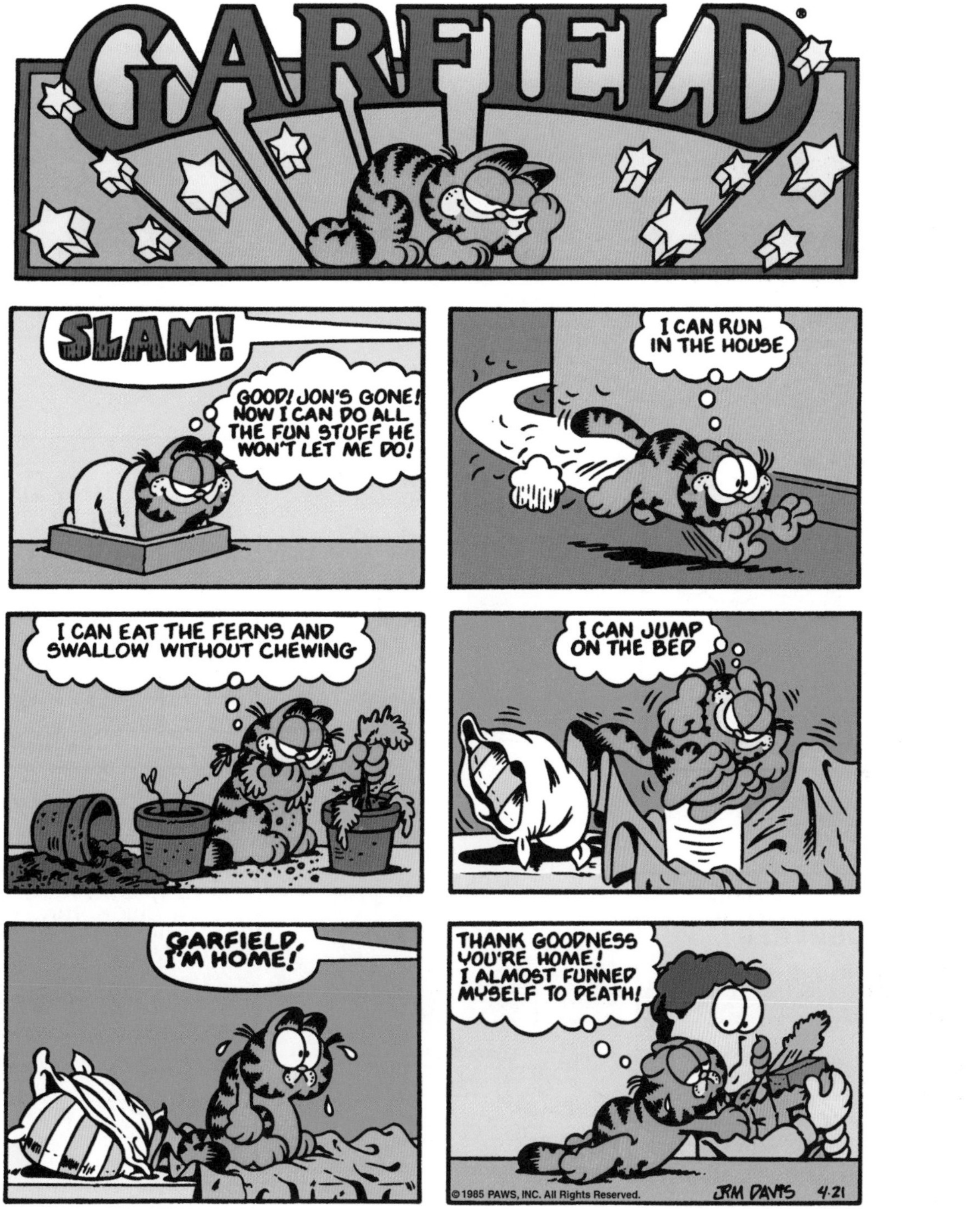
GARFIELD®
SLAM!
GOOD! JON'S GONE! NOW I CAN DO ALL THE FUN STUFF HE WON'T LET ME DO!
I CAN RUN IN THE HOUSE
I CAN EAT THE FERNS AND SWALLOW WITHOUT CHEWING
I CAN JUMP ON THE BED
GARFIELD, I'M HOME!
THANK GOODNESS YOU'RE HOME! I ALMOST FUNNED MYSELF TO DEATH!
©1985 PAWS, INC. All Rights Reserved.
JIM DAVIS 4·21

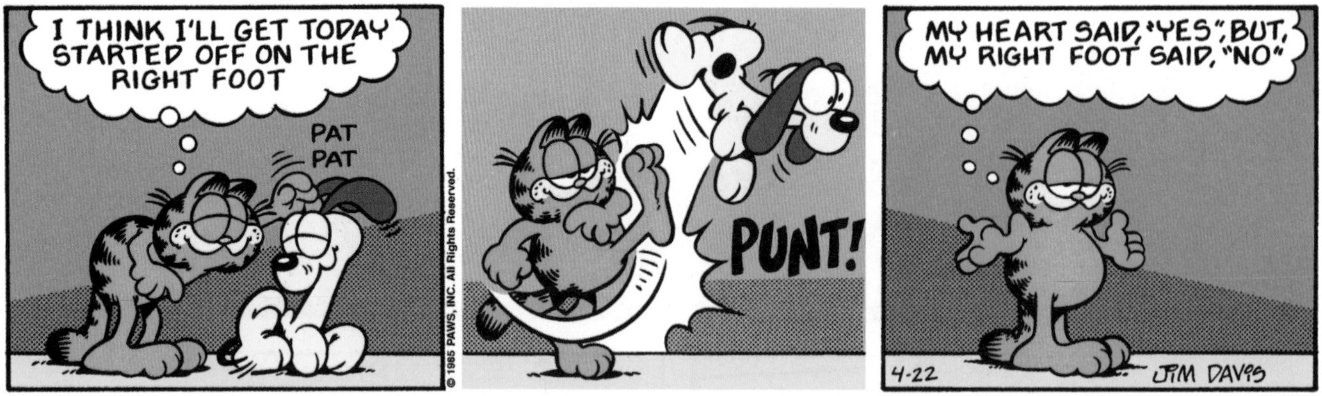
I THINK I'LL GET TODAY STARTED OFF ON THE RIGHT FOOT
PAT PAT
PUNT!
MY HEART SAID, "YES", BUT, MY RIGHT FOOT SAID, "NO"
4-22
JIM DAVIS
© 1985 PAWS, INC. All Rights Reserved.

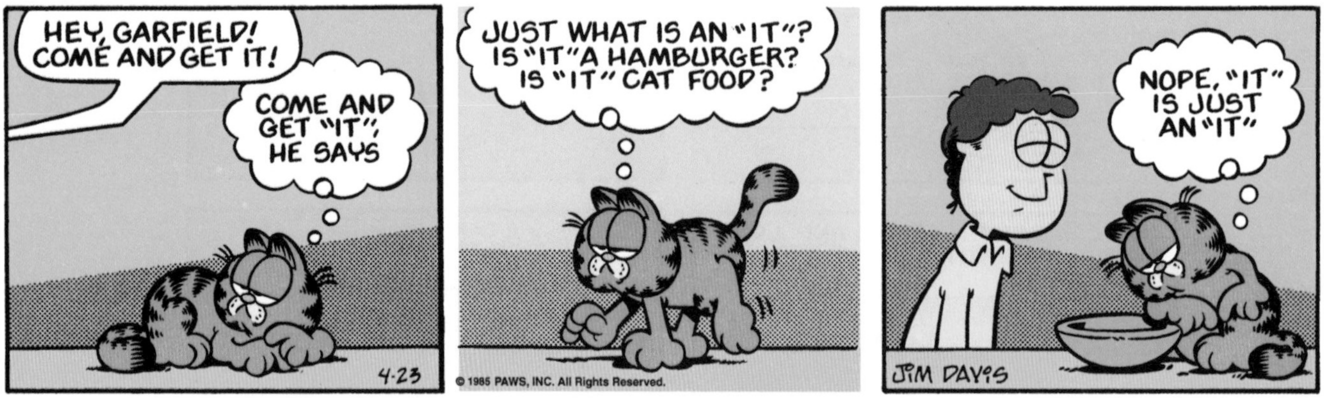
HEY, GARFIELD! COME AND GET IT!
COME AND GET "IT", HE SAYS
4-23
JUST WHAT IS AN "IT"? IS "IT" A HAMBURGER? IS "IT" CAT FOOD?
© 1985 PAWS, INC. All Rights Reserved.
NOPE, "IT" IS JUST AN "IT"
JIM DAVIS

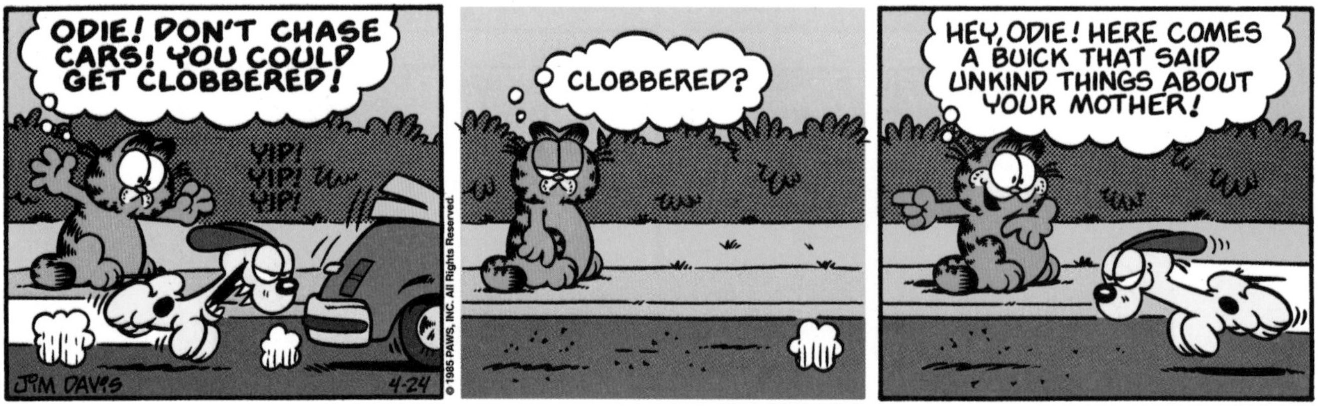
ODIE! DON'T CHASE CARS! YOU COULD GET CLOBBERED!
YIP! YIP! YIP!
JIM DAVIS
4-24
CLOBBERED?
HEY, ODIE! HERE COMES A BUICK THAT SAID UNKIND THINGS ABOUT YOUR MOTHER!
© 1985 PAWS, INC. All Rights Reserved.

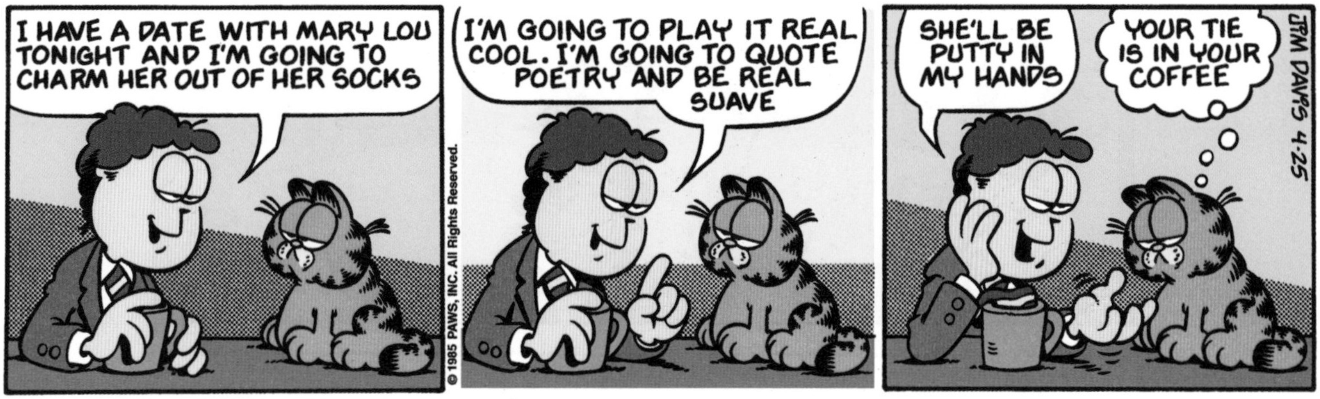
I HAVE A DATE WITH MARY LOU TONIGHT AND I'M GOING TO CHARM HER OUT OF HER SOCKS
I'M GOING TO PLAY IT REAL COOL. I'M GOING TO QUOTE POETRY AND BE REAL SUAVE
SHE'LL BE PUTTY IN MY HANDS
YOUR TIE IS IN YOUR COFFEE
© 1985 PAWS, INC. All Rights Reserved.
JIM DAVIS 4-25

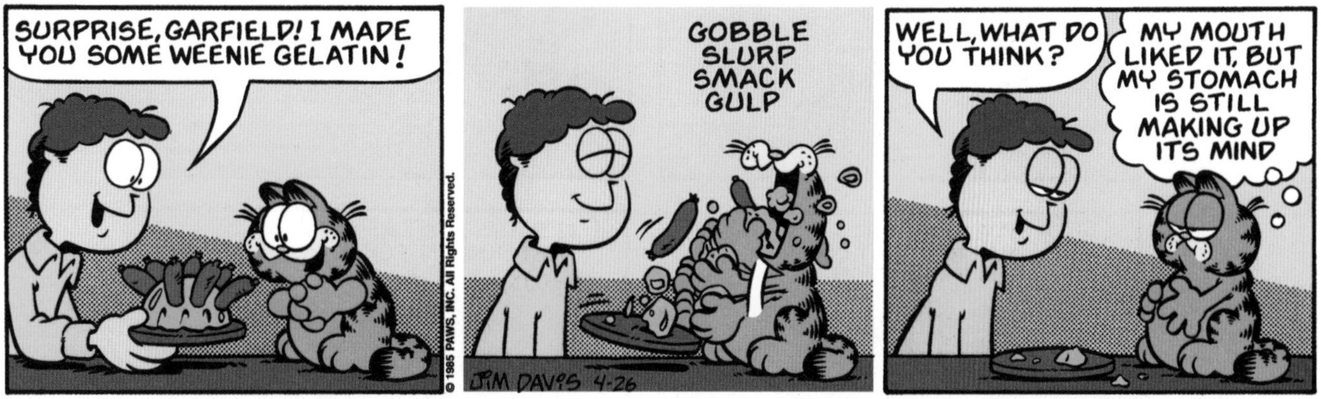
SURPRISE, GARFIELD! I MADE YOU SOME WEENIE GELATIN!
GOBBLE SLURP SMACK GULP
WELL, WHAT DO YOU THINK?
MY MOUTH LIKED IT, BUT MY STOMACH IS STILL MAKING UP ITS MIND
© 1985 PAWS, INC. All Rights Reserved.
JIM DAVIS 4-26

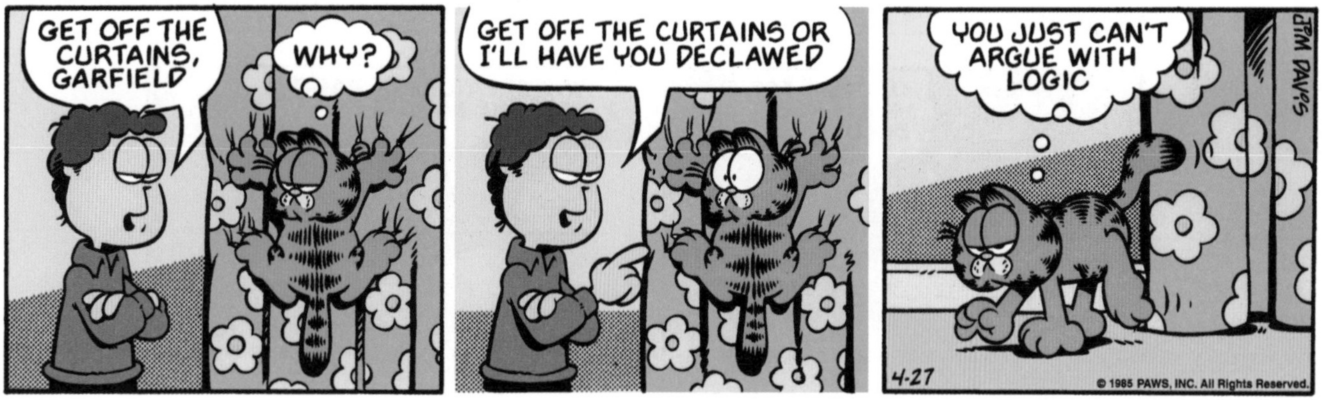
GET OFF THE CURTAINS, GARFIELD
WHY?
GET OFF THE CURTAINS OR I'LL HAVE YOU DECLAWED
YOU JUST CAN'T ARGUE WITH LOGIC
JIM DAVIS
4-27
© 1985 PAWS, INC. All Rights Reserved.

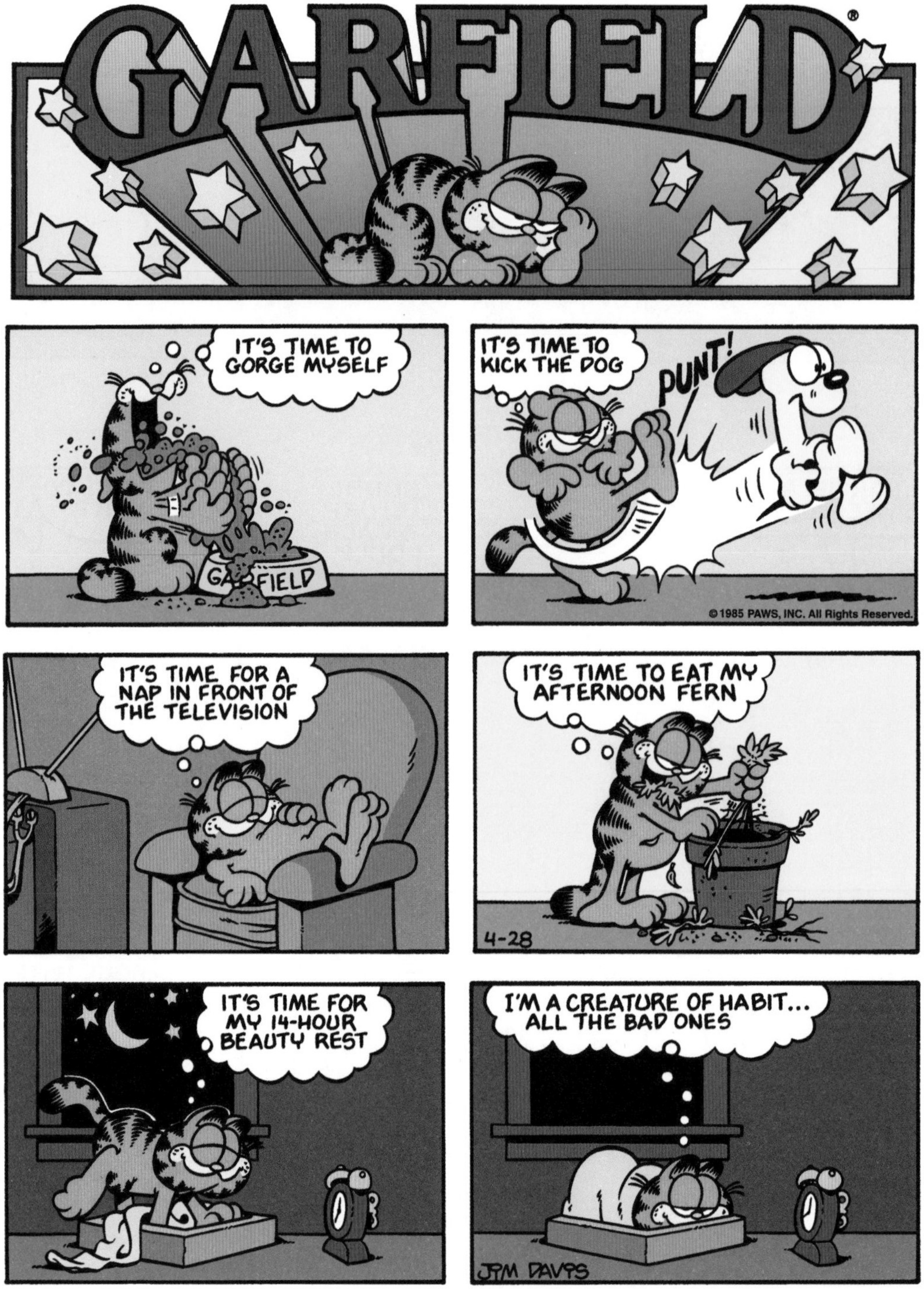
GARFIELD
IT'S TIME TO GORGE MYSELF
GARFIELD
IT'S TIME TO KICK THE DOG
PUNT!
© 1985 PAWS, INC. All Rights Reserved.
IT'S TIME FOR A NAP IN FRONT OF THE TELEVISION
IT'S TIME TO EAT MY AFTERNOON FERN
4-28
IT'S TIME FOR MY 14-HOUR BEAUTY REST
I'M A CREATURE OF HABIT... ALL THE BAD ONES
JIM DAVIS

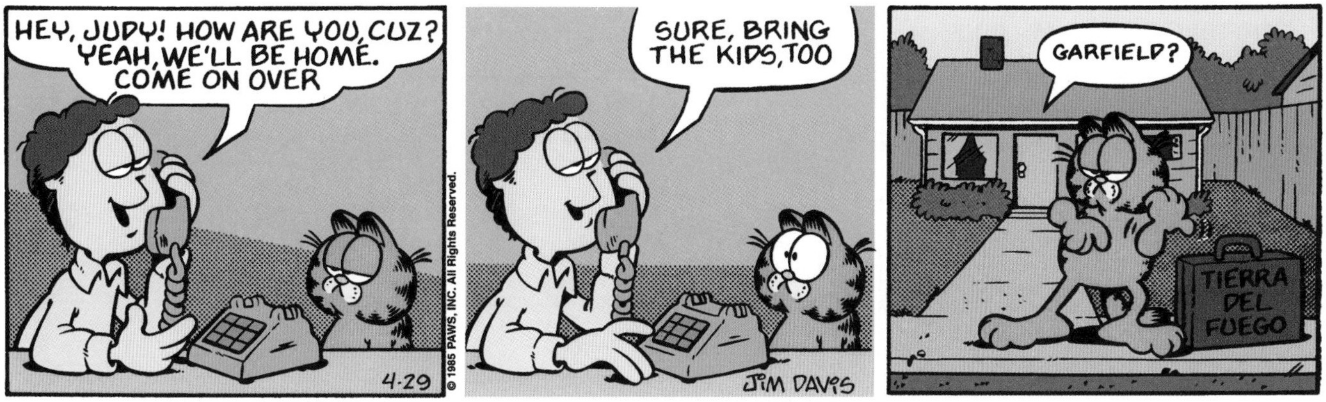
HEY, JUDY! HOW ARE YOU, CUZ? YEAH, WE'LL BE HOME. COME ON OVER
4-29
© 1985 PAWS, INC. All Rights Reserved.
SURE, BRING THE KIDS, TOO
JIM DAVIS
GARFIELD?
TIERRA DEL FUEGO

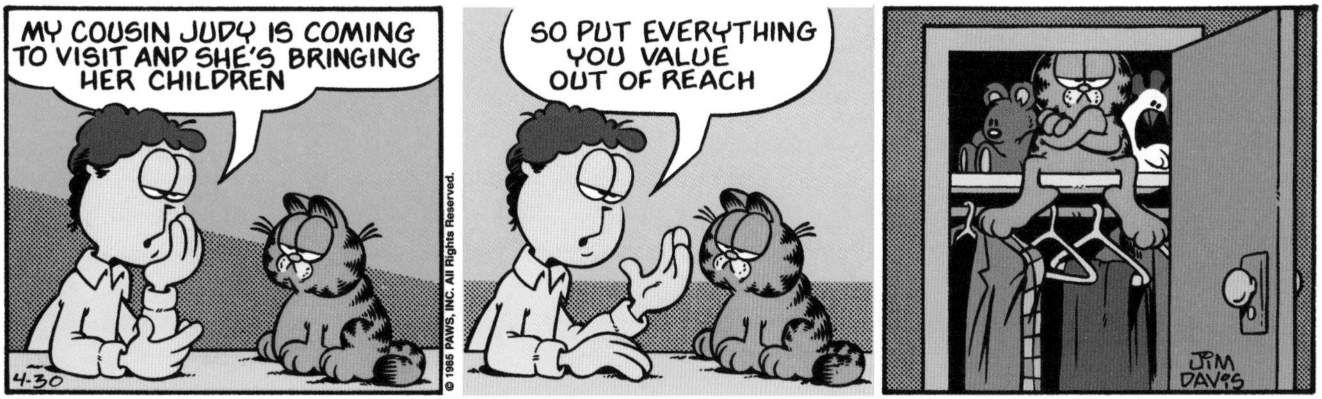
MY COUSIN JUDY IS COMING TO VISIT AND SHE'S BRINGING HER CHILDREN
4-30
© 1985 PAWS, INC. All Rights Reserved.
SO PUT EVERYTHING YOU VALUE OUT OF REACH
JIM DAVIS

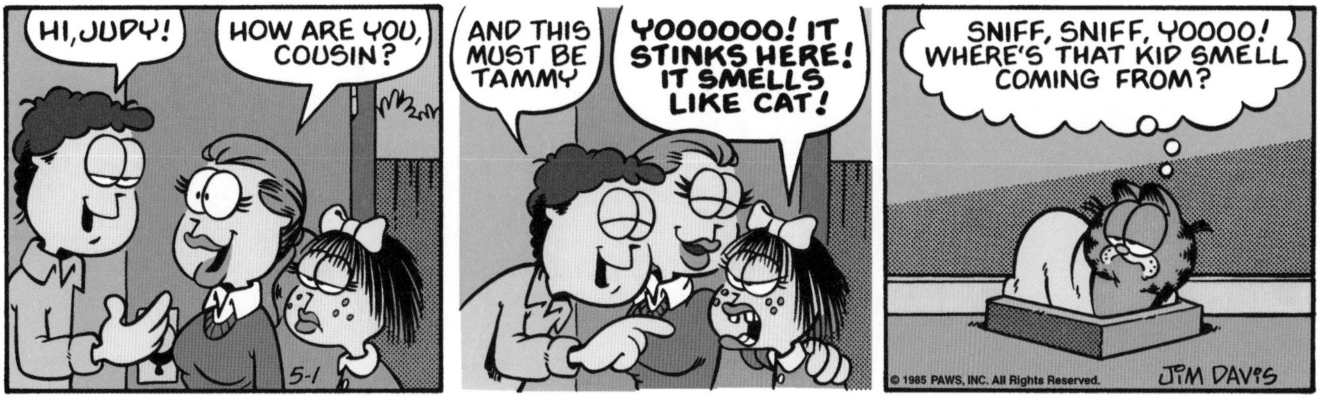
HI, JUDY!
HOW ARE YOU, COUSIN?
5-1
AND THIS MUST BE TAMMY
YOOOOOO! IT STINKS HERE! IT SMELLS LIKE CAT!
SNIFF, SNIFF, YOOOO! WHERE'S THAT KID SMELL COMING FROM?
© 1985 PAWS, INC. All Rights Reserved.
JIM DAVIS

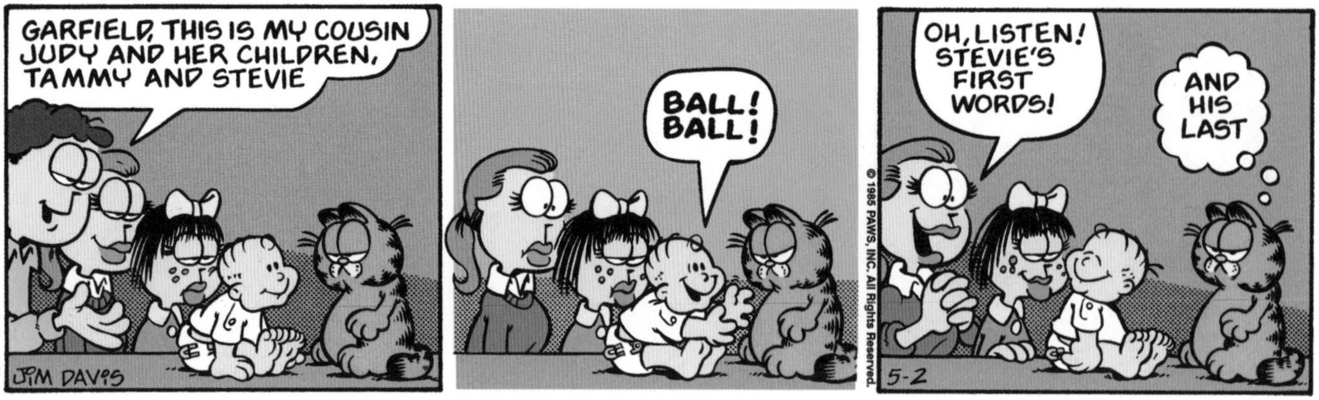
GARFIELD, THIS IS MY COUSIN JUDY AND HER CHILDREN, TAMMY AND STEVIE
JIM DAVIS
BALL! BALL!
© 1985 PAWS, INC. All Rights Reserved.
OH, LISTEN! STEVIE'S FIRST WORDS!
AND HIS LAST
5-2

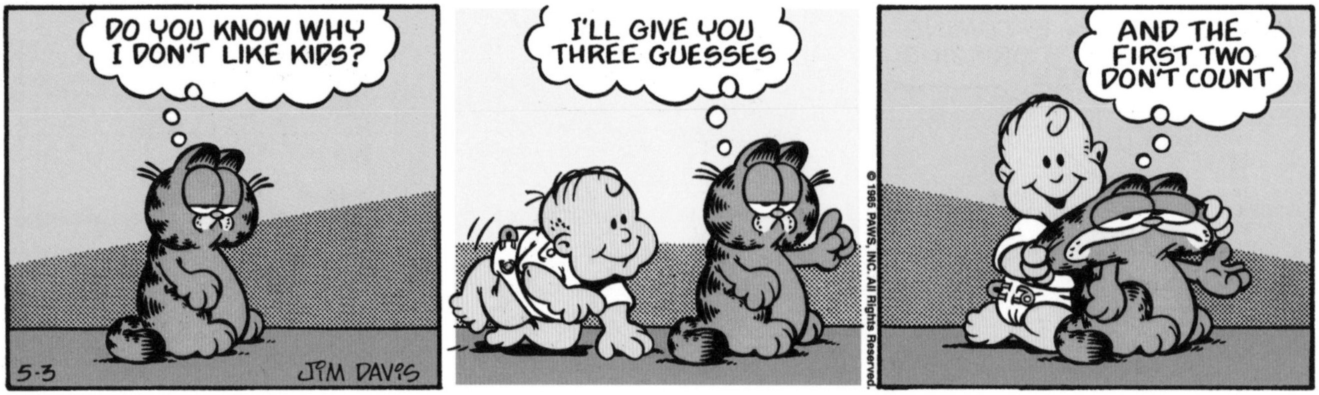
DO YOU KNOW WHY I DON'T LIKE KIDS?
5-3
JIM DAVIS
I'LL GIVE YOU THREE GUESSES
© 1985 PAWS, INC. All Rights Reserved.
AND THE FIRST TWO DON'T COUNT

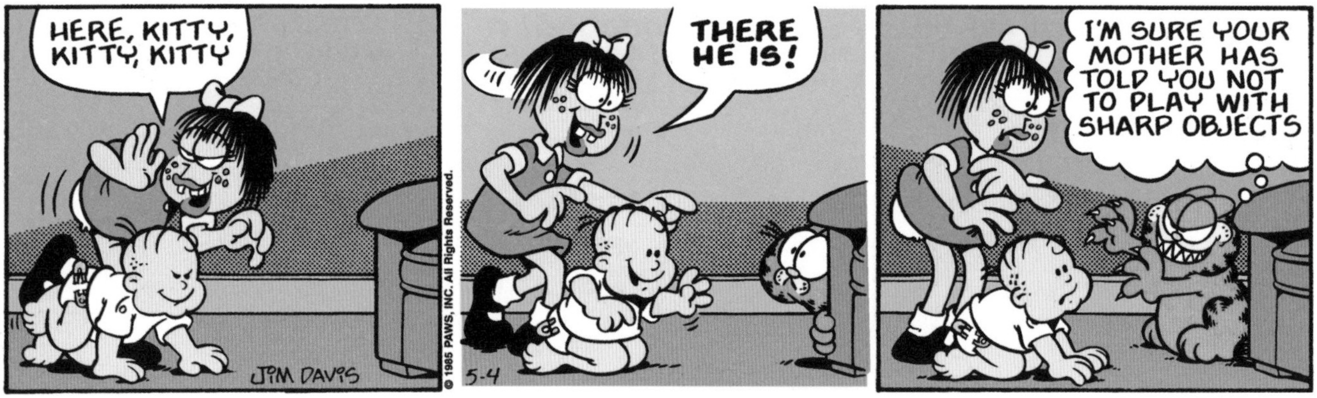
HERE, KITTY, KITTY, KITTY
JIM DAVIS
© 1985 PAWS, INC. All Rights Reserved.
THERE HE IS!
5-4
I'M SURE YOUR MOTHER HAS TOLD YOU NOT TO PLAY WITH SHARP OBJECTS

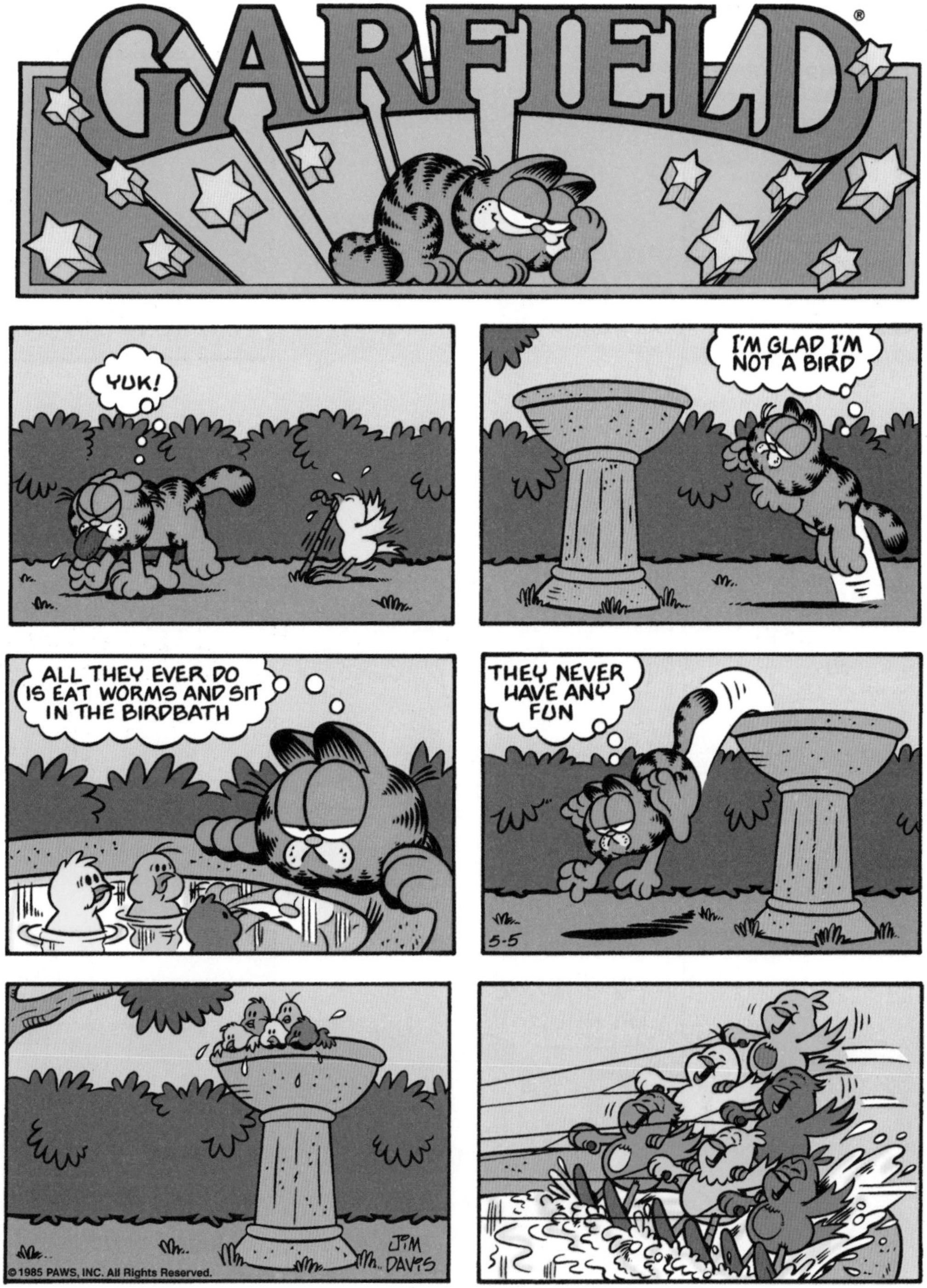
GARFIELD
YUK!
I'M GLAD I'M NOT A BIRD
ALL THEY EVER DO IS EAT WORMS AND SIT IN THE BIRDBATH
THEY NEVER HAVE ANY FUN
5-5
JIM DAVIS

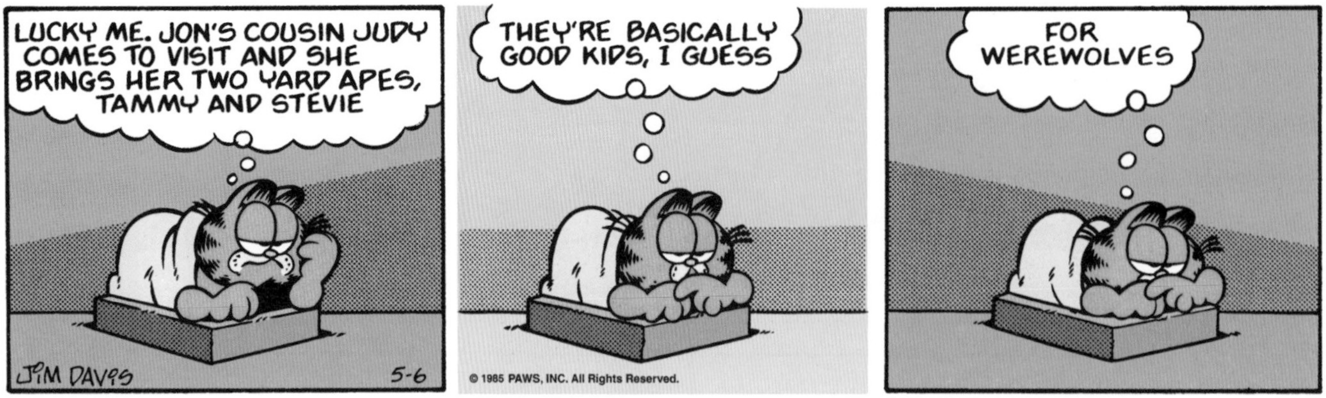
LUCKY ME. JON'S COUSIN JUDY COMES TO VISIT AND SHE BRINGS HER TWO YARD APES, TAMMY AND STEVIE
JIM DAVIS
5-6
THEY'RE BASICALLY GOOD KIDS, I GUESS
© 1985 PAWS, INC. All Rights Reserved.
FOR WEREWOLVES

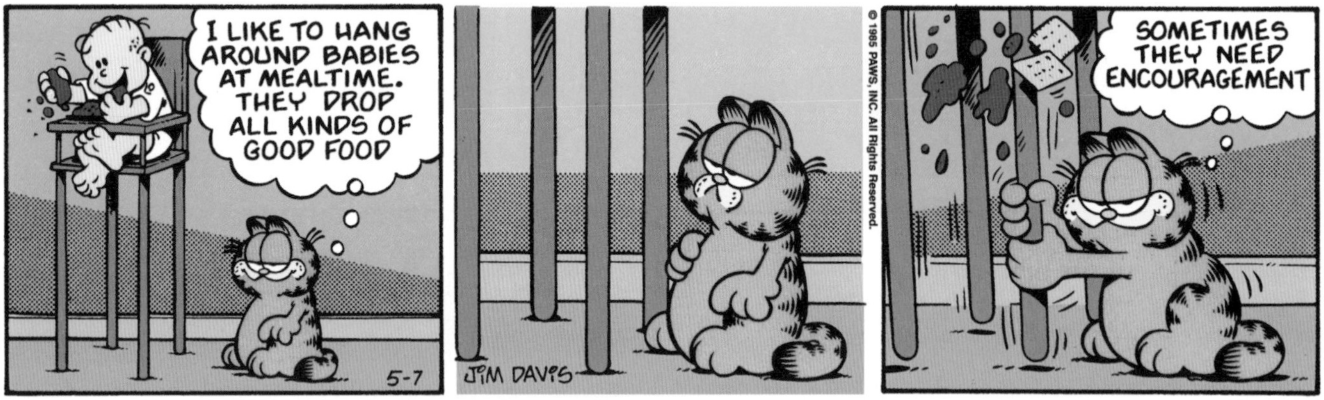
I LIKE TO HANG AROUND BABIES AT MEALTIME. THEY DROP ALL KINDS OF GOOD FOOD
5-7
JIM DAVIS
© 1985 PAWS, INC. All Rights Reserved.
SOMETIMES THEY NEED ENCOURAGEMENT

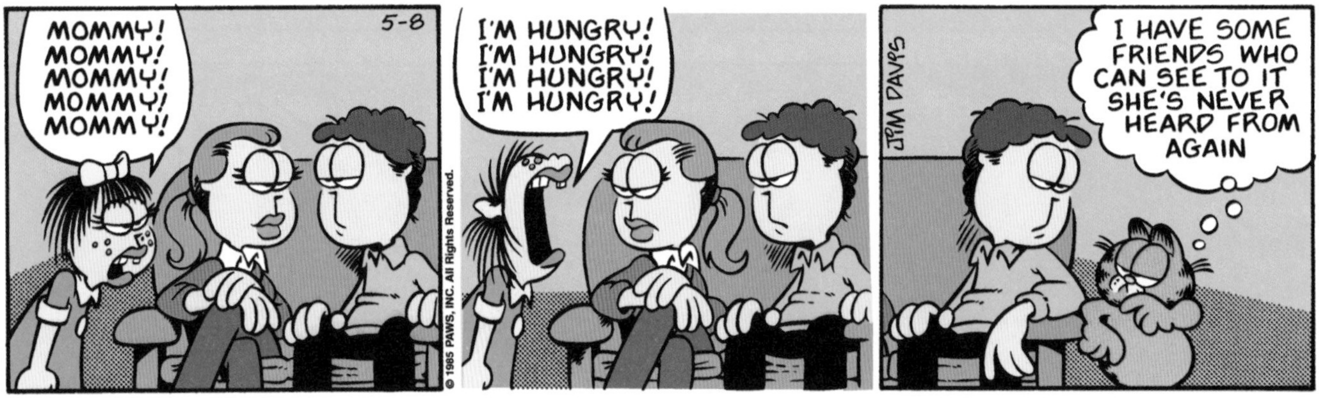
MOMMY! MOMMY! MOMMY! MOMMY! MOMMY!
5-8
© 1985 PAWS, INC. All Rights Reserved.
I'M HUNGRY! I'M HUNGRY! I'M HUNGRY! I'M HUNGRY!
JIM DAVIS
I HAVE SOME FRIENDS WHO CAN SEE TO IT SHE'S NEVER HEARD FROM AGAIN

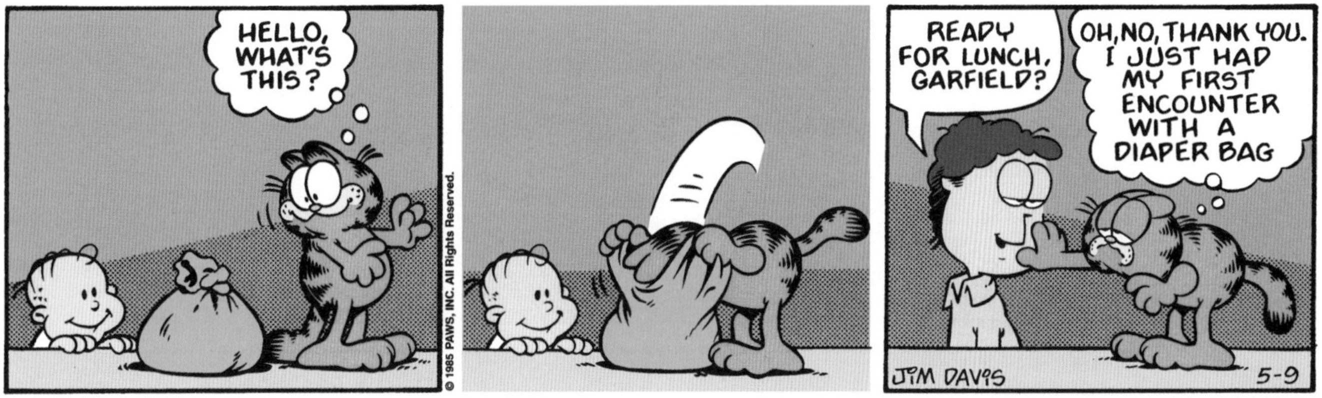
HELLO, WHAT'S THIS?
© 1985 PAWS, INC. All Rights Reserved.
READY FOR LUNCH, GARFIELD?
OH, NO, THANK YOU. I JUST HAD MY FIRST ENCOUNTER WITH A DIAPER BAG
JIM DAVIS 5-9

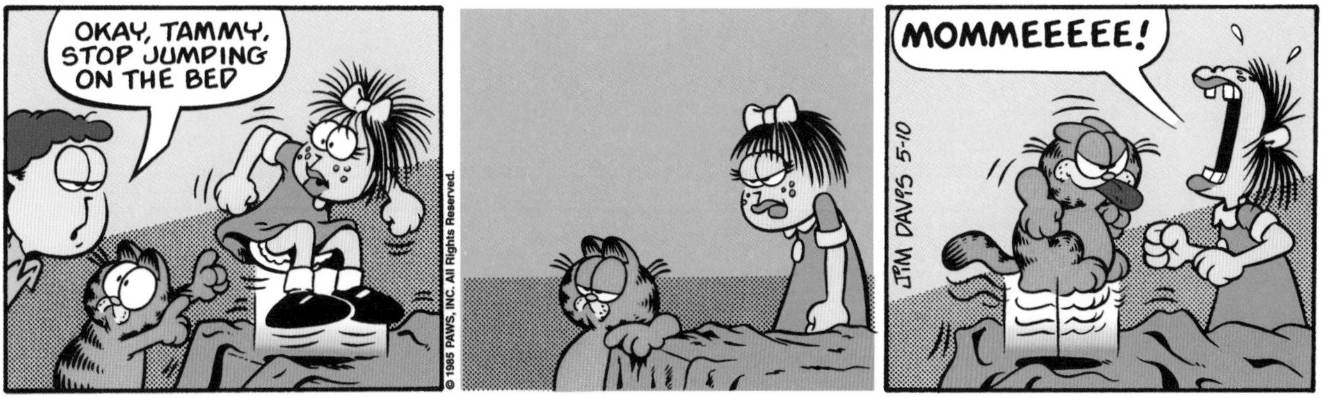
OKAY, TAMMY, STOP JUMPING ON THE BED
© 1985 PAWS, INC. All Rights Reserved.
JIM DAVIS 5-10
MOMMEEEEE!

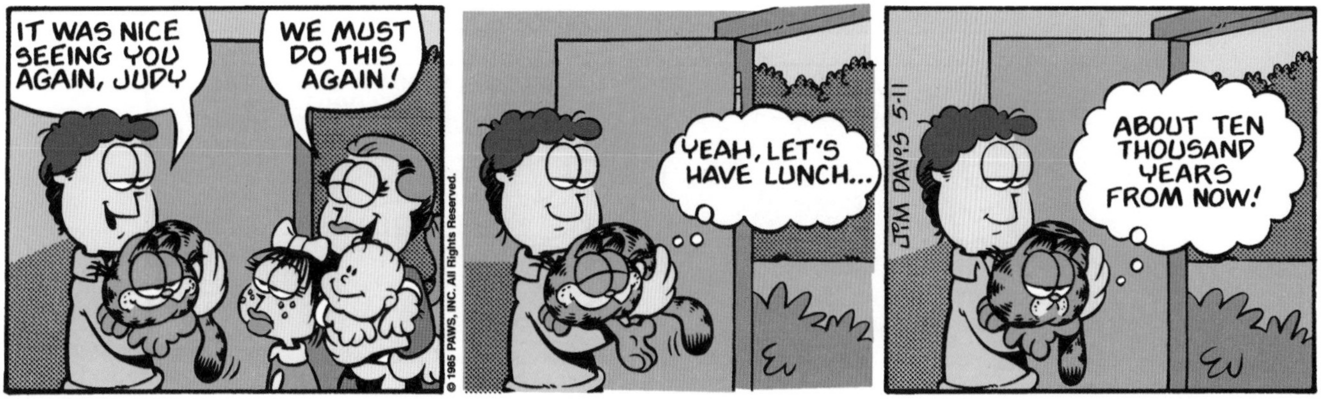
IT WAS NICE SEEING YOU AGAIN, JUDY
WE MUST DO THIS AGAIN!
© 1985 PAWS, INC. All Rights Reserved.
YEAH, LET'S HAVE LUNCH...
JIM DAVIS 5-11
ABOUT TEN THOUSAND YEARS FROM NOW!

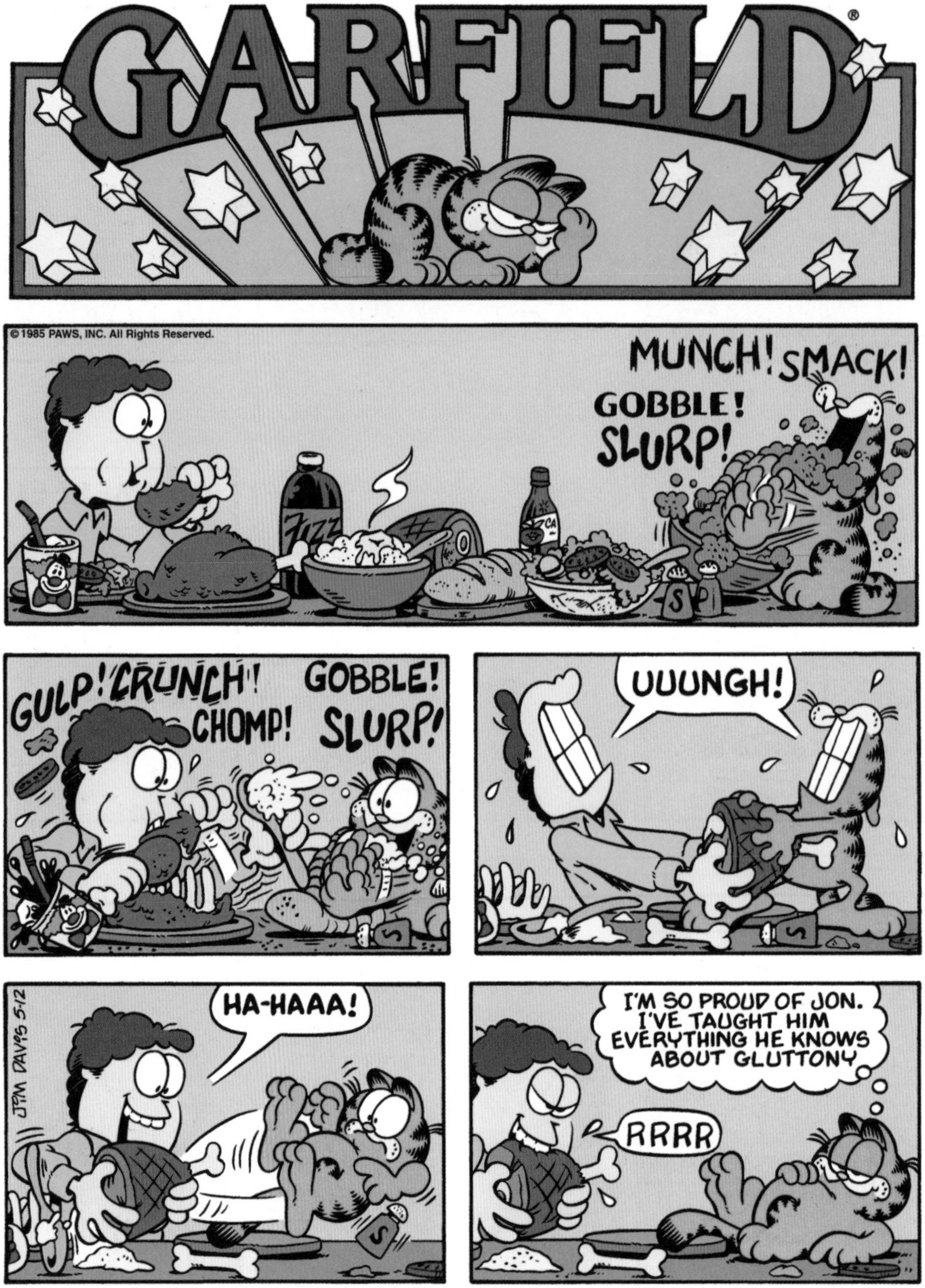
GARFIELD®
© 1985 PAWS, INC. All Rights Reserved.
MUNCH! SMACK!
GOBBLE! SLURP!
GULP! CRUNCH! CHOMP!
GOBBLE! SLURP!
UUUNGH!
JIM DAVIS 5-12
HA-HAAA!
I'M SO PROUD OF JON. I'VE TAUGHT HIM EVERYTHING HE KNOWS ABOUT GLUTTONY
RRRR

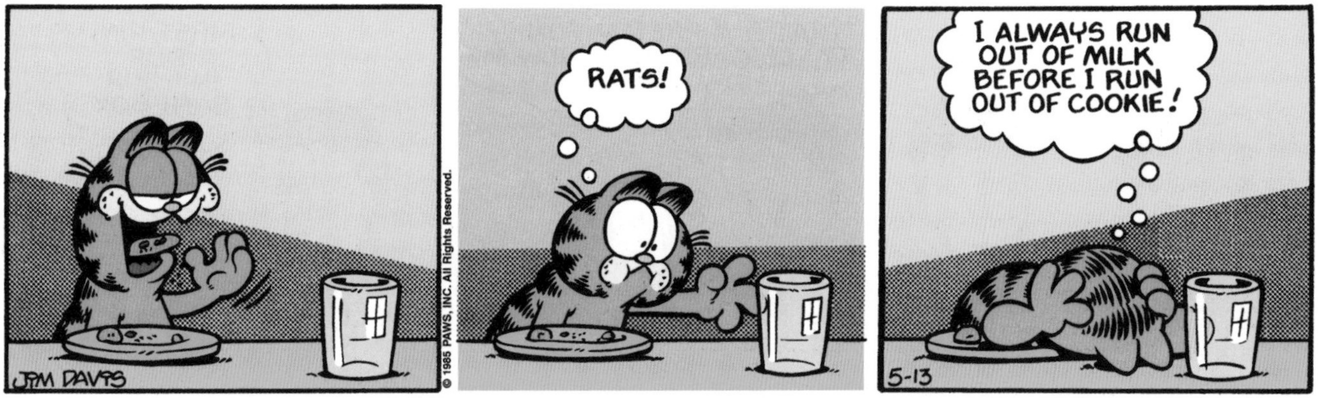
RATS!
I ALWAYS RUN OUT OF MILK BEFORE I RUN OUT OF COOKIE!
JIM DAVIS
© 1985 PAWS, INC. All Rights Reserved.
5-13

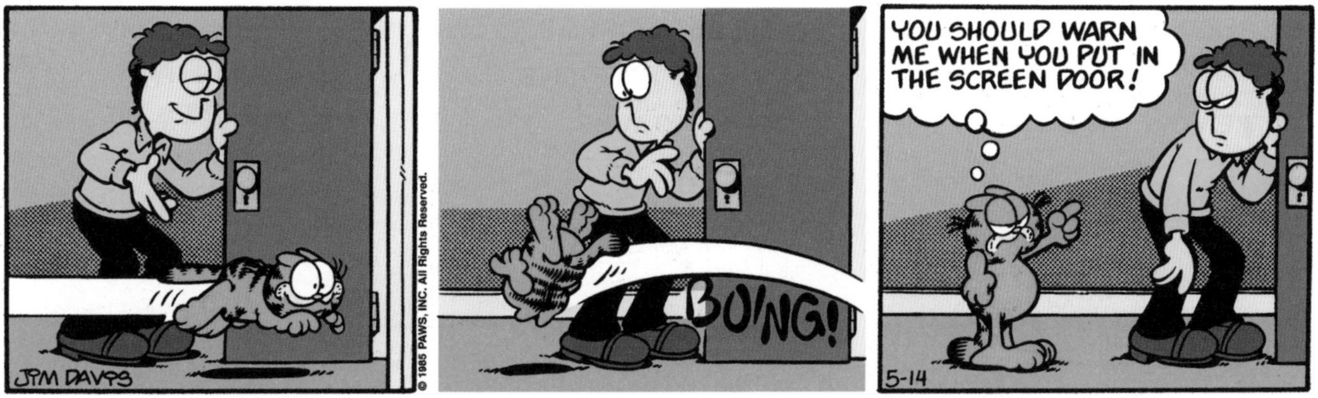
BOING!
YOU SHOULD WARN ME WHEN YOU PUT IN THE SCREEN DOOR!
JIM DAVIS
© 1985 PAWS, INC. All Rights Reserved.
5-14

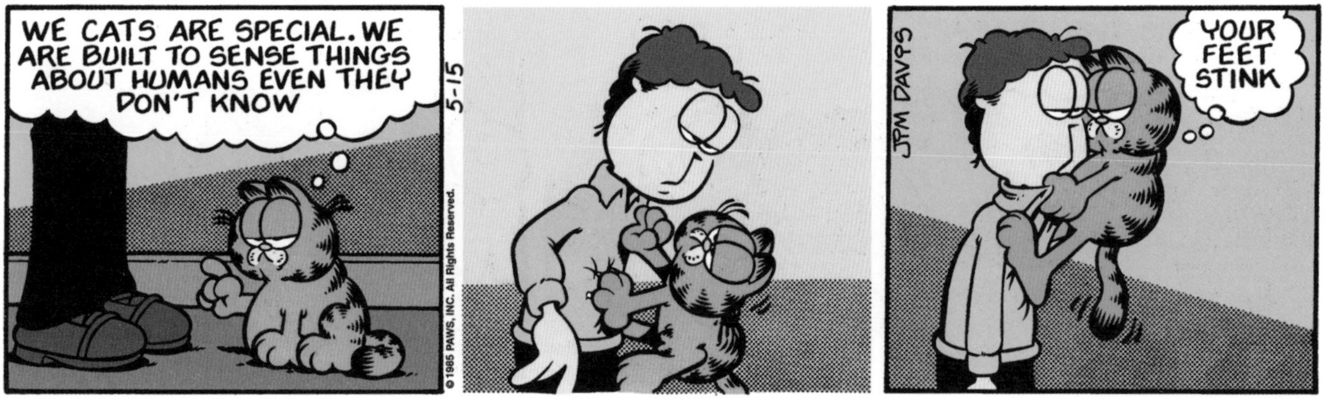
WE CATS ARE SPECIAL. WE ARE BUILT TO SENSE THINGS ABOUT HUMANS EVEN THEY DON'T KNOW
YOUR FEET STINK
5-15
JIM DAVIS
© 1985 PAWS, INC. All Rights Reserved.

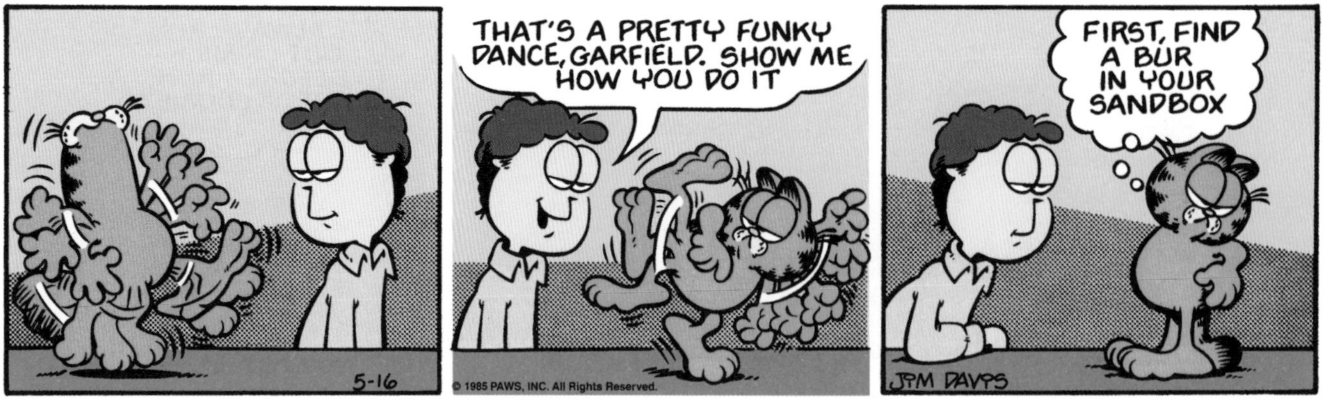

5-16
THAT'S A PRETTY FUNKY DANCE, GARFIELD. SHOW ME HOW YOU DO IT
© 1985 PAWS, INC. All Rights Reserved.
FIRST, FIND A BUR IN YOUR SANDBOX
JIM DAVIS

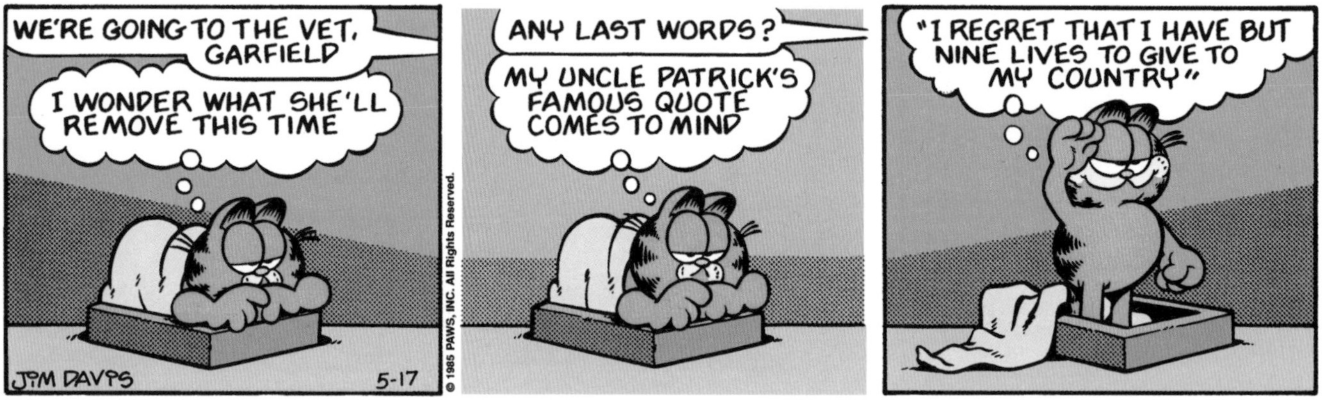

WE'RE GOING TO THE VET, GARFIELD
I WONDER WHAT SHE'LL REMOVE THIS TIME
JIM DAVIS
5-17
© 1985 PAWS, INC. All Rights Reserved.
ANY LAST WORDS?
MY UNCLE PATRICK'S FAMOUS QUOTE COMES TO MIND
"I REGRET THAT I HAVE BUT NINE LIVES TO GIVE TO MY COUNTRY"

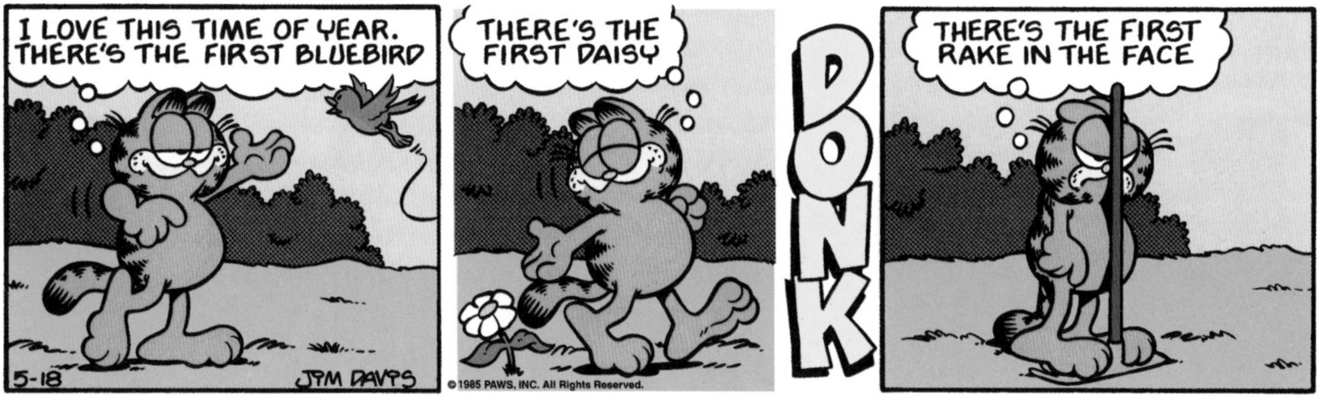

I LOVE THIS TIME OF YEAR. THERE'S THE FIRST BLUEBIRD
5-18
JIM DAVIS
THERE'S THE FIRST DAISY
© 1985 PAWS, INC. All Rights Reserved.
DONK
THERE'S THE FIRST RAKE IN THE FACE

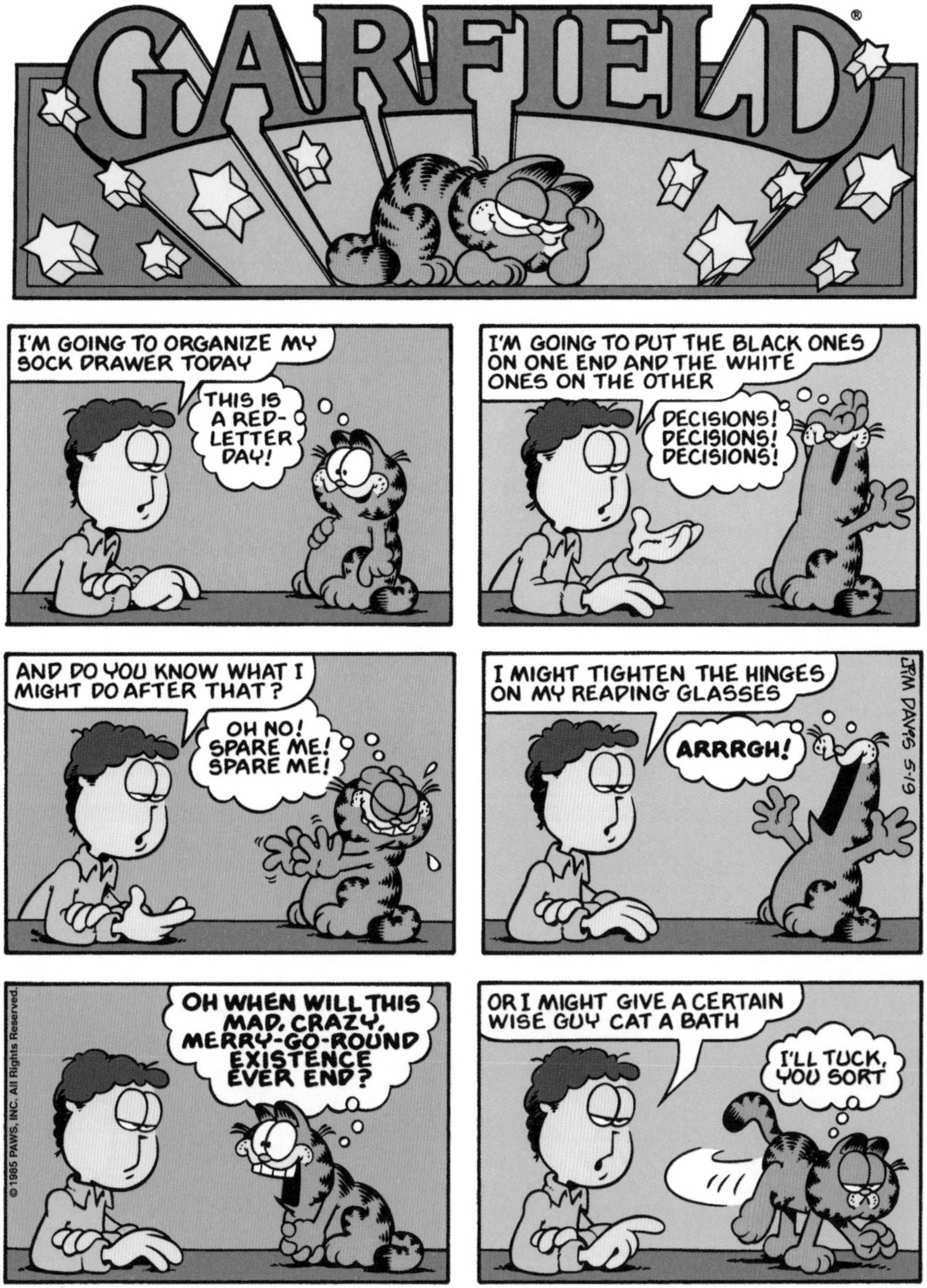
GARFIELD®
I'M GOING TO ORGANIZE MY SOCK DRAWER TODAY
THIS IS A RED-LETTER DAY!
I'M GOING TO PUT THE BLACK ONES ON ONE END AND THE WHITE ONES ON THE OTHER
DECISIONS! DECISIONS! DECISIONS!
AND DO YOU KNOW WHAT I MIGHT DO AFTER THAT?
OH NO! SPARE ME! SPARE ME!
I MIGHT TIGHTEN THE HINGES ON MY READING GLASSES
ARRRGH!
JIM DAVIS 5-19
OH WHEN WILL THIS MAD, CRAZY, MERRY-GO-ROUND EXISTENCE EVER END?
OR I MIGHT GIVE A CERTAIN WISE GUY CAT A BATH
I'LL TUCK, YOU SORT

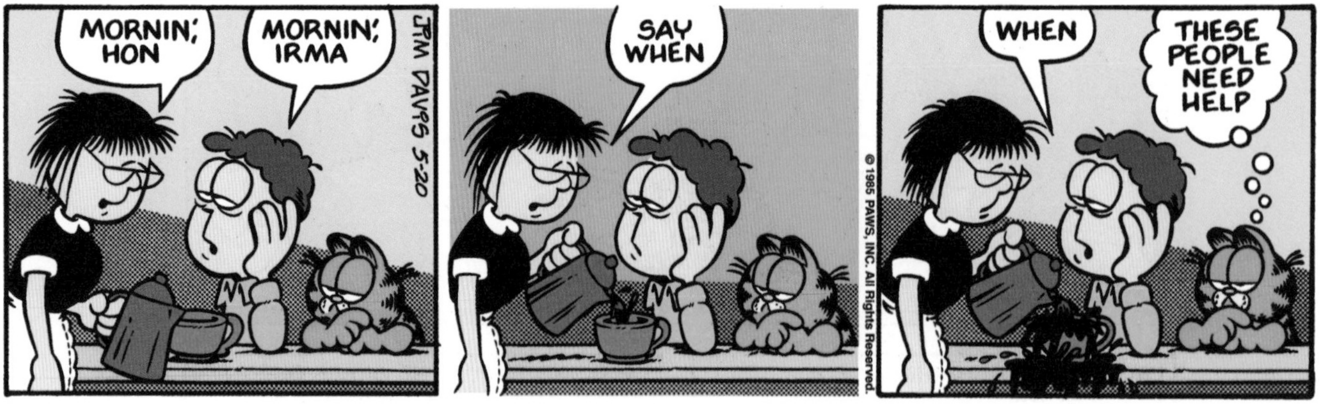
MORNIN', HON
MORNIN', IRMA
JIM DAVIS 5-20
SAY WHEN
© 1985 PAWS, INC. All Rights Reserved.
WHEN
THESE PEOPLE NEED HELP

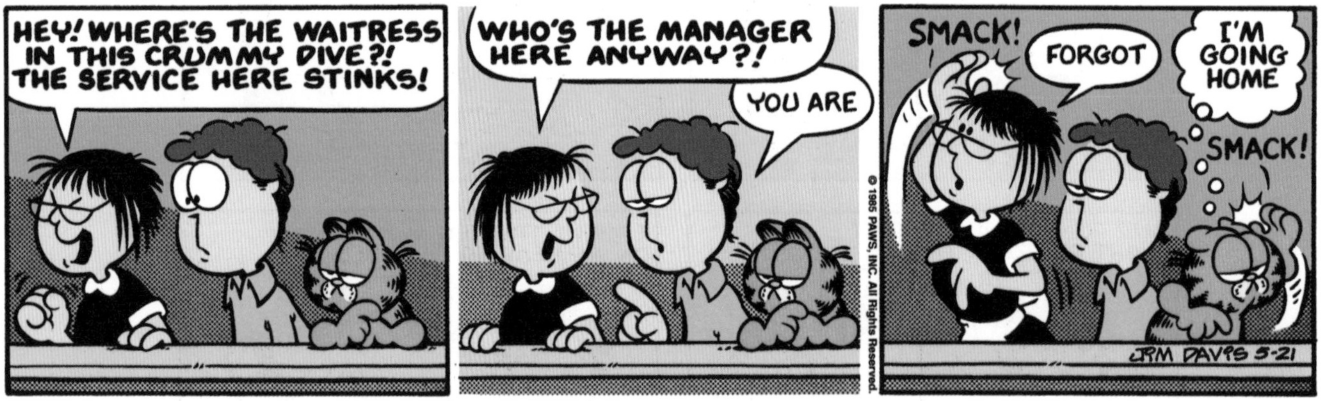
HEY! WHERE'S THE WAITRESS IN THIS CRUMMY DIVE?! THE SERVICE HERE STINKS!
WHO'S THE MANAGER HERE ANYWAY?!
YOU ARE
© 1985 PAWS, INC. All Rights Reserved.
SMACK!
FORGOT
I'M GOING HOME
SMACK!
JIM DAVIS 5-21

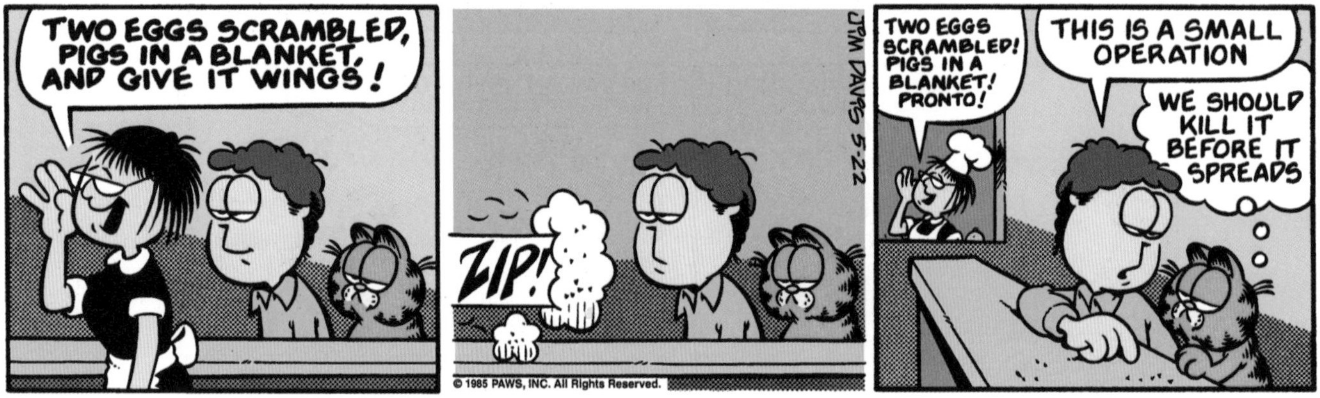
TWO EGGS SCRAMBLED, PIGS IN A BLANKET, AND GIVE IT WINGS!
JIM DAVIS 5-22
ZIP!
© 1985 PAWS, INC. All Rights Reserved.
TWO EGGS SCRAMBLED! PIGS IN A BLANKET! PRONTO!
THIS IS A SMALL OPERATION
WE SHOULD KILL IT BEFORE IT SPREADS

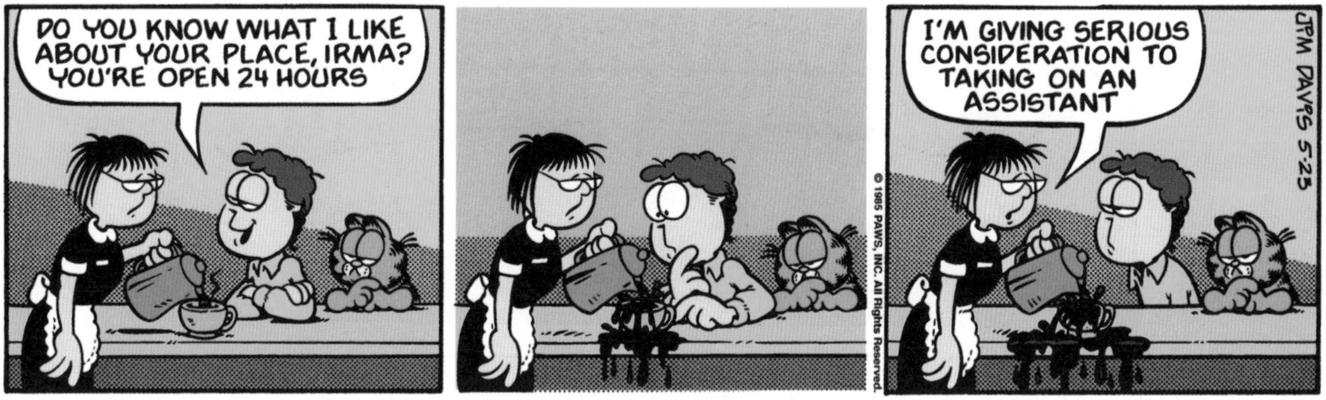
DO YOU KNOW WHAT I LIKE ABOUT YOUR PLACE, IRMA? YOU'RE OPEN 24 HOURS
© 1985 PAWS, INC. All Rights Reserved.
I'M GIVING SERIOUS CONSIDERATION TO TAKING ON AN ASSISTANT
JIM DAVIS 5-23

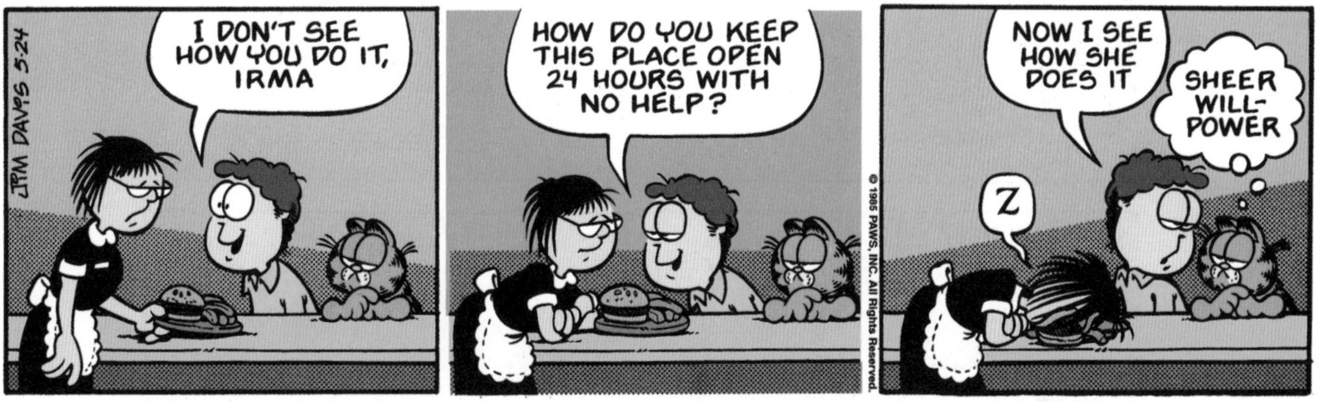
JIM DAVIS 5-24
I DON'T SEE HOW YOU DO IT, IRMA
HOW DO YOU KEEP THIS PLACE OPEN 24 HOURS WITH NO HELP?
© 1985 PAWS, INC. All Rights Reserved.
NOW I SEE HOW SHE DOES IT
SHEER WILL-POWER
Z

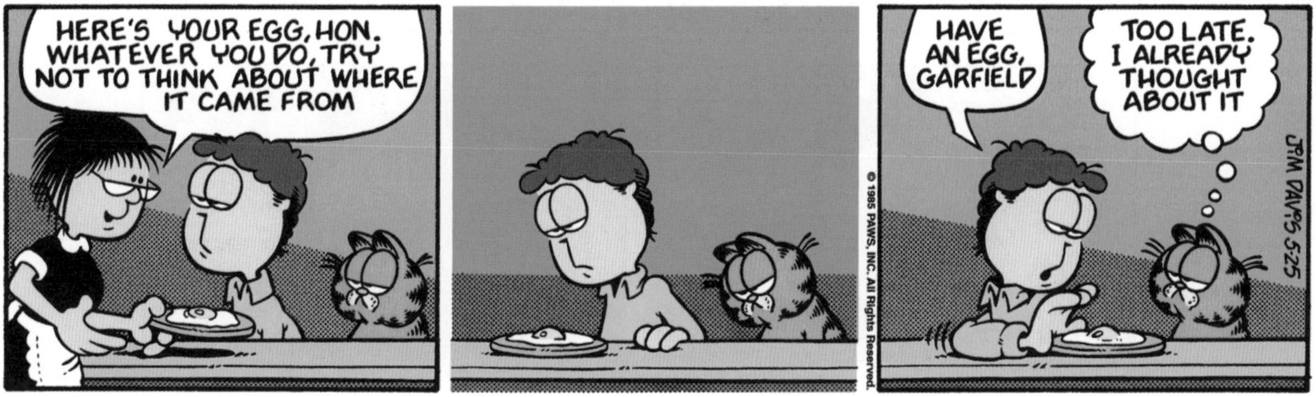
HERE'S YOUR EGG, HON. WHATEVER YOU DO, TRY NOT TO THINK ABOUT WHERE IT CAME FROM
© 1985 PAWS, INC. All Rights Reserved.
HAVE AN EGG, GARFIELD
TOO LATE. I ALREADY THOUGHT ABOUT IT
JIM DAVIS 5-25

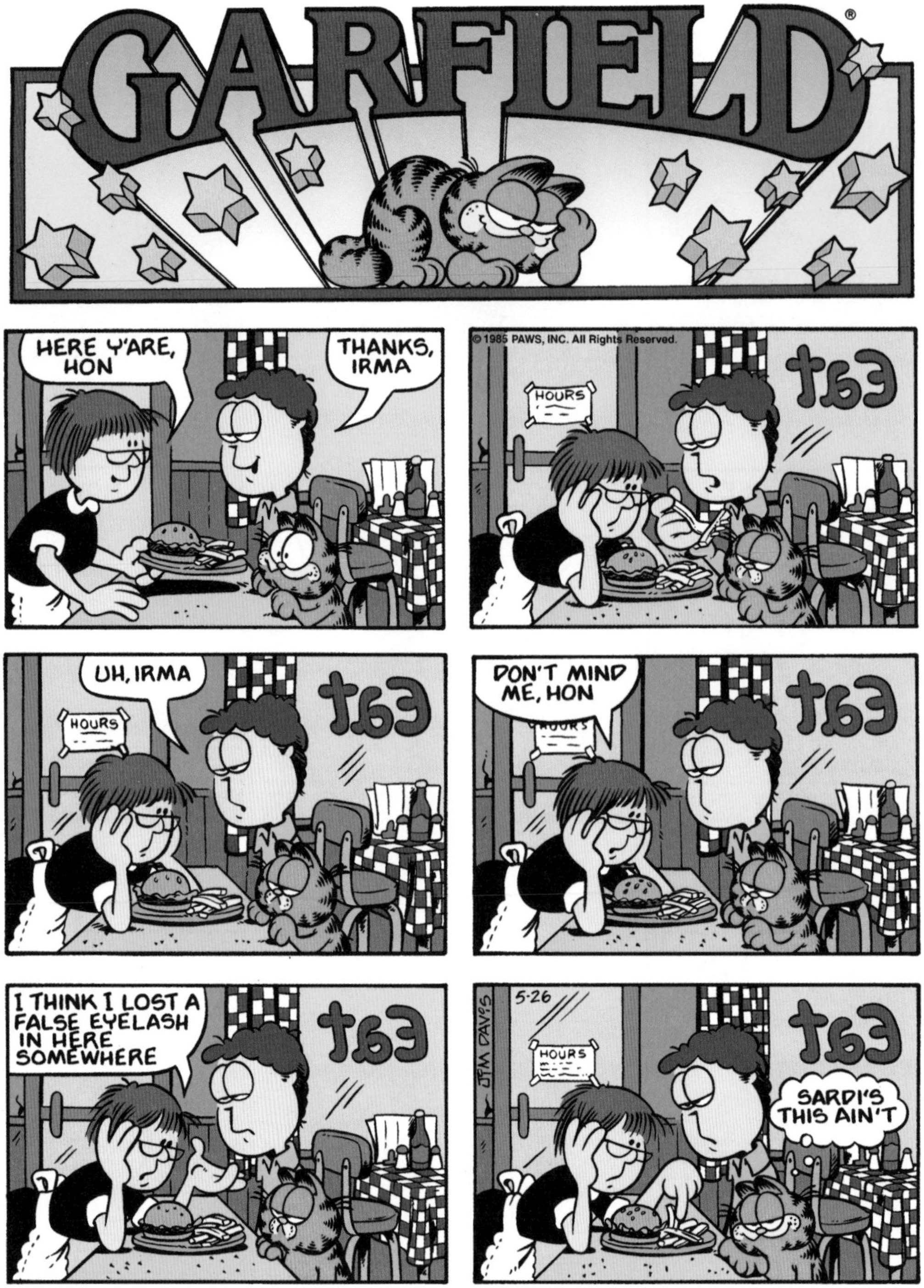
GARFIELD®
HERE Y'ARE, HON
THANKS, IRMA
© 1985 PAWS, INC. All Rights Reserved.
HOURS
UH, IRMA
HOURS
DON'T MIND ME, HON
HOURS
I THINK I LOST A FALSE EYELASH IN HERE SOMEWHERE
JPM DAVIS 5-26
HOURS
SARDI'S THIS AIN'T

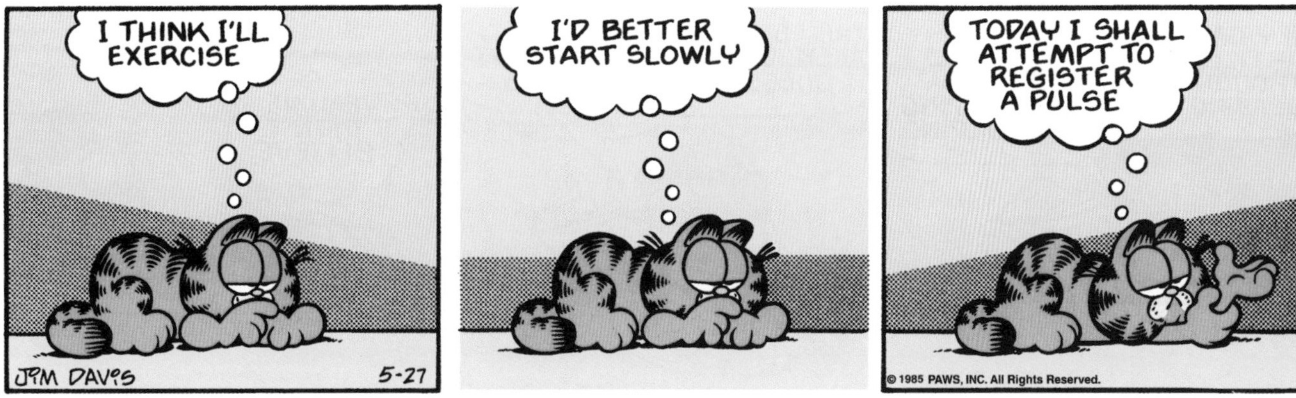
I THINK I'LL EXERCISE
JIM DAVIS
5-27
I'D BETTER START SLOWLY
TODAY I SHALL ATTEMPT TO REGISTER A PULSE
© 1985 PAWS, INC. All Rights Reserved.

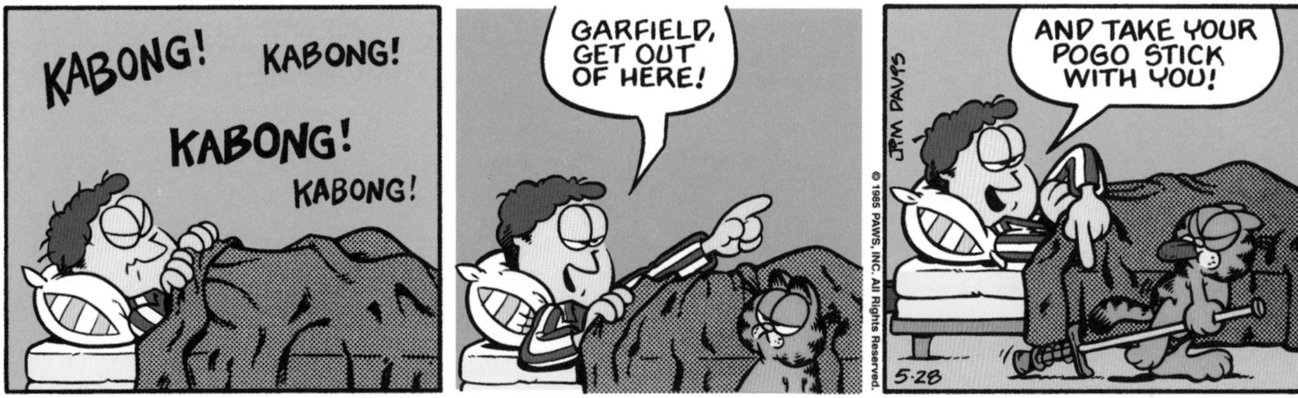
KABONG! KABONG!
KABONG!
KABONG!
GARFIELD, GET OUT OF HERE!
© 1985 PAWS, INC. All Rights Reserved.
JIM DAVIS
AND TAKE YOUR POGO STICK WITH YOU!
5-28

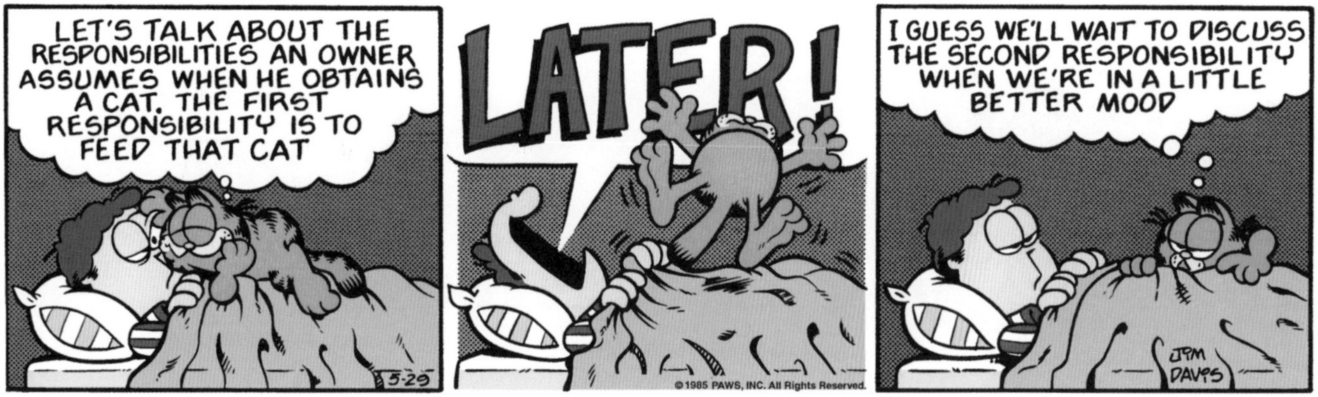
LET'S TALK ABOUT THE RESPONSIBILITIES AN OWNER ASSUMES WHEN HE OBTAINS A CAT. THE FIRST RESPONSIBILITY IS TO FEED THAT CAT
5-29
LATER!
© 1985 PAWS, INC. All Rights Reserved.
I GUESS WE'LL WAIT TO DISCUSS THE SECOND RESPONSIBILITY WHEN WE'RE IN A LITTLE BETTER MOOD
JIM DAVIS

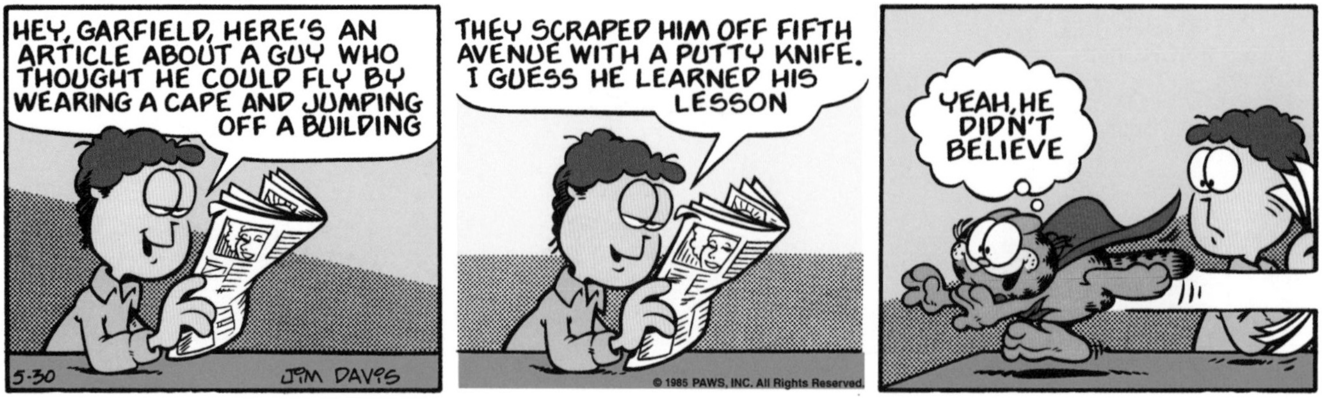
HEY, GARFIELD, HERE'S AN ARTICLE ABOUT A GUY WHO THOUGHT HE COULD FLY BY WEARING A CAPE AND JUMPING OFF A BUILDING
5-30
JIM DAVIS
THEY SCRAPED HIM OFF FIFTH AVENUE WITH A PUTTY KNIFE. I GUESS HE LEARNED HIS LESSON
© 1985 PAWS, INC. All Rights Reserved.
YEAH, HE DIDN'T BELIEVE

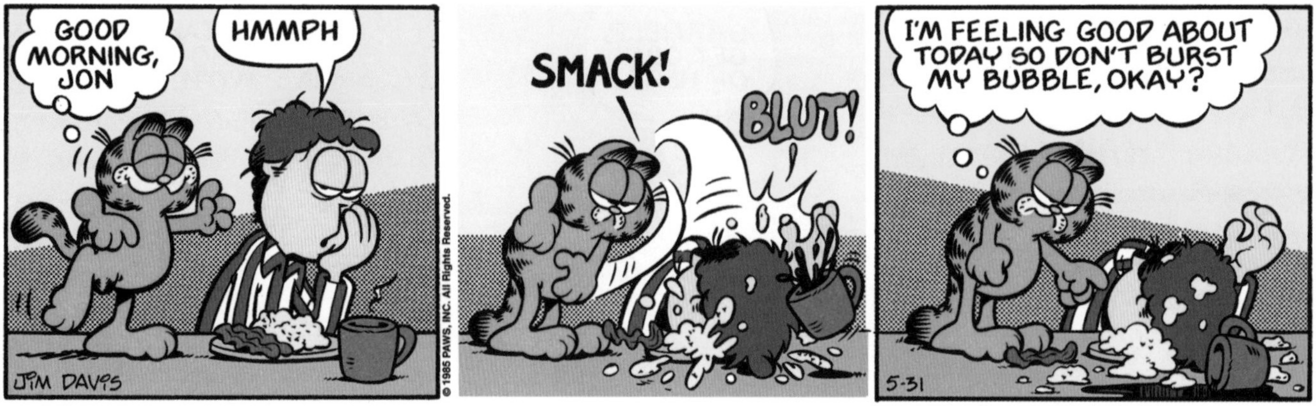
GOOD MORNING, JON
HMMPH
JIM DAVIS
© 1985 PAWS, INC. All Rights Reserved.
SMACK!
BLUT!
I'M FEELING GOOD ABOUT TODAY SO DON'T BURST MY BUBBLE, OKAY?
5-31

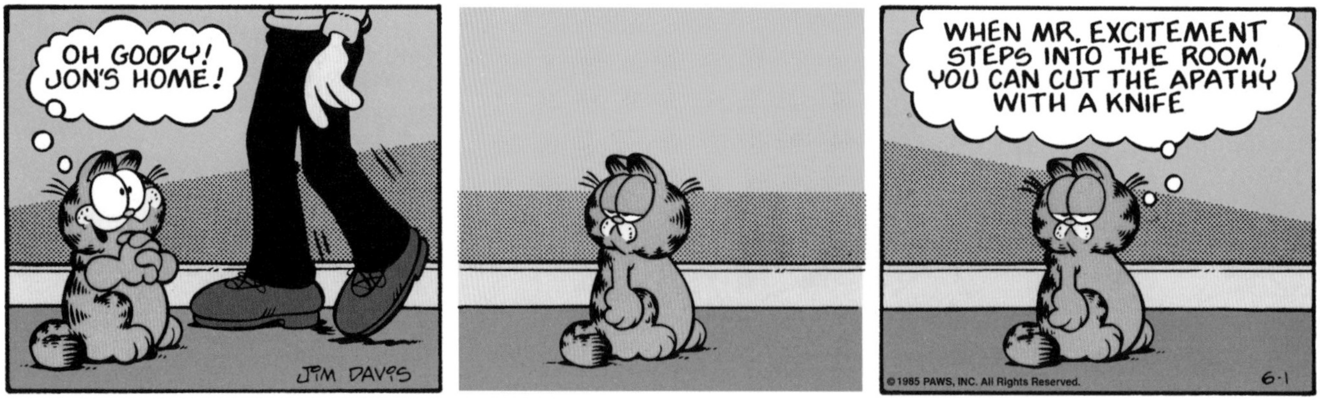
OH GOODY! JON'S HOME!
JIM DAVIS
WHEN MR. EXCITEMENT STEPS INTO THE ROOM, YOU CAN CUT THE APATHY WITH A KNIFE
© 1985 PAWS, INC. All Rights Reserved.
6-1

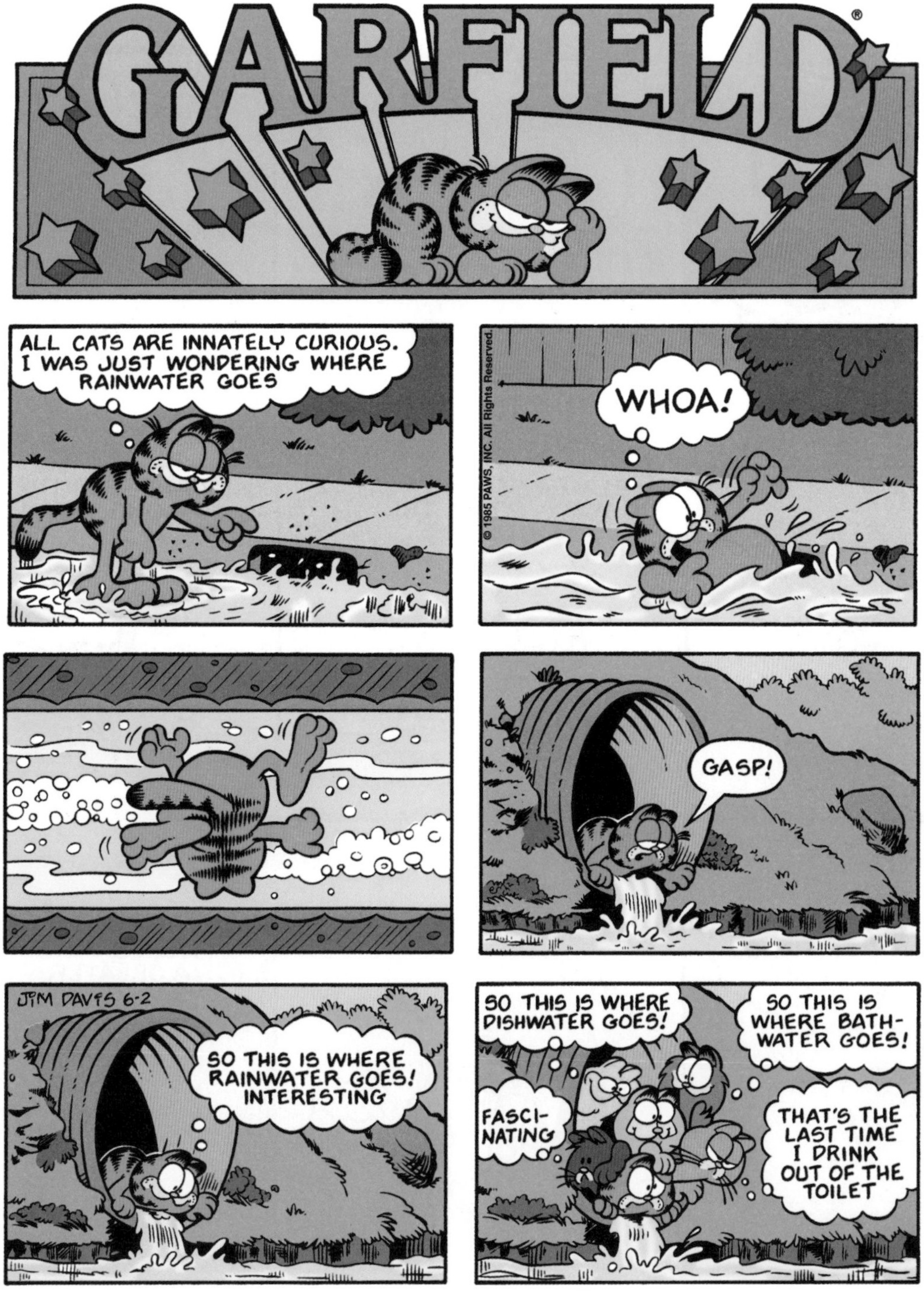
GARFIELD
ALL CATS ARE INNATELY CURIOUS. I WAS JUST WONDERING WHERE RAINWATER GOES
© 1985 PAWS, INC. All Rights Reserved.
WHOA!
GASP!
JIM DAVIS 6-2
SO THIS IS WHERE RAINWATER GOES! INTERESTING
SO THIS IS WHERE DISHWATER GOES!
SO THIS IS WHERE BATH-WATER GOES!
FASCI-NATING
THAT'S THE LAST TIME I DRINK OUT OF THE TOILET

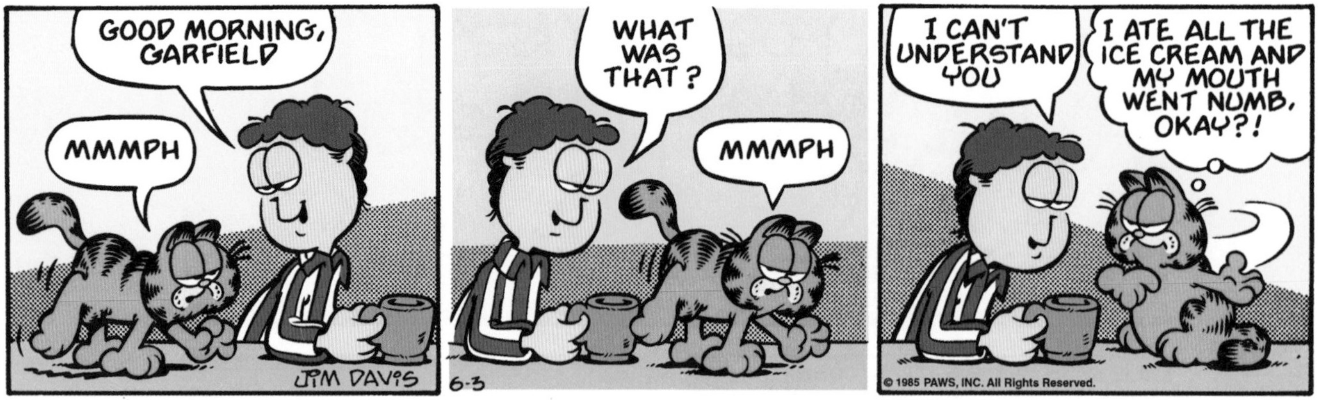
GOOD MORNING, GARFIELD
MMMPH
JIM DAVIS
WHAT WAS THAT?
MMMPH
6-3
I CAN'T UNDERSTAND YOU
I ATE ALL THE ICE CREAM AND MY MOUTH WENT NUMB, OKAY?!
© 1985 PAWS, INC. All Rights Reserved.

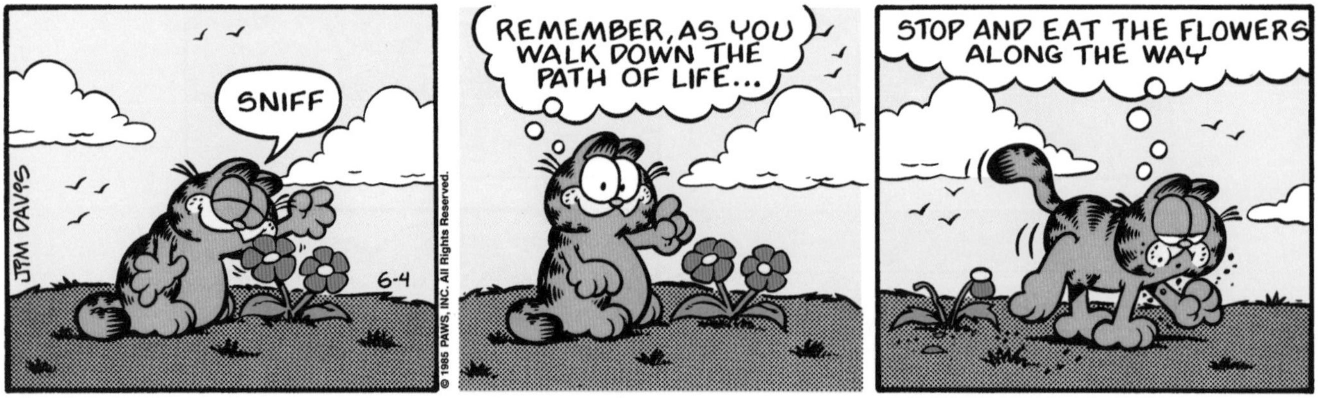
JIM DAVIS
SNIFF
6-4
© 1985 PAWS, INC. All Rights Reserved.
REMEMBER, AS YOU WALK DOWN THE PATH OF LIFE...
STOP AND EAT THE FLOWERS ALONG THE WAY

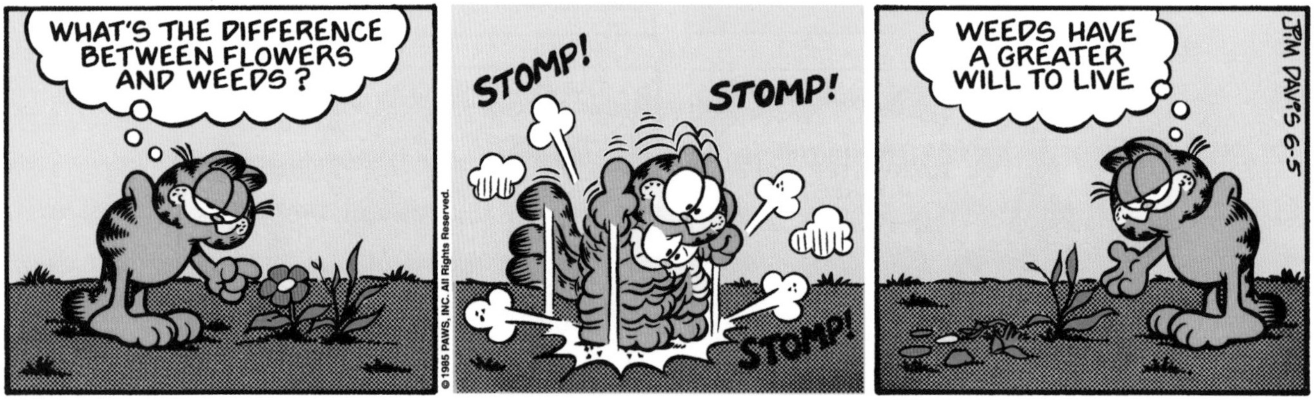
WHAT'S THE DIFFERENCE BETWEEN FLOWERS AND WEEDS?
© 1985 PAWS, INC. All Rights Reserved.
STOMP!
STOMP!
STOMP!
WEEDS HAVE A GREATER WILL TO LIVE
JIM DAVIS 6-5

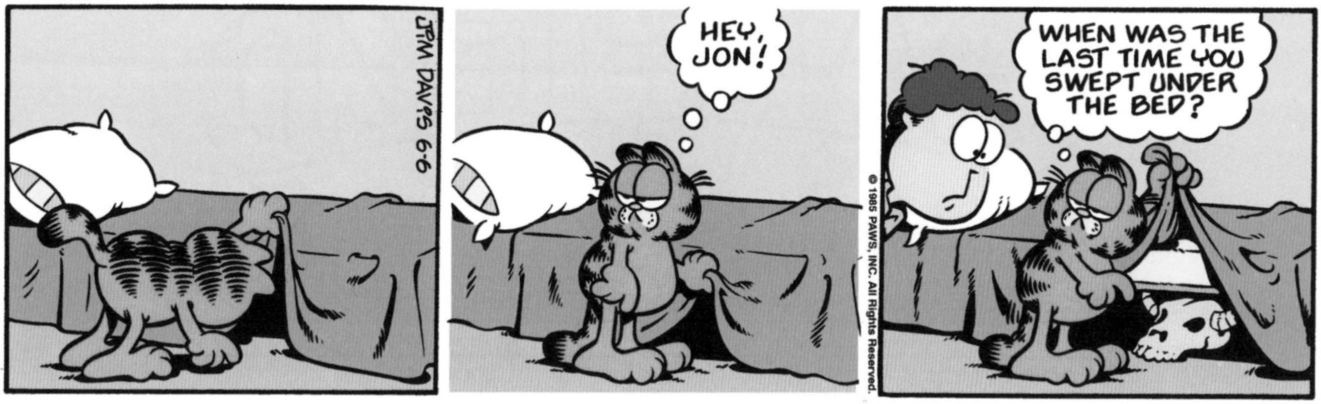
JIM DAVIS 6-6
HEY, JON!
© 1985 PAWS, INC. All Rights Reserved.
WHEN WAS THE LAST TIME YOU SWEPT UNDER THE BED?

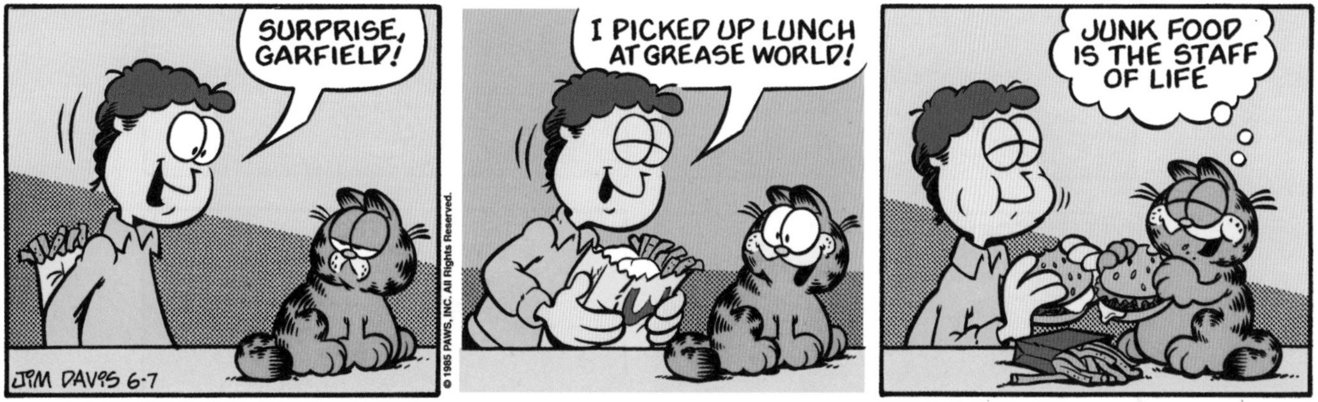
SURPRISE, GARFIELD!
JIM DAVIS 6-7
© 1985 PAWS, INC. All Rights Reserved.
I PICKED UP LUNCH AT GREASE WORLD!
JUNK FOOD IS THE STAFF OF LIFE

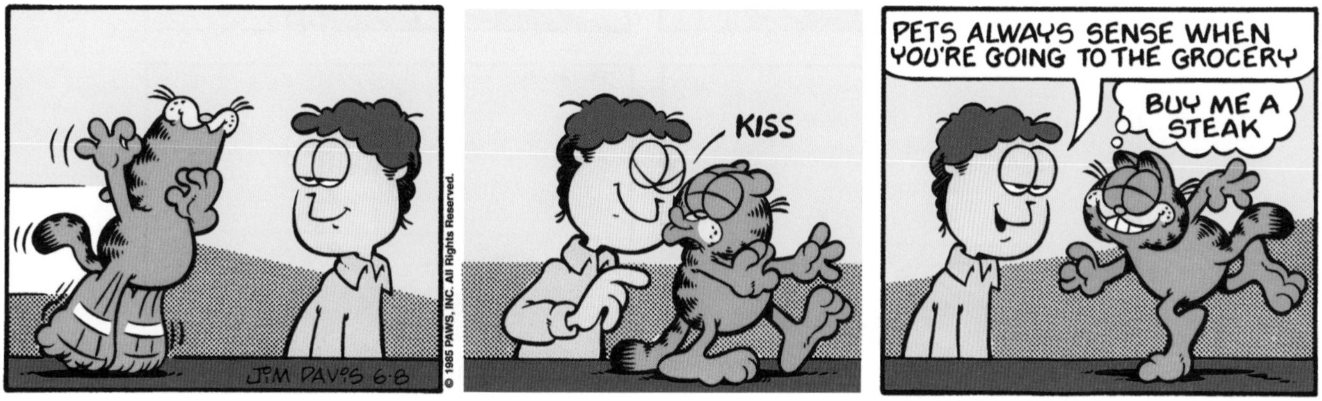
JIM DAVIS 6-8
© 1985 PAWS, INC. All Rights Reserved.
KISS
PETS ALWAYS SENSE WHEN YOU'RE GOING TO THE GROCERY
BUY ME A STEAK

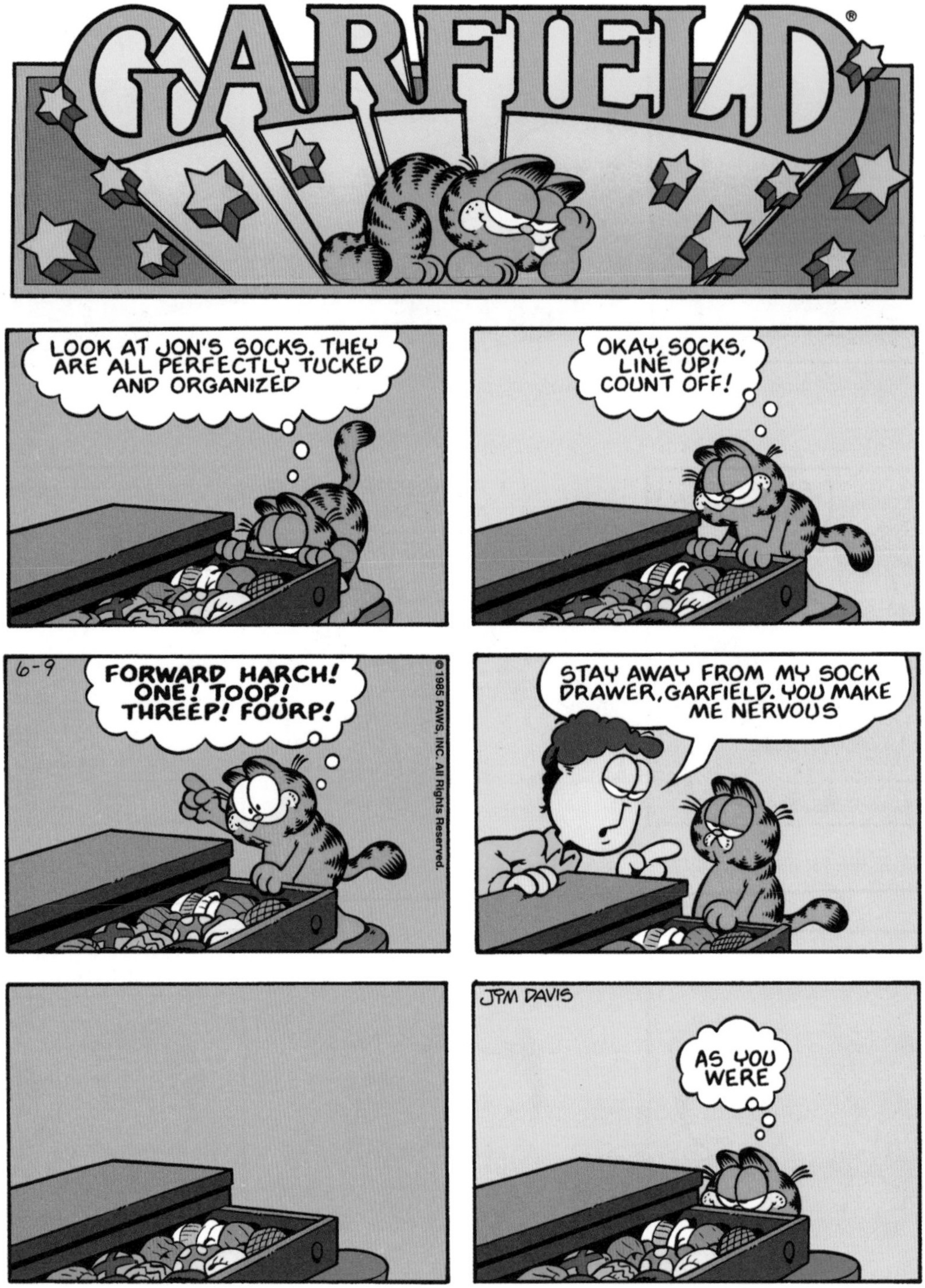
GARFIELD®
LOOK AT JON'S SOCKS. THEY ARE ALL PERFECTLY TUCKED AND ORGANIZED
OKAY, SOCKS, LINE UP! COUNT OFF!
6-9
FORWARD HARCH! ONE! TOOP! THREEP! FOURP!
© 1985 PAWS, INC. All Rights Reserved.
STAY AWAY FROM MY SOCK DRAWER, GARFIELD. YOU MAKE ME NERVOUS
JIM DAVIS
AS YOU WERE

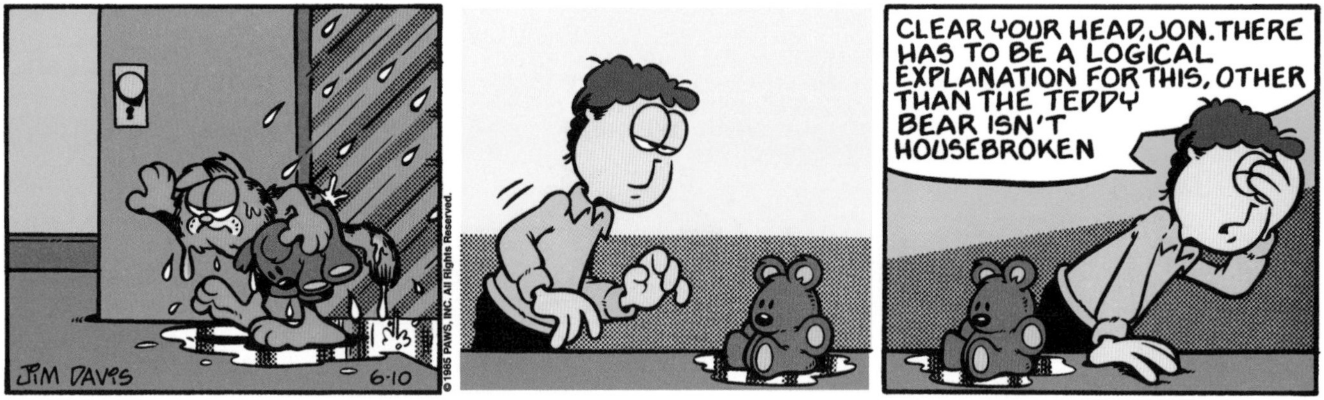
JIM DAVIS
6-10
© 1985 PAWS, INC. All Rights Reserved.
CLEAR YOUR HEAD, JON. THERE HAS TO BE A LOGICAL EXPLANATION FOR THIS, OTHER THAN THE TEDDY BEAR ISN'T HOUSEBROKEN

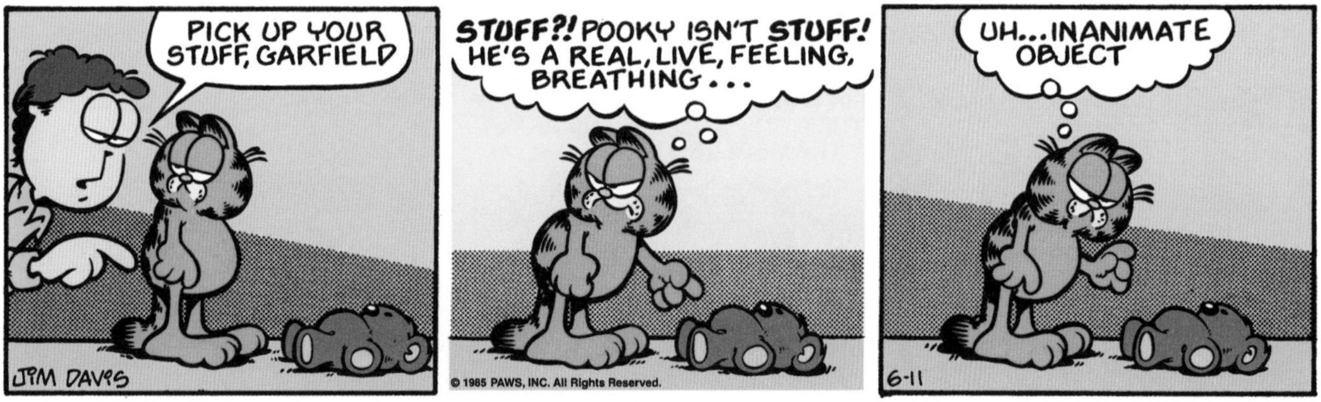
PICK UP YOUR STUFF, GARFIELD
JIM DAVIS
STUFF?! POOKY ISN'T STUFF! HE'S A REAL, LIVE, FEELING, BREATHING . . .
© 1985 PAWS, INC. All Rights Reserved.
UH...INANIMATE OBJECT
6-11

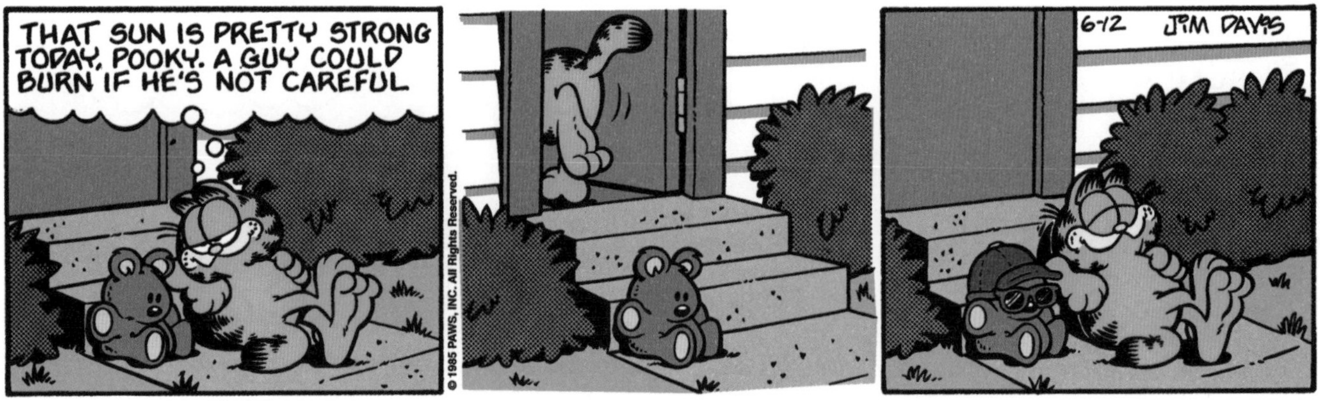
THAT SUN IS PRETTY STRONG TODAY, POOKY. A GUY COULD BURN IF HE'S NOT CAREFUL
© 1985 PAWS, INC. All Rights Reserved.
6-12 JIM DAVIS

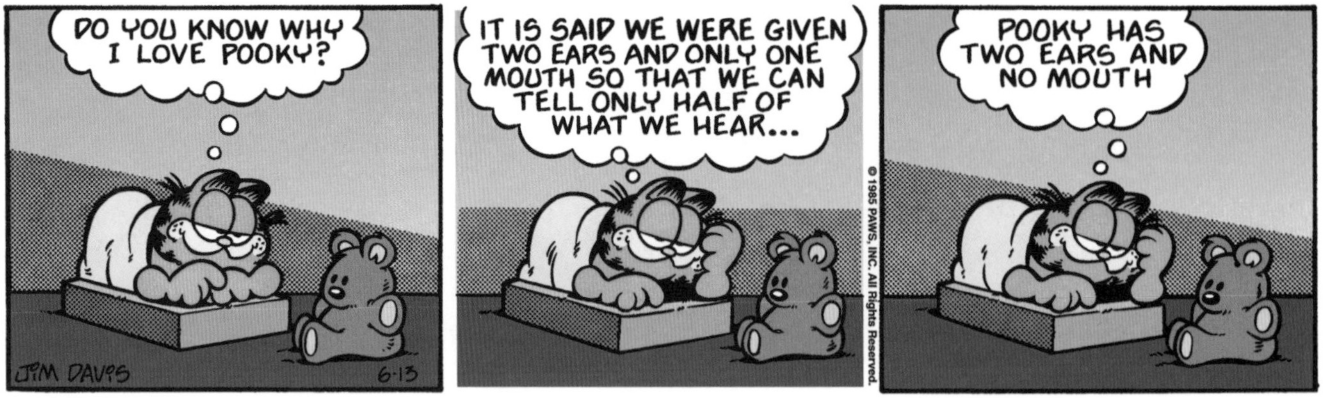
DO YOU KNOW WHY I LOVE POOKY?
JIM DAVIS
6-13
IT IS SAID WE WERE GIVEN TWO EARS AND ONLY ONE MOUTH SO THAT WE CAN TELL ONLY HALF OF WHAT WE HEAR...
© 1985 PAWS, INC. All Rights Reserved.
POOKY HAS TWO EARS AND NO MOUTH

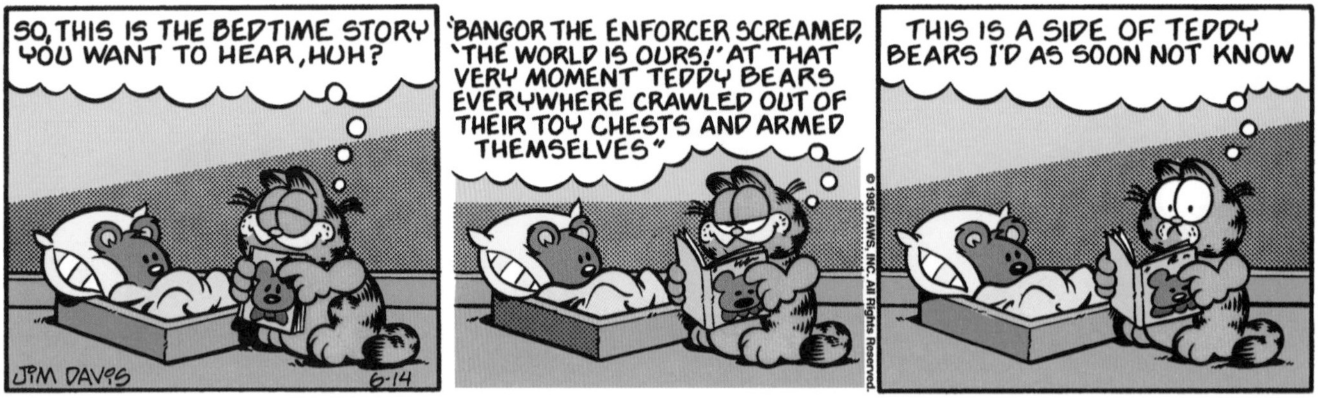
SO, THIS IS THE BEDTIME STORY YOU WANT TO HEAR, HUH?
JIM DAVIS
6-14
'BANGOR THE ENFORCER SCREAMED, 'THE WORLD IS OURS!' AT THAT VERY MOMENT TEDDY BEARS EVERYWHERE CRAWLED OUT OF THEIR TOY CHESTS AND ARMED THEMSELVES"
© 1985 PAWS, INC. All Rights Reserved.
THIS IS A SIDE OF TEDDY BEARS I'D AS SOON NOT KNOW

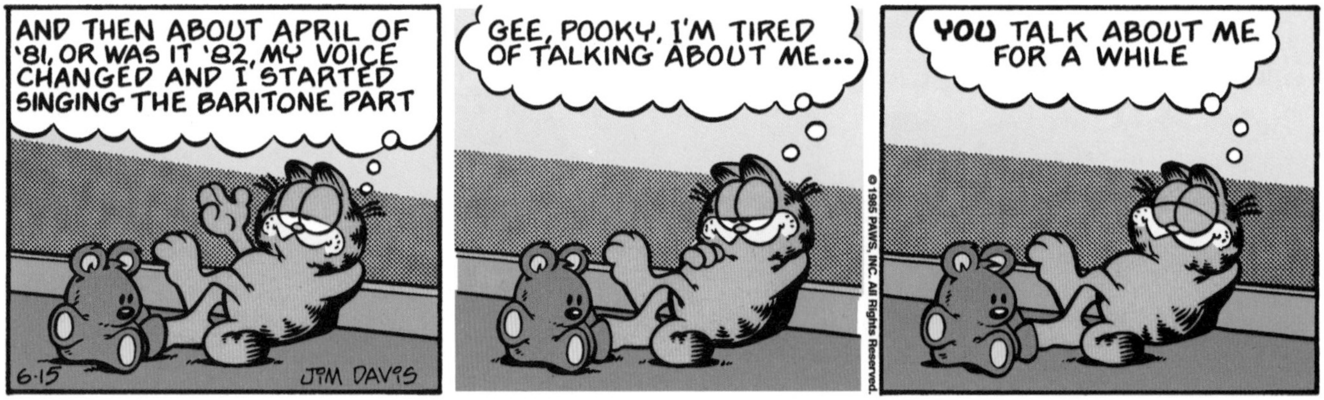
AND THEN ABOUT APRIL OF '81, OR WAS IT '82, MY VOICE CHANGED AND I STARTED SINGING THE BARITONE PART
6-15
JIM DAVIS
GEE, POOKY, I'M TIRED OF TALKING ABOUT ME...
© 1985 PAWS, INC. All Rights Reserved.
YOU TALK ABOUT ME FOR A WHILE

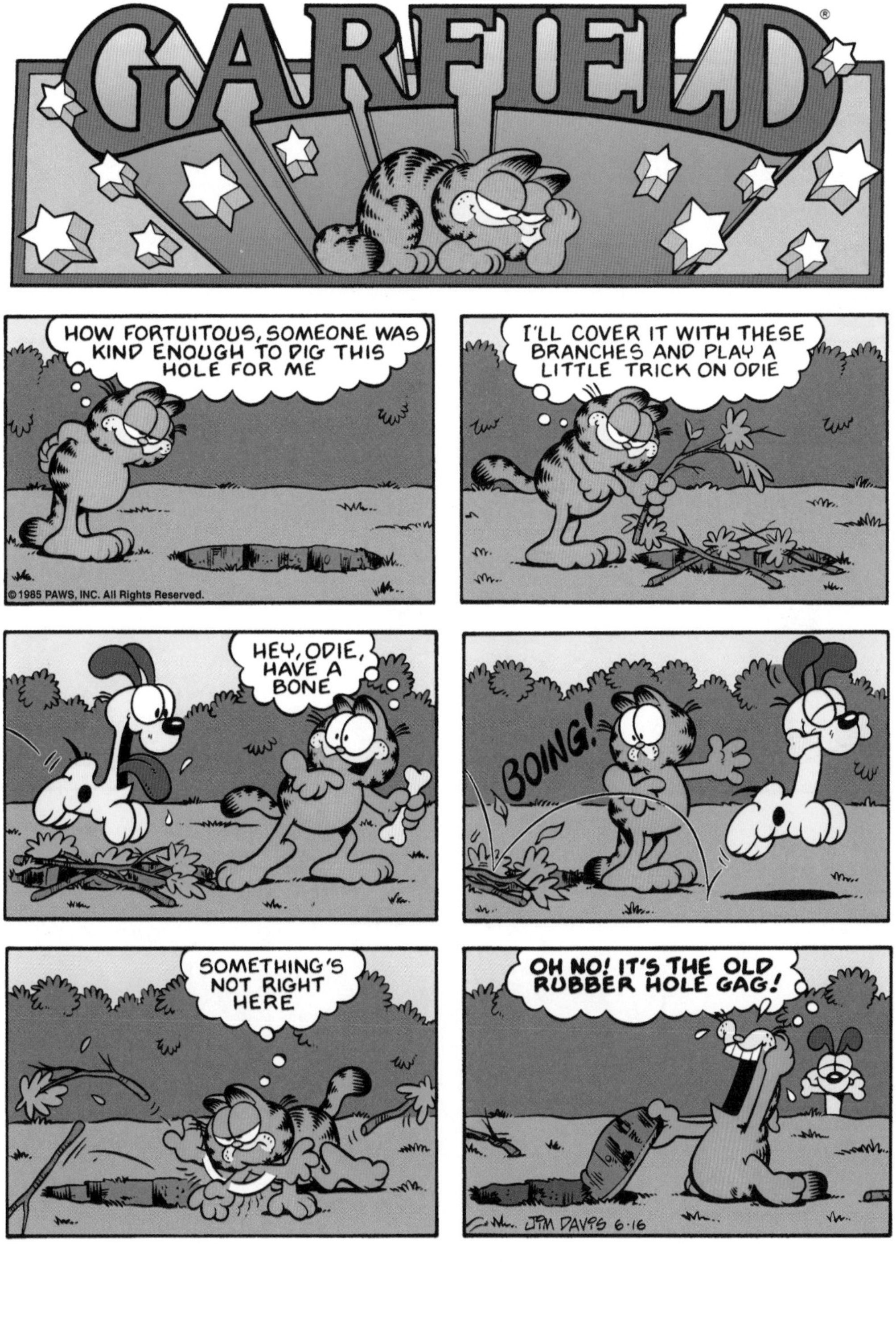
GARFIELD
HOW FORTUITOUS, SOMEONE WAS KIND ENOUGH TO DIG THIS HOLE FOR ME
© 1985 PAWS, INC. All Rights Reserved.
I'LL COVER IT WITH THESE BRANCHES AND PLAY A LITTLE TRICK ON ODIE
HEY, ODIE, HAVE A BONE
BOING!
SOMETHING'S NOT RIGHT HERE
OH NO! IT'S THE OLD RUBBER HOLE GAG!
JIM DAVIS 6-16

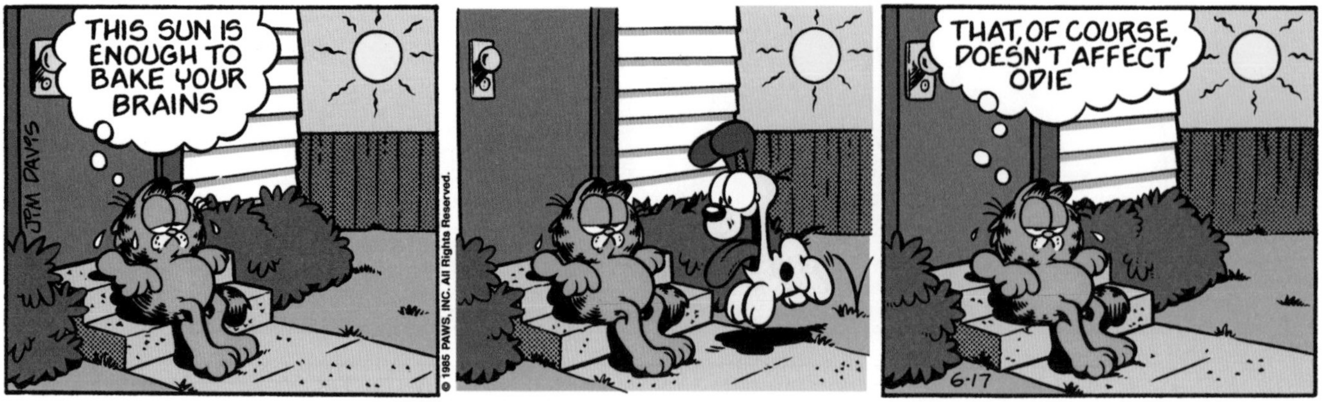
THIS SUN IS ENOUGH TO BAKE YOUR BRAINS
JIM DAVIS
© 1985 PAWS, INC. All Rights Reserved.
THAT, OF COURSE, DOESN'T AFFECT ODIE
6-17

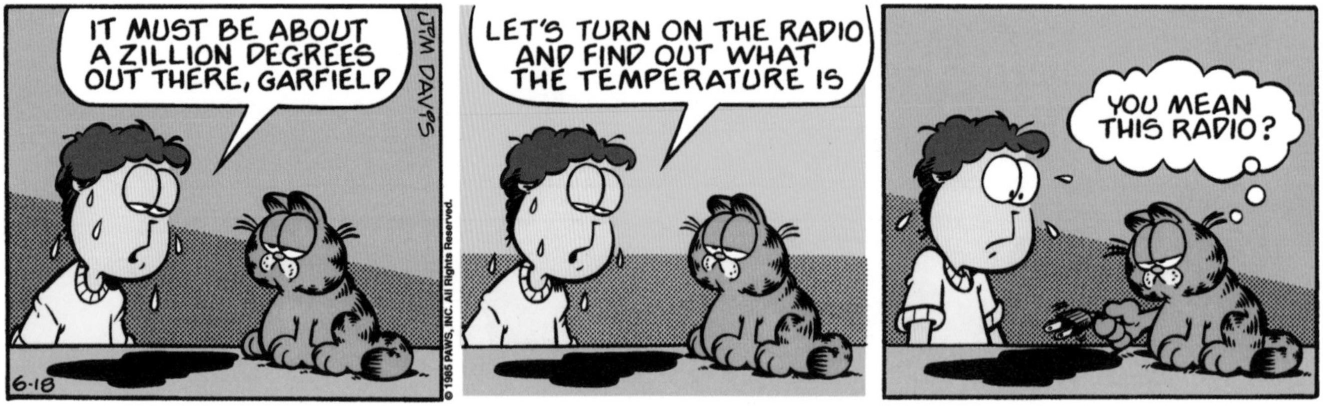
IT MUST BE ABOUT A ZILLION DEGREES OUT THERE, GARFIELD
JIM DAVIS
6-18
© 1985 PAWS, INC. All Rights Reserved.
LET'S TURN ON THE RADIO AND FIND OUT WHAT THE TEMPERATURE IS
YOU MEAN THIS RADIO?

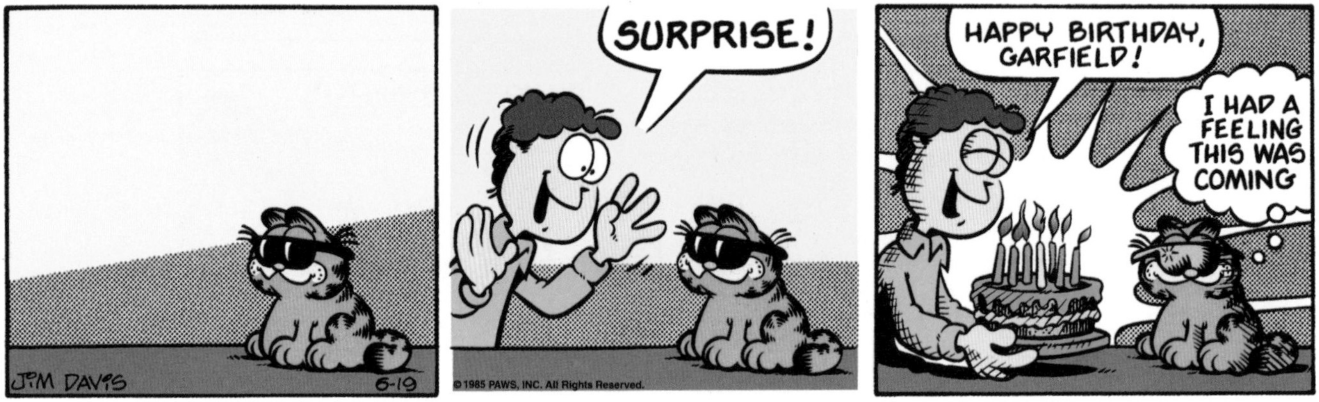
JIM DAVIS
6-19
SURPRISE!
© 1985 PAWS, INC. All Rights Reserved.
HAPPY BIRTHDAY, GARFIELD!
I HAD A FEELING THIS WAS COMING

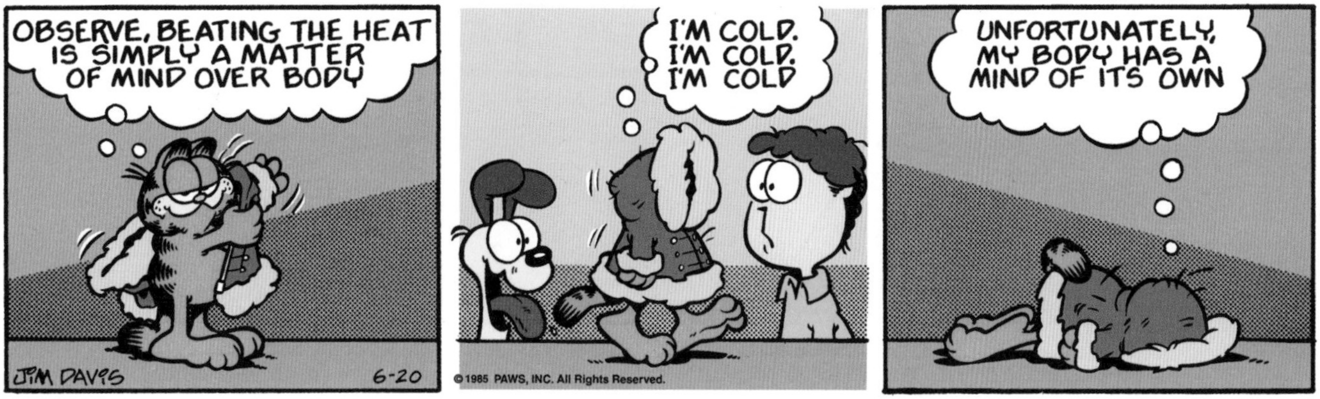
OBSERVE, BEATING THE HEAT IS SIMPLY A MATTER OF MIND OVER BODY
JIM DAVIS 6-20
I'M COLD. I'M COLD. I'M COLD
© 1985 PAWS, INC. All Rights Reserved.
UNFORTUNATELY, MY BODY HAS A MIND OF ITS OWN

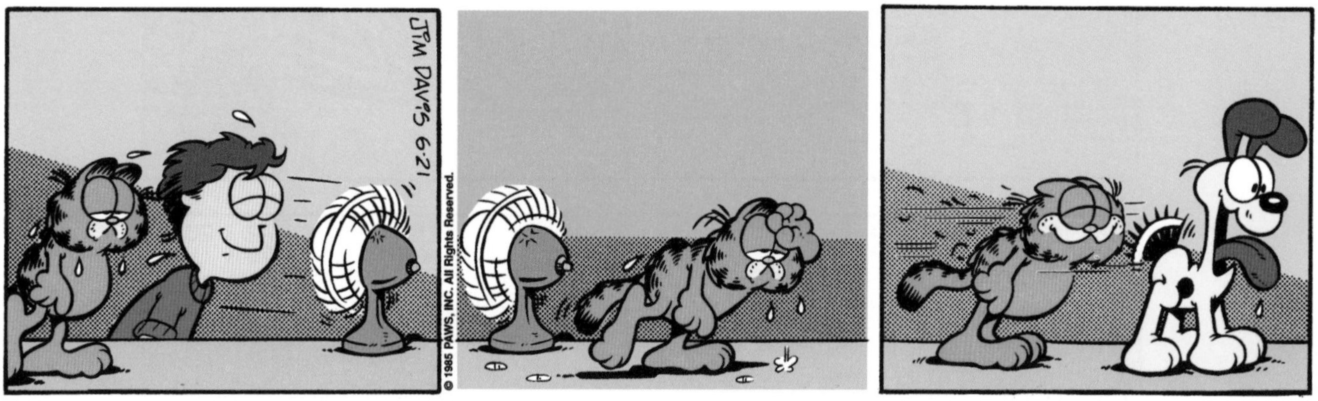
JIM DAVIS 6-21
© 1985 PAWS, INC. All Rights Reserved.

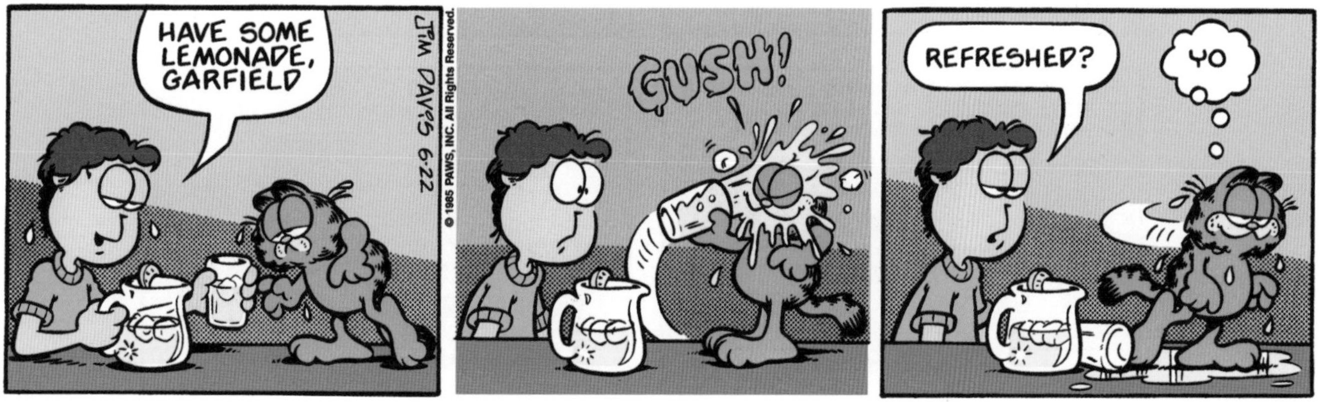
HAVE SOME LEMONADE, GARFIELD
JIM DAVIS 6-22
© 1985 PAWS, INC. All Rights Reserved.
GUSH!
REFRESHED?
YO

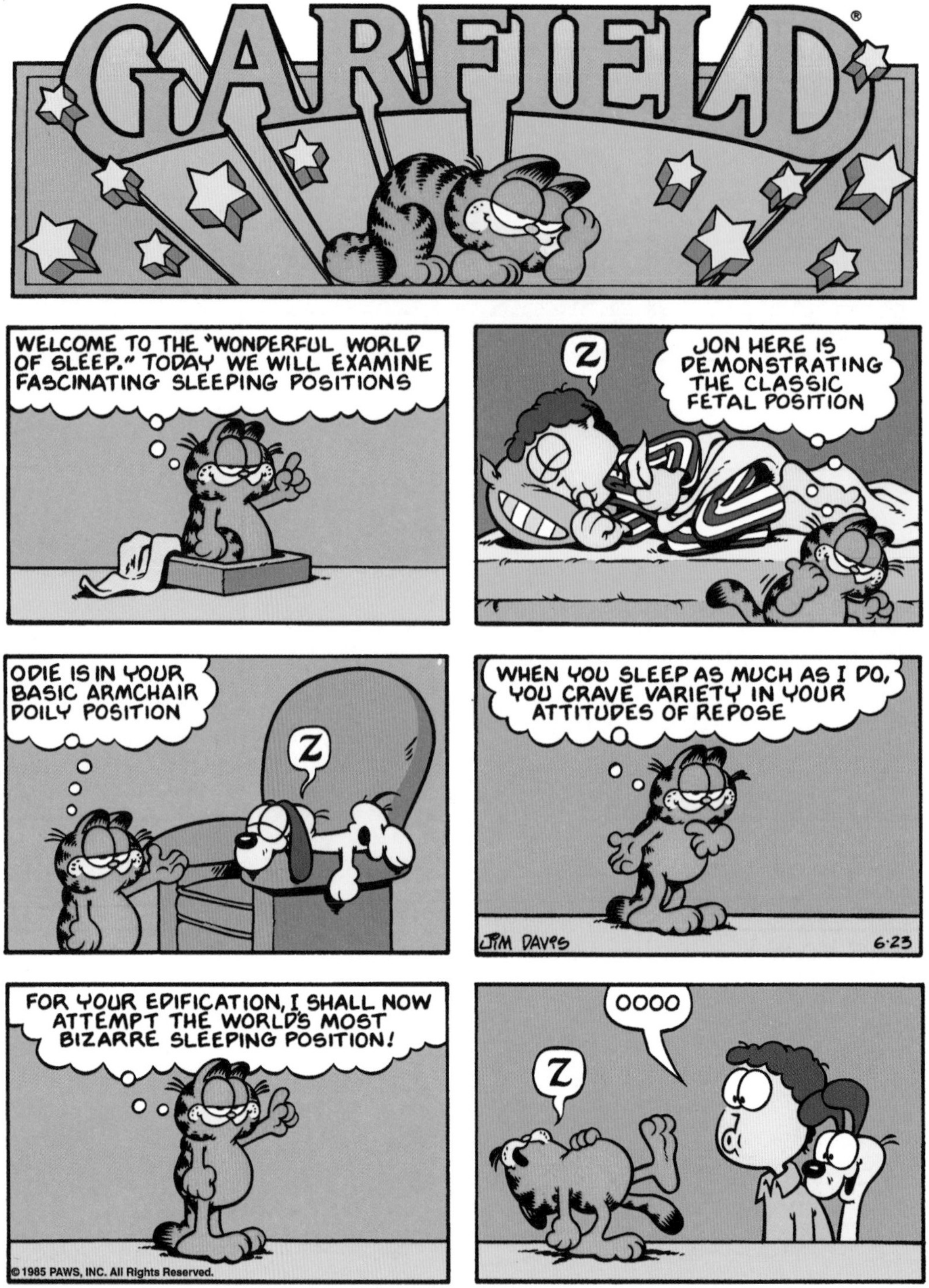
GARFIELD
WELCOME TO THE "WONDERFUL WORLD OF SLEEP." TODAY WE WILL EXAMINE FASCINATING SLEEPING POSITIONS
Z
JON HERE IS DEMONSTRATING THE CLASSIC FETAL POSITION
ODIE IS IN YOUR BASIC ARMCHAIR DOILY POSITION
Z
WHEN YOU SLEEP AS MUCH AS I DO, YOU CRAVE VARIETY IN YOUR ATTITUDES OF REPOSE
JIM DAVIS
6·23
FOR YOUR EDIFICATION, I SHALL NOW ATTEMPT THE WORLD'S MOST BIZARRE SLEEPING POSITION!
© 1985 PAWS, INC. All Rights Reserved.
Z
OOOO

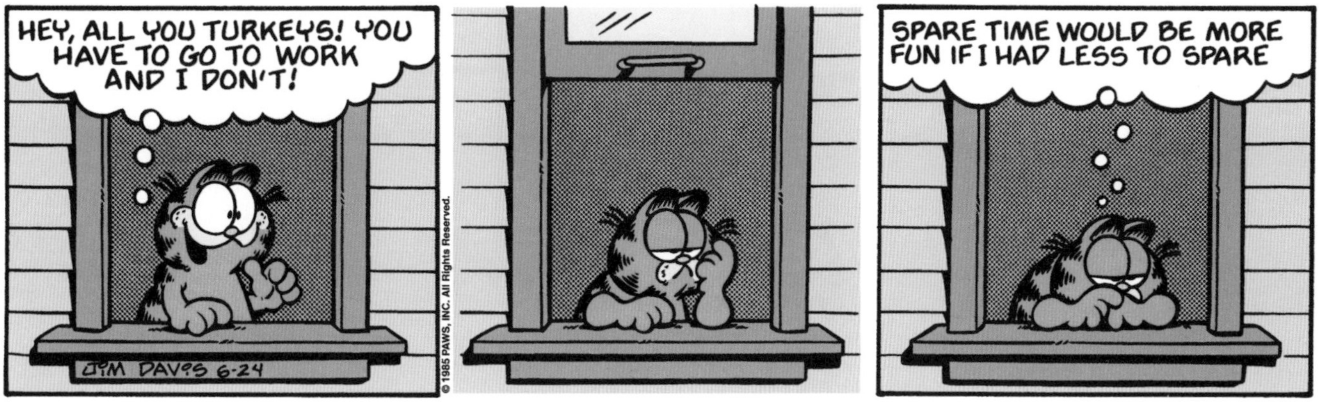
HEY, ALL YOU TURKEYS! YOU HAVE TO GO TO WORK AND I DON'T!
JIM DAVIS 6-24
© 1985 PAWS, INC. All Rights Reserved.
SPARE TIME WOULD BE MORE FUN IF I HAD LESS TO SPARE

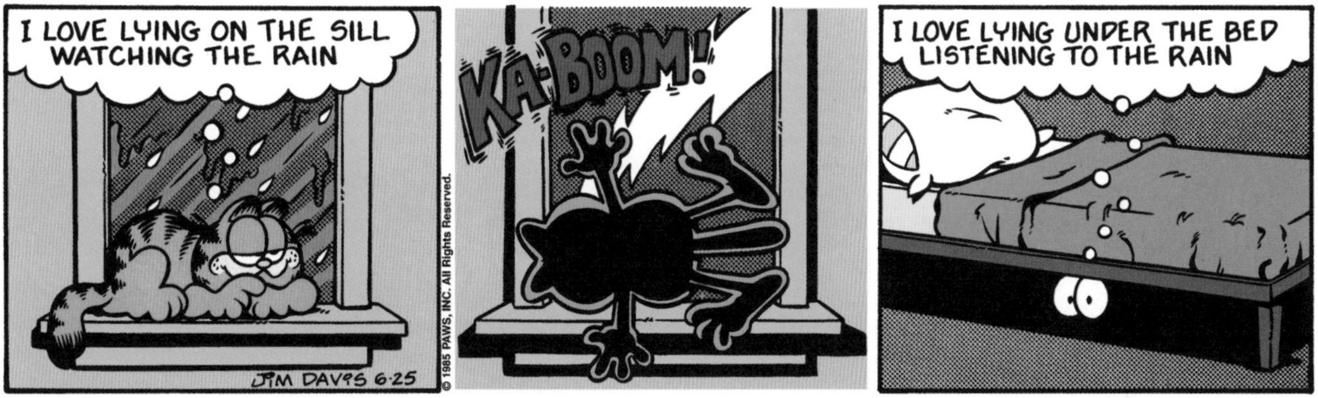
I LOVE LYING ON THE SILL WATCHING THE RAIN
JIM DAVIS 6-25
© 1985 PAWS, INC. All Rights Reserved.
KA-BOOM!
I LOVE LYING UNDER THE BED LISTENING TO THE RAIN

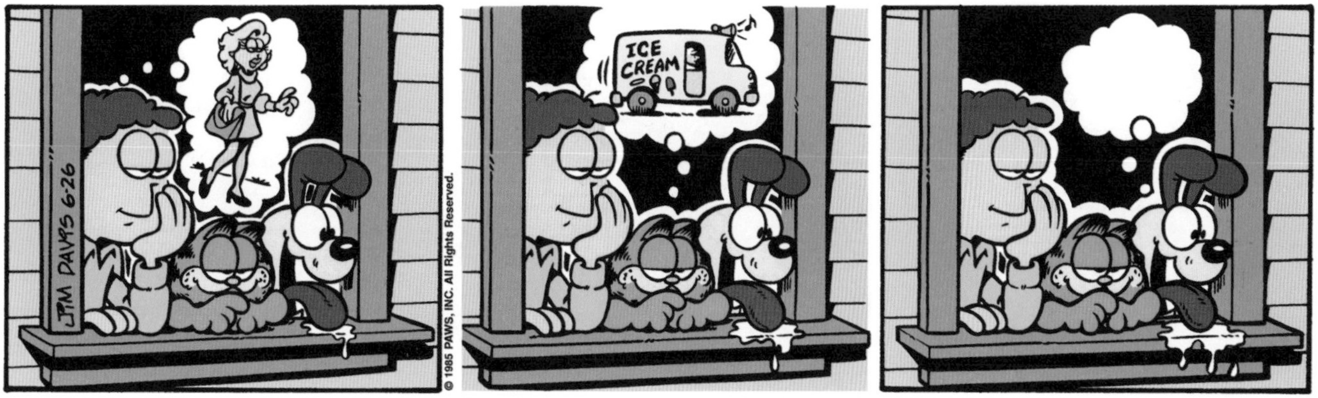
JIM DAVIS 6-26
© 1985 PAWS, INC. All Rights Reserved.
ICE CREAM

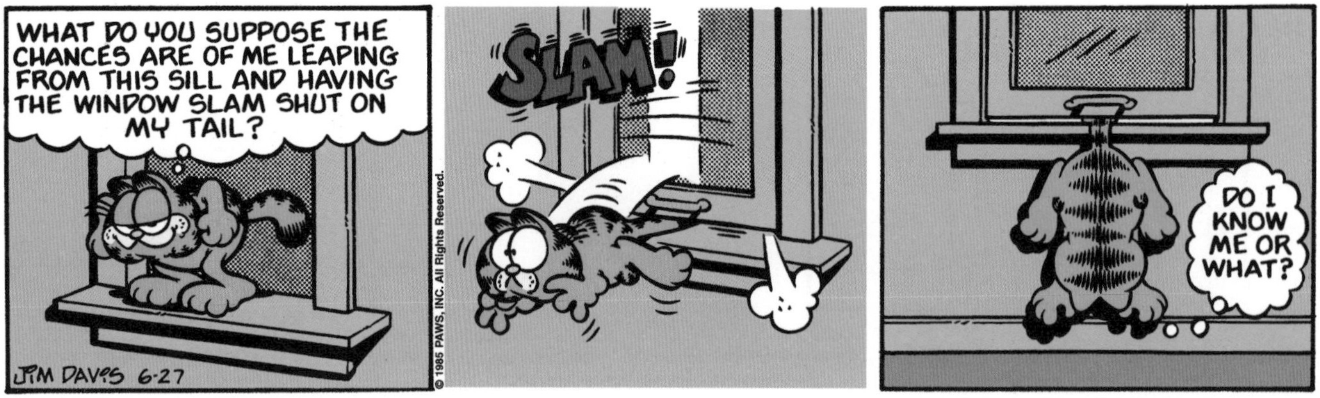
WHAT DO YOU SUPPOSE THE CHANCES ARE OF ME LEAPING FROM THIS SILL AND HAVING THE WINDOW SLAM SHUT ON MY TAIL?
JIM DAVIS 6-27
SLAM!
© 1985 PAWS, INC. All Rights Reserved.
DO I KNOW ME OR WHAT?

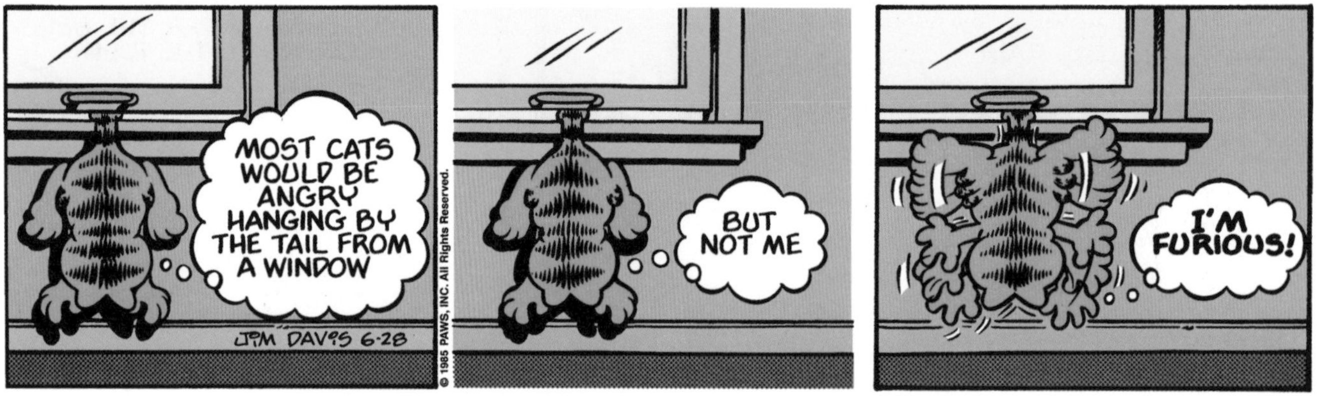
MOST CATS WOULD BE ANGRY HANGING BY THE TAIL FROM A WINDOW
JIM DAVIS 6-28
© 1985 PAWS, INC. All Rights Reserved.
BUT NOT ME
I'M FURIOUS!

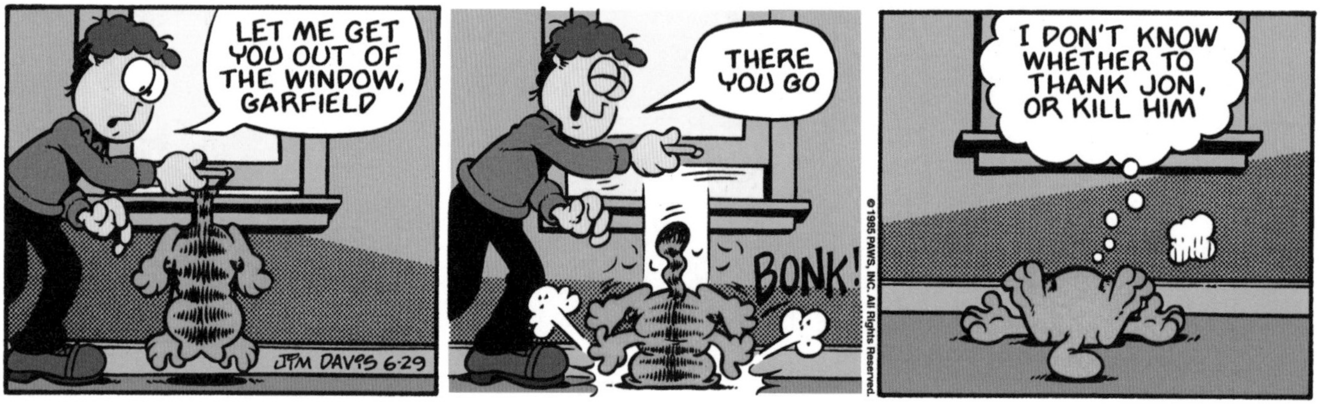
LET ME GET YOU OUT OF THE WINDOW, GARFIELD
JIM DAVIS 6-29
THERE YOU GO
BONK!
© 1985 PAWS, INC. All Rights Reserved.
I DON'T KNOW WHETHER TO THANK JON, OR KILL HIM

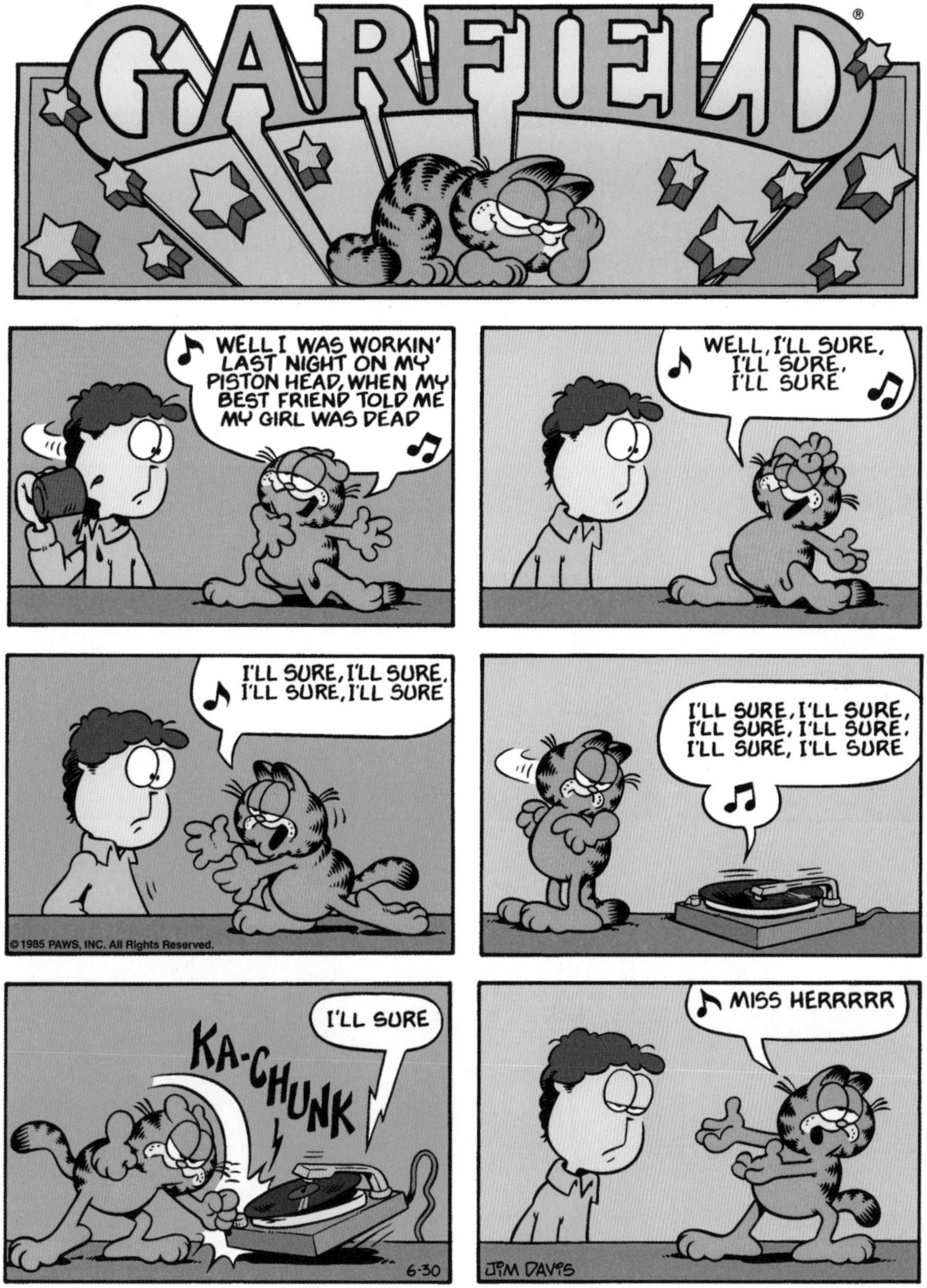
GARFIELD
WELL I WAS WORKIN' LAST NIGHT ON MY PISTON HEAD, WHEN MY BEST FRIEND TOLD ME MY GIRL WAS DEAD
WELL, I'LL SURE, I'LL SURE, I'LL SURE
I'LL SURE, I'LL SURE, I'LL SURE, I'LL SURE
I'LL SURE, I'LL SURE, I'LL SURE, I'LL SURE, I'LL SURE, I'LL SURE
I'LL SURE
KA-CHUNK
MISS HERRRRR
6-30
JIM DAVIS

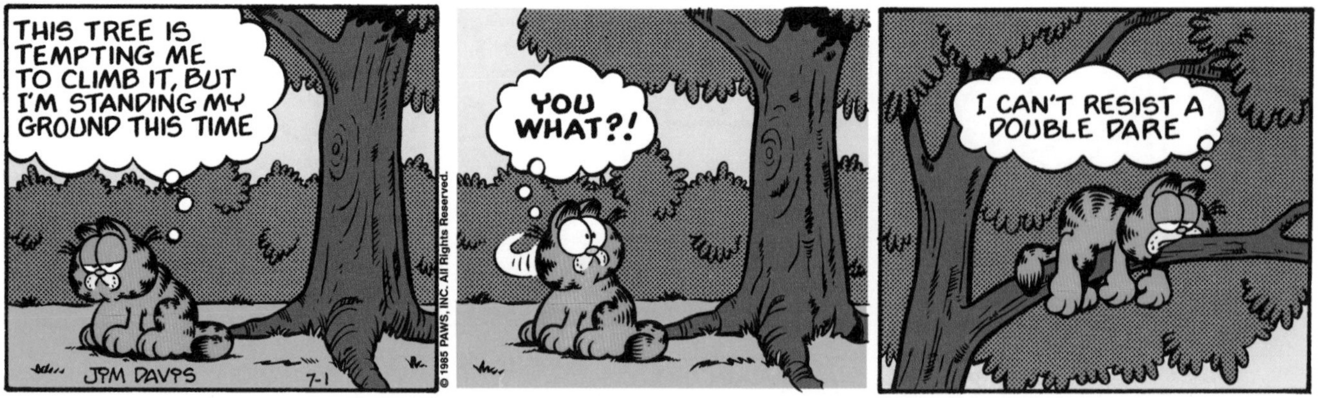
THIS TREE IS TEMPTING ME TO CLIMB IT, BUT I'M STANDING MY GROUND THIS TIME
JIM DAVIS
7-1
© 1985 PAWS, INC. All Rights Reserved.
YOU WHAT?!
I CAN'T RESIST A DOUBLE DARE

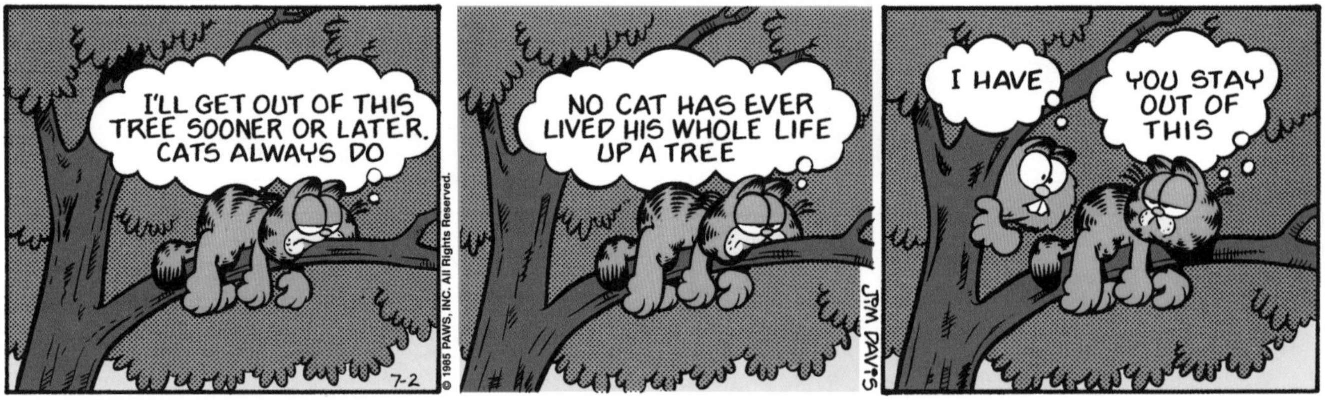
I'LL GET OUT OF THIS TREE SOONER OR LATER. CATS ALWAYS DO
7-2
© 1985 PAWS, INC. All Rights Reserved.
NO CAT HAS EVER LIVED HIS WHOLE LIFE UP A TREE
JIM DAVIS
I HAVE
YOU STAY OUT OF THIS

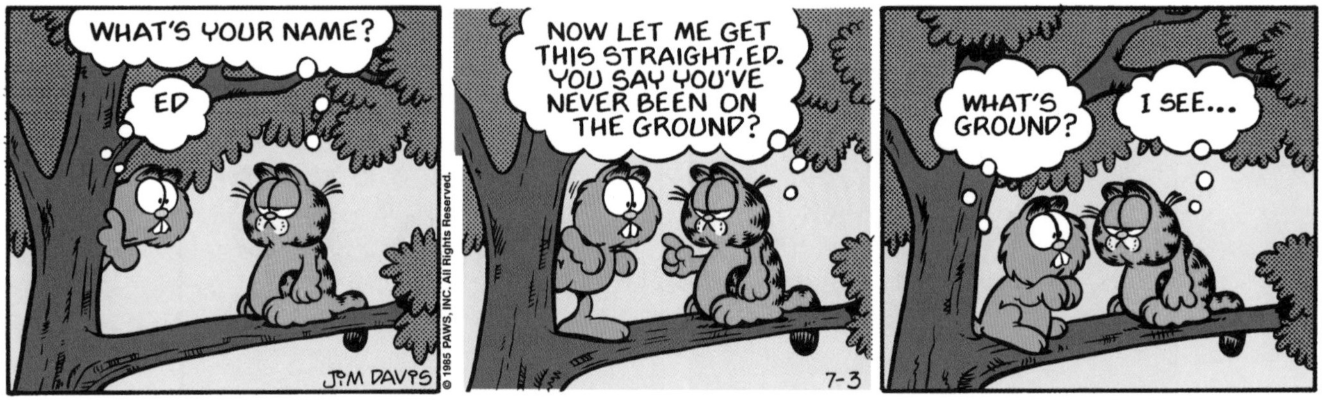
WHAT'S YOUR NAME?
ED
JIM DAVIS
© 1985 PAWS, INC. All Rights Reserved.
NOW LET ME GET THIS STRAIGHT, ED. YOU SAY YOU'VE NEVER BEEN ON THE GROUND?
7-3
WHAT'S GROUND?
I SEE...

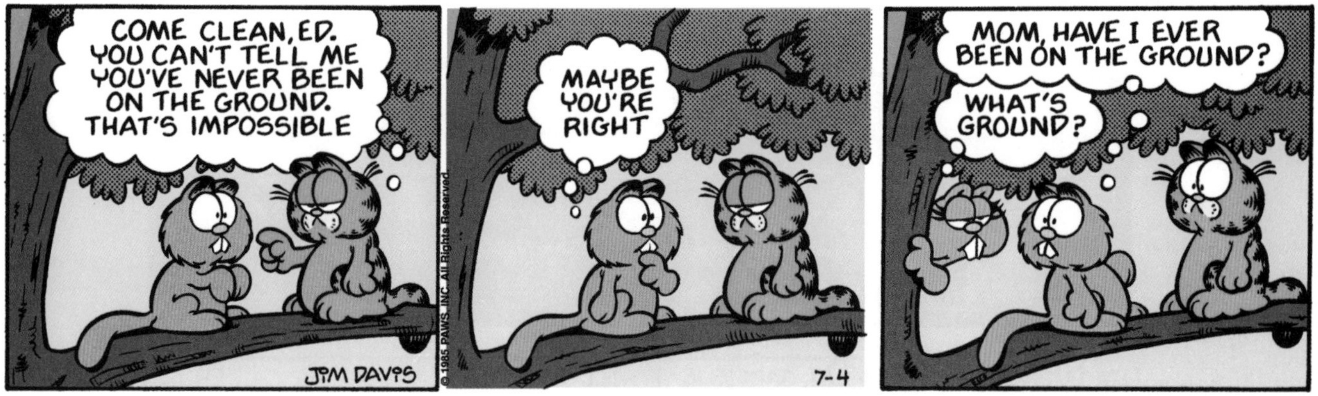
COME CLEAN, ED. YOU CAN'T TELL ME YOU'VE NEVER BEEN ON THE GROUND. THAT'S IMPOSSIBLE
JIM DAVIS
MAYBE YOU'RE RIGHT
© 1985 PAWS, INC. All Rights Reserved.
7-4
MOM, HAVE I EVER BEEN ON THE GROUND?
WHAT'S GROUND?

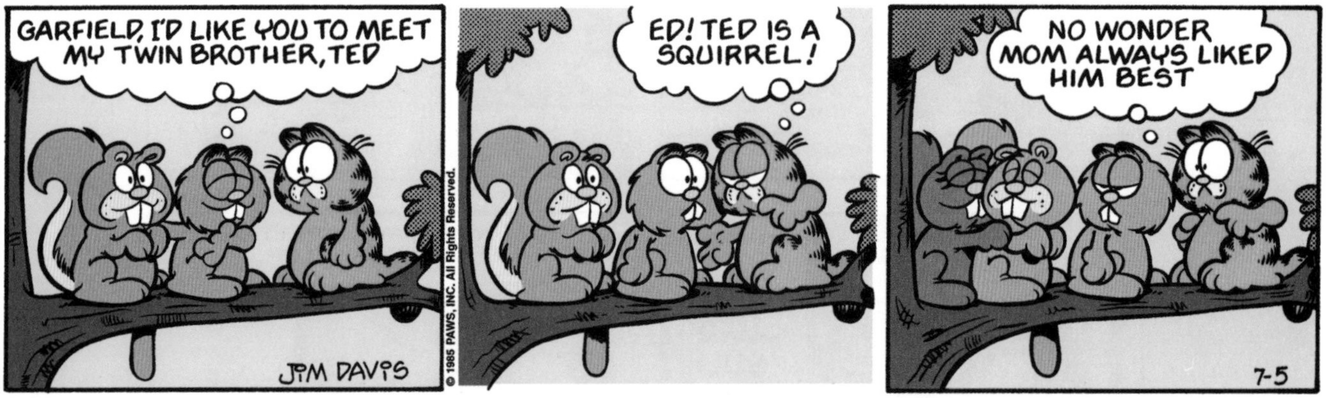
GARFIELD, I'D LIKE YOU TO MEET MY TWIN BROTHER, TED
JIM DAVIS
© 1985 PAWS, INC. All Rights Reserved.
ED! TED IS A SQUIRREL!
NO WONDER MOM ALWAYS LIKED HIM BEST
7-5

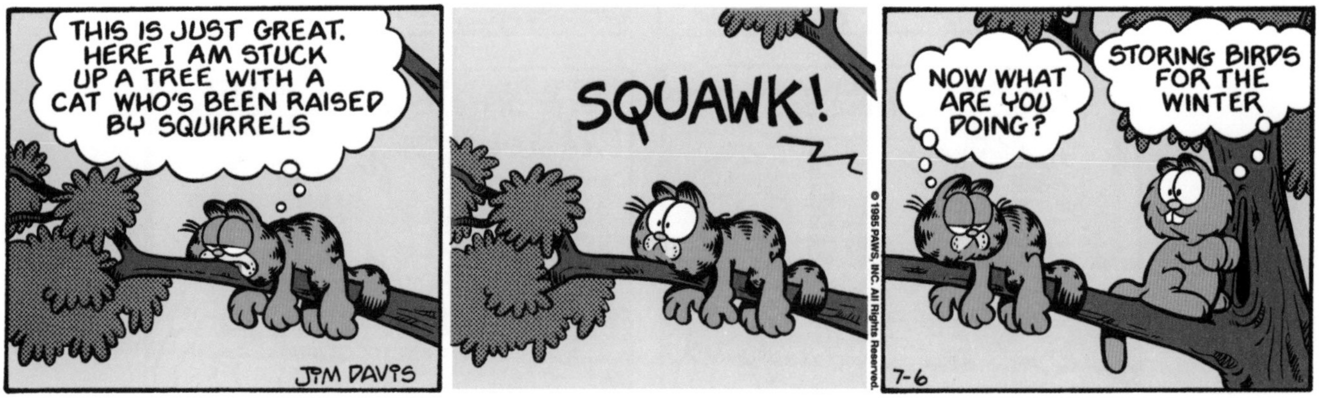
THIS IS JUST GREAT. HERE I AM STUCK UP A TREE WITH A CAT WHO'S BEEN RAISED BY SQUIRRELS
JIM DAVIS
SQUAWK!
© 1985 PAWS, INC. All Rights Reserved.
NOW WHAT ARE YOU DOING?
STORING BIRDS FOR THE WINTER
7-6

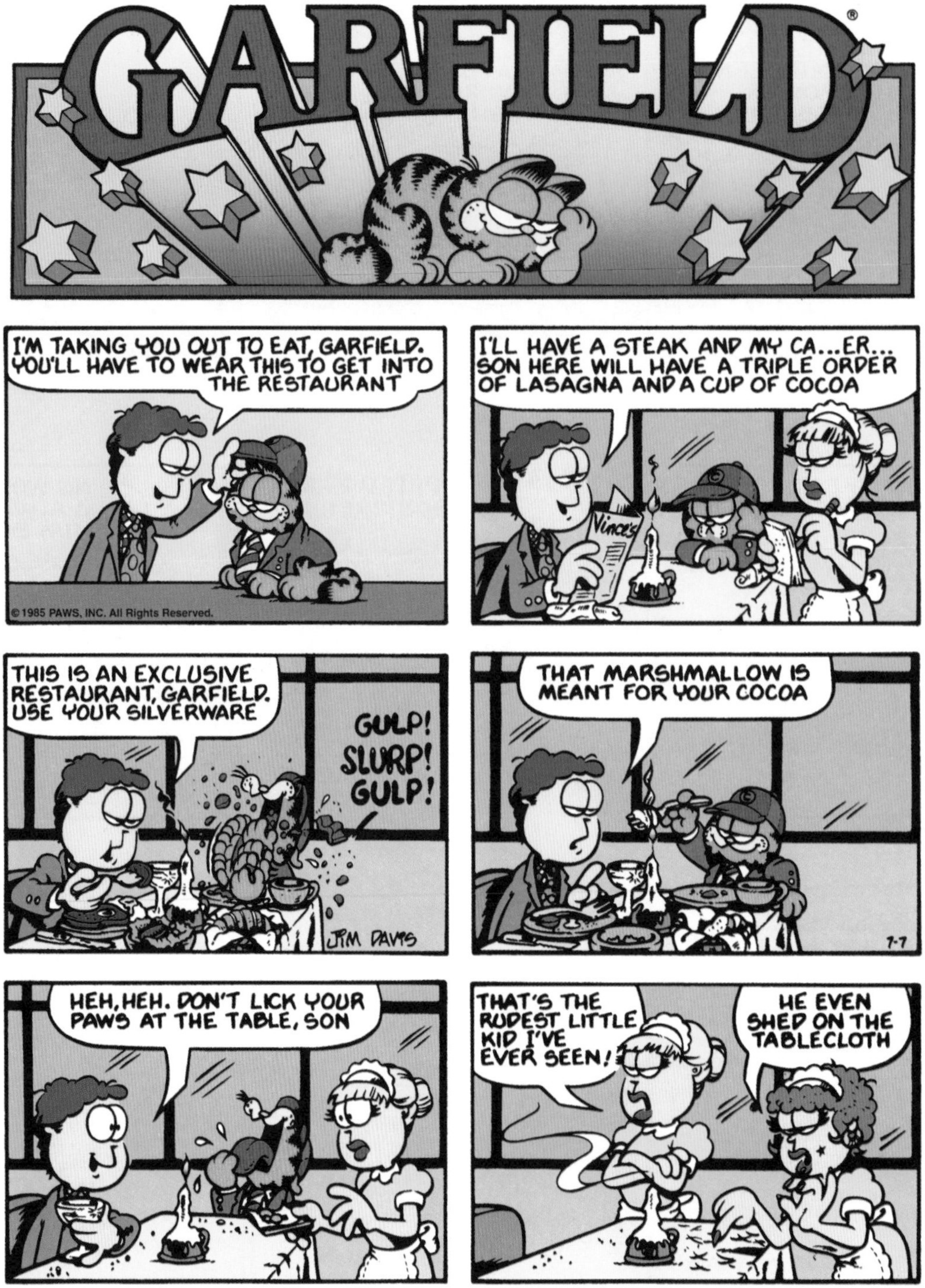
GARFIELD
I'M TAKING YOU OUT TO EAT, GARFIELD. YOU'LL HAVE TO WEAR THIS TO GET INTO THE RESTAURANT
© 1985 PAWS, INC. All Rights Reserved.
I'LL HAVE A STEAK AND MY CA...ER... SON HERE WILL HAVE A TRIPLE ORDER OF LASAGNA AND A CUP OF COCOA
Vince's
THIS IS AN EXCLUSIVE RESTAURANT, GARFIELD. USE YOUR SILVERWARE
GULP! SLURP! GULP!
JIM DAVIS
THAT MARSHMALLOW IS MEANT FOR YOUR COCOA
7-7
HEH, HEH. DON'T LICK YOUR PAWS AT THE TABLE, SON
THAT'S THE RUDEST LITTLE KID I'VE EVER SEEN!
HE EVEN SHED ON THE TABLECLOTH

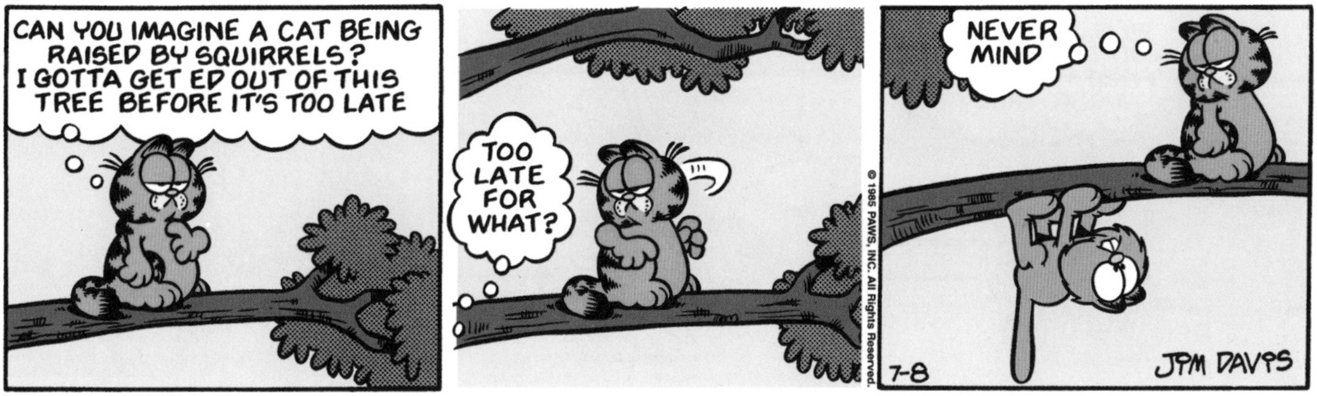
CAN YOU IMAGINE A CAT BEING RAISED BY SQUIRRELS? I GOTTA GET ED OUT OF THIS TREE BEFORE IT'S TOO LATE
TOO LATE FOR WHAT?
© 1985 PAWS, INC. All Rights Reserved.
NEVER MIND
7-8
JIM DAVIS

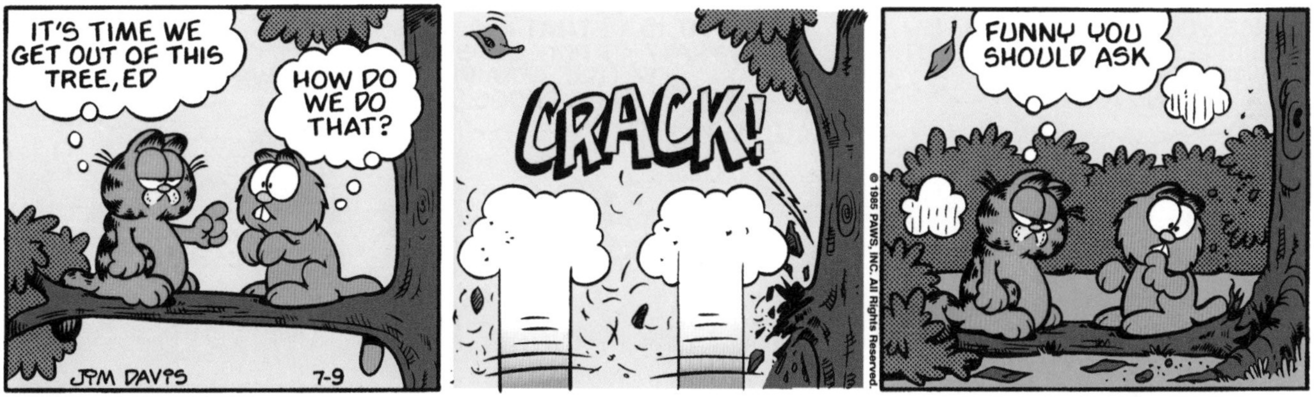
IT'S TIME WE GET OUT OF THIS TREE, ED
HOW DO WE DO THAT?
JIM DAVIS
7-9
CRACK!
© 1985 PAWS, INC. All Rights Reserved.
FUNNY YOU SHOULD ASK

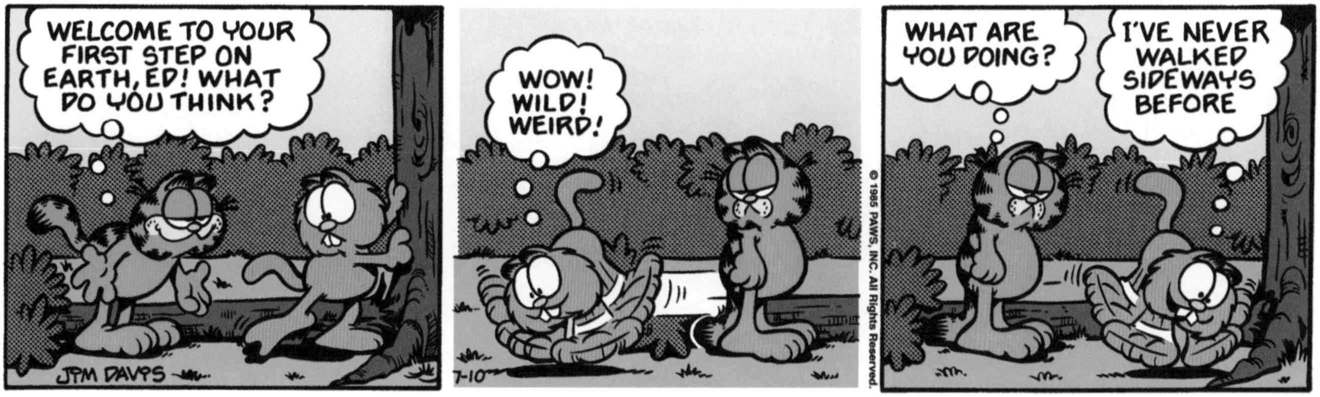
WELCOME TO YOUR FIRST STEP ON EARTH, ED! WHAT DO YOU THINK?
JIM DAVIS
WOW! WILD! WEIRD!
7-10
© 1985 PAWS, INC. All Rights Reserved.
WHAT ARE YOU DOING?
I'VE NEVER WALKED SIDEWAYS BEFORE

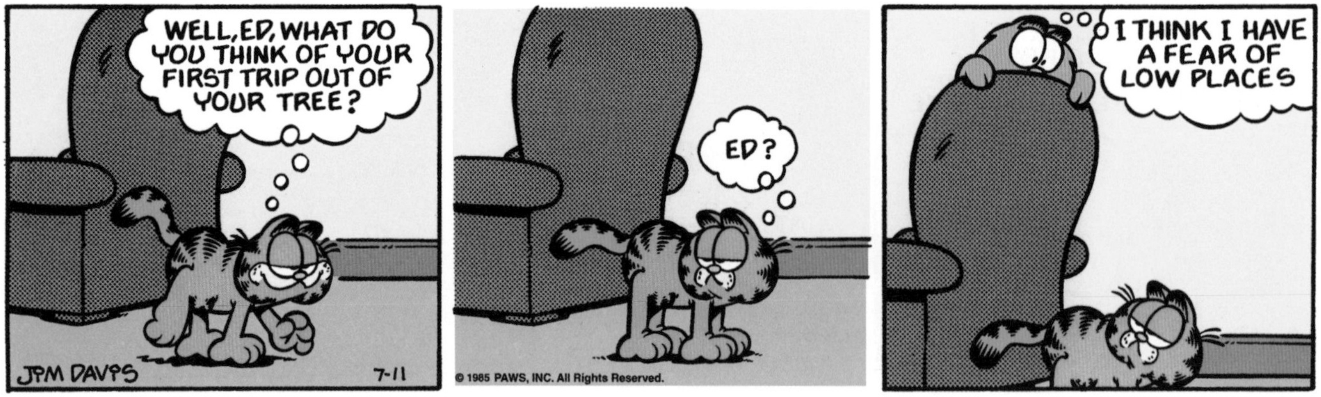
WELL, ED, WHAT DO YOU THINK OF YOUR FIRST TRIP OUT OF YOUR TREE?
JIM DAVIS
7-11
ED?
© 1985 PAWS, INC. All Rights Reserved.
I THINK I HAVE A FEAR OF LOW PLACES

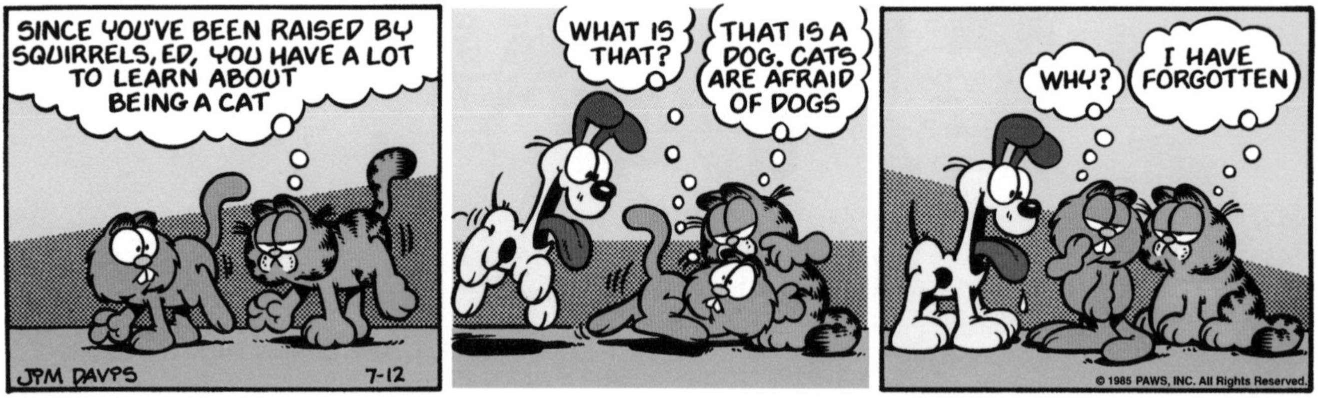
SINCE YOU'VE BEEN RAISED BY SQUIRRELS, ED, YOU HAVE A LOT TO LEARN ABOUT BEING A CAT
JIM DAVIS
7-12
WHAT IS THAT?
THAT IS A DOG. CATS ARE AFRAID OF DOGS
WHY?
I HAVE FORGOTTEN
© 1985 PAWS, INC. All Rights Reserved.

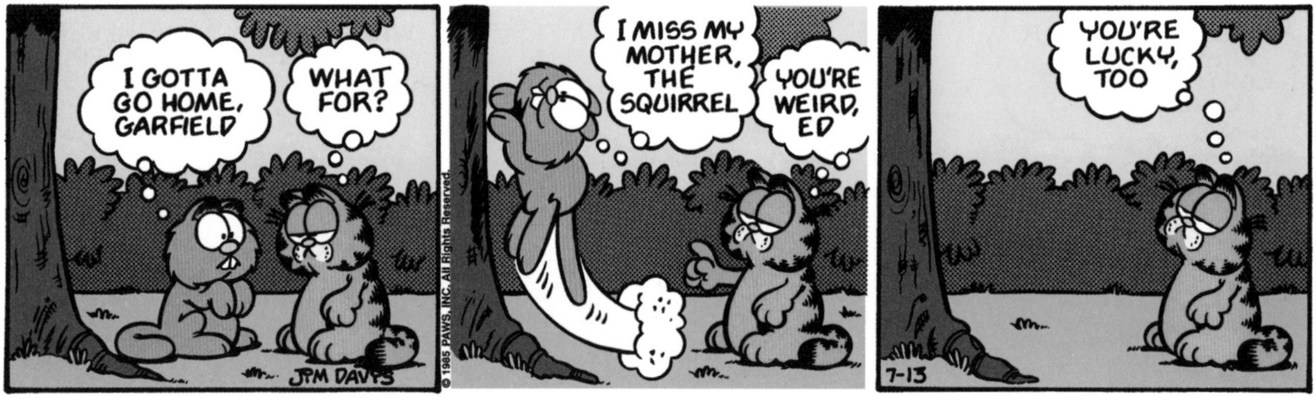
I GOTTA GO HOME, GARFIELD
WHAT FOR?
JIM DAVIS
© 1985 PAWS, INC. All Rights Reserved.
I MISS MY MOTHER, THE SQUIRREL
YOU'RE WEIRD, ED
YOU'RE LUCKY, TOO
7-13

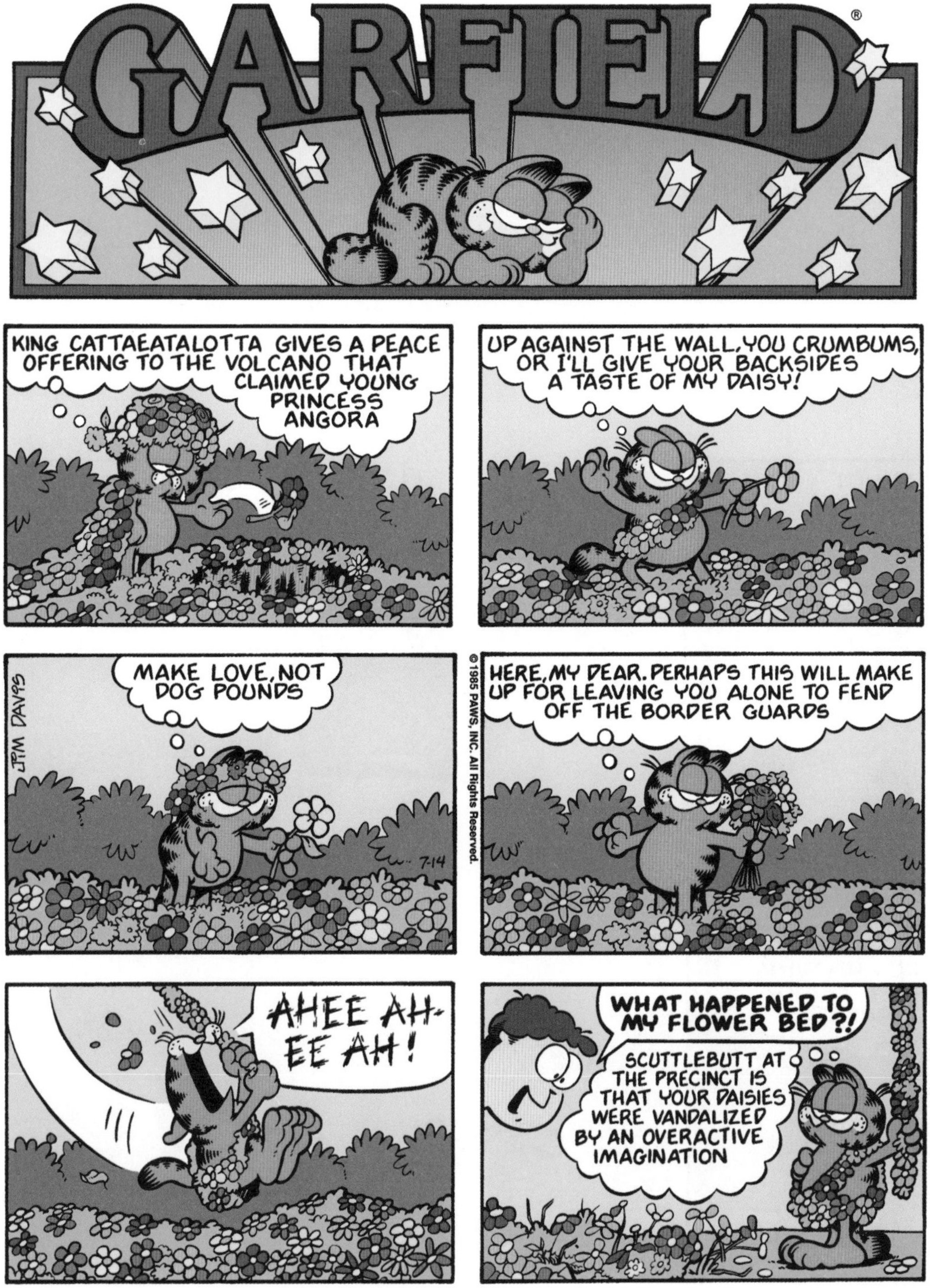
GARFIELD®
KING CATTAEATALOTTA GIVES A PEACE OFFERING TO THE VOLCANO THAT CLAIMED YOUNG PRINCESS ANGORA
UP AGAINST THE WALL, YOU CRUMBUMS, OR I'LL GIVE YOUR BACKSIDES A TASTE OF MY DAISY!
MAKE LOVE, NOT DOG POUNDS
JPM DAVPS
7-14
© 1985 PAWS, INC. All Rights Reserved.
HERE, MY DEAR. PERHAPS THIS WILL MAKE UP FOR LEAVING YOU ALONE TO FEND OFF THE BORDER GUARDS
AHEE AH-EE AH!
WHAT HAPPENED TO MY FLOWER BED?!
SCUTTLEBUTT AT THE PRECINCT IS THAT YOUR DAISIES WERE VANDALIZED BY AN OVERACTIVE IMAGINATION

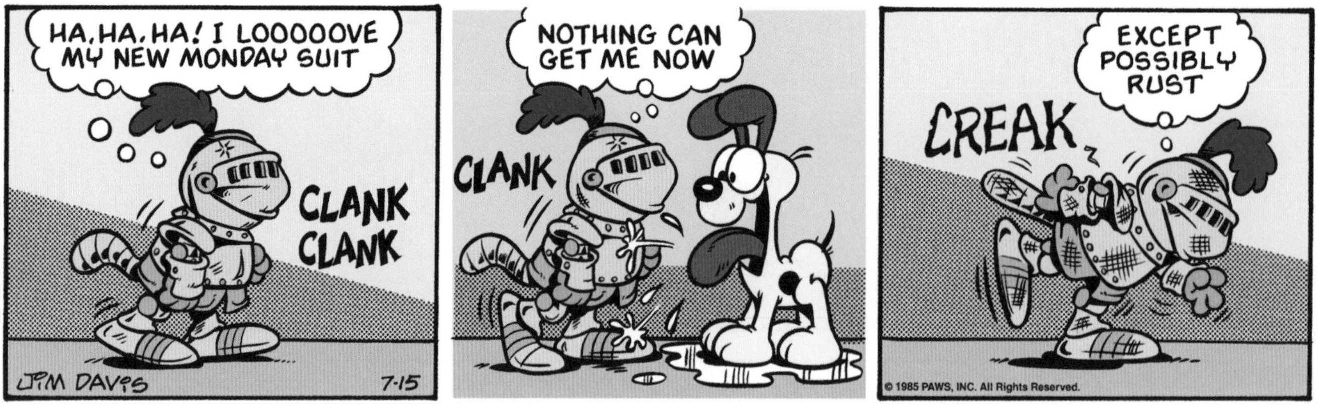
HA, HA, HA! I LOOOOOVE MY NEW MONDAY SUIT
CLANK CLANK
JIM DAVIS
7-15
CLANK
NOTHING CAN GET ME NOW
CREAK
EXCEPT POSSIBLY RUST
© 1985 PAWS, INC. All Rights Reserved.

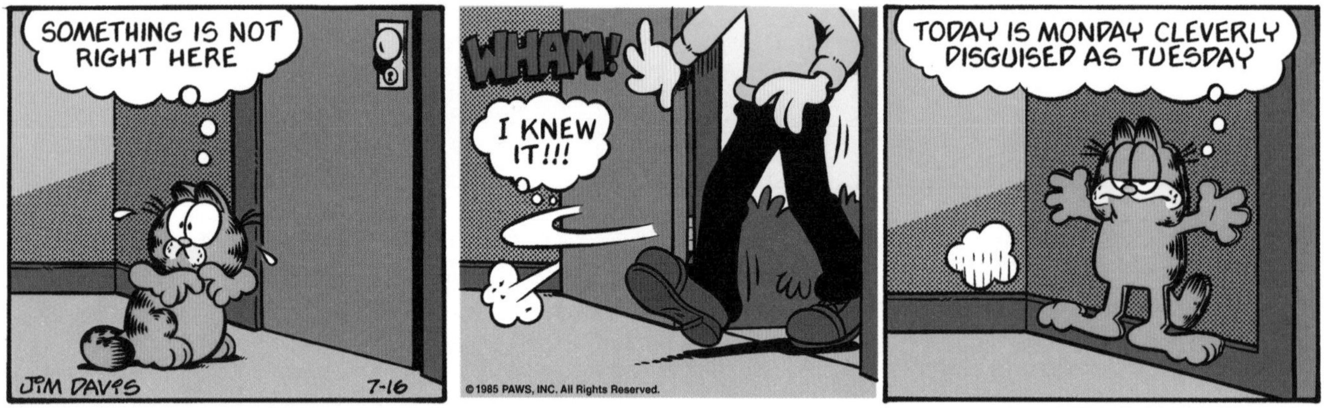
SOMETHING IS NOT RIGHT HERE
JIM DAVIS
7-16
WHAM!
I KNEW IT!!!
© 1985 PAWS, INC. All Rights Reserved.
TODAY IS MONDAY CLEVERLY DISGUISED AS TUESDAY

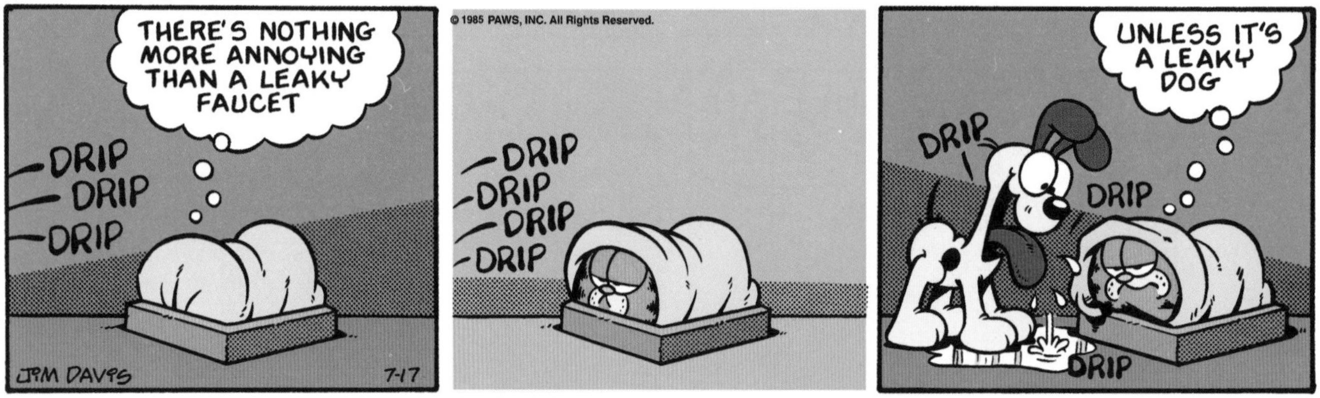
THERE'S NOTHING MORE ANNOYING THAN A LEAKY FAUCET
DRIP
DRIP
DRIP
JIM DAVIS
7-17
© 1985 PAWS, INC. All Rights Reserved.
DRIP
DRIP
DRIP
DRIP
UNLESS IT'S A LEAKY DOG
DRIP
DRIP
DRIP

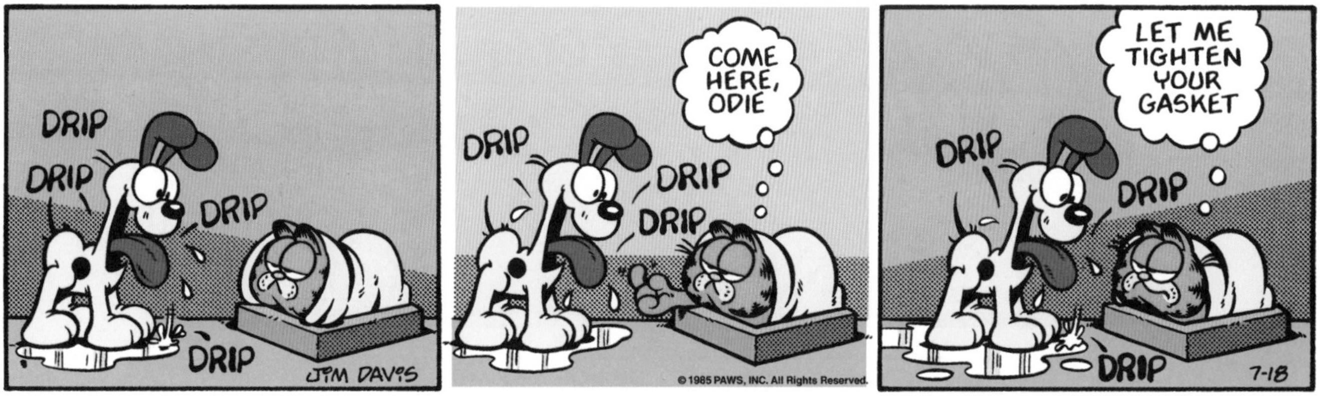
DRIP
DRIP
DRIP
DRIP
JIM DAVIS
COME HERE, ODIE
DRIP
DRIP
DRIP
© 1985 PAWS, INC. All Rights Reserved.
LET ME TIGHTEN YOUR GASKET
DRIP
DRIP
DRIP
7-18

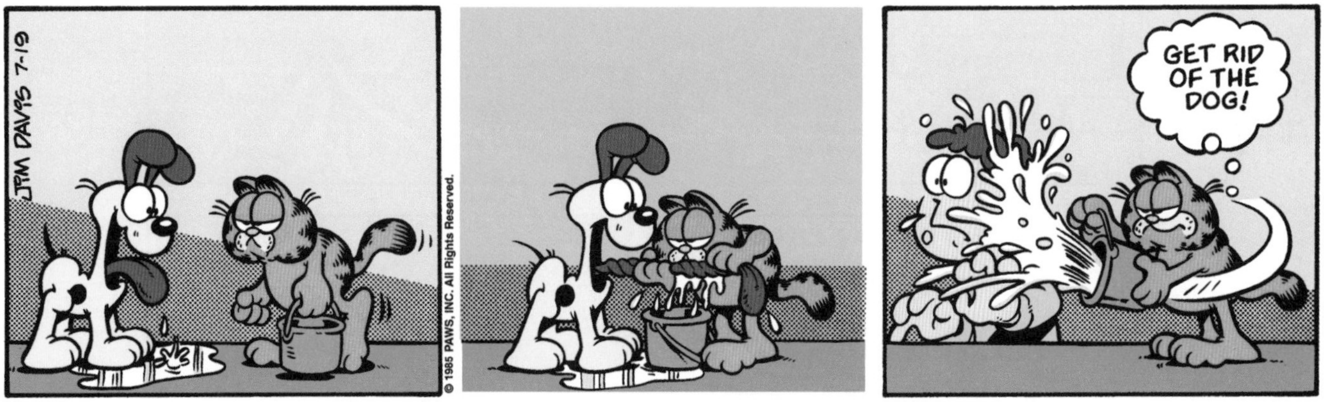
JIM DAVIS 7-19
© 1985 PAWS, INC. All Rights Reserved.
GET RID OF THE DOG!

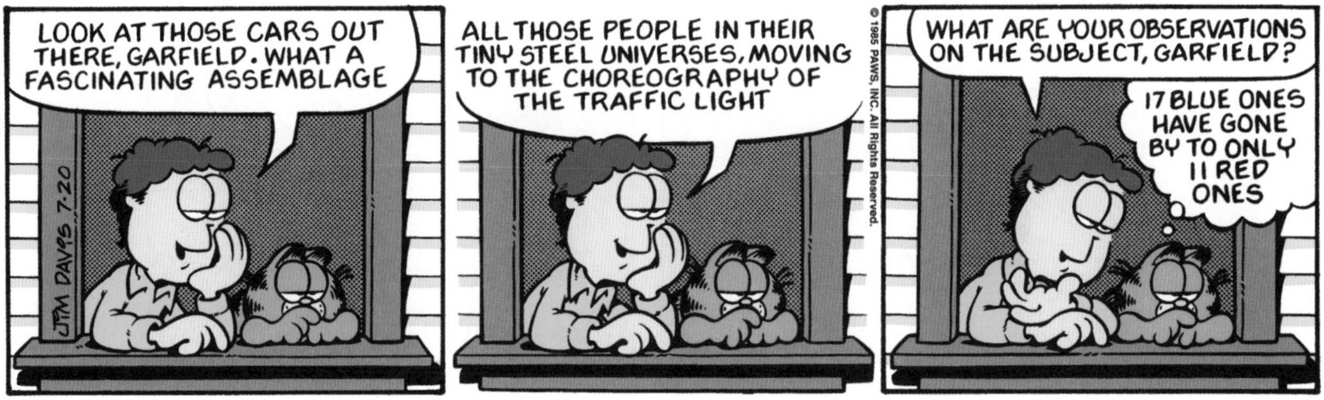
LOOK AT THOSE CARS OUT THERE, GARFIELD. WHAT A FASCINATING ASSEMBLAGE
JIM DAVIS 7-20
ALL THOSE PEOPLE IN THEIR TINY STEEL UNIVERSES, MOVING TO THE CHOREOGRAPHY OF THE TRAFFIC LIGHT
© 1985 PAWS, INC. All Rights Reserved.
WHAT ARE YOUR OBSERVATIONS ON THE SUBJECT, GARFIELD?
17 BLUE ONES HAVE GONE BY TO ONLY 11 RED ONES

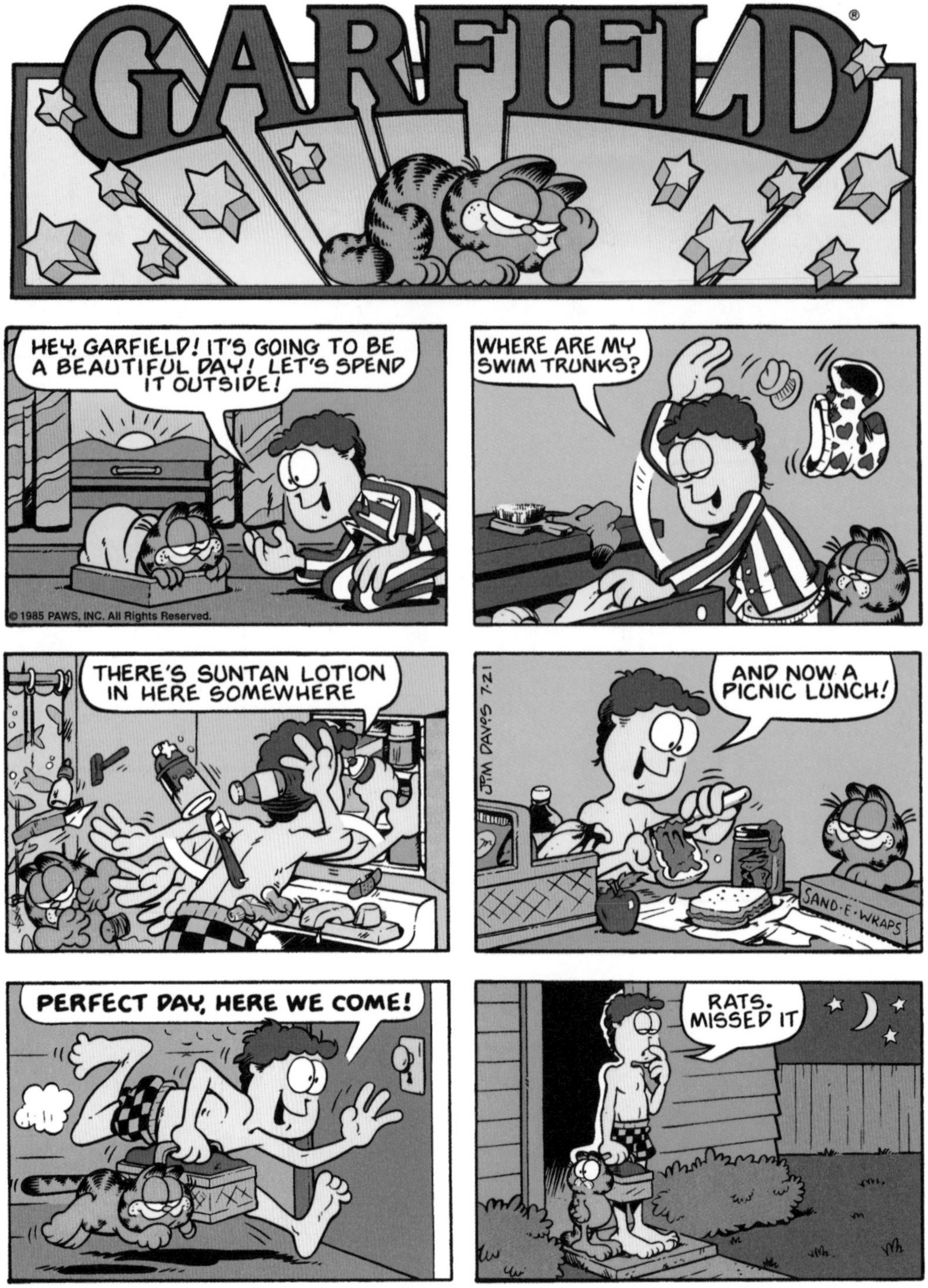
GARFIELD
HEY, GARFIELD! IT'S GOING TO BE A BEAUTIFUL DAY! LET'S SPEND IT OUTSIDE!
© 1985 PAWS, INC. All Rights Reserved.
WHERE ARE MY SWIM TRUNKS?
THERE'S SUNTAN LOTION IN HERE SOMEWHERE
JIM DAVIS 7-21
AND NOW A PICNIC LUNCH!
SAND-E-WRAPS
PERFECT DAY, HERE WE COME!
RATS. MISSED IT

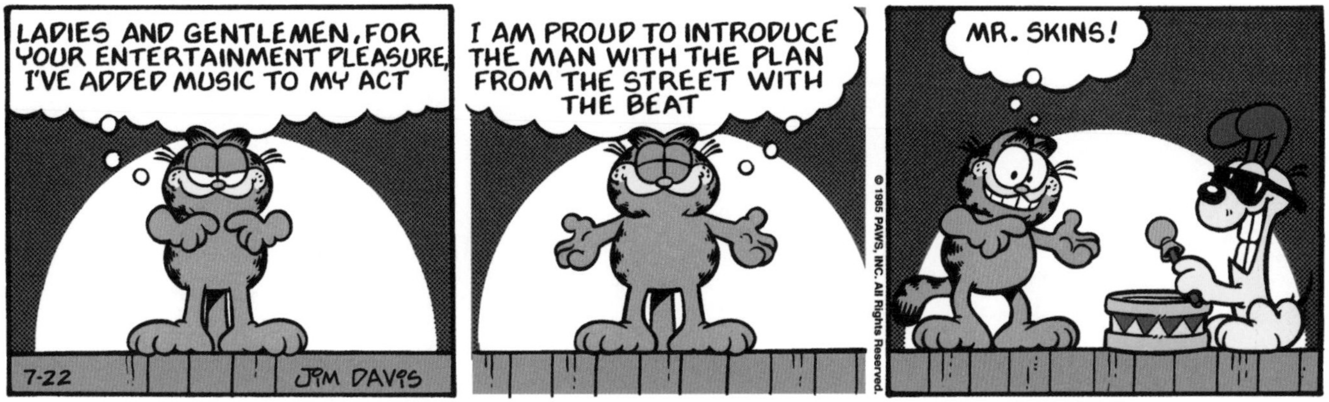
LADIES AND GENTLEMEN, FOR YOUR ENTERTAINMENT PLEASURE, I'VE ADDED MUSIC TO MY ACT
7-22
JIM DAVIS
I AM PROUD TO INTRODUCE THE MAN WITH THE PLAN FROM THE STREET WITH THE BEAT
© 1985 PAWS, INC. All Rights Reserved.
MR. SKINS!

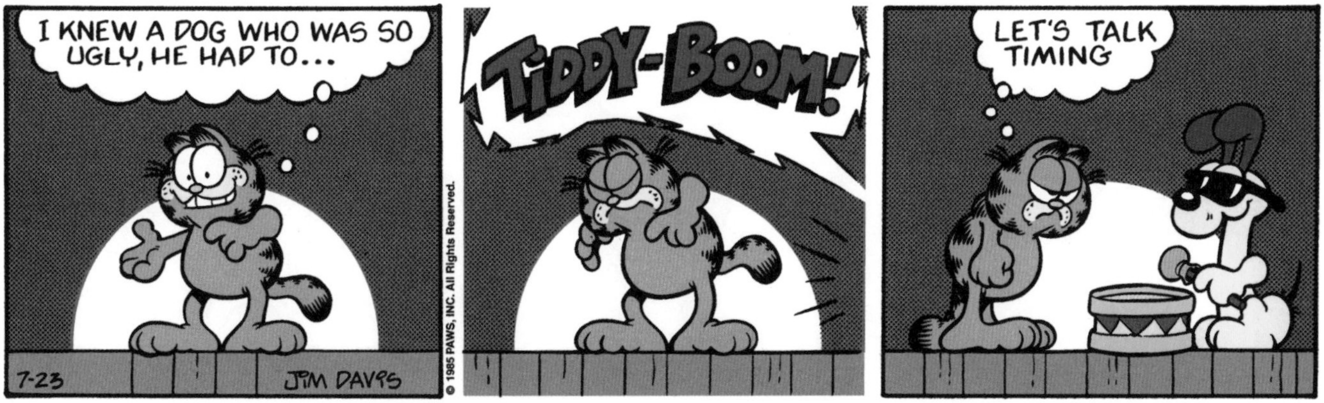
I KNEW A DOG WHO WAS SO UGLY, HE HAD TO...
7-23
JIM DAVIS
© 1985 PAWS, INC. All Rights Reserved.
TIDDY-BOOM!
LET'S TALK TIMING

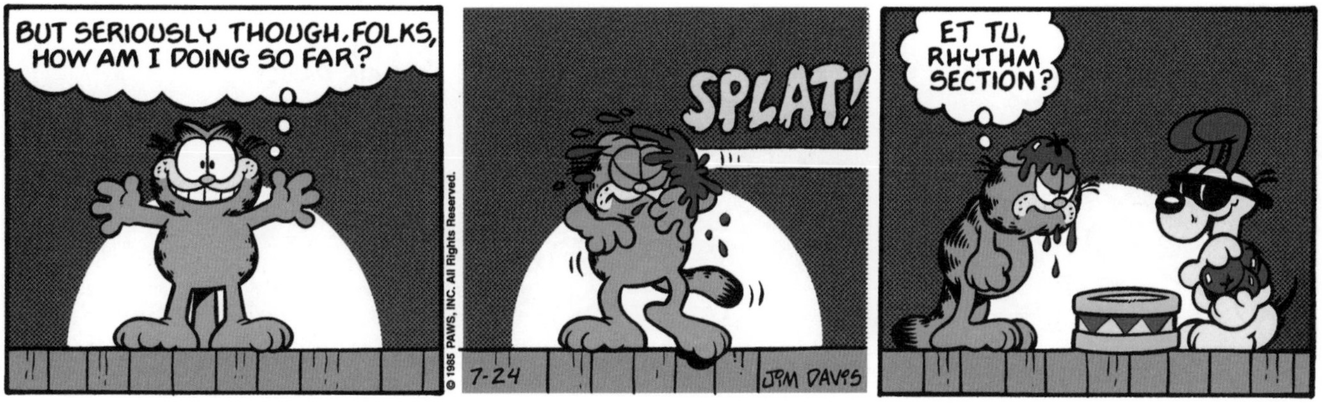
BUT SERIOUSLY THOUGH, FOLKS, HOW AM I DOING SO FAR?
© 1985 PAWS, INC. All Rights Reserved.
SPLAT!
7-24
JIM DAVIS
ET TU, RHYTHM SECTION?

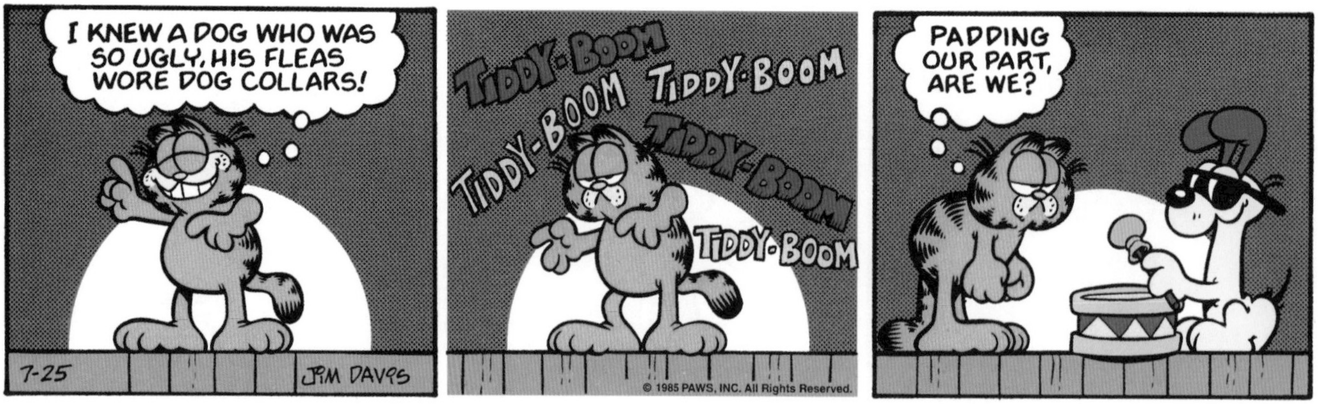
I KNEW A DOG WHO WAS SO UGLY, HIS FLEAS WORE DOG COLLARS!
7-25
JIM DAVIS
TIDDY-BOOM TIDDY-BOOM TIDDY-BOOM TIDDY-BOOM TIDDY-BOOM TIDDY-BOOM
© 1985 PAWS, INC. All Rights Reserved.
PADDING OUR PART, ARE WE?

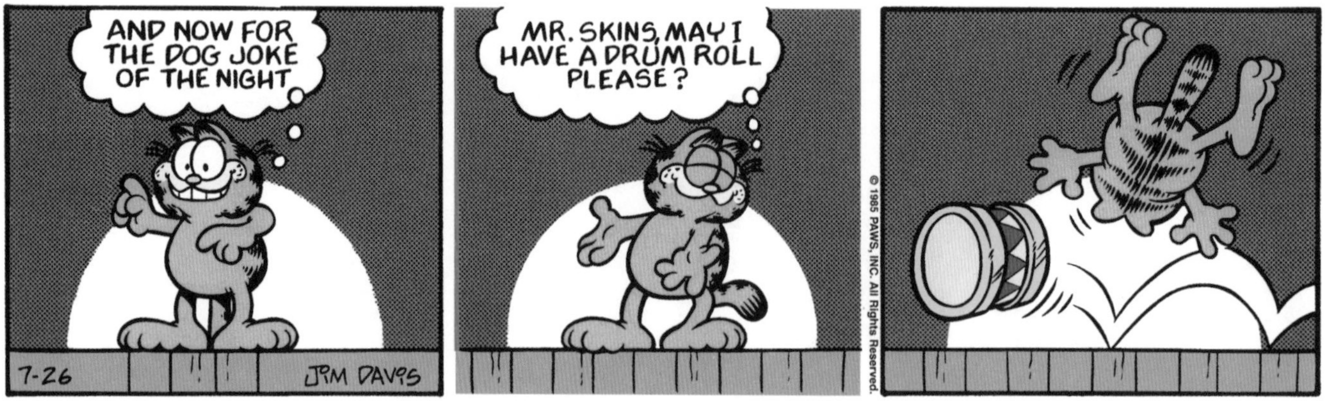
AND NOW FOR THE DOG JOKE OF THE NIGHT
7-26
JIM DAVIS
MR. SKINS, MAY I HAVE A DRUM ROLL PLEASE?
© 1985 PAWS, INC. All Rights Reserved.

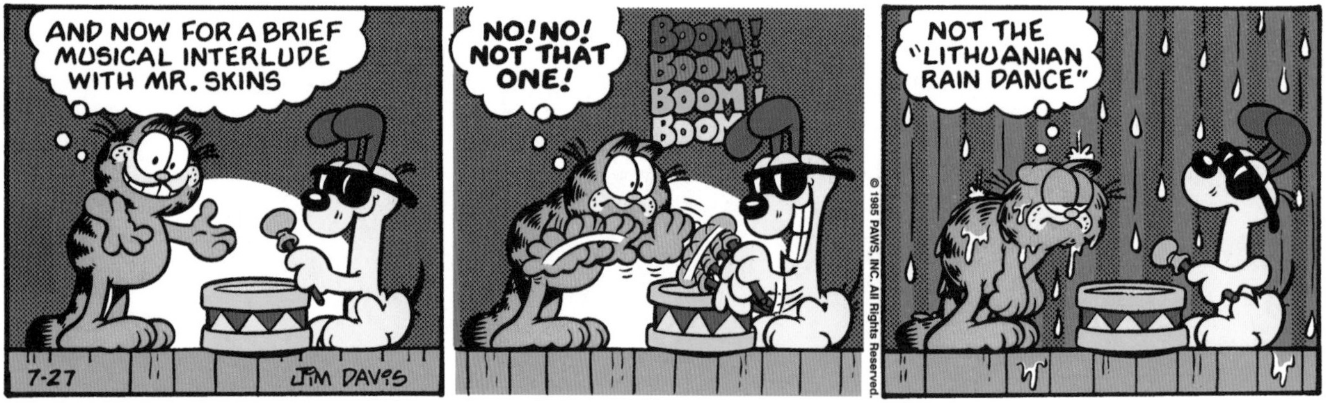
AND NOW FOR A BRIEF MUSICAL INTERLUDE WITH MR. SKINS
7-27
JIM DAVIS
NO! NO! NOT THAT ONE!
BOOM! BOOM! BOOM! BOO
© 1985 PAWS, INC. All Rights Reserved.
NOT THE "LITHUANIAN RAIN DANCE"

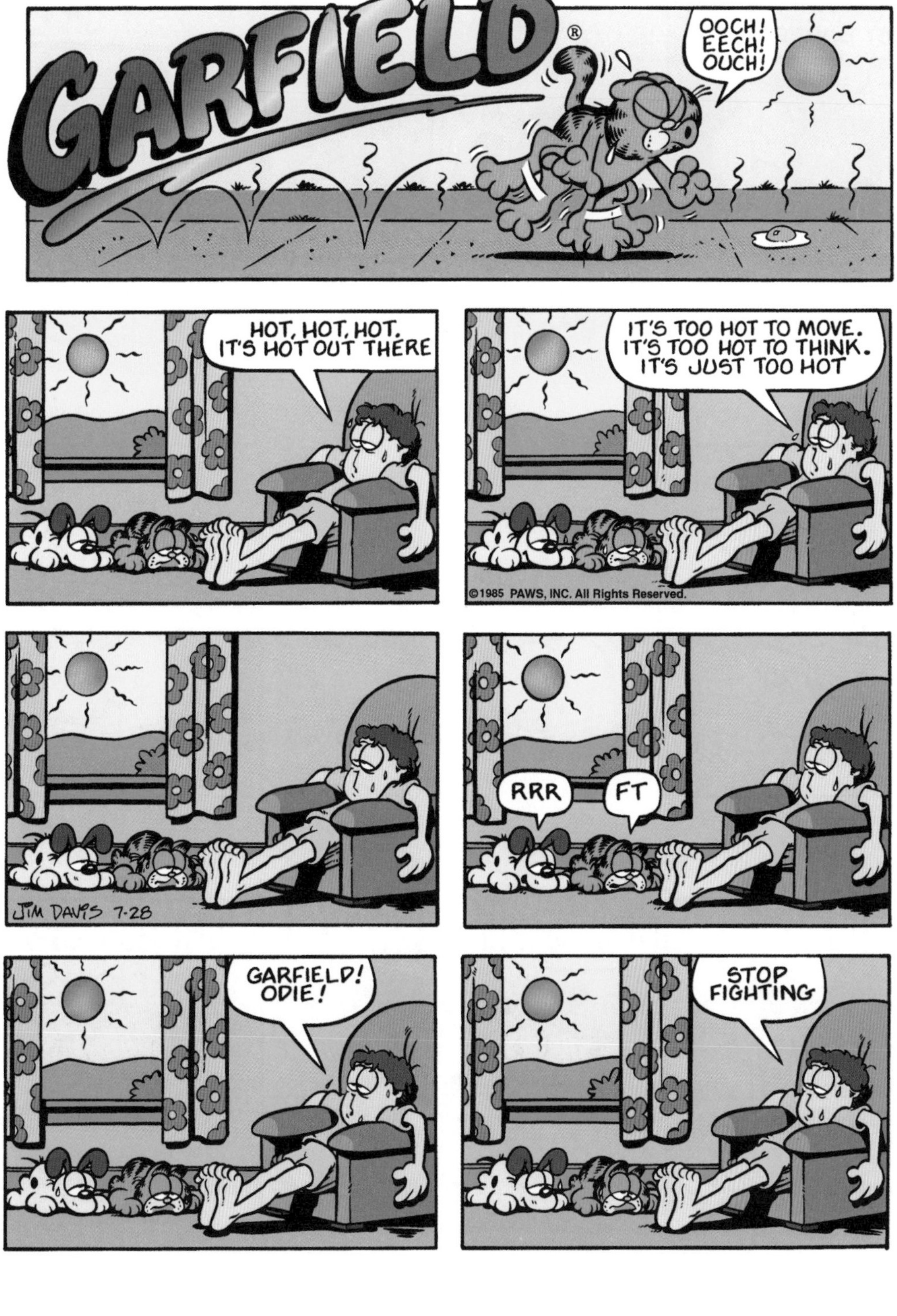
GARFIELD®
OOCH! EECH! OUCH!
HOT, HOT, HOT. IT'S HOT OUT THERE
IT'S TOO HOT TO MOVE. IT'S TOO HOT TO THINK. IT'S JUST TOO HOT
©1985 PAWS, INC. All Rights Reserved.
JIM DAVIS 7-28
RRR
FT
GARFIELD! ODIE!
STOP FIGHTING

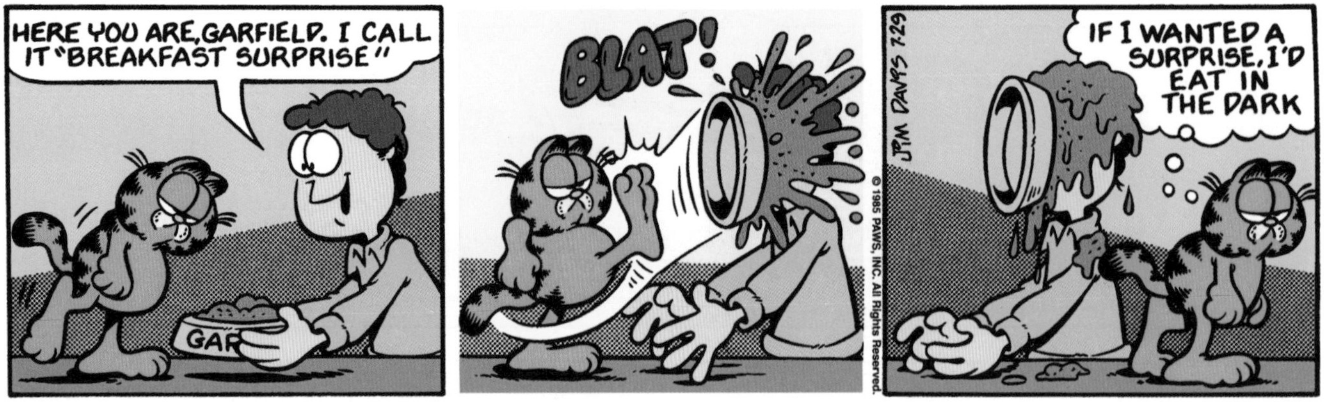
HERE YOU ARE, GARFIELD. I CALL IT "BREAKFAST SURPRISE"
BLAT!
JIM DAVIS 7-29
© 1985 PAWS, INC. All Rights Reserved.
IF I WANTED A SURPRISE, I'D EAT IN THE DARK

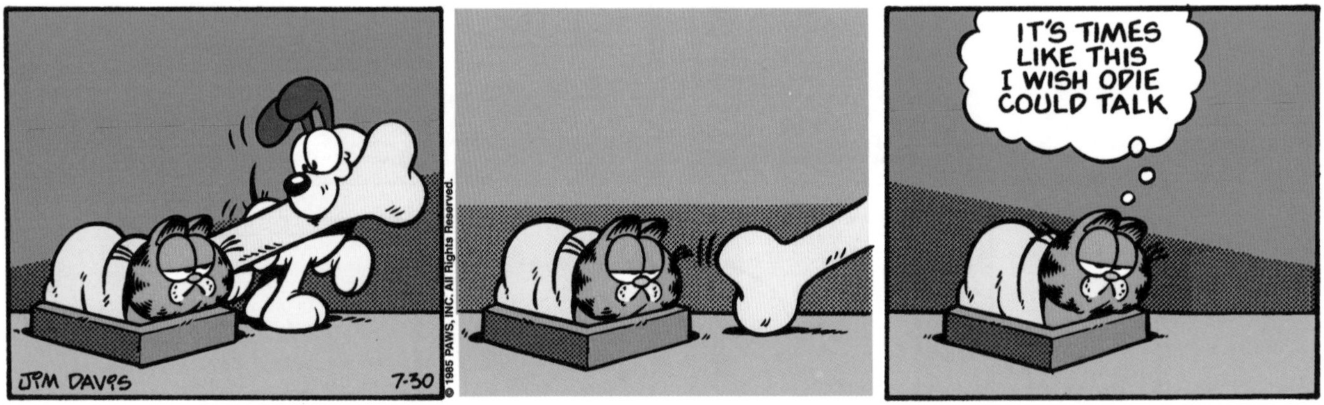
JIM DAVIS
7-30
© 1985 PAWS, INC. All Rights Reserved.
IT'S TIMES LIKE THIS I WISH ODIE COULD TALK

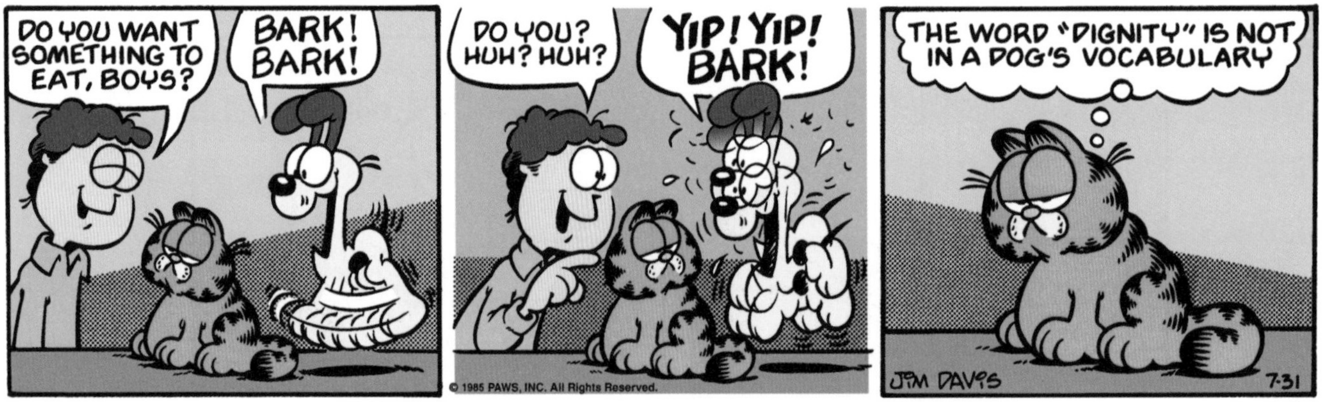
DO YOU WANT SOMETHING TO EAT, BOYS?
BARK! BARK!
DO YOU? HUH? HUH?
YIP! YIP! BARK!
© 1985 PAWS, INC. All Rights Reserved.
THE WORD "DIGNITY" IS NOT IN A DOG'S VOCABULARY
JIM DAVIS
7-31

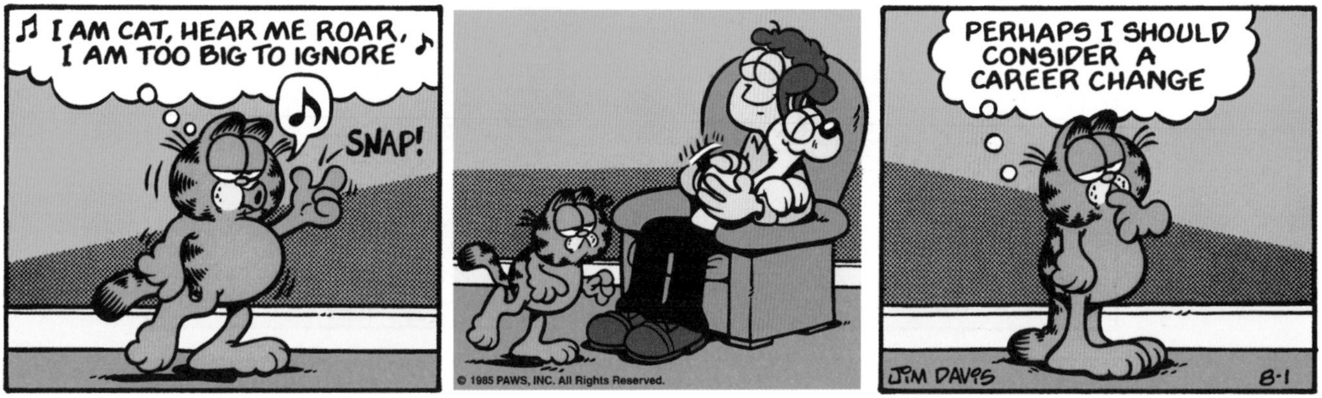
I AM CAT, HEAR ME ROAR, I AM TOO BIG TO IGNORE
SNAP!
© 1985 PAWS, INC. All Rights Reserved.
PERHAPS I SHOULD CONSIDER A CAREER CHANGE
JIM DAVIS
8-1

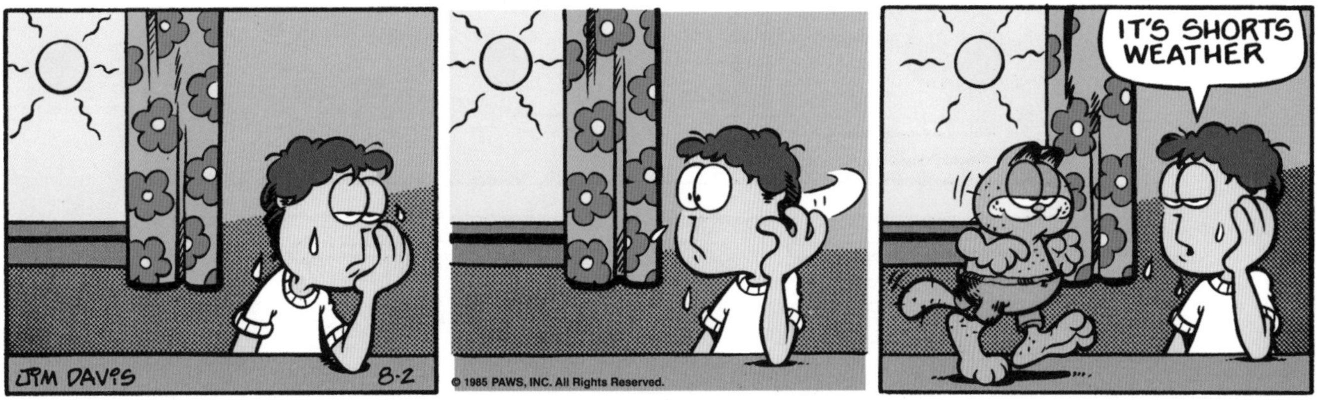
JIM DAVIS
8-2
© 1985 PAWS, INC. All Rights Reserved.
IT'S SHORTS WEATHER

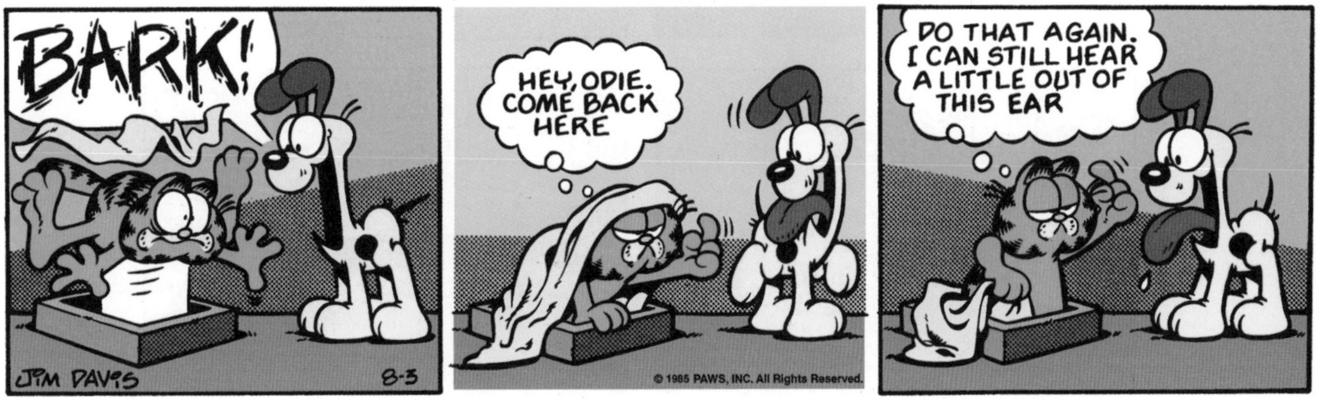
BARK!
JIM DAVIS
8-3
HEY, ODIE. COME BACK HERE
© 1985 PAWS, INC. All Rights Reserved.
DO THAT AGAIN. I CAN STILL HEAR A LITTLE OUT OF THIS EAR

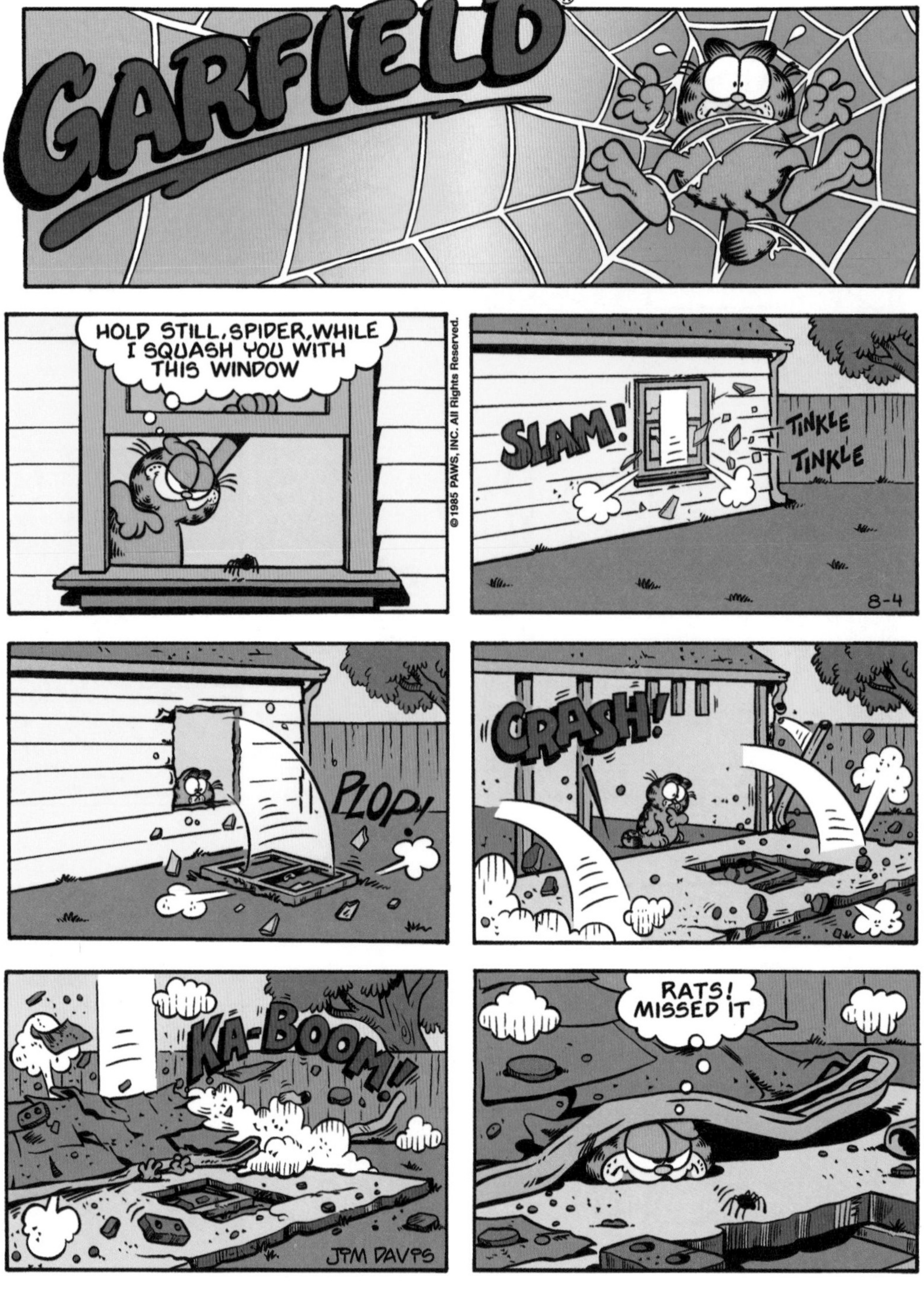
GARFIELD®
HOLD STILL, SPIDER, WHILE I SQUASH YOU WITH THIS WINDOW
© 1985 PAWS, INC. All Rights Reserved.
SLAM!
TINKLE
TINKLE
8-4
PLOP!
CRASH!
KA-BOOM!
JPM DAVPS
RATS! MISSED IT

EARLIEST KNOWN GARFIELD!

Presented here for the first time anywhere is the earliest known Garfield strip.

This 12 lb. block dates to around 2300 b.c. during the rule of Sumerian king Naram-Sin. Jim Davis' name appears in lower right.

typysyttwng wn psy, npyr- tn chxrxctyrs,

r
y
d
y
'd
nr
by
m
wg
xw
nn
wy
yd
ry
hw
fnr
spl
nd
fnr
nd
m
xw
nn
wy
dyx

NEWS FLASH!

Jim Davis a Fraud!

Teddy bear Pooky recently revealed that Jim Davis did not create the Garfield comic strip. Garfield himself writes and draws the world-famous cartoon. Garfield has been sitting at a drawing board for the last six years as Davis has gained notoriety through national television and print. Davis was not available for comment, but Garfield was. "The way I figured it, who would ever believe a cat could do a comic strip. So, I hired this down-and-out, hack cartoonist to take the credit for it. Sure . . . he looked good and said all the right things, but it's time the truth were known."

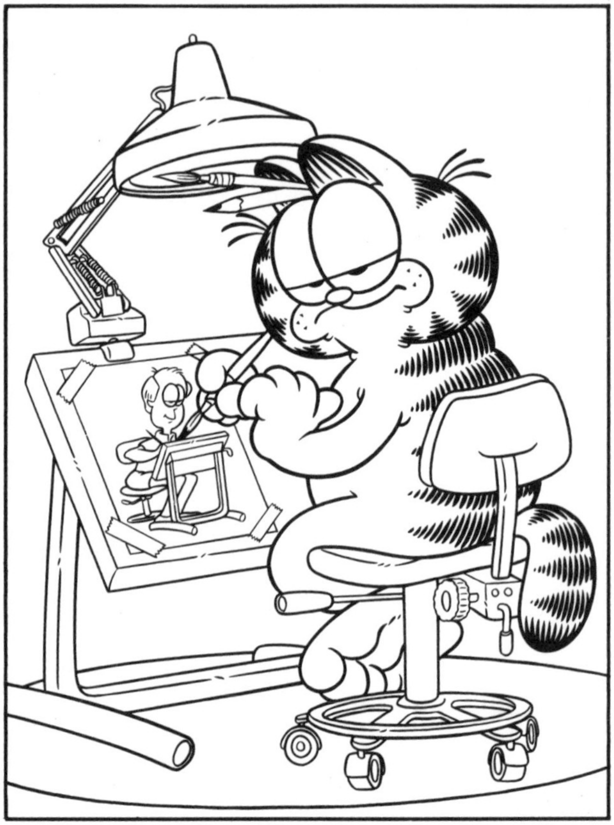

The Big Cheese, the Head Honcho, the Chief Muckamuck . . .